THIS LAND WAS THEIRS

A SAHAPTIN
B SPOKANE
C KALISPEL
D COEUR d'ALENE
E CAYUSE
F NEZ PERCE
G BANNOCK
H CHEYENNE

I HIDATSA
J MANDAN
K ARIKARA
L PONCA
M MENOMINEE
N WINNEBAGO
O POTAWATOMI
P E. OJIBWA

Q OTTAWA
R HURON
S SENECA
T CAYUGA
U ONONDAGA
V ONEIDA
W MOHAWK
Y MAHICAN

x Unoccupied areas   xx Unclassified

POLAR ESKIMO

EAST GREENLAND ESKIMO

WEST GREENLAND ESKIMO

EAST GREENLAND ESKIMO

IGLULIK ESKIMO

NETSILIK ESKIMO

BAFFINLAND ESKIMO

End maps adopted from Goddard, 1996; Courtesy of the *Handbook of North American Indians*, Vol. 17, Smithsonian Institution, Washington, DC.

CARIBOU ESKIMO

SALLIRMIUT

QUEBEC ESKIMO

LABRADOR ESKIMO

Hudson Bay

NASKAPI

CREE

MONTAGNAIS

BEOTHUK

WEST MAIN CREE

EAST CREE

NORTHERN OJIBWA

MICMAC

SAULTEAUX

MALISEET

ALGONQUIN

PASSAMAQUODDY

SOUTHEASTERN OJIBWA

LAURENTIAN

ABENAKI

ATLANTIC OCEAN

YANKTON-YANKTONAI

SANTEE-SISSETON

P

M

O

Q

R

V
S
U
W
Y

N

SAUK FOX

S. NEW ENGLAND ALGONQUIANS

IOWA

MIAMI

xx

KICKAPOO

DELAWARE

SHAWNEE

. . . so long as the waters shall flow
and the sun shall shine . . .

THIS LAND WAS THEIRS

A Study of Native North Americans

EIGHTH EDITION

Wendell H. Oswalt
University of California, Los Angeles

New York   Oxford
OXFORD UNIVERSITY PRESS
2006

Oxford University Press

Oxford   New York
Auckland   Bangkok   Buenos Aires   Cape Town   Chennai
Dar es Salaam   Delhi   Hong Kong   Istanbul   Karachi   Kolkata
Kuala Lumpur   Madrid   Melbourne   Mexico City   Mumbai   Nairobi
São Paulo   Shanghai   Taipei   Tokyo   Toronto

Published by Oxford University Press, Inc.
198 Madison Avenue, New York, New York 10016
www.oup.com

Oxford is a registered trademark of Oxford University Press

Library of Congress Cataloging-in-Publication Data
Oswalt, Wendell H.
 This land was theirs : a study of Native North Americans/Wendell H. Oswalt.—8th ed.
   p. cm.
 Includes bibliographical references and index.
 ISBN-13: 978-0-19-517810-4 (paper : alk. paper)
 ISBN 0-19-517810-6 (paper : alk. paper)
 1. Indians of North America.   I. Title.

E77.O8 2005
970.004'97—dc22   2004042373

Printing number: 9 8 7 6 5 4 3 2
Printed in the United States of America
on acid-free paper

In memory of
Edward H. Spicer
and
John J. Honigmann

Contents

Preface xv

Chapter 1   Questions about Native Americans   1

Bison and Americans 2
Indians in Popular Culture 4
Who Is a Native American? 6
Population Figures 9
Where Did Native Americans Originate? 10
Precontact History North of Mexico: An Overview 13
How Have Native American Cultures Been Studied? 17
What Do We Know of Native American Languages? 21
Grouping Tribes 24
Additional Sources 29
Selected Bibliography 29

Chapter 2   Indian–Non-Indian Relations   32

Early Contact 33
Destruction and Displacement of Peoples 36
U.S. Treaties 38
Administration of U.S. Indian Affairs 40
Canada, the First Nations 41
Greenland in Brief 43
Landmark U.S. Indian Policies 43
Forces Fostering Native American Identity 46
Recent History 54
Native Americans and Anthropologists 62
Comparing Cultures 65
Additional Sources 66
Selected Bibliography 67

Chapter 3   The Netsilik: Seal Hunting and Snowhouse Eskimos 69

Aboriginal Life 72
Historical Developments 94
Recent Changes 98
Additional Sources 102
Selected Bibliography 102

Chapter 4   The Chipewyan: Subarctic Hunters 104

Aboriginal Life 106
Early History 117
Becoming Modern at Snowdrift (Lutselk'e, Lutsel K'e) 120
Contemporary Lutselk'e 128
Additional Sources 135
Selected Bibliography 136

Chapter 5   The Lower Kootenai: Plateau Fishers and Hunters 138

Aboriginal Life 141
Historical Changes 155
Select Comparisons: Bonners Ferry Kootenai (BFK)
    and Creston Kootenay (CK) 167
Additional Sources 168
Selected Bibliography 168

Chapter 6   The Western Shoshone: Subduers of the High Desert 170

Aboriginal Life 173
Early Historical Developments 184
Later History 188
The Battle Mountain Colony 191
Additional Sources 199
Selected Bibliography 200

Chapter 7   The Crow: Plains Raiders and Bison Hunters 202

Baseline Ethnography 203
Early History 224

Later History 226
Other Dimensions 233
Additional Sources 236
Selected Bibliography 237

Chapter 8   The Cahuilla: Gatherers in the Desert 239

Aboriginal Life 240
Historic Changes 255
The Agua Caliente Band 258
Additional Sources 266
Selected Bibliography 266

Chapter 9   The Tlingit: Alaskan Salmon Fishers 268

Aboriginal Life 269
Early History 292
Later History 293
Additional Sources 303
Selected Bibliography 304

Chapter 10   The Hopi: Farmers of the Desert 306

Aboriginal Life 307
Early History 327
Later History 328
Emergence of the Modern Hopi 331
Additional Considerations 335
Additional Sources 338
Selected Bibliography 338

Chapter 11   The Navajo: Transformations among a Desert People 340

The Background 342
Traditional Life 350
The Comparatively Recent Past 366
Modern Developments 369
Additional Issues and Concerns 375
Additional Sources 378
Selected Bibliography 378

Chapter 12   The Iroquois: Warriors and Farmers of the Eastern Woodlands 381

Early Historic Life 382
Later History 401
The Six Nations Reserve 404
Nationalism and Sovereignty 414
Additional Sources 416
Selected Bibliography 417

Chapter 13   The Eastern Cherokee: Farmers of the Southeast 419

People, Population, and Language 420
Early Historic Life 420
Early History 431
Later History: The Eastern Band of Cherokee 435
The Contemporary Scene 440
Additional Sources 444
Selected Bibliography 444

Chapter 14   The Natchez: Sophisticated Farmers of the Deep South 447

Aboriginal Life 448
Ceremonies 457
Tattooed Serpent's Oration 463
Recorded Natchez History 464
Additional Sources 467
Selected Bibliography 467

Chapter 15   Overviews 469

Indian Casino Highlights 470
Federal Administration 476
Urban Indians 479
Unrecognized Tribes 482
Diabetes and Native Americans 484
Indians as Environmentalists 485
Tribalism 486

National Museum of the American Indian 488
Tribal Sovereignty 488
Summarizing Thoughts 493
Additional Sources 493
Selected Bibliography 493

Appendix A: A Sample of Widespread Artifact Types 495
Appendix B: Resources about Native Americans 503
Glossary 509
Pronunciation Guide 519
Name Index 523
Subject Index 528

Preface

The first edition of *This Land Was Theirs,* published in 1966, introduced a different approach to the study of Native Americans living north of Mexico. The emphasis was, and remains, on traditional and changing Indian lifeways. The tribes with chapter-length presentations represent culture areas and varying degrees of cultural complexity. The tribal accounts include scientific and humanistic approaches to anthropological data. Likewise, ecological, ethnohistorical, functional, structural, and other perspectives are included as appropriate. Thus, no single orientation dominates.

The two opening chapters address questions commonly asked about Native Americans, such as their prehistory, history, and current issues, including Indian casinos. This and additional background material are followed by twelve chapters about specific populations. After brief introductions, most chapters begin with early ethnographic accounts. The Navajo chapter is an exception because most information available is ethnohistorical, and the Navajo emerged as a tribe in the comparatively recent past. Each chapter plots historical developments to the fall of 2004. The concluding chapter offers an overview of Native American life with emphasis on the present and the near future.

The tribal chapters reflect differences in sociopolitical life (band, tribe, chiefdom), and particular aspects of their lifeways are accented. The presentation sequence is as follows. The Netsilik (Eskimo, Inuit) of north-central Canada, with their dog teams, seal hunting, and snowhouses, represent a "classic" Eskimo group in the Arctic culture area. Considerable emphasis is placed on their material culture and the impact of food stress. The Chipewyan of northwestern Canada represent Subarctic hunters and fishers; their adaptations to the fur trade are highlighted. The Lower Kootenai in Idaho and British Columbia represent hunters and fishers in the Plateau culture area; they provide an opportunity to examine the impact of Canadian and U.S. policies on a single group. The Western Shoshone in the Great Basin culture area represent a "classic" example of gatherers; their land claims against the federal government are emphasized. The Crow of the northern Plains represent foragers, and their historic emphasis on horse-related activities. The Cahuilla, with an aboriginal economy focused largely on wild plant products, inhabit an arid sector of the California culture area. The circumstances leading to the vast present-day wealth of the Palm Springs group are reviewed. The Tlingit of southeastern Alaska represent Northwest Coast culture area salmon fishers. Their attitudes toward property and wealth are central concerns. The Hopi of the Southwest, as arid-area farmers, in numerous ways typify the complexities of Pueblo Indian life. For the Navajo in the Southwest, historical roots are stressed. Their varied biological and cultural background and comparatively recent emergence as a tribe attract considerable attention. The Iroquois of the Northeast depended largely on domestic crops; their political life is featured. The Cherokee as farmers are one of the few major Indian populations that continue to occupy their homeland in the Southeast. Finally, the Natchez of Mississippi reflect one of the most complex lifeways among Indians north of Mexico. The stages leading to their demise receive particular attention.

The concluding chapter has multiple goals, which include addressing general issues and recent developments among tribes in the United States that do not fit comfortably in most tribal chapters. Examples include urban Indians, tribalism, and sovereignty. Current developments among the First Nations of Canada are presented in the pertinent chapters (3, 4, 5, and 12).

In closing, it is gratifying to acknowledge a resurgent interest in Native Americans among non-Indians. Hopefully, this edition will lead to further understanding of Indian life, *past and present.*

| New to This Edition

One major difference distinguishes this edition from previous editions. A Great Basin culture area people, the Western Shoshone, is presented in a new chapter. Thus for the first time each culture area is represented by at least one tribe. The Yurok chapter, however, has been deleted.

The opposition of some Pentecostal church congregations to Indian lifeways past and present is a startling and relatively recent development among the Crow and Tlingit.

A major change in northern Canada has been the discovery of vast diamond deposits in Chipewyan country and Nunavut territory, which includes the Netsilik.

For each tribe described at chapter length, except the Natchez, greater attention is placed on recent social and political changes.

Timely subjects of interest or concern among Native Americans include prehistoric cannibalism in the Southwest, anthropological involvements resulting from the discovery of Kennewick Man, individual Indian trust fund accounts managed by the Bureau of Indian Affairs, and the 2004 *Lara* case ruling by the U.S. Supreme Court about an aspect of tribal sovereignty.

Finally, Indian casinos in general are examined in greater detail.

| Acknowledgments

I am most grateful for the help of Sharlotte Neely, the coauthor for the fifth and sixth editions. Without her devotion, the fifth and later editions would not have appeared. Many thanks, Sharlotte.

My debt to Helen Louise Oswalt for copyediting the revisions for this edition is ardent and heartfelt.

Two reviewers of manuscript drafts deserve special recognition. The Western Shoshone chapter was read by Catherine S. Fowler. She kept me from making clear errors, clarified ambiguous statements, and added desirable particulars. Timothy P. McCleary provided critical and otherwise inaccessible data about the modern Crow.

Although the core of this book is based on published sources, some of the information about the recent past has been obtained in conversations with Indians and non-Indians. In brief or sometimes long and repeated discussions, their help was essential and profoundly appreciated.

PAT BARKER	JANET HOLLEY	CHRIS LUKE
LOWELL J. BEAN	FELIX IKE	DEBORAH K. MENDEZ
TINA L. BEGAY	ALISON ITZA	TERRY MORGART
DONALD BREMNER	GELFORD JIM	LARRY MYERS
THOMAS D. BURKE	MARTHA J. JOHNNIE	CINDY NUNEZ
CHERYL CARPENTER	MIRIAM JOHNSON	PATTY PERRY
TRIB CHOUDHARY	LEON D. JONES	MIKE PRICE
ARVILLA CONETAH	RENAE KEITH	GLORIA J. THOMAS
GARY FEIMAN	LEWIS KNIGHT	JERRY TSOSIE
EUGENE M. HATTORI	STANFORD KNIGHT	TOM TURPIN
ROGENE HILL	BERNICE LALO	BILL WEST
GREG HOLLEY	VICKI LEDFORD	DAVID WISEMAN

Janet M. Beatty, executive editor at Oxford University Press, has guided this book through five editions. I honor her insight, combined with her flexibility and firmness.

The following colleagues provided insightful prepublication reviews of the manuscript for this edition: Thomas S. Abler, University of Waterloo; Kirstin Erickson, University of Arkansas; Sergei Kan, Dartmouth College; and Robert Sanderson, University of Arkansas, Little Rock.

Unattributed photographs are by Wendell H. Oswalt.

1 Questions about Native Americans

*We ask only an even chance
to live as other men live.
We asked to be recognized as men.*

Chief Joseph, Nez Perce Tribe, 1877

THIS ANTHROPOLOGICAL STUDY begins by focusing on general questions about American Indians living north of Mexico. How have we been influenced by Indians? Who is a Native American? How long have their ancestors been in the New World, and where did they originate? The answers to these questions and others are the subject of this chapter. They provide essential background for the next chapter about what happened as Indians became deeply involved with non-Indians.

The use of the word *Indian* requires initial comment. The term originated with Christopher Columbus, who thought he had reached the East Indies, islands off Asia. He called the people *los Indios,* and even after the error was realized, the Spanish continued to use the word *Indios* for all New World peoples; the word became *Indian* in English. Alternatively, the words *savage, heathen,* and *barbarian* became commonplace in the 1600s to identify Indians and to emphasize their "noncivilized" and "non-Christian" status. By the late eighteenth century, the "Noble Savage" designation became an increasingly popular way to glorify and romanticize traditional Indian life, especially in art and literature.

By the early 1970s the word *Indian* was becoming politically incorrect because it was increasingly identified as a racist term. *Native American,* whose earliest usage appears to date from the 1880s, became the most popular alternative, although it can apply to anyone born in the United States. Historically the word *native* dates from ca. 1450 and initially was applied to a person born in bondage. At present, the neutral term *indigenous American* appears to be expanding in usage. In Canada, *First Nations* is the well-established designation for Eskimos and Indians. A recent survey in the United States indicates that about 50 percent of Indians sampled preferred the term "American Indian" over "Native American" as the major alternative. In this book the words *Indian* and *Native American* dominate when referring to aboriginal New World peoples. Indians often call themselves *Indians* or *Skins* in casual conversations.

| Bison and Americans

If one animal is chosen to symbolize early Native American life, it probably is the bison ("buffalo"). Bison literally meant life itself for numerous Indian tribes, and they have a great deal of romantic appeal to Americans in general. In some respects a brief overview about bison, past and present, effectively encapsulates indigenous American history.

Bison are the largest terrestrial animals in North America. Both sexes have horns, and an especially large bull may weigh more than 2,000 pounds. One subspecies, the plains bison, grazed throughout the United States except for the region adjacent to the Pacific (see Figure 1-1). A second subspecies, the wood (mountain) bison, lived in northwestern Canada. No one knows the total bison population at the arrival of Europeans, but estimates range from thirty to sixty million animals. One clear fact is the immensity of plains bison herds. At times they literally blackened the landscape for miles on end and made the ground tremble as they ran. Among many Plains Indians, bison were, or be-

Figure 1-1 | A plains bison bull. (From Catlin 1841.)

came, *the* basic food. Furthermore, they provided most of the raw material from which to make diverse artifacts ranging from tepee covers to garments. Other items made from their skins, bones, and tissue included containers, horn spoons, glue, medicines, and objects with supernatural meaning.

As food for Indians, bison provided meat, marrow, blood, and milk. Favored edibles included fetuses, humps, tongues, and meat from females. A single kill could involve hundreds or more of these impressive animals. When abundant, bison might be harvested just for their tongues and humps or as sport. Hunting methods included driving herds over cliffs to their death and into box canyons, where they could be killed with bows and arrows. A change came in the late 1700s when domestic horses were being introduced from the south and trade became a reliable source of firearms. Indians with guns and horses harvested expanding numbers of plains bison.

Kills of even greater scope and intensity began as the transcontinental railroad brought great numbers of Euro-Americans into the Plains from 1869 onward. As a result of rail shipment, bison and their products could be rapidly shipped to growing markets to the east. Between 1872 and 1874, as the bison trade boomed, some 3.5 million animals were killed by white and Indian hunters. In addition, white ranchers and settlers killed bison to make way for cattle and for farms. Federal authorities widely favored the extermination of bison as one means of destroying the basis for Plains Indian life, and in this they were successful. Major kills by whites were for sport and for meat, robes, hides, and especially tongues. Bison bones were processed into fertilizers and also were used in the manufacture of bone china.

In sum, Indians and Euro-Americans alike hunted Plains bison to wasteful excess and contributed directly to the population decline. Other factors leading to the near extinction of bison included droughts, drownings, diseases, and competition for winter grass with vast herds of horses. In addition, both Indians and non-Indians emphasized killing cows, whose hides made the best blankets for trading purposes; this act reduced the breeding population. By 1833 bison had disappeared east of the Mississippi River. By 1869 the plains bison of the heartland may have numbered 4.5 million, but by 1890 they verged on extinction.

One historical aspect of plains bison recovery began in the 1870s when a Pend d'Oreille (Kalispel) Indian, Samuel Walking Coyote, coaxed five orphaned calves from the Plains over the continental divide and into the Flathead Valley of Montana. When he had about a dozen animals, he sold them to two ranchers. Years later, they in turn sold part of the herd to the Canadian government. Another portion became the nucleus of the herd at the National Bison Range, Montana, established in 1908. (The most widely known herd is in Yellowstone National Park.)

The boreal forests of northwestern Canada were the original home of the wood bison, which is larger, darker in color, and more reclusive than the plains bison. By 1893 only about 250 of them had survived, and plains bison were brought in to help restore the bison population. Thus some portions of the modern herds are of mixed genetic background, but others are wood bison. The best known herd in Canada is at the Wood Buffalo National Park established in 1922.

The plains bison in the United States totaled about 30,000 by the early 2000s. They are concentrated in the Great Plains area on public, private, and Indian lands. Reservation Indian bison herds have great symbolic significance to the people involved and provide a local source of meat for food and for sale. Bison meat has a low fat content, which is important because the diabetes rate among Native Americans is much higher than in the general American population. Low-fat diets can aid diabetes prevention. Beef has as much as three times the amount of fat per ounce as bison meat, and bison has about a quarter of the calories. Bison meat is also promoted as contributing to the remarkable strength of the aboriginal American hunters and is thought to be related to the inherent strength of bison.

| Indians in Popular Culture

Discomfort and ambivalence characterize the widespread views of Indians among white Americans. The European roots of their perspective have been nurtured for centuries in American soil. In straightforward language, Native Americans are most commonly judged "good" and "bad," as obvious stereotypes. Stereotyping is an important facet of popular culture and reveals deep-seated American values (a value is a shared concept of what is desirable or undesirable). Negative views of Indians are especially evident in numerous American English words and phrases. Early general examples refer to Indians as *barbarians, heathens,* and *infidels.* Subsequently there arose such terms and phrases as *Indian giver, speaking with a forked tongue, squaw, wild Indian,* the racist designation *redskin,* and, finally, *lo! the poor Indian.* Notably ambivalent terms include *Noble Savage* and *good Indian.* Finally there is the positive term used in Canada, *First Nations,* and the popular label, *America's first environmentalists.* If you personally have mixed feelings about Indians, there are good historical reasons. Yet gross misrepresentations of Native Americans are both sad and real.

In a less prejudicial popular-culture context, non-Indian American understanding of Indians is affected by typically superficial presentation in schools. A prominent example is emphasizing Thanksgiving-feast foods introduced by Indians, such as cranberries, maize (corn), pumpkins, and turkey. Stereotypes of Indians were conveyed in the once-popular radio and television shows about the Lone Ranger and Tonto. Boy Scouts, Girl Scouts, and Camp Fire Girls strive to mimic Indian arts, crafts, and dances. They may learn also that birchbark canoes, moccasins, and toboggans first were items of Native American material culture.

Likewise, popular culture is evident in early American literature. No subject had greater appeal than the Indians, but their literary image has been far from uniform. The Indian entered into American literature through speeches recorded during treaty deliberations. The oratorical skills of Indians were appreciated, and the texts were printed for general circulation in the eighteenth century. Because Indians were close at hand in the eastern states and were an obstruction when whites coveted more land, they soon were viewed as foes. As the frontier expanded westward in the first half of the nineteenth century, the image of the Indian reverted to that of a nonantagonist, in fact to a romantic figure. Drawing on accounts about Indians, James Fenimore Cooper wrote his great novels and conceived the character of Leatherstocking, a white Indian without literary equal. Henry Wadsworth Longfellow's *Hiawatha* too is a literary monument of this era. The earliest play about Indians, *Metamora,* was first produced in 1829 by the actor-playwright John Augustus Stone, and it became one of the most popular plays for the remainder of the century. Included in the first American opera, *Tammany,* performed in 1794, was a Cherokee melody, and the Indian exists in such American folk songs as Charles Cadman's "From the Land of Sky Blue Waters" and "Red Wing" by Thurland Chattaway and Kerry Mills.

By the 1810s, west of the Mississippi River, Indians began to be regarded as they had been in the East by non-Indian Americans who sought land. According to these settlers, the Indian impeded progress and was a form of vermin to be exterminated. Never mind that the settlers traveled west over trails and pathways established by Indians. After Indians had been defeated in skirmishes and wars and remnant Indian populations were confined to reservations, these people again could be viewed romantically; even before the West was colonized, the Indian was a figure in nearly half of the 320 dime novels originating in the 1860s. The Indian theme never died.

Indians played an important role in shaping the belief system of one of the few large and important religions originating in the United States, the

Church of Jesus Christ of Latter-day Saints, or Mormons. *The Book of Mormon* relates that Indians originated from a Jewish population that entered the New World before Christian times. According to Mormon beliefs, Indians descended from the Lamanites; although these were thought to be a degenerate people, the Mormons have been kind in their dealings with Indians. As noted by A. Irving Hallowell (1958, 461), the inclusion of population theory in a religious dogma "could hardly have occurred anywhere but in early nineteenth-century America."

It may be asked why, from a global perspective, North American Indian cultures were comparatively less elaborate than those further south. It was not from any lack of intelligence among Indians but rather because of the nature of their environmental setting and its possibilities for development. The New World was largely devoid of animals with great potential for domestication, such as cows and pigs; nor did there exist such grains as barley and wheat. More important, in the New World the animals and plants that did have potential as domesticates were *not* concentrated in one restricted geographical area. A contrary situation existed in the Old World, in which the basis for most of Old World civilization emerged in the Near East about 8000 B.C. New World developments, however, are not to be cast aside as failures. One must recognize that in aboriginal Mexico and Peru, complex societies emerged with large populations and elaborate lifestyles; in these regions the environmental potential for indigenous cultural developments was far greater than in settings to the north.

Who Is a Native American?

In the sixteenth century, as ever-increasing numbers of European maritime explorers ventured to the Americas, there was no difficulty in establishing who was a Native American. The biological, linguistic, and cultural differences separating Africans, Europeans, and indigenous Americans were apparent to all observers. Indians spoke languages that differed widely from one tribe to another, but none could be understood by the explorers. Indians looked different, dressed in an unfamiliar manner, and wore bodily adornments that were unusual, if not bizarre, to a traveler from England, France, or Spain. Then, too, the main crops that Indians raised, maize and beans, were not cultivated in Europe. Thus the people of the New World stood in striking contrast to Europeans and their ways.

The problem of classifying a person as an American Indian became complex with the arrival of African slaves and European adventurers, fishermen, missionaries, settlers, traders, and trappers. Three conditions resulting from these contacts were important. First, outsiders mated with Indian women to produce persons of mixed genetic heritage; second, Indians sometimes captured blacks and whites and made them "Indians"; and third, some Indians lost their identity by assimilation into the intrusive society. To identify an Indian with clarity after the period of early historic contact, we must deal primarily with racial and sociocultural factors. Socially, we can imagine that foreigners who were assimilated into an Indian tribe became Indians, despite their genetic heritage. Likewise, Indians who disassociated themselves from other Indians came to be judged as non-Indian. For individuals of mixed Indian and white or black ancestry, the distinctions were clear as long as they consistently followed one lifestyle or the other. Such persons could, however, behave as Indian in one context and non-Indian in another, as Indian or non-Indian exclusively throughout their lives, or as Indian at one time in life and non-Indian at another. The identification of a Native American has become a matter of definition and is most reasonably considered in a legal sense.

Before we consider Indian identity further, one point requires clarification. Non-Indians classify Aleuts and Eskimos* as separate from Indians because of their physical appearance and cultures. In biological terms, Aleuts and Eskimos are the most Asiatic of indigenous New World peoples, having been the last to arrive from Asia, and their economic adjustments stand apart from those of other aboriginal Americans. However, the cultural differences separating some Indian tribes from each other are greater than those that separate Aleuts and Eskimos from many Indians. Thus Aleuts, Eskimos, and Indians all may reasonably be called Native Americans.

It merits note that in North America by the early seventeenth century, Native Americans commonly were called "blacks" or "negroes." Subsequently, Indians also might be termed "free people of color," in the manner of some blacks, or "mulattoes." Likewise, individuals of Native American and African ancestry could be called "negroes." In the 1980 U.S. census, a person who checked the "black" and "Indian" categories on the census form was counted as "black." Until recently the official classification of Native Americans and blacks clearly was a product of Euro-American racism.

In the history of United States Indian law, there has been no uniform definition of an Indian. In general, if a person is considered an Indian by other individuals in the community, he or she is an Indian. The degree of a person's Indian genetic heritage may be important, but under most circumstances it is secondary to sociocultural standing in the community in which she or he resides. Regardless of heredity, a person who "acts white" may not be regarded as a "real Indian" in a settlement. Examples will illustrate why there is so much confusion. If an individual is on the roll of a federally recognized Indian group, the person is Indian; the degree of Indian genetic heritage is of no consequence. On some reservations a tribal member is Indian even if records show that fifteen of sixteen immediate ancestors were not Indian. However, the real need for defining an Indian is with reference to a specific piece of legislation at a particular time. A person who is on the federal roll of a tribe and lives on a reservation clearly is an Indian; if that person moves from a reservation but

---

*Canadian Eskimos and numerous white Canadians are adamant that Eskimos be called Inuit, their name for themselves, and not Eskimo. In this book, *Eskimo* is used as the generic designation of these northern peoples because all Eskimos are *not* Inuit; many who live in Alaska and small numbers in Siberia are *Yuit,* a designation comparable to Inuit yet distinct from it. Therefore, to use the word *Inuit* for Eskimos in general is incorrect.

remains on the roll, he or she continues to be an Indian. If he or she receives a clear title to allotted reservation land, he or she may or may not subsequently remain an Indian, depending on the circumstances. Indian status also is lost by voluntary disassociation from other Indians and by identifying with some other segment of society (see also Chapter 15).

DNA testing is another relatively new aspect of enrollment procedures for new applicants among some tribes. The applicants are usually the offspring of an existing member or members. In theory an enrollment committee may ignore whether parents are legally married, claims of paternity made by unmarried or married women, and birth certificate evidence. For example, an enrolled man may claim to be the father of a child to ensure her or his enrollment whether or not he knows the paternity of the offspring. DNA tests of all existing enrolled members of a tribe has the potential of redefining who is biologically an Indian. Not only would members of some tribes be disenrolled, but present-day nonmembers could also make a case for membership. Widespread DNA testing along family lines obviously is fraught with profound sociocultural implications.

In the United States, all Native Americans did not become citizens until 1924, when the Indian Citizenship Act was passed by Congress. Previously, about 250,000 Indians had become citizens by other means; the act made citizens of about 125,000 more persons. As early as 1817 individuals were granted citizenship under treaty arrangements if they met certain provisions, such as the acceptance of title to individual lands in contrast to living on tribal lands. For many years the prevailing opinion of the federal government was that Indians who followed tribal customs and were not under the control of the state or territory in which they lived could not be citizens. Becoming a citizen was given a different basis with the passage of the Dawes Act in 1887 (see Chapter 2 for details). In 1888 a law was passed making Indian women citizens if they married citizens, the assumption being that these women were following the path of "civilization." As noncitizens, Indians were not inducted into the armed services during World War I. However, those who volunteered were made citizens by congressional action. By 1938 seven states still refused to allow Native Americans to vote, and only in 1948 were voting rights granted to Indians in Arizona and New Mexico. Opposition to Indian suffrage was based on their special relationship to the federal government.

One provision in the Canadian Indian Act of 1876 was that any Indian who had a university education or its equivalent thereby became a citizen. In other instances an individual, or the band by majority vote, initiated enfranchisement proceedings; this method required a probationary period before becoming effective. When a man with a wife and unmarried minor children became enfranchised, his family was granted the same legal status. These provisions were not generally applied to the Indians of British Columbia, Manitoba, or the Northwest Territories. For the next fifty years Canadian Indian policy fluctuated between voluntary and forced enfranchisement. Finally, as a result of the Indian Act of 1951, Canadian Indians became subject to the same general laws that applied to other Canadians. They could vote in national elections and could consume intoxicants legally for the first time. In 1985 a dramatic change was made in Canadian Indian law. One result was that Indians who had become non-Indian could once again regain their Indian identity (see Chapter 2 for details).

| Population Figures

The indigenous American population north of Mexico may have included as many as seven million individuals in the late 1400s. The total is exceedingly tenuous, if only because the earliest figures pertaining to tribal numbers usually are crude at best. Nonetheless, it is certain that the aboriginal population declined abruptly as Europeans became well entrenched. The introduction of new diseases, such as smallpox, dramatically reduced tribal membership in many regions. A combination of additional factors may have been equally or more detrimental. These include armed conflict with other Indians and with whites, forced labor, dietary changes, tribal disorganization as a result of relocation, and a disruption in family life leading to a decline in fertility (see also Chapter 2). In any event, the lowest population total, an estimated 250,000 Indians, occurred around 1900.

The current number of Native Americans in the United States is again a complex issue, as illustrated by the federal census of 2000. As in the past, the key identifier for someone filling out the census form was her or his self-determination of race. (Designation by race is, or at least has been, as American as apple pie.) However, for the first time in a decimal (ten-year) census, an individual now could list genetic heritage based on either one race or more races for a "combination" listing. Just as in earlier decimal census reports, Census Bureau decisions may be arbitrary. For example, a Cherokee woman with a white father was classified as American Indian even though she claimed a combination heritage. The reported Indian population was 110 percent greater then in 1990. One possible reason is that the birthrate for Indians is relatively high compared with the national average. Then, too, being Indian appears to have greater national acceptance since 1990 as a result of the success of Indian casinos. By 2000 an unknown number of whites listed themselves as Indians, or part Indian, based on "family tradition" without documented evidence. At least some of them were "wannabe" (want-to-be) Indians. Tangentially the definition of Indians varies from one federal agency to another, as well as from one state to another. Furthermore, an unknown number of Indians did *not* consider themselves Indian in the census self-definition. Finally, formal tribal membership is widely based on Indian blood quantum, which varies widely, or primarily based on the record of a particular tribal roll. These factors contribute to the problems with identifying Native Americans in the 2000 census. A brief summary of pertinent census data follows.

The total U.S. population was some 281.4 million, and the Native American (American Indian and Alaska Native) total was about 2.5 million, 0.9 percent of the total. Native American population percentages by geographical regions were greatest for the western states (43), the South (31), the Midwest (17), and the Northeast (9). The states with the greatest numbers of Indians were California (627,562), Oklahoma (391,949), Arizona (292,552), and Texas (215,599). Cities with the most Native Americans were New York (87,241), Los Angeles (53,092), Phoenix (35,093), and Tulsa (30,227). Tribes with the greatest Indian populations were the Cherokee Nation (Oklahoma) (228,307) and the Navajo (298,215).

In the United States during 2001, there were 562 federally recognized Native American entities ("tribes"), of which 230 were in Alaska. In that year, 468 tribes (83 percent) responded to the Bureau of Indian Affairs population and labor report. The reported total population was 1,524,025.

In the 2001 national Canadian census, the aboriginal population total was about 975,000, including Métis, persons of mixed genetic heritage. About half of the First Nations people lived on reserves (reservations). The Inuit population total in Greenland was about 48,000 in 2001.

| Where Did Native Americans Originate?

Speculations about the origins of Native Americans have had lasting romantic appeal. Humanists, the general public, and scientists alike have long puzzled over the original Indian homeland. The theories advanced to explain their derivation involve something that is lost to modern times; thus the supportive evidence can only be indirect.

It is appropriate at this point to dispose of the most fanciful theories related to Indian prehistory. Conjecture about a lost continent of Atlantis (or *Antillia*, the word on which Antilles is based) predates the discovery of the Americas. After Europeans learned about the existence of Native Americans, it seemed logical that the latter had used Atlantis as a stepping-stone from the Old to the New World. The presumed occupants of Atlantis had developed a complex civilization that was lost when the continent was destroyed by a cataclysm after the population had departed. Authors who supported this theory were struck by the presumed cultural similarities between American Indians, usually those in Mexico, and some Old World civilizations, usually that of Egypt. It was not yet known that broadly similar cultural developments such as pyramids, writing systems, and pottery had emerged among different peoples around the world independently of one another. Furthermore, there is *no* geological evidence for a lost continent in the Atlantic Ocean nor in the Pacific Ocean, which had also been postulated as a theory but now has been disproven by geologists.

Others have supposed seafaring peoples such as the Carthaginians or Phoenicians to be responsible for the original occupation. Another theory was that Indians were descendants of the Lost Tribes of Israel who were defeated by the Assyrians and wandered into Asia until they ventured to the point nearest the Americas, crossed the waters into the New World, and subsequently became the initial Indian population. Cotton Mather, in colonial New England, advanced a unique explanation for the origin of Indians. He wrote that "probably the *Devil* decoyed those miserable salvages* hither, in hopes that the gospel of the Lord Jesus Christ would never come here to destroy or disturb his absolute empire over them" (Drake 1837, 9).

The earliest tightly reasoned theory was by a Jesuit missionary, Father Joseph de Acosta, who worked in Peru. After returning to Spain, he wrote a book, *Historia natural y moral de las Indias,* which was published in 1590. Acosta reasoned that because Adam was the original ancestor of humanity and because Indians were humans, they must have come from the Old World, which Adam's descendants had peopled. He contended that the New World and Old World had been connected by a narrow strait, because certain land mammals were the same in the respective hemispheres. He felt that people and animals alike had traveled along the same route. The human entry was visualized as having taken place slowly, caused by overpopulation, famines, or the loss of former living areas. Thus Acosta was the first to advance a land-bridge theory to explain why and how people entered the New World. He also theorized that the original occupants were hunters who later developed a more complex way of life. Therefore, any comparisons between New and Old World civilizations could not be very meaningful.

Modern anthropologists support the general thesis of Indian origins first advanced by Acosta. People did not evolve in the New World but migrated there. The bones of *all* the distant human ancestors that have been found are reported in the Old World. Bones that are clear markers along humankind's evolutionary trail have been repeatedly discovered in Africa. In the same context, the earliest cultural remains in the New World appear to date about fourteen thousand years ago and were produced by people who were essentially modern in physical appearance. From the fossil record in the New World, we must currently conclude that people arrived in comparatively recent times.

The New World human fossil record became complicated in 1996, when the remains of Kennewick Man were found at Kennewick, Washington. The nearly complete skeleton is about 9200 years old and is among the earliest such remains in the Americas. An expensive, drawn-out, and complex legal battle over the skeleton pitted tribes in the region and the U.S. Department of the Interior against a group of anthropologists. The immediate issue was whether the find should be reburied by local tribes or studied in depth by anthropologists. The court cases ultimately were won by the anthropologists. Measurements were made by anthropologists as the controversy deepened. They have been compared with a broad sample of relatively recent skulls throughout most of the world. On a morphological basis, Kennewick Man was *not* a direct ancestor of any present-day tribe in the region. His closest physical similarities appear to be with the ancestors of the Ainu of Japan and Polynesian peoples.

Another line of evidence about the original peopling of the New World is mitochondrial DNA (mtDNA) studies, which can broadly plot relatively recent genetic inheritance along matrilineal lineages in a chronological manner. These studies, however, raise troublesome issues related to the number of mi-

*Middle English spelling of "savages."

grations, sample size, the calibrations of mutations, divergence rates and their possible errors, and conceivable sample contamination. Irrespective of these issues, it currently appears that the migrants originated in central Asia, moved into eastern Siberia in a single initial migration, and began entering the New World about fourteen thousand years ago. They may have lingered in Alaska, eventually followed western mountains southward into the western United States, and continued on to South America.

In recent years a competing theory has gained greater attention. It holds that one or more maritime peoples sailed from northeastern Asia to the West Coast and traveled along it to populate the Americas at various points.

The only pre-Columbian voyages currently beyond reasonable dispute are the ones made by Viking, or more properly Norse, explorers. Iceland was settled in the ninth century by Scandinavians, and within a hundred years the Icelanders had discovered Greenland. This occurred after Eric the Red, who was involved in a series of homicides, was exiled from Iceland for three years. He spent the time, A.D. 982–985, exploring southwestern Greenland, and on his return he organized a colonizing expedition. It left for southwestern Greenland in 986, and additional settlers arrived later. The Greenland colony was occupied by the Norse until about 1540 and had a maximum population of about five thousand persons. Given the turbulent weather in the north Atlantic, many ships heading toward Greenland were lost or blown off course. One vessel strayed to the coast of North America but did not land. About the year 1000, the son of Eric the Red, Leif Erikson, purposely sailed for continental North America. In the centuries to follow, a number of planned trips were made to northeastern North America from Greenland, especially to obtain building timber. The Norse appear to have settled briefly in northern Newfoundland at L'Anse aux Meadows, which was discovered and partially excavated by Helge Ingstad. Radiocarbon dates indicate that the site was occupied about A.D. 1000. The presence of a few Norse artifacts and wrought iron at the site leaves little doubt that these were Norse remains. However, no clear evidence exists to suggest that these Europeans had any influence on the cultures of aboriginal Americans.

If voyagers from the Old World, apart from the Norse, did arrive in the New World during pre-Columbian times, we might expect to find artifacts that they brought with them. Conversely, if travelers ventured in the opposite direction, we would expect to recover objects in the Eastern Hemisphere that were made in the Americas. Despite the thousands of excavations in which millions of artifacts have been recovered, not one such artifact has been found in a clearly valid context. Admittedly, these objects may exist in unexplored sites, and if any are found, our thinking will need to be revised or reversed.

If there were substantial Old and New World contacts, we would expect to find evidence in linguistic ties. Relationships between languages cannot be postulated based on a small number of words with the same form and meaning, because such parallels may be accounted for by chance alone. To demonstrate historical connections between languages, clear phonemic (sound) and grammatical (structural) similarities, as well as numerous parallels among words, must exist. Is there any evidence of this nature to link pre-Columbian peoples of the two hemispheres? The answer is a cautious "yes." The Eskimo–Aleut language family that spans the American Arctic and the Chukchi–Kamchatkan family in northeastern Siberia are possibly related. The same is true for Nadene languages in North America and Yeniseian languages in Siberia. These and other language comparisons suggest Native American linguistic ties with peoples in northern Eurasia.

Another approach to the problem centers on evidence of a different nature: domestic plants and animals transported by pre-Columbian peoples to the New World. In a symposium that he organized, Carroll L. Riley and his associates considered cultigens. A quotation from their summary remarks follows (Riley et al. 1971, 452–453): "The consensus of botanical evidence given in this symposium seems to be *that there is no hard and fast evidence for any pre-Columbian human introduction of any single plant or animal* across the ocean from the Old World to the New World, or vice-versa. This is emphatically *not* to say that it could not have occurred." Thus the case rests on a largely negative note.

| Precontact History North of Mexico: An Overview

The earliest human migrants to the New World came from Siberia, and they were hunters. These statements seem beyond reasonable doubt. By early historic times, Indians had made innumerable adaptations, depending on localized resources, contact with other Indians, and other factors. This section provides a brief synopsis of pre-Columbian cultural developments, with the emphasis on the regions north of Mexico.

PALEO-INDIANS   Controversy surrounds the question of when the earliest migrants first entered the Americas. It is widely accepted that in the vicinity of the Bering Strait a land bridge, called Beringia, existed from about 20,000 to 11,600 years ago, and it was during this time span that the earliest humans probably entered northern North America. During this and earlier cold periods, glacial ice covered large areas of the Northern Hemisphere, and worldwide sea levels were lowered by as much as 300 feet. In eastern Siberia and western Alaska, there were no major glaciers, because conditions were unfavorable for their formation: the amount of annual precipitation was low, and the land was relatively flat. When the land bridge loosely connected the continents, it served as a pathway and a cultural filter. Hunters who lived by killing large herbivores, such as bison, caribou, mammoth, and horses, were possibly among the earliest migrants.

A critical year in the discovery of evidence about prehistoric humans in the Americas was 1926. It was then that J. D. Figgins, a paleontologist excavating a site in northern New Mexico, uncovered the bones of an extinct bison that was much larger than modern bison. The site had been located in 1908 by George McJunkin, an African American cowboy who was the foreman at the ranch on which the discovery was made; unfortunately, McJunkin died before the site was investigated. Ultimately, Figgins found four flint points near bison bones, and a fifth point was embedded *in* bone. This evidence has never been seriously challenged. The projectile points were named Folsom, after the discovery site, and date around 10,500 years ago.

Excavations at the Folsom site demonstrated that Native Americans had considerable antiquity in the New World. The next question was and remains: When did people begin to occupy the New World? Unfortunately, we do not know. Archaeologists are rather confident that the sporadic claims that some sites were occupied 30,000 years ago or in the even more distant past are incorrect. Pre-Folsom artifacts made from flaked stone occasionally have been found in the far north, but relatively far from Beringia. Artifacts from the Bluefish Caves in the Yukon Territory, Canada, date around 15,000 years ago, although this date has been questioned by some researchers. Much farther south, especially in Arizona, distinctive projectile points, termed Clovis, repeatedly have been excavated in association with mammoth bones and are now dated around 11,000 years ago. Finally, there is the Monte Verde site in southern Chile. The occupants hunted small game and collected plant products; they lived there at least 12,500 years ago.

Considering the location and earliest date for the Monte Verde site, if the ancestors of these Native Americans traveled by land from Siberia and Alaska, they probably arrived in the Americas much earlier than 12,500 years ago in order to reach southern South America by this time. One reasonable explanation might be that there are older and yet-to-be-discovered inland sites. Another, more speculative, possibility is that at least some early migrants traveled by water, not by land. In this context, it is widely accepted that the initial human occupation of Australia was by watercraft at least 60,000 years ago. Could it be that watercraft existed long ago along the eastern fringe of Siberia? The possibility exists. If so, early migrants may have boated along the Siberian coast, island-hopped along the north Pacific area of Alaska, and continued southward in the Americas.

THE ARCHAIC TRADITION   As the West and the Southwest became drier, hunting diminished in importance. By about 6000 B.C. a way of life adapted to the western deserts had developed, one that has been termed the Desert culture. The primary foods were wild plant products and small game. As small groups of people moved about to exploit varied resources, they occupied open sites or camped in caves and rock shelters on an opportunistic basis. Grinding stones became key technological forms in processing seeds, nuts, and other plant or animal products to render them edible. Small animals were stunned with missile sticks or captured in fencelike nets, and spears harvested large game, such as antelope or bison. Basketry became important for winnowing wild seeds, for cooking foods, and for storage. This eminently successful lifeway, the Archaic tradition, persisted in many parts of the West until after the arrival of Europeans. The Western Shoshone (Chapter 6) and Cahuilla (Chapter 8) represent this lifestyle as it continued into historic times. In the north-western Plains, Archaic tradition bison hunters persisted into historic times, but their lives changed dramatically beginning about A.D. 1730, when domestic horses, of colonial Spanish origin, were introduced from the south. The Crow (Chapter 7) represent one such people.

Along the northwest coast from the Gulf of Alaska to northern California, prehistoric maritime cultures emerged, probably from an Archaic base. By 1000 B.C. people hunted sea mammals and fished for salmon with expanding intensity. Woodworking tools were well established by about A.D. 200, suggesting the manufacture of plank houses and large dugout canoes. These developments provided the general background for the emergence of historic Northwest Coast Indian cultures such as the Tlingit (Chapter 9).

In the eastern United States and Canada, along rivers and coastal areas, Indians lived as hunters and gatherers from about 8000 to 1000 B.C. These Archaic economies varied widely because of differences in local resources. In some areas, shellfish, fish, or large game were the dominant foods, whereas in many others, wild plants predominated. The oldest sites had relatively brief spans of occupation, but by about 3000 B.C. some settlements, especially those along major rivers with abundant food resources, had been occupied for generations. These people are noted especially for their ground and polished stone woodworking tools, such as adzes, axes, and gouges. The technology of these people was far more diversified than that reported among Paleo-Indians.

THE NORTHERN HUNTERS The distant descendants of some pioneer hunters in the north remained hunters or became hunters and fishers. Early evidence about them is associated with inland areas and dates from as long ago as 13,500 years. Some reasonably early finds recall Archaic tradition artifact types. Other tools are similar to finds in Siberia and thus support an archaeological link with northeastern Asia. It is thought that the Nadene Indians, the northern hunters who were the ancestors of modern Athapaskan Indians, were living in interior Alaska and northwestern Canada by at least 5000 B.C. These distinctly inland people hunted caribou or moose, depending on the locality, and fished; for most of them, their fishing activities increased during times of food stress. The Chipewyan Indians (Chapter 4) are a historic example of Athapaskans who were hunters and fishers, and the Lower Kootenai (Chapter 5) employ that strategy much farther south. The Navajo (Chapter 11) were northern hunters before they entered the western United States, where they became part-time farmers in prehistoric times and herders during the historic era.

The oldest known maritime economy in the New World appears to have emerged along the northern and western Pacific coast of Alaska about 6000 years ago. Their probable descendants moved north in the Bering Strait area of Alaska some 3000 years ago and became Eskimos, who filtered eastward into Greenland. About A.D. 1000 other Alaskan Eskimos, identified with Thule culture, soon occupied the northern fringe of North America from Alaska to Greenland. The Netsilik (Chapter 3) are their direct descendants.

THE FARMERS   Among Indians in many areas, the most radical prehistoric economic change occurred when hunting and gathering were replaced by a primary dependence on domestic plant products. Maize was domesticated in Mesoamerica about 4000 B.C.; the common bean may have been domesticated at about the same time in Peru, where squash could have been a cultigen somewhat earlier. By about 1000 B.C., the cultivation of maize had spread from the south into the American Southwest; later, beans and squash were planted there as the primary crops raised north of Mexico. Some western Indians developed more productive hybrid strains of maize that enabled them to become increasingly sedentary. In the Southwest this led to the Hohokam cultural tradition in the deserts of Arizona and the Mogollon tradition best associated with highland areas of Arizona and New Mexico. The Anasazi tradition represents the ancestors of modern Pueblo Indians such as the Hopi (Chapter 10) and arose primarily from various groups of gatherers identified with the Basketmaker culture. The Pueblo Indian cultures that emerged between A.D. 700 and 1400 are most often associated with pueblo-type dwellings, separate ceremonial chambers or *kivas,* and elaborate pottery.

In recent years a major archaeological controversy in the United States has centered on possible evidence for cannibalism in the Southwest culture area. Compelling evidence occurs in an Anasazi (Pueblo) site along Cowboy Wash in southwestern Colorado. It seems to have been abruptly abandoned around A.D. 1150. Disarticulated human bones were found on the living floors of pithouses in which typical household artifacts were found intact, suggesting sudden death of their owners. Human blood residues were attached to two butchering tools, and myoglobin (a protein molecule) of human origin had adhered to potsherds. In addition, an unburned human coprolite (fossil excrement) was found that apparently had been deposited in a fireplace after the last fire was built there. This excrement included human myoglobin. The combination of this evidence strongly indicates cannibalism.

In the eastern United States, some Archaic peoples became gardeners, and by 2000 B.C. they were raising sunflowers for food, as well as a variety of squash, maygrass, and sumpweed. By A.D. 100, maize was cultivated, but beans did not become evident until about A.D. 1000. The Woodland tradition began to coalesce about 1000 B.C., with its burial mounds and distinctive pottery. The Adena people, concentrated in the Ohio River drainage area, became prominent mound builders who flourished until about A.D. 100. They traded widely for raw materials and probably were well organized, possibly with chiefs as leaders of political and religious life.

In the same general area, the successors to the Adena people represented the Hopewell tradition that flourished from about 200 B.C. to A.D. 500. They were probably farmers living in relatively permanent communities, and they are famous for their elaborate earthworks. They were organized into distinctive social classes and accorded prominent attention to certain of the dead. We do not know why the Adena and Hopewell traditions declined rather abruptly at their centers, although disease may have been a contributing factor. Hopewell branches persisted in the Northeast, and one group probably provided the background for Iroquois Indian culture (Chapter 12).

Prehistoric Indian culture in the United States reached its greatest complexity in the Mississippian tradition, found in parts of the Midwest and Southeast from about A.D. 900 to 1500; their economy was based on the cultivation of maize, beans, and squash. The Mississippians probably were organized into complex social and political units, each with a clear sense of national identity. Social ranks existed, with priests and other elites topping the hierarchy. Their ceremonial centers must have required years to plan and construct, with the labor of many people required to build their elaborate terraced temple mounds, as well as the house mounds of the elite. The Natchez Indians (Chapter 14) represent a remnant population within the Mississippian tradition. It had spread widely in the Southeast, and a more peripheral manifestation led to the emergence of the Cherokee (Chapter 13).

SUMMARY This brief review of the prehistory of Native Americans north of Mexico should demonstrate that the original American Indian culture developed from that of Asian migrants who were hunters. Farming emerged much later and was based primarily on crops domesticated in Mexico and Peru. The diversity of American Indian life observed by early Europeans represented adjustments to different ecological and social settings as these groups occupied the continent. Eventually, hundreds of distinct Indian cultures appeared. Thus no fanciful lost continents, lost tribes, or large-scale shipborne migrations in prehistoric times are required to explain the presence and diversity of Indians in the New World.

| How Have Native American Cultures Been Studied?

No matter where Europeans settled in North America, it soon became apparent that Indians were well entrenched and quite different culturally. Some Native Americans were primarily fishers, whereas others farmed and still others hunted or gathered. They spoke many different languages and organized themselves in diverse ways, ranging from small, mobile family groups to large, stable nations or confederations. To better understand this variability and how it has been described, it is helpful to introduce a number of concepts.

Any reasonably systematic account of the lives of a people is called an *ethnography*. Their artifacts, language, social and political organization, art, knowledge, and myths are each an ethnographic dimension. An ethnography is overwhelmingly descriptive and pertains to a brief period of time. In more exact terms, an ethnography is a descriptive framework for behavioral information about a population at a particular point in time. Ethnographic data are collected as systematically as possible and are checked for internal consistency; for these reasons, most accounts by explorers, travelers, or journalists do not qualify. There are two general categories of ethnographies: baseline studies made about life at the time of historic contact and others made for later points in time. A *baseline ethnography* describes a people before they had any significant contact with representatives of Western societies. Thus the data represent conditions *before* the people studied were influenced or disrupted by Europeans, Euro-Americans, or the members of other clearly foreign groups. In a strict sense, a baseline ethnography should be compiled before European trade goods or diseases of European origins prevail. Yet capable observers seldom were present to record a broad range of information about a Native American population in a systematic manner before their customs were altered by agents of Western culture. The first comprehensive ethnography of an Indian tribe, or of any aboriginal people for that matter, that made a significant impact on anthropology appeared in 1851. The author was Lewis Henry Morgan, and his study was of the Iroquois Indians in the state of New York. Thus ethnography as a distinct intellectual pursuit is comparatively recent in origin. When narrow or broad generalizations are drawn from ethnographies, the study is termed *ethnology,* which is the comparative analysis of ethnographic data.

Trained investigators did not begin making thorough studies of American Indians until around 1900. Usually they attempted to collect verbal information about Native American life at the time of historic contact, or at least for a period as far back in time as an informant could recall. An ethnographer talked with Indians about the past, observed current customs, and consulted written sources. By using these data he or she assembled a *reconstructed baseline ethnography.* The primary difficulty in such an enterprise was obtaining reliable information about the early historic period. Most ethnographies written by anthropologists about American Indians are reconstructions made long after the first historic contacts of the groups studied. A major problem was to validate informants' statements, especially when documentary sources had not been studied thoroughly, a typical failing of early ethnographers. The time factor often could not be held constant for the early historic period, and as a result many descriptions were actually composites of customs at various times. Traditional ethnographies began changing character by the early 1930s, but it was not until much later that most anthropologists realized what had happened. The long-term ideal of reconstructing aboriginal baseline accounts rarely could be realized after about 1940.

As the lives of Native Americans changed following prolonged firsthand contact with exotic complex societies, the Indians were said to be undergoing the process of acculturation; the end product was either stabilized pluralism or assimilation into the dominant society. Thus we may consider *acculturative ethnographies* as a type of ethnography. They present a description of life relating to a brief span of historic time, usually based on documents, observations, and interviews. Margaret Mead (1932) was the first person to focus a field study on contemporary Indian life. She worked among the Omaha Indians in 1930. This was a watershed in North American Indian studies and anticipated hundreds of broadly similar accounts about Indian acculturation. Over the years, as ethnographers became more methodologically sophisticated, the emphasis shifted further. Problem-focused studies began to dominate, with one or more aspects of Indian life identified for detailed attention.

Clearly, the data base of old has disappeared, and the study of urban Indians or certain aspects of modern reservation life, such as health or land tenure, has been one response. Other aspects of modern studies are presented in Chapter 2. Noteworthy here, however, is another approach, called *ethnohistory*. Favored by persons more interested in traditional Indian life, this is the study of pertinent historical documents, often with accompanying field studies for additional information, to plot changes in a people's lifeway. The study of historical records long has been the purview of historians, and some of them, such as William T. Hagan, Roy H. Pearce, Lewis O. Saum, and Wilcomb E. Washburn, have a keen understanding of the Indian in American history. For American anthropologists concentrating on Indians north of Mexico, an appreciation of historical developments has been comparatively recent. One of the earliest studies was that carried out in 1928–1930 by Felix M. Keesing (1939) concerning the Menominee of Wisconsin. The next major work was by Oscar Lewis (1942) and dealt with Blackfoot culture change. Thus ethnohistory as an anthropological focus is a comparatively new development; *Ethnohistory,* a journal devoted to the subject, originated in 1954.

Ethnohistory has emerged as a significant focus among anthropologists. In addition to archival and library research, field studies often are recognized as valuable; some Native Americans clearly remember many customs and historical events that had never found their way into written records. The study of historical records has led to major revisions in our understanding about some tribes early in their history. It probably is true that every tribal ethnography for aboriginal or early historic times could be more accurate after a careful study of existing archival and published records. Thus superior accounts for many tribes are yet to be written.

Thus far the units for study have not been defined precisely, but their clear identification is desirable. Different groups of Indians usually are termed tribes, yet no one set of criteria for a tribe accommodates all North American Indians. The difficulties in deriving a concept that encompasses the diversity of social norms and cultural forms may be illustrated by a rather typical definition. Alfred L. Kroeber (1925, 474) stated that a true tribe "has a name, a dialect, and a territory." Yet among the nearly fifty major Indian groups in California, only the Yokuts of the San Joaquin Valley had all three characteristics. Most California Indians did not have a distinct tribal name; they identified themselves only as members of a particular community. Efforts to define a tribe on the basis of political cohesiveness are equally unrewarding. As John R. Swanton (1953, 1–2) pointed out, the variability seems to defy the use of a single label. The Creek confederation comprised dominant and subordinate tribes; the name Powhatan embraced about thirty tribes or subtribes united by conquest; the name Ojibwa (Chippewa) included small groups of people who had little if any sense of political unity; each Pueblo village governed its own affairs and was in a sense a small tribe.

Kroeber (1955, 303) attempted to bring some order to the terminological maze. He wrote, "What are generally denominated tribes really are small nationalities, possessing essentially uniform speech and customs and therefore an accompanying sense of likeness and likemindedness, which in turn tended to prevent serious dissensions or internal conflicts." Within such nationalities were smaller sovereign states, usually termed bands or villages, that were economically self-sufficient and had a recognized territory and political independence. Kroeber reasoned that a tribe was rather like a German state before the consolidation in 1871: each state functioned independently although they shared a common language, culture, and ideology. In the United States these Indian units were more properly regarded as nations in the seventeenth and eighteenth centuries. Actually, the concept of a tribe or nation most often was a product of white contact; government officials grouped tribes, bands, or villages so they could more conveniently negotiate treaties, arrange resettlements, and so on. Aboriginal decision making most often was at the band or village level, although some peoples were consolidated into larger political aggregates. In the subsequent chapters, the difficulties in defining a tribe are not overwhelmingly important, but the reader should be aware that the label *tribe* does not always mean the same thing when applied to different peoples. Those interested in pursuing the topic further are referred to a volume on the subject edited by June Helm (1968).

Over the years, for administrative purposes in the United States, Indian groups have acquired numerous labels. In 1993 the federal government identified 543 recognized "Indian entities." Those in the contiguous states numbered 315, most of whom were identified as tribes or bands. Alternative names included colonies, communities, nations, rancherias, reservations, and tribal towns. In Alaska 228 entities most often were designated as villages. In each instance these administrative units have the same legal status vis-à-vis the federal government.

Another aspect of studying Native Americans that has led to confusion because of its overall inconsistency is any attempt to view the time of historic contact collectively. Historic contact with Indians differed widely in time from one region to another. Many tribes in the eastern United States had been destroyed by disease and homicide or displaced from their lands before others to the north and west ever heard of white people or knew of the diseases that they carried. Historic contact began about A.D. 1000 in northern Newfoundland, whereas in the Southwest it was 1540, and it was 1885 in one sector of central Alaska. Thus no single decade or century represents the contact period. This means that there is a *sliding historical baseline* (chronological skewing) for the beginnings of Indian history on a regional basis. Swanton (1953, 3–6) has suggested that if A.D. 1650 is taken as a base date, it is possible to establish many indigenous Indian boundaries for the southern and eastern United States, as well as for eastern Canada. In the northwestern sector of the continent, no major relocations of peoples appear to have occurred between 1650 and the time of their actual historic contact, making it possible to tentatively include them under this date as well. For the balance of the continent north of Mexico, the date of 1650 is less satisfactory. An adjustment backward in time to around A.D. 1540 might be more accurate to accommodate the peoples of the Southwest. The Plains area would require several dates over a considerable time span. The most important conclusion is that the boundaries and positioning of many tribes on standard ethnographic maps, including those in this volume, are not entirely accurate for any single time period. Instead, they attempt to represent the area of any particular tribe at the moment in history when it was surveyed and located on a map.

The maps at the beginning and end of this book identify the general areas occupied by tribes after taking into consideration a sliding historical baseline. These maps are based largely on the monumental language classification by Ives Goddard (1996) that appears in volume 17 of the *Handbook of North American Indians*. The tribal names and distributions reported in other volumes in this series published by 2001 also were consulted. These maps do not include all of the smallest tribes nor the tribes about which little is known.

| What Do We Know of Native American Languages?

Seven million Native Americans may have lived north of Mexico at the time of Columbus, and they spoke about four hundred languages. In some sectors, such as among Eskimos (Inuit) along the Arctic rim, the same language was spoken over a wide area. In other regions, as in northwestern Canada, people spoke different but closely related languages. Elsewhere, highly distinct languages might exist in a limited area. In California, for example, far greater linguistic diversity existed than is found in all of modern Europe.

European settlers could ignore Indian customs if they wished because they lived in separate communities, but they could not ignore Indian languages if they hoped to communicate with them. Because typical colonists felt superior to Native Americans, they seldom attempted to learn an Indian language; most often Indians or persons of mixed heritage became bilingual. Yet, for Christian missionaries intent on converting Indians, it was essential to learn the languages of peoples among whom they worked. The first landmark in American Indian linguistics was the publication in 1663 of a Bible translated into Massachuset, an Algonquian language, by the missionary John Eliot; in 1666 he published an Algonquian grammar.

The first prominent student of Indian linguistics was Thomas Jefferson. He was concerned that Native American languages were disappearing rapidly, and before he became president in 1801 he had collected considerable linguistic information. Jefferson (1801, 149) reasoned that preserving linguistic data from Indians in the Americas would make it possible to trace the relationships among these peoples. Subsequent linguistic studies by Peter S. Du Ponceau and Albert Gallatin enabled John Wesley Powell to publish a definitive classification of Native American linguistic families in 1891. Powell's classification was revised by C. F. Voegelin and F. M. Voegelin (1966) and more recently by Goddard (1996, 4). The major language families are those identified by Goddard, and they appear in simplified form as Figure 1-2.

Figure 1-2 | The dominant Native American linguistic groups north of Mexico at the time of early regional contacts with Europeans. Hokan and Penutian represent superfamilies; they include nine and eleven language families, respectively. These superfamilies and the major families are presented in capital letters. Lan-

ESKIMO-ALEUT

Hudson
Bay

ALGIC   ALGIC

Beothuk

Atlantic
Ocean

SIOUAN-CATAWBA

IROQUOIAN

ALGIC

C

CADDOAN

A

KIOWA-
TANOAN

Yuchi

S-C

S-C

Tunica   S-C

S-C

N   CADDOAN

IROQUOIAN

U-A   MUSKOGEAN

TIMUCUAN

Tonkawa xx

xx

N

S-C   xx

Solano

Adai   Natchez

ATAKAPAN   xx

Aranama   Chitimacha

Coahuilteco   Calusa

Cotoname

COMECRUDAN

Major family abbreviations:
ALGIC (A)
CADDOAN (C)
ESKIMO-Aleut (A-E)
IROQUOIAN (I)
KIOWA-TANOAN (K-T)
NADENE (N)
SALISHAN (S)
SIOUAN- CATAWBA (S-C)
UTO-AZTECAN (U-A)
UNOCCUPIED (x)
UNCLASSIFIED (xx)

guages in upper- and lowercase type generally refer to families represented by a
single language. "x" indicates an unoccupied or poorly known area. (Adapted
from Goddard, 1996; Courtesy of the *Handbook of North American Indians*,
Vol. 17, Smithsonian Institution, Washington, DC.)

By 1995 about forty-five of the nearly four hundred Native American languages north of Mexico in early historic times continued to be spoken by adults and learned by significant numbers of children. These included Chipewyan, Cherokee, Navajo, and Eskimo (Inuit and Yupik). Some ninety other languages were spoken by adults but few or no children, for example, Crow, Kootenai, Tlingit, and Iroquoian languages (Cayuga, Mohawk, Oneida, Onondaga, and Seneca). About seventy languages were spoken only by small numbers of older people; examples include Cahuilla, Yurok, and Tuscarora, an Iroquoian language.

For many tribes a rapid decline in the number of aboriginal language speakers is a pressing concern. A typical response is to launch an indigenous language program in the primary grades. These efforts have been successful only with adequate funding and devoted staff in immersion schools. Another program involves pairing an indigenous language speaker with a younger member of the tribe who does not speak the language. This method was set forth in 1992 by the Advocates for Indigenous California Language Survival. The program is an intense and demanding master–apprentice relationship involving as many as twenty hours each week. It appears to be promising. By 1999, sixteen California tribes had from one to fifteen master–apprentice teams to help ensure language continuity.

Radio broadcasts in tribal languages are increasingly common and provide another context for learning. News items about Native Americans have been broadcast since the early days of commercial radio in the 1920s, but regularly scheduled programs for Indians did not begin until the 1960s. Native-owned radio stations and noncommercial public and tribal stations began to appear in 1971. By 1998 in the United States there were thirty tribal radio stations, including eight in Alaska. Canada has about two hundred stations dominated by First Nations peoples. In Canada and the United States, many Indian-dominated stations air native-language programs. They increasingly broadcast programs that emphasize cultural revitalization. Another systematic approach to learning indigenous American languages originated in 1993. The company Audio-Forum in Guilford, Connecticut, released its first audiocassettes for Navajo language instruction. Since then they have prepared learning tapes for diverse languages, for example, Apache, Cherokee, and Mohawk.

The only nationwide Indian–related talk show in the United States is *Native America Calling,* which originates at the University of New Mexico. It is carried by about thirty-five tribal radio stations and a lesser number of public radio stations. Topics include political issues, diabetes, language preservation, and gambling. The programs attract hundreds of thousands of Indian and non-Indian listeners.

| Grouping Tribes

The relationships among tribal languages provide valuable insight into their linguistic evolution, yet tribes belonging to a single language family sometimes have contrasting lifeways. As a result researchers found it desirable to group tribes based primarily on nonlinguistic factors. Their goal was to classify some four hundred tribes into a small number of meaningful units. By 1896 Otis T. Mason had advanced a means for grouping all tribes by culture area based on environmental and cultural characteristics. A *culture area* is a gegraphical sector of the world whose aboriginal occupants exhibited greater similarities with each other than with the peoples in other such areas. Ideally, culture areas are established from baseline accounts of each tribe within an area, considered on a sliding historical scale. The culture area concept was applied systematically to North American Indians by Clark Wissler (1938, 1942). We find, however, that one culture area may include peoples with different ways of life and that tribes along the boundaries may share the characteristics of two or more areas.

It is reasonable to assume that tribal names and their specific boundaries are well established. This is often, but not universally, the case, for multiple reasons. As European explorers or others entered a new area, they might learn the name of a particular tribe from the members of an adjacent tribe, and this name could be different from the target tribe's name for themselves. Likewise, the name of a target tribe might be mistranslated into a European language. Furthermore, a population initially identified as a tribe might prove to be a subtribe or band. Conversely, two tribes could later be combined on the basis of more complete information or, at times, for administrative convenience. In relatively recent years, some tribes have insisted on their original self-identification as their official name when it differs from their standard ethnographic name.

Tribal geographic boundaries may pose greater problems. The normal dynamics of tribal expansion and contraction meant that boundaries could have been unstable when non-Indians first appeared. And the indirect impact of European presence in a region could rapidly change aboriginal boundaries. For instance, prior to direct European contacts, the mortality rate from exotic diseases led to the contraction of some tribes, to the expansion of others, and to tribal extinctions. Likewise, early explorers typically had more on their minds than the distribution of tribes. Queries about boundaries could result in confusion from an inadequate understanding of an Indian language or from inaccurate translations by interpreters. Later, with systematic inquiries, aboriginal boundaries might be revised. Another widespread difficulty is that early non-Indians did not establish boundaries for many tribes. As a result, their aboriginal land holdings are uncertain and based on comparatively recent information. Additional cautionary observations are required. Although tribal boundaries for culture area maps are precisely drawn, they are not fully reliable for other reasons. The area between two tribes can be a contested "shatter zone," sometimes occupied by neither claimant. Finally, ethnographers may have honest but unresolved disagreements about some boundaries.

For aboriginal Native Americans living north of Mexico, ten culture areas are identified. The major sociocultural characteristics for each area are listed in Table 1-1. Their geographical locations are shown in Figure 1-3.

TABLE 1-1. Summary of characteristics of the ten culture areas

Culture Area	Examples of Tribes	Languages	Subsistence	Descent
Arctic	Aleut Eskimos 　Caribou 　Copper 　Mackenzie 　Netsilik 　Pacific	Eskimo-Aleut	sea mammals caribou fish	bilateral
Subarctic	Beaver Chipewyan Dogrib Eastern Cree Han Hare Ingalik Naskapi	Nadene in west Algonquian in east	caribou moose fish	matrilineal in west patrilineal in east bilateral in both
California	Achumawi Cahuilla Chumash Gabrielino Yana Yokuts	highly varied	acorns mesquite beans game marine resources	bilateral
Great Basin	Bannock Northern Paiute Ute, Washo Western Shoshone	Uto-Aztecan	pine nuts rabbits antelope	bilateral
Plateau	Coeur d'Alene Flathead Kootenai Spokane	Salishan	salmon game roots	bilateral
Plains	Arapaho Blackfoot Comanche Crow Osage, Santee	Siouan-Catawba	bison in west maize in east	bilateral patrilineal matrilineal
Northwest Coast	Bella Bella Haida Kwakiutl Nootka Tlingit Tsimshian	Nadene in north Salishan in middle varied in south	salmon land mammals sea mammals	matrilineal in north patrilineal in south
Northeast	Abenaki Algonquin Delaware Fox Huron Iroquois Micmac Winnebago	Algic Iroquoian	maize, beans, 　squash game fish	matrilineal patrilineal

Political Organization	Religion	Housing	Manufactures & Other
charismatic leaders bands	shamans good & evil spirits ceremonies in west	wood, stone, sod in east & west snowhouse in central area	tailored clothing elaborate harpoons umiaks, kayaks, dogsleds sinew-backed bows feuds over women infanticide
charismatic leaders bands	shamans Nakani in west shaking tent divination in east	double lean-to & rectangular log-frame in west conical tent in east	semitailored clothing toboggans, snowshoes bark canoes deadfalls & snares birch-bark baskets cannibalism during famines spruce-root baskets in west hunting dogs in east
bands	shamans diverse supernaturals elaborate female puberty ceremonies	impermanent brush, bark, grass	developed basketry seed-grinding stones sinew-backed bows
bands	shamans elaborate female puberty ceremonies	impermanent brush, bark, grass	basketry seed-grinding stones sinew-backed bows nets for land mammals
villages	shamans diverse spirits	semisubterranean winter reed- or mat- covered summer	basketry important bark fiber clothing
bands band alliances military societies raiding important	vision quest guardian spirits emerging ceremonialism	skin tepee	developed bone & skin working dog-drawn travois game surrounds hide shields
villages	potlatch elaborate ceremonial round complex masks	rectangular, plank multifamily	elaborate woodworking dugout canoes social classes, slaves
tribes confederations	developed ceremonial round harvest stress secret societies dogs eaten ceremonially	dome-shaped wigwam longhouse multifamily palisades	hide clothing bark canoes

(*Continued*)

TABLE 1-1. (*Continued*)

Culture Area	Examples of Tribes	Languages	Subsistence	Descent
Southwest	Acoma Apache Hopi Laguna Mohave Navajo Zuni	Nadene Uto-Aztecan	maize, beans, squash game	matrilineal bilateral
Southeast	Cherokee Chickasaw Choctaw Creek Natchez	varied	maize, beans game fish	matrilineal

Figure 1-3 | Native American culture areas north of Mexico.

Political Organization	Religion	Housing	Manufactures & Other
villages	elaborate ceremonial round kiva masked dancers	pueblo-type	developed pottery & basketry cotton garments domestic turkeys irrigated farmland
tribes confederations warfare important	complex ceremonies sun worship priests	rectangular multifamily fortified	feathers over netting for clothing houselike storage facilities "black drink" emetic

| Additional Sources

The best bibliographic sources by tribe are the fourth edition of the *Ethnographic Bibliography of North America* by George Peter Murdock and Timothy J. O'Leary (1975) and its 1990 supplement, by M. Marlene Martin and Timothy J. O'Leary. The best widely available anthropological and historical source about Native Americans is the new multivolume *Handbook of North American Indians* (Washington, DC) under the general editorship of William C. Sturtevant. The first of the proposed twenty volumes appeared in 1978. Brian M. Fagan's (1995) *Ancient North America* is an excellent source for North American prehistory. Evidence for cannibalism in a Pueblo Indian site is detailed by Richard A. Marlar et al. (2000). Jack Weatherford (1988) chronicles Indian contributions to the world.

The book *Ancient Encounters* by James C. Chatters (New York, 2001) places Kennewick Man in context. Articles in the journal *Evolutionary Anthropology* (2003, vol. 12, no. 1) examine the initial peopling of the New World at length. A standard source about bison is by Jerry N. McDonald (1981). Charles L. Cutler (1994) provides a wonderful review of Native American loanwords in modern English. Michael Yellow Bird (1999) examines the alternative names for Indians. Alfred W. Crosby, Jr. (1972) describes the impact of Old World diseases, animals, and plants on American Indian life. The book by Jack D. Forbes (1988) is the key source about black Americans and their Indian relationships. Russell Thornton (2000) presents a recent overview about population history. A key and essential source about languages was edited by Ives Goddard (1996) as volume 17 of the *Handbook of North American Indians*.

| Selected Bibliography

Barth, Fredrik, ed. 1969. *Ethnic groups and boundaries: The social organization of cultural difference.* Boston.

Catlin, George. 1841. *Letters and notes on the manner, customs and conditions of the North American Indians, written during eight years' travel among the wildest tribes of Indians in North America.* New York.

Crosby, Alfred W., Jr. 1972. *The Columbian exchange*. Westport, CT.

Cutler, Charles L. 1994. *O brave new words!* Norman, OK.

Denevan, William M., ed. 1992. *The native population of the Americas in 1492*. Madison, WI.

Drake, Samuel G. 1837. *Biography and history of the Indians of North America*. Boston.

Driver, Harold E. 1939. *Culture element distributions: VII. The reliability of culture element data*. Anthropological Records, vol. 1, 205–19.

Driver, Harold E., and William C. Massey. 1957. *Comparative studies of North American Indians*. Transactions of the American Philosophical Society, n.s. 47, pt. 2.

Fagan, Brian M. 1995. *Ancient North America*. New York.

Forbes, Jack D. 1988. *Black Africans and Native Americans*. Oxford, England.

Fritz, Gayle J. 1994. Are the first American farmers getting younger? *Current Anthropology* 35:305–09.

Goddard, Ives, ed. 1996. Languages. Vol. 17, *Handbook of North American Indians*. Washington, DC.

Hagan, William T. 1961. *American Indians*. Chicago.

Hallowell, A. Irving. 1957. The impact of the American Indian on American culture. *American Anthropologist* n.s. 59:201–17.

———. 1958. *The backwash of the frontier: The impact of the Indian on American culture*. Annual Report of the Smithsonian Institution, 1957–58, 447–72.

———. 1963. American Indians, white and black: The phenomenon of transculturalization. *Current Anthropology* 4:519–31.

Haven, Samuel F. 1856. *Archaeology of the United States*. Smithsonian Contributions to Knowledge, vol. 8, 1–159.

Helm, June, ed. 1968. *Essays on the problem of tribe*. Seattle.

Holmes, William H. 1893. The World's Fair Congress of Anthropology. *American Anthropologist* 6:423–34.

Jefferson, Thomas. 1801. *Notes on the state of Virginia*. New York.

Keesing, Felix M. 1939. *The Menomini Indians of Wisconsin*. Memoirs of the American Philosophical Society, vol. 10.

Kinkade, M. Dale. 1991. The decline of native languages in Canada. In *Endangered languages,* R. H. Robins and E. M. Uhlenbeck, eds., 157–76. New York.

Kroeber, Alfred L. 1925. *Handbook of the Indians of California*. Bureau of American Ethnology Bulletin 78.

———. 1955. Nature of the land-holding group. *Ethnohistory* 2:303–14.

Lewis, Oscar. 1942. *Effects of white contact upon Blackfoot culture*. Locust Valley, NY.

Marlar, Richard A., et al. 2000. Biochemical evidence of cannibalism at a prehistoric Puebloan site in southwestern Colorado. *Nature* 407 (7 Sept.):74–78.

McDonald, Jerry N. 1981. *North American bison: Their classification and evolution*. Berkeley.

Mead, Margaret. 1932. *The changing culture of an Indian tribe*. New York.

Morgan, Lewis Henry. 1851. *League of the Ho-De-No-Sau-Nee or Iroquois*. 2 vols. New York. (Editions published in 1901 and 1904 were edited and footnoted by

Herbert M. Lloyd and were reproduced in 1954 by the Human Relations Area Files.)

Murdock, George Peter, and Timothy J. O'Leary. 1975. *Ethnographic bibliography of North America.* 4th ed. (Supplement, 1973–1987 by M. Marlene Martin and Timothy J. O'Leary. 1990). New Haven.

Pearce, Roy H. 1965. *The savages of America.* Baltimore.

Powell, John W. 1891. *Indian linguistic families of America north of Mexico.* Bureau of American Ethnology, 7th Annual Report, 1–142.

Powers, William K. 1988. The Indian hobbyist movement in North America. In *History of White-Indian relations,* Wilcomb E. Washburn, ed., vol. 4, 557–61. *Handbook of North American Indians.* Washington, DC.

Riley, Carroll L., et al. 1971. *Men across the sea.* Austin.

Saum, Lewis O. 1965. *The fur trader and the Indian.* Seattle.

Swanton, John R. 1953. *The Indian tribes of North America.* Bureau of American Ethnology Bulletin 145.

Thornton, Russell. 2000. Population history of Native North Americans. In *A population history of North America,* Michael R. Haines, and Richard H. Steckel, eds., 9–50. New York.

U.S. Department of the Interior. 1958. *Federal Indian Law.* Washington, DC.

Voegelin, C. F. and F. M. 1966. *Map of North American Indian languages.* American Ethnological Society.

Washburn, Wilcomb E. 1984. A fifty-year perspective on the Indian Reorganization Act. *American Anthropologist* n.s. 86:279–89.

Wauchope, Robert. 1962. *Lost tribes and sunken continents.* Chicago.

Weatherford, Jack. 1988. *Indian givers.* New York.

Wissler, Clark. 1938. *The American Indian.* New York.

———. 1942. *The American Indian and the American Philosophical Society.* Proceedings of the American Philosophical Society, vol. 86, 189–204.

Yarnell, Richard A. 1978. Domestication of sunflower and sumpweed in eastern North America. In *Early food production in North America,* R. I. Ford, ed., 285–99. Ann Arbor.

Yellow Bird, Michael. 1999. What we want to be called. *American Indian Quarterly* 23(2):1–21.

Zepeda, Ofelia, and Jane H. Hill. 1991. The condition of Native American languages in the United States. In *Endangered languages,* R. H. Robins and E. M. Uhlenbeck, eds., 135–55. New York.

2 Indian – Non-Indian Relations

"We've never been a nation of conquerors."

George W. Bush
(C-SPAN broadcast,
December 4, 2002)

SOON AFTER DISCOVERY of the New World, a great debate raged in Spain about the humanness of Indians. Regardless of the manner in which the conquistadores were received, they argued that Indians were irrational, heretical, and tainted with mortal sin. This attitude served to justify inhumane treatment of Indians and seizure of their land or property. Francisco Vitoria, a professor at Salamanca and a founder of international law, argued against this thesis. He noted that in Europe heretics were privileged to own property and could not be punished for sins without a trial. Implicit in Vitoria's argument was the acceptance of Indians as human beings. When the exploiters of Indians maintained that the pope of the Roman Catholic church had granted title to all newly discovered lands to the kings of Spain and Portugal, Vitoria countered that the pope had no power over the aborigines and their land and that title by discovery could apply only to unoccupied lands. In a papal bull of 1537 Pope Paul III proclaimed "that the Indians are truly men and that they are not only capable of understanding the Catholic faith, but according to our information, they desire exceedingly to receive it" (Cohen 1960, 290). Considering Indians as human beings gave the church new millions of immortal souls to be saved. This acknowledgment of Indian humanness, combined with an acceptance of Native American land ownership, served as a guide for colonial governments in the Americas. In the years to come, the course of Indian–non-Indian relations was to take many twists and turns, as this chapter demonstrates.

| Early Contact

European maritime explorers found the Indians fascinating because they felt that Indians embodied what people could be like when stripped of Christian and "civilized" behavior (see Figure 2-1). Indians were considered savages; although human in form, they were barely human in their customs, according to these biased observers. The land they owned was attractive, and many intruders felt that Indians were a blight on it. A brief review of early contact in different areas provides an overview of Indian–white relations that fosters greater understanding of the subsequent course of history.

The Virginia Charter of 1606 provided for bringing God to Indians because adopting Christian ways was equated with being civilized. Land was purchased from the Indians, and settlers were certain that they could live in harmony with Indians who would soon be Christianized. Before long, about fifty missionaries were sent to work primarily with children because it was felt that children would learn more readily than adults. The colonists were convinced that their efforts were succeeding, because there were no serious hostilities. Actually, the most powerful Indian leader in the region, Powhatan, was waiting and hoping that the colony would fail, but the English grew more firmly entrenched with each year. In 1622 Powhatan's successor decided he had waited long enough and attacked the colonists. Nearly 350 whites were killed, and the only reason the colony was not destroyed was that a Christian Indian warned the English at the last moment. To the colonists the massacre

Figure 2-1 | This 1493 woodcut accompanied the Italian printing of the first letter by Christopher Columbus about his New World discoveries. In the background is one of the earliest representations of aboriginal Americans. (From Winsor 1889.)

was clear evidence of inborn Indian treachery, and the settlers now felt justified in destroying these savages whom they no longer sought to understand. The Indians in Virginia were viewed as an impediment to the march of civilization, and within the next fifty years they were systematically destroyed or displaced. This pattern was repeated time and again.

"The Indian experience" of each colony was different because of the settlers' backgrounds and the Indians encountered. It might be anticipated that the Quakers, granted the land comprising Pennsylvania in 1681, would be more successful in making Indians into Christians, given their commitment to nonviolence and humanistic tolerance of others. The Quakers stressed the common denominators that unite all people and did not seek to identify differences between themselves and Indians. They offered the Indians love and peace; nevertheless, they were unable to win many converts. Moreover, the Quakers remained neutral when non-Quakers fought the Indians in their midst and at their frontiers.

The Puritans of New England believed that God would guide their affairs with Indians, who were viewed as fallen people in the grip of Satan. When many Indians died in a "wonderful plague" of smallpox, the Puritans saw it as

God's way of furthering the goals of the settlers. The Puritans believed that Indian lands were intended for Christian English use. Nevertheless, to keep peace they purchased land from the Indians rather than taking it. On the other hand, they did not hesitate to initiate raids and wars against the Indians or to foster dissension for their own purposes. They also insisted that Indians should be "civilized." Missionaries such as John Eliot began working among Indians in 1632, but the number of converts was small and success transient. Puritan efforts to integrate the Indians into transported Western European culture failed for obvious reasons.

The Spanish who first entered the Southwest in 1540 expected to find barbarians or savages and felt a strong obligation to civilize them. Church and civil authorities accepted this as their primary goal after realizing that the area was not going to yield great riches. The gross pattern of Spanish life was to be introduced, and the advance agents usually were Roman Catholic missionaries. They built churches and quarters near established pueblos, instructed certain individuals in Catholic doctrine, and soon recruited Indians as catechists and helpers. The missionaries especially were responsible for introducing new crops and novel crafts; their goal was to create self-sufficient Roman Catholic communities. The missionaries in New Mexico usually were accompanied by soldiers who reinforced Spanish authority. In general, the Spanish treatment of Indians was harsh, and on occasion brutally cruel. In New Mexico a major and temporarily successful Native American response to their mistreatment led to the Pueblo Revolt of 1680. Most missionaries were killed, plus some four hundred colonists. The Spanish, however, regained at least partial control in 1692.

Apart from the mission environment, Spanish frontiersmen impinged on the Indians of New Mexico through the policy of giving land grants to soldiers for services rendered. The great *encomienda* grants, made to Spanish colonists in New Mexico as a reward for services rendered, did not include any of the large pueblos; but the people who lived in the small communities in the midst of such grants were forced to work these lands for the Spanish, usually with little or no compensation. Before long, Spanish employees of encomenderos were marrying Indians and acquiring their lands. Abuses of the encomienda system engendered a great deal of hostility in some pueblos and eventually led to its abandonment. Spanish towns, with Santa Fe as the prime example, formed another setting for cultural contact, but because the Indians were drawn to them only for services, their impact was relatively minor.

When the Mexican War for Independence ended in 1821, Indians in the Southwest were granted the full rights of Mexican citizens. All persons born in Mexico became citizens, irrespective of their culture or race, and efforts were made to incorporate Indians into national life. This goal was not achieved in New Mexico, however. Anglo-Americans began to penetrate New Mexico in the 1840s, and their attitudes contrasted rather strikingly with those that previously had prevailed. The mission settlement had no place in their plans. They regarded the pueblo-dwellers as moderately "civilized" but considered most of the less sedentary Indians "wild." The American policy was to push Indians aside, either peacefully or by force, to facilitate westward expansion.

Effective Spanish intrusion into California in 1769 was guided by the same policies that the Spanish had introduced to the Southwest. A primary purpose of the Spanish colony in California was to Christianize Indians and to settle them at self-sufficient missions; thus Indians were very much a part of the economic order. Yet most of the people who were drawn to the missions, either voluntarily or by force, were unlikely to adapt to a sedentary life in crowded conditions with a rigid work routine. The experiment had clearly failed by the time the missions were secularized, beginning in 1834. Souls had been saved, but the cost in human life had been great.

In the northern portions of the continent, the English, French, and Russian ventures were of a different order. Here the fur trader, not the settler or missionary, usually was the most important advance agent of Western culture. Irrespective of their national origins and time of contact, fur traders viewed Indians very differently from most other white intruders. Indians and traders were *joined* by economic ties that profited them both. The areas where the fur trade dominated longest were those unsuitable for large settlements of whites, and thus the Indians' way of life was not disrupted by large groups of intruders. Furthermore, the fur trader and the Indian could maintain their relationship only as long as the Indians remained trappers and retained the essence of their aboriginal economy. Regardless of nationality, fur traders could be intolerant or tolerant, cruel or kind, depending on their personalities and their experiences with Indians.

| Destruction and Displacement of Peoples

It seems likely that after initial historic contact far more Indians were killed by diseases introduced by whites than by bullets. It also appears that more Indians were killed by other Indians than by outsiders, although many such murders unquestionably were abetted by whites. Every tribe probably was subjected to at least one severe epidemic, and there were very few Indians whose way of life was not altered dramatically, or even destroyed outright, soon after contact.

Throughout this volume, the impact of disease on specific peoples is documented, and its disruptive force should not be underestimated. Certain diseases long prevalent among Europeans eventually became less virulent among them but deadly to a virgin population; measles and whooping cough are examples. Other diseases, such as malaria, raged through Indian and white populations alike. Tuberculosis was a dreadful killer of Indians but was less lethal among whites.

Records of tribes destroyed by diseases are not difficult to locate; one depressing example will illustrate the speed of impact. The Massachuset, with an estimated population of three thousand in 1600, were reduced to five hundred by 1631 as a result of a terrible epidemic, possibly smallpox. By 1663, when John Eliot published the Bible in their language, they were nearly extinct.

Even though an epidemic might not destroy a tribe, it could kill so many people that they could not defend themselves against outsiders or continue their cultural traditions. For example, a malaria epidemic struck in the Central

Valley of California and along the Columbia River in the early 1830s. A mortality rate as high as about 75 percent made it impossible for the survivors effectively to resist subsequent white intrusions or to maintain their ways of old.

The extinction of a population unquestionably is tragic, but another consequence of white dominance was nearly as sad. Because of the intimate associations of Indians with their traditional homelands, their displacement to other areas was often heartrending. One example will suffice. In aboriginal times the Delaware lived in New Jersey and adjacent areas, but in the early 1700s the Iroquois dominated them politically and sanctioned their displacement by white settlers. Before long many Delaware settled in eastern Ohio, but only after wandering largely homeless for some time. By 1820 some lived in Arkansas, and others had ventured on to Texas. Some fifteen years later many of them had settled on a reservation in Kansas, from which they were moved to Oklahoma in 1867. Most of them remain there today, but Delaware Indians are scattered from eastern Canada to Montana, far from each other and from their eastern homeland.

The personal and cultural trauma wrought by purposely displacing a tribe from its home is tragic in itself. But the federal policy of moving all the Indian tribes from one vast area into another violates the very principles on which the United States was founded. Yet this happened, and the drama began to unfold with clarity about 1800. One overwhelming argument was advanced to justify assuming control of Indian lands, and it *never* has changed: Indians obstructed the progress of whites who could use land much more effectively, and thus it was the God-given right of the settlers or real estate promoters to obtain such ground. Displacement became a blanket policy with the Indian Removal Act of 1830. New England whites could deplore this policy elsewhere because they had long ago resolved their "Indian problem" by killing many local Native Americans, displacing them, or tolerating small remnant Indian populations. It was the residents of the southeastern states and settlers in the Midwest who became the wanton destroyers of Indian rights. Most surviving tribes with large landholdings east of the Mississippi River were bribed and intimidated into moving west. By 1831, the states of Alabama, Georgia, and Mississippi had forced the removal of the Choctaw, Chickasaw, and Creek. Cherokee resistance to removal was strong but largely unsuccessful (see Chapter 13).

Among the epic sagas of displacement, the Fox (Mesquakie) represent a fine example of tribal resiliency. One Fox homeland was in Wisconsin, where they were nearly destroyed by the French in the 1730s and from which they fled to Illinois. Here they clashed with white settlers in the early 1800s. The Fox received a parcel of land in Iowa, but most of them were forced to relocate to Kansas. However, in 1857 a small group *purchased* eighty acres of land near Tama, Iowa, where they were joined by others. Gradually they bought additional land. By the early 1900s they were desperately poor and conditions did not change dramatically until 1992, when they opened a casino. From the profits the Fox were able to provide a substantial steady income to all enrolled members. Their land holdings now include about seven thousand acres. Although most Indian tribal governments in the east central United States disappeared long ago, the Fox are a notable exception; and the land is their own, not a reservation in the usual sense.

U.S. Treaties

Virtually all inhabitable land in North America was occupied by Native Americans when Europeans arrived. By the 1990s, Indian reservations in the United States represented about 2.5 percent of the country. A study of treaties reveals the changing nature of Indian and white relations.

Until the early 1800s, treaty negotiations were between governments, which established the basis for Indian laws and policies. The sovereignty of tribes was fully recognized by European colonial powers and, initially, by the United States. Negotiators sought to stabilize the white–Indian relationship through equitable treaties containing mutual accommodations. They established boundaries, often issued passports, and attempted to develop means to avoid military conflict. In the process, Indian conventions became a part of negotiations. A prime example was the ritual in which both parties smoked a peace pipe as a solemn gesture of trust. For at least some tribes, a treaty was more than a political document; it became a sacred text. The first treaty enacted by the federal government was with the Delaware in 1778. It provided that the Delaware and other tribes might form a state and have congressional representation, a provision that was never realized (see Table 2-1).

Between 1778 and the early 1800s, federal power over Indians expanded dramatically, especially in the eastern states. Eventually all tribes came to be regarded as quasi-sovereign peoples, not national equals. This view led to diminished tribal control over their destiny, their increasing exploitation, and federal paternalism. Tribes came to be regarded as dependent nations, and treaties were considered in the same light as other statutes of the U.S. Congress. It may come as a surprise that, despite military conflicts between the federal government and various tribes, the United States never formally declared war on hostile Indians.

Many treaty obligations continue to be met by the federal government, although no new treaties have been made with Indians since 1871. In later treaties the federal government reserved the right to regulate Indian affairs, and seldom was this right relinquished to a state. Once a treaty was negotiated and ratified, it could not be nullified by the Indians, even if duress, fraud, or improper Indian representation occurred during the negotiations. Treaties might be renegotiated by mutual federal and Indian consent. Treaties or treaty rights also have been repealed by Congress, with or without the consent, involvement, or agreement of Indians; this is called abrogation. Indian treaties, like all other treaties, have the same status as any other federal statute and can be repealed or modified by a later statute. Yet it has been a general policy of the government to interpret ambiguities in treaties in favor of Indians and to consider the circumstances under which a treaty was negotiated. The courts could not interpret a treaty in a manner not intended in the original wording, however.

Treaties with Indians were negotiated by the president of the United States and were binding when approved by the Indians and two-thirds of the U.S. Sen-

TABLE 2-1. Major events in Native American relations with the federal government of the United States

1778	The first U.S. treaty with Indians, the Delaware tribe
1824	The Bureau of Indian Affairs was created to "civilize" Indians (also termed the "Office of Indian Affairs")
1830	The Indian Removal Act was designed to relocate southeastern Indians to land west of the Mississippi River; the purpose was to open the land to white settlers
1849	A Navajo treaty permitted the federal government, for the first time, to influence the internal affairs of a tribe
1871	The last treaties with Indians
1879	The Carlisle Indian School was founded and became the most famous Indian boarding school; its purpose was to acculturate children rapidly
1887	The Dawes Severalty Act was designed to allot reservation lands to individual Indians and thus break up reservations; "surplus" land was opened to Euro-American settlers
1924	The Indian Citizenship Act granted U.S. citizenship to indigenous Americans who had not previously become citizens by other means
1934	The Indian Reorganization Act attempted to reverse the impact of the Dawes Act by restoring land to reservations and to encourage tribes to form federally recognized tribal governments
1946	The Indian Claims Commission Act was created to settle outstanding Indian claims as a step toward ending federal responsibilities to Indians
1953–1962	House Concurrent Resolution 108 included a timetable for ending federal obligations to Indians; Public Law 280 transferred civil and criminal jurisdiction to select states as a major step in terminating federal responsibilities
1974	The federal government policy to terminate responsibilities toward Indians was itself terminated
1975	The goals of the Indian Self-Determination and Education Assistance Act were to foster tribal self-government and to transfer many of the functions of the Bureau of Indian Affairs to individual tribes
1983	President Ronald Reagan declared that the termination of federal responsibilities to Indians was no longer a goal and proposed greater funding for tribal self-government and resource development
1988	Indian Gaming Regulatory Act launched Indian casinos
1990	The Native American Graves Protection and Repatriation Act provided for the return of skeletal remains and artifacts by universities and museums to the tribes requesting them

ate. It is important to note that a treaty could not provide funds for Indians; monetary commitments required separate congressional action. Nearly 400 treaties were negotiated. The greatest number, nearly 260, were arranged during the great westward expansion of white settlers following the War of 1812. The majority of these treaties, 230, involved Indian lands. A block of 76 treaties called for Indian removal from their lands and resettlement on other lands. Two tribes, the Potawatomi and Ojibwa (Chippewa), negotiated 42 treaties each, a record number.

The first treaty in which the federal government sought to control the internal affairs of a tribe was with the Navajo in 1849. It stipulated that the federal government could "pass and execute in their territory such laws as may be deemed conducive to the prosperity and happiness of said Indians" (U.S. Department of the Interior 1958, 163). By the mid-1800s, it was becoming apparent that treaties with tribes were unrealistic because of the increasing dependence of Indians on the federal government. Treaty making ended when the U.S. Senate and the House of Representatives could not agree on treaty appropriations.

Indians have land rights based on aboriginal possession, treaty, congressional act, executive order, purchase, or the action of some colony, state, or foreign nation. Reservations were created by treaty arrangements before 1871, by acts of Congress after that time, and by executive orders of the president. In almost every instance the federal government retained the title to reservation lands. Statutory reservations usually consisted of public domain or land purchased by the federal government for use by designated Indians. Reservations were created by executive order between 1855 and 1919. This practice met resistance from Congress, however, and was brought to an end except for the addition of some Alaskan reservations. From time to time Indians have purchased lands with their own funds for the group as a whole, and these properties have been supervised by the federal government (see Chapter 13). Because nearly all of the land that is now the United States was held earlier by European-based powers, the rights of Indians under British, Dutch, French, Mexican, Russian, and Spanish rule have been taken into consideration when a transfer of sovereignty has occurred. In each instance at least some recognition has been given to aboriginal rights of occupancy by the Indians.

Treaties with Indians after about 1800 usually were not negotiated in a meaningful sense. Representatives of a particular tribe or tribes were assembled, and a treaty was offered for their approval. Furthermore, and of critical importance, treaties were based on Euro-American political concepts, *never* on tribal legal norms. As treaty signers, Indians had little control over the terms. Then, too, treaties often were made through "chiefs" who were sympathetic to the whites, and in certain areas of the United States it was not uncommon for intoxicants to be distributed freely at treaty-making sessions. In addition, the interpreters often could not or did not set forth the fine points of an agreement in true detail or spell out the implications of what the Indians were losing and what they were gaining.

| Administration of U.S. Indian Affairs

In 1775 the Continental Congress created three agencies, on a geographical basis, to deal with Indians. Among the commissioners were Benjamin Franklin and Patrick Henry, an indication of the importance attached to Indian matters. The commissioners were to make treaties, to establish friendly relations with Indians, and to prevent them from aiding the British. In 1786 Indian administration was placed under the secretary of war. With adoption of the Constitution, the War Department maintained jurisdiction over Indians. The first Congress in 1789 appropriated funds for negotiating treaties and placed the governors of territories in charge of local Indian affairs. The next year Congress, in an important step toward federal control, began licensing traders among Indians. The Bureau of Indian Affairs (BIA) was created in 1824 within the War Department, and its administration passed into civilian control at the newly created Home Department of the Interior in 1849. Flagrant corruption and mismanagement within the bureau led to the creation of the Board of Indian Commissioners that functioned from 1869 to 1933. They oversaw the expenditure of funds and made policy decisions.

The BIA remains the federal agency most responsible for Indian affairs. However, bureau mismanagement again was endemic by the 1980s. A federal study in 1984 demonstrated that *two-thirds of the BIA budget was consumed by the bureau itself.* As a result of this finding and the excessive regulatory power of the bureau, administrative changes were launched. Despite revelations about inefficiency, by 1994 only an estimated twenty cents of each dollar received by the BIA actually reached the Indians for whom it was intended. The worst BIA scandal concerns individual Indian trust accounts (see Chapter 15). The BIA budget in 2003 was $2.34 billion.

| Canada, the First Nations

In recent years "First Nations" and "Aboriginals" have emerged as accepted terms for the indigenous peoples of Canada. The earliest significant grant of land to Indians was made in 1680 by the French to a band of Iroquois. The first large British grant was in 1784 to the Six Nations (Iroquois), who received about 675,000 acres in Ontario as a reward for their loyalty to the British during the American Revolution (see Chapter 12).

A cornerstone of British policy was embodied in the Proclamation of 1763. It included the guiding principles for Indian–white relations: Indians possessed the rights to all lands *not* formally surrendered; land could be surrendered only to the Crown; Indians could not grant land to individual whites unless it had been surrendered. Under these terms, settlers in what is now the United States could not readily occupy Indian lands; this provision later emerged as a cause of the American Revolution. Large sectors of Canada have *never* been legally ceded by Indians to the Crown.

In the first series, eleven treaties were arranged between Indians and the British from 1781 to 1921. They involved relatively few tribes, and as a result the status of most land belonging to aboriginal Canadians was unsettled (see also Chapter 4).

With the confederation of Canada in 1867, Indian administration passed to the Dominion of Canada, which became responsible for relief, education, health services, Indian-based farming, industry, and enfranchisement (full Canadian citizenship). Under the Canadian Act of 1871, reserve (reservation) land could be held by an Indian under an allotment system, with the allottee having the exclusive right to use and occupancy. An allotment could be passed on to heirs or sold to another Indian within the group. "Surplus" land could be sold by a tribe and the money received used for tribal welfare. Then, too, an

Indian could obtain clear title to land by requesting and being granted enfranchisement. A Department of Indian Affairs, founded in 1880, underwent numerous administrative changes, and in 1967 the Department of Indian Affairs and Northern Development was created. It must be emphasized that Canadian provinces have far greater control over Indian lands than do states in the United States.

Canadians with European and Indian ancestry were treated differently from full-blood Indians in some contexts. In general, people of mixed heritage, or Métis, were given the rights of Indians, and those Métis who lived as Indians had the right to be treated as Indians. Efforts by the Métis to protect their land rights were partially responsible for the Red River Rebellion of Manitoba in 1869. As a result of this uprising, the rights of Métis were more fully recognized in that province. In 1982 the Métis received greater recognition and became comparable to First Nations peoples in many respects.

One far-reaching administrative change occurred in the eastern portion of the former Northwest Territories. In 1999 it became a separate territory, Nunavut ("our land"). The region includes about one-fifth of all Canadian land. The population at that time was about 28,000, of whom about 85 percent were Inuit (see also Chapter 3). The residents received surface title to the land and the subsurface title to a portion of it; the latter is important with respect to the development of mineral resources.

Canadian Indian efforts to obtain control of aboriginal landholdings are by far the least successful in British Columbia (see also Chapter 5). A small number of limited-scope treaties had been negotiated in British Columbia before it became a province in 1871. From then until the present, this provincial government seldom has acted in good faith with respect to Indians. Serious negotiations began with the federal and provincial governments in 1991. The first major change, which was completed in 1998, was with the Nishga (Nisga'a), a band (the Canadian administrative label for "tribe") in the northwestern sector. Approximately ninety bands in the province have yet to sign treaties. Some British Columbian Indians feel that they have little chance of receiving a just settlement and have turned to the courts for adjudication. One major incentive for this shift was the 1997 Delgamuukw case in which the Supreme Court of Canada ruled that aboriginal title exists. However, to obtain court settlements is a more complicated, uncertain, expensive, and drawn-out process than the current negotiations.

Elsewhere a number of important land and self-government settlements have been made. In one of these, the Dogrib (Ticho) First Nation settled with the Northwest Territories in 2003. Then, too, the Labrador Inuit, who extend into a portion of Quebec, began their effort for greater autonomy in 1977 and reached a "final agreement" in 2003. Of far greater significance, the Canadian government set forth a new Indian Act in 2003, one that would result in greater federal control over the First Nations. It was formulated with little band input and has been challenged in federal courts by tribes, who declare it a violation of treaty rights (see also Chapter 12).

| Greenland in Brief

Norse people, largely from Iceland, settled Greenland beginning in A.D. 986, but Eskimos had occupied portions of the island since at least 2000 B.C. The original Norse colony was neglected over the years and had disappeared by about 1540. Greenland began to be resettled in 1721 by Norwegian Lutheran missionaries; at that time Norway was under the political control of Denmark. Danish sovereignty over much of Greenland, however, was not established until 1921, and it was a closed country until after World War II. The Danes dominated most aspects of Eskimo life from the beginning and were concerned primarily with saving souls and with commercial profits. The deplorable health and living conditions of the Eskimos did not begin to be acknowledged in a realistic manner until 1953, when the colonial status of Greenland was abolished. In that year, Greenlanders became full citizens of Denmark, and their living conditions began to improve dramatically. Finally, home rule was extended to Greenland in 1979. Contemporary Greenland is occupied by about 56,000 Greenlanders, 86 percent of whom are Eskimo (Inuit).

| Landmark U.S. Indian Policies

Indian tribes were relatively free and independent nations until the War of 1812 ended. Soon thereafter they became "domestic, dependent nations" and lost realistic control over their destiny. The Indian Removal Act of 1830 was a clear indication of the change in relations between Indians and the federal government. The end of treaty making in 1871 was another plateau, but the General Allotment Act (Dawes Severalty Act or Dawes Act) of 1887 had the greatest impact on changing Indian life.

THE DAWES ACT Under the terms of this act, the president was authorized to allot most reservation land to individual Indians. Indians were to select their acreage, and the federal government was to hold a trust title for at least twenty-five years, during which time the land could not be encumbered. Surplus reservation lands then were sold, and the funds derived were held in trust for the tribe, subject to use for educating and "civilizing" the tribe when Congress approved these uses. The Dawes Act was modified over the next ten years to allow allotted land to be leased. Indian education began to be stressed. Schools were provided, and the attendance of children virtually was forced; but federal support for church schools was withdrawn. An important supplement was made to the act in 1906 that permitted the president to extend the trust period for allotted lands. The aim of the Dawes Act was to bypass tribal organizations and make land allotments to individual Indians. The act was designed to *destroy* the tribes by doing away with the land base held collectively and, at the same time, to integrate Indians into the dominant society. Many whites who truly were concerned with Indian welfare felt that the sterile and depressing quality of reservation life should be destroyed and that the best means to accomplish this goal was to make individual Indians property holders and farmers.

THE INDIAN REORGANIZATION ACT (IRA) The goals of this act were the direct opposite of those of the Dawes Act. The IRA of 1934 was intended to end the alienation of Indian lands through the allotment process. In fifty years of allotments, Indians had lost nearly 90 million of their 138 million acres of land, and about half of the remaining land was desert. The most effective means to permit retention of the land base was to extend the period of trust holding, which the act did. Furthermore, the act acquired additional land for Indians, declared it exempt from taxation, and placed it under federal control.

Two guiding principles of the IRA were self-government with democratic ideals and parliamentary procedures and communal enterprises as the best avenue to bettered economic conditions. Tribes were encouraged to form chartered corporations and to operate essentially as local governments; revolving credit funds helped those choosing to incorporate. One key condition of the original law was that it would apply only to those tribes that by majority vote decided to come under its provisions. Initially, 181 tribes accepted and 77 rejected the IRA. Fourteen groups came under it because they did not vote, and the act was extended in 1936 to include Alaskan and Oklahoman peoples without their vote of approval. Because Indians in general had come to distrust the federal government, the Indian response to this enlightened legislation was not as positive as had been hoped for by its creators. Some tribes favored allotments and were able to obtain clear title to their land in spite of the IRA (see Chapter 8). Other tribes, such as those that stressed individual wealth, did not even agree with the principles behind the IRA.

World War II disrupted the implementation of IRA goals, and in the period between the end of this war and the late 1960s the federal government generally pursued policies designed to assimilate Indians into the greater American "melting pot." However, the IRA has remained the legislation with the most critical effect on reservation Indian life. As Wilcomb E. Washburn (1984) observed, acceptance of the IRA by reservation Indians in general over the years has led to the revival of tribal life or its creation among them. The act has contributed significantly to the vitality of tribal political structure. As will become evident in numerous chapters to follow, many tribes probably would have been destroyed by now had it not been for the IRA (see Chapter 6).

U.S. TAXATION HIGHLIGHTS A great deal of misunderstanding surrounds the subject of Indians and taxes; the topic merits review. In the United States, the taxation of Native Americans focuses on land identified as "Indian Country" by the federal government. *Indian Country* is defined as reservation and nonreservation land owned by a tribe or its members and held in trust by the federal government.

By treaties and statutes, tribes cannot be taxed, and tribal members may not be taxed unless there are exemptions by treaty or statute. States, in theory, cannot tax in Indian Country. Tribes, as sovereign entities, have the inherent right to tax Indians and non-Indians in Indian Country, because the power to tax is an essential element for self-government (i.e., infrastructure). Tribes, just as all other units of government, are not taxable, nor are tribal businesses taxable by federal or state governments.

Specific examples illustrate application of the pertinent treaties and statutes.

When an Indian or tribe obtains a patent in fee to land (a clear title), such as under the Dawes Act, the land is subject to state property taxes. This does not apply to trust lands.

Tobacco products or gasoline sold at reservation businesses by Indians to non-Indians or nontribal members are subject to state taxes. This is an area of continuing conflict between tribes and states.

Indians, just as any other citizens, are subject to federal and state taxes beyond the boundaries of Indian Country.

Neither federal nor state income taxes apply to fishing rights set forth in treaties.

With reference to Indian gaming operations, the wages of *all* employees are subject to federal income taxes, but tribal members do not pay state income taxes. Winnings at an Indian gaming enterprise are taxable by the federal and state governments, except when a winner is a member of the tribe operating the establishment. If a tribe with a casino distributes a portion of the earnings to tribal members, they become subject to federal income taxes. In theory, a tribe with a casino cannot be taxed by a state. However, *and most important,* states have increasingly devised means to tap casino profits (see also Chapter 15).

Tribes have been encouraged by the federal government to establish "industrial parks" on reservation lands, which may be an advantageous situation for non-Indian companies. A company is permitted accelerated depreciation rates on capitalized buildings and equipment.

FEDERAL INTRUSION AND INDIAN IDENTITY   In the 1930s the concept of acculturation became prominent in anthropology. It came to mean the steps by which native peoples are gradually absorbed into the dominant sociocultural pattern. With assimilation, acculturation is complete. Yet few anthropologists are satisfied with the concept because it fails to define the stages leading to assimilation or to explain the persistence of tribal identity in the face of hundreds of years of pressures to negate it. Quite clearly, the idea of acculturation does not allow for the lasting quality of Indian identity. A bold and innovative approach to the general problem was articulated by Joseph G. Jorgensen (1971).

The central concept of Jorgensen's thesis is that tribes were assimilated into national economic and political life as soon as they came under U.S. control; Indian identity was strongest where federal intrusion was weakest. Jorgensen attributed the deplorable conditions on most reservations to what is essentially a colonial political system. The metropolis is the center at which economic and political power are concentrated. Thus the politically weak areas in which reservations usually are located are exploited by the metropolis for its own growth. Indians also are subject to the same laws that apply to everyone else, *in addition to* those imposed by federal control through the BIA. In the 1950s the BIA launched a program to "relocate" Indians to urban areas, and the program came to include vocational and on-the-job training. The goal was to force their assimilation into the mainstream national workforce. The BIA maintained that the program was voluntary, which was untrue; people were encouraged to participate and quotas were established for relocating Indians. By the mid-1970s the failings of the program and changing views of Indians by non-Indians led to an end of the experiment (see also Chapter 15).

Compatible with the goals of the relocation program, the federal government made a move to "get out of the Indian business" by settling old claims with the Indian Claims Commission Act of 1946. Then in 1953 a federal policy was launched that had a far more immediate impact—House Concurrent Resolution 108. It was designed with a timetable for ending federal responsibilities to Indians. As Randall H. McGuire (1992, 825) noted, "If Indian people would not vanish, then the Congress would terminate them." Termination of the Klamath and Menominee reservations was one result; these reservations included major stands of timber that were being sought by lumber companies. In addition, other reservations were terminated, such as those in western Oregon. For some Indians, Public Law 280 in 1953 transferred civil and criminal jurisdiction to select states, including California, Minnesota, Nebraska, and Oregon. Largely through efforts by the Menominee, the termination policy was itself terminated in 1974, and reservation status was restored to such tribes as the Menominee and Klamath.

| Forces Fostering Native American Identity

Compared with European intruders, early historic cultural diversity among Native Americans north of Mexico was great. Indians not only spoke many unrelated languages and had varied social conventions but also reflected different social and political norms. By contrast, the cultural background of Europeans was homogeneous; their linguistic differences were minor, and social and political ideals were broadly similar. Thus, compared with Europeans, the Indians were fractured and fragmented along many dimensions. The agents of Western civilization often exploited these differences to divide Indians still further. In the face of European threats to their cultural integrity, Indians came to recognize what different tribes had in common and to develop a new sense of identity as Indians that transcended tribal lines.

PAN-INDIANISM   This concept refers to a general sense of Indian cultural identity that unites the members of different tribes. *Pan-Indianism* is a term that gained prominence in the 1950s and was applied to a condition that had originated much earlier. More accurate designations might be intertribalism or pantribalism, because participation brings together Indians with different tribal backgrounds. Pan-Indianism began in the mid-1700s and eventually emerged as a movement that has become a primary source of Indian identity for many of its members. This has been true especially for those Indians with a weak sense of tribal identity, such as those raised off reservations, and for other persons who consider themselves Indian although they lack the customary biological or cultural heritage.

Varied factors contributed to the rise of pantribalism, especially the influence of Indian prophets who predicted what must be done to free themselves of control by whites. Prominent and relatively recent prophets are associated with the Ghost Dance. As Indians in the western United States came into increasing conflict with non-Indians, the first Ghost Dance was originated in 1869, but it did not have wide impact. The Ghost Dance of 1890 that originated with a Paiute from Nevada named Wovoka (Jack Wilson) became far more important. Wovoka reportedly died during an eclipse of the sun in January 1889 and went to heaven, where he saw dead Indians living in an idyllic state. God reportedly said that if Wovoka returned to earth and taught the people to perform the Ghost Dance, the dead and living would be reunited. He cautioned people not to fight with each other or with non-Indians; neither should they lie or steal. If these instructions were obeyed, there would be no more illness, old age, or death. Performing the Ghost Dance was to hasten the dawning of this new world. Although some tribes embraced the dance with fervor, it inevitably failed.

Much of the background for Pan-Indianism may be traced to Indian prophets, but there were essential non-Indian elements as well. The most important of these was the formal education process imposed on Indians. In government and mission schools instruction was in English, which became the language for communication between the members of different tribes. Boarding schools likewise had a profound influence. None was more famous than the Carlisle Indian School in Pennsylvania. It was founded in 1879 by Richard H. Pratt, an army officer, whose philosophy was encapsulated in his slogan, "Kill the Indian and save the man!" The school was organized along military lines and attended by the members of far-flung tribes. It was intended to be a way station between the reservation and assimilation. Carlisle often is thought of as a college because its football team played university teams, but it was largely a secondary school that stressed vocational training and the fundamentals of English. Indians who attended Carlisle and other boarding schools often had a difficult time readjusting to reservation life. Although some went "back to the blanket," meaning that they reverted to Indian ways, others were assimilated into the white world, and many worked for the federal government in Indian administration.

The boarding schools in the United States and residential schools in Canada were *the most powerful institutions for the systematic destruction of traditional Native American cultures*. The military model, with its repressive environment, is as sad as it was dreadful. Children, young and old, might be confined to a school for years on end. Furthermore, and of singular importance, many children were unable to learn the subsistence activities, social norms, or religious conventions of their parents. It appears that much of the social disorganization on contemporary reservations and reserves may be traced directly to these schools (see Chapter 12). It was not until the Indian Child Welfare Act in 1978 that the education of Indian children reverted to tribal control.

Christianity was an especially important influence on Indians in the late 1800s in a number of ways. Indians from different tribes came to be identified with each other because they were members of the same church denomination. Likewise, mission advocates helped foster Indian identity by working for their well-being. Missions maintained many schools, and diverse white organizations with Christian backing were concerned with Indian life. The members sought to *assimilate* Indians, and most of them had little tolerance for Indian customs. These white activists in Indian affairs supported the principles of the Dawes Act but deplored the injustices of its administration. As Hazel W. Hertzberg (1971, 22) has noted in the best study of this era, "All unwittingly the reformers—the Indians' chief friends in court in the white world—thus helped to break down Indian self-respect and Indian attempts at self-help." Many Indian leaders were Christian, but at the same time they often were unwilling to abandon their Indian heritage. They sought accommodation with Euro-American customs, and their general approach has endured among many Indians seeking to retain their identity. For many others assimilation into white society was desired and realized.

Indians of many tribes with different historical backgrounds were drawn into Pan-Indianism through the peyote cult. The peyote plant, which grows in southern Texas and northern Mexico, is a spineless cactus with "buttons" containing alkaloids that are stimulants or sedatives in varying proportions. When consumed, buttons produce a wide range of reactions. A common response to taking peyote is exhilaration and an inability to sleep for about twelve hours; depression and hallucinations, sometimes including color visions, follow. This non-habit-forming drug was consumed in Mexico in aboriginal times but was not widely used in the United States until more recently. It became popular among Indians of the southern Plains between 1850 and 1900 and spread to other western tribes. Early use in the Plains appears to have been associated with warfare, and it was taken only by men. Indians began using peyote more widely when they were suffering in the dismal aftermath of military defeat, physical displacement, and confinement to reservations. The Bureau of Indian Affairs, Christian missionaries, and white reformers all were actively opposed to the peyote cult, and its adherents were harassed. Despite the oppression by whites and some Indians, there were about twelve thousand members in 1918. Efforts were made in 1916 and again in 1917 to pass a federal law against the use of peyote, but these bills failed. In 1918, as a response to white opposition, a group of participants incorporated as a formal religious institution, the Native American church. Although a number of states soon passed laws against the use of peyote (for example, Kansas, 1920; Arizona, 1923), seven states had chartered Native American churches by 1925. As members of a formal religious organization, Indians were afforded far greater protection from persecution than previously.

According to Hertzberg, the peyote religion had appeal because old tribal religions had lost their meaning and Christian teachings seemed remote from reality. Furthermore, this was an Indian religion that united members of different tribes in a common sense of brotherhood. Peyote often was considered a powerful medicine for the diseased, and the rituals also provided an opportunity for social gatherings. Some Indians, such as the Pueblo peoples, Five Civilized Tribes in Oklahoma, and Iroquois, were relatively untouched by the peyote religion, but it had become *the* religion for many Indians by 1934 (see Chapter 11).

The anthropologist James H. Howard (1955) was one of the first to identify the Pan-Indian movement and to define the traits associated with it. He identified the movement's roots as being in Oklahoma, especially among the small tribes originally from the East. Howard felt that racial discrimination against Indians was an important factor fostering solidarity among them. Coupled with poverty, apartheid tended to bind Indians of diverse backgrounds. Howard viewed Pan-Indianism as a breakdown of tribalism and a major step leading to the assimilation of Indians into the greater Euro-American matrix. As William K. Powers (1990) vividly conveys, empirical evidence does not support Howard's assimilation model. Instead, Powers suggests, tribalism represents one dimension of modern Native American life and intertribalism another. The most important implication is that tribalism represents sociocultural continuity of the distant past *with and into the present,* as opposed to the slow death of tribal conventions. Widespread systematic studies about *modern* tribes are few.

THE INDIAN IMAGE The Plains Indian has come to symbolize Indians to most Americans, and we might take a moment to consider how it has happened that Indians in one sector of the country have become representative of all Indians.

Indians of the Great Plains were seen first by Spanish and then by French and English explorers, yet they were nearly unknown until after the Louisiana Purchase of 1803. In 1821 members of Plains tribes visited Washington, DC, and none was more popular than Petalesharo, the Pawnee who rescued a Comanche girl from being sacrificed to the Morning Star. In three paintings of him by different artists, he wore a flowing feather headdress (see Figure 2-2), and according to John C. Ewers (1965) this probably was the first pictorial record of the feather "war bonnet." Many other Indians in the same party had their portraits painted, and their exhibit long was a popular attraction in Washington. The earliest picture of a Plains tepee appeared in 1823 (see Figure 2-3), and the first illustration of a Plains Indian on horseback was printed in 1829 (see Figure 2-4). This beginning possibly never would have led to the emergence of the Plains tribes in popular fancy were it not for the efforts of Karl Bodmer, George Catlin, and Charles M. Russell, who painted Plains Indians in the 1830s.

Figure 2-2 | This 1821 painting of Petalesharo, a Pawnee, is one of the first illustrations of a Plains Indian headdress. (From Ewers 1965.)

Catlin especially was important, for he not only painted many pictures of Indians but also exhibited his Indian gallery widely in the United States and then in London and Paris. His book *Manners, Customs and Condition of the North American Indians,* first published in 1841, had a wide distribution, and this two-volume work with over three hundred engravings was reprinted again and again. To Catlin the noblest Indians clearly were those of the Plains. His paintings and those of Bodmer were copied or modified and also inspired other artists to venture west to paint Indians.

The Plains Indian symbol crystallized in Buffalo Bill's Wild West Show, which opened in 1883. It was seen by millions of people in Canada, the United States, and Europe during its run of more than thirty years. William F. Cody, or "Buffalo Bill," was a colorful frontier figure who became the hero of innumerable dime novels. The show, a reenactment of episodes in Plains life, was highlighted by an Indian attack on a stagecoach and its dramatic rescue by cowboys led by Buffalo Bill. Other Wild West shows that imitated the original and Indian medicine shows intensified and spread the image of the Plains Indian. By the turn of the twentieth century Indians all over the country were beginning to dress as Plains Indians for special occasions.

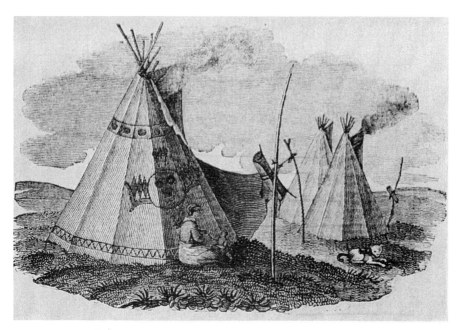

Figure 2-3 | The first illustration of a Plains Indian tepee to be published, appearing in 1823. (From Ewers 1965.)

Figure 2-4 | Probably the first published illustration of a Plains Indian warrior on horseback, appearing in 1829. (From Ewers 1965.)

POWWOWS   In Canada and the United States some two thousand pow-wows are presented each year. For many non-Indians, powwows and reserva-tions have been prominent keys to modern Indian identity. *Powwow* is a Narraganset Indian word that originally referred to the activities of shamans; the earliest citation in English appears to date from 1624. By the 1950s the word became identified with an Indian ceremonial configuration of regalia, dance, and music among Oklahoma tribes. The regional styles in Oklahoma during the 1960s had essentially amalgamated by the 1980s and spread throughout much of Canada and the United States.

Powwows are hosted by tribes or organizations within tribes in associa-tion with Indian fairs, on patriotic holidays, and for other celebrations. Typi-cally, a powwow committee organizes the event. A princess may be chosen, a convention dating from the 1960s. A paradelike procession of non-Indian ori-gin introduces dancers to the performance area. Six major costume and dance styles are presented, three each for females and males. Performance contests for each dance style highlight a modern powwow. The two major types of dances are the relatively slow and dignified "straight" dances and the fast and furious "fancy" dances. Four-part songs, old and new, are sung repeatedly to the accompaniment of a drum. Participants consider the drum as the heart of dances, and a powwow is said to be only as good as the drummers. Songs may include words or be represented by sound combinations without meaning. In dance contests the performers must know the songs so well that they are able to stop dancing at the last drumbeat for a song.

For powwow visitors the most striking initial impression is the variety of colorful and elaborate costumes worn by the participants, male and female, young and old. The most popular dance style is the War Dance, especially the Fancy War Dance (Fancy Dance), which may have originated around 1920 for a Wild West show but has little to do with war. Men dominate as fancy dancers. The headdress, or roach, is of porcupine guard hairs and dyed hair from deer tails. Armbands, a choker, and moccasins are adorned with matched bead-work. Anklets have bells attached, important for keeping time to the music. The most spectacular features are the neck and back "bustles" dominated by turkey or eagle feathers (Figure 2-5). In dance contests a stick may be held in each hand and decorated with hair or ribbons. This dance, like all the others, is individualized, meaning that participants perform as they choose; thus the coordination of dancers and practice sessions are not required. Among the largest powwows is the one held at the Foxwoods Resort Casino in Connecti-cut. This four-day gathering is inspired by a traditional corn festival. In 1997 it attracted more than two thousand dancers.

For non-Indian observers, a powwow is highlighted not only by the dance performances but also by vendor sales of Indian arts and crafts. For Na-tive American participants, a major highlight is the "giveaways." Individuals and families present gifts, sometimes quite valuable, to persons who had been helpful in particular contexts, an old convention among Plains tribes. Presents now acknowledge aid received at passage rites, notable leadership, and other

Figure 2-5 | The Fancy Dancer, Wilber Beebe, a Canadian Blackfoot (Blood subtribe), at the Kootenai Casino Powwow, Bonners Ferry, Idaho, in 1999.

events important in the lives of the givers. Among the Indians involved, pow-wows provide an opportunity to exhibit and strengthen their Indian identity in a public context.

A powwow may include an aboriginal form of gambling, the stick game (stickgame, hand game), especially on Indian land in the Canadian and American west. It often is played in tournaments held separately from powwows. A tournament may be local or may be a major regional one that attracts avid players who have driven hundreds of miles to participate. The stick game, which combines chance and skill, unquestionably is the most popular and wide-spread game among traditionalists. Children sometimes begin to play among themselves at four years of age and become competent players by the time they are nine. Traditionally the more formal games were played only by men, but the modern version may be played by men and women, young or old, and children. Historically, federal Indian agents prohibited the game on Indian lands because the stakes could be high, such as horses and saddles. Irrespective of the prohibition, the game was played often and widely. Modern players may seek the supernatural aid of a shaman for gaming power, just as in the past. To enhance winning, they may sing old and new songs as the game is played. Alcohol and drugs are strictly prohibited at many tournaments but are tolerated at others. Drum accompaniment and costumed cheering sections in the audience are relatively recent aspects of the game.

Stick game rules follow a basic pattern, although they vary in detail by locality. Two teams with five members each sit opposite one another on folding chairs (see Figure 2-6). For a major tournament the entry fee for a team may be $150, and the prize money may total thousands of dollars. A coin is tossed to determine which team first handles the "bones." They are relatively small sections of bone, plastic, or metal readily concealed in one hand. The "female" piece is white and plain, and the "male" one has a black strip around the middle. With seemingly closed fists, a bone handler manipulates the gaming pieces while facing the opponents. At the same time, a drummer plays, and team members sing. Fundamentally, the guesser on the opposite team seeks to identify the fist that holds the white bone. If the guess is correct, both the white and black bones are forfeited; if incorrect, the guesser forfeits a stick. This continues until one team has won all of the sticks, usually ten in number, and thus wins the stakes. For an outsider the most engaging aspects of the hand game are the clever and often complicated bone manipulations and the conviviality of the participants, as well as of their supporters and opponents. The many jokes, asides, groans, and cheers are infectious and appreciated by the entire audience.

The Coeur d'Alene Casino in Idaho held a stick game tournament in 2003 that attracted eighty-nine teams for the three-day event. The winning team won six successive games and the $10,000 first prize; the team included four women and one man.

| Recent History

The feelings of non-Indians toward Native Americans seem to swing between sympathy and resentment. During the height of the civil rights movement in the 1960s and early 1970s, many Americans regarded Indians with sympathy, if not with compassion. Motion-picture stars, such as Marlon Brando, rallied to tribal causes; the depressed economy of Indians was the subject of television documentaries; and the Indian folksinger Buffy Sainte-Marie, who recounted old and new injustices, became popular. Members of the U.S. Congress less often urged Indian assimilation into the American "melting pot." Indians flexed their political muscles in an unprecedented manner: Native Alaskans formed an "ice block" in the statehouse, the Iroquois wanted their wampum

Figure 2-6 | Stick game drummers and bone handlers at the Yakama Nation Legends Casino Stick Game Tournament at Toppenish, Washington, in 2003.

back from museums, and Canadian Eskimos (Inuit) sought to establish their own political unit in the Arctic. Indian demands received more thoughtful attention from politicians and administrators than they had previously.

As the 1970s drew to a close, the civil rights movement had lost its thrust, and social justice diminished as a major American concern. With this new climate and a downturn in the economy, Native Americans and other minorities began to elicit more resentment than sympathy. One particular development in 1977 seems to have decreased American support for Indians. In that year a special White House study group issued a report about the land claims of the Passamaquoddy and Penobscot Indians of Maine. A settlement was proposed that would have given four thousand Indians millions of dollars and vast tracts of land. Officials in Maine labeled the proposal as "really outrageous" and "crazy." The suggested settlement received widespread and intense media attention, and many non-Indians shared the attitudes expressed by Maine officials. In the 1980 settlement, the Indians received $81.5 million from the federal government, a decision that elicited ill feelings toward Indians in general, especially among people not familiar with the merits of the case.

Anti-Indian feelings crystallized during this time, especially after other tribes realized that the Maine settlement represented legal precedent and pressed their own claims against illegal land seizures. Non-Indian constituents urged members of Congress to do something, and there was a serious proposal that the United States abrogate *all* Indian treaties. This approach failed, and in the 1980s a concerted federal effort was made to vitalize reservation life that continued through the 1990s. In the early 2000s, however, a shift in federal Indian policies and programs began to emerge. These changes are examined in Chapter 15.

POLITICAL ACTIVISM   The Pan-Indian movement of the 1930s appears to have been a source for the Red Power movement of the late 1960s. A major contributing factor was the impact of World War II and the Korean War on Indians who were members of the armed services and who afterward refused to fit back into the Indian stereotype. Some began to search for their cultural roots. College-educated Indians resented the way the BIA treated them. The most radical group to emerge was the American Indian Movement (AIM) in 1968; its goal was to seek equality for Indians in the civil rights arena. The most dramatic confrontation, and one that has stuck in the minds of non-Indians, began in 1973. AIM seized the small town of Wounded Knee on the Pine Ridge Reservation in South Dakota. (At Wounded Knee Creek, about 300 Siouan men, women, and children were massacred by U.S. Army troops in 1890; this episode and the site have long symbolized white injustice.) In a seventy-one-day standoff, between 250 and 400 Indians held out against 125 Federal Bureau of Investigation agents, 40 BIA police, and 150 U.S. marshals. The siege resulted in hundreds of arrests, and the two major leaders, Dennis Banks and Russell Means, spent fifteen years in court trying to vindicate themselves in politically motivated trials by the federal government. By the end of the 1970s, AIM had few members and diminished political impact. (In 1979 the Federal Bureau of Investigation files in Washington, DC, contained 17,725 pages of information bearing on the activities of AIM, which was said to be a revolutionary organization.)

In 1978 Congress passed the American Indian Religious Freedom Act (AIRFA), which was designed to review and update federal policies so that Native Americans would have the legal right to practice their traditional religions, possess sacred objects, and gain access to sacred sites. Policies were reviewed, and several recommendations were made. However, in 1988 and again in 1990, the U.S. Supreme Court ruled that AIRFA is a policy statement and not law, and as such it does not afford rights to the protection of sacred sites or the religious use of peyote in the Native American church. The Native American Graves Protection and Repatriation Act (NAGPRA), passed in 1990, was a notable exception.

NAGPRA requires that all federal agencies and all organizations receiving federal funds (most museums and universities, for example) conduct an inventory to determine what Native American skeletal remains and sacred objects are in their collections and which modern tribes are affiliated with the remains and objects. The tribes involved must then be consulted about what is to be done with the remains and objects. Although some groups have elected to leave items with museums and universities, others have requested their return for tribal museums or reburial (see Chapter 11).

TRIBAL SELF-DETERMINATION   Relatively recent historical emphasis on greater tribal control over Indian lives may have been an indirect response to the civil rights movement, with its stress on ethnic diversity. In 1968 President Lyndon Johnson spoke of Indians as "The Forgotten Americans" and proposed changes in policies, including self-determination. Yet it is an old concept for Indians to manage their own affairs. Government-to-government negotiations took place in colonial times and in early U.S. history, when Indians had full jurisdiction over their internal affairs. As noted earlier in this chapter, tribal autonomy began to be eroded with a Navajo treaty in 1849. The current policy is set forth in the Indian Self-Determination and Education Assistance Act of 1975. It was designed to foster greater self-government and to free Indians from pervasive BIA control. A major barrier to self-determination had been the Alaskan Eskimo and Indian land claims that were resolved in 1971 (see Chapter 9). In 1983 President Ronald Reagan stressed that termination of federal responsibilities to Indians was no longer a goal, and he proposed that a greater percentage of the federal budget be earmarked for tribal self-government and resource development. However, the money for Indian programs actually was decreased.

The label "self-determination" is deceptive, because it does not mean that Native Americans are gaining unlimited control over their destiny. It does mean that the federal government has taken a somewhat more humane political attitude toward Indians. Again, the concept of "tribal sovereignty" is misleading. It is inconceivable that Indian reservations will become sovereign in a strict sense, despite a 1940 U.S. Supreme Court ruling that sovereign immunity is necessary for self-governance. Sovereignty really has come to mean that in some contexts Indians are regaining a degree of local autonomy at the state and federal levels. These changes, however, are set against a complex historical backdrop: there are nearly four hundred ratified Indian treaties; some five thousand federal statutes deal with Indians; and some two thousand court decisions have been rendered. The constitutions of tribes and lesser Indian political entities must be considered as well (see also Chapter 15).

Courtrooms increasingly have become a prominent Indian battleground, and sovereignty issues have been salient. In general, federal courts have been sympathetic to Indian rights, whereas state courts have been, and remain, largely anti-Indian. For example, in 1980 the White Mountain Apache in Arizona, together with a timber company, sued the state, maintaining that state motor carrier and fuel taxes did not apply on the reservation. The U.S. Supreme Court agreed on the basis that the federal government controlled such taxes on reservations. In 1996, the U.S. Supreme Court ruled that in Oklahoma tribal-owned service stations were exempt from paying the state gasoline tax. Thus federal court rulings have, on occasion, made non-Indians subject to Indian laws and regulations on reservations. Further examples are presented in later chapters.

A long-established aspect of sovereignty is represented by tribal courts that arose during the treaty-making era; initially they emerged from traditional Indian customs and laws for particular tribes. By the latter part of the nineteenth century, Indians on reservations were typically resolving their own internal legal disputes. In 1883 the BIA formally launched the Courts of Indian

Offenses with Indian judges appointed by the federal government. These courts sometimes, possibly often, were used to suppress traditional Indian laws and were under the control of local Indian agents. The contemporary court system emerged in 1934 with the Indian Reorganization Act. This system was far more responsive to Indian customs and legal norms and was controlled by each tribe. These courts seek to resolve civil disputes and have limited jurisdiction over criminal law on reservations. Most cases seem to be alcohol-related or concerned with child custody and divorce. One recurrent problem is the difference between Indian customary law and the demands of the Euro-American legal system.

An unexpected and positive aspect of self-determination has been the emergence of tribal colleges. The Navajo Community College (now Diné College) was founded in 1968 because tribal leaders realized that formal education was one key to the future. Leaders were frustrated because many young people lacked the knowledge and skills to cope with Euro-Americans. Before long the federal government acknowledged the potential of Indian colleges, especially in the Tribally Controlled Community College Assistance Act of 1978. As a result, twenty-four tribal colleges were founded, most of which are in Montana and the Dakotas. Typically, the libraries have relatively few books, most faculty have been non-Indian, and the physical plants are inadequate. But because most reservations are located in rural areas with no ready access to four-year colleges, tribal community colleges provide an exceedingly valuable post–high school learning environment (see also Chapter 7).

INDIANS AND ALCOHOL   Treaties and laws referring to Indians in Canada and the United States often made reference to the consumption of intoxicants. In Canada, Indians who were not enfranchised could not buy liquor legally for ordinary consumption until 1951. The Canadian Indian Act of 1951 permitted the provinces or territories, with the approval of the governor in council, to allow Indians to consume intoxicants in public places. This condition existed over most of Canada until 1958. Between 1958 and 1963 the restriction was lessened in most provinces and territories to permit Indians to buy alcoholic beverages in the same manner as Canadian citizens in general—that is, either in a public place or from a package store. A band has the option of prohibiting intoxicants on its reserve lands.

In the United States the first federal regulation of intoxicants among Indians occurred in 1802. The law was modified periodically to ease enforcement and to cover loopholes. The federal government did not repeal this law until 1953. Prohibition still was possible on any reservation under local option. Before Indians could consume intoxicants in some states, state laws against the sale of liquor to Indians had to be changed.

To Native Americans the right to drink has been important symbolically as well as literally. For hundreds of years whites have expressed the opinion that Indians have a tolerance of alcohol lower than their own. Some whites have gone so far as to use the stereotype of the drunken Indian to rationalize not attempting to resolve depressed social and economic conditions among Indians. The question of Indian tolerance of alcohol has been the subject of many studies, but the one by Lynn J. Bennion and Ting-Kai Li (1976) deserves particular attention. They compared the rate of alcohol metabolism in thirty whites and thirty full-blooded Indians who had had some prior exposure to alcohol. They wrote, "Since our study showed no significant difference between American Indians and whites in rates of alcohol metabolism, the conclusion cannot be drawn that racial variations in proclivity to alcohol abuse can be accounted for by racial variations in alcohol metabolic rates" (1976, 12). Subsequent comparable studies validate these findings.

Thus the effects of excessive alcoholic beverage consumption by Indians are best attributed to nonbiological factors, but, as Philip A. May (1994) has stressed, alcohol abuse by Indians is a complex issue. Recent comprehensive studies date from the late 1980s, when about 18 percent of Indian deaths were attributed to alcohol use compared with 5 percent for the general U.S. population. As these percentages are compared, it is essential to be fully aware of the major contributing factors. First, the Indian population is quite young, with a median age in the early twenties compared with a median age in the early thirties for the United States in general. As in the general population, young Indians are the most likely age group to be risk takers and careless drinkers. Second, many Indians live in rural areas of western states, and when they are involved in accidents, aid often is delayed. Third, many Indians live in poverty, which makes them prime candidates for alcohol abuse that leads to accidents, suicides, and homicides. In addition, although broadly based statistics about Indian drinking suggest that the vast majority of Indians are heavy drinkers, this does *not* seem to be the case. The reason is that heavy drinkers inflate the apparent total number of drinkers in arrest and treatment records. That *non-Indians are probably heavier drinkers than are Indians* is suggested in one study: 52 percent of Navajo adults in 1984 drank, whereas at the same time 67 percent of adults in the United States in general drank.

The federal government has recognized the problem of Indian drinking, and by 1986 it had established more than two hundred programs in thirty-four states to combat it. Increasing numbers of these programs have been turned over to Indian management and adjusted to local conditions. Alcoholics Anonymous (AA) is a widely popular alcoholic therapy program for Indians and other U.S. citizens. However, by the late 1990s, there never had been a scientific study of the AA success rate; it appears that AA is no more successful in general than are other approaches to alcoholism.

RESERVATION GAMING OPERATIONS   Although bingo is hardly an ancient American Indian game, it attracted intense Indian interest beginning in 1979 when the Florida Seminoles initiated high-stakes bingo. A 1982 U.S. Supreme Court decision held that reservation Indians could sponsor bingo if the game was permitted elsewhere in the state. There was no direct state or federal control over Indian gambling, nor were Indians subject to any taxes on gambling except those that Indians approved. As a result, the Indian gaming industry was born.

In 1988 Congress passed the Indian Gaming Regulatory Act (IGRA), which made Indian gaming the most rigidly controlled form of legal gambling in the United States. The act identified three categories of gaming that could take place on "Indian lands." Class I is regulated by a tribe and consists of social games or traditional forms of Indian gaming. Class II is controlled by the tribes and the National Indian Gaming Commission established by the act. It includes bingo and card games that are authorized by the state or legally played somewhere in the state and regulates hours of operations and bet or pot limits. Class III facilities are controlled by the tribes and the states in formal compacts. Included are all lotteries, card games, and games of chance apart from bingo. Class III operations are, in essence, casinos. They are considered with reference to specific tribes in Chapters 5, 7, 8, 12 and 13, plus an overview in Chapter 15.

OUTSTANDING INDIANS   At present and in the comparatively recent past, innumerable Indians have achieved prominence in many fields. It is feasible to include only a small cross-section of individuals here. (Indians who have been successful anthropologists are discussed in the next section of this chapter.)

Sherman Alexie (1966–), of Spokane and Coeur d'Alene ancestry, is a prominent young author. His books of poetry have been widely praised, as has his collection of short stories, *The Lone Ranger and Tonto Fistfight in Heaven* (New York, 1993). His novels *Reservation Blues* (New York, 1995) and *Indian Killer* (New York, 1996) are humorous and heartrending. In 1998 Alexie also wrote and coproduced the widely praised film *Smoke Signals*. Robert L. Bennett (1912–), an Oneida, was the BIA commissioner of Indian affairs from 1966 to 1969 and later became the director of the American Indian Law Center at the University of New Mexico. Benjamin Nighthorse Campbell (1933–), a Northern Cheyenne, is an artist, former judo champion, and politician. He was the only Native American in the U.S. Senate. The person of Native American heritage who achieved the highest political status in the United States is Charles Curtis (1860–1936). His mother was a Kaw (Kansa) Indian, and his father was white. He served in the House of Representatives and the Senate before becoming vice president (1929–1933) under Herbert Clark Hoover. Curtis believed strongly in the assimilation of Indians into the greater society.

Ada Deer (1935–), a Menominee, played a critical role in the restoration of the Menominee Reservation after it and other reservations had been terminated by the federal government. Her efforts led to the reinstatement of additional terminated reservations. She later became an assistant secretary of Indian affairs in the Department of the Interior. Deer is currently the chair of American Indian studies at the University of Wisconsin, Madison. Vine Deloria, Jr. (1933–), a Standing Rock Sioux, is possibly the most celebrated Indian writer. He is an attorney and professor best known for his book *Custer Died for Your Sins* (New York, 1969; reprinted Norman, OK, 1988), which includes a vigorous attack on anthropologists. Deloria is an author of ten additional books, and the ones that address the legal issues involving Indians are especially notable. Walter Echo-Hawk (1948–), a Pawnee, is a lawyer with the Native American Rights Fund, the most important advocacy group managed by Indians for Indians. Joy Harjo (1951–), a Creek, is most recognized for her award-winning poetry. She also is a screenwriter and plays saxophone with her band, "Poetic Justice."

Ira Hamilton Hayes (1923–1955), a Pima, was a U.S. Marine hero during World War II. He participated in the assault on the island of Iwo Jima and was one of the marines (in a famous photograph) who raised the U.S. flag at the summit of a volcano under heavy Japanese fire. William L. Hensley (1941–), an Eskimo (Inuit), was born in northern Alaska and played a significant role in resolving native claims in Alaska during the 1960s. He later served in the Alaska House of Representatives and remains an outstanding spokesman for native Alaskan issues. John Bennett Herrington (1958–), an enrolled Chickasaw born in Oklahoma, is a commander in the U.S. Navy. In 1996 he became the first Native American astronaut in the National Aeronautics and Space Administration and was a member of the *Endeavour* crew on a thirteen-day flight in 2002. Maria Montoya Martinez (ca. 1887–1980) was born at San Ildefonso Pueblo and attended an Indian school at Santa Fe, New Mexico. She returned home and married a pueblo member, Julian Martinez. The couple became interested in pottery when they worked for an archaeologist excavating a pueblo site. Their interest intensified over the years, and the couple developed the black-on-black pottery style. By the 1920s her pottery began to be appreciated by collectors, and she became the most famous pueblo potter.

Russell Means (1940–), an Oglala–Yankton Sioux, is best known as one of the American Indian Movement leaders who confronted federal agents at Wounded Knee, South Dakota, in 1973. He also played a dominant role in subsequent confrontations while supporting Indian causes.

N. Scott Momaday (1934–) is a Kiowa raised in the Southwest who attended the University of New Mexico and became an outstanding novelist. His best-known book is *House Made of Dawn*. Momaday also is a widely respected poet. William Lewis Paul, Sr. (1885–1977), a Tlingit, became a lawyer and did more than any other individual to further Tlingit rights and those of other native peoples in Alaska. He was a pioneer in the 1920s in addressing civil rights issues.

William Penn Adair Rogers (1879–1935) was an Oklahoma Cherokee; known as Will Rogers, he was one of the most famous American humorists. He also was a prominent writer and actor. Buffy Sainte-Marie (1942–), a Canadian Cree, is an award-winning folksinger and a songwriter of note. She is an articulate advocate of Indian rights as well. Will Sampson (1934–1987), an Oklahoma Creek, was a notable motion picture actor best known for his role in the 1975 film *One Flew over the Cuckoo's Nest*.

James Francis Thorpe (1888–1953), a Sauk and Mesquakie (Fox) from Oklahoma, was regarded as the greatest athlete in the world after winning gold medals in the 1912 Olympics. Although he was later stripped of his medals on a technicality, they were restored posthumously. From 1907 to 1912,

Thorpe played football for the Carlisle Indian School in Pennsylvania; at that time there were only about 250 students in the school old enough to play football. Carlisle football teams played against major universities and seldom lost a game. The teams of 1911 and 1912 were among the best in the history of football.

SMITHSONIAN INSTITUTION The federal government first became involved with anthropology on a formal and enduring basis in an unexpected manner. James Smithson (1765–1829), a British chemist with considerable wealth, spent much of his life in France. Although he had no obvious ties with the United States, he bequeathed his property to found the Smithsonian Institution (SI), "for the increase and diffusion of knowledge among men." Congress accepted the one-half million dollars in 1846 and built the new institution in Washington, DC. The SI is administered as a private foundation under federal trust. Currently the SI is supported largely by congressional appropriations. Within it the Bureau of Ethnology emerged in 1879; later its name was changed to the Bureau of American Ethnology. Over the years its publications have become a *key* ethnographic source about Native American cultures. An early synthesis, the two-volume *Handbook of North American Indians North of Mexico,* was compiled and edited by Frederick W. Hodge and published in 1907–1910. A second major achievement is the nearly completed twenty-volume *Handbook of North American Indians,* produced under the general editorship of William C. Sturtevant. The first volume appeared in 1978, and the last volumes are now being prepared. The SI also has numerous anthropological subdivisions, including museums, a repatriation office, and an archives program. One important new addition is the National Museum of the American Indian, which opened in 2004.

| Native Americans and Anthropologists

American anthropologists have had a deep and abiding interest in American Indians for obvious professional and less obvious personal reasons. Because Indians in the United States and Canada have been quite accessible and usually considerate hosts, they have served as the subjects for thousands of ethnographic studies. A well-established tradition in cultural and social anthropology is the study of people in at least one other society as a part of professional training. In this manner the observer not only gains meaningful cross-cultural experience but also assembles a body of information that contributes to a broader understanding of humanity. The personal dimension is important because ethnographers typically develop a great affinity for the people among whom they work; they empathize with Native Americans in a way that most others do not. The field study of an ethnographer has two primary goals: to record the activities of people and to employ this information for the solution of theoretical or practical problems. Some Indians are resentful of anthropologists, and we need to ask: What do anthropologists do that may displease Indians?

Describing Native American life, the main purpose of ethnographers, would seem to be a relatively neutral activity. It is important if only because customs are reported that otherwise might go unrecorded and be lost to history. To preserve disappearing information has been a real concern of many investigators, especially those convinced that they were witnessing the rapid disappearance of aboriginal ways of life. Some ethnographers, especially those in the early 1900s, became secular crusaders who devoted their lives to recording cultural ways before they were gone forever. Surely this is a worthwhile, if not noble, goal.

With aboriginal customs as their focal point, many ethnographers recorded behavior that lived only in the memories of Indians. Counting coup (showing bravery by striking or touching a live enemy), scalping an enemy, bison hunts, and feather headdresses were given emphasis in descriptive accounts, conveying the impression that these forms and norms typified Native American life in the recent past. Modern Indians may justly object, because in their lifetimes or during the lives of their grandparents these customs no longer existed. Such ethnographers misrepresented Indians because they froze them in time; this was true of most pre-1930 studies. In retrospect, we can say that anthropologists did not lack compassion, but, unfortunately, they did produce a distorted picture of past practices lasting into the present.

Directly contributing to this misunderstanding is the fact that aboriginal or more recent Indian life often was described in terms of the "ethnographic present." This means that even though an ethnographer was describing extinct customs, the information was reported in the present tense as a literary technique to impart vitality to an account. Criticisms of this technique clearly are valid, especially because so much has happened to Indians historically and in the recent past. It distorts contemporary realities and contributes further to unrealistic views of Native Americans.

D'Arcy McNickle (1970) suggested that the use of the ethnographic present and the failure by ethnographers to present the *adaptive* changes in Indian lifeways has led to another unfortunate result, that of abetting the advocates of Indian assimilation. Acculturation studies became important in ethnographic fieldwork during the early 1930s, and usually stressed the negative aspects of reservation life. This hardly has been a criticism of the Indians involved, however, nor was it intended as a prop for assimilation programs. Instead it often was an expression of dismay about federal programs as they were administered at the time.

Older Indians often are quite sympathetic when an eager ethnographer arrives to collect information about the past, but younger ones often have neutral or hostile attitudes toward these efforts. The older people see what they regard as the essence of Indian life disappearing, and they are well aware that their children or grandchildren often have little or no interest in their cultural heritage as Indians. Thus an old man or woman finds it very satisfying to talk about the past to an ethnographer and have the conversations recorded with care. The attitude of many younger Indians about such information can be one of disinterest or of shame about old customs. If or when these younger people decide to learn about their past as Indians, it is probable that they will have to rely on the writings of the very ethnographers that they now resent.

In a discussion of anthropologists and Native Americans, it should be noted that a number of Indians have emerged as outstanding anthropologists with ethnography as a specialization. Anthropologists long have encouraged—and continue to encourage—Indians to join their ranks. Ethnographers are keenly aware that in many contexts a perceptive insider may be a better reporter and interpreter of Indian life than an outsider. The names of a number of Indian anthropologists come to mind. Francis La Flesche (1857–1932), an Omaha, first collected information about Indians with Alice Fletcher and then worked for eighteen years at the Bureau of American Ethnology. William Jones (1871–1909), of Mesquakie and white ancestry, earned a PhD at Columbia in 1904 and is noted for his research among Algonquian Indians. He was killed by the Ilongots on a field trip in the Philippine Islands. J. N. B. Hewitt (1859–1937), of Tuscarora and white ancestry, was an authority on the Iroquois. Edward P. Dozier (1916–1971), born at Santa Clara Pueblo, was noted for his writings about Pueblo Indians. Alfonso Ortiz (1940–1997) was a part-Hispanic member of the San Juan Pueblo and a specialist in Indians in the Southwest.

Prominent Indians today who are professional anthropologists are numerous. They include Edward D. Castillo (1947–), a Cahuilla and Luiseno, who holds a PhD in anthropology and is best known for his studies of California Indians. Nora Dauenhauer (1927–), a Tlingit, is recognized for her voluminous and insightful studies of the Tlingit. Jack D. Forbes (1934–), Powhatan and Lenape, earned a PhD degree in anthropology and is the chair of Native American Studies at the University of California, Davis. He is best known for his insightful historical studies of Indians. Shirley Hill Witt (1940–), a Mohawk, earned her PhD in anthropology and became a member of the U.S. Commission on Civil Rights. She has been especially active in supporting the rights of women. These are but a few examples.

An important question remains: If anthropologists know so much about Indians, why have they not played a more prominent role as "experts" on culture change among Indians? The basic reason is straightforward. For many years the guiding principle behind federal Indian policy in the United States was assimilation, the sooner the better—a position that anthropologists found distasteful. When the Indian Reorganization Act of 1934 became law, a number of outstanding anthropologists did work for the BIA to further the provisions of the act, because it was designed to restore vitality to reservation life. However, World War II diverted national attention from this program, and the early 1950s ushered in the termination policy, which found little support among anthropologists. In theory and in fact, the BIA was long committed to Indian assimilation, but like most bureaucratic organizations, it has in truth devoted a great deal of energy and funds to its own expansion. Furthermore, bureau personnel often regarded anthropologists as "Indian lovers" and neither sought nor welcomed their advice. Anthropologists in turn have had little sympathy with the bureau policies in general and have preferred not to become involved in most of their programs.

Anthropologists clearly have served Indians in useful and positive ways. They spoke out against the termination policy, although in retrospect not as strongly as they might have. They have worked to increase the effectiveness of health programs, given evidence to support Indian land claims and identity, testified in vigorous support of the Native American church, and often served as advisors to Indians in economic development programs. In recent years anthropologists have aided Native Americans in their efforts to obtain aboriginal resource utilization rights opposed by the federal and state governments. Furthermore, anthropologists have played an important role in interpreting Native American life to non-Indians, both in and out of the classroom.

| Comparing Cultures

In each of Chapters 3–14, a particular tribe is discussed in detail. You will be reading about Indian conventions that seem quite ordinary, reasonable, and even self-evident. In these cases, your reaction no doubt will be one of appreciation and understanding, because you are familiar with these Indian ways; they will seem "normal." On the other hand, you will also be reading about Indian behavior that seems strange, bizarre, and possibly barbaric. In these cases, your response probably will range from negative to abhorrent. Examples will help you realize that behavior associated with human biology is not the same everywhere but rather the result of cultural learning. Among traditional Navajo, for instance, youthful males stand to urinate, whereas older men kneel on one or both knees. Young Navajo women squat, but older women urinate while standing. Then, too, you may regard swearing as universal among peoples around the world. This again is not true. When first contacted by outsiders, Native Americans, Japanese, and some other peoples did not swear. Thus one must be cautious when making broad statements about specific cultural behavior. Our own biases may distort our evaluations.

To better understand American Indians—or any other unfamiliar people—it is desirable to be as objective as possible. Three concepts are introduced for your consideration. The first is ethnocentrism, meaning that one's own lifeway is the basis for judging all other lifeways. This is a commonplace human reaction when exposed to persons in other cultures, especially those quite different from the one in which you were born and raised. Ethnocentrism is "good" in some ways; it gives you a strong sense of personal identity with a particular culture (or subculture). But ethnocentrism is "bad" in other ways; it fosters irrational prejudice, contempt, or hostility toward other peoples. The phrases "a good Indian is a dead Indian," "America right or wrong," and "ethnic cleansing" serve as examples. The "bad" of ethnocentrism overwhelms the "good."

The second concept is cultural relativism, which holds that human behavior always occurs within the context of a particular culture and should be considered within such a framework. Thus every culture has its own standards, attitudes, and particular logic. Stated differently, a culture is considered from an insider viewpoint. We might say that the people in some cultures "smell bad," and we in turn may be accused of "smelling bad." There is no universally accepted standard for how people smell. Euro-Americans cut wood with a handsaw on the push stroke, whereas the Japanese would cut with a handsaw on the pull stroke; the contrast represents different motor habits to achieve the same goal. The people in one culture may believe that "little people" inhabit a hinterland, whereas another people may label such an idea as "nonsense." Is one right and another wrong? No, because the ideas are culture-bound. Ethnographers embraced cultural relativism because it helped them avoid biases built into their own culture. However, as Paul R. Turner (1982) points out, the concept of cultural relativism is in essence ethnocentric.

Turner suggests a third approach. Universalism holds that certain categories of values are universal; they are found in all cultures. A value is a shared concept of what is desirable or undesirable by a people; when combined, all of their values provide a worldview. The universal value categories are the following:

1. power (participation in decision making)
2. enlightenment (access to information)
3. wealth (income, including goods and services)
4. well-being (health and safety)
5. skill (proficiency in any practice)
6. affection (love, friendship, and loyalty)
7. respect (recognition by others)
8. rectitude (ethical behavior)

With this list of value categories in mind, it becomes possible to view the behavior of people, any people, without reference to culture-specific standards. It encourages nonbiased comparisons. In sum, I would encourage you not to be ethnocentric as you read about Indian life. You may take a cultural relativist view, or, better yet, consider universalism as an approach to understanding human lifeways.

| Additional Sources

The best widely available general source about Indians in historical perspective is volume 4 of the *Handbook of North American Indians,* edited by Wilcomb E. Washburn (1988) and published by the Smithsonian Institution. A brief but effective history about Native Americans is by William T. Hagan (1961). For the colonial era the best ethnohistory is by James Axtell (1981). The best presentation about treaties is by Robert A. Williams (1990). The Ghost Dance study by Alice Beck Kehoe (1989) should be consulted for revitalization movements. The emergence of the Pan-Indian movement is detailed best in the volume by Hazel W. Hertzberg (1971). The wide-ranging study of dance, music, and powwows, with emphasis on the Plains, by William K. Powers (1990), is excellent. A relatively recent source concerning tribal government is by Sharon O'Brien (1989). *Indian Reservations in the United States* by Klaus Frantz (Chicago, 1999) is excellent, especially with reference to socioeconomic developments. The classic study of Indian law is by Felix S. Cohen, published originally in 1942 and republished by Lucy K. Cohen (1960) and Charles Wilkinson, editor (1982). An outstanding source about Indian law is by Vine Deloria, Jr., and Clifford M. Lytle (1983). The sovereignty issue in particular is addressed by Francis Paul Prucha (1985). Settlement of Passamaquoddy and Penobscot claims against the federal government is presented by Paul Brodeur (1985). Donald L. Fixico's book (1991) focuses on contemporary issues. The education of Native American children in Canada is presented in a volume edited by Marie Battiste and Jean Barman (1995). A book edited by David Alan Long and Olive Patricia Dickason (1996) examines diverse aspects of modern First Nations developments. W. Dale Mason (2000) provides a book-length presentation about Indian gaming.

| Selected Bibliography

Axtell, James. 1981. *The European and the Indian*. New York.

Battiste, Marie, and Jean Barman, eds. 1995. *First Nations education in Canada*. Vancouver, British Columbia.

Bee, Robert L. 1982. *The politics of American Indian policy*. Cambridge, MA.

Bennion, Lynn J., and Ting-Kai Li. 1976. Alcohol metabolism in American Indians and whites. *The New England Journal of Medicine* 294:9–13.

Brodeur, Paul. 1985. *Restitution*. Boston.

Brookings Institution. 1928. *The problem of Indian administration*. Baltimore.

Cohen, Felix S. 1960. *The legal conscience*. Lucy K. Cohen, ed. New Haven. Reprinted 1982 as *Felix S. Cohen's handbook of federal Indian law*, Charles Wilkinson, ed. Charlottesville, VA.

Cook, S. F. 1955. *The epidemic of 1830–1833 in California and Oregon*. University of California Publications in American Archaeology and Ethnology, vol. 43, no. 3.

Deloria, Vine, Jr., and Clifford M. Lytle. 1983. *American Indians, American justice*. Austin.

Donaldson, Thomas. 1886. *The George Catlin Indian Gallery in the U.S. National Museum*. Annual Report of the Board of Regents of the Smithsonian Institution, 1885, pt. 2, appendix.

Ewers, John C. 1965. *The emergence of the Plains Indian as the symbol of the North American Indian*. Smithsonian Report for 1964, 531–44.

Fixico, Donald L. 1991. *Urban Indians*. New York.

Foreman, Grant. 1932. *Indian removal*. Norman, OK.

Hagan, William T. 1961. *American Indians*. Chicago.

Hearne, Samuel. 1958. *A journey from Prince of Wales's Fort in Hudson's Bay to the Northern Ocean*. Richard Glover, ed. Toronto.

Hertzberg, Hazel W. 1971. *The search for American Indian identity.* Syracuse, NY.

Howard, James H. 1955. Pan-Indian culture of Oklahoma. *Scientific Monthly* 81:215–20.

Jorgensen, Joseph G. 1971. Indians and the metropolis. In *The American Indian in urban society,* Jack O. Waddell and O. Michael Watson, eds., 66–113. Boston.

Kehoe, Alice Beck. 1989. *The Ghost Dance.* Fort Worth.

Kroeber, Alfred L., and Edward W. Gifford. 1949. *World renewal.* Anthropological Records, vol. 13, No. 1.

La Barre, Weston. 1960. Twenty years of peyote studies. *Current Anthropology* 1:45–60.

Long, David Alan, and Olive Patricia Dickason. 1996. *Visions of the heart.* Toronto.

Mason, W. Dale. 2000. *Indian gaming: Tribal sovereignty and American politics.* Norman, OK.

May, Philip A. 1994. The epidemiology of alcohol abuse among American Indians. *American Indian Culture and Research Journal* 18(2):121–43.

McDonnell, Janet A. 1991. *The dispossession of the American Indian, 1887–1934.* Bloomington, IN.

McGuire, Randall H. 1992. Archeology and the first Americans. *American Anthropologist* n.s. 94:816–36.

McKenney, Thomas L., and James Hall. 1933. *The Indian tribes of North America.* Vol. 1. Edinburgh.

McNickle, D'Arcy. 1970. American Indians who never were. *The Indian Historian* 3(3):4–7.

Mooney, James. 1896. *The Ghost Dance religion and the Sioux outbreak of 1890.* Bureau of American Ethnology, 14th Annual Report, pt. 2, 641–1110.

O'Brien, Sharon. 1989. *American Indian tribal governments.* Norman, OK.

Pearce, Roy H. 1965. *The savages of America.* Baltimore.

Powers, William K. 1990. *War dance.* Tucson.

Prucha, Francis Paul. 1985. *The Indian and American society.* Berkeley.

Saum, Lewis O. 1965. *The fur trader and the Indian.* Seattle.

Sorkin, Alan L. 1971. *American Indians and federal aid.* Washington, DC.

Spicer, Edward H. 1962. *Cycles of conquest.* Tucson.

Taylor, Theodore W. 1972. *The states and their Indian citizens.* Washington, DC.

Turner, Paul R. 1982. Anthropological value positions. *Human Organization* 41:76–80.

U.S. Department of the Interior. 1958. *Federal Indian law.* Washington, DC.

Washburn, Wilcomb E. 1984. A fifty-year perspective on the Indian Reorganization Act. *American Anthropologist* n.s. 86:279–89.

———, ed. 1988. *History of Indian–white relations.* Vol. 4, *Handbook of North American Indians.* Washington, DC.

Williams, Robert A. 1990. *The American Indian in Western legal thought.* New York.

Winsor, Justin. 1889. *Narrative and critical history of America.* Vol. 2. Boston.

3 The Netsilik:
Seal Hunting and
Snowhouse Eskimos

*Life is so with us that we are never
surprised when we hear that someone
has starved to death. We are so used to it.
It sometimes happens to the best of us.*

(Rasmussen 1931, 134)

ESKIMOS* QUITE POSSIBLY are one of the most exotic peoples anywhere. In the widely accepted stereotype, they lived in a land of perpetual ice and snow, ate raw meat, wore skin clothing, built snowhouses, and sledded behind dog teams. They were a gentle and happy people who shared wives and never punished their children. Statements such as these are reasonably correct for some Eskimos but not for others who were equally noteworthy in less familiar ways. For instance, Eskimos along the Pacific littoral of Alaska usually went barefoot throughout the year, wore sleeveless garments, and took steam baths. They never saw a polar bear or "mushed" a dog team, and the wooden houses of some villages were backed by great forests. Sadly, perhaps, relatively few Eskimos lived in snowhouses. These observations have far-reaching implications. First, they indicate that Eskimos lived in more varied ecological settings and in different ways than generally recognized. Second, as suggested in Chapter 1, the culture area concept masks regional differences among the peoples within a single culture area. The failings of the classification are well illustrated by the Arctic culture area, which is occupied only by Eskimos. Typical conventions among some Eskimos are foreign to others. This chapter examines a "classic" Eskimo population.

One man, Robert E. Peary, an American naval officer and explorer, is most responsible for the view of Eskimos that prevails in the United States. Between 1886 and 1909 Peary repeatedly voyaged to a base camp in northwestern Greenland in his attempts to reach the North Pole, a goal that he falsely claimed to have accomplished by 1909. For a U.S. citizen to become the first person to stand at the top of the world became a national obsession. Peary's efforts received intense press coverage for more than twenty years. The Polar Eskimos he encountered lived in snowhouses, hunted seals, and had dog teams. They provided Peary with essential help in his quest, and because so much was written about them most Americans came to regard the Polar Eskimos as typical of all Eskimos.

Of the nearly 52,000 aboriginal Eskimos, fewer than 5000 lived in the manner of the Polar Eskimos. The Netsilik (NET-silik) are one people who did. When discovered by Europeans, they possibly numbered 700. Their particular lifeway was one of the most remarkable sociocultural adaptations anywhere on earth.

Eskimo may mean "eaters of raw flesh" in a language of Indians in northeastern Canada. *Netsilik,* or more correctly *Netsilingmiut,* means "the people

---

*The word *Esquimawes,* from which Eskimos is derived, was introduced into English in 1584 and thus is long established. Yet it is considered offensive among some present-day Eskimos because it is not their self-identification. Eskimos in Canada prefer the word *Inuit* or a variant, which means "people" in their language, whereas those in northern Alaska call themselves Inupiat. Greenlandic Eskimos call themselves Kalaallit, meaning "Greenlanders," not Inuit, although this term would be fitting. Most Eskimos in southwestern Alaska and others in Siberia call themselves Yuit or a variant, meaning "people" in their Eskimoan languages. Some Alaskan Eskimos regard themselves as Koniag, and others consider themselves Aleut. In sum, the only generic designation that embraces *all* of these people is Eskimo.

of the ringed seal"; their name is largely an anthropological label. They spoke Inuit (IN-yoo-it) also termed Inuktitut (in-NOOK-t-toot), a language with sixteen dialects ranging from east Greenland to the Bering Strait area of Alaska. It is related to the Yupik (YOO-pik) language of Eskimos elsewhere in Alaska and eastern Siberia. Inuit and Yupik are distantly related to Aleut, the language spoken on the Aleutian Islands. These three populations make up the Eskimo–Aleut language family.

The Netsilik homeland is tundra country dominated by lichens, mosses, and other low-growing plants. The tree line is far to the south, a critical factor with respect to their material culture. Driftwood was their major source of wood; the people thought trees grew at the bottom of the sea and surfaced as driftwood after they died. The coastline of Netsilik country is convoluted with many inlets; rivers are common and lakes innumerable (see Figure 3-1). Virtually all of their domain is north of the Arctic Circle. Thus for part of each year there is no alternation between daylight and darkness. Instead there is continuous daylight in midsummer, and the darkness of winter is relieved only by moonlight and reflected sunlight. The winters are long and cold, with the mean daily temperature in January about −20° F; −40° F temperatures are common. On average there are twenty frost-free days a year.

The Netsilik spoke Inuit with minor local differences. They had neither a tribal name nor a clear sense of tribal identity. Instead, an individual was a member of one of nine named bands (a relatively small sociocultural group), each identified with a hunting area. Band membership was somewhat fluid, and rigid boundaries between bands did not exist; a sense of oneness among bands was lacking.

Eskimo biology is of interest, if only because of where they live. Compared with contemporary Euro-Americans, early historic Eskimos usually were of medium stature, not short, with large chests and relatively short legs. They were typically *not* fat, although their bulky garments and muscular build might suggest corpulence. Their heads and faces were relatively large, whereas their hands and feet were somewhat small. Eskimo physiological adaptations to the cold are evident in relatively recent studies. Their basal metabolism was elevated from 13 to 33 percent above the Du Bois (normal) standard and was highest among those living under essentially aboriginal conditions. Their higher metabolic rate was attributed primarily to diet, not to genetic differences from Europeans. Core body temperatures were much the same as among whites, possibly because Eskimo skin garments protected their bodies from extreme cold. When exposed to cold under test conditions, however, Eskimo finger and hand temperatures rose quicker than those of Europeans, and Eskimos had a greater cold tolerance at low temperatures. Their capacity to withstand low peripheral temperatures probably included a genetic factor. Summarily, Eskimos stand somewhat apart from most other peoples in their capacity to withstand cold. When genetic identity, language, and culture are weighed in combination, these Arctic peoples exhibited greater homogeneity than is known for any other North American culture area.

Figure 3-1 | The early historic Netsilik homeland.

| Aboriginal Life

In this and most other chapters about specific Native American groups, I follow much the same format. I first emphasize and present Indian life before intense contact with Westerners, followed by a relatively brief presentation of major historical changes. Each chapter concludes with an account of contemporary developments and issues.

Aboriginal Netsilik life was exceedingly different from contemporary American life. For example, a Netsilik lived all of her or his life with about fifty or fewer persons who were exceedingly well known to each other and usually related by blood or marriage. In a lifetime a person might never see more than two hundred other Netsilik at any one time and seldom had contact with non-Netsilik. Knowledge was self-gained or verbally transmitted across the generations; they were nonliterate, not illiterate. A family moved often from one camp to another and had no permanent home. A person could carry most of his or her belongings from one camp to the next. Furthermore, an individual wore one set of garments until they were outgrown or disintegrated. Illness was thought to be caused by evil spirits, and life expectancy may have averaged about thirty years. Intermittent hunger was a fact of life, and starving to death was an ever-present possibility. These realities should be considered as you read about their aboriginal lives.

ORIGIN MYTH Unlike most people around the world, the Netsilik did not have a unified account about the beginning of life on earth. Instead, a number of nonsequential myths addressed particular origins, and they did not attempt to reconcile inconsistencies or contradictions.

The earth always existed and was dark when the earliest people appeared; they survived without pleasure or suffering. Then people crossed a body of water on kayaks lashed together to form a raft. As they approached their destination, the children anxiously jumped into the water to go ashore. A little orphan girl was thrown into the water because she had no relatives. As she clutched a side of the raft, her fingers were cut off, and she disappeared beneath the water. Her detached fingers became alive, bobbed about, and turned into seals. The orphan girl emerged as the Sea Goddess who controlled everything on which the people depended for food. The Weather God was ill-disposed toward people and could, with his great power, produce storms to prevent men from hunting. The Moon God, the third major deity, was not especially powerful but was reasonably sympathetic toward people. The Sun and Moon were thought to be brother and sister who had an evil mother. She planned to kill them but they murdered her instead and became lovers who ascended into the sky.

In primeval times, spoken words produced immediate results. When the fox repeatedly said "darkness," it became dark, enabling him to raid human food supplies. The hare repeatedly said "day" to find a place to feed. Subsequently, darkness and light alternated. All animals and people died in a flood except for two male shamans. They copulated, and one man gave birth to males and to females.

MATERIAL CULTURE Among aboriginal North Americans, only Eskimos and some northern Indians wore tailor-made garments. Most Netsilik clothing was cut from caribou fur, an exceptional material for cold-weather apparel. Caribou fur is soft, light, and dense; each hair is hollow to provide excellent insulation. The caribou fur of a man's outer parka, worn for hunting and traveling, faced outward, and the fur on his inner parka faced inward. Parkas had hoods and sometimes front and back flaps with border trim. Decorative panels

Figure 3-2 | An engraving of three Netsilik. The man lost a lower leg in an encounter with a polar bear. The ship's carpenter on the Ross expedition in 1830 fitted him with a wooden leg. Note the facial tattoos of the women. (From Ross 1835.)

of light-colored fur adorned the arms and shoulders (see Figure 3-2). Inner and outer trousers reached from the hips to the knees, and two pairs of boots protected a man's feet. The fur of mittens faced outward; gloves were introduced to Native Americans by Europeans. A child wore a hooded combination suit that was put on and removed through a laced opening at the chest; this garment also had an opening at the groin for elimination.

A woman dressed much the same as a man, but her garments were more bulky. A woman wore a single pair of trousers with boots attached that was held up with a belt. It is sometimes thought that a baby was carried in the hood of a mother's parka, but this was not so; a roomy pouch at the back of the parka accommodated an infant. On the outside of the parka, a cord that ran beneath the baby and over the mother's breasts held the infant in place. As a naked infant began to relieve itself, the mother quickly released the cord and rapidly removed the baby, holding it by its arms until it eliminated, irrespective of the weather.

Females were tattooed around the time of puberty and later, a painful process. Sinew threaded through an eyed needle was covered with soot and plant juice and laced beneath the skin. Alternatively, the skin could be punctured and the wounds rubbed with the tattooing substance to produce a blue color. Relatively simple facial tattoos were complemented by others on the hands, arms, and thighs that could be quite elaborate.

Two qualities in particular characterized Netsilik material culture: the limited nature of the raw materials available and the relative technological simplicity of the finished artifacts. The two major clusters of raw materials were flexibles (e.g., sinew and skins) and solids (e.g., antler, bone, snow, stone, and wood). In addition, the most valuable material of a plastic nature was a blood-based glue.

The preparation of skins was dominated by women and had emerged as the most integrated, complex, and time-consuming technological process. After a man had killed and skinned a caribou, the skin could be processed in varied ways. To prepare skins for inner garments, for example, a woman placed a raw skin on the ground with the flesh side down and anchored it with stones for preliminary drying. Subsequently, people slept with the underside of these skins around their naked bodies. In this manner skins were softened for scraping and stretching. A skin then was placed outside to freeze, and the subcutaneous (beneath the skin) layer was removed with a sharp-edged bone scraper. Finally, because of the strength required, a man thinned a skin with a scraper before it was cut and sewn by women.

Sealskin is more durable than caribou skin and has far greater resistance to water. A key use of sealskins was for kayak covers. A woman scraped the underside of these skins with a semilunar-bladed knife made from ground slate and set into an antler handle. She scraped the skin further and chewed it until all of the fat was removed. Skins were then rolled up and placed in a snowhouse on a drying rack that was suspended over a soapstone lamp fueled with seal oil. After a number of days the hair rotted and was scraped free. Kayak covers were stored in the snow until they were cut, fitted, and sewn over a kayak frame. Women used bone needles and thread made from caribou sinew. To make a waterproof seam, they used a blind stitch, one that was carried halfway through the skins; but for fur clothing a simple overcast stitch was satisfactory. Sealskins were the best not only for summer boots and kayaker parkas but also for tent covers, packsacks for dogs, and containers for oil or water. Sealskin thongs (*babiche*) served many purposes, especially as binders for composite tools and weapons.

Snow as a solid was a key raw material. It is often observed that Eskimos had many words for snow, depending on its particular qualities (e.g., snow in the air, soft and watery snow), an obvious indicator of its importance. The snowhouse unquestionably is the best-known Eskimo structure. It is widely thought that *igloo* means a snowhouse, but the word refers to any type of dwelling. The availability of snow, the nomadic nature of Netsilik life, and the scarcity of wood made snow an ideal building material. When constructing a house of snow, a man first tested a snowfield with a long, slender antler probe to make certain that the snow was sufficiently deep and of acceptable consistency. A large snowhouse, about fifteen feet in diameter, could be completed by a skilled craftsman in about an hour. The builder first drew a circle in the snow with his antler snow knife to outline the size and location of the structure. Enough blocks for the house could be removed from within the circle. Each block was about twenty inches long, twenty-five inches wide, and four inches thick. Lower blocks were cut with a basal slant to form a circular wall that spiraled upward as a dome. A long tunnel to trap cold outside air was added, as was a dome-shaped entryway. The builder shoveled snow over the new structure to fill cracks and provide additional insulation. He made a small ventilation hole in the ceiling and used a block of clear river ice to replace a snow block above the entrance to serve as a window. A sleeping platform was constructed of snow blocks at the rear of a dwelling, and another platform held a soapstone lamp with a drying rack suspended above it. The occupants of a snowhouse attempted to keep the temperature inside somewhat *below* freezing. Otherwise the snow froze on the inside and turned to ice, making the house colder.

Snow served additional construction purposes. Snow-block windbreaks protected men in the winter as they fished or hunted seals, and snow blocks piled on one another served as platforms for meat storage. In the fall, before satisfactory snow became available for a snowhouse, blocks of river ice were cut to form the vertical walls of a dwelling roofed with tent skins.

With the scarcity of wood, caribou antler emerged as a major raw material. Antler is relatively soft but strong and easily worked, and after being heated it may be bent into various shapes. Bone by contrast is hard, brittle, and more difficult to process. A primary tool for working antler or bone was an adz with a ground and polished stone blade lashed to an antler handle. The blade of an adz is set at right angles to the handle, whereas an ax has a blade parallel to the handle; greater cutting control is possible with an adz. To cut antler or bone into sections, a man fit a small stone blade into an antler handle. For refined cuts, an antler-handled knife was fitted with a stone blade in a groove near one end. Holes were made with a bow drill, and blood-based glue served to join two pieces of wood for tent poles and weapon shafts.

Another critical solid material was soapstone, available in one sector of their country. It is comparatively soft and was cut from the source with an ice pick and then shaped with an adz, drill, and knife. A soapstone lamp was about twenty inches long, oblong in shape, and had a flat bottom with low sides. The final key soapstone artifact was a woman's cooking pot, her most valued possession. It was rectangular, about twenty inches long, and steep sided, with holes in the corners for suspension over an oil lamp.

Figure 3-3 | A man completing a sled with runners of frozen fish wrapped in sealskins. The caribou antler crossbars are lashed in place with sealskin lines. (Courtesy Canadian Museum of Contemporary Photography, 65-2696. NFB Collection. Photograph by Doug Wilkinson.)

Technological ingenuity is in the eyes of the beholder, and most beholders would agree that the dominant Netsilik sled was an ingenious artifact. The first step in construction was to cut sealskins from a summer tent in half and soak them in river water to soften. Next, the two sections of skins were spread flat, and on each one, overlapping fish were placed along one edge. The fish on each portion were rolled tightly, bound with thongs, flattened, turned up at one end, and left to freeze to form the runners. Caribou antler crosspieces were placed at right angles between the runners and bound in place with thongs (see Figure 3-3). Crosspieces occasionally consisted of frozen meat. To protect the skin runners at the bottom, a thick mixture of moss, snow, and water was frozen in place. Finally, to make the sled shoes, a man squirted mouthfuls of water on a piece of polar bear fur and rubbed it on the bottoms of the runners to create a shoeing of ice that would slide freely over the snow.

Kayaks were narrow, about twenty feet long, and had round manholes. Frames preferably were made from driftwood, although components might be fashioned from antler. Bent sections of dwarf willow formed the ribs. Thongs joined the components, resulting in flexible joints that tended not to break with hard use. Each fall a kayak was stripped of its cover and cached (stored) on piles of stones near areas in which caribou would be hunted the following year. That spring women prepared and sewed new kayak covers.

As will become evident, the Netsilik were relatively mobile in their subsistence round. Although the foregoing inventory of artifacts is not complete, it does suggest that their material culture was limited. Most everything a family owned could be sledded from one camp to the next or carried in packs by dogs and people. The portability of their artifacts is remarkable, especially considering how and where they lived.

THE SUBSISTENCE ROUND* A key to food-getting success for a family was to be at an optimal location at the right time to harvest edibles. This was a strategy of interception, as opposed to the pursuit of quarry. During a normal year the habits and availability of most key species could be predicted, and a man was free to hunt anywhere. Caribou migrated north from the tree line in the spring, and most of them returned south in the fall. Arctic char descended rivers to the sea each spring and returned in the fall. Seals do not migrate, and people began to hunt them after ice formed on the sea.

Localized food resources varied considerably; only the major subsistence methods are detailed here. Beginning in the fall as the weather turned cold and blustery, small groups of families moved to riverbank camps to fish for char. Because by then their tepeelike skin-covered tents were cold, men chipped blocks of river ice to form walls for houses roofed with tent skins. To fish, a man chipped a hole in the river ice with an ice pick and removed the small pieces of ice with an antler scoop. He knelt close to the hole, and with one hand he jiggled an ivory lure attached to a sinew line in the water. In his other hand he held a two-pronged leister (fish spear). As a char approached the lure, the fisherman impaled the fish on the leister. A man fished in this manner for hours, days, and weeks. Char provided daily food, and any surplus was stored in ice-block caches. By November, as the river ice thickened, this fishing method became unrewarding; families lived on cached char or previously harvested caribou meat until the sea ice thickened.

By January several scattered extended families sledded with their belongings from riverbank sites to camp on an expanse of sea ice. (An extended family consists of two or more consanguineal families spanning a number of generations; e.g., two brothers, their wives, and children.) The move by dogsled was slow and often arduous, especially over fields of broken ice. Only one or two dogs, with the help of people, pulled a sled; larger teams could not be fed. Very young children rode on a sled, while all others, young or old, walked. Women usually walked in front of a team to encourage and help guide the dogs. After reaching the sea ice, hunters searched for an expanse of flat ice likely to include a concentration of seal breathing holes. Families built their

---

*For this and the other tribal chapters, some of the widely used artifacts are described and illustrated in Appendix A.

Figure 3-4 | Men at a sealing camp on the sea ice in 1923 as they prepare to hunt seals at their breathing holes. Each man has a dog on a leash. (Courtesy of The National Museum of Denmark, Department of Ethnography. Photograph by Knud Rasmussen.)

snowhouses nearby. Seals are active throughout the year and must maintain a series of holes in the ice to breathe through about every fifteen minutes. As the ice thickened, a seal scratched and gnawed the ice at a breathing hole to create a funnel-shaped opening. On the surface the hole was covered with snow and frost from seal's breath. Most important, a seal used numerous breathing holes over a comparatively wide area. It was strategically desirable for as many hunters as possible to be stationed at a cluster of breathing holes to increase the probability that a seal might be harpooned at a particular hole.

Hunting ringed seals at their breathing holes required skill and patience and was physically demanding. The most capable hunter at a camp decided where they would concentrate their effort. After a hearty meal the men set off, each with a dog on a leash (see Figure 3-4). Snow concealed the breathing holes, but dogs could sniff out their approximate locations. When his dog had found such a spot, a man signaled to the others, who came running. Each man attempted to find the hole with a snow probe. The finder of the hole, irrespective of whose dog made the preliminary discovery, became the hole "owner," and with his snow knife he cut the snow away from above the hole. Using a long slender breathing hole probe of antler, he determined the hole's configuration so that he could launch his harpoon at a key point if a seal appeared. The small exposed hole was re-covered with snow to deceive a seal, and a seal indicator was placed in the hole. This indicator consisted of a split section of sinew attached to a sinew thread, with a small piece of swansdown tied at the end. When a seal entered the hole to breathe, the delicate indicator would move. After the indicator was in place, a man made as little noise as possible, because seals have a keen sense of hearing. To keep his feet warm and to muffle any sounds of movement, the man stood on the fur bag in which he had carried his sealing equipment. Next he stuck two peglike harpoon rests in the snow adjacent to the hole. Fur on the harpoon rests muted the noise as he lifted the harpoon to strike a seal. Bending slightly and leaning forward with his hands up his sleeves, the hunter waited with his eyes fixed on the seal indicator; and so he might remain, statuelike, for hours. According to one account, fifteen men bent over breathing holes for eleven hours and harvested a single seal.

If the seal indicator moved, a man grabbed his harpoon in one hand and held the coiled line attached to it in the other hand. He thrust the harpoon as hard as possible into the breathing hole, and the pointed bone harpoon penetrated the seal's body. A basal hole in the harpoon head was fitted to a foreshaft, which was designed to receive the impact of the thrust without breaking the harpoon head. The foreshaft was attached to a wooden shaft with an ice pick at the base. As a seal attempted to escape, the harpoon head toggled in its body in the manner of a button in a buttonhole. The harpoon head was attached through a hole to the handheld line, and the seal was played until it was exhausted. The last step was to enlarge the breathing hole with the ice pick and pull the seal onto the ice. Other hunters soon arrived, and, after making a cut in the seal's underside, the liver and some blubber were removed and eaten raw. After the incision was closed with a wound plug, dogs dragged the seal to camp. Each family shared in the catch. (Their elaborate distribution system is described later.)

Hunters sometimes discovered fresh polar bear tracks on the ice and anxiously followed them after turning their dogs loose. The dogs brought the bear to bay until the hunters arrived. If it was possible the men used a variety of weapons, including lances, bows and arrows, and harpoons, to dispatch the bear. Men and dogs alike were often maimed and sometimes killed. The man who actually killed a bear received the skin, and all of the others shared the highly desirable meat.

By late spring families abandoned the sea ice and sledded to the adjacent coast, where small groups camped together. After erecting their summer tents, they began sealing on the melting sea ice. By then the breathing holes of seals were large, and seals sunned themselves near holes for long periods. Under these circumstances, women and children stood at breathing holes and drove off seals as they surfaced to breathe. Thus hunters at other breathing holes were more likely to make a kill. This, the most rewarding sealing method, was employed as long as ice conditions permitted.

During the summer, and to a lesser degree in the winter, the subsistence pursuits varied depending on the edibles available to a particular band. Band members might collect seagull eggs, fish for lake trout with barbless hooks, fish for char with leisters at stone weirs (see Figure 3-5), hunt musk ox, and pick berries. Yet during the late fall, caribou hunting typically dominated.

As caribou congregated for their southward migration, they were hunted intensively because the animals were fat and their fur made prime garments. One prominent hunting method involved the cooperation of entire families. People camped on high ground near the narrows of lakes habitually crossed by migrating caribou. From a campsite they could see caribou far off and prepared

Figure 3-5 | Men and a woman fishing at a stone weir. Each person held a line in his or her mouth to string captured fish. (Courtesy Canadian Museum of Contemporary Photography, 64-2345. NFB Collection. Photograph by Doug Wilkinson.)

to intercept them. As animals entered the lake water, concealed men launched their kayaks and paddled furiously to lance as many animals as possible. As frightened and wounded caribou approached the opposite shore, women and children appeared on the bank waving skins and imitating the cry of wolves. The confused caribou turned back, only to again face the kayakers. At the end of a hunt each man paddled to his kills, tied them together, and slowly made for the shore. Hundreds of animals could be taken in this manner. Soon after they were beached, children feasted on the eyes as adults ate raw meat. After butchering the harvest, everyone enjoyed cooked meat at leisure and cached excess raw meat beneath piles of stones.

The foregoing accounts of subsistence activities may suggest that these people thrived, especially considering the aptness of their technology, their knowledge as hunters, and their persistence. But this was not the case. If for any reason migrating caribou did not appear at a lake crossing as expected, then the waiting families went hungry. With little or no food at hand, they might be unable to reach another hunting site, and to fish locally could prove unsuccessful. Likewise, when hunting seals on the winter ice, severe storms could force men to remain idle for long periods. If there were few seals locally, the families camped nearby were forced to scatter before they starved. When a family waited too long, a man might not have the strength to hunt at a new sealing site, or the site could prove unrewarding, and they starved. Around 1920, from a population of 259, 25 people starved to death within two years. Starvation led to cannibalism. "Hunger holds terrors; hunger is always accompanied by dreams and visions that may destroy even the strongest man and make him do things he would otherwise detest. So we never condemn those who have eaten human flesh; we have only pity for them" (Rasmussen 1931, 136).

DESCENT, KINSHIP, AND MARRIAGE Who are one's most meaningful relatives? This is a key question regarding one's kinship rights, duties, and obligations. In some societies the closest kinship ties (bonds based on descent) are traced primarily through females (matrilineal), whereas other peoples stress genealogical bonds primarily along the male line (patrilineal). Still others trace kinship ties through both females and males. This patterning prevails in the United States today and among the Netsilik; it is identified as a bilateral descent system. (The bilateral descent system in contemporary America must not be confused with our pattern of typically taking our father's surname. This practice may give added stress to the father's line, but a mother's line may be equally or more important in the lives of some individuals. The Netsilik did not have family names in early historic times.)

Among the Netsilik and contemporary Euro-Americans, close relatives belong to personal kindreds. A *personal kindred* consists of the consanguineal (blood) relatives of a person on his or her generational level, as well as junior and senior generations. In brief, blood relatives on both sides of your family to whom you trace step-by-step kinship ties represent your personal kindred. Significantly, *only* your siblings (biological brothers and sisters) share your personal kindred. The personal kindreds of your cousins differ from your own.

Why is a personal kindred important in many societies with bilateral descent? Most of all, it expands close kinship bonds beyond the nuclear family (a husband, wife, and their children) because it includes extended family members (minimally the families of two siblings). These family types provide a person with a network of meaningful relatives through the female and male lines for security in social, economic, and other contexts. As is typical for the Netsilik, members of one's personal kindred did not live together, nor did they usually assemble as a group. In addition, the members of a personal kindred with whom one never interacted were ignored. However, contrary to the definition of a personal kindred, some Netsilik relatives by marriage (affinal relatives) could be included when they lived with or had other close social ties with the kindred's members. In the Netsilik case, marriage was with a member of one's personal kindred.

We take our kinship terminology (the configuration of words used to identify relatives) for granted and may assume that peoples in other societies share our system. Some do, but most do not, as is evident in this and later chapters. If we begin by acknowledging that no particular kinship terminology is "natural" or "universal," understanding the differences among peoples is less difficult.

In a worldwide study of kinship terms, it was established that the words used by a male ego ("I") for female first cousins provides one useful guide for understanding a particular kinship terminology. A second, equally important, guide is provided by the terms used by a male ego for his parents and their siblings.

In the basic Netsilik cousin terminology (ego's generation), the term for "brother" was extended to all male first cousins, and the word "sister" included all female first cousins. Obviously, their sibling terms had broader meaning than ours do. In normal conversation a Netsilik did not distinguish between his or her brothers and sisters and cousins, but a person could identify these individuals precisely when necessary (e.g., my biological sister, my father's sister's daughter). Technically, the Netsilik cousin terminology is called Hawaiian because that patterning prevailed in Hawaii, and it came to be identified as a classic type in anthropological writings.

For the parental generation (the first ascending generation above ego), the Netsilik had separate words for mother, mother's sister, father's sister, father, father's brother, and mother's brother. The Netsilik system for the parental generation is termed bifurcate collateral, meaning that collateral lines are separated and termed differently.

The *basic* Netsilik system of kinship terminology appears as Figure 3-6. The symbols in this and all subsequent kinship diagrams follow the same pattern. A circle symbolizes a female; a triangle, a male. Short parallel lines represent marriage. The long horizontal lines and short vertical lines represent descent. The point of departure for examining a diagram is a male "Ego." Each letter represents a different kinship term.

The kinship terminology of these people was more complex than indicated in the figure, and all of the particulars need not be detailed. A number of observations, however, are pertinent. They identified older and younger sisters and brothers by different terms, depending on whether the speaker was male or female. They distinguished between blood relatives and those by marriage; once again the terms varied depending on the gender of the speaker. Nuclear family members were terminologically separated from other relatives except for cousins of the opposite sex, an important exception. We already have seen that uncle and aunt terms on each side of a family were different. Yet ideally a father's brother's relationship with this nephew was emphasized because the boy lived with or near both his father and his father's brother, who formed the core of an extended family. Likewise, relative age was important within an extended

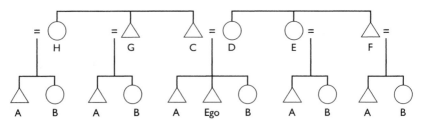

Figure 3-6 | The *basic* early historic Netsilik kinship terminology.

family, with younger persons deferring to older ones as reflected in the sibling and some cousin terms. Although it is not recognized in their cousin terminology, a Netsilik ideally married a first cousin. Thus for a man a "sister" became a "wife," and preferably she was a member of the husband's local group. Finally, a married couple typically lived with or near the husband's family (patrilocal marriage residence).

SOCIAL DIMENSIONS Eskimos may not have been the most congenial people in the world, but they had few serious rivals. For one Netsilik band, Jean L. Briggs (1970, 311–366) provided a preliminary review of emotional concepts and their social implications. Eskimos usually are judged as shy or nonaggressive, except for small children, and so it was with the group studied by Briggs. People tended to be bashful, withdrawn without being hostile. In fact, hostility in various forms was strongly disapproved, again with the exception of small children. Ill temper and aggression were associated with Euro-Canadians, who, like small Netsilik children, angered easily, became moody, and had strange ideas. Aspects of ill temper included jealousy, envy, and verbal or physical aggression.

Humor assumed many forms but may be best associated with pervasive laughter, either at oneself or someone else. The context in which people laughed varied, from behavior that was unacceptable or inappropriate to simply amusing. Eskimos who spoke a different dialect or the sounds of a foreign language caused laughter. The English word "affection" also had multiple dimensions. Its most crucial aspect was protectiveness; to feed the hungry, warm someone who was cold, or safeguard a person from harm were its manifestations. This rubric also was reflected in wanting to be with a loved person, as when a husband remained in bed with his wife because she was ill. Then there was happiness. To smile, laugh, and joke were personally satisfying and infectious for others. Happy experiences included play, telling stories, or sharing pleasant company. Happy individuals were worthy.

Given the texture of social life, emotional expressions such as these focused on a relatively small number of persons. The basic social unit was the nuclear family. The different and yet complementary work of women and men within a nuclear family is typical around the world. Netsilik men primarily obtained food because it would be unwise to expose women to the dangers of the hunt. Women cared for children, cooked the food, and processed skins for various purposes. Yet a nuclear family could not be self-sufficient for very long and was fully integrated into an extended family. In the Netsilik case an extended family usually consisted of an elderly father, his married sons, and their children—possibly fifteen individuals—who lived in adjoining tents or snowhouses and aided one another. A number of extended families occupied a winter sealing camp; as many as about fifty persons lived near one another.

At a large camp on the sea ice a dance house was often built, and it symbolized group cohesion. As snowhouses were constructed, four of them could be arranged as a square that became the base for a large, high-domed dance house that partially encompassed the original structures. As the central dome neared completion, portions of the inner walls of the adjoining houses were removed so that the activities of the occupying families were visible to one another at the periphery. The central dome area served as a community hall in which people danced, sang, and observed the seances of shamans.

The mutual dependency between hunters was institutionalized in a system of partnerships illustrated by the sharing of a seal at a large winter camp on the sea ice. In the snowhouse of the successful hunter, his wife butchered a seal into fourteen precise, named units that she distributed. The hunter received little meat but was given choice blubber. A man's sharing partner was unrelated, or distantly related, because to share with near relatives was a normal expectation. The choice of a partner was made by the parents of a boy, and sons tended to replace their fathers in particular partnerships. Thus dyadic (paired) socioeconomic integration spanned generations. A hunter addressed a sharing partner by the term for the portion of a seal that the partner received (e.g., my shoulder, my hindquarters). Behind this and other sharing was potential or real hostility felt toward persons outside of one's extended family. Partnerships tended to mute potential ill feelings between men and bound them to one another for food and thus for survival.

POLITICAL LIFE Concepts such as chief, honored elder, or judge were unknown. To write about Netsilik political life almost seems wrong. A more appropriate label could be "social control." In a strict sense each band was autonomous and had neither a formal leader nor a sense of political unity with another band. To the contrary, bands generally were hostile to one another. In late prehistoric times a state of "war" prevailed among bands that led to murders and massacres. The people were suspicious of strangers and would attack them when it seemed advantageous.

Within a band the leaders were older hunters who guided the activities of their extended families. Typically an extended family represented a bloodline of males, but it could be adjusted to include outsiders, especially by adoption. In this kin-based society, an extended family head was identified as "the one who thinks," but for important decisions the opinions of all adult males were welcome; a consensus was sought. In a decision age distinctions, specific kin ties, and the personalities of those involved were weighed.

Conflict between individuals took varied forms. A common means to express displeasure was to withdraw from a vexing situation and thereby avoid potential conflict. Gossip and ridicule also were powerful means to induce conformity, especially considering how few people lived together. Personal differences likewise could result in fistfights or in formal song duels (explained subsequently); in an extreme case, a deviant might be killed. The reactions of individuals varied widely in what appeared to be similar situations, such as a theft or an insult. One man could ignore such an episode, whereas another might contemplate the perpetrator's murder. In addition, a grudge could be harbored for many years before erupting. The cases that follow are drawn largely from the fieldwork of Geert van den Steenhoven (1959).

To avoid potential disharmony in a camp, newcomers were obligated to obtain permission to live there from those already established. This rule may have applied primarily to strangers. In one instance a man and his family from farther north moved near Pelly Bay. Although the residents distrusted outsiders, they permitted the family to remain there. They laughed at the man and abused him nonetheless. They knocked him over as he hunted at seal breathing holes. They poked fun at him for not having local relatives, and before long he and his family left. In his anger he performed sorcery to cause starvation at Pelly Bay, and many of those who had laughed at him slowly starved to death. As a postscript the sorcerer later died of starvation.

Songs were popular in many contexts. There were songs for hunting, joking, and magic; however, derisive songs were highlighted. The community hall at a winter camp typically was the setting for a derisive song exchange. A "song duel" could be either spontaneous or prearranged, with no clear-cut division between the two. One man sang and danced and might beat a tambourinelike drum as he poked fun at another man. The victim sang in response, and the man whom the audience applauded the most became the informal winner. To win approval, the text of a song might be based on fact, such as a theft, or on an accusation of avarice. Being henpecked was another subject for a song, as was murder. In addition to their value as pure entertainment, these exchanges represented social criticism and served to release tensions between individuals. At the same time, songs could mend ruptured friendships. But all exchanges did not end well; a "boxing" match might result. In this case the opponents faced one another and alternated in delivering blows, but neither man attempted to defend himself. The winner was the man who continued to strike blows longer.

The sanctioned murder of an adult resulted when band welfare was considered in jeopardy. In one instance an angry man killed another without provocation. Subsequently, he threatened everyone and wounded his wife with a knife. The man's instability posed a threat, and his logical executioner, in Netsilik thinking, was his brother, the oldest family member. The older brother told the murderer that he planned to kill him and asked how he wanted to

Figure 3-7 | This Netsilik man shot and killed his brother, who was a menace to the group. (Courtesy of The National Museum of Denmark, Department of Ethnography. Photograph by Knud Rasmussen.)

die—with a knife or a bullet or by hanging. The victim chose a bullet and was shot to death (see Figure 3-7). Likewise, a sorcerer might be killed for common good. For killings of this nature, "execution" is an acceptable label. The most common cause for murder, however, was when one man desired the wife of another man and killed for her. A woman sometimes married two men (polyandry), and one husband might kill the other. Occasionally a woman killed her husband, in one case because the husband was hot-tempered. Surprisingly, in historic times the relatives of a murder victim did not seek blood revenge, but judging from legends that practice had prevailed in late prehistoric times. In sum, and admittedly the evidence is not the best, social control customarily was achieved by individuals and families, not by band members as a collective.

RELIGION A minimal definition of religion, "the belief in Spiritual Beings," was proposed by the first modern professional anthropologist, Edward B. Tylor (1871, 23). Among the many more detailed definitions, the one by Melford E. Spiro (1966, 96) is notable. He defined religion as "an institution consisting of culturally patterned interaction with culturally postulated superhuman beings." Within the parameters of either definition, Netsilik religion was quite different from what a modern Euro-American might expect. The Netsilik did not have an integrated body of dogma and ritual, structures devoted to religious purposes, or an annual calendar of ceremonial events, and priests (full-time specialists in supernatural matters) were unknown. Notwithstanding, religion was convoluted and complicated; it dominated their lives.

The conceptual basis for religion is encapsulated in accounts about the world's creation as summarized early in this chapter. In daily life the Sea Goddess, Weather God, and Moon God were the most powerful deities. Additionally, a host of greater and lesser spirits existed, and supernatural forces generally were hostile toward humankind. Fear more than solace characterized their religion. Amulets were thought to aid their owners, young or old, female or male, to gain protection from negative forces and thereby foster prosperity. Within each amulet resided a beneficial spirit force; the physical object was not important in itself. Amulets might be animal teeth, small bones, or miniature artifacts. They were attached to a parka or to an amulet belt. Some amulets were thought to produce hunting success and to promote physical skills. Others fostered personal well-being, and a third group protected one from evil and aided in shamanistic activities. One individual had eighty amulets. As Asen Balikci (1970, 203) noted, "[a]mulet spirits clustered around each person like a ring of supernatural protectors and helpers. They were individually owned and aided only their owner." Closely akin were magic words that were covert and highly personal and that worked to achieve a specific goal. These words were either learned from one's father or obtained by payment to a shaman. They could not be heard by anyone else and were said in secret or when alone. Such words helped to ensure success in caribou hunting or in fishing for a particular species.

A man derived his strength, health, and power from his immortal soul, usually conceived as an intangible replica of his physical body. Little information is available about the personal souls of women. Despite the positive qualities of a personal soul, it was vulnerable to evil forces. In one means used to avoid harm, a shaman would perform rituals at the time of a male's birth to remove his personal soul from his body. The soul was magically placed beneath a soapstone lamp, usually one belonging to a close relative of the mother. Here his personal soul remained and strengthened.

Each person, female and male, possessed name souls based on personal names; names were not identified with gender. The greater the number of sequential personal names, the greater the protection. The inventory of traditional names varied a great deal. Examples include "the unlucky one," "leister," "butterfly," "the round one," and "the one who just shit." Many names for males especially were thought to make them more manly, and for a woman they helped to ensure the health of her children.

Ordinary and extraordinary happenings in Netsilik life were bound by a rigid network of taboos. A *taboo* is something that is both sacred and forbidden. Taboos had become a major basis for the religious system. To ignore or to break a taboo invited disaster for individuals or potentially for an entire band. In the broadest terms, a land—sea dichotomy was fundamental and best reflected in the hunting of caribou as opposed to seals. To mix edibles from the land and the sea was antipathetical to the Sea Goddess and was surrounded by innumerable taboos. Taboos applied not only to people and animals but also to key localities in the subsistence round. A specific site for hunting caribou, or a stone weir for fishing, could be sacred and enveloped by restrictions that promoted successful harvests.

The rituals surrounding the harvest of a seal on the winter ice illustrate one set of taboos. The soul of a seal was thought to be highly sensitive to how its body was treated. To pacify a soul and help ensure its reincarnation into the body of another seal, a particular procedure was followed. Clean snow was placed on the floor of the snowhouse before a seal was taken inside for butchering. The animal was given a drink of water, and as long as it remained there adults were prohibited from most routine work. The skull of each seal was kept. As the people left the site, the accumulated skulls were faced in the direction that the people would travel. These and other conventions were rigidly observed. Innumerable taboos likewise were associated with caribou and polar bear kills. By observing taboos, some of the stresses in food-getting were reduced, but success was never assured.

Although adults in general had the individual ability to deal with supernatural forces, two major groups of specialized practitioners dominated. Those associated with lesser powers, head lifters, had no formal training. Their goals were to establish what taboo had been broken to cause illness in a family and to determine where game was located. Customarily a wife stretched out on her back, and her husband tied a thong around her head. He questioned the ghost (helping spirit) of one close relative after another to identify the broken taboo. The husband pulled upward on the thong. If his wife's head was "light," the answer to a particular question was negative; if "heavy," the head indicated a positive response. Thus evil spirits were forced to abandon a sick person, while helpful spirits aided in the food quest. This technique was used only when the aid of family ghosts was sought.

Shamans, as part-time specialists in supernatural matters, focused on spirits as individuals. Unlike all other persons, shamans integrated the natural and supernatural spheres at the highest level. A shaman's daily routine was the same as for other males, but he stood apart because of his superior abilities. A boy identified as having potential to become a shaman was instructed by a practicing shaman. The apprentice was constrained by many food taboos and prohibited from having sexual intercourse. As he began to receive visions of spirits, a snowhouse was built for his further instruction. Here he learned secret words from his instructor, and his parents presented him with a shaman's headdress and belt. The power of a shaman focused on one group of protective spirits that he attempted to control; such a spirit was called a *tunraq*. After completing his long and arduous training, the apprentice was given a tunraq by his teacher; but initially the spirit controlled the novice. He became a practicing shaman within a band only after he learned to control this spirit.

As a shaman aged, additional spirits came to his aid, and still others were gifts from other shamans. Some of these supernaturals were easily manipulated, whereas others were unreliable and potentially dangerous. The latter might rage out of control and in their fury cause illness and death. These dangers were real enough, yet another class of spirits were especially hostile toward people, the *tupiliq*. The tupiliq was round to the point of bursting its blood-filled body and was inherently evil. Thus the greatest challenges confronting a shaman were to cope with tunraqs gone astray and with tupiliqs.

One primary function of a shaman was to counteract hostile spirits after a broken taboo, which was viewed as the cause of all illness. His goal was to drive one or more evil spirits from the patient's body. Normally the rituals were held in the victim's dwelling with an audience in attendance. After the lamps were extinguished, the shaman covered himself with a caribou skin. He called for a protective spirit to enter his body through his mouth. After the spirit arrived, the shaman went into a trance. He began to speak in his secret vocabulary to re-move the tupiliqs from the patient with the aid of his helpful spirits, but the tupiliqs hid outside. The audience lured them to return. When they appeared, the shaman fought them with a snow knife. He killed as many as possible, as evidenced by the blood on his hands. If the patient died, however, the rea-son was that the shaman had failed to kill all of the evil spirits. This became the explanation for failure to heal.

Miraculous travels to the underworld and to the moon and encounters with monsters provided evidence of a shaman's capacity to go far beyond the ordinary. Shamans also called forth their spirit helpers to attract game, to con-trol the weather, and to avert famines. In situations such as these, as well as when curing, public confession of taboo breaking played an intimate part in shamanistic efforts to rectify the imbalance in nature or among people. Arbitra-tion clearly was a shaman's major function. Another was to resolve differences between individuals, most often arising from envy and jealousy. Sometimes shamans used their power for personal goals and thus behaved in an antisocial manner. For example, a shaman who was sexually attracted to an unwilling woman might threaten her with illness to achieve his end.

To maintain and reinforce their positive authority, shamans singly or in competitions gave public demonstrations of their powers. To apparently wound oneself with a spear and thereby bleed or to suddenly grow a beard impressed an audience. And so it is elsewhere in the world when an audience does not know the basis for the trickery. Deception of this nature was real among the Netsilik, but to identify shamans as simply tricksters is mistaken. They believed in their powers, as did other Netsilik. In a sense shamans were incipient psy-chologists and scientists as they sought to understand cause and effect in the world.

LIFE CYCLE An ethnographic account of any people is enhanced by an overview of the lives of individuals. The transitions from one stage to the next deserve special attention. Passage ceremonies (rites of passage) in particular acknowledge changes in status that permanently alter the relationships of an individual with members of the greater community. Birth, puberty, marriage, old age, and death are prominent examples. As the Netsilik life cycle is compared with those of peoples described in later chapters, the differences in Native American lifeways will become abundantly apparent.

As the time of a birth approached for a pregnant Netsilik woman, a small snowhouse was built for her in which she remained alone for about four days. Isolated and unassisted, she gave birth on her knees. During an especially difficult delivery, she recited various personal names (name souls). When delivery followed the calling forth of a particular name, it meant that a specific name soul had entered the body of the newborn. The mother cut the umbilical cord with a special knife and cleaned the neonate with a special piece of skin that became a potent amulet. The baby soon was placed in the pouch at the back of the mother's parka. For the next month the mother and baby moved into a new snowhouse built for them. Sometimes she was visited by females, but she could eat only certain foods and observed, many other taboos for the next year.

Female infanticide prevailed widely among Eskimos, but the Netsilik rate was unusually high. Apparently as many as half of the Netsilik females born were killed or permitted to die. An unnamed and unwanted baby girl might be suffocated, placed in the entrance of a snowhouse to freeze to death, or buried alive in a shallow grave. The name souls of these dead were thought to seek reincarnation. A baby named before or soon after birth was permitted to live. The father usually made the infanticide decision. An abandoned baby could be adopted by anyone who found it alive, and a newborn was not killed if the baby was promised in marriage.

Why was the rate of female infanticide so high? It was not because children were unloved, as will soon be apparent, or because these were a cruel and heartless people. One reason may be that women made no significant and direct contribution to food getting. Another is that local group solidarity increased if women did not become the wives of outsiders; first-cousin marriages and female infanticide strengthened a local group. Betrothing an offspring before she or he was born to a near relative likewise furthered group cohesion. Still other variables have been noted. Not only did girls not become hunters, but when a mother nursed a girl for the usual two or three years, the woman was less likely to conceive and was thus possibly unable to bear a male offspring. During famines families could not support a newborn. Likewise, when a starving family was on the move, any child, male or female, who could not keep up with the others was abandoned to die. More formal child killings also are reported. In one instance a mother in her fury stabbed her son after he broke her valuable soapstone pot; the child soon died.

Life and death decisions such as these were a family concern, not a matter of religion or morality. The physical survival of a family had precedence over the life of an individual. Thus there were many more boys than girls. Nonetheless, the adult sex ratio was nearly balanced. One major reason was that numerous men died in hunting accidents. Then, too, men were more likely to die from starvation or to commit suicide than were women.

An Eskimo stereotype is that small children were neither punished nor told "no," an exaggeration with more than a grain of truth. Briggs (1970) recorded many insightful particulars about traditional child rearing when she lived with a small isolated group of families in the 1960s. She found that young children often raged, screamed, cried easily, and were unreasonably demanding. The adult reaction was to appease them, to respond by amused laughter, but not to be critical. Little children had "no mind," meaning that they were incapable of reasoning. They began to gain this capacity as they learned to walk, to talk, and to remember. A child soon learned that a parent's raised eyebrows indicated "yes" or a wrinkled nose meant "no." As a child approached the age of six, an expanding ability to reason was expected. Instruction was by example, and to succeed or to fail in a task produced laughter from adults. Children and adults alike commonly used a phrase comparable to "just a minute," rather than saying no.

In the life of a small child, the birth of a sibling could be initially traumatic. To nurse on demand and to be carried in the back of a mother's parka had provided comfort and security. As a small child competed with a newborn, the mother distracted and comforted the child. The child in turn soon became more self-aware and self-sufficient. Maturing years brought absorption in solitary play and behavior comparable to "let's pretend." By the age of ten a girl helped her mother in meaningful ways, and by the age of twelve a boy was becoming a hunter.

A girl's menarche (first menstruation) involved innumerable taboos, as was the case for a woman in childbirth. Netsilik women did not have what modern Americans would consider a regular menstrual cycle. The reason was that a woman of childbearing age was usually either pregnant or nursing. When a woman did menstruate, she made the fact known to adults in a camp because she was regarded as impure. She stayed in her dwelling, avoided talking about game animals, and observed other prohibitions deemed essential for personal and community good.

In societies around the world, life tends to focus on birth, marriage, and death with differential emphasis. For the Netsilik, complications centered on marriage. Problems that contributed to the complexity were the scope of female infanticide, accidental deaths among adult males, deaths from starvation, low population numbers, and the physical proximity of a potential mate. Ideally a mother arranged a betrothal of a son soon after his birth to a young girl or to one as yet unborn. This was not always possible, and some marriages could not be arranged until a male was older. Additional alternatives existed. Widows and widowers were potential mates. Another man's wife might be stolen, or on rare occasions one man might kill another and take his wife. Plural marriages (polygamy), although uncommon, added another dimension of complexity. A woman might have more than one husband (polyandry) because of the scarcity of women, or an outstanding hunter might have more than one wife (polygyny); women were attracted to a man partially because of the security he provided as a hunter.

Marriages preferably were between first cousins, as described previously. A girl was expected to be married by the age of fifteen. For a male the age was about twenty because so many years were required for him to become a skilled hunter. A marriage ceremony did not exist, but a woman was expected to have property of her own, most important a soapstone cooking pot and soapstone lamp. The bride with her possessions customarily joined the family of her husband, or else the couple lived nearby (patrilocal marriage residence). Marriages were unstable until an offspring was born, and a woman could have had numerous trial marriages. A young husband continued to hunt and fish with relatives and friends in the same area in which he was raised, an obvious economic advantage.

A Netsilik couple was typically loving and caring, although having sexual relations outside of marriage was institutionalized. The arrangement was typically made by men who were friends or partners. Their presumption was that the wives would cooperate, which was usually the case. Concurrently, wives might informally arrange an exchange but leave the formalities to their husbands. Sexual desire may have produced many such arrangements, but a practical aspect existed. For instance, when a man planned a long trip and his wife was pregnant, he could arrange to take his partner's wife to perform womanly obligations on the trail. Wife exchange could be for a night or for a lifetime. A permanent exchange of spouses might result, or the practice might lead to jealousy, bitterness, and sometimes murder.

In the routine of adult life, food and children dominated, with the specter of death from starvation ever present. In this regard it is essential to realize that these people could not meaningfully stockpile food from one year to the next. As a result each subsistence year began anew, irrespective of how productive or poor the previous year had been. The trials of living did not lead to personal bitterness and dissatisfaction with life. Quite to the contrary, social geniality prevailed; warmth, good humor, and laughter dominated. Admittedly, jealousy, envy, and animosities could and did exist beneath the surface and could erupt in violence, to the travail of all.

As Knud Rasmussen (1931) noted, men dominated in marriages, but wives were not passive; quite the opposite. Wives not only were outspoken but also appear to have been more mentally agile in arguments. A couple did not customarily use given names when talking with one another. Pet names prevailed. These included "my new wife" and "my dear little elder brother." Likewise, children were called by names of affection, such as "my bit of a child," and children addressed their parents in a similar manner. In addition, an intimate sign of affection, nose rubbing, was a form of kissing between a man and woman or an adult and a child.

Living in a snowhouse or other structure was confining because the dwellings were small. Each person, young or old, was allotted a little space toward the back of a residence where people lounged and slept. Inside, at the rear of a dwelling, garments and equipment were stored. At the front were food and household items. As vividly conveyed by Briggs (1970), family members were inordinately considerate of one another, with the exception of small children. Bedtime was decided by the man of the house, who undressed and slipped into the sleeping skins, followed by all the others. This was the time when a man talked about the distant or recent past, times of trauma and times of joy, as family members fell asleep.

A death in a family could be planned, as in the case of infanticide, or it could be devastating, as when a hunter–husband–father died in an accident. Additionally, deaths of adult males from suicide were common. Balikci (1970, 163–172) examined thirty-five cases of suicide in a population of less than three hundred people. He found that there was about one suicide each eighteen months, an extremely high rate. Most suicides were committed by married men between twenty-four and fifty years of age who had children. A man was most likely to hang himself as a result of personal distress, such as the violent death of someone close to him, personal illness, or other misfortune. These data are contrary to the suicide pattern associated with Eskimos in which older people killed themselves because they felt useless; comparatively few Netsilik suicides were of this nature. Balikci suggests that Netsilik religious beliefs best explain most suicides. They believed that the manner of death influenced afterlife. The soul of a person who died a violent death, including suicide, dwelled in the most desirable afterworld.

After a person died the soul lingered with the body for a number of days, and household members were prohibited from normal work. They feared that the soul would become an evil spirit and do harm. During this period of mourning the people observed numerous taboos, such as not combing their hair or feeding dogs. In the winter, following the mourning period a body was sledded out on the ice by close relatives and left there without ceremony. During the summer a corpse was placed on the tundra with one stone at the head and another at the feet, and the person's earthly possessions might be left nearby. After disposing of a body, the people of a camp moved elsewhere. A soul was thought to be immortal, and it journeyed to one of three afterworlds.

The souls of notable hunters, especially those who died violent deaths, and of women who had suffered the pain of having large and beautiful tattoos went to a place high in the sky in which life was good and they never aged. Deep beneath the earth existed another favorable afterworld entered by the same persons, but here the seasons were reversed. Finally, women without exceptional tattoos and lazy hunters existed just beneath the surface of the earth, where they huddled with closed eyes and hanging heads and with only butterflies as food.

| Historical Developments

Written history is young in the Netsilik region. Their homeland is in the far north, and the adjoining seas are ice clogged most of the year. The first European explorer to venture there was John Ross, the leader of a British expedition. In 1829 he set out to find a northwest passage to the Orient. He failed in this effort, although he did discover the magnetic pole and the Netsilik. The passage was first navigated by the Norwegian Roald Amundsen in 1903–1906, and he was the first person to describe the Netsilik in reasonable detail. By then Netsilik life had begun to change as commercial whalers ventured to north-western Hudson Bay in the 1880s. Many Netsilik soon moved east from their homeland to Repulse Bay to take advantage of trading opportunities.

The people were amazed at the wealth of artifacts aboard the ships of explorers and whalers. Most of all, they coveted iron to replace the stone blades for their weapons and tools. The amount of wood on ships astounded them. In addition to iron and wood, they were anxious to obtain rifles and ammunition. Cloth was desired for summer garments, and tobacco and tea became desirable but previously unknown stimulants. Matches, exotic foods, kerosene-burning stoves, and metal containers likewise were greatly appreciated. As imports became widely available, the people gave up their traditional material culture with little hesitation. They were technological empiricists. By the early 1950s the Netsilik had abandoned their traditional way of life, and sooner or later all of the Netsilik were drawn into the fur trade.

Cooperative seal hunts on the sea ice declined in the 1920s as rifles became more readily available; a lone man with a gun could also harvest caribou throughout the year. The introduction of gill nets made fishing easier and more productive. A gill net looks rather like a tennis net with floats attached at the top and sinkers at the bottom. When a fish of appropriate size swam into a net, it was held in the mesh by its gills. Their traditional fish spear (leister) required the presence of a fisherman, whereas a gill net "worked" all of the time. With changes in hunting and fishing methods, food sharing was confined to near relatives. Likewise the earlier dependence on spirit aids, amulets, and magic in the food quest declined; hunting and fishing became mundane concerns. Yet to obtain rifles, nets, and other imports from the south, men were obligated to trap fur animals, especially white fox, and as a by-product of hunting seals for food, the skins were sold to traders. They obtained these animals on an individual basis, and each man kept his earnings.

Effective social control over the Netsilik by outsiders gained momentum in the 1930s. The Roman Catholics built a mission at Pelly Bay in 1935 that included a small store stocked with staples. It was not unusual for missionaries in isolated communities in the far north to operate trading posts. By the 1940s most Netsilik had become Christians. Missionaries were respected and were probably feared as rich and powerful white shamans. The conversion to Christianity was rapid and met no serious opposition. A major contribution of missionaries in the Canadian Arctic, beginning in 1876, was the development of an Eskimo (Inuit) syllabary. As a result literacy was rapidly achieved outside of a formal educational context. This syllabary in a modified form continues to be widely used in newspapers, as well as government and mission publications.

The Hudson's Bay Company established a post at Gjoa Haven in 1927, and a Royal Canadian Mounted Police (RCMP) station was founded at Spence Bay in 1949. In the early 1950s the Canadian government for the first time launched

Figure 3-8 | A hunter from Pelly Bay (Kugaaruk) searching the sea ice for seals in June 1997. (Photograph courtesy of David F. Pelly.)

serious programs to maintain sovereignty in the far north. Concurrently, the influence of missionaries and company traders began to decline. Many Canadian outposts were centered at or near Distant Early Warning stations (DEW Line radar units). A radar station and airfield were built near Pelly Bay between 1955 and 1957. Local Netsilik built houses at Pelly Bay from materials retrieved from the DEW Line dump site. Likewise snowmobiles would soon replace dog teams; the "iron dog" only "ate" when it worked (see Figure 3-8). As a result, hunting pressure on caribou and seals declined as the need for dog food diminished.

By the early 1960s the people lived primarily at Gjoa Haven, Pelly Bay (Kugaaruk), and Spence Bay (Taloyoak). Canadian government programs began to make an expanding impact on Netsilik life. Each family with children received monthly Family Allowance funds (now Child Tax Credit), depending on the number of offspring and their ages (see Figure 3-9). This was a major source of income for these cash-starved communities. In addition, anyone over sixty-five years of age received old-age assistance, and numerous welfare programs aided needy families. Schools, nursing stations, and family homes were built in the three major communities. Families also received electricity, heat, and water delivery and had waste facilities as municipal services at low cost. Jobs maintaining the infrastructure increasingly dominated the local economy, but most families continued to hunt, fish, and trap for a living. By the 1970s

Figure 3-9 | Spence Bay (Taloyoak) children in 1999. (Photograph courtesy of David F. Pelly.)

animal-rights advocates in Europe and the United States rejected the use of *all* animal pelts and skins in any context, a devastating blow to the local economy. Likewise Westerners successfully campaigned to stop the use of jaw traps because of the suffering of captured animals. With these developments, combined with the price fluctuations for pelts and skins, the people lost control of their economy in the world marketplace.

As aboriginal conditions and those in the relatively recent past are compared, one conclusion is self-evident: traditional artifact production as a means of making a living had nearly disappeared. Manufactured products from the "south" had won in the "north." The most important locally produced artifacts are for the art and tourist markets. If nothing else, this demonstrates modern Inuit technological adaptability. Before the arrival of whites, as mentioned previously, the Netsilik made cooking pots and lamps from a local source of soapstone. It is the primary raw material for their art and craft productions. From 1948 to 1962, the Canadian artist James Houston encouraged the Inuit of the eastern Arctic to produce soapstone carvings for sale. Some Netsilik began to participate, although the effort did not have a major impact at Gjoa Haven until about 1970. By 1990 about nine hundred people lived there, most of whom were Netsilik. A few years later thirty-two men and seventeen women were soapstone carvers; for ten men it was a full-time occupation. To obtain soapstone located some ninety miles away required a number of snowmobile trips each year to the source, and men often attempted to combine quarrying with caribou hunts. Soapstone was processed with hand tools and electrical equipment. The inspiration for a carving was typically drawn from oral traditions, especially legends. Carvers attempted to impart the spiritual qualities of their subjects—human, animal, or the combination. Thus the basis for their art was intimately associated with traditional cultural knowledge. Carvings by the bestknown Netsilik artists are in museum collections and are sold at galleries in Canada and elsewhere.

| Recent Changes

Historically, the most momentous change to affect the Netsilik occurred on April 1, 1999, when they, along with other tribes in the eastern portion of the Northwest Territories, were granted their own territory, Nunavut ("our land"). The capital is Iqaluit (Frobisher Bay) on Baffin Island. The Nunavut area represents about one-fifth of the Canadian land surface, and in 1999 it had a population of about 28,000, some 85 percent of whom were Inuit living in twenty-seven widely dispersed communities (see Figure 3-10). In Canada a territory is under far greater federal control than a province, which meant that the federal government was largely responsible for this step toward greater autonomy of the Inuit involved. The federal start-up commitment was C$1.1 billion (Canadian dollars), beginning in 1993 when the claims agreement was negotiated.

Figure 3-10 | Patrick Qaggutaq, a Pelly Bay (Kugaaruk) resident in 1997. (Photograph courtesy of David F. Pelly.)

In 2000–2002, more than 90 percent of the C$640 million was from the national government. (By 2001 a single person living in Iqaluit received C$259 a month as income support from the territorial government; a family of three received C$665 a month. The residents of more isolated communities received greater cost-of-living funds.)

The creation of Nunavut as an Inuit territory was a long and involved process. Life in the three Netsilik communities, as in other scattered villages, is dominated by the seat of government at Iqaluit and, equally important, by the federal government in Ottawa. In the first Nunavut election for the new legislative assembly, 88 percent of the eligible voters turned out to elect the nineteen-member legislative body. Paul Okalik, at thirty-four years of age, became the first leader of the assembly, the youngest person to hold the office of premier in all of Canada.

Inherent conditions contributing to the current Nunavut growing pains merit review. First is its remoteness from the rest of Canada—the relatively small and widely scattered communities, limited traditional economic resources, prohibitive transportation costs, and poor living standards when compared with these aspects of living in the remainder of Canada. Second, and of critical importance, the federal government remains in control of funding, especially unanticipated budgetary needs—for example, the rebuilding of schools if they are destroyed by fire. Third, the federal government has been critical of the Nunavut government for the manner in which it spends some funds and is vigorously seeking greater efficiency. In one instance the Nunavut spent C$2.3 million on a computer payroll system that they soon abandoned. A fourth concern is whether many Nunavut officials have the capacity to meet administrative needs, because of their inexperience and inadequate educational backgrounds.

Considering the newness of the Nunavut government, however, its initial accomplishments are praiseworthy, if only because the new administration is functioning without any deplorable consequences. The legislators are struggling to achieve one major long-range cultural goal, that of restoring their aboriginal language, Inuktitut (Iñupiaq). The founders of Nunavut knew full well that much of their cultural identity was intimately associated with their language. It was the first language of virtually all of the older people, but it had been played down by Euro-Canadians over the years. The Inuit were determined to ensure the perpetuation of Inuktitut once they had greater control of their land. They felt that making it *the* language for government administration could help to better achieve self-rule.

Accomplishing their goal of teaching Inuktitut systematically in their schools will not be easy. In practical terms, one initial barrier is the newness of federal schools, in which English has been established as the language of instruction. Currently the quality of Inuktitut classroom instruction suffers, because there are not enough qualified language teachers. Furthermore, at present large numbers of preschool children speak English as their first language, and although they may be taught Inuktitut in school, they tend not to speak it outside of the classroom. Most youths under fifteen years of age had not progressed beyond the ninth grade. One reason appears to be that to obtain an adequate family meat supply, boys must learn to hunt. This means that they will miss school as they become hunters. (An estimated 80 percent of the males continue to be full-time hunters.) Given these circumstances, it appears that most Inuit males will not have had sufficient education, or desire, to become Inuktitut speakers by 2020. In sum, the current educational time, administrative effort, money, and future allocations of funds may be able to perpetuate this aspect of Inuit life most effectively for females. At best, males may thwart these efforts unless they accept the legislators' desire for government to be conducted in Inuktitut.

The major natural resource for the far northern peoples had long been identified as the harvest of wild animal skins, especially those of seals and white fox. The fur trade was the primary reason that the Hudson's Bay Company opened trading posts in Netsilik country. The Nunavut Inuit in general depended almost entirely on these stores to obtain Canadian edibles, manufactures, and other imports. The international market for furs diminished in the late 1900s because of changing fashions in Western garments, as well as campaigns by animal rights advocates in the United States and Europe. The U.S. market for marine animal skins closed following the Marine Mammal Protection Act of 1972, which prohibited the import of such skins, as well as any items manufactured from them. By the early 2000s the market for animal skins remained depressed in Nunavut, leaving the current generation poor and more dependent than ever before on federal resources.

In the 1980s the region that became Nunavut was being successfully promoted as a tourist destination by the government of Canada and the Northwest Territories. After Nunavut emerged, the early attempts to attract these visitors were modest, and they failed. A far greater effort was financed again in 2000–2002 when Nunavut Tourism received about C$1 million to attract visitors. The impact of this financing is yet to be determined. A serious obstacle in attracting large numbers of tourists at present is the expense. A seven-day guided kayak trip to Kugaaruk (Pelly Bay) costs over C$4000 per person, including air fare from Winnipeg.

Thus far Nunavut financial survival has resulted from being understaffed. When Paul Okalik became premier in 1999, the government headquarters had only 20 percent of the anticipated and funded number of employees. By 2003 the staffing was 81 percent, of whom 43 percent were Inuit. For the short term, the understaffing proved advantageous. The money from unspent salaries was used to cover operating deficits. By April 1, 2004, the surplus was gone.

Contrary to prevailing economic conditions, the Inuit future in Nunavut is coursing in an unexpected direction. Why? *Diamonds.* They are crystals of pure carbon, the hardest naturally occurring substance. Geologically, diamonds originate in ancient kimberlite pipes formed deep within the earth. These pipes typically rise above the present-day ground surface, but in the far north glacial erosion has characteristically destroyed the upper portions of pipes. Evidence for potential diamond finds is associated with the recovery of G-10 garnets, which were found in the Northwest Territories of Canada in the late 1980s. Based on this and other evidence, five promising pipes were drilled in 1994, and diamonds of gem quality were recovered. This discovery launched the current diamond rush in northern Canada. The existing finds in Nunavut, plus the productive mines in the Northwest Territories (see Chapter 4), have resulted in the greatest known mineral rush in the world.

In 2003, diamonds were found near the western border of Nunavut. The property of one mine is valued at C$1.25 billion. Furthermore, the diamond prospects on Melville Peninsula to the east are excellent. In 2003, some C$82 million was spent there by prospecting companies. Irrespective of this, Nunavut government expectations are cautious because they do not hold mineral rights in all of their country. Thus Inuit royalities from diamonds may not be as great as anticipated.

Perhaps the earnings from diamonds will help resolve the social and economic difficulties faced by the Netsilik and the other Inuit in Nunavut. These have had a serious impact in recent years. The 2001–2002 federal statistics report a crime rate four times higher in Nunavut than elsewhere in Canada and a sexual offense rate ten times greater. Also, five times more children under fourteen years of age were living with grandparents. The suicide rate is also a major concern. Statistics from a different source show that thirty-one suicides occurred in October 2003, a record for one month in the territory. Quite often the Inuit who kill themselves are between the ages of fourteen and twenty-four, with romantic relationship breakups as a major cause. Suicide prevention efforts intensified in 2001, when the suicide rate had become one of the highest in the world. As noted earlier in this chapter, however, suicide was well entrenched among the historic Netsilik.

A pilot study of suicide in two non-Netsilik communities was made in the recent past by Michael J. Kral (2003). His findings may be applied with caution to Nunavut villages in general. In interviews and questionnaires, Kral obtained systematic information about Inuit concepts of social harmony and what constitutes a good life. (The ultimate goal was to identify means to prevent the high suicide rate.) One key to harmony centers on frequent positive interactions with one's immediate family members (i.e., the ability to communicate) and on developing positive bonds with other relatives. Wellness is identified with talking over problems within families, and acquiring traditional knowledge from older persons ranks very high. Prominent reasons for self-murder among youths in particular are hurtful romantic relationships and serious family problems. In many ways this indicates a desire to return to the values of parents and grandparents.

Other problems seem to best account for the high incidence of self-destruction. Housing is often inadequate, and homes may be grossly overcrowded. The relatively new pattern of cluster housing in relatively large villages is unprecedented. Compared with the past, neighborhoods often appear to represent new social combinations of friends, relatives, and acquaintances living among strangers and even foes as a relatively recent development. It also is clear that compared with the rest of Canada many Nunavut homes are grossly substandard.

If poor housing is indeed a major factor underlying suicide, reasonably productive diamond mines could yield sufficient money to implement programs to build houses, help resolve other social difficulties, and restore harmony. A possible danger is that the Nunavut government may absorb most of the diamond profits in administrative expansion, yet underfund conditions that causing unrest and fail to provide housing aid to the many poor families. This would further erode what it means to be Inuit. Diamonds may be forever, but their contribution to general Nunavut well-being could be far less meaningful than anticipated.*

| Additional Sources

The best book-length presentation about the variability in aboriginal Eskimo culture unquestionably is by Edward M. Weyer (1932). The most durable popular and authoritative discussion of Eskimos is by Kaj Birket-Smith (1936). Early accounts about Eskimos by explorers and others are examined in my book on the subject (Oswalt 1999). The best overview about North American Eskimo prehistory, ethnography, and history into the early 1980s is the widely available *Arctic* volume of the *Handbook of North American Indians* edited by David Damas (1984) and published by the Smithsonian Institution.

It was not until 1923 that Knud Rasmussen (1931), of Greenlandic Eskimo and Danish descent, compiled his wonderful, yet eclectic, baseline Netsilik ethnography. The second seminal study to focus on traditional life was by Asen Balikci (1970) based on fieldwork from 1959 to 1965. His book is a key source for the presentation in this chapter. Balikci's ethnographic film reconstructions of traditional culture are excellent. A third major study, based on fieldwork in the 1960s, is by Jean L. Briggs (1970), whose presentation about traditional family life is superior. The monograph by Geert van den Steenhoven (1959) is the best source concerning traditional Netsilik legal concepts. The key presentation about Eskimo kinship terminology is by Marc G. Stevenson (1997).

| Selected Bibliography

Amundsen, Roald. 1908. *The North West Passage.* 2 vols. London.

Balikci, Asen. 1970. *The Netsilik Eskimo.* Garden City, NY. (Other edition: 1989).

Birket-Smith, Kaj. 1936. *The Eskimos.* London. (Other editions: London, 1959; New York, 1971).

Briggs, Jean L. 1970. *Never in anger.* Cambridge, MA.

Damas, David, ed. 1984. *Arctic.* Vol. 5, *Handbook of North American Indians.* Washington, DC.

---

*Judging from experiences at some Canadian reserves and at reservations in the United States, a major new source of a great deal of money may not meaningfully help a typical family.

Kral, Michael J. 2003. *Unikkaartuit: Meanings of well-being, sadness, suicide, and change in two Inuit communities.* National Health Research and Development Programs, Health Canada, Project #6606-6231-002. Np.

Nunatsiaq News. 2001–2004. (Inuit newspaper).

Oswalt, Wendell H. 1999. *Eskimos and explorers.* Lincoln, NE. (Other edition: 1979).

Rasmussen, Knud. 1931. *The Netsilik Eskimo.* Report of the Fifth Thule Expedition, 1921–24, Vol. 7, pts. 1–2. Copenhagen.

Ross, John. 1835. *Narrative of a second voyage in search of a North-West Passage.* London.

Spiro, Melford E. 1966. Religion. In *Anthropological approaches to the study of religion,* Michael Banton, ed., 85–126. London.

Stevenson, Marc G. 1997. *Inuit, whalers, and cultural persistence.* Toronto.

Svensson, Tom G. 1995. Ethnic art in the northern Fourth World. *Études/Inuit/Studies* 19(1):69–102.

Tylor, Edward B. 1871. *Primitive culture.* Vol. 1. London.

Van de Velde, Franz, Trinette S. Constandes-Westermann, Cornelius H. W. Remie, and Raymond R. Newell. 1993. One hundred and fifteen years of Arviligjuarmiut demography, central Canadian Arctic. *Arctic Anthropology* 30(2):1–45.

van den Steenhoven, Geert. 1959. *Legal concepts among the Netsilik Eskimos of Pelly Bay N.W.T.* (Report no. NCRC-59-3). Northern Co-ordination and Research Centre, Department of Northern Affairs and Natural Resources.

Wenzel, George. 1991. *Animal rights, human rights ecology, economy and ideology in the Canadian Arctic.* London.

Weyer, Edward M. 1932. *The Eskimos.* New Haven.

4 The Chipewyan: Subarctic Hunters

*Before the flood, caribou were easy to
hunt with the bow and arrow, but after
it the arrows could not pierce them: it
was just as if they were nothing but
bone. The hunters had to aim at their
heads and hit a vein to make them
bleed to death. Then the raven said,
"We cannot kill the caribou because
they are only bone," and while all
others were asleep it stayed up and
made magic all through the night. It
was the raven that gave the caribou their
present form with flesh on their bones,
through which the arrows could go.
After that they were easy to hunt. This is
what we know about the raven.*

A myth about caribou and the
raven (Birket-Smith 1930, 88)

THE CHIPEWYAN HAVE been chosen to represent the Subarctic culture area for cultural, ecological, historical, and social reasons. They are one of the numerous Athapaskan tribes that inhabit interior Alaska and northwestern Canada. Most Subarctic peoples depended on caribou and fish for food, and the Chipewyan were reasonably typical in this respect, although caribou were far more important in their diet. We know more about them than about most other Northern Athapaskans largely because of historical chance. They were reasonably well described by Europeans soon after historic contact, and beginning in 1960 a thorough study was made of a modern community. Furthermore, there are comparatively recent ethnohistorical studies and additional field research among these people. We do not have information of comparable scope for any other Northern Athapaskan tribe. The sociocultural reasons for describing the Chipewyan are equally significant because their lifeway was considered one of the least complex reported for North American Indians. Typically described as a band-level society, they formed temporary groups of extended families and exhibited marked local variability in social organization. Furthermore, the Chipewyan provide an opportunity to analyze the impact of the fur trade, which changed them from caribou hunters to beaver and marten trappers.

Chipewyan (chip-uh-WI-uhn) is a Cree word meaning "pointed skins," a reference to the dangling point at the front and back of the poncholike garment worn by men. These people called themselves Dene, meaning "humans," and were unified on the basis of language and lifestyle. The major subgroups were territorial and based on the exploitation of regional caribou herds. By the time of contact with Europeans, the Chipewyan possibly numbered forty-five hundred, one of the lowest Native American population densities.

The Chipewyan language belongs to the Nadene linguistic family and the Athapaskan subfamily. The Nadene are concentrated from near the Bering Strait to the western shore of Hudson Bay. They were primarily inland peoples. Some Nadene spread south to form the Pacific group concentrated in sections of coastal Oregon and California. Another cluster settled in the Southwest. The close cultural and linguistic bonds between the Chipewyan and the Yellowknife lead some modern ethnologists to consider them as a single people, as I do in this book.

The early historic range of the Chipewyan is shown in Figure 4-1. Chipewyan country is a vast expanse of tundra extending as much as seven hundred miles from east to west and nearly six hundred miles from north to south. The climate is continental, with long, cold winters and short, hot summers. The extremes range from the high 80s °F in summer to −60°F in winter. Everywhere networks of waterways—foaming as well as hesitant streams and rivers, great lakes, and countless smaller lakes—interlace. Barren rocks show obvious signs of glacial wear on their smoothed or striated surfaces. Results of glacial action are especially evident in the north, where rolling masses of bedrock give way to boulder-strewn valleys with adjacent lines of eskers. Lichens dominate the highlands, but valleys are covered with dwarf birch, mosses, lichens, and willows. This region is known to the Chipewyan as the Barren Grounds, a fitting term

Figure 4-1 | Early historic range of the Chipewyan Indians.

incorporated in geographical writings. Along river bottoms on the southern Barrens, stands of white spruce appear as outriders of their species; this is the taiga, where the tundra and northern forest meet. Still farther south the spruce are dense, and aspen, birch, and juniper stands are fringed by marshy bogs and upland tundras. The forested area was foreign to the aboriginal Chipewyan, but it became important to them in historic times. Above all, Chipewyan country was dominated by great caribou herds that meant survival for these Indians. Interestingly, and contrary to the title of this book, the Chipewyan maintained that they did not own the land but that the land owned them.

| Aboriginal Life

When the Chipewyan first encountered Europeans, their economy, based on caribou and fish, was well established and probably had been much the same for thousands of years. The baseline ethnographic account that follows examines each major aspect of their sociocultural lives. Although much of the information is based on observations by Samuel Hearne, his findings are supplemented by those of later observers as they relate to aboriginal conditions.

ORIGIN MYTH   The Chipewyan regarded the primordial world as centering about a woman who lived in a cave and subsisted on berries. As the myth unfolds, a doglike creature followed her into the cave to live with her. She thought that she dreamed this animal turned into a handsome young man who had sexual intercourse with her, but it was no dream, and the woman became pregnant. At this juncture a giant man approached; he was so tall that his head reached nearly to the clouds. With a stick he outlined the bodies of water and caused them to fill. The giant tore the doglike being to shreds and threw its internal organs into the water, creating fish. He tossed the flesh on the land in bits and it became land animals, and he tore the skin and threw it into the sky to become birds. The giant told the woman that her offspring would be able to kill as many of these creatures as they required and she need not worry about the animals' abundance, as it was his command for them to multiply. The giant returned from whence he had come and was never seen again.

In this way, order in the world emerged, and the abundance of game was assured. This tale justified the Chipewyans' indiscriminate killing of game and led to a supernatural association with dogs, because the woman's human offspring were descended from a creature related to the dog. The creation myth was not only taught to children but also used to guide thoughts about the adult world.

CLOTHING   Chipewyan garments were made from the skins of caribou killed in the early fall when the hides were strong and the hair dense but not long. Eight to ten skins were required to outfit an individual for winter. The upper garment of a man consisted of a loose-fitting, sleeved poncho with the hair side out and the skins cut to a point in front and back. He sometimes wore a fur boa when the temperature was low, and his ears might be protected by a fur band or cap. His ankle-length leggings were of dehaired skins, with moccasins sewn at the bottom. In severe weather he draped a caribou skin cape over his shoulders. The garb of a woman included a sleeved dress that reached her knees or ankles; to hold a long dress up from the ground she wore a belt around her waist. Her leggings reached from below the knee to the ankle and may or may not have had attached moccasins. She also wore a cape, and both sexes used mittens of double thickness. They could slip their hands out of the mittens without the chance of losing them because each was attached to a leather harness that hung about the neck.

SETTLEMENTS AND MANUFACTURES   Habitations ranged from isolated family dwellings to clusters of as many as seventy units, but large aggregates usually were of brief duration. The size of a community depended on the time of year and the local availability of food. People lived in a Subarctic variety of the tepee best known from the American Plains. A Chipewyan tent was framed with poles set in a circle and bound near the top. The cone was covered with as many as seventy sewn caribou skins, and it measured over twenty feet across at the base. An opening at the apex of the cone permitted smoke from the central fireplace to filter upward. If spruce boughs were available, they were placed around the fire and covered with caribou skins; on these people relaxed, worked, and slept.

Most manufactures could be found in and around the tents. A well-supplied camp included tripods of poles from which hung caribou-skin bags filled with meat. Among the possessions of women were cooking and storage containers of birch bark or skin. The women commonly used a basket of folded and sewn bark for cooking by filling it with water, preheated stones, and raw meat. They probably had skin bags in which they kept sewing awls and thread of caribou sinew. The men's tool kits included antler wedges for splitting planks from logs; a crooked knife with a copper blade and antler handle, the most important form of knife; a curved, wooden-handled knife with a beaver incisor for a blade, another highly useful tool for cutting small sections of wood; and a hand drill with a copper bit and an antler handle, the only drill form known. Awls were of copper, and a copper ax head was hafted on a wooden or antler handle. These uses of native copper, and its use in icepick points, arrow points, spearheads, and spoons, reflect a reliance on this metal. The copper tools were made by pounding a raw lump of the metal into shape. These people never heated or smelted copper but processed it as they did stone.

CONVEYANCES The little that is known about aboriginal Chipewyan boats suggests that they had only small skin-covered canoes with wooden frames (see Figure 4-2). These vessels were used to hunt caribou as they swam across lakes, and canoes lashed together formed rafts to ferry people across rivers. The toboggan for winter transport was up to fourteen feet long and about fourteen inches wide. It was made from thin juniper planks that were steamed and bent upward at the front. The planks were joined to crosspieces, probably with thongs. Chipewyan men, or women if the occasion arose, pulled

Figure 4-2 | A man carrying a small birch-bark canoe in early historic times. (From Hearne 1795.)

the toboggans; they presumably did not use dogs as traction animals because of their supernatural associations. If wood was unavailable, the people could make toboggans by using sewn caribou leg skins as a substitute.

Snowshoes were essential for travel over deep snow, and men jogged along for hours on end at a pace faster than a walk. Snowshoes were made by lashing babiche through holes in birch-wood frames. A snowshoe had a slightly turned-up tip and was asymmetrical in outline; the outer edge flared, but the inner edge was relatively straight. Men prepared the frame, and women laced the babiche with an eyed snowshoe needle. Curiously, although women made snowshoe webbing with an eyed needle, they used awls to sew garments. This would appear to be an instance of "cultural blindness."

HOUSEHOLD LIFE In camp, women prepared meals and cared for children, as did their counterparts throughout most of the world. To these obligations was added one of their most important activities, the task of processing skins, particularly those of caribou. After a man had killed a caribou, his wife recovered it, skinned it, and removed bits of flesh and fat with a bone scraper. If the hair was to be removed, the woman propped a wooden beam obliquely in the ground, draped the skin over it with the hair side up, and removed the hair with a scraper. A dehaired skin often was smoke-cured by hanging it over a pole framework under which decayed wood smoldered. A skin to be used with the hair intact was scraped, softened in water, and wrung out and dried, and a paste of partly decayed caribou brains was rubbed on the inner surface. Later the skin was dried once again and finally scraped with a copper-bladed end scraper. The skin probably was rubbed by hand to make it pliable and relatively soft. This process of skin preparation was a key technological complex for the Chipewyan, who relied on caribou skins not only for clothing but also for bedding, dwelling covers, containers, and ropes. American Indians did not tan skins in the technical sense.

Favorite foods largely were caribou products: the head and fat from the back, a fetus, and grubs from beneath the skin. The Chipewyan did not consider steaks and chops luxuries. They ate caribou meat or fish both raw and cooked. In addition to boiling it in a birch-bark container, they roasted flesh over an open fire. The diet rarely included plant products, although a moss soup is reported and moss could season meat soup.

Although women prepared meals at camp, men ate first. This was customary because if men were not reasonably well nourished, especially in times of food stress, they could not hunt or fish as effectively. The women received what the men had not consumed, which might at times be nothing. However, because women typically prepared meals, we might assume that they ate at least some food in the process.

Pemmican was an important food in the Subarctic, although it usually is associated with Plains Indians. Pemmican, from a Cree word meaning "manufactured grease," was made from lean meat that had been cut into strips and dried by the sun or near a fire. The dry meat was pounded into a powder, mixed with fat, and stuffed into caribou intestines; this highly concentrated food was a favorite of travelers. Dried meat had the advantage of being light and portable. Many Chipewyan considered it more desirable than fresh meat.

SUBSISTENCE ACTIVITIES   Aboriginal Indian life on the Barren Grounds probably would have been impossible without the presence of caribou as a basic food and an essential raw material for manufactures. The Chipewyan words for "meat" and "caribou" are quite similar, which is in itself revealing. Caribou migrating north in the spring were typically lean, and men hunted them largely as day-to-day food. In the early fall the herds began to wander south; at this time they were usually abundant with prime skins, a thick fat layer, and the most nourishing meat. That was the time for the most intense hunts. The subsistence cycle began anew in the early spring with caribou hunt preparations. Band members gathered at birch groves along the northern forest border, where they cut tent poles and built canoes for summer travels in the Barrens. The primary goal was to intercept caribou, and some people reported that they preyed on caribou in the manner of wolves.

As many as two hundred people might assemble for the trip north over the snows of spring. Women and young girls pulled the heavily loaded toboggans along the most direct route, and men and boys hunted on snowshoes adjacent to the toboggan trail. Dogs, burdened with parcels of tent skins, containers, and poles, accompanied the women. The female–male division of labor at this time might appear to have been more arduous for females, but this may not have been the case. Females pulled toboggans along the most direct route, and their noise scattered any game along the way. Men covered far greater distance in their pursuit of edibles. Thus a reasonable balance of energy expended may have prevailed between the genders.

In the eastern sector, winter and early spring camps were established on promontories along the forest edge, in localities frequented by caribou and near lakes containing fish. People moved only once or twice during the winter from an ideally situated camp, one accessible to lakes or wide rivers along which caribou normally passed. Here funnel-shaped caribou surrounds were built. Converging lines of brushy poles were erected, with poles at about twenty-yard intervals. When caribou approached the wider end of a funnel, they were unaware of the poles, which sometimes spanned three miles. As animals entered the surround, the women, boys, and some men appeared from behind to herd them. The caribou were driven into a trap, which was a large enclosure of branches at the end of the funnel, with snares set at narrow exits. After the entrance was blocked with trees, snared caribou were speared, and arrows were shot at loose animals.

In the fall, six hundred people might gather at well-known caribou crossings and camp in a single locality. Families seeing each other for the first time in months or years followed an established etiquette at their reunion. At first they sat apart from each other and said nothing. Then an older person of one party recounted all of their personal traumas since the last meeting, and women of the other group wailed on hearing of the misfortunes. The fate of the second party next was recounted and responded to. Men then greeted one another, and women exchanged presents as well as good news. When caribou appeared, their number might be truly fantastic. Sometimes so many were killed that only the skins, long bones, fat, and tongues were taken, and the carcasses were left to rot. As the caribou moved, the Indians followed, drying as much meat as they could conveniently carry.

When caribou rutted in October, a hunter sometimes attached lengths of caribou antler to his belt so that they rattled as he walked. A bull caribou in the vicinity would think he heard two other bulls fighting over females and would boldly approach, expecting to lead off the females. A bull could be killed more readily this way than by the usual method of stalking against the wind. At these times hunters used the self bow, a one-piece wooden shaft strung with babiche. Caribou-killing arrows had unbarbed bone or stone points and were vaned with feathers. An alternative and preferable fall hunting method was to drive large herds of caribou into water and kill them from canoes with lances.

When the snow was soft and deep, men, on snowshoes, sometimes tracked caribou. This meant following a single animal until it was exhausted from floundering in the snow. In the winter, the men might set gill nets beneath the ice of lakes or jig for fish through holes in the ice with hooks. In the western area of Chipewyan country, fishing was more important than among the eastern bands. Secondary means for taking game included the use of deadfalls for bear, marten, squirrels, and wolverine. The Chipewyan used nets for taking beaver in summer, but in winter, after they had broken open the beaver lodges, they took the animals from retreats beneath the ice along stream or lake edges. They set babiche snares to entangle hares or ptarmigan. Even though these Indians reached Hudson Bay at Churchill, they did not hunt the sea mammals abundant there at certain seasons.

It is important to note the advantage, in food-getting activities, of using devices that do not require the presence of a person. Set nets, snares, traps, and deadfalls are examples of "untended facilities" that operate when no one is present and no danger, waiting, or pursuit are required in their use. By contrast, lances and bows and arrows must be operated by hand and may be dangerous for the user—for example, against a bear. Thus, under most circumstances, it is preferable to use untended facilities when possible. Note that the Chipewyan used snares and deadfalls.

When the people could not harvest sufficient caribou, irrespective of the season or reason, they turned to their only other meaningful food source—fish, especially lake trout, northern pike (jackfish), and whitefish. Gill nets had emerged as the principal fishing method. The netting of babiche was strung with wooden floats at the top and stone sinkers at the bottom. Set across narrow streams, at river eddies where fish typically pause, and at spots in lakes, fish of appropriate size for a net were held by their gills. The people attached charms to nets designed to attract fish. Additional fishing methods included the use of dip nets that looked somewhat like our butterfly nets; fish trapped by weirs made from brush in shallow streams or rivers were caught with these nets. Likewise, men might shoot fish with barbed arrows from bows or impale them on leisters (fish spears) from canoes.

Additional details of Chipewyan hunting and fishing activities could be presented, but it already is obvious that caribou, and fish to a lesser extent, were the primary staples. Although recent studies suggest that the Subarctic may have been more productive than previously realized, relying on comparatively few species meant that food sometimes was scarce and that people might starve. At these times they ate berries, mosses, and other plant products and later consumed items of clothing; under extreme conditions they turned to cannibalism.

SOCIAL DIMENSIONS   The Chipewyan were described in less than glowing terms by Europeans, who characterized men as patient and persevering but also as morose and covetous. The Chipewyan firmly believed that they were more intelligent than the intrusive outsiders. The Chipewyan were peaceful within their own community, at least in terms of not shedding blood. When angry with one another, the men wrestled, pulled their opponent's hair or ears, or twisted his neck. As far as honesty went, among the eastern tribes of the Northern Athapaskans, the Chipewyan were ranked as superior to all others; they abhorred a thief. However, they considered whites to be not quite human and did not really consider taking their property to be theft.

No description of these people would be complete without commenting on the status of women as recorded by Samuel Hearne, the first white explorer in the region. According to him, women were subordinated in every way, were treated cruelly, and were held in gross contempt by men. Female infants were occasionally permitted to die, a practice viewed by adult women as kindly. In fact, they are said to have wished their mothers had done it for them. Women were beaten frequently, and although it was considered an odious crime to kill a Chipewyan man, it was regarded as no crime for a man to beat his wife to death. We probably will never know whether this was typical behavior toward women, but we may suspect that Hearne exaggerated or that his description was based largely on the behavior of his guide Matonabbee. This man had six wives and was obviously a highly successful hunter and a charismatic leader; he unquestionably was a very powerful and self-centered person. The treatment of women as recorded by Hearne seems inordinately severe and out of character for Indians north of Mexico. Furthermore, a similar pattern did not exist among the Chipewyan in more recent historic times. Contemporary researchers have suggested that although women may have been devalued symbolically, in everyday life they had considerable influence and power (Sharp 1988).

As was typical for many collectors, fishermen, and hunters around the world, the constraints on individual behavior were defined largely on the basis of age and gender. Each household was self-sufficient and could exist in isolation until a member sought a spouse. Group responsibilities or community cohesion hardly existed, and individuals had a great deal of flexibility in their behavior. Environmental resources were open to exploitation by everyone on an equal basis; family hunting or trapping territories did not exist.

POLITICAL ORGANIZATION   Aggregates of people structured in a formal manner and functioning as cohesive units did not exist among the aboriginal Chipewyan. Instead, as studies by James G. E. Smith (1970; 1976a; 1976b) and others have indicated, local groups were somewhat amorphous and highly flexible. In ecological terms, it is important to note that regional bands were defined largely on the basis of the separate herds of caribou exploited, and a regional group was divided further into localized bands of one hundred or more people who hunted together. Seasonally, when great numbers of caribou were available, several localized bands might assemble for a hunt. However, when caribou did not follow their expected migration routes, people divided into smaller hunting groups. Conditions influencing the movements of caribou included fires, weather variations such as sudden thaws or blizzards, and, in all likelihood, cyclical variations in their number. The most important observation about the nature of a band was its flexibility in number as a function of local food resources.

Families might unite under the aegis of a charismatic leader. Such a man was above all else an outstanding provider with an inordinate ability to take game and fish. Hearne's guide, Matonabbee, is an example. Once a man's reputation as a leader was established, fathers of marriageable daughters sought him as a son-in-law. This was to the personal advantage of the father-in-law because the pattern of marriage residence was for a husband to join his wife's natal household (matrilocal residence). Subsequent wives could be sisters (sororal polygyny) of the first, but other women could also be chosen. Such a man had to be physically strong because he was obligated to validate his claim to a wife, especially a younger wife, by wrestling if challenged by another man. Less successful hunters, relatives, and nonrelatives cast their lot with him for greater security. An important characteristic of this form of leadership was its transient nature. A man could keep his wives and other followers only as long as his powers of persuasion, hunting skills, and physical strength endured. As he began to fail physically, he sometimes could retain his position of authority by craft and intrigue, but this was only a temporary respite before he slipped into obscurity.

The Chipewyan were a tribe, but only in a general sense, and comparatively little political integration existed among the member bands. Conflicts with non-Chipewyan took the form of raids and generally were carried out by the members of a single band. An account by Hearne illustrates this type of hostility. He was accompanying a group of Chipewyan to the Coppermine River mouth when they raided an Eskimo (Inuit) camp. Matonabbee was the undisputed leader, and the raiders were unusually cooperative as they lent equipment to one another. Beforehand each man painted his shield in black and red, adding one or more figures representing supernatural aids. They painted their faces red, black, or with a combination of these colors and took off most of their clothing or lightened it so that they could run fast. They launched the attack in the middle of the night and caught the Eskimos asleep. Once alarmed, the twenty or so Eskimos ran naked from their tents only to be speared to death by the attackers. Afterward the Indians plundered the camp and departed. As was typical among northern Indians, the Chipewyan attacked these Eskimos for individual prestige, plunder, potential glory, and tribal security; territorial gain was not a goal.

DESCENT, KINSHIP, AND MARRIAGE   The Chipewyan calculated their ancestry through both female and male relatives (bilateral descent); the descent group (kindred) was like that which prevails in the United States today. When a man married, he attached himself to the household of his parents-in-law (matrilocal residence), and his ideal mate was his father's sister's daughter (patrilateral cross-cousin). In *recent* times at least some Chipewyan called a father's sister's daughters and mother's brother's daughters (cross-cousins) by the term for sweetheart, a convention that gives strength to the assumption of cross-cousin marriage. As the anthropologist Fred Eggan (1937) pointed out, a man relied on his son-in-law for support, and the son-in-law in turn was aided by his wife's brother's son. Although there was regional variation, it appears that, in general, in the aboriginal system of kinship terminology, the cousin terms were of the Iroquois type.

Their system of kinship terminology is diagrammed in Figure 4-3. Father's brother's children and mother's sister's children were termed the same as siblings, but different terms were employed for a father's sister's children and mother's brother's children. This terminology would be compatible with cross-cousin marriage. For the generation above an individual, the kinship terms for father and father's brother are alike (bifurcate merging), and mother's brother is distinct. Mother, mother's sister, and father's sister are all termed differently (bifurcate collateral). This terminology indicates that probably siblings and parallel cousins of the same sex (who were terminological siblings), particularly if they were males, extended mutual aid to one another and regarded their cross-cousins as possible mates. With the further presence of wife exchange, we find

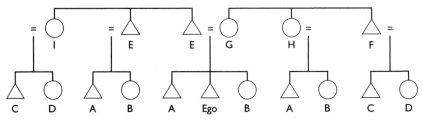

Figure 4-3 | The early historic Chipewyan system of kinship terminology.

an integrated network of blood relatives on an individual's generational level. On the parents' generation the same social distance separated aunts and uncles from one another as from parents. The inference is that these individuals were not as important socially or economically as near relatives of one's own generation.

SUPERNATURALISM   External threats to the Chipewyan came from the neighboring Cree and Eskimos. The hostility stemmed in part from the belief that the shamans of these people sent evil by supernatural means to cause illness. The Chipewyan believed that death or disease occurred from natural causes only among the aged. Thus in theory each physical disorder of a younger person resulted from the hostile activities of a foreign shaman. Chipewyan shamans attempted to negate the effects of such evil by acting through personal spirits that they controlled. When someone fell sick, a shaman sang and danced to summon his supernatural aids or "shadows," who were animal, bird, or imaginative familiars. He then sucked and tried to blow the intrusive disease substance from the patient. For serious cases a shaman treated an ill person in a special small square tent built with no opening at the top.

Death and disease led the Chipewyan to frequent hostilities with non-Athapaskan neighbors, and they made sporadic forays into the lands of their tormentors. In the raid on Eskimos reported earlier, the attackers carried wooden shields on which they had painted designs representing their individual guardian spirits. After the encounter the raiders observed numerous taboos to placate the spirits of those they had killed. A raid of this nature united the participants against a common enemy but did not require elaborate organization.

In the Chipewyan view of the supernatural world, spirits hovered about constantly; some more potent than others. Because the spirits of wolves and wolverine were considered dangerous, these animals usually were not hunted or killed. The bear, too, was considered dangerous; when one was killed, its skin might be burned and the large bones scattered in the four directions. A woman could not touch or step over a bearskin; thus, one placed before a door was a means of keeping women from entering a tent. The spirits of a shaman were powerful, and the spirit of an ordinary person was sometimes feared. Only a vague notion existed of a future life, a life like that on earth but free from cares, according to one observer. Not all accounts agree, however. One states that the Chipewyan believed that the soul of the deceased crosses a river and that if the individual has been good on earth he reaches an island on which life is free from worry. If he has been evil, he struggles in the river forever.

LIFE CYCLE   The Chipewyan, like all other North American Indians, realized that conception resulted from sexual intercourse. As the time of delivery approached, a small tent or brush-covered structure was erected away from the main camp for a pregnant woman. Here she bore her offspring and remained apart from normal camp routine for about a month. Her isolation was enforced whether the group was traveling or at a relatively permanent camp. The mother was cared for by other women, but she had no contact with men. The father did not see his infant until the period of isolation had ended. Similar isolation was the norm for menstruating women and for girls at menarche. The blood associated with women at these times was considered antipathetic to fish and game, and men avoided contacts with females in these conditions. Apparently the women were successful in keeping the true nature of the menstrual cycle a secret from men. When a woman sought to avoid her husband, which might be several times in one month, she simply crawled out of the tent beneath a side, to indicate that she was beginning to menstruate, and went to the menstrual hut.

During the first year of life an infant was carried on its mother's back next to her skin; the baby was held in place by a belt that passed from the middle of the mother's back over her breasts. In this secondary "womb," a baby wore only a moss-padded diaper. A female infant was typically named after a form or characteristic of a marten, such as Marten's Heart, Summer Marten, or White Marten. The names for males were taken from the seasons, places, or animals. Unfortunately, little is known about the social environment of children. Males clearly occupied a favored position compared with their sisters, but children in general were treated as adults. Conversations in the presence of children were free and frank.

Childhood betrothals were customary, and parents were careful to prevent a girl from participating in sexual intercourse before she married. Matches were made by parents or other relatives; a girl had no choice. The usual marriage was between a pubescent girl and a man who was at least twice her age. There was no marriage ceremony; the man simply attached himself to his wife's household. A marriage assumed stability only after an infant was born. Offspring seldom were born during the early years of marriage, and from this it may be presumed that the young bride's adolescent sterility tended to delay conception. A nuclear family (a husband, wife, and children) was neither a stable nor a long-lasting unit. The possibility of death by accident, disease, or starvation always existed, and life expectancy was probably less than thirty years on an average. (High infant mortality rates often account for a statistic such as this one.) Dislike of a spouse could rupture a household, and the practice of wrestling to retain one's wife whenever challenged did not lead to familial stability. Skill in wrestling was developed during youth, and the rule was that the man first thrown to the ground was the loser. An opponent could be downed most readily by grabbing his hair—thus it was cut short—or by seizing his ears—so they were greased. The woman being fought over had no voice in these matters but was expected to follow the winner dutifully.

A wrestling match for a wife did not always end well. In one case the husband killed a potential rival. He and his wife then were forced to live in isolation, and whenever other Chipewyan happened on the couple, they would take everything they owned except their clothing. Women deserted their husbands, but because of the physical isolation of most camps this was a dangerous undertaking. The woman might be caught and beaten by her husband or seized by another man before she found safety with a man she desired. Men guarded their wives jealously, not allowing them out of their sight if the opportunity for adultery existed. Wives generally were faithful to their husbands, but a particular wife sometimes shared her husband with as many as seven co-wives. The exchange of wives for a night perhaps helped temper any urge to seize a woman for sexual purposes alone. Wife exchanges were made by men and had implications that were more economic than sexual. The bonds between men resulted in continuing friendship and mutual aid. If one of the men died, his partner assumed the responsibility, at least temporarily, of caring for the widow and her children.

Games and other forms of amusement were few, and the only dancing was a step borrowed from the Dogrib Indians. A widely popular pastime was the hand game, a guessing game in which two opponents sat opposite each other with ten to twenty counters beside them. One man had an object in one hand and, behind a skin, shifted it. His opponent then guessed the hand that contained the gaming piece. A correct guess gave the winner one counter, and the game was won when one man had all of the counters.

As individuals aged and became less capable of caring for themselves, they were regarded as a burden. Old people had the poorest of tattered clothing and were given the most undesirable food. When a camp was moved, they might be left behind in a small shelter where they would starve alone. The corpse of a person who had died in isolation was not buried when it was found, and the corpse of one who died in camp was simply placed on the ground. In both cases, the bodies were eaten by animals. Property of the deceased was destroyed, and immediate relatives also destroyed their personal property. A widow cut her hair short as a sign of bereavement, and the shorn hair might be placed beside the deceased. She wailed about camp, stripped of her clothing and other possessions, to be aided and soothed by relatives and friends but not to remarry for a year.

In drawing the Chipewyan life-cycle discussion to a close, it is appropriate to comment on the manner in which these people behaved toward one another, especially on men's treatment of women and the general treatment of the aged. We should realize fully that the area in which these people lived offered either feast or famine. It was one of the most difficult sectors of North America in which to live in aboriginal times because of food uncertainties. The men, as the hunters and primary providers, presumably were often anxiety-ridden about their capacity to feed their families. This at least provides a partial explanation for their harsh treatment of women and the aged. We also must recognize that early writers about the Chipewyan were European men whose own attitudes toward these segments of the population possibly colored their accounts.

| Early History

According to nearly all standard sources, the Chipewyan lived in the northern forests at the beginning of their history and were driven into the Barren Grounds by the Cree after the latter received firearms. However, ethnohistorical studies by Beryl C. Gillespie (1970; 1976) have shown this was not the case. Instead, the Chipewyan lived in the taiga and tundra during early historic times and began to exploit interior forests only under fur traders' influence.

A Hudson's Bay Company post was built at Churchill along western Hudson Bay in 1717. From here agents launched the most important and lasting trading contacts with adjacent Northern Athapaskans. As Chipewyan began trading at Churchill, they told of a major copper deposit to the northwest. The Chipewyan, however, were making tremendous profits as middlemen in the trade with more distant tribes and were reluctant to guide company explorers. As a long-term Hudson's Bay Company employee, Samuel Hearne attempted to locate the copper deposit. In this endeavor his name became intimately associated with Chipewyan ethnography and with explorations in northwestern Canada.

Hearne made two abortive attempts to penetrate Chipewyan country and succeeded on his third effort. His ultimate success in this venture hinged on the Chipewyan guide Matonabbee, who had his own opinions about how to travel. The key to his plan was to take women along to relieve the men of the many burdensome chores. Matonabbee had six wives at that time. The trip to the Coppermine River and Coronation Gulf was completed successfully in mid-1772 and is one of the most noteworthy feats of individual exploration anywhere at any time. Hearne's maps were not accurate, and for this he has received periodic criticism, but, far more important, his book (1795) is a classic in exploration literature and the first comprehensive account of the Chipewyan. Hearne died a month after his manuscript was accepted by a publisher in October 1792.

The map Hearne prepared and his knowledge of the country facilitated further expansion to the northwest. The first trader to settle in the midst of Chipewyan territory was Peter Pond, who established himself near Athabasca Lake in 1778. The organization of the North West Company in 1783 introduced an era of fierce competition with the Hudson's Bay Company, and not until their amalgamation in 1821 did trading conditions become stabilized. The history of Chipewyan country centered about a failed quest for mineral wealth, the expanding fur trade, and disappointing searches for a water passage to the Pacific Ocean. Later, missionaries began the search for souls to save. In 1846 Roman Catholic missionaries founded a permanent mission at Lake Ile a la Crosse, and the Anglicans located at Churchill in 1912. Thus fur and souls attracted most outsiders to Chipewyan country.

As the people were drawn into the fur trade by the mid-1700s, some of them ventured south into the boreal forest, where they trapped beaver and marten to exchange for trade goods. The quest for beaver in particular led to a decline in caribou hunting, a major change from their aboriginal subsistence pattern. As contacts with Europeans intensified, the people were exposed to new diseases. A severe smallpox epidemic struck in 1781, and an estimated 90 percent of the people died. Although this estimate may have been exaggerated by whites who only observed Chipewyan living near the trading posts, there is no doubt of the horrendous effect of the 1781 epidemic. In 1819, another smallpox epidemic "carried away whole bands" (Simpson 1938, 81). Thus they had become a remnant people early in their history. With the emphasis they placed on trapping, they sometimes were unable to obtain enough food and faced starvation.

Famines made devastating inroads into the vitality of this society; although famines were not new, they now occurred more often. At Fort Resolution in 1833 some "forty of the choicest hunters" died in a famine (Back 1836, 209), and between 1879 and 1881 many people died of hunger.

The increased seasonal mobility required by the fur trade led to the construction of large birch-bark canoes to transport pelts and to obtain trade goods from Churchill or elsewhere. As the fur trade matured, a new leadership pattern emerged. Traders preferred to deal with representatives of a group, not with individuals, and this attitude led to the emergence of trading chiefs (see Figure 4-4). Traders strengthened a trading chief's standing by deferring to him

Figure 4-4 | A 1913 photograph of Chief Pierre Squirrel, a Chipewyan trading chief. (Courtesy of the Canadian Museum of Civilization, neg. no. 26070.)

and presenting him with clothing, medals, and a formal reception on his arrival at a post. By the late 1880s, the "chiefs" were distributing the meat of caribou and moose to whomever they chose, irrespective of the wishes of the men who killed the game, although the hunters personally kept the skins of animals. If this was the norm, we must conclude that a chief possessed authority and some form of power. By 1908 chiefs represented groups in dealings with officials of the federal Indian Affairs Branch, but, as we would expect, they were not very effective.

It is revealing to consider the changing status of dogs. Recall that a dog-like creature was thought to have fathered these people, and the dog, along with bears, wolves, and wolverine, had strong supernatural associations (Sharp 1988). In the 1820s the people were convinced by a powerful man that they should not use such closely related animals to do their work, and consequently they destroyed all of their dogs. For this reason, during the early period of contact the people had very few dogs or none at all. Apparently, dogs were not widely used as beasts of burden, nor did they pull toboggans, until sometime in the mid-1800s. Yet Hearne mentioned that in his time dogs hauled birch poles as hunters moved into the Barrens. Certain taboos still surrounded dogs in the early 1930s. For example, dogs were not shot, and to feed a dog a moose head or bear intestines was thought to bring ill fortune.

The unformalized supernatural system of the aboriginal Chipewyan population absorbed Cree concepts, and by the early 1800s they had borrowed the concept of *manitou,* a supernatural force that pervades the natural world. An evil manitou was blamed for sickness, disease, or bad luck. By 1908, some Chipewyan had learned Cree folktales, including tales that involved a trickster-hero. In these accounts, one animal tricks another, or a supernatural force creates something, and thus becomes a mythological hero. Christianity was introduced by Roman Catholic missionaries, and most Chipewyan became converts by the 1920s, at least in name. Yet many traditional supernatural beliefs continued to prevail; Catholicism was integrated with the old religion, a typical pattern among Indians.

In early historic references to caribou hunting, taboos were rarely reported. Later in history, caribou remained the key food, but numerous taboos surrounding them appeared. For example, in one area, if a woman's skirt were to pass over a hunting knife, there was fear that the caribou would not migrate in that direction during that year. A woman was supposed to pierce the caribou's eyeball before she butchered the carcass to prevent the spirit of the deceased animal from reporting its fate to others. The implication might be that these taboos emerged as caribou hunting became less dependable.

| Becoming Modern at Snowdrift (Lutselk'e, Lutsel K'e)

1960 was a watershed year in Chipewyan history. It was then that a professional anthropologist, James W. VanStone, began his study of a contemporary settlement, Snowdrift. At this time also the people were just beginning to undergo the most dramatic changes since the introduction of the fur trade. To examine this transitional period provides insight into the nature of present-day Chipewyan life in one sector of their domain.

Snowdrift, along eastern Great Slave Lake, is a sparsely forested area that borders on tundra country. The people in the vicinity traditionally traded at Fort Resolution, founded in 1786, before a Hudson's Bay Company post was built at Snowdrift in 1925. In 1928 a devastating influenza epidemic struck the region, and families scattered widely in an unsuccessful hope of avoiding the disease. An estimated 20 percent of the regional population died from either influenza or pneumonia.

It was not until 1954 that most people began to settle there in response to pressure from the federal Indian agent. In 1960 about 150 people lived at Snowdrift, including 38 school-age children. The village consisted of twenty-six predominantly log houses, a Hudson's Bay Company store, a Roman Catholic church, and cabins of Euro-Canadian sports fishermen and mining enterprises. The commitment to settled village life represented a dramatic shift in residence pattern for these previously mobile hunters and trappers. With so many people in one community, it was difficult to obtain enough food locally. Their previous standard of living appears to have declined, and they came under far greater control by federal authorities.

THE PEOPLE AND THE SETTLEMENT In striking contrast with the not-so-distant past, clothing typically came from the local store. Most men wore imported shirts, trousers, underwear, and footwear. Older women wore imported underwear, stockings, dresses, skirts, sweaters, and shoes. Girls favored slacks, colorful lightweight jackets, brooches, earrings, finger rings, and curled hair. Younger males favored ornamental black leather jackets. The most important locally made items included skin moccasins for men and slippers for women as summer wear. Money obviously was required to purchase most clothing.

After 1950, with federal support, most families constructed substantial houses or renovated existing cabins. Some people participated with reluctance in the housing program because they hesitated to commit themselves to permanent village life. Most of the dwellings were one-room cabins with board floors and furnished with homemade beds, chairs, tables, and shelves. Light was supplied by kerosene lamps, and heat was furnished by wood-burning sheet-iron stoves. Trunks or bags for extra clothing and bedding, a battery-powered radio, a hand-operated sewing machine, and utensils were common household items. In nearby log storage sheds they kept frozen or dried fish, dog harnesses, outboard motor parts, traps, snowshoes, fishnets, and rifles. Quite clearly, with all of the new material goods, a family became far less mobile.

Each family owned a large imported canoe, an outboard motor, and a small canvas-covered canoe. A type of toboggan existed that was purchased from the store and that was more correctly a *cariole* with a rear panel and canvas sides. A family had about five dogs to pull its cariole. Dog teams and outboard motors unquestionably increased the mobility of a family in subsistence activities. The canvas-covered canoes were being replaced by aluminum boats that required a substantial cash outlay.

MAKING A LIVING Traditional Chipewyan economic life had centered about caribou and fish, and with the addition of trapping furbearers, these foci persisted. Although trapping was an important major source of cash, hunting remained a significant part of family welfare. Most men would abandon their traplines if caribou appeared in the vicinity.

Trapping was difficult and surrounded by uncertainties. To reach a trapline required one to three days of dog-team travel. Steel jaw traps or wire snares were set for the most valuable species: lynx, marten, mink, white fox, and wolverine. Wolverine sometimes ate the animals caught in traps or sprung a line of sets and ate the bait. Gray jaybirds or other creatures might also spring traps. A canvas trapping tent was small and impossible to heat for comfort, and men found it difficult to work alone for weeks on end. Previously the family of a man accompanied him on a trapline; this was no longer possible because school-age children were obligated to attend classes. Thus men tended to trap only for short periods in the late fall when the pelts of most furbearers were prime. The price of fur was not very high, and a trapper's average take was about C$320. Income from trapping remained the only source of cash for many families.

In the early 1960s dependence on caribou remained great, and the late summer hunt was of prime importance. A household head believed that he required about one hundred caribou per year, yet harvests of this magnitude were no longer realized. In the fall when caribou were absent locally, which usually was the case, families traveled in large canoes in search of game. Burdened by large amounts of equipment, they could not reach the best hunting grounds. Thus the rewards were meager. The meat they obtained was smoked, brought back to the village, and stored in the Indian Affairs Branch cold-storage unit. In 1960 nearly half of the households were unrepresented in the fall caribou hunt. For unsuccessful hunters and others, fishing with gill nets for lake trout and whitefish in the fall might be intense (see Figure 4-5). The catch was partially dried and stored as winter food for dogs and people.

Men began to prefer wage-labor employment, but jobs were few and usually temporary. As a result, making a living by wage labor was more uncertain than the subsistence pursuits of old.

Aboriginal foods were increasingly replaced by purchased edibles. People preferred fish and meat with every meal, but because these often were unavailable, the staple was *bannock*. This is an unleavened baked bread of Scottish origin, and it was usually made from barley or pease (peas). A variety of bannock ("fry bread" or "Indian bread"), the standard fare of poor Eskimos

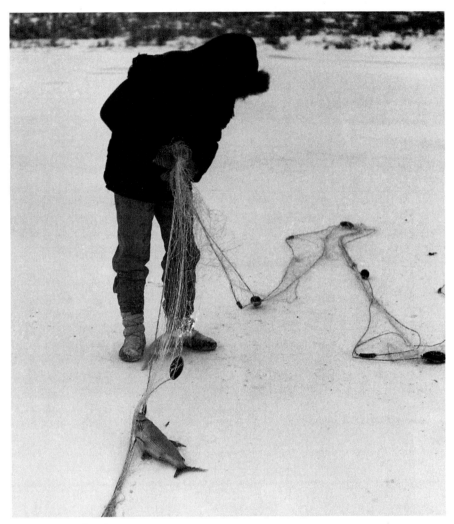

Figure 4-5 | A Snowdrift man, Louison Abel, checking a gill net set beneath lake ice in 1960. (Photograph by James W. VanStone, © The Field Museum, Neg. no. A107886.)

and Indians throughout Alaska, Canada, and elsewhere, is made from white flour and baking powder mixed with water into a paste and spread on a greased skillet to fry. Often this was the only food at a meal; bannock and tea are the bread and water of depressed Subarctic living. When families were able, they bought prepared foods from the store. The most desired imports were flour, sugar, tea, coffee, crackers, peanut butter, canned meats and fruits, evaporated milk, and seasonings.

SOCIAL DIMENSIONS   Along with the changes in subsistence activities and material culture since aboriginal times, we likewise find significant differences in other aspects of living. The old attitudes and harsh treatment toward women described by Hearne were no longer reported. VanStone conveyed the impression that domestic harmony existed. Certain activities, such as food preparation and child raising, remained female obligations, but men performed these tasks as the need arose. Women could profit monetarily from their own labors. A woman who processed a moose or caribou hide or sewed skin garments for someone outside her family was paid directly and retained the profits. The favorable position of women at Snowdrift may have resulted from the fact that they were a distinct minority; for unknown reasons there were fewer young women than men. Because it was difficult to obtain a wife, she was treated with care (see Figure 4-6).

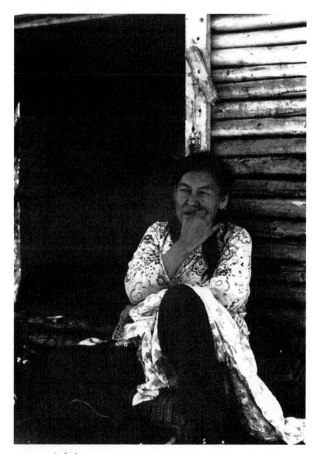

Figure 4-6 | A Snowdrift woman, Mary Louise Rabesca, sitting in front of a smokehouse in 1976.

The people continued to trace their descent along both the female and male lines (bilateral descent), as they had in early historic times. Cousin terminology, however, was of the Eskimo type (similar to the current classification of cousins in the United States). Preferential cousin marriage no longer existed; in fact, people did not recall it as an aboriginal practice. The one hundred years of contact with Roman Catholic missionaries who spoke against cousin marriage probably had produced the change, yet premarital fornication between cousins continued.

When a person married, he or she was most likely to select a mate within the community (village endogamy), and immediately after marriage the couple lived with the in-laws who were best able to receive them (temporary bilocal residence). As soon as possible the couple built a separate dwelling and lived alone (neolocal residence). In 1961 most households were nuclear or nuclear core families, the latter comprising a nuclear family to which were added a near relative or two of the husband or wife. Plural marriages no longer existed, and capable providers did not attract followers who lived with them. The overall impression is that the nuclear family remained the most important social unit, although it was not as autonomous as before.

Social bonds beyond those based on kinship were new and of expanding importance. Village life produced feelings of unity, and people thought of themselves as economically, morally, and physically superior to persons in adjacent settlements. Other evidence of village cohesion was the widespread sharing of locally available foods. By the time a successful moose hunter beached his boat, he had given away most of the meat, and the same applied to a catch of fish. Food had been shared in aboriginal times, but apparently not in as pervasive or egalitarian a manner. Furthermore, an intensive pattern of reciprocal borrowing had developed, and this included major as well as minor items of material culture. These attitudes and their behavioral manifestations clearly were integrating the community on a social and economic basis.

Square dancing was a popular pastime. The people probably had learned the steps from commercial fishermen, who often stopped for a few days of relaxation during the summer. Men played guitars or violins and learned dance music by listening to village phonographs or broadcasts from the Yellowknife radio station. The square dances were called expertly by village men, and participation at dances was good. Less formal entertainment included nightly card games, which were extremely popular, particularly blackjack and gin rummy. Men and women often played together, and the stakes ranged from small change and ammunition to three-dollar hands in gin rummy games if men were affluent. While adults were playing cards, children sometimes gambled by pitching coins to a line. The hand game of old was known but seldom played; card games were considered more exciting (see Figure 4-7).

The consumption of alcohol was as much a ritual as a form of entertainment, and prescribed drinking patterns were rarely ignored. The only alcoholic beverage regularly consumed was home brew, produced from yeast, raisins, sugar, and water. It was made secretly by two or three men and allowed to age

Figure 4-7 | A summer card game at Snowdrift circa 1960. (Photograph by James W. VanStone, courtesy of the Field Museum, Chicago, neg. no. A107881.)

for about twenty-four hours. It was thought better if it aged longer, but anticipation negated the possibility. The men drank the brew in the home of one of the makers or in the brush during the summer; the object was to become intoxicated. A man would dip a cup into the three-gallon pail, drink the beverage, and pass the cup to the next participant. Normally, some brew was stored in bottles, to be consumed after the brew pail had been drained. When participants became reasonably intoxicated, they visited one house after another, regardless of the time, and drank as they chatted with their reluctant hosts. Sometimes they offered to share their brew, but this practice was not consistent. The conversations of intoxicated men were about village life, and they became more outgoing during drinking sprees than at any other time of their adult lives.

POLITICAL LIFE The Snowdrift Chipewyan were included in Treaty Number 11, which was signed by the Indians in 1921 and provided them with direct monetary and other benefits. The Indians gave up their aboriginal rights to the land but at the same time were protected in their exploitation of local resources. In exchange, they received tangible benefits such as formal education, health services, and material goods. Each year a band member received a cash payment of five dollars, the band chief received twenty-five dollars, and counselors, fifteen dollars each. The Indian Affairs Branch began to provide fishnets, ammunition, and items such as roofing and doors for house construction.

Furthermore, families in need, as defined by the Indian agent, received a "ration" from the Indian Affairs Branch through the store. A national program of old-age assistance provided for the welfare of persons sixty-five years of age or older. Even more important was the "baby bonus," or Family Allowance, which was a national program. Every month, each family received six dollars for each child under ten and eight dollars for those ten through sixteen. The program was designed to improve child care, and it probably served this end at Snowdrift.

One result of living in a stable community was intensified contact with the Indian agent. Stationed at Yellowknife, he visited Snowdrift and called meetings on matters of villagewide concern. Attendance usually was poor, and it was difficult to conduct a general meeting because each Indian was inclined to raise issues of personal interest, usually specific requests for aid. Thus the process of democratic group action failed. Unity, when it was manifested, consisted of a stand against a proposal rather than any positive approach. The Chipewyan preferred to deal with the agent on a private, almost secret, basis concerning specific requests. They felt that an agent was in a position to grant favors, and for him not to do so was regarded as pure stubbornness.

Visits to the village by the Royal Canadian Mounted Police (RCMP) in the 1960s represented a show of federal power rather than a response to crime. Crimes in the Canadian legal system were rare and centered most on the manufacture of home brew. The people felt that it was wrong to appeal to Canadian legal authorities and rarely did so, although they might threaten such action.

In 1960 the bands of the region were reorganized, and the villagers received their own chief and two counselors. The people expected the chief not to interfere with village life but to adopt a stern attitude toward Euro-Canadians in general and the Indian agent in particular. An Indian agent, by contrast, expected a chief to be cooperative; if he was not, the chief was bypassed and the agent acted through the trader or teacher and thereby undermined Indian authority. During this period the federal government encouraged local band political development. Yet in 1969 governing obligations shifted to the Northwest Territories, whose representatives fostered the democratic process through local settlement councils in direct competition with the band organization. These competing institutions intensified local factionalism and divided the community politically.

THE BELIEF SYSTEM Villagers were participating but nominal Roman Catholics. A priest visited the settlement frequently and was always present during the Christmas and Easter seasons. Church dogma and beliefs were poorly understood, but attendance at ceremonies was high. In general, the Church was regarded as wealthy and as obliged to pay for labor performed on its behalf. Thus the feeling of belonging to a church and strengthening its purposes was not understood by the members. Interestingly enough, it was in the supernatural sphere that the Chipewyan admitted openly that they were different from whites.

The concept of a "bush man" prevailed here as among other Northern Athapaskans. In their conceptualization, this creature was a man who wore manufactured shoes and appeared at a distance during the summer. He kidnapped children, but apparently he did not harm adults as long as they remained beyond his reach. The Indians believed that certain supernatural beings could harm them but did not affect whites. They also held beliefs about trapping practices, but these were unknown by whites.

By the early 1960s, reliance on shamans as healers was declining. At least some people continued to believe in the power of spirit aids of shamans to cure illness and predict the future. As a secular cure, spruce gum may have been the dominant traditional medicine. Disease treatment was passing into the domain of the Indian and Northern Health Services and a lay dispenser, usually the Hudson's Bay Company manager. If a case was considered serious, the nurse at Yellowknife was contacted by radio, and she decided what course of action was to be followed. This nurse, sometimes accompanied by a medical doctor, visited the village at intervals. These Indians were concerned about their health but did not use patent medicines or turn freely to Euro-Canadians for aid. They seemed to enjoy talking about their aches and pains, but they sought treatment only when they were quite ill.

| Contemporary Lutselk'e

Settled village life was above all else an artifact of federal policies, but the community had no realistic control over government decisions. During the early 1980s in particular the federal government launched innumerable programs to change the texture of village living. Homes were becoming better built, and water and fuel delivery were provided, along with sewage disposal, electricity, and roads (see Figure 4-8). By 1996 the 286 residents included 10 Euro-Canadians. With federal and territorial support, buildings had been constructed for band administration. There was a school that educated students through the ninth grade, along with a permanently staffed nursing station, a local RCMP office, and an airport with mail service six days a week (see Figure 4-9). Accompanying these developments, old-age assistance benefits were provided, in addition to varied forms of relief for the needy. The Child Tax Credit (previously Family Allowance) was a nationwide program to foster the welfare of children; the amount received depended on family income. Quite obviously, government policies and practices had dramatically altered what it meant to be a Chipewyan. In sum, the federal goal had been to recast the people into a generalized Euro-Canadian mold.

In the government effort to transform villagers into "standard" Canadians, the system of formal education became a major catalyst. In 1935 families began to be encouraged by the Indian agent to send children ranging in age from three to seventeen to a residential (boarding) school at Fort Resolution that was managed by Roman Catholic missionaries. Instruction was in English, and children

Figure 4-8 | The community of Lutselk'e (Snowdrift) in 1996.

Figure 4-9 | By 1996 Lutselk'e had mail service six days a week.

were discouraged from speaking Chipewyan. Thus during their formative years these children spent only about two months at home each year. Residential schooling intensified after school attendance became compulsory in 1960. The fund of traditional cultural knowledge conveyed to a child depended to a great extent on his or her family background and ranged from being comprehensive to comparatively superficial. A federal village school was opened in 1960 that ended residential schooling for most young children. However, by 1996 a free high school education could be obtained only at the government residential school in Fort Smith; during that year, thirty-four high school students studied there. The school system in general, with its stress on Euro-Canadian values, did little to foster or sustain traditional Chipewyan life. A partial indicator is that most younger people do not speak Chipewyan.

For many, possibly most, adults, life had lost its purpose; they could no longer pursue their old ways, nor could they truly become Euro-Canadians. A widespread reaction was a pervasive dependence on the government to provide. A by-product of this situation was a growing dependence on the consumption of alcoholic beverages imported from Yellowknife. The situation became critical in the 1970s, and in 1980 the band council passed an ineffective prohibition law. In the 1980s multiple deaths and violence as a result of excessive drinking became alarming. By the mid-1990s intoxicant consumption had *decreased* significantly. By then about 25 percent of adults had been abstinent for about five years. During the first eight months of 1996, most of the police action cases involved alcohol, and about twenty individuals were the most frequent offenders. The following year a survey indicated that the community drug and alcohol counselor was regarded as helpful by numerous persons but of little value by others. There appears to be at least a short-term trend toward less social turmoil associated with intoxicants.

Recent years have introduced major changes in federal Indian policies. Greater administrative authority shifted to the local level, but not to local control. In 1991 a symbolic but meaningful change was made. The official village name was changed from Snowdrift to Lutselk'e, Chipewyan words meaning "the place of small fish," a nearby locality. In that same year we also find that an effort was being made by the First Nations (Indians, Inuit, and Métis) in the Northwest Territories to renegotiate their treaty rights, including a transfer of land ownership to the indigenous peoples. The federal government has been reasonably sympathetic with these efforts, and a shift toward more administrative power is taking place. A major change in the local economy has already occurred. The Hudson's Bay Company store closed in 1973, and, after a brief period of private ownership and with financial assistance from the government, it became a member of a network of northern cooperative stores. Thus the people became the store owners. Management of the local school is supervised by a community educational authority that administers the budget and hiring. With respect to local government, a band manager was trained, and the band council has emerged as a municipal government with territorial funding and expanding administrative control over local affairs. The band council includes representatives from the major family groups, as well as women, and the council has been working together far more harmoniously than ever before. Likewise, a Chipewyan held the office of justice of the peace, and a local Dene was trained as a law enforcement officer. In sum, changes in federal policies have led to far more local responsibilities than would have been conceivable thirty years ago.

Socially, it is not insignificant that five white women had married Chipewyan men by 1996, and four Dene women once were married to white men. Furthermore, although we do not associate respect for most older persons with the early historic Chipewyan, the villagers appeared to be changing

Figure 4-10 | Lutselk'e men in 1996: Alfred Boucher (left) and his father, Joe Boucher.

their attitudes toward their elders (see Figure 4-10). Finally, the position of women was strong. This may be a product of a higher sex ratio for men, as in the early 1960s. More women than men had post–high school training; one local Chipewyan woman earned a college degree.

By the mid-1990s local food resources remained of critical importance for many families. In the early 1960s game was scarce in the vicinity, and the area continues to be a "land of feast or famine." Since about 1980 the fall caribou migration has shifted to nearby localities and has included many animals; in addition, some caribou winter locally. Moose likewise have become more readily available as a source of meat. Coupled with an abundance of lake trout, this had become a land of plenty. Accompanying these increases was a decrease in pressure on food resources from hunting and fishing in the settlement area from a generation ago, because a smaller number of families depend on these activities for their primary food supply. Others depend far more on federal and territorial monies, both earned and unearned. Historically, the harvest of furbearers was the major source of cash for the local people, but by 1996 trapping was a primary activity for only ten men.

Although employment opportunities were limited by the mid-1990s, the number of year-round jobs was far greater than previously. The band employed some twenty persons, including an elected chief, a social worker, and a drug and alcohol abuse counselor. The cooperative store grossed about one million dollars a year and employed seven persons on a full-time basis. The school employed four teachers. To maintain the infrastructure, workers provided water and heating oil delivery and power plant and airport maintenance. In addition, summer construction projects were a source of employment, and ten men were available to fight forest fires. There previously had been commercial fishing at the eastern end of Great Slave Lake, but it was discontinued to help preserve lake trout. There were a number of local fishing lodges for sport fishermen, and some men in the community worked as guides for these fishermen.

The relatively recent discovery of diamonds in northern Canada, as outlined in the previous chapter, affects not only the Inuit of Nunavut but also Northern Athapaskans in the region. During the search for diamonds, Lutselk'e residents guided the prospecting parties, who staked claims at the most promising sites. This work provided an alternative source of income to the trapping of furbearers and had vast economic implications.

Before the mines could open, negotiations were required with the national government, with numerous mining companies, and with Native Americans who lived where diamonds had been found. From a Canadian legal perspective, the Chipewyan and Dogrib involved had ceded their lands to the Crown in 1899 and 1921 treaties. These Indians, however, now contend that the treaties did not extinguish their aboriginal title to their lands. Irrespective of this, the federal government with its pervasive political power and the mining companies with their vast financial resources dominated negotiations that began in the 1990s; Indian interests were regarded as "third party" and clearly subordinate. At the planning meetings, Indian concerns were only modestly addressed. One reason was that Ottawa did not grant them sufficient funds to hire experts to testify on their behalf (e.g., biologists, geologists, and hydrologists). Furthermore, Lutselk'e leaders did not fully understand the technical language used by the Canadian government and mining company specialists who spoke at the hearings. Consequently, any problems basic to an Indian perspective, especially environmental ones, were ignored, played down, or avoided. The following synopsis suggests how Indian concerns were inadequately addressed.

Before the mines could operate, it was critical to establish water rights in the area. The mining companies needed to obtain access to mines by "dewatering" lakes, but the long-term impact of draining lakes was not meaningfully discussed. Nor were concerns about returning the mined-out lands to a reasonable facsimile of their pre-mine condition addressed systematically. The problems of wastewater pollution from mines (e.g., acidic waste work discharges and tailings) and the impact of the mines on fish and game, especially on migrating caribou, were not resolved. The fact that the federal timetable established for drafting an impact and benefits agreement was relatively short and rigid caused negotiations between Ottawa and the mining companies to be rushed to a conclusion. This was not helpful to the Indians.

Employment of some people from the community began affecting Indian life after BHP Billiton Diamonds, Inc., was granted land and water permits in 1996 to operate the Ekati Diamond Mine some 140 miles north of Lutselk'e. It was there that the most mine workers from the community were employed. The open-pit and subsequent underground operations at the Ekati mine soon became both intense and extensive. Diamonds were mined for twenty-four hours each day of the year. By 2002 the yearly support operations cost more than C$400 million. Of the 2859 employees in that year, about 25 percent were drawn from the indigenous population. Because most Native American applicants did not have the minimal skills required in math, English, and computer literacy, the company provided a scholarship program for the postsecondary education of its potential employees.

A quantitative and qualitative community-based monitoring study at Lutselk'e by Evelyn Marlowe et al. (2002) analyzed the perceptions of villagers about employment at the mines, especially in relation to the traditional subsistence efforts. The study included a follow-up workshop for participants after the survey results became available.

Twelve Lutselk'e residents, representing 30 percent of the workforce, were employed at the mines in early 2002. Pertinent comments by workshop participants were:

- I think part-time and casual employment is better for people; mining companies don't like this it costs more
- there are hardly any women working from Lutsel K'e
- working is better than being on welfare
- most of the jobs are just labour jobs; you feel like you are at the bottom
- if someone from here screws up—it makes a bad name for everyone and its harder for anyone from Lutsel K'e to find a job; they aren't supposed to blacklist people but I think they do
- prior to employment individuals should be taught very well about the differences between the home and work environment

With respect to mining careers, youths with a parent working at a mine were lonely when that person was absent and would not want their children to face this possibility. Yet in the follow-up workshop, adults felt that increasing numbers of students were interested in mine employment.

In a broad overview, a dichotomy remains between caribou hunting and full-time mine employment. In the 1960s, a household ideally obtained 100 caribou each year for food, material items, and construction materials. Even then, numerous men no longer had the equipment essential to hunt caribou intensively. By August 2002 about 60 percent of the potential hunters did *not* hunt caribou, and the most animals killed (more than thirty), were taken by only 2 percent of the hunters. This suggests that the intensity of caribou hunting will continue to decline without radical economic changes.

In this general context, two statistics are critical. Despite the high unemployment rate, 41 percent, twelve individuals worked full time at the mines in January 2002. Why so few? The mines apparently refused to hire greater numbers of villagers because they had the reputation of excessive alcohol and/or drug use. In addition, those who adhered to the traditional value system avoided highly scheduled routine work. If the cultural values of villagers remain the same and mine hiring practices do not change, large-scale employment at mines appears unlikely in the future. The single large-scale involvement in mining activities at Lutelk'e was in 2002, when the community received a contract for C$285 thousand from BHP to produce stakes for company survey crews. The manufacture of the stakes did not inherently require a rigid work schedule for the workers involved.

In general terms, speaking their indigenous language fluently at home is one indicator of traditional culture vitality, as noted in other chapters. At Lutselk'e, in a 2002 survey, 10 percent of the householders spoke the aboriginal language all of the time or at least frequently. English is the dominant language, however, which means learning it would better prepare youth for eventual mine employment. An elder workshop participant said:

- If kids don't speak Chip, it is the parents' fault. At one time nobody understood English, everyone spoke Chip. It's the other way around now.

The future of caribou hunting obviously is central to this interpretation, especially with respect to the next generation. Between early 2000 and early 2002, most youths, some 72 percent, *did not participate in these hunts*. This suggests that most of this generation would be ill prepared to harvest caribou intensively and successfully as adults even if they had the essential equipment required, which is unlikely given their economic circumstances. Participants in a feedback workshop for elders commented:

- it's definitely better for kids to learn about their culture from their parents
- we should try and focus on the family in educating youth about their culture
- in the past—no one had money for things; nowadays everyone says they need money to go out on the land—this is a really big change

About three-quarters of the youths would prefer to work in the community to be near their families. At the same time, nearly all of them said they were willing to further their education away from home.

A statement from an elder workshop participant summarizes the negative effect on the community of focusing on mining in the future:

- Overall, I think the mining developments are having a negative effect on the community. The whole thing is very short-sighted. There may be instant financial gratification but it is only short term. There is not enough understanding of what impact it is having on families. And the benefits are not happening for everyone. There is not enough training, no day-care support for families. If you look at it that way, the benefits don't measure up to all the problems . . . Some employment has been created but at what cost?

The community-based monitoring findings are valuable even though they are occasionally unclear or contradictory. This is to be expected when the age, gender, and experience of older Lutselk'e residents are taken into account. With respect to the future, the attitudes of young people also are critical, but how they will actually respond to economic conditions in the short term is unknown. Because so many of them are ill prepared to engage in traditional subsistence pursuits, especially caribou hunting, they may be forced into wage-labor employment, primarily minework at present. In sum, Lutselk'e residents appear to be trapped by a learned helplessness as a result of their past livelihood as subsistence hunters and fishers being inappropriate because of federal policies (e.g., cluster residences, comprehensive welfare programs), of the present economic conditions (e.g., depressed fur market, diamond mines), and of their negative individual reactions to the future as they see it (e.g., excessive alcohol and drug uses). It would appear that to remain in the village and engage in mine-related employment may be the best solution in the near future. The large-scale project in 2002 to manufacture surveyor stakes for a mining company is a recent example.

A key concern not addressed in the community-based monitoring presentation centers on the final contract between the villagers and BHP Billiton Diamonds, Inc. Judging from the preliminary meetings, Lutselk'e residents probably were not satisfied with the final contract, including diamond mine royalties. The final agreement is confidential and thus unknown.

Some cultural anthropologists have a reputation for emphasizing the changes in Indian life that were introduced by Westerners at the expense of traditional Indian culture. One reason is that the changes are often so overwhelmingly evident and important. One result of this focus has been to downplay or ignore the continuing vitality of traditional Indian ways that may be far less obvious. An example from Lutselk'e will illustrate the point. As a long-term observer of Athapaskan (Dene) Indians in the Northwest Territories, Father René Fumoleau, noted, "the most important thing in life is mobility." The capacity to move about remained a fundamental value in the 1990s, just as it was in much earlier historic times. To go to Yellowknife by airplane, boat, or snowmobile on the spur of the moment, to suddenly decide to hunt, fish, or visit someone, or to allow a child not to attend school on a particular day encapsulates a worldview held by villagers.

| Additional Sources

The best overview about Northern Athapaskans is the widely available volume edited by June Helm (1981) and published by the Smithsonian Institution. The best comparative analysis of Northern Athapaskan tribes is by James W. VanStone (1974) who also is the author of an in-depth study of Snowdrift (1965). An anthropologist, Ellen Bielawski (2003), conducted ethnographic studies at Lutselk'e from 1992 to 1997. She also became a village representative in the diamond mine negotiations. The community-based monitoring report by Evelyn Marlowe et al. (2002) about Lutselk'e involved villagers trained to administer the surveys with the full cooperation of community leaders. Home visits by Chipewyan speakers was a key data-gathering method. For relatively recent and authoritative studies about the Chipewyan and their neighbors, the reader is referred to the selected bibliography that follows. The writings of Beryl C. Gillespie, Robert Jarvenpa, Henry S. Sharp, David M. Smith, and James G. E. Smith are especially important. For a conservative band of Chipewyan in the Barren Grounds, the key studies are by Sharp. The background to Indian and Inuit treaties (8 and 11) in the Northwest Territories of Canada, plus the treaties themselves and developments to 1939, are insightfully reported by René Fumoleau (2004).

| Selected Bibliography

Back, George. 1836. *Narrative of the Arctic Land Expedition*. London.

Bielawski, Ellen. 2003. *Rogue diamonds: The rush for northern riches on Dene land*. Vancouver, British Columbia.

Birket-Smith, Kaj. 1930. *Contributions to Chipewyan ethnology*. Report of the Fifth Thule Expedition, Vol. 6, no. 3. Copenhagen.

Eggan, Fred, ed. 1937. *Social anthropology of North American tribes*. Chicago.

Fumoleau, René. 2004. *As long as this land shall last: A history of Treaty 8 and Treaty 11, 1870–1939*. Calgary, Alberta.

Gillespie, Beryl C. 1970. *Yellowknives*. Proceedings of the 1970 Annual Spring Meeting of the American Ethnological Society, Robert F. Spencer, ed., 61–71.

———. 1976. Changes in territory and technology of the Chipewyan. *Arctic Anthropology* 13:6–11.

Hearne, Samuel. 1795. *A journey from Prince of Wales's Fort in Hudson's Bay to the Northern Ocean*. London. (Other editions: Dublin, 1796; Toronto, 1911; Toronto, 1958).

Helm, June, ed. 1981. *Subarctic*. Vol. 6, *Handbook of North American Indians*. Washington, DC.

Jarvenpa, Robert. 1976. Spatial and ecological factors in the annual economic cycle of the English River band of Chipewyan. *Arctic Anthropology* 13:43–69.

———. 1977. Subarctic trappers and band society. *Human Ecology* 5:223–59.

———. 1982. Intergroup behavior and imagery. *Ethnology* 21:283–99.

Jenness, Diamond, ed. 1956. The Chipewyan Indians: An account by an early explorer. *Anthropologica* 3:15–33.

Lowie, Robert H. 1909a. The Chipewyans of Canada. *Southern Workman* 38: 278–83.

———. 1909b. An ethnological trip to Lake Athabasca. *American Museum Journal* 9:10–15.

Marlowe, Evelyn, et al. 2002. *A community-based monitoring in the Slave Geological Province: Case study Lutsel K'e,* West Kitikmeot/Slave study, Part 2.

Mason, John A. 1946. *Notes on the Indians of the Great Slave Lake area*. Yale University Publications in Anthropology, no. 34.

Rich, Edwin E. 1960. *Hudson's Bay Company, 1670–1870*. 3 vols. Toronto.

Sharp, Henry S. 1975. Introducing the sororate to a northern Saskatchewan Chipewyan village. *Ethnology* 14:71–82.

―――. 1977. The Chipewyan hunting unit. *American Ethnologist* 4(2):377–93.

―――. 1979. *Chipewyan marriage*. Mercury Series, Canadian Ethnology Service Paper, no. 58.

―――. 1986. Shared experience and magical death: Chipewyan explanations of a prophet's decline. *Ethnology* 25(4):257–70.

―――. 1988. *The transformation of Bigfoot: Maleness, power, and belief among the Chipewyan*. Washington, DC.

―――. 1991. Memory, meaning, and imaginary time: The construction of knowledge in white and Chipewyan cultures. *Ethnohistory* 38(2):149–76.

―――. 1995. Men and women among the Chipewyan. In *Women and power in native North America*, L. Klein and N. Ackerman, eds., 46–74. Norman, OK.

Simpson, George. 1938. *Journal of occurrences in the Athabasca department, 1820 and 1821*. Publications of the Champlain Society, Hudson's Bay Company Series, no. 1.

Smith, David M. 1973. *INKONZE: Magico-religious beliefs of contact-tradition Chipewyan trading at Fort Resolution, NWT, Canada*. Mercury Series, Ethnology Division Paper, no. 6. National Museum of Man, Ottawa.

―――. 1976. Cultural and ecological change: The Chipewyan of Fort Resolution. *Arctic Anthropology* 13:35–42.

―――. 1982. *Moose-Deer Island house people: A history of the native people of Fort Resolution*. Ottawa.

Smith, James G. E. 1970. The Chipewyan hunting group in a village context. *Western Canadian Journal of Anthropology* 1:60–66.

―――. 1976a. Introduction: The historical and cultural position of the Chipewyan. *Arctic Anthropology* 13:1–5.

―――. 1976b. Local band organization of the caribou eater Chipewyan. *Arctic Anthropology* 13:12–24.

Smith, James G. E., and Ernest S. Burch, Jr. 1979. Chipewyan and Inuit in the central Canadian Subarctic, 1613–1977. *Arctic Anthropology* 16(2):76–101.

Tyrrell, Joseph B., ed. 1916. *David Thompson's narrative*. Publications of the Champlain Society, vol. 12.

VanStone, James W. 1963. Changing patterns of Indian trapping in the Canadian subarctic. *Arctic* 16:159–74.

―――. 1965. *The changing culture of the Snowdrift Chipewyan*. National Museum of Canada Bulletin no. 209.

―――. 1974. *Athapaskan adaptations*. Chicago.

5 The Lower Kootenai: Plateau Fishers and Hunters

A 1929 photograph of Kiuki, a Lower Kootenay in the Creston area of British Columbia. (Courtesy of Creston & District Museum & Archives.)

It was after the strangers came, more and more of them everywhere, that [life] began to change.

(Elders of the Kootenai Nation 1990, 19)

THE PLATEAU CULTURE area is an inland sector of the Pacific Northwest in Canada and the United States in which Euro-American settlement has been comparatively recent. Of all the culture areas north of Mexico, the Plateau tribes probably are the least known. Unfortunately, yet typically, they were exposed to exotic diseases with devastating impact, both before and following the arrival of whites. In addition, after the boundary between the United States and Canada was determined in 1846, land-hungry white settlers soon began to pour into the Oregon Territory. Some tribes in the southern Plateau sector were nearly destroyed, whereas others were displaced or confined to relatively small tracts of land. As a result of new diseases and white intruders, their aboriginal cultures typically declined rapidly. More northern Plateau tribes, however, were affected somewhat later and less intensively by Euro-Americans. As a result, ethnographic accounts about some of these people are reasonably satisfactory. The Kootenai (Kootenay, Ktunaxa, Kutenai) are an example. Because they lived and continue to live on both sides of the international boundary, they also provide an opportunity to consider the national policies of Canada and the United States for a single Native American population.

These Indians had a number of names for themselves, but their self-identification is now *Kootenai* (KOOT-nee), a word of uncertain origin. No one knows their number in early historic times; two thousand may be a reasonable guess. They appear to have lived farther to the east before occupying their historic homeland. Their language is a "language isolate," meaning that it is not clearly related to any other linguistic group. The Kootenai are divided into the Upper (upriver) and Lower (downriver) dialect groups, depending on where they lived along the Kootenay River system. This geographical division is somewhat confusing; the Upper Kootenai occupy the eastern sector, and the Lower Kootenai are to the west and north of Kootenai Falls (see Figure 5-1).

The baseline ethnographic reconstruction presented in this chapter must be accepted with caution. Ethnographers did not begin to assemble comprehensive information about the aboriginal Kootenai until generations after historic contact. Investigators were forced to rely heavily on what people remembered about their earlier lifeway. The general tendency is for people to idealize their culture of old, and it can be difficult or impossible to verify what they remember. Life in the past no doubt seemed "good" to these people, especially in retrospect after outsiders had seized most of their land and had destroyed much of their culture. At least some of their oral history is questionable. Furthermore, verbal information about the past may produce contradictory statements. For instance, one person may report that a particular ceremony was aboriginal, whereas another person with a more recent knowledge base might deny that the ceremony existed. Contradictions of this nature produce interpretive challenges and may defy resolution.

Figure 5-1 | Early historic Kootenai.

Aboriginal Life

This chapter, as far as the data permit, focuses on the Lower Kootenai. They are considered a subtribe by ethnologists, yet a case can be made for identifying them as a separate tribe. They occupied a clearly defined geographical area, spoke a distinct dialect, and had a separate economic base. The terms used to characterize the Lower Kootenai likewise are distinct. They include *Valley Indians, River People, Canoe Indians,* and their own traditional term, *Marsh People.* They were divided into two bands, the people of the modern Bonners Ferry area in Idaho and those of the Creston sector in British Columbia. The habitat was well suited to their economy, which was based on fishing, harvesting waterfowl, and deer hunting.

The Upper Kootenai to the east placed much greater emphasis on big game. Soon after domestic horses became available in the 1730s, providing greater mobility, big game became even more important. Furthermore, they expanded their hunting range eastward into the Plains, and bison became increasingly significant in their economy. This pattern did not prevail among the Lower Kootenai because bison did not frequent their area, nor were they readily accessible elsewhere. In brief, the Upper Kootenai became equestrian hunters in the manner of many Plains Indian tribes (see Chapter 7 on the Crow).

The Kootenay River and a fingerlike lake, Kootenay Lake, dominated the Lower Kootenai homeland. The valley bottom is relatively broad in the south and characterized by ponds, marshland, and meadows. The southern extreme is a forest of hemlock, cedar, fir, and pine. The valley narrows to the north and becomes a subalpine forest setting. Prominent trees include hemlock, fir, and spruce. Throughout the area winters can be cold, with deep snow and subzero temperatures, and the summers are typically hot. Average precipitation is about fifty inches a year. At the same time the climate is relatively mild, considering the geographical location.

ORIGIN MYTH   The Kootenai did not have a specific account to explain their beginnings. Their rich and varied corpus of tales, however, does emphasize prehuman and humanlike animal spirits. Particular spirits produced an orderly world as precedent and as a model for human life. Some myths include specific creative episodes, such as when Doe and Lynx mated to produce two sons, the Sun and Moon. Numerous tales involve the adventures of Coyote as a trickster and transformer in his associations with various animals and birds. When humans emerged, spirit beings withdrew from the earth. Yet spirits continued to have a profound influence on human life, particularly as individuals obtained supernatural aid in personal vision quests.

APPEARANCE AND ARTIFACTS   The Marsh People bathed often and favored perfumes produced from dried and crushed plants mixed with beaver musk and grease. A woman parted her hair in the middle, with braids on each side. A man

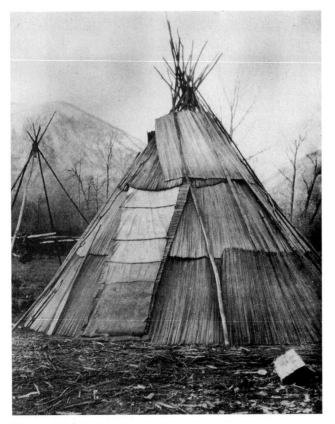

Figure 5-2 | A Lower Kootenai tepee covered with matting. (Courtesy of Glenbow Archives, Calgary, Alberta: neg. no. NA-1141-4.)

wore a braid on both sides of his head and had another at the back of his head and a braided scalp lock. Buckskin garments dominated. A woman wore a frock fringed at the bottom and leggings. A man's clothing included a breechclout, shirt, and leggings in cold weather. The people typically went barefoot in the summer, especially when working in wet areas. Otherwise they wore moccasins. Both sexes wore hats, mittens, and robes of fur in cold weather.

Summer dwellings accommodated small family groups. Mats sewn from rushes typically covered pole-framed tepees (see Figure 5-2). The winter home, termed a longhouse, accommodated multiple, closely related families. Paired poles bound near the top and spread at the base formed A-shaped frames arranged as an elongated triangle; horizontal support poles provided framework stability. Rush mats covered a longhouse, and the interior included a separate fireplace for each family.

A small, dome-shaped structure framed with bent saplings and covered with mats served as a sweat house. A pit dominated the interior. Stones, heated in a nearby fire, were transferred to the pit. Naked bathers sprinkled water on the hot stones to produce steam. People bathed for cleanliness, to cure illness, and, equally as important, to achieve or retain spiritual well-being. A small, probably mat-covered, conical menstrual hut completed the structures represented at a settlement.

Each family owned a number of dogs, their only domestic animal. Dogs guarded camps against intruders and served to drive big game toward concealed hunters. To train a hunting dog, a person might wrap a young puppy in the fresh skin of a big game animal, such as a deer, for a relatively brief period. In theory the puppy later became especially capable of pursuing that species. As families moved from one camp to another, dogs might serve as pack animals. A dog carried two loaded packs, one on each side of its back; binders beneath an animal secured the packs.

The most common tools included a variety of multipurpose knives with flaked flint blades, rodent-tooth knives, elk horn chisels, whetstones, and wooden wedges. They likewise had hafted and grooved stone axes and mauls of similar construction. To produce fire, a wooden fire drill was hand rotated on a fireboard made of a dry piece of poplar. Fungus on the board ignited, and dry grass caught the flames. The people attempted to keep at least one fire burning in a camp because of the labor required to produce a new fire.

Containers are a prominent cluster of artifacts. They fulfilled many functions, including collecting and processing plant products, cooking, serving foods, and storing edibles. The most common types consisted of folded sections of bark stitched to retain the vessel shape. A popular storage container, especially for fish and berries, consisted of a square cedar box with a lid. Foods stored in these boxes had a pleasing taste. Old containers of this type were torn apart by children and used as sleds. Deep coiled baskets were designed for food storage, and shallow ones were favored as plates. The bladders of big game held grease and oil. Note that most artifacts were highly portable and well adapted to a mobile way of life.

Skin processing by women had become the most integrated and complex technological process, just as among the Netsilik and Chipewyan. Women went to great lengths to whiten skins, as they were especially desirable for garments. After the preliminary preparation of a skin, it was soaked in a mixture of brains and water to remove blood stains, to break down the tissue, and to soften it. After this process was repeated as often as necessary, a skin finally was sun dried and scraped with a knife before being cut and sewn.

The Kootenai canoe is their most prominent aboriginal artifact type, primarily because of its distinctive outline. Canoes were indispensable in the lifeway of the Marsh People. The framework of a canoe consisted of cedar stringers some twelve feet in length and bent wooden ribs bound to the stringers with plant fibers. The vessel was covered with spruce bark, and pitch concealed any holes in the bark. Wooden strips bound the gunwales to the cover, and a wooden crosspiece fitted across the top and middle of a vessel helped retain the shape. The beam was about thirty inches. A protruding ramlike bow and

Figure 5-3 | A Lower Kootenai bark-covered canoe. (Courtesy of Glenbow Archives, Calgary, Alberta: neg. no. NA-1141-5.)

stern are the canoe's most distinctive features (see Figure 5-3). The leaf-shaped paddles lacked handgrips. To prevent leakage when traveling through ice, the canoer fitted the bow with a section of green hide.

SUBSISTENCE CYCLE   Permanent settlements did not exist, and yet families generally camped at the same localities from one year to the next, depending on the availability of edibles. The primary staples consisted of fish, deer, and ducks, in that order of importance. The cooperative harvest of these edibles had emerged as most rewarding, and each major food source was under the supervision of a formal leader. Aided by a personal spirit, a leader had the reputation of being skillful and successful. Nonetheless, a fear of famine was always present, and people depended heavily on the aid of spirits to obtain most edibles. This religious dimension suggests that food could not be procured on a reliable basis with the existing technology.

Cooperative fishing reportedly was most rewarding when supervised by a leader aided by either kingfisher or mink spirits; the mink spirit was classified as part fish and part clawed animal. The leader guided the activities of others in constructing weir-trap combinations, especially soon after the spring runoff. The weirs and traps were placed in streams and sloughs leading to the main river. At each fishing site ceremonial preparations spanned three nights. The fishing leader "divined for fish trap" to predict fishing success and foresee potential misfortune or deaths. First they prepared a weir, a damlike obstruction. Crotch-topped poles were cut and driven into the bottom of a water course. In the crotches they lashed long stringer poles. Next mats fashioned from fir boughs were lashed to the poles and stringers on the upstream side; three openings were left, one for each trap. In fast water they fashioned wickerwork weir sections from willow branches. A cylindrical fish trap with willow branch stringers was about nine feet in length, and the mouth was some two feet in diameter. The stringers at the opposite end were lashed together. Willow hoops bound around a trap helped retain the cylindrical design. At the trap mouth a funnel-shaped opening of willows was tied in place. Fish that swam into the funnel seldom could escape from a trap. After the weir-trap combination was completed, the fishing leader checked it each morning. He then returned to a camp to announce the number of men and canoes required to retrieve the catch. For supernatural reasons, fish could not be killed as they were removed from a trap. Trout, burbot, whitefish, or suckers were most often harvested, depending on the season. The catch was distributed to each family at a camp, irrespective of whether men from a particular family participated in the harvest. Fresh fish were placed in cedar root baskets with water and hot stones to cook. At the morning meal everyone ate together, whereas an evening meal was shared in small family groups. All fish bones were collected, saved, and returned to the river.

During the winter families fished especially for burbot, a large fish that was often plentiful. Traps and weirs for winter use were of heavier construction, and any ice that formed was crushed with a stone maul so that the traps could be set and tended from canoes.

A deer-hunt leader knew the habits of deer and the local terrain, and with the aid of spirits he reportedly could establish the location of deer. A hunt preferably was organized from a base camp in February following a heavy snow. On instructions from the leader, men and boys prepared their equipment, including small, round snowshoes of the bear-paw type. From high ground along each side of a stream at a hunting site, males yelled to drive deer into deep snow at lower elevations where the animals foundered. Self bows and arrows with needle-sharp heads dispatched the deer. Hunters made every effort to kill the lead deer first and thereby confuse the others. Following a harvest some meat was prepared for immediate consumption. The surplus meat was dried and cached on wooden platforms adjacent to large conifers to protect it from rain, snow, and predators.

A duck-hunt leader received spirit power from Two-Year-Old-Goose, and on summer mornings he supervised the harvest of ducks, swans, and geese. A twined bark net some twenty-five feet long and fifteen feet high was knotted with four-inch mesh to capture and hold ducks. Stretched between two stout poles with a rope arrangement, the net rested on the ground but could be raised abruptly by net tenders. Duck decoys were placed near the net, and a man imitated the cry of a feeding duck. If all went well, a flock landed nearby. The hunt leader watched the ducks until one of them stopped eating, an indication that they were preparing to fly off. The leader signaled the net tenders to raise the net abruptly as other men in strategic spots made a great deal of noise. After ducks flew into the net, it was dropped, and the net tenders broke the necks of the captives. Hunters hoped to harvest four flights in a morning. Larger-gauged nets served to tangle geese and swans. Waterfowl was processed soon after a kill for immediate consumption and storage because these birds spoiled rapidly. Some waterfowl nets could be converted into gill nets.

Women dug two species of camas (lily) bulbs as their primary contribution to the food supply. Before removing the bulbs with a fire-hardened digging stick, women recited prayers for a successful harvest. The bulbs retained their original flavor for a long while after being baked. A particular woman supervised the collection of salmonberries and huckleberries. Some berries were consumed fresh, and others were dried and stored for winter.

Tobacco was the only cultivated plant. A man dreamed that the Grizzly Bear, a supernatural, instructed him to sow the seeds and direct the plantings of others. Apparently the tobacco was harvested without ceremony. It was smoked in pipes during rituals, but not for pleasure.

Some families, apparently comparatively few, were known as "drifters." They were poor, had no fixed territory, and wandered about throughout the year in search of food. It would appear that they were not successful in enlisting the aid of spirits. They subsisted mainly by fishing with hooks and lines, and sometimes robbed the food caches of others. Such thefts were ignored, not punished.

These basic foods were augmented by a variety of others. For example, caribou provided a favorite meat and the best bedding. Mountain goats were difficult to hunt, but again the meat was appreciated, and the hides made fine robes. For sturgeon, a large and powerful fish, a baited hook was bound to a stout line. Finally, deadfalls served to trap furbearers.

Over the generations extended families typically exploited a particular locality for raw materials and edibles. Unclaimed land could be utilized by anyone. In at least some cases a particular spirit granted a man ownership of a specific locality in which he and his family might remain. A son or grandson who took care of his father or grandfather was likely to become the subsequent owner if the same spirit presented itself to that person.

DESCENT, KINSHIP, AND MARRIAGE   The descent system of these people was bilateral, as has also been reported for the Netsilik and Chipewyan. Accounts about the traditional Kootenai kinship terminology are not consistent. The variations may represent local differences, historic changes, or a combination of these factors. Yet it is clear that numerous terms differed depending on whether the speaker was male or female (e.g., a woman and man used different terms for a younger brother). However, numerous terms were reciprocals, meaning that they were the *same* for different sets of relatives (e.g., a grandparent and grandchild used the same word for each other). The brother and sister terms were extended to first cousins (Hawaiian cousin terminology) with obvious implications; cousins were treated essentially the same as biological siblings. With siblings and cousins termed alike, we would expect that the

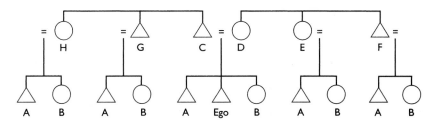

Figure 5-4 | Reconstruction of the basic early historic Kootenai kinship system.

mother term would be extended to mother's sister and father's sister, but this was not the case. Instead separate terms existed for mother, mother's sister, and father's sister (bifurcate collateral parental generation terms). Presumably the basic terminology was changing when it was recorded (see Figure 5-4).

A newly married couple initially lived with the parents of the bride, and they later established an independent household nearby (matrilocal residence). The clearest joking relationship was between a man and his wife's sisters. Their jokes could be ribald, and sexually suggestive horseplay took place. This patterning was understandable because when a man's wife died it was customary for him to marry her oldest unmarried sister (the sororate). Similarly, a widow was expected to marry her deceased husband's brother (the levirate). In this general context, the death of a spouse tended not to disrupt the continuity of family life within marriages.

SOCIAL DIMENSIONS   During the summer band members dispersed, and small family groups occupied tepees near one another. In the winter closely related families ideally lived in a single longhouse. By early historic times an estimated twenty families lived in the Bonners Ferry sector. The annual settlement pattern meant that comparatively few people lived in close contact with near biological relatives and in-laws. Yet in-law taboos prevailed. Parents-in-law did not directly address a son-in-law or daughter-in-law of the opposite gender. For example, a man never looked at his mother-in-law or communicated directly with her. When he had something to say to this woman in the presence of his wife, the message was conveyed by the wife. We also find that after puberty biological brothers and sisters avoided one another. These taboos may have emerged to prevent any hint of sexual relations that could disrupt the harmony within small, closely cooperating family groups.

Social bonds within a band found strength through male cooperation, with clearly defined subordinate and superordinate statuses, in key subsistence pursuits. In many social contexts, however, egalitarian relations were the norm. Young and old adults, as well as children, offered their opinions freely, without hesitation, and in straightforward language. Concurrently, people were exceedingly hospitable with other Kootenai and foreign friends. Families vied with one another to feed and lodge guests. It was rude not to offer someone food and in equally poor taste not to accept it.

Social control does not appear to have been a major problem, because band members were few and familiar with one another. Possibly the most powerful means of control was ridicule, as commonly is the case in small-scale societies. A persistently antisocial man might be ostracized until he conformed. Possibly the most disturbing situation resulted when one band member murdered another. Relatives of the deceased were obligated to seek justice. The murderer might be challenged to combat with an outstanding warrior, and whatever resulted could end the case, although enduring family feuds are reported.

If there was one Kootenai passion, it surely was gambling, and the hand game dominated; it was played separately by men, women, and children. Two players at a time were involved and backed by their supporters, who sang medicine songs for success and wagered on the outcome. A well-known gambler represented each side. The goal was to guess the hand that held a small white bone. Hand manipulations were extremely rapid, and ten counting sticks kept score until all were won or lost. When the stakes were high, a game might last through the night. Reportedly, in precontact times marten and fisher pelts represented the standard of wealth, especially for gambling. One might suspect that this emphasis on pelts was a product of the fur trade.

POLITICAL LIFE   Early in their history, two Marsh People bands existed. A band of related families in a particular sector was presided over by a band leader. He was not the stereotype of a powerful "chief." Instead he possessed special rapport with spirits and represented moral authority. The people obeyed his decisions, not because of any threat but because he acted for the common good. A band leader was chosen by men who had achieved status through personal vision quests and had proven abilities. A band council consisted of leaders representing each of the three major subsistence complexes, a war leader, and the band leader.

When a band leader failed in his duties or died, an institutionalized procedure was followed. A new leader was chosen in council, but he could be a consensus leader before his formal appointment. A patrilineal emphasis prevailed in the selection, because the candidate seems most often to have been the wisest son of the previous leader. A candidate, irrespective of his background—or so it appears—went alone into the forest and sought spiritual instructions to become the successor. If he achieved his goal, he returned to camp singing a new song to validate his leadership role. He might then become the interim leader and the council-approved leader if the band thrived under his guidance. If not, the process was repeated until the council agreed on a replacement. The band leader alone officiated throughout the year.

The Marsh People are said not to have fought offensive wars. Their reasonably well-developed warfare complex was apparently a response to encroachments by other Indians. The Blackfoot were their greatest enemy. Campsites were chosen partially on the basis of defendability. The war leader for a band had proven abilities and spirit protection.

When preparing for combat, a warrior might wear only a breechclout and white body paint or body paint alone. Alternatively, he could wear an animal pelt with personal supernatural associations. A fourth possibility was to wear armor made from wooden slats bound tightly to protect the front and back of his body. Additional panels shielded his upper arms and lower legs. Over the body armor he could also wear a spirit-protected animal pelt. All of this variability was dictated by spirit aids. The primary weapon was the bow and arrow, but a war club or coup stick, used to touch or strike a live enemy, might be carried. In an open confrontation enemy warriors formed opposing lines, and a conflict began as they shot arrows at one another from a distance. Only the bravest warriors took quivers of arrows into battle. One such man after another approached the enemy, singing his protective song as he shot and dodged arrows. The most prestigious and dangerous form of combat was to strike an armed enemy with a coup stick and live to tell about the event. Dead enemies were scalped, but a scalp had no supernatural associations; it was a trophy. Ethnographic accounts suggest that counting coup and scalping were uncommon among the Lower Kootenai, unlike the Upper Kootenai, who were strongly influenced by the Plains Indian war complex.

RELIGION Earth, Water, and Sky represented the basic components of the natural world. Water with its aquatic life surrounded the Earth to sustain people, their artifacts, rocks, terrestrial plants, and animals. Sky was a dome occupied by avifauna; by the Sun, Moon, and other celestial bodies; and by natural phenomena such as thunder and lightning. Stars were human souls in the Sky, the Milky Way was the path of ghosts, and the Northern Lights represented the dead dancing. Each life form and every other earthly configuration possessed physical and spirit reality. A person became absorbed into the cosmological system through a vision quest.

Males and females alike sought visions, although those of males were judged more powerful. The people felt that a young person, ten years of age or somewhat older, possessed the potential for strong visions. To encourage a vision an object from the spirit (medicine, sacred) bundle of a relative might be taken on a quest. Yet the nature of spirit contacts was largely unpredictable. A father decided when a child would seek a vision, and preparations included purification with a smudge of dried juniper needles—the spirits were said to be attracted by the odor. A child sought spirit guidance at a body of water, in the mountains, or elsewhere. The successful novice had a vision, or less often a dream, in which an animal or sometimes a human spirit entered the person's body; supernatural power was conferred in a song. A particular spirit remained with an individual until he or she died. It then returned to the locality of its origin as a spirit ghost.

A successful quest by all men and many women was associated with a personal medicine bundle prepared under spirit guidance. An owner sang to his or her bundle and received instructions from it. A sacred bundle usually was buried with its owner. They thought that most people "only got cheap spirits," whereas those of shamans were powerful. Young people, female or male, could become shamans following an initial vision. Shamans served no apprenticeships, nor did they represent a distinct social group. Several shamans usually lived in a community, and each of them retained a respectful reputation as long as his or her spirit aids were successful in curing illness.

The major shamanistic ceremony was the curing ceremony, termed "putting-up-the-blanket," meaning that blankets were suspended from a rope across one section of a lodge where a juniper smudge burned for the evening event. In the darkened room a male shaman clad only in a breechclout sat with the blankets at his back facing the audience-participants. He beat a drum and sang a song to summon a spirit. After the spirit arrived, he went behind the blankets. The blankets began to shake, sometimes violently, and footfalls might be heard on the roof. After being tied up by a spirit, the shaman rolled out from behind the blankets. Someone placed a whistle in his mouth that was used to summon as many as four spirits, and he returned to behind the blankets. Next he appeared before the onlookers freed of his bonds. He again returned behind the blankets, from where a spirit was said to carry him off. The blankets shook so violently that the viewers could see that the shaman had disappeared. From behind the blankets spirits advised the audience in low and sometimes confusing voices. A seance ended when the shaman reappeared from behind the blankets in a dazed state. For his services in curing a patient he received no compensation. A number of shamans could perform in a single seance.

The most elaborate religious observance of the aboriginal Marsh People was the Grizzly Bear Ceremony. The veneration of bears prevailed widely among peoples of the northern forested regions in the northern hemisphere. A number of compelling reasons have been offered to account for this emphasis. Bears, like people, usually are omnivorous, they can stand on their hind legs, and they behave in other humanlike ways. Equally important, a skinned bear looks quite human. Bears can be dangerous, and their ability to hibernate is yet another impressive characteristic. Among the Marsh People black and brown bears had supernatural associations, but systematic ritual attention focused on the grizzly. They are impressively large, agile, and elusive; they maul or kill people when they feel threatened. People apparently hunted grizzly bears after a man dreamed that a friend or relative would be killed by a grizzly. If a shaman confirmed the dream, the dreamer sought to kill the animal. Dogs tracked the bear in the late fall or early winter, and they held it at bay for the hunter to make the kill with his bow and special magical arrows. Fresh bear meat was roasted over a fire, and any surplus was dried for the future; bear oil was valued as a condiment. Dogs were prohibited from gnawing on bear bones.

The grizzly bear was accorded special recognition in similar ceremonies held twice each year: before the bears emerged from dens in the spring and before they denned in the fall. The Grizzly Bear Ceremony "was characterized by petitions, propitiatory songs and mimetic dances, tobacco offerings, food sacrifices and other gifts made to the bear, with prayers by women that they not be molested during the root- and berry-gathering season, and by men that the spirit not be angry if one of its 'children' was killed, since the flesh was to be used as food" (Schaeffer 1966, 17).

The observances were held in an especially large tepee. Facing the entrance was the representation of a grizzly bear, possibly made from earth and including a bear skull. The male participants, and sometimes women with spiritual powers, appear to have had their medicine bundles included at the bear altar. The ceremony began with supernatural songs about the grizzly bear, other songs were sung in its honor, and some men and women danced for the same purpose. Gifts to the grizzly bear were made by the participants and accompanied by prayers. These presents were buried as offerings to the animal. The ceremony concluded with a feast of berries, a favored food of bears.

Sorcery also was associated with the grizzly bear and performed by shamans empowered by the bear's spirit. A sorcerer sent the spirit against a victim, and it reportedly entered a camp as a bear to seek the victim and attack him. A shaman-sorcerer also could cause illness, and the victim sought another shaman to sing over him; if he was cured, it was a sign that the malice of the shaman-sorcerer had caused the illness. The victim might in turn ask the helpful shaman to kill the evil one by supernatural means.

LIFE CYCLE A pregnant woman observed many taboos to help ensure the well-being of her offspring. She slept with few blankets, she could not pause in a doorway to look outside, nor could she break bones. These, plus many other prohibitions, set her apart from other women—in anthropological terms. Delivery occurred in her dwelling, where she knelt and held onto cords suspended from upright poles as a midwife supported her from behind. A midwife reportedly began her career following a dream in which she helped a particular woman. A midwife received no compensation. A shaman was called in for a difficult delivery; his aid appears to have been more supernatural than purely medical. After childbirth the mother wore a buckskin belt to bind her abdomen; she remained in the dwelling for ten days and drank through a drinking tube. For a month she was prohibited from having sexual intercourse. The major restriction of a husband was to drink through a drinking tube for that month.

A neonate was named at birth and usually retained the same name throughout life; however, names and the naming process are unclear. For a few days a new baby was wrapped in a robe and later carried in a cradleboard that hung from the mother's back; a piece of the umbilical cord was dried and sewn into a bag that was attached to the cradleboard. The inside of a cradleboard was lined with fur from which urine and feces could be removed. A baby initially slept between its parents, a symbolic prohibition against their sexual intercourse.

Indulgence characterized adult behavior toward small children, who were expected to speak Kootenai reasonably well at about fourteen months of age; soon thereafter she or he began to be taught. They emphasized being silent and reserved; loudness was associated with antisocial behavior. Parents did not hesitate to spank their children, and older siblings disciplined younger ones, irrespective of gender. The following story for children appears to have been conceived to induce conformity: A brother and sister once lived as husband and wife, but their descendants became dullards and "wild people." Only their tracks were ever seen, and they became extinct. The story of these wild people appears to have been used as a "bogeyman" and may represent an effort to prevent brother-sister incest.

A small girl played with dolls and increasingly mimicked her mother's behavior. Thus the child learned to acquire womanly habits at a young age so that she could help her mother following the birth of a sibling. An eight-year-old girl was expected to be capable of preparing a simple meal. People likewise felt that a boy must begin to learn adult skills early in life. By the time he was six, a boy had his own bow and arrows. He was expected to kill birds and thereby make at least a symbolic contribution to the family food supply.

A child crossed a major threshold when he or she sought a lifelong protective spirit, as discussed previously. For a girl, her first menstruation represented another milestone. She was isolated under the supervision of an old woman and lived in a menstrual hut away from a camp. The girl drank little water and ate sparingly. Her hair was braided and painted red, and her face was painted the same color. When she itched, she scratched with a piece of wood. In the hut she sat on a low platform, and outside of it she walked over poles placed on the ground. Her ten days of isolation were followed a year later by the same set of conventions, but the isolation was for only five days. During subsequent menstrual periods she was not isolated. All of this ritual attention obviously separated her from other, more youthful, females and emphasized her new status as a woman. Comparable ceremonial involvement at puberty did not exist for a male. Yet as indicated earlier, a brother and sister avoided contact with one another upon reaching puberty.

Ideally a woman remained a virgin before marriage, and her close relatives attempted to prevent premarital sexual intercourse. Nonetheless, "mischief men" seduced maidens and then ridiculed them; rapes also occurred. Spirits reportedly ceased to aid such men. No stigma fell on a woman or her offspring if she conceived before marriage, and the biological father was responsible for supporting the child. The existence of such standards suggests that this pattern may have been relatively common.

Monogamy dominated in marriages, and a young couple had comparative freedom in making their own arrangements as long as the families involved did not strongly disapprove. A youthful male could take the initiative by composing and singing a love song for the one he desired. A young woman in turn could respond with a song if she looked favorably on the singer. Flute music likewise could be a part of courting behavior. Alternatively, if a girl desired a particular man and had the support of her mother, the older woman could initiate the arrangements. A few days following a marital agreement, the couple received gifts from each set of parents. No formal marriage ceremony existed, and a couple usually lived with the wife's family for a year or more to absorb the routine of adult life. Subsequently, they set up their own tepee in the summer near the wife's parents, and a feast was held to honor the couple, the only public recognition of their change in status.

Circumstances in all societies led to alternative marital arrangements. Among these Indians, for instance, an orphan girl could be taken into a family as a servant. A young man who desired her for a wife might creep silently at night into the dwelling where she lived. If the girl allowed him to remain, their cohabitation became a marriage. Divorce was common when a partner found the marriage difficult; this was a private decision, not a public concern, and children remained with the mother.

The concept of purity found prominent expression in the sweat bath, known to some people as Grandfather Sweat House. A person bathed for physical cleanliness, to obtain spirit blessing in prayers, to reinforce spirit songs, for gambling luck, and to cure illness under a shaman's supervision. In at least some bathing, a person with Sweat-House Spirit power put water on the hot stones. He dipped one handful of water at a time from a container and threw it on the rocks. Twenty-one handfuls produced so much moist heat that some bathers would be forced from a bathhouse.

Apart from shamans, female herbalists employed plant products under the guidance of spirits to cure physical ailments. Secular curers appear to have been instructed by spirits about how to use most plant products in this manner. Shamans, male or female, treated illness that was thought to be of supernatural origins. Their goal was to locate and remove a foreign substance from a patient's body by sucking.

It was anticipated that a fatally ill person could predict what would happen to the living. Following a death the body was attended by relatives and remained in the dwelling during the day of death, and that night all mourners were present. People cried and sang weeping songs. The following day the corpse was bathed and later removed from the dwelling headfirst. Burial was in a shallow grave and without ceremony. They had little interest in an afterlife.

ONE-STANDING-LODGE-POLE-WOMAN Early in Marsh People history, this woman unquestionably was the most famous individual in highly varied ways. She was a courier, guide, prophetess, warrior, shaman, peacemaker, and possibly the only Kootenai female at that time to assume the role of a man. She was a transvestite, a woman-man, or berdache (meaning a woman-man or more often a man-woman). Firsthand accounts about her by white explorers and traders, as well as secondhand reports, are relatively numerous. She became famous from along the Columbia River to the sea.

As she matured, it appears that Lodge-Pole-Woman was large and heavy boned. She apparently had hoped to marry, but because of her size she could not obtain a Kootenai husband. Before long the first white traders appeared locally, and Lodge-Pole-Woman became the wife of one of them. They spent the winter of 1808–1809 at Kootanae House, where she appears to have learned to speak limited Cree. As a result of "loose" behavior, she was obligated to leave the trading post and her husband.

More than a year later she rejoined the Marsh People and told of her remarkable transformation. In dances she related that her former husband had performed an operation to change her sex—evidence for the great powers of whites. As a result of her sex change, she assumed a new name, Gone-to-the-Spirits. It was then that she began to wear a man's garments and carry weapons. She soon attempted to obtain a wife, but without success, despite her claim of supernatural powers. At this point people began to regard her as threatening, or possibly dangerous. Eventually Gone-to-the-Spirits began living with a woman abandoned by her husband. The woman-man beat her partner for having an open affair with a man, which led to their separation. Gone-to-the-Spirits, who was thought to have fashioned a leather phallus, subsequently had a sequence of wives.

In keeping with her male status, she became a warrior, although few details are known about this role. We do know that she accompanied her brother and others on foot to raid for horses. Whenever they came to a stream it was customary to cross it naked and to carry clothing on one's head. The brother noticed that his sister lagged behind the others at these crossings. On one occasion he saw his sister in the water below the waist and knew that she was not a man, but he said nothing. She apparently realized that her gender was now known to her brother and quickly squatted in the water, pretending to have turned her ankle. As a result of this feigned misadventure, she changed her name to *Qánqon kámek klaúla* (Sitting-in-the-Water-Grizzly). Following the abortive raid she obtained a new wife and treated her poorly. During one noisy confrontation heard by the brother, he announced to the people of the camp that she really was a woman and that he would call her Qanqon, a derisive nickname, a reference to her squatting in the stream. Despite ridicule she continued to live with her band and obtained a new bride. Before long the woman was mistreated and threatened to use her supernatural powers against the woman-man. To test her power Qanqon shot the wife in the wrist with an arrow. The woman pulled out the arrow, rubbed the wound, and it reportedly healed immediately. She left Qanqon following this incident, but the woman-man treated subsequent wives with greater consideration.

In 1811, and with a new wife, Qanqon journeyed to Spokane House, a British outpost of the North West Company. Here she was asked by the trader to deliver a letter to a distant post. Qanqon and her spouse made a truly remarkable trip to the mouth of the Columbia River and the new Pacific Fur Company post at Astoria, an American enterprise. The contents of the delivered letter are unknown, and where it was to be delivered is confused. Nonetheless, Qanqon told the Astoria traders a great deal about the fur resources along the middle reaches of the Columbia. As a result a party of Astoria traders, loosely guided by Qanqon, was sent to build an inland post to rival Spokane House.

As they traveled inland, Qanqon asked the whites to protect her because as a prophetess on the downstream trip she had predicted disease among the Chinook Indians, who feared a smallpox epidemic. The whites whom she guided assured the Chinook that they did not carry smallpox and probably saved Qanqon's life.

On the trip up the Columbia, Qanqon and her spouse pushed ahead of the whites as "bold and adventurous amazons." She claimed to be an advance agent of "the great white chief" (Schaeffer 1965, 206). She reported to Indians along the way that their desires for trade goods would be fulfilled, at no cost to them, by white men who were following her. By the time Qanqon and her wife were some distance up river, they had received twenty-six horses, many of them loaded with robes, and other spoils from foreign Indians. She had gained a reputation as a prophetess and was at least partially responsible for the Prophet Dance movement. It focused, as did the later Ghost Dance (see Chapter 2), on world renewal, a return of the dead, and a blissful life after a particular dance was performed repeatedly.

The next mention of Qanqon is in 1825, when she visited the Flathead Post and became "tipsy" on rum. Claude E. Schaeffer (1965, 214) suggested that by this time she was gaining a reputation as a shaman, possibly as a result of her transvestite status. Twelve years later, in 1837, she again emerges in history. By then she was about forty-seven years old and sought to make peace between the Blackfoot and Flathead. The same year she participated in an unsuccessful raid for horses with other Kootenai. According to Blackfoot and Kootenai oral traditions, the raiders were ambushed by a party of Blackfoot. A Kootenai who had lagged behind the others concealed himself before the attack. He heard one Blackfoot war whoop after another, indicating Kootenai deaths. He then heard a woman scream and knew it was Qanqon. Reportedly she was shot a number of times before being subdued in a sitting position. Blackfoot warriors slashed at her midsection with knives, but the wounds were said to close each time a knife was withdrawn from her body. One Blackfoot then cut open her chest and ate a piece of her heart, an ultimate tribute to a great warrior. She could not heal this wound, according to tradition, and died. Some time later when a Kootenai party located her body, they found that predators had not disturbed the corpse.

Historical Changes

Early in their history the number of Marsh People is uncertain. Before whites arrived, smallpox epidemics had struck repeatedly. Other early epidemics of exotic diseases in the region included whooping cough, a strain of cold or influenza, and probably measles; each could prove deadly to a virgin population. From the cumulative impact of these diseases, it is reasonable to assume that older people, infants, and children most often died. If so, this would mean that few elders survived to pass on cultural traditions and that relatively few children lived long enough to learn the old ways. Population numbers and cultural knowledge must have diminished a great deal within a few generations.

Two great fur trading companies dominated early explorations and control of the Plateau region. In the late 1700s North West Company agents reported that the Kootenai were attempting to reach their distant posts, but Plains Indians barred the way. The first local post was Kootanae House, founded in 1807. By then the Kootenai had few guns or ready access to other trade goods; they were delighted when this post was opened. The competing Hudson's Bay Company absorbed the North West Company in 1821 and controlled the region until after 1846, when the boundary between the United States and Canada was established. The international boundary divided the Marsh People into two groups: those around Bonners Ferry, Idaho, and others in the vicinity of Creston, British Columbia. Their total population in 1830 reportedly was close to three hundred, a third of whom were children. Oregon Territory was created in 1848 with Indian rights acknowledged but poorly respected. The major treaty with Indians of the region was the Hell Gate Treaty of 1855, but it did *not* involve the Lower Kootenai (see Figure 5-5).

The earliest prominent historical leader among the Marsh People was Three Moons, their last great warrior and first "chief." He died about 1840. Three Moons had prophesied the arrival of men with light skin who would bring peace and salvation. His revelations, similar to those of other Indians in the region, resulted in the Prophet Cult movement. The earliest missionary was

Figure 5-5 | The earliest known Kootenai photograph made by the North American Boundary Commission Survey, 1860–1861. (Courtesy of the National Anthropological Archives, Smithsonian Institution, photo number 96-10679.)

Father Pierre-Jean de Smet, a Roman Catholic. During an extended stay among the Lower Kootenai in 1845, he converted everyone to Catholicism and had a cross erected at the site that came to be known as Mission Hill near the future town of Bonners Ferry, Idaho.

The cosuccessors of Three Moons, christened Thomas and Moses, emerged as assertive Roman Catholic advocates. They sought to destroy the traditional religion. People who did not conform with Church teachings were confined to their dwellings or flogged, practices introduced by priests. Yet by about 1890 some people became disillusioned with the new religion. Successive chiefs vacillated between acceptance and rejection of Catholicism. The first church was built on Mission Hill in 1890, and people began to settle nearby. A new church was completed in 1907, but soon thereafter so many people were reverting to the old religion that the priests no longer visited them. The Marsh People obviously had mixed feelings toward the "strangers" among them.

THE KOOTENAI OF BONNERS FERRY, IDAHO   This band of Kootenai emphatically and justifiably stress that they were not represented at the Hell Gate Treaty of 1855. As a direct result, these people had neither early nor formal recognition by the United States. Because their valley bottom land was prime for farming and grazing, it was coveted by white settlers and land speculators and regarded by the federal government as public domain. The Bonners Ferry Kootenai were strongly encouraged by federal agents to settle on the Flathead Reservation in Montana, and a small number of families relocated there. Those who refused to move finally were allotted the local land on which they lived by a presidential executive order in 1887. These holdings did not constitute a formal reservation but came to be regarded as the Kootenai Reservation.

The federal goal was to have families farm their allotments, but in the absence of any Kootenai farming tradition, most families continued to fish, hunt, and collect plant products on a miniscule and clearly inadequate land base. Nonetheless, a few men began to farm and raise cattle. Over the years, as the original allottees died, their plots repeatedly were divided by inheritance and became so small that a family could not farm even if they so desired. The federal government solution was to lease the land to white farmers. Oral tradition indicates that some "leases" negotiated by whites actually were bills of sale. Eventually the federal government leased most allotments to white farmers; band members received ⅓ of the lease profits.

By the early 1930s the people were largely landless, and addiction to alcoholic beverages had become endemic. (Indians in Idaho could not legally consume alcohol until 1955, when the state repealed their prohibition law.) In 1934 a federal response to their plight was to build new houses for families at Mission Hill. In another development the people sought compensation for land they had lost, and in 1960 they received a settlement of $425,000 based on the 1859 value of 125,000 acres in northern Idaho. According to the Elders of the Kootenai Nation (1990, 23–24), none of the money could be used to buy back land. Each person was to receive $4700 for the settlement, but they were

Figure 5-6 | A war bond issued by the Kootenai of Idaho to help fund their confrontation with the United States in 1974.

obligated to put it in trust accounts to repay the state for welfare benefits, as was a common policy for states.

Pressured by the BIA, an elected tribal government emerged in 1947 as the Kootenai Tribe of Idaho. In anthropological terms, these people represent a band, not a tribe, but their identification as a tribe in this legal context is accepted in the following text. Tribal membership initially included all local Kootenai with at least one-fourth Kootenai genetic heritage who were not affiliated with any Canadian Indian group. By 1999 nearly half of the 126 tribal members were under eighteen years of age. About 90 tribal members lived either on their tribal lands or in the vicinity of Bonners Ferry. The same year, the tribe and its members held about two thousand acres, most of which was leased to white farmers.

Dissatisfaction with their land settlement led to the next major development. In 1974 the tribe declared a "nonviolent war" on the United States, and in it they sought all of their rights to lost land. The single "battle" was a roadblock at Bonners Ferry. The Indians attempted to restrict access to one road and charged a toll of 10¢ per car from drivers willing to pay. The state responded by sending a large number of Idaho State Police to the town. The threat of arrest ended the roadblock. These Kootenai also issued "war bonds" to finance their cause (see Figure 5-6). In meetings with local, state, and federal represenatives, the confrontation was defused but not resolved, in part because the national press paid scant attention to their war. The people were

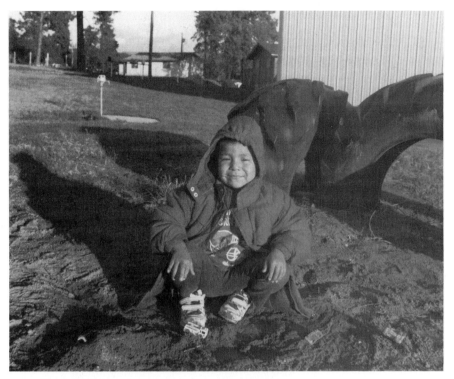

Figure 5-7 | Paul Abraham, a Lower Kootenai, playing near his home on Mission Hill in 1998.

awarded 12.5 acres at the Mission Hill site and assured that additional efforts would be made to obtain more land for them; by the early 2000s this promise had remained unfulfilled. The federal government did, however, build new houses for the people and a community hall. A state of war continues to exist with the United States.

The most positive change of recent years began in 1986 when the tribe opened a motel, the Kootenai River Inn, on allotted land in Bonners Ferry. More important, in 1993, they launched at the same site a gaming facility with bingo and pulltabs ("slot machines" that issue receipts for winnings as opposed to cash). By 1999 the inn and casino had 150 employees, of whom 4 temporary student workers were Kootenai; the annual payroll was $1.5 million. By 2003 the inn and casino had become the major employer in Boundary County, Idaho. Each tribal member, irrespective of age, receives a significant quarterly income from the inn and casino investments. The earnings of underage members are held in trust (see Figure 5-7). They begin to receive their money at age eighteen if they graduate from high school or at age twenty-one for nongraduates.

Before opening the inn, it appears that most whites in Bonners Ferry were intermittently helpful and sympathetic to local Kootenai and quite willing to

Figure 5-8 | A 1964 celebration at Bonners Ferry, Idaho, included Lower Kootenai participation. Chief Eneas Abraham posed on a horse. (Photograph courtesy of Paul Flinn.)

honor and to exploit them in promotional contexts (see Figure 5-8). In general, however, a socioeconomic chasm separated local Indians from residents of the town, and no Kootenai worked there. A widespread Indian stereotype prevailed. With some exceptions these Indians were characterized as lazy, unreliable, poor, and drunkards; they were most often to be pitied. Following the business acumen of the tribe in developing the inn and casino, the attitudes of most townspeople changed, but not a great deal. The Indians continued to be regarded as lazy and unreliable but *rich*. In this sense Kootenai economic success became yet another *divider* between Indians and Euro-Americans. In a major effort to gain greater acceptance by local whites, a three-day Kootenai Casino Powwow was presented in June of 1999 as a part of the Bonners Ferry Centennial celebrations. The powwow attracted some seven hundred Indian dancers representing diverse tribes, and about twelve

Figure 5-9 | These dance participants are awaiting their turn at the 1999 Kootenai Casino Powwow.

hundred visitors attended the event. The tribe spent well over $100,000 on the powwow, which was considered by most whites and Indians as a great success (see Figure 5-9).

Casino profits earned by Native American tribes have been negatively labeled as a "quick fix" for their many problems, and this may be true. Yet it must be reemphasized that the Bonners Ferry Kootenai land holdings are minuscule and that they had no secure economic base. Likewise, their relationship with all levels of the U.S. government has been disappointing at best. Yet the short-term positive benefits from inn and casino earnings are impressive:

1. Tribal members collectively have unprecedented economic security. How lasting it will be is unknown, especially considering continuing efforts in the U.S. Congress to tax gaming operations one way or another and/or to withdraw federal support from tribes with successful gaming operations.
2. The tribe now provides full college scholarships for eligible members.
3. The tribe helps fund the Indian Health Service for benefits received.
4. In 1997, when the county school district was in desperate need of funds, the tribe contributed $93,000.

5. They also have their own welfare program to aid members confronted by temporary economic adversity; the tribe receives neither federal or county welfare aid.
6. They contract with the county for general law enforcement.
7. To expand the land base, the tribe is buying back land that once was theirs.
8. The casino attracts local patrons and tourists alike to provide much needed economic vitality to the *town* of Bonners Ferry. This Kootenai contribution possibly amounts to millions of dollars each year.
9. Finally, the success of the inn and casino provide a newfound pride among tribal members as Indians, especially as Kootenai.

The "good" derived from the inn and casino operations understandably is accompanied by the "bad."

1. Historically, the Kootenai have been avid gamblers, a cultural focus that remains strong. As a direct result, for some members their income from the tribe has fueled their gambling passion. Thus a comparatively small number are worse off than previously. In addition, children and youth continue to be enculturated with a gambling emphasis. There is reason to believe that as adults at least some of them will become compulsive gamblers.
2. A county official familiar with the youth of the Bonners Ferry area reported that Indian and non-Indian youths have much the same rate of involvement with substance abuse. The motivation for individuals in both groups to obtain a high school education is mixed. Some youthful Kootenai see no reason why they should graduate from high school, acquire job skills, or attend college. They assume that as adults they will always have income from casino profits.
3. The long-standing historical pattern of heavy adult consumption of alcoholic beverages remains a major concern. For some adults among whom the problem was acute, it is now greater as a result of their economic security. The tribe employs a counselor who focuses largely on the excessive drinking of youths; adults usually have not been responsive to the program.
4. The unclear legal status of Indian gaming in Idaho was settled by a statewide ballot in 2002, when voters approved a gambling initiative to legalize electronic machines. Challenges were rejected by the Idaho Supreme Court in 2003. The governor and state legislators approved a law that casinos must annually share 5 percent of their net revenues with the state. This is "bad" because it represents yet another direct and successful weakening of tribal sovereignty.

What did it mean to be an Idaho Kootenai in the late 1990s? A knowledgeable female, a tribal leader, considered the question. She noted that about half of the adults continued to speak Kootenai and that about the same number were considered genetically as Kootenai. The vast majority of the tribal members lived nearby, and marriages to non-Indians were rare. Although most members were nominal Roman Catholics, the traditional religious system, although far from intact, was strong. This was reflected especially in the vision quests of some youths and a few adults. Likewise, for some persons the sweat bath remained a dimension of religious life. Their own brand of humor still prevails, along with an emphasis on gambling. She readily conceded as well that a few families had become Euro-American in their lifestyles.

The clear economic and political insight of the Idaho Kootenai leaders led not only to the establishment of a successful casino but also to other prominent achievements. One example is the 1989 contract with the Bonneville Power Administration to study the decline in the Kootenai River system of white sturgeon, a species subsequently identified as an endangered fish by the federal government. In close cooperation with state and federal agencies, the Kootenai now comanage a program to breed these sturgeon and to reintroduce them in waters where they no longer exist. This effort has expanded to include broader programs for revitalizing the general ecological setting of other valuable species.

A closely related landmark decision was reached in 2002, when they negotiated a joint powers compact with Boundary County and the City of Bonners Ferry. This led to the creation of the Kootenai Valley Resource Initiative (KVRI), with participants from pertinent state and federal agencies, as well as business and industrial groups, working with the Kootenai. The goals include water quality improvement, wetland conservation, fish and game recovery and restoration, and other closely related issues. One early tangible result is a successful burbot (i.e., a freshwater cod) recovery program. Initiated by the Kootenai in 2001, it was the *major* KVRI pilot project. In sum, the Kootenai of Idaho have become "movers and shakers," active in improving the regional environment.

THE CRESTON AREA KOOTENAY   As indicated in Chapter 2, Native American administration in Canada has been quite different from that in the United States. The Canadian provinces have far more authority and power in dealing with Indians than the states of the United States. In theory, the major document regulating Indian affairs in Canada is the Royal Proclamation of 1763. It recognized exclusive Native American title to their land and declared that land could only be alienated with Indian permission and only to the Crown. For most Canadians of aboriginal ancestry, this document has proved meaningless, especially in British Columbia. A review of Indian policy in British Columbia is revealing.

The British North American Act, Canada's federal constitution, led to the creation of the Dominion of Canada in 1867, and the political status of British Columbia changed from a colony to a province in 1871. Apart from a relatively few small reserves (reservations) established on Vancouver Island in colonial times, the province denied the legal right of Indians to their land. An exception was for the Peace River area Indians in 1899. Despite intermittent efforts of other British Columbia Indians to have their claims recognized, they failed to gain a reasonable hearing until 1927. In that year a federal report responded to claims by declaring that Indians of British Columbia had *no* claims to their aboriginal land holdings! Separate legislation prohibited Indians from raising money to support their claims, and this prohibition was not lifted until 1951. Status (officially recognized by the federal government) and nonstatus Indians organized in 1969 and vigorously fought for their rights with some success. Village and tribal councils, with federal support in the 1970s, gained expanded control over the everyday administration of reserves.

Federal policy began to change from denial of the rights of First Nations to an acceptance of land claims in principle in 1972. Yet it was not until the Constitutional Act in 1982 that Native American rights received contemporary legal acceptance at the national level. The response in British Columbia in the 1980s was that a province had the right to deny special rights for Indians but that if these rights did exist, they were a federal, not a provincial, responsibility. First Nations goals were primarily to obtain land and its resources under their ownership, financial compensation, and self-government. Despite resistance in British Columbia, a treaty with the Nishga (Nisga'a) in the northwestern sector of the province was signed in 1998. Immediately thereafter the provincial government began to resist implementation of this treaty. Notably, by 2003 the First Nations people represented about 4 percent of the British Columbian population.

Beginning in 1970 the Canadian Lower and Upper Kootenay formed the Kootenay District Council to negotiate a treaty with the British Columbian and federal governments. Their goals were to obtain control over Crown lands that had been part of their aboriginal landholdings, to receive a monetary settlement, and to establish a greater self-government that would include hunting and fishing rights. In 1991 the organization expanded, and the name was changed to Ktunaxa/Kinbasket Tribal Council, thus consolidating their claims with the Kinbasket, Shuswap Indians who had settled among the Canadian Kootenay. Treaty negotiations began with the British Columbia Treaty Commission in 1994, and an agreement in principle was reached between the parties. However, in October 2003, the Creston band withdrew from the cover organization and sought a separate treaty; they regarded the council as ineffective in pursuing their goals. The Creston band hope that their treaty will be signed in about ten years.

Traditionally, and at present, the Lower Kootenai near Bonners Ferry in Idaho and those in the Creston sector of British Columbia represent a single, integrated population. Systematic ethnographic information about the Creston area people is not available, but the existing record strongly suggests that they have been and are similar to those near Bonners Ferry. The Lower Kootenai Indian Reserves (reservations) in British Columbia were created in 1877. They include about seven thousand acres in seven parcels along the Kootenai River.

Figure 5-10 | Headquarters in 1998 for the Lower Kootenay Indian Band near Creston, British Columbia.

The land is held collectively by enrolled (status) Indians (see Figure 5-10). In general, historical developments for the Idaho and British Columbia populations are similar in numerous respects. White farmers and ranchers obtained most of their land, and eventually small sectors were set aside for the Kootenai. With a much diminished land base, they could not continue to exploit their homeland in a traditional manner. They also were distinctly disadvantaged by their cultural background and by the negative attitudes of local Euro-Canadians toward them.

A revealing book about Kootenay life in the Creston area is the autobiography of Chris Luke (2003). The text spans that part of his life from birth in 1948 to the early 1970s. His mother and stepfather were Kootenay, and both died when Luke was a teenager. He continued to be raised in tradition-oriented households and spoke Kootenai as his first language. It was not until he was an adult that he learned his biological father was a Euro-Canadian. Luke's book focuses on memorable events involving his family and friends, his fellow students in schools, his wife, and his coworkers. In anthropological context the most poignant information centers on what it meant to be a member of the Indian minority living near a small Canadian town in southern British Columbia soon after the 1950s.

Luke (2003, 36) summarized some of the prejudices white Canadians expressed against Indians:

My parents were not allowed to enter restaurants, licensed premises [bars], the liquor store, and other retail stores. When I was born, much of this type of

Figure 5-11 | Christopher Luke, the Lower Kootenay elected chief and band manager, Creston, British Columbia, in 2003.

discrimination was still happening. We were not even allowed to get a taxi home. In 1954 we were given permission to enter stores and cafés through the front door. A year earlier, Native children were allowed into public schools, provided they had short hair and were decently dressed. In 1962 Native people gained the right to purchase alcohol and were admitted to licensed premises, and in 1969 we regained the right to practice our beliefs.

In 1970 Luke, who was by then twenty-two, became the elected chief of the Lower Kootenay Band in Canada (see Figure 5-11). In 2003 he was still the elected chief and band manager, although he had taken a few years off in the 1980s.

Formal legal status of Indians in the Lower Kootenay band is based on federal government rolls, irrespective of blood quantum. By 2003 they numbered 260, and the vast majority lived in houses on reserve lands. A few families had left the area. The people had no farming tradition, and their landholdings were small and scattered among the farms of whites.

As individuals, some Kootenay leased their land, totaling some five thousand acres, to white farmers. Most men worked in the local timber industry until its abrupt decline in recent years. Other job opportunities were few, and the unemployment rate climbed to 40 percent. The band administration consisted of twelve persons, most of whom were Kootenay women.

In light of federal and provincial government efforts to suppress the Kootenay culture of old for many years, the band members became concerned about perpetuating their traditional conventions. Because the loss of their aboriginal language became a major issue in the early 1970s, the local band's school launched an instructional program for language revival in 1976. It began with preschool children, ended at the seventh-grade level, and included particulars about their culture, as well as language training. By 2000 only ten individuals spoke Kootenai fluently, and most of these were older persons. Numerous young adults had gained a working familiarity with their indigenous language as a result of the school program, but the number of fluent speakers has remained small. (After completing their years at the band school, students attend the Creston high school, and in recent years each of them has graduated.)

Select Comparisons: Bonners Ferry Kootenai (BFK) and Creston Kootenay (CK)

DIFFERENCES The British Columbian and federal authorities currently have far greater direct control over the CK than the U.S. government has over the BFK in Idaho. In addition, BFK membership is based on blood quantum, whereas CK membership is based on direct historical identity. This means that out-marriages in the respective groups have very different implications. BFK Indians usually marry within their group, in part to reduce the likelihood that offspring will be disenfranchised as a result of their insufficient Indian-blood quantum. It appears that CK marriages are almost entirely within the group also, but the Indian-blood quantum is not a deciding factor in their case. They appear to have a stronger sense of their Kootenay identity.

Aboriginal language loss by the BFK is abundantly apparent; virtually all remaining Kootenai speakers are elderly. As noted previously, the CK have a well-established and moderately successful Kootenay language program for their children.

The successful BFK casino, which is a result of local initiative, provides a firm basis for its greater economic security. The recently launched Upper Kootenay casino at Cranbrook, British Columbia, is unlikely to profit the CK because they separated from the Ktunaxa/Kinbasket Tribal Council in 2003.

For the CK, the social and health programs of the provincial and federal governments are more comprehensive than those covering the BFK. However, BFK casino earnings have been directed to those areas and appear to be contributing to the general well-being of band members.

SIMILARITIES The most striking historic similarity was the seizure of most Lower Kootenai and Kootenay land in both countries with the tacit or open approval of the respective federal governments. This led to the rapid destruction of the aboriginal subsistence base in both instances. This in turn contributed to Indian feelings of hopelessness and widespread alcoholism, which abated as economic hardships became less severe.

An issue in both the United States and Canada is Native American sovereignty, a special concern of the Kootenai because they span the international boundary. In the 1980s these Indians began to be arrested if they crossed the international border without reporting to border authorities. Canadian and U.S. officials delayed and hassled the Kootenai who insisted that they had the legal right of free passage. The Indians also objected on religious grounds when customs officers prohibited the export or import of medicinal plants and animal parts used in ritual contexts. Together they pursued an acceptable solution, and the problem was resolved by 2003. Customs officials now recognize the identity cards issued by the Kootenay reserve and Kootenai reservation and allow all of these individuals free movement across the border. This was a significant achievement because it reflects international recognition of tribal sovereignty.

The Lower and Upper Kootenay bands in Canada and their U.S. counterparts affirm and reenforce their cultural ties yearly at Kootenai Falls in Montana. Spiritual and political leaders, among others, meet there to affirm the importance of these Falls in their collective myths, tales, and historical experiences. These meetings provide the best symbolization of their tribal unity in contemporary context.

| Additional Sources

Unfortunately, an inordinate number of Kootenai studies are unpublished and not readily available. In addition, ethnographic accounts sometimes are contradictory, which makes it difficult or impossible to reconcile numerous differences. The best brief published report is by Bill B. Brunton (1998), and the best overview about tribes for the Plateau culture area is the Smithsonian Institution volume edited by Deward E. Walker, Jr. (1998). Walker (1982), in his book about Idaho Indians, devotes considerable text to the Kootenai, and his material culture illustrations are superior. The major published Kootenai monograph is the reconstruction by Harry Holbert Turney-High (1941). Claude E. Schaeffer worked among the Kootenai intensively from 1935 to 1937 and continued his field studies among them into the 1960s. His major published contribution is about bear ceremonialism (1966). Schaeffer's field notes are a major source and were consulted for this chapter. An account of the "war" at Bonners Ferry in 1974 by Timothy R. Pembroke (1976) is excellent. Information about the Kootenai woman-man is based primarily on articles by O. B. Sperlin (1930) and Schaeffer (1965). The best studies about Indian policies in British Columbia are by Forrest E. LaViolette (1973), Christopher McKee (1996), and Robert J. Muckle (1998).

| Selected Bibliography

Baker, Paul E. 1955. *The forgotten Kutenai*. Boise.

Boas, Franz. 1918a. *Kutenai tales*. Bureau of American Ethnology Bulletin 59.

———. 1918b. Kinship terms of the Kutenai Indians. *American Anthropologist* n.s. 20: 98–101.

Boyd, Robert T. 1998. Demographic history until 1900. In *Plateau,* Deward E. Walker, Jr., ed., vol. 12, 467–83. *Handbook of North American Indians.* Washington, DC.

Brunton, Bill B. 1998. Kootenai. In *Plateau,* Deward E. Walker, Jr., ed., vol. 12, 223–37. *Handbook of North American Indians.* Washington, DC.

Cassidy, Frank, and Norman Dale. 1988. *After native claims?* Victoria, British Columbia.

Elders of the Kootenai Nation. 1990. *Century of survival.*

Garvin, Paul L. 1948. Kutenai I. *International Journal of American Linguistics* 14(1): 37–42.

Lahren, Sylvester L., Jr., 1998. Reservations and reserves. In *Plateau,* Deward E. Walker, Jr., ed., vol. 12, 484–98. *Handbook of North American Indians.* Washington, DC.

LaViolette, Forrest E. 1973. *The struggle for survival.* Toronto.

Luke, Chris. 2003. *Drags Grizzly.* Creston, British Columbia.

McKee, Christopher. 1996. *Treaty talks in British Columbia: Negotiating a mutually beneficial future.* Vancouver, British Columbia.

Muckle, Robert J. 1998. *The First Nations of British Columbia.* Vancouver, British Columbia.

Nisbet, Jack. 1994. *Sources of the river.* Seattle.

Pembroke, Timothy R. 1976. *An anthropological analysis of conflict and confrontation among the Lower Kootenai of Bonners Ferry, Idaho.* Master's thesis, Washington State University.

Ray, Verne F. 1939. *Cultural relations in the Plateau of northwestern America.* Publications of the Frederick Webb Hodge Anniversary Publication Fund 3. Southwest Museum, Los Angeles.

Sapir, E. 1918. Kinship terms of the Kootenay Indians. *American Anthropologist* n.s. 20: 414–18.

Schaeffer, Claude E. 1935–1969. Claude Everett Schaeffer Papers. Glenbow Archives, Calgary, Alberta.

———. 1965. The Kutenai female berdache. *Ethnohistory* 12(3):193–236.

———. 1966. *Bear ceremonialism of the Kutenai Indians.* Studies in Plains Anthropology and History, no. 4.

Sperlin, O. B. 1930. Two Kootenay women masquerading as men? Or were they one? *Washington Historical Quarterly* 21:120–30.

Turney-High, Harry Holbert. 1941. *Ethnography of the Kutenai.* American Anthropological Association Memoir 56.

Walker, Deward E., Jr. 1982. *Indians of Idaho.* Moscow, ID.

———, ed. 1998. *Plateau.* Vol. 12. *Handbook of North American Indians.* Washington, DC.

Walker, Deward E., Jr., and Helen H. Schuster. 1998. Religious movements. In *Plateau,* Deward E. Walker, Jr., ed., vol. 12, 499–514. *Handbook of North American Indians.* Washington, DC.

6 The Western Shoshone: Subduers of the High Desert

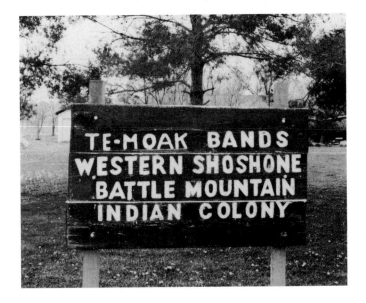

"We of the Western Shoshone Indian people
have known that our ancestors were shot, the
springs poisoned, germs were spread among our
people and we even today are subject to every
deceitful and dishonest trick of attorneys who
are supposed to represent us and do not,
together with Indian agents in order to steal our
lands from us, under the pretence of buying
these lands which they say on the other hand
that we do not own. . . ."

Statement by Chief Frank Temoke
at an Indian meeting, Elko, Nevada,
in 1965 (Clemmer 1974, 38)

THE GREAT BASIN is a vast and largely arid sector of the American West, so named because the waterways flow into lakes, playas, and sinks but not into the sea. The Great Basin culture area is larger than its geographical designation and includes portions of rivers that flow into the Pacific Ocean. The rigors of aboriginal American life here in the homeland of the Western Shoshone and some of their neighbors were in numerous ways comparable to those of Native Americans in the Arctic and Subarctic regions.

Centered in Nevada, the Western Shoshone call themselves *Newe,* meaning "people." Early in their history they depended primarily on widely dispersed native plant and animal products as food. Reliable water sources for domestic needs were essential but often widely scattered. Typically the food quest focused on small groups, especially nuclear families, whose members walked from one anticipated food source to the next. Because families often were on the move, their material possessions were few in number, lightweight, highly portable, and eminently practical. Their lifeway often has been stereotyped as "simple" or "impoverished." However, their innovative sociocultural adaptations more truly merit praise, if not acclaim. For this reason, as well as for additional compelling ones, they are presented here as representative of environmental adaptation that led to sustained survival in notably austere surroundings.

The Great Basin culture area was the last major sector of the contiguous states to be settled by Euro-Americans. For this reason, the Indians living there provide particular insight into maturing federal policies. The early historic Western Shoshone homeland included some 24 *million* acres, centered largely in Nevada. At present their land holdings are minuscule as a result of land seizures by the federal government, in particular, and to a lesser extent by states, white settlers, and miners. Despite this treatment, these Indians have struggled one hundred and fifty years to again control their homeland. Most tribal members know this is a fanciful goal, but their continuous efforts to seek a just land settlement make up a historically significant endeavor. This is one of the last major indigenous American claims against the federal government, and it recently resulted in a partial resolution.

This chapter pays particular attention to the historical impact of small land holdings for one cluster of Western Shoshone. Fortunately, Steven J. Crum (1994), a Western Shoshone tribal member and professional historian, has provided special insight into the problems of his people in a book-length study.

All Shoshone are members of the Central Numic branch of the Uto-Aztecan language family. No one knows the origin of the word *Shoshone.* The Western, Northern, and Eastern Shoshone all spoke dialects of the same language. Additional speakers of Numic languages in the Great Basin culture area include the Ute, Northern Paiute, and Southern Paiute. Because rigid ethnoboundaries did not exist, the Western Shoshone married across dialect and language lines. For example, the Northern Paiute and Western Shoshone often intermarried, giving rise to families whose members spoke both languages.

Western Shoshone habitat is semidesert country (see Figure 6-1), with annual precipitation typically ranging from 10 to 15 inches per year. The

Figure 6-1 | The early historic Western Shoshone homeland.

north-south mountain ranges, sometimes over ten thousand feet in height, are separated by high valleys some five thousand feet above sea level. This fractured landscape had a profound impact on aboriginal life, because plant and animal distributions depended largely on local precipitation and temperature. The temperature is lower at high elevations, which increases precipitation.

Above timberline are herblands, and below them are highland trees, including juniper, pinyon, fir, and spruce. Watercourses along the valleys nourish willows and cottonwood and diverse grasses. The dominant ecological setting, however, is sagebrush-grass steppe country, also termed basin and range. Significant populations of bighorn sheep and pronghorn antelope prevailed in some localities, but in general animals represented secondary edibles. More widespread sources of meat included waterfowl and rodents. Animals and plants alike provided raw materials for most artifacts.

| Aboriginal Life

Professional Euro-American trappers employed primarily by fur companies began to penetrate Western Shoshone country from the north in the 1820s. These transients moved on after depleting the beaver population and other furbearers in any area. Next, beginning in the late 1840s, thousands of westward-bound whites in wagon trains traveled through the region as they followed the Humboldt River. By the 1860s local Indian life had undergone dramatic changes as a result of these contacts and those with traders. However, systematic efforts by ethnographers to compile baseline accounts about aboriginal conditions date largely from the late 1920s and 1930s, long after most traditional Western Shoshone conventions declined, became modified, or disappeared. This was largely "salvage" ethnography, based on what was becoming a "memory culture" in many of its aspects. Beginning in the 1960s and down to the present, other studies were launched as details of aboriginal life were compiled by talking with knowing Indians, by more thoroughly analyzing documentary sources, by ecological studies, and by reevaluating early accounts. In recent years the federal Bureau of Land Management (BLM) has sponsored numerous reports about the identification, evaluation, and protection of properties associated with Native Americans. These studies, based largely on federal legislation and executive orders since the 1970s, add further insight into the Shoshone past.

What does all of this mean in terms of this chapter? First, the available information about the early historic Western Shoshone is less satisfactory than for other tribes included in this book. Second, localized cultural variability was greater than once had been assumed. Therefore, and note with care, this chapter focuses on those Western Shoshone who lived along the Humboldt River, from the lower Reese River drainage eastward to and including Ruby Valley. Justification for concentrating on this sector is that about half of the aboriginal Western Shoshone lived there. The modern residents of the sector are now identified as the Te-Moak Bands of Western Shoshone Indians.

Finally, the information about traditional life is based primarily on the many publications by Julian H. Steward, the most prominent ethnographer to study the Western Shoshone. Steward has been faulted in recent years for obtaining his information from comparatively few persons with whom he spent relatively little time and for failing to appreciate the extent of localized cultural variability (e.g., Thomas 1979; 1981). Nonetheless, Steward remains the standard primary source. Although he may have failed to grasp the complexity of ethno-historical developments, these are available in other sources, such as Crum (1994).

ORIGIN MYTH Localized Western Shoshone accounts about their emergence as a people have similar basic plots but include differing details. The following synopsis was recorded at Battle Mountain in 1939 and was narrated by Jim Tybo (Smith 1993, 150–51).

Coyote, who lived alone in a dwelling, was preparing a rabbit net when a girl named Water Girl looked in momentarily before leaving. (Among many tribes, Coyote was regarded as a creator and trickster who also was often licentious.) Coyote thought she was beautiful and decided to follow her. He caught up with her when she arrived at a body of water. Water Girl said Coyote could sit on her back for the crossing, but he slipped down her body and did not "behave himself." Coyote then changed himself into a water strider and arrived at her home before she did. The girl lived with her mother. After supper they all went to bed. Coyote visited Water Girl in the night and felt an opening with some teeth between her legs. (The concept of a toothed vagina is a reasonably common belief among numerous aboriginal peoples.) Coyote put his thumb in but quickly withdrew it when the teeth snapped. After this episode, the women unsuccessfully attempted to kill him. He then found a stone pestle, forced it into the vagina of one woman and then the other to dislodge the teeth, and had sexual intercourse with them that night and the following one. The next morning Water Girl was obviously pregnant, and her multiple offspring were born within a few days.

One day the older woman gave Coyote a jug to obtain water at springs. When the jug leaked, he soaked it in water until it sealed itself. By the time Coyote returned with water, the children of Water Girl had matured. The women divided them into two groups based on their physical appearance. The mother and daughter went off with the handsome ones, who became non-Shoshone Indians. Coyote put the ugly ones in the jug and closed it with a stopper. He left for home carrying the jug, but the offspring became noisy, and Coyote tired of carrying them. He opened the jug, and the smaller ones ran off. Coyote took the remaining ugly people home, where he cleaned and released them. They became the original Western Shoshone.

MATERIAL CULTURE AND SUBSISTENCE Both sexes cut their hair below the shoulders and dressed it with marrow. Earlobes were pierced and commonly decorated with a shell bead attached to a string. Necklaces of animal claws or bone tubes were popular. Dry pigment applied to the face and body had decorative value and may also have served as protection from the elements. Some people, whether young or old and female or male, typically went naked except during cold weather, when they wore woven fur robes. What a person wore at other times depended largely on the availability of appropriate skins, which was an indication of the hunting skills of males in a family. A successful man wore a sleeved shirt and leggings made from skins; his wife wore a long gown of skins. A less fortunate man wore a belted buckskin breechclout, and his wife apparently wore either a small apron in front or a large one at the back. People commonly went barefoot except when traveling. Then hard-soled skin moccasins lined with shredded bark protected their feet.

The most substantial structure by far was the cone-shaped winter house built over a shallow pit. Interlocking poles were placed over the foundation or were bound together at the top. This framework was covered by layers of grass tied to the poles. Over it was a layer of earth except at an opening for a door, which was covered with a bark mat. An opening in the roof allowed smoke to escape from a central fireplace. Residents slept on twined bark mats covered with blankets either of woven fur or plant fibers. Storage pits were dug beneath the floor. In most localities two to ten family groups wintered near permanent water sources and exploited a twenty-mile surrounding area.

Structures for summer use included windbreaks and sun shades made from brush. A sweathouse that served a local group was owned by its maker. It consisted of a dome-shaped frame of willows covered with grass except at the entrance. Men or women carried heated rocks into the structure to bathe or to cure illness. Women used a building similar to the sweathouse in construction during menstrual periods and to give birth.

As was noted earlier, aboriginal life centered on the collection of plants for food. The names for local populations often were derived from their most prominent edibles, such as "eaters of redtop grass" and "eaters of rye seed grass," even though the resources exploited by a family fluctuated seasonally and from year to year. In early historic times local groups moved often to exploit a variety of plant products. As the primary food providers, women possibly obtained as much as 80 percent of the day-to-day diet. They utilized a broad range of edible plants, some of which also became raw materials for artifacts. Their systematic scientific knowledge about the local flora, plus intimately related labor and harvesting skills, had a profound impact on the quality and texture of life. For example, to gather stickweed seeds successfully, it was essential to be in the area where plants grew to near maturity and just before the seeds dispersed. Because dispersal occurred only a few days a year, precise scheduling was a critical factor. Likewise, to obtain some edible seeds or berries in different ecological niches required well-timed moves. The people also carefully pruned some plants, such as those used for arrowshafts and basketry, in anticipation of future uses for the harvests.

They collected wild tobacco seed, and it appears that some of the seeds were scattered for future growth. This plus some broadcast sowing of other edible seeds are possible instances of horticulture among these people. They had two types of pipes: One was tubular with a stone bowl and wooden stem; the other was a stone elbow pipe stemmed with wood. A less desirable means of smoking was to fill pieces of cane with tobacco, in effect making cigarettes.

Figure 6-2 | A woman gathering rice grass in the mid-1930s. (Photograph by Julian H. Steward. Courtesy of the Department of Anthropology, University of Illinois, Urbana.)

Old men smoked most often, and they passed a pipe from one smoker to another. Apparently women did not begin to smoke until historic times.

Great Basin culture area basketry has justifiably received particular attention, in part because of the varieties of utilitarian types produced. The women in the area twined baskets. One type that had become especially prominent was the large, open twined conical carrying basket with an attached tumpline for ease of transport. It was lightweight, durable, and highly portable, which made it ideal for collecting and for general transport. The conical carrying basket with its tumpline freed a woman's hands to use a digging stick; these two artifacts best symbolize food procurement and the economic activities of women. With a digging stick, edible roots could be harvested throughout the year. They used a pointed stick to impale lizards, snakes, and rodents and their hands to collect leaves, grasshoppers, and crickets. Women also set traps and snares for ground squirrels and cottontail rabbits and likewise obtained ground squirrels by pouring water down their burrows.

To harvest some plant seeds, they dislodged them from the seed heads with a basketry seed beater (shaped somewhat like a modern tennis racket) and caught them in a conical basket that was pointed at the bottom and placed upright in the sand. Seed heads could be detached by hand (see Figure 6-2) or cut with a stone knife, later threshed with a stick and then separated from the chaff with a winnowing basket, which also served to parch seeds (see Figure 6-3).

Figure 6-3 | The women to the left are threshing grass with sticks, and the woman to the right is separating seeds by shaking and tossing them in a winnowing basket; photographed in the mid-1930s. (Photograph by Julian H. Steward. Courtesy of the Department of Anthropology, University of Illinois, Urbana.)

Given family mobility, a cradle for an infant was especially useful. It was oval or elliptical in outline and twined at the back, and the sun shade was made of willow. A twined sagebrush bark and jackrabbit fur blanket covered an infant.

Ruby Valley requires particular attention as one of the most productive food-getting areas, as is evident in an early population estimate of one person per each 2.8 square miles. For the Great Basin culture area in general, the average was one person for each 15.6 square miles; for the Great Salt Lake Desert, it was one person for each 30 to 40 square miles.

Early in their history, Ruby Valley quite possibly supported about one-half of all the Western Shoshone, in part because of the widely available and reliable water sources: scattered springs; a relatively large lake, Lake Ruby; smaller lakes; and extensive marshlands. These made the valley an especially attractive setting for pronghorn antelope, small game, and migratory and year-round bird populations. Here diverse species of wild seed plants grew in abundance. At higher elevations, innumerable stands of pinyon pine served as a key food source. Pine nuts had emerged as a rich and nutritious edible. However, the trees in any particular stand produced abundant harvests only at intervals of three to four years. In the fall, family groups worked together with hooked sticks to dislodge the cones. The cones were tapped or heated to release the nuts. As with seeds from other plants, the nuts were spread on a metate (milling stone), and their seeds were cracked with a mano (hand stone) and winnowed away. The nut meats were ground between the same two implements. The flour was cooked in water-filled pottery vessels placed over open fires. Local residents, as well as families from afar, such as those along the Humboldt River and to the west, collected pine nuts in this area, making repeated trips home to store the nuts as food for winter. In this context it is notable that valley residents did not regard the pinyon stands as their exclusive property.

Ruby Valley residents habitually reaped enough nuts to carry them through the winter in homes at higher elevations, where juniper could be used for heating. In the spring, they moved to the valley floor to obtain seeds and other edibles. This settlement pattern had critical social, economic, and political implications that soon will be considered.

When women harvested plant food, it was on an individual basis, apparently with little ritual involvement except following the pine nut harvest. By contrast, the most important and complex hunting by men was in cooperative drives accompanied by formal rituals. When pronghorn antelope became abundant in an area, hundreds of people from near and far gathered at a preselected site. At that time the hunt leader, a male shaman, received power (*puha*) through dreams and performed integrated rituals deemed essential for success. In one account, he first sent a scout to precisely locate the target antelope. While he was gone, the people built an oblong ceremonial enclosure of brush with one fire kindled at the entrance and another at the back near where the shaman sat. Participants, who ranged along the inner walls, ceremonially smoked tobacco, passing a large-bowled pipe from one to the next. After dark the scout returned to report where the antelope slept. The shaman held up a stick with a stuffed antelope hide attached and sang his particular song for about two hours. At the same time, a line of boys imitated the behavior of antelope as they danced. When the boys appeared to tire, this was a sign that the shaman had captured the souls of the prey. The shaman soon fell to the ground, his nose bled, and he lapsed into a trance, which meant that he now controlled the antelopes' souls.

Early the next day the people used poles or brush to build guide lanes to the mouth of a surround fashioned from brush and stone. When this work was completed, adults and children guided the antelope into the surround, and the shaman closed the entrance with fire. The best bowman shot the lead antelope with an arrow; this reportedly prevented the others from escaping. The bow he used was made from sheep horn backed with sinew and included a sinew bowstring. Vaned arrows carried in quivers had foreshafts fitted with points. Following the death of the lead antelope, other men killed the remaining captives with bows and arrows. Additional drives followed a successful one. If the initial drive was unsuccessful, the explanation for failure was likely to have been a broken taboo. In order not to offend the souls of the antelope, dead animals were handled in a respectful manner. The meat and skins were shared equally among participants, including the shaman. Successful hunts included feasting, singing, dancing, and visiting people seldom seen at other times of the year.

Another important cooperative hunt centered on black-tailed jackrabbits. (Although jackrabbits commonly are called "rabbits," they are hares. Hares are fully developed at birth and not raised in nests in the manner of rabbits. Unlike rabbits, hares have a divided upper lip, large ears, powerful hindlegs, and live in open country. In ethnographic accounts rabbits and hares commonly were termed "rabbits.") In the fall or winter, when jackrabbit fur was prime, a male hunt leader, who was not a shaman, organized a drive without ritual involvements. Nets owned by individuals were set at a favorable location, and people drove hares toward the nets. Along the way, on an opportunistic basis, they killed some of the animals with clubs or blunt arrows shot from bows. A primary purpose was to obtain fur for blankets. Families assembled for days or weeks, depending on harvest success. They feasted on the meat after a drive or drives and enjoyed themselves in the manner reported following cooperative antelope hunts.

Snares and traps served to capture prey on an individual basis, with multiple sets used for a target species if food stress was critical. Spring-pole snares held birds, and simple noose snares strangled cottontail rabbits, as well as rodents such as squirrels and chipmunks. Deadfalls crushed any small creatures that took the bait.

Additional examples of food procurement reflect localized variability. In one area men hunted mountain sheep and mule deer with bows and arrows, thereby providing skins and meat for their families. Elsewhere men disguised as antelope drove courting sage grouse into nets. Along the Humboldt River people fished for chub, suckers, and trout using nets and basket traps set in conjunction with weirs. They also fished with hooked lines and relied on barbed harpoons. With respect to killing animals for food, the people made offerings, such as a piece of gall, to the animal and to the forces of nature in general. Taboos prevented eating specific animal parts, such as the heart of a deer. To preserve meat and fish, they might hang the flesh in trees for drying, but they did not process these edibles by other means, such as smoking.

Early Euro-American travelers and later ethnographers have stressed Western Shoshone poverty, considering them as living at a minimal subsistence level. Social indicators for such judgment include abandonment of the ill and aged, death by starvation, and cannibalism. How commonplace these occurrences were in the area considered is unknown. It seems that extreme hunger may well have been an acknowledged cultural condition and an accepted aspect of life. However, many of these observations were made after the region had experienced considerable environmental degradation.

SOCIAL DIMENSIONS Among these Shoshone in early historic times, local groups represented unstable social units. The nuclear family, however, could be, and often was, self-sufficient on a day-to-day basis, as well as over longer periods. This fact had far-reaching implications because it encouraged individualism within a biological family as a means for survival, although it was somewhat

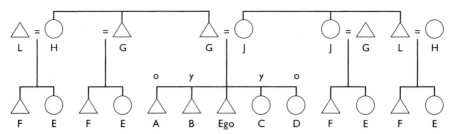

Figure 6-4 | The basic Reese River Western Shoshone kinship terminology.

tempered by relations with neighboring families. In varied combinations they had developed "family clusters" whose members shared access to and exploitation of local resources. Notably more inclusive social institutions, such as clans, moieties, or sodalities, did not exist. Only small numbers of nuclear families could cluster in a typical locality because the resource base was not dependable enough to sustain larger aggregates.

When tracing one's relatives, equal emphasis was placed on the female and male blood lines (bilateral descent). Thus in theory a person could seek aid or comfort from near relatives on either side of a family. Pertinent considerations included physical proximity, personalities, and previous contacts. A close relative was addressed with the appropriate kin term, which in itself became formal recognition of socially defined expectations. The kinship terms for parents and their siblings were the bifurcate merging type, whereas cousin terminology was the modified Eskimo type. The preferred marriage pattern in some localities was for a man to marry his father's sister's daughter (patrilineal cross-cousin marriage). This convention meant that patrilineal aunts and uncles became in-laws, which may partially explain why in-law avoidance did not prevail, contrary to the pattern in many small-scale societies. The fact that the kin term used by a man for his most desirable bride was the same as for his other cousins suggests that the terminology may have been in a state of flux (Figure 6-4).

During the first year of marriage, the groom ideally lived with his wife's family (initial matrilocal residence) and contributed to their welfare (bride service). Later the couple would choose to settle permanently with the set of parents whose resource potential could provide for them all (bilocal marriage residence). Sometimes a woman might become a man's wife by abduction. Aided by friends, an abductor would carry her off, regardless of whether she was already married. If she was, her husband and the abductor might fight, although this was done without weapons or lethal intent. Marriage conventions also included polyandry and polygyny (a composite family). Brothers in some localities married one sister (fraternal polyandry), a pattern that is rare worldwide. A man was expected to marry his deceased wife's unmarried sister (sororate), and it was desirable for a woman to marry her deceased husband's brother (levirate).

Varied amusements provided a break in the routine, especially when they were part of large gatherings, such as cooperative hunts. The hand game was most popular, and stakes commonly were bet on the outcome (see Chapter 2). Dice games centered on either four or eight flat sticks, each painted red on one side and white on the opposite side. When each tossed die turned up red, it was a win. Some of the alternative combinations were neutral, whereas others represented one count toward the total for winning. Again, bets were made on the outcome.

At Battle Mountain young girls made small houses for dolls and animal figures fashioned from unfired clay. Teams of boys competed by throwing poles at a moving hoop until a member of one team failed to pierce the hoop and lost the game. Boys made willow whistles that they played for amusement; the only adult musical instrument, a bone flute with three to six holes, also was played for pleasure.

The Circle (Round) Dance was part of several social events that included a supernatural aspect. A dance held in the spring encouraged the development of seed plants, and in the summer it hastened the ripening of seeds. A fall dance that was held before the collection of pine nuts helped ensure a plentiful nut harvest, as well as an abundance of deer. The pleasure of the dances loomed large because they provided an opportunity to visit with friends and relatives seldom seen. Males and females danced alternately around a central post, although in some localities men and women danced together, with women selecting their partners. One person was the principal singer, but the dancers also might sing as they executed a shuffle step in a clockwise direction. Historically the Circle Dance became associated with Euro-American celebrations in this area.

POLITICAL LIFE   The economic basis for family clusters appears to have impeded the emergence of aboriginal bands or a sense of tribal identity. Instead, in-marrying family clusters had become small sociopolitical units. A male with proven decision-making abilities became a family cluster leader. However, "chiefs" with authority by common consent emerged in the Ruby Valley, yet they lacked coercive powers, a key attribute of a chief as typically defined. In Ruby Valley, leadership preferably passed along the paternal line, but a male antelope shaman could also become a local leader. The key role of such a person was to coordinate the collection of pine nuts, the most productive storable winter food source. Once a satisfactory supply of pine nuts was at hand, family clusters settled in winter villages. Here they had reasonably intense mutual day-to-day contacts, and problems arising from group living were resolved by chiefs. Elsewhere in this general region, chiefs did not exist because the dispersed food sources prevented large aggregates of people from wintering together on a regular basis.

Armed conflict between family clusters did not exist in aboriginal times. Important reasons appear to be that spouses commonly came from adjacent ethnic groups and, equally important, that they regarded their resource base as open to exploitation by anyone. Yet family feuds occurred occasionally.

One cause was a death in which supernatural causes were suspected. Deviant shamans were most susceptible to these accusations, especially when they were thought to have disliked the person who died. If this happened, the accused might be murdered. Wife abduction may have been the most common basis for disputes between neighbors, but these were resolved by the families involved rather than becoming a general concern.

RELIGION The text of myths provided the spiritual basis for being a Western Shoshone. They taught that Coyote was a creator and sometimes evil trickster, and in Western Shoshone thinking they united by blending into one another. In similar fashion humans and animals were thought of as integrated because animals once were human. In this desert region *puha,* the life force, was represented by the diverse immortal spirits primarily associated with water, including those in lakes, rivers, and marshlands. Hot springs, geysers, and fumaroles embodied another cluster of water-related spirits. Water Babies, especially those associated with springs, were thought to embody dangerous and powerful spirits confined to specific localities. They reportedly were some three feet in length, with long hair and a shell-like skin. One example of spirit power was their capacity to lure women and children to water and death by drowning. Other features on the landscape, such as caves and unusual rock formations, had powerful spirit occupants. In a similar vein, established animal and human trails were thought to guide the flow of *puha.*

Spirits were said to appear in unsought recurrent dreams of children or adults, males more often than females; notably, these dreams did not involve pain or sacrifice. In a sense, an immortal spirit helper, usually a bird or animal, adopted the dreamer. From this helper the person acquired a sacred song and learned ritual practices and prohibitions, as well as the use of ceremonial equipment. By transmission of this material, the capacity of the dreamer was determined by a spirit.

The recipients of the greatest knowledge became shamans (general practitioners, doctors). One major role of this person was to remove a foreign object that had invaded a patient's body. Severe pains were thought to result from such invasions. As treatment, a curing session took place in a special brush enclosure where an audience had gathered. The doctor sang a sacred song of power, and the audience participated by singing the same song. The shaman smoked a pipe, walked about, and danced before sucking the harmful object from the patient's body. The object was blown or brushed away from the body and then exhibited to the audience as evidence of success. Treatment for apparent soul loss was the second major context for which a general practitioner was employed. The patient was stretched out on the ground in the same general setting. Unconsciousness was the symptom thought to evidence his or her condition. The doctor shook a rattle adorned with dewclaws and the down of an eagle and followed this by going into a trance. As he entered an altered state of being, he was held up by men and then placed by them beside the patient. The shaman spoke in a low voice to a silent audience to indicate he had reached the land of the dead and found the lost soul. As his journey ended, the doctor rose, danced, and then blew on the patient's head to rub in the soul. If he was successful, the individual recovered. If a shaman failed repeatedly, he might be killed, at least in theory. A separate group of curers dreamed about dealing with other concerns, which varied widely. These might be curing rattlesnake bites and aiding in childbirth, as well as more environmental problems such as weather control and harvesting antelope.

In addition to using supernatural means to cure illnesses, these Shoshone employed plant products in highly varied contexts, as evidenced in an extensive ethnobotanical study, from 1937 to 1941, of medicinal plants used by Nevada Indians (Train et al. 1957). Excepting the treatment of those diseases introduced by Euro-Americans, such as smallpox and venereal diseases, Western Shoshone folk medicine was well developed and the scope of treatments wide. Frequently plant products were prepared in hot water, and the decoction was taken in specific doses. Treatments for colds and coughs varied widely. Boiled sagebrush, for instance, was one preparation thought to be effective against bad colds, coughs, and fevers. Treatment for other illnesses included the use of prepared prickly poppy root to relieve a toothache, as well as processed seeds used as a salve for cuts, burns, or sores. Big sagebrush branches that had been boiled and were still hot relieved the pains of rheumatism and were considered a blood tonic or purifier. Finally, a favored contraceptive was prepared from the boiled roots of skunk cabbage. The effectiveness of most herbal medicines employed in small-scale societies has neither been proven nor disproven.

Sweat baths appear to have been taken as another means to cure illness in late prehistoric times. A dome-shaped sweathouse, which looked somewhat like a small winter house, was owned by its builder. Within the structure a pit held rocks that had been heated in a outside fire; water was poured on the hot rocks to produce steam. Naked men or women bathed for cleanliness or to cure colds, lessen the pains of rheumatism or treat more general ailments and also for spiritual purposes.

Unlike most of the other tribal chapters in this book, which devote a section to the aboriginal life cycle, this topic is not included for the Western Shoshone. The reason is that ethnographic accounts for the area examined do not present well-rounded description. It is possible, however, to outline the major rites of passage in the life of an individual from birth to puberty, marriage, and death. Marriage is considered earlier in this chapter.

Little is known about the behavioral conventions for a pregnant woman and the father. Presumably the fathers were involved, judging from the postpartum customs. As the time of delivery approached, a woman moved into a comparatively secluded childbirth structure, where she remained for as many as thirty days. Any woman could help the birthing woman, who knelt to deliver an offspring. Afterwards the ground inside the structure was warmed by a fire made from wood collected by the new father, and here the mother rested as she began her recovery. Following the birth, both the mother and father bathed separately, meat and grease were taboo, and they could only scratch with sticks. The man ran daily and was prohibited from gambling. The father's involvements of this nature lasted five days. The mother obeyed her taboos for at least thirty days. At the end of her seclusion, the mother painted herself before returning home early one morning. In combination, these observances set new parents apart from all others and emphasized their status change. They also introduced the offspring to the group. According to the sketchy reports, infanticide existed and the mother made the decision.

Menarche signaled another abrupt transition toward achieving adult status. A girl lived alone in a childbirth/menstrual structure for as many as thirty days and was visited only by women. She was instructed by older women about future appropriate behavior, she scratched only with a stick, and she excluded meat, grease, and fish from her diet. She was expected to rise early and speak little, in addition to working hard, best illustrated by her collecting firewood and carrying it at a rapid pace. Subsequent menstruations required more repetitive rituals than a Western Shoshone would follow in any other context. A woman lived alone in a menstrual structure for at least five days and followed dietary restrictions, scratched with a stick, and avoided hunters. Male puberty had no clear recognition.

Death customs were the same for everyone. When a death occurred in a dwelling, the structure usually was burned. Property of the deceased might be burned, although relatives could receive various artifacts. A corpse was painted and adorned, and any man could be the undertaker. At the burial site an old man gave a positive speech about the deceased. The site was preferably among rocks, although in some localities a body was simply covered with earth. Female relatives cut their hair as the major sign of mourning. The people had relatively little interest in afterlife and ghosts, yet burial sites typically were avoided.

Early Historical Developments

The first sustained contacts with intruding whites began in the 1820s, as trappers for British and American fur companies moved into the area, expanding their quest for pelts, beaver in particular. In 1828–1829, a Hudson's Bay Company party led by Peter S. Ogden trapped along the Humboldt River drainage and became a harbinger of the subsequent negative relationships with whites. Ogden described the Western Shoshone as poor and miserable people who depended on roots for food; this early description became the enduring stereotype for Great Basin Indians. Before long competing trappers essentially destroyed the beaver population that had been a significant source of food and fur for the local Indians. Ogden's livestock ate plants on which the people depended as edibles. Within a few years, an American trapper, Joseph R. Walker, arrived in the Humboldt area and understandably faced hostility from the residents, who demanded food and horses from the encroachers on their land.

The Walker Party responded by killing a number of Western Shoshone, which further strained early contacts.

At the conclusion of the Mexican-American War in 1848, the Treaty of Guadalupe Hidalgo granted the United States formal control over a vast region of the West, including Shoshone lands. Before long some 200,000 or more migrants in wagon trains began to travel the main westward trail, termed the Overland Route or Humboldt Trail, along the Humboldt River. They were bound for the gold fields of California and Oregon, as well as other western destinations. Their livestock further depleted the grasslands on which the Western Shoshone were so dependent. Whites generally had little or no respect for the local people. Indians typically were disparaged and sometimes feared. Occasionally they were lured into wagon train camps and killed. Indians in turn stole the livestock of whites for food and killed the newcomers on an opportunistic basis.

Although the Western Shoshone did not have an aboriginal pattern of warfare, they rapidly developed political means to deal with the intruders. Family clusters and extended families began to consolidate into bands, with prominent men informally chosen as the leaders. By then some people had obtained horses, firearms, and ammunition from traders or had raided or traded with migrants in wagon trains. The availability of horses provided unprecedented mobility. To avenge injustices and obtain exotic goods, the Indians developed an increasingly successful campaign of guerrilla warfare by the 1850s. Whites in turn appealed to the federal government to stem what they considered dangerous Indian militancy.

In 1851 a federal agent met with the Western Shoshone and white transients along the Humboldt River to assess conflicts between them. He found the Indian complaints about transient deprivations justified, presented the Western Shoshone with gifts, and assured them that the federal government was concerned about their well-being. The first major intrusion of whites who intended to settle in the general region began in 1847 as Mormons, members of the Church of Jesus Christ of Latter-day Saints, arrived in the Salt Lake City area; it was part of Utah Territory, established in 1850, that included Utah and Nevada. At that time territorial governors were responsible for Indian matters through the Bureau of Indian Affairs (BIA). The area was increasingly settled by white ranchers and farmers, who chose the best lands, those with reliable water sources. This development expanded as the livestock of whites destroyed still more land on which the Indians depended.

The westward population expansion led to the creation of Nevada, which was a territory in 1861 but became a state in 1864. Another major development was passage of the federal Homestead Act of 1862, which had a critical and immediate impact on life in northern Nevada. It enabled settlers to claim 160 acres of surveyed federal public land on which to build a house, live for three years, and then pay a fee and receive clear title. Innumerable whites claimed the best well-water lands. As these were unsurveyed, they could establish a legal claim after the area had been surveyed, which was much later, generally in the 1880s.

Technically most homesteaders were illegal squatters, but this proved to be immaterial, as they eventually received title to their homesteads.

Prospectors and miners arrived to exploit the dispersed and relatively rich mineral deposits in this sector. In 1861 white prospectors saw Western Shoshone collecting placer silver in gulches southeast of Battle Mountain. The whites proceeded to displace the Indians without compensation and subsequently tapped the deep hardrock silver deposits with costly and complex equipment typically owned by large mining companies. From this time into the early 2000s, the Western Shoshone received *no compensation* for the millions of dollars of silver, gold, and copper plundered from their homeland. Over the years the environmental impact of the mining practices of whites was profound. Great quantities of water were required, and these were sometimes piped for many miles, with obvious implications. Then, too, the charcoal kilns required to fuel the ore smelters devastated the pinyon and juniper stands along the mountains, thus depriving the people of pine nuts and fuel. These takeovers, combined with grassland depletions by livestock, doomed the Indian lifeway of old by the late 1860s.

The fertile, well-watered Ruby Mountain area in particular attracted early white farmers and ranchers, especially Mormons. Here the federal government proposed the creation of a major reservation, hoping that the Indians could be taught to farm. Federal agents appointed charismatic leaders as "captains" and "chiefs" to facilitate dealing more effectively with the people. An unknown number of Western Shoshone moved to this area under the guidance of a band leader, Tsokkope (Sho-kub), who was friendly with whites and realized that the old Indian ways could not be sustained. However, most Western Shoshone appear to have rejected the prospect of becoming farmers, and some of them continued to prey on whites. Chief Te-moka (Temoka), the most prominent leader in Ruby Valley, had a cooperative attitude toward whites and favored establishing a reservation site in the valley. His proposal was favored by the BIA and numerous Shoshone, and a "six-mile-square" reservation was formed in 1859. It soon was abandoned because of its size and because of pressure from white settlers who sought more farmland. Further government decisions led the U.S. Army to build Fort Ruby in 1862. The original fort commander pursued a vigorous policy of killing Indians whenever possible, leaving their unburied bodies to rot as an example to others. When Western Shoshone men were captured, an alternative to death was to become an army scout and help locate resisting Indians. In one location the cavalry killed fifty-two Indians to avenge the deaths of two whites. After these policies had weakened the population, Shoshone militancy declined, which contributed to abandonment of the fort in 1869. In this same year the transcontinental railroad was completed. To finance the railroad, the government awarded the companies involved every other section of land within the twenty-mile strip along the right-of-way. Again, this federal action directly affected the Western Shoshone, who lived near the Humboldt River.

The key document in Western Shoshone dealings with the United States was the 1863 Treaty of Ruby Valley. It was a treaty of "peace and friendship." The Indians did *not* surrender their aboriginal land title to the United States.

This issue has remained critical into the early 2000s. The Western Shoshone *did* agree to recognize the *existing* property rights of Euro-Americans, and they promised not to interfere with the activities of wagon train transients, prospectors and miners, farmers, and ranchers. They also agreed not to disturb the existing telegraph line or railroad construction. Only about one-fourth of the Western Shoshone were represented at the treaty negotiations, and Chief Te-moka was the most prominent signer. Furthermore, the treaty text included a provision for the creation of a reservation on which they could live in a traditional manner as they became herders and farmers.

A major treaty provision was for the Indians to receive goods, supplies, and livestock valued at $5000 each year for twenty years. However, federal agents did not designate a time and place for the distribution of payments, which led to confusion and underpayment. Then, too, the transportation costs to Shoshone country were charged against the fund, as were the salaries of those involved in the transfer and other administrative costs. If no Indians were present at the place where an annuity payment was made, the goods were left with whites for distribution, which led to problems. When treaty goods were left at Fort Ruby, soldiers are known to have sold them to the Indians.

With sporadic and relatively minor exceptions, the Western Shoshone honored their treaty obligations. There were conflicts with whites over water rights for farming, and the theft of livestock by hungry Indians posed intermittent problems. More serious were the isolated murders for which both sides were responsible.

Contrary to the contact setting for most Native Americans, when a smallpox epidemic struck the Shoshone in the late 1860s and soon thereafter, it did not prove devastating, because most of the people lived in small isolated family groups and the disease did not spread rapidly with frightful results. In addition, federal agents vaccinated some of the people before the disease reached them. In subsequent years tuberculosis was a significant killer, possibly the greatest.

Following failed efforts to create a major reservation locally, the federal representatives sought to relocate all Western Shoshone in the region to an existing reservation at Fort Hall, Idaho. This met with staunch opposition by the Indians involved. Finally in 1877 the Duck Valley Indian Reservation was created at the northwestern fringe of their traditional homeland. This was the only relatively enduring large Western Shoshone reservation. Chief Te-moka and his band refused to leave the Ruby Valley, but the "White Knives," Western Shoshone who lived north of the Humboldt River, became occupants of the Duck Valley reservation. In sum, at least two-thirds of the Western Shoshone did not relocate. A disgraceful consequence was the federal classification of those who did not move to the reservation as "landless." They were classified as "non-wards" of the federal government, and their indigenous American rights were denied for many years to come.

A second reservation, Carlin Farms, was established in 1877 for those Shoshone who lived in an unoccupied area not far from the town of Carlin. Indians moved there and began to develop productive farmland. However, it appears that the land records subsequently were falsified to enable whites to obtain the land. At any rate the reservation was cancelled, and the Indian occupants were forced to leave.

During the 1860s the people had increasingly accepted select aspects of Euro-American culture, especially items of material culture such as garments, firearms, and metal tools. To make a living, some men learned to work as cowhands, farm laborers, or herders. More often, however, they settled at the fringes of white settlements and intermittently found employment doing odd jobs for whites. Women commonly worked as domestics in white households; because of this pattern they became more familiar with Euro-American culture than did the men.

| Later History

By the early 1880s only about three hundred Western Shoshone lived on the Duck Valley reservation, and the BIA unsuccessfully proposed its abandonment and the relocation of residents to Fort Hall. In the same decade, Paiute from Oregon and Nevada, many of them refugees from the aftermath of the Bannock War (1878), began to relocate in the Duck Valley reservation; they found it preferable to settling on other reservations. To better accommodate the newcomers, the government added sixty-nine thousand acres to the reservation. Initially a certain amount of hostility prevailed between the Shoshone and Paiute as they sought to retain their distinctive lifeways while allowing for advantageous compromises with the BIA in particular and whites in general. During this time bureau policies fluctuated, reflecting the attitudes of various reservation superintendents and changes in federal funding. A consistent goal, however, was to absorb indigenous Americans into the Euro-American matrix (see Figure 6-5).

The introduction of schools represented a major federal means to destroy Indian cultures. The first Duck Valley school opened in 1881, but the government came to realize that its localized Indian schools provided an inadequate education. Soon these schools were integrated into the Nevada state school system. Initially, and typically, Indian students were separated from whites in the classrooms. By 1910 the BIA sent children to distant boarding schools. Reservation and nonreservation children alike were forcibly sent to these schools, despite the vigorous objections of most parents. The most famous boarding school was the Carlisle Indian School in Pennsylvania (see Chapter 2). Contrary to government expectations, children sent there did not typically accept white ways. To the contrary, when they returned home, they often became political leaders who effectively contested federal regulations. In general the students retained diverse aspects of their traditional culture but utilized their new skills as well. In 1911 they were at least partially responsible for the organization of a reservation council at Duck Valley, where a tribal constitution soon was approved, enabling the local people to achieve a certain degree of political power. In addition, delegations went to Washington, D.C., to lobby for varied projects.

Figure 6-5 | George Yowell, Elko, Nevada, ca. 1910. (Courtesy of the Nevada Historical Society.)

A decline in the Western Shoshone population in the 1880s paralleled the ever-expanding numbers of whites in Nevada. A feeling of helplessness prevailed among the Indians. They did not know where to turn, as the federal government had not fulfilled its obligations, and most whites were hostile. Then a Northern Paiute, Wovoka (Jack Wilson), originated the Ghost Dance of 1890 (see also Chapter 2). Reportedly, he died and went to heaven, where he saw other dead Indians living an idyllic life. Wovoka reportedly talked with God, who told him to return to earth and teach the people to hold Ghost Dances. This would hasten the emergence of a new world in which the living and dead Indians would be united. Furthermore, disaster would destroy the whites. Despite strong federal objections, Ghost Dances were widely held, but a new world failed to materialize.

Figure 6-6 | Fandango dancers at Battle Mountain, ca. 1930. (Courtesy of the Nevada Historical Society.)

Significant changes in traditional ceremonial life gradually emerged. Previously localized rituals were held by family groups, especially rituals intended to encourage successful food harvests and at cooperative hunts. A prominent feature was the Circle Dance, with its songs and associated hand games. By the late 1880s, whites called these celebrations "fandangos," based on the Spanish word for lively dances accompanied by fast music. The Shoshone soon began to apply the word to traditional ceremonies held at large gatherings, including those for Euro-American holidays, especially Fourth of July celebrations (see Figure 6-6). Fandangos took place in other contexts as well, such as when band leaders were installed. The gatherings provided an opportunity to exchange information and develop strategies for dealing with whites, particularly those representing the federal government. In time fandangos accompanied baseball games and rodeos, thereby integrating old and new institutions.

In 1906 the federal government created the Ruby Mountains Forest Reserve, which soon became a part of the vast discontinuous Toiyabe National Forest. A relatively small number of Shoshone families lived on land within this new forest at individual allotments encompassed by the General Allotment Act of 1887 (see Chapter 2). They were allowed to remain, and eleven additional allotments were made in Ruby Valley within the proposed "six-mile-square" reservation. The ability of Nevada Indians to exploit fish and game at traditional times changed abruptly in 1908. They were required by state law to obtain hunting and fishing licenses and to abide by the accompanying restrictions.

This was yet another blow to aboriginal subsistence patterns, and those who did not comply were arrested.

| The Battle Mountain Colony

The remainder of this chapter places considerable emphasis on the Western Shoshone living adjacent to the town of Battle Mountain, Nevada. It was so named following a skirmish with wagon train migrants by Western Shoshone and Northern Paiute, possibly in 1857. The locality had long been a traditional area for antelope drives and socioreligious activities. Construction of a nearby Central Pacific Railroad station in 1869 led to the creation of the town of Battle Mountain, which initially consisted of a store to serve white ranchers, farmers, prospectors, and miners. Before long some Shoshone worked on local ranches and farms, where some wives became domestic servants. Others who were more impoverished lived near the town, and still others attempted to live off the land and intermittently found employment with whites.

The Battle Mountain Colony (BMC), the first Indian "colony" in Nevada, was established by a presidential executive order in 1917. According to this order, the enrolled members of the colony had the same legal status as reservation Indians. The BMC's land, 680 acres, represented a modest but significant federal effort to improve the "landless" condition of numerous Western Shoshone. In 1934 the federal government provided funds for the colony members to build ten houses, but they were without running water, electricity, or sewage disposal facilities.

Another pertinent development was the federal Indian Citizenship Act of 1924. It granted U.S. citizenship to indigenous Americans who had not previously become citizens by other means, such as by being members of the armed services during World War I. The act did not change existing federal laws regarding Indian rights. Based on the Treaty of Ruby Valley, most Western Shoshone initially regarded accepting citizenship as a denial of their sovereign status. They considered themselves to be noncitizens and resented the United States' unilaterally making them citizens. From this time forward, successive leaders attempted to assert their treaty rights. A major achievement in this respect occurred in 1932, when they created a formal treaty council to address pertinent issues with the BIA. However, the federal Bureau of Land Management (BLM) that was created in 1934 began to oversee most public lands in Nevada. This meant that yet another agency controlled lands of the Western Shoshone based on aboriginal occupancy and the 1863 treaty.

New Deal programs launched by President Franklin D. Roosevelt in 1933 resulted in diverse work projects and relief agencies as a major response to the Great Depression. However, officials of Lander County, where Battle Mountain is located, systematically denied Indian federal relief funds and jobs on the varied federal projects. This was a good indicator of how Indians were regarded by whites in the area.

Figure 6-7 | Residents of Ruby Valley, ca. 1936. (Courtesy of the Northeastern Nevada Museum.)

The New Deal introduced a major change in Indian policy, and most Western Shoshone now accepted their status as U.S. citizens. In 1934, the Indian Reorganization Act (IRA) was passed by Congress (see Chapter 2). Perhaps its most critical initial consequence for Nevada Indians was the appointment of Alida Bowler, the first woman to become a BIA superintendent, as the head of the Carson Indian Agency. Her initial goal—to establish relatively large blocks of public land for nonreservation Shoshone could not be realized. Opposition by Nevada whites and the BLM, plus limited federal funds and the conflicting hopes, desires, and demands of the Shoshone, doomed Bowler's forward-looking plans. A major provision of the IRA was to create local governments and thereby break the BIA stranglehold on reservation life. Among the widely dispersed Shoshone in northeastern Nevada, only the Battle Mountain and Elko colonies initially obtained recognition under the IRA. Others felt that acceptance of the IRA provisions would diminish their land claims (see Crum 1994 for details). Summarily, after Bowler's initial efforts, the Battle Mountain and Elko colonies of Western Shoshone formed elected councils under the IRA and together became the Te-Moak Bands of Western Shoshone Indians, named after Chief Te-Moak. Eventually the relatively small South Fork Indian Reservation and much smaller Wells Colony also became members. The major purpose of their consolidation was to gain greater political power, which has been moderately successful (see Figure 6-7).

Figure 6-8 | Mary Hall (1868–1956) was born at Austin, Nevada. She was a spiritual leader and the most prominent historic Western Shoshone basket-maker. (Courtesy of the Northeastern Nevada Museum.)

The Indian Claims Commission Act (ICC) in 1946 was passed to award money, not land, for successful claims by tribes. The aim was to resolve all outstanding claims as a step toward ending federal paternalism. For the Western Shoshone, the 1863 treaty was once again the critical basis for their claim, which was vigorous, prolonged, and divisive along many tangents. The dispersed nature of the population, reservation versus nonreservation claimants, traditionally oriented versus more acculturated families, disputes among lawyers, and the need to create a cover organization to press their claim became exceedingly complex. The ICC decision, which was made in 1962, ruled against the Western Shoshone based on its conclusion that Euro-Americans had taken possession of most of their land gradually and that no transitional date could be established. The people were astounded at the decision because it was so blatantly unfair. In retrospect, the hostility engendered by the ICC ruling strengthened Western Shoshone identity and resolve to pursue the matter further.

In 1953, "getting out of the Indian business" became a national policy. Congress established a timetable to end the special status of Native Americans, largely and initially by turning many BIA responsibilities over to other federal agencies and to the states. Repeated efforts to "terminate" Nevada Indians failed, even though counties gained broader jurisdiction over the federally recognized Indian entities. In one sense an *opposite* approach was taken in 1975 with the Indian Self-Determination and Education Act, which was designed to foster tribal self-government by transferring many BIA responsibilities to tribal political units. President Ronald Reagan declared in 1982 that termination of responsibility was no longer a federal goal, although the Western Shoshone generally regarded the self-government effort as yet another step toward eventual termination.

Sociopolitical life among the Te-Moak bands (Battle Mountain, Elko, South Fork, and Wells) has been partially shaped by the IRA and its amendments. Enrollment was based on the rolls recorded in 1937 and is confined to persons with at least one-quarter Shoshone blood, their descendants with one-quarter or more Shoshone blood, and some others who qualified but were unlisted on these rolls. By 2002, the 2521 enrolled members were widely scattered. Relatively few lived on federally designated Indian lands; some others lived relatively nearby, and still others at distant communities. In general Te-Moak economic life has been depressed and remains that way. A major cause of poverty is that colony landholdings are too small to support numerous families. The only colony enterprises that provide meaningful income are convenience stores, which emphasize tobacco sales, and gasoline stations; their earning potential for a band is limited.

The recession that began in the early 2000s made it increasingly difficult for employable persons to find jobs outside the colonies, especially at mines in the region. Currently the most desirable jobs are as firefighters, but these are temporary and sporadic. The best stable employment opportunities are a product of the 1975 Indian Self-Determination and Education Act. By accepting the act's guidelines, the colonies receive federal aid, largely as contracts with the BIA. This enables local people to assume many former BIA administrative responsibilities and to enter the federal bureaucratic labyrinth. In addition to completing training programs, Western Shoshone employees need years of experience to grasp federal programs, especially as they are affected by procedural changes and budgetary constraints. Despite these difficulties, numerous Te-Moak have become dedicated career employees. They have learned how the system operates, and even though job descriptions change frequently, these individuals remain a reliable administrative core. To date far more women than men are colony employees, in part, it would appear, because they have become the better educated segment of the population. An additional factor probably is that over the past twenty years the male mortality rate has been about twice that of females.

Historical Western Shoshone housing established near white settlements was described as deplorable. It appears that people did not begin to live on BMC land until 1934, when they built a small number of homes under BIA sponsorship. Traditionally, family dwellings were widely scattered, but the Euro-American model of cluster housing was introduced by the BIA and became well established in subsequent housing developments.

The next dramatic change in family homes resulted from the creation of the federal Department of Housing and Urban Development (HUD) in 1963.

Figure 6-9 | From 2000 to 2003 Stan Knight was the chairman of the Battle Mountain Colony. This is a 2002 photograph.

To facilitate a new HUD housing program, the Te-Moak Western Shoshone Housing Authority was created in 1965. In the early 1960s BMC received funds for a right-of-way across colony land to build a section of Interstate Highway I-80. This enabled the colony to move fifteen houses from an area near a mine to their colony land. Following this step, twenty-seven new homes funded by HUD were constructed south of the new highway. Appreciation of this better housing by adults who had grown up in substandard dwellings is still apparent in their frequent comments that life has become far better as a result of these housing programs. They particularly noted that an inside bathroom with modern plumbing made a great difference in their comfort. By 2003, two families had paid for their houses, ten were occupied as rentals, fourteen others were being bought in a mutual-help program, and one was vacant. In each instance payments were income based, and many of the homes were being bought by women. In sum, housing has become far more satisfactory than ever before, despite complaints about its quality.

In 2004 the Western Shoshone enrolled at the BMC numbered 580, but only 165 lived there. The 2003 unemployment rate approached 40 percent, and 13 percent of employed persons lived below the poverty-level guidelines. Most jobs were with the colony administration; these employed thirty persons. One of the major tasks of the colony social worker has been to help the unemployed become aware of job opportunities and to drive them considerable distances for interviews, but few jobs were available. This meant that the unemployed seeking work, sometimes as many as twenty, could only rely on limited short-term economic assistance from federal funds. The only other aid was through the food stamp program, plus state and church commodity distributions. These are good reasons why enrolled members have moved away for employment.

Very few colony members worked in the town of Battle Mountain. Whites living there commonly said that local Indians were treated just like anyone else, and they may add, "some of my best friends are Indians." However, colony members felt that white prejudice was widespread and real and affected about forty colony children who attended public schools in particular. Some teachers in these schools had the reputation of "picking on" Indian students. White classmates, especially those in junior high, sometimes referred to Indians in terms such as "wagon burners" or "burnt toast." The dropout rate for Indians was highest in the first year of high school. About a third of the Indian children graduated; eight who had graduated recently were attending college on supplementary scholarship money.

Adult colony members often lamented the failure of children to learn about and appreciate the Shoshone ways of old, but there was no formal effort to impart such information at the colony. Programs started there to teach the aboriginal language have failed. Parents sometimes commented that they felt out of touch with their children, and parental neglect, especially by those who were alcoholic, was widely recognized.

Because the BMC landholdings are so small, few options exist for the colony itself to accumulate funds. Tobacco sales are a profitable source of income because in theory no state tax is charged. States frequently contest this Indian advantage in courts. By 2003 the three reasonably accessible Te-Moak bands, one being the BMC, each had convenience stores at which tobacco sales were emphasized (see Figure 6-10). Contrary to the widespread pattern in other states with reservations, the law in Nevada was quite liberal. The state

Figure 6-10 | The Battle Mountain Colony Smoke Shop in 2002.

excise tax on a pack of cigarettes was 35¢. Everyone who bought cigarettes, a Te-Moak or an outsider, was charged this tax. The colony was allowed to keep all the tax money for colony purposes. At the BMC store, gross tobacco sales were about $92,000 a month early in 2003. The profits were shared by enrolled members, each of whom received a $30 voucher to be redeemed at the convenience store or a local grocery store before Thanksgiving and a $40 voucher before Christmas. Elders could request payment of utility bills and burial benefits from the profits.

ROCK CREEK CANYON For some forty years, white residents of Lander County, Nevada, sought to build a dam at the canyon entrance on BLM and county land northeast of the town of Battle Mountain. Their goal was to stimulate the local economy by attracting vacationers to camp, fish, swim, and water ski at the anticipated reservoir. In 1984 the county residents passed a $2 million bond issue to fund the project.

BMC members and other Western Shoshone objected to this proposed dam because the canyon had profound traditional associations with their *puha* (power). The steep rocky canyon entrance is marked by Eagle Rock, embodying the Eagle spirit, which reportedly had healing powers. Here people prayed and left offerings. The creek running through the canyon is fed by springs, which also are considered sacred. Bathing in one particular heart-shaped pool was a popular means to cure varied ailments. People customarily collected plants growing in the canyon; these provided food as well as medicine. Furthermore, the canyon had served as a place for burials within the memory of older persons.

An unclear number of Western Shoshone claim that the proposed dam would inundate sacred land, and this led to adamant objections. One spiritual leader in particular, Corbin Harney (1995), organized resistance to the dam, as did the medicine women at the BMC. The seasonal gatherings held in the canyon attracted numerous Indians, as well as whites who supported the environmental movements or Indian spiritualism. As a result the BLM identified the canyon as Traditional Cultural Property and supported Indian objections. The dam project was abandoned in the late 1990s as a major recognition of Western Shoshone religious and traditional cultural rights. In the early 2000s traditionalists fully supported holding rituals there that centered on Mother Nature. Other colony members, however, felt that the canyon ceremonies, while important in the past, now were dominated by religious leaders with questionable qualifications. Some also considered the white participants to be a "bunch of hippies."

THE LAND DISPUTE Unquestionably the most critical issue in this ongoing conflict is traced to the previously described 1863 treaty. Early in their history the Western Shoshone lived primarily in Nevada with small enclaves in California, Idaho, and Utah; the total amount of land was about 24 million acres. Currently federal agencies (e.g., BLM, U.S. Park Service, and U.S. Forest Service) manage over 80 percent of Nevada land. The Western Shoshone political units are dominated by the Te-Moak bands, but they also include other bands (i.e., Duck Valley reservation, Duckwater, Ely, Fallon, and Yomba). This land *never* has been formally transferred by the Western Shoshone to the federal government of the United States.

A major hurdle in resolving the land issue developed in 1962, when the Indian Claims Commission was dissolved. The pending Western Shoshone case was moved to the jurisdiction of the U.S. Court of Claims. In 1979 this court authorized the payment of some $27 million to settle the case. The Western Shoshone refused to accept the settlement and continued to pursue their claim in the federal courts. The U.S. Supreme Court ruled that the money already authorized represented just compensation for land losses by "gradual encroachment" by the United States, thereby extinguishing any further claim. The Western Shoshone maintained that the federal government had no legal title to their land and therefore had no right to offer compensation.

In 1984 a major effort to achieve a unified position before settling with the federal government led to the creation of the Western Shoshone National Council (WSNC). The most critical and enduring questions were whether to accept a monetary settlement for lost lands, to press for recognized ownership of a major land claim, or to seek money plus a relatively modest amount of land. In the mid-1990s Secretary of the Interior Bruce Babbitt favored returning some of the disputed land to the Shoshone, but because the WSNC could not agree on what type of settlement to accept, the proposal became moribund.

Of all the present-day Western Shoshone land rights advocates, none stand more visible and firm than members of the Dann family. Dewey Dann, a staunch supporter of aboriginal Shoshone land rights, bought a homestead in Crescent Valley in the 1920s. Over the years his politically active daughters, Carrie and Mary, have taken their father's land claim position. In the late 1950s the sisters began grazing livestock on nearby BLM land without the required permits. In protracted court battles, especially since 1974, they have fought for what they consider Shoshone treaty rights. In the early 1990s the WSNC established the Western Shoshone Defense Project, whose goals included a proposal to end seizures of Dann livestock. The sisters were dominant in the defense project, which raised money from sympathic individuals and foundations. Their efforts also have been a rallying point for environmental activists. Another prominent supporter of a land settlement was Raymond Yowell of the WSNC.

By the early 2000s, western state newspapers, and to a lesser extent the national press, featured articles sympathetic to the sisters. Beyond that, they gained international attention. The Inter-American Commission on Human Rights of the Organization of American States concluded that the rights of the Dann sisters, as well as those of other Western Shoshons, had been violated by inequity before the law, lack of freedom from discrimination, and no fair trials. In 2002 federal agents seized 227 of their cattle for grazing on BLM land without permits. Their unpaid grazing fees were nearly $1 million.

In 2003 resolution of this long-standing land dispute began to boil over. A key unanswered question was how and when the Western Shoshone gave up their aboriginal homeland rights to the United States. This issue was not seriously considered in the congressional debates. One thing was clear, however: Powerful mining enterprises in Nevada actively sought a solution in order to develop new gold mines with vast potential and to gain control over water resources and geothermal energy sources. Most national and state politicians in Nevada have always been and remain beholden to mining interests. Not surprisingly, they sought a money, *not a land,* settlement.

The Western Shoshone in turn remained deeply divided. To settle with the ICC-based decision or reject it was a primary issue. With interest added to the ICC fund awarded, the total was about $145 million, and a congressional bill was proposed to *forcibly* distribute most of the money to "judgment roll" members on a per capita basis and secondarily for educational purposes. In 2003 nearly identical settlement bills were considered by Congress. (The Indians involved would be compensated about 15¢ per acre for their land losses.) One bill was sponsored by Representative Jim Gibbons (R-Nev.) and another by Senator Harry Reid (D-Nev.). Some Indians favored acceptance, whereas others pressed for a major land settlement.

A contentious Western Shoshone issue was who represented them as a tribe. The head of the Te-Moak Tribal Council, Felix Ike, supported a monetary settlement in testimony before a congressional committee, but this was a position contrary to that held by most leaders of constituent bands. Ike testified that in a 2002 referendum 65 percent of the twenty-five hundred voters favored a money settlement, but this vote was not certified, and opponents tended not to vote. Yet another issue raised by the Te-Moak leadership was that Ike did not have the authority to speak for the tribe, nor did he have the approval of the band leaders. Between 2002 and 2004 colony and reservation leaders (Battle Mountain, Elko, South Fork, and Wells) passed resolutions rejecting the settlement proposal. In sum they objected to the ICC and related decisions for a monetary settlement, and the same was true for most of the other bands. Then in an October election Ike was removed from the Te-Moak Tribal Council, and his major supporters were not reelected.

In July 2004 the Western Shoshone Distribution Act had been passed by Congress without significant opposition, and it was signed by the president. It was a monetary settlement of about $145 million forced on the people—so much for meaningful government-to-government negotiations. However, the distribution bill did not waive existing treaty and other rights. This means that the Western Shoshone may continue to press their land claims. Judging from past experience, their hopes for a reasonable land settlement in the near future are unlikely given the national political climate in 2004.

| Additional Sources

The best readily available anthropological source is *Great Basin,* volume 11 of the *Handbook of North American Indians,* edited by Warren L. D'Azevedo (1986) and published by the Smithsonian Institution. Included in that volume are chapters about prehistory, ethnography, ethnohistory, and topics such as subsistence, kinship, music, and basketry. A Western Shoshone chapter by David H. Thomas et al. provides the best brief summary into the 1970s. The key reconstructed aboriginal baseline monographs about the Western Shoshone are by Julian H. Steward (1938; 1941). The 1994 book by Steven J. Crum is the standard source about ethnohistory. A comparatively brief ethnohistorical presentation is by the Western Shoshone Sacred Lands Association, *Newe Sogobia* (1981). A concise review of Western Shoshone historical land claims into the early 2000s is by Michelle Nijhuis (2002).

| Selected Bibliography

Bengston, Ginny. 2002. *Northern Paiute and Western Shoshone land use in northern Nevada: A Class I ethnographic/ethnohistoric overview.* SWCA Cultural Resources Report no. 02-551, prepared for Bureau of Land Management, Nevada State Office, Reno.

Bowers, Martha H., and Hans Muessig. 1982. *History of Central Nevada: An overview of the Battle Mountain District.* Cultural Resource Series, Monograph no. 4, Bureau of Land Management, Nevada State. Office, Reno.

Clemmer, Richard O. 1974. Northern and Eastern Nevada, 1858–1971: Land use patterns and aboriginal rights. *The Indian Historian* 7(1):24–41, 47.

Crum, Steven J. 1994. *The road on which we came: A history of the Western Shoshone.* Salt Lake City.

Eggan, Fred. 1980. Shoshone kinship structures and their significance for anthropological theory. *Journal of the Steward Anthropological Society* 11(2):165–93.

Fowler, Catherine S. 1986. Subsistence. In *Great Basin,* Warren L. D'Azevedo, ed., vol. 11, 64–97. *Handbook of North American Indians.* Washington, DC.

Fowler, Catherine S., and Lawrence E. Dawson. 1986. Ethnographic basketry. In *Great Basin,* Warren L. D'Azevedo, ed., vol. 11, 705–37. *Handbook of North American Indians.* Washington, DC.

Fowler, D. D. 1966. Great Basin social organization. In *The current status of anthropological research in the Great Basin: 1964.* Warren L. D'Azevedo et al., eds. Desert Research Institute Technical Report Series S-H, Social Sciences and Humanities Publications, no. 1, 57–74.

Fowler, D. D., and Catherine S. Fowler, eds. 1971. *Anthropology of the Numa: John Wesley Powell's manuscripts on the Numic peoples of Western North America, 1868–1880.* Smithsonian Contributions to Anthropology no. 14.

Harney, Corbin. 1995. *The way it is: One water, one air, one Mother Earth.* Nevada City, CA.

Harris, Jack S. 1940. The White Knife Shoshoni of Nevada. In *Acculturation in Seven American Indian tribes,* Ralph Linton, ed., 39–118. New York.

Holliday, J. S. 1981. *The world rushed in: The California Gold Rush experience.* New York.

Inter-Tribal Council of Nevada. 1976. *Newe: A Western Shoshone history.* Reno.

James, Steven R., ed. 1981. *Prehistory, ethnohistory, and history of eastern Nevada: A cultural resources summary of the Elko and Ely districts.* Cultural Resource Series no. 3, Bureau of Land Management, Nevada State Office, Reno.

Malouf, Carling. 1966. Ethnohistory in the Great Basin. In *The current status of anthropological research in the Great Basin: 1964,* Warren L. D'Azevedo et al., eds. Desert Research Institute Technical Report Series S-H, Social Sciences Humanities Publications no. 1, 1–38.

Miller, Jay. 1983. Basin religion and theology: A comparative study of power (Puha). *Journal of California and Great Basin Anthropology* 5(1–2):66–86.

Newton, Virginia, and Molly Rhodenbaugh. 2000. *The Williams I-80 Fiber Optic Project: Native American consultation and identification of traditional cultural places.* SWCA Cultural Resources Report no. 99-270, prepared for Bureau of Land Management, Nevada State Office, Reno.

Nijhuis, Michelle. 2002. Land or money? *High Country News* 34(14):1, 8–11.

Rusco, Elmer R. 1982. The organization of the Te-Moak Bands of Western Shoshone. *Nevada Historical Society Quarterly* 25(3):75–96.

———. 1999. Julian Steward, the Western Shoshones, and the Bureau of Indian Affairs: A failure to communicate. In *Julian Steward and the Great Basin,* Richard O. Clemmer et al., eds., 85–116. Salt Lake City.

Smith, Anne M. 1993. *Shoshone tales* (collected and edited by Anne M. Smith, assisted by Alden Hayes). University of Utah Publications in the American West, vol. 31.

Steward, Julian H. 1936. Shoshoni polyandry. *American Anthropologist* n.s. 38:561–64.

———. 1938. *Basin-Plateau aboriginal sociopolitical groups.* Bureau of American Ethnology Bulletin 120.

———. 1941. *Culture element distributions: XIII Nevada Shoshoni.* Anthropological Records, vol. 4, no. 2.

———. 1943. *Some Western Shoshoni myths.* Bureau of American Ethnology Bulletin 136, Anthropological Papers, no. 31, 249–99.

———. 1958. *Cultural change: The methodology of multilinear evolution.* Urbana.

———. 1970. The foundations of Basin-Plateau Shoshonean society. In *Languages and cultures of Western North America,* Earl H. Swanson, Jr., ed., 113–51. Pocatello.

Stewart, Omer C. 1978. The Western Shoshone of Nevada and the U.S. Government, 1863–1950. In *Selected papers from the 14th Great Basin Anthropological Conference,* Donald R. Tuohy, ed., 77–109. Socorro, NM.

———. 1980. Temoke Band of Shoshone and the oasis concept. *Nevada Historical Society Quarterly* 23(4):246–61.

Thomas, David H. 1979. On Steward's models of Shoshonean sociopolitical organization: A great bias in the Basin? In *The development of political organization in Native North America.* 1979 Proceedings of the American Ethnological Society, Elizabeth Tooker, ed., 59–68.

———. 1981. Complexity among Great Basin Shoshoneans: The world's least affluent hunter-gatherers? In *Affluent foragers: Pacific coasts East and West,* Shuzo Koyama and David H. Thomas, eds. Senri Ethnological Studies, no. 9, 19–52.

Train, Percy, et al. 1957. *Medicinal uses of plants by Indian tribes of Nevada.* Lawrence, MA.

Western Shoshone Sacred Lands Association. 1981. *Newe Sogobia.* Battle Mountain, NV.

7 The Crow: Plains Raiders and Bison Hunters

I wonder how my grandchildren will turn out. . . . They have only me, an old woman, to guide them, and plenty of others to lead them into bad ways. The young do not listen to the old ones now, as they used to when I was young. I worry about this, sometimes.

Observations by Pretty-shield, an elderly woman in the early 1930s (Linderman 1932a 23)

PLAINS INDIAN LIFE has long captivated Euro-Americans and Europeans, sometimes to the point of indifference to all other Native Americans. The image of warriors astride horses recklessly chasing herds of bison or enemies across the plains conveys a sense of daring and freedom. The Crow typify this life-style shared by other Siouans* and Algonquians, such as the Blackfoot, Cheyenne, and Gros Ventre. The Crow are presented because any book about American Indians would be incomplete without including a people of the Plains culture area. The Crow also dramatically illustrate how a tribe could change rapidly early in its history. The chapter ends with a focus on the problems of modern Crow tribal government.

Traditional Crow accounts about their tribe's late prehistory are at least partially contradictory; for this reason anthropological findings will be emphasized here. From linguistic evidence, it appears that the Crow began to separate from the Hidasta tribe somewhere along the upper Missouri River in the 1500s and gradually filtered westward. By 1850 the Mountain Crow and the River Crow had emerged, each with its distinct identity, and soon thereafter the Kicked in the Bellies clan separated from the other Mountain Crow (see Figure 7-1). Collectively, the Crow tribe called itself the *Absaroke,* spelled in various ways but always referring to a "large-beaked bird," not a crow as we know it but apparently a mythological being. (By the 1900s most of these people accepted *Crow* as their name.) The introduction of domestic horses in Mexico during the early 1500s led to the movement of these horses northward, and by 1730 the Crow received horses in trade from nearby tribes. By the 1750s the horse was becoming a catalyst for remarkable changes, to the extent that for the next 140 years horses, bison (buffalo), and warfare dominated a new Crow way of living.

| Baseline Ethnography

The far-reaching mobility achieved with domestic horses, combined with the particular location of Crow country, affected historical developments in the region. In the late 1700s the Crow were becoming middlemen in the continental Indian trade. From the south and east they received European manufactures such as metal axes, glass beads, and blankets. From the west they obtained salmon oil, pemmican, and raw materials such as shells. Their subsequent trade distributed desired items in each direction. Concurrently they developed superior craft skills locally that provided more trade items, such as those decorated with porcupine quill work. The Crow also contributed beaver skins to the trade. However, this led to open conflict with neighboring tribes, such as the Assiniboine and Mandan. These factors in combination made the Crow prey for surrounding tribes, who began to plunder for goods and for horses. By the mid-1800s the Crow realized that it was in their best interest to establish

---

* The Crow are Siouan in the sense that they are linguistically related to the Sioux, the popular name for the Dakota Indians who more correctly are the Santee, Yankton-Yanktonai, and Teton tribes.

Figure 7-1 | Historic homeland of the Crow Indians.

alliances with whites in order to survive attacks by their host of tribal enemies. This section seeks to describe Crow life before white influences became intense.

ORIGIN MYTH According to the Crow, they originated with Old Man Coyote. While most of his adventures reflect his trickster character, Old Man Coyote also was the creator of the world. In the Crow origin account, there was first Old Man Coyote, who was traveling alone in a cold, wet world with no place to rest. He asked three species of duck to dive beneath the waters and bring up earth, but each failed. At last he asked a grebe to bring up some earth. The grebe dove deep, was down a long time, and surfaced with a small piece of mud. With this earth, Old Man Coyote was able to travel from east to west to make the land, its mountains and rivers, and its animals and plants and to give them life. The world remained a lonely place. So Old Man Coyote molded from the earth an image he liked and blew a small breath into it. The first man moved. Old Man Coyote still was not satisfied. He tried again and made an image he liked even more. The first woman moved. Now Old Man Coyote was no longer alone. He taught the people how to live and pray. He gave them their language and clans. Finally, with the help of mice, Old Man Coyote taught people the Sun Dance.

Additional names for Old Man Coyote include the One Who Has Made Everything, the First Doer, and the Maker. He was, and remains for many Crow, the ultimate supernatural. He directly or indirectly receives prayers, pledges, and requests and is instrumental in vision quests. He is "appropriately conceived as a pervasive agent, omnipotent over all natural forces, the ultimate life-force, and the perennial meaning in the cosmos" (Frey 1987, 63).

APPEARANCE AND CLOTHING   The earliest Crow encounter with whites probably was with the French in 1744, who called them Beaux Hommes (Handsome Men). To the Crow a handsome man was tall and had a straight nose and a face free from blemishes or scars. The noble appearance and bearing of Crow men attracted favorable comment from most early travelers. Men greased their long hair and sometimes made it even longer by gluing on additional human or horse hair. One great chief, Long Hair, especially was concerned about the length of his hair because his extraordinary abilities were attributed to his long hair. Thus he grew it to about ten feet in length. Men plucked their whiskers, and both sexes apparently removed axillary hair. Strings of ornaments hung from the hair on each side of a man's head, and his ears were adorned with abalone-shell earrings cut into angular designs. Men painted their faces red and highlighted their eyelids with yellow paint. Bear-claw and bone-disk necklaces, as well as bone pendants, were popular. Men in general, and young men in particular, were fastidious about their appearance. Men wore hair-trimmed leggings held up by tucking the tops into a belt. Other items of male clothing included a shirt, moccasins, and a bison robe.

The gartered skin leggings of a woman reached her thighs. A sleeved skin dress had an opening on each side for nursing. Her long dress fringed at the bottom was trimmed with porcupine quills. A woman's robe, unlike the painted ones of men, had decorative quills. A woman in mourning for a relative, which could be often, cut her hair short and had dried blood smeared on her face from self-inflicted wounds; her face was spotted with clay. Young boys went naked until they were about nine years old and then wore the clothing of men; girls dressed in the manner of women.

SETTLEMENTS   The Crow had no permanent villages but moved from one campsite to the next in search of game. After so many people died from smallpox, most of the tribe camped together for protection against enemies.

Camps were dominated by tepees framed with about twenty poles, each some twenty-five feet long, set in the form of a cone and covered with bison skins. An opening was left at the top as a smoke hole, and two external poles were attached to flaps at the top of the cover to open or close the smoke hole (see Figure 7-2). Before the Crow had horses to haul tepee poles and covers, it appears that their dwellings were much smaller. There was a fireplace at the center of a tepee, and along the sides toward the back were hide mattresses beneath sleeping robes; the seat of honor was at the back and center. Other structures of importance were circular arbors with conical roofs made from boughs and used as sun shades and small dome-shaped sweat lodges where men bathed in a ritual context by pouring water over heated stones.

When a band moved, the caravan might extend for miles. Scouts kept a lookout for enemies, and hunters scattered in search of game. Men wore their best buckskin garments and carried their weapons in case of a sudden attack. Women rode astride horses, as did men, and from the saddle of a wife's horse hung her husband's shield and sword, if he owned one. Small children were tied to saddles, but five-year-olds rode alone. Meat, tools, utensils, and other property were packed in skin containers tied to horses. One horse carried a tepee cover and another dragged the poles. Some horses pulled pairs of tent poles with a frame attached to carry wounded or ill persons; this conveyance, a travois, was in earlier times pulled by dogs. The most important purpose of dogs appears to have been to warn of the approach of enemies or strangers.

Figure 7-2 | A Crow tepee, after a painting by Catlin. (From Donaldson 1886.)

HORSES   Wild horses lived on the North American Plains during the Pleistocene era, but they disappeared about 8000 B.C. or perhaps in more recent times, possibly hunted to extinction by Indians. The domestic horses used by Indians in North and South America were descendants of those introduced by Europeans in historic times. The Spanish took domestic horses to Mexico in A.D. 1519, and by the end of the century large herds of domestic and feral animals ranged over northern Mexico. Thus North American Indians did not begin to use domestic horses until the early 1500s.

By the mid-1800s the Crow had more horses than any other tribe east of the Rocky Mountains. A poor person owned at least twenty animals, and a middle-aged man had up to sixty. Horses represented the major form of wealth and became a medium of exchange; a horse was worth from sixty to one hundred dollars. In a proper marriage, a groom presented horses to the bride's brothers. Personal conflicts in a camp, usually involving women, might be settled with horses.

Crow men, women, and children always were described as excellent riders who depended on horses so much that their ability to endure long periods of walking had diminished (see Figure 7-3). Their saddles were high in the

Figure 7-3 | A Crow woman on horseback. (Courtesy of the Field Museum, Chicago, neg. no. 2784.)

front and back but were not used for hunts or during war. Most horses could be guided without a bridle. A rider leaned in the direction in which she or he wanted to turn, and the horse turned in that direction until the rider sat upright.

Horses were obtained in trade, but far more often they were seized in raids. When an enemy raid was expected, the best horses were tethered at the entrance of their owners' tepees so that riders could pursue horse thieves quickly at any time. Once they realized that horses had been stolen, Crow warriors gave pursuit, each riding his fastest horse and leading another. They rode day and night, and when the first horse was exhausted they rode the other; when that horse gave out they might continue on foot. If they caught up with the thieves, they first attempted to recover their horses and then killed and scalped an enemy if it was possible to do so without the threat of losing one of their number.

SUBSISTENCE ACTIVITIES   Part of the Crow habitat in the 1840s was described by Edwin T. Denig (1961, 139) as "perhaps the best game country in the world." He reported immense herds of bison from the Rocky Mountains to the mouth of the Yellowstone River and herds of hundreds of elk along the river, as well as many black-tailed and white-tailed deer. Antelope covered the prairies and badlands near the mountains, while in the mountains were many bighorn sheep and grizzly bears. The truly majestic Rocky Mountains, high valleys, fast-flowing streams and rivers, meadows, hot springs, and great forests characterized this idyllic land.

The Crow economy was based on hunting large game, especially bison, deer, elk, and antelope; in fact, they did not eat fish or berries. Except for the maize that they obtained by trading with the Hidatsa, the most important use of plant products was as seasoning for meat dishes. Cooperative hunts were the norm, and the purpose was to kill or maim herd animals by driving them over cliffs or riverbanks. Alternatively, animals were driven into a valley with a single narrow exit, and a fence was erected after the animals were confined. The planning and coordination required for large-scale hunts was supervised by the members of military sodalities, and hunting rituals were performed to further ensure success.

The bow and arrow was the primary weapon for the hunt or for war. The wood-shafted arrows were tipped with points of bone or stone. Bows were fashioned from horn or antler; pieces were cut, smoothed, spliced, glued, bound together, and then backed with sinew (composite, sinew-backed bow). Arrows were carried in skin quivers that were ornamented with porcupine quills.

A woman's life was physically demanding. She supplied the household with firewood and water, cooked the food, cared for children, collected plant products, and made and repaired all the clothing, skin containers, and tepee covers. Women were also responsible for erecting and taking down tepees. A woman groomed her husband, saddled his horse, and took off his leggings and moccasins in the evening. Women usually followed men on bison hunts and skinned the animals killed. One of women's most highly developed skills was working skins. Depending on the skin involved and the purpose served, hides or skins were dehaired, prepared on one or both sides, smoked or not smoked. To break down its texture and make it supple, a skin was spread with a preparation made from bison brains and liver. In addition to processing bison hides for tepee covers and skins for clothing, women made small skin pouches for pipes and sacred objects. The best-known rawhide container, termed a parfleche, was folded, often painted with designs, and used primarily for storing and transporting dried meat or pemmican. Although other American Indians were skilled in basketry, pottery, weaving, and elaborate wood carving, the Crow did not practice these crafts.

For men, camp life was as leisurely as it was busy for women. They made tools and equipment, but these were not time-demanding activities. Some men were part-time specialists in making bows or arrows. The major pursuits of men, hunting and fighting, usually took place at a distance from a campsite.

DESCENT, KINSHIP, AND MARRIAGE   Descent was traced through women (matrilineal system), since each person was identified primarily with the mother's clan (matriclan). Thus an individual was a member of the same clan as his or her mother, mother's sisters and brothers, mother's mother, mother's mother's brothers and sisters, and so on. The thirteen named Crow clans reported for both the Mountain and River Crow included Thick Lodge, Sore-Lip Lodge, Tied-in-a-Knot, and Bad War Honors. Clan members usually were dispersed over a broad area; in other words, Crow clans were not localized.

It appears that by the seventeenth century the Crow lived farther north, and their primary economic focus was on crops raised by women. Presumably the cultivated plots were relatively stable. Daughters learned horticultural skills from their mothers. In this reconstruction, women produced the food staples; when a man married he went to live with his wife. The resulting focus on the female line led to or sustained a matrilineal descent system with matrilocal marriages. However, as the Crow became bison hunters on horseback in the mid-eighteenth century, the emphasis dramatically shifted to men, and the Crow began to be patrilocal. Because whites were fast becoming a dominant force in Crow life, subsequent changes in their descent system and kinship terminology were forced rather than occurring naturally and logically.

Pairs of clans (or in one case three clans) were grouped into units (phratries) that were not named; one of the two-clan clusters may have been a single clan. It was most common for a spouse to be from another clan (clan exogamy). Yet the bonds between some paired clans seem to have been so close that members could not marry each other (phratry exogamy).

The kinship terminology employed by the Crow came to be called the Crow type, and it is shared by other people around the world. The Crow termed father and father's brother alike and used a different word for mother's brother.

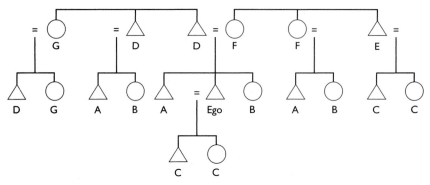

Figure 7-4 | The early historic Crow system of kinship terminology.

Likewise, father's sister was termed differently from mother and mother's sister, who were termed alike (bifurcate merging). Furthermore, father's sisters' daughters and their daughters' daughters were termed as father's sister; the term really designated women of the father's clan from his generation downward. The same logic applied when father's sister's husband was termed father, as was his son. The ignoring of generational distinctions in these contexts made clan members equivalents. In a like manner, the term mother was extended to her clan sisters (see Figure 7-4). The most rigid behavioral taboo prohibited a man from talking with or having any contact with his wife's mother or her grandmothers. Likewise, a woman did not interact with her daughter's husband or her daughter's daughter's husband.

SOCIAL DIMENSIONS The worst possible insult was for one Crow to say to another, "You are without relatives," meaning that the accused had no merit. Supportive relatives protected one from slander, came to one's defense in times of conflict with others, and provided material aid in times of stress. A matriclan was the largest integrated social unit, and one's obligations to it were great. Although members of the same clan do not appear to have camped adjacent to one another, they often ate together.

As Rodney Frey (1987) emphasized, clan solidarity represented the essence of social life. Their word for "clan" translates to "as driftwood lodges." The symbolism is telling. In a fast-flowing river a single piece of wood is battered, destroyed, or washed away. Along a riverbank, however, driftwood may accumulate in a compact, long-lasting mass. So it was with the Crow as individuals. Each person found security with other members of the same clan. Because the members of a single clan were dispersed, an individual was welcome among strangers belonging to the same clan. The bonds within a clan were most severely tested when a person from one clan killed someone from another clan. In these rare instances, the members of the murdered person's clan were obligated to kill either the offender or one of his clansmen. Despite their matrilineal focus, a father had close ties with his sons. When someone asked a special favor, a common phrase was, "By the love you bear your children, I beg you" (Lowie 1935, 18).

"Sodalities" are special-purpose groups in which membership might be either voluntary or required. Among the Crow most men were either Lumpwoods or Foxes. These were military sodalities into which young males were recruited by established members. Each sodality had distinctive adornments, dances, and behavioral characteristics.

In the fall after the first snow, Lumpwood men met and ate in the tepees of one member and then another. The membership was distinguished partially on the basis of age grades, and officers served for one year. The four pairs of officers were called elders, straight-staff bearers, hooked-staff bearers, and rear men. Being offered a pipe and smoking it were symbolic of selection and acceptance of an office. Men often were reluctant to become staff bearers because after a straight shaft was planted in the ground by its bearer during a battle he could not retreat from the spot unless another Lumpwood rode between him and the enemy. After a hooked staff had been placed in the ground, it could not be moved, and the bearer defended it until he was killed. Because of the danger involved, the bearers of these staffs counted a double coup if they struck an enemy.

Sodality members extended mutual aid to fellow members in stressful times; they sometimes fought together, and they honored by excessive mourning a member killed in battle. One Lumpwood behavioral peculiarity was that when a member mourned the loss of certain relatives, the other Lumpwoods had the right to make jokes about the loss to his face. This behavior would have been insulting to anyone else, irrespective of the circumstances.

The Foxes were organized much the same as the Lumpwoods, and competition between the two sodalities was keen. This was most dramatically expressed in the abduction of wives. In the spring either group could initiate the proceedings, and any man was free to abduct the wife of a member in the other fraternity if he had been her lover. Sometimes a woman was kidnapped without cause, and women sometimes hid to avoid abduction. A wife might also successfully plead with a potential abductor and not be taken away. Men who suspected that their wives would be abducted often made a point of being away because they had no desire to see their wives seized. Yet, if a man was present, custom dictated that he should make no effective effort to prevent his wife's capture. These women were paraded about and were received as brides by their abductors' families. A stolen wife could not return to her husband; a man caught sleeping with such a woman was tied up and smeared with feces. This period of license lasted about two weeks, and then the Lumpwoods and Foxes went on the warpath, each attempting to count coup (touch a live enemy) first so that they could ridicule their opposites. After the first snows fell the rivalry abated, only to surge again the next spring.

WARFARE   The Plains Indian stereotype is that of a bloodthirsty killer for whom war was by choice a dominant cultural focus. Yet economic factors best account for the intensity of warfare on the plains and prairies. We find that the Crow rarely killed whites, even though they often had ample opportunity and just cause, especially for killing white trappers in their midst. This situation contrasted with the animosity between whites and the members of surrounding tribes. Furthermore, when the Crow were at peace with another people, they appear never to have initiated a new conflict. Their primary reason for launching a raid was to avenge the death of a Crow killed by the members of another tribe. Unlike most Plains Indians, the Crow killed men but usually captured women and children; the children were adopted and captive women worked beside Crow wives. An adopted boy who was raised as a Crow did not hesitate to kill men from the tribe of his birth. In rational terms, by not initiating a war and by assimilating captives, the Crow compensated for their relatively small number and their losses in war. They went to war most often for a combination of three purposes: revenge, glory, and horses.

The word translated as "chief" really meant "good, valiant," and to achieve this title a man had to perform four feats: lead a successful raid, capture tethered horses from an enemy camp, be the first to count coup, and take a bow or gun from a live enemy. Warriors who performed each of these deeds at least once were chiefs; but this did not mean that they were political leaders. The greatest living chief in 1910 was Bell-rock; he had led at least eleven war parties, taken at least two tethered horses, counted coup six times, and seized five guns. Such a man boasted of his achievements at public gatherings, depicted his brave deeds on a robe that he wore, and had distinctive adornments on his clothing. To take a scalp was important to the tribe but was not ranked as a major personal achievement, and when a man listed his war honors he did not mention scalps. It should be noted that scalping an enemy was especially widespread in the Northeast culture area (see Chapter 12).

The foremost weapon of war was the bow and arrow, but it soon was replaced by the gun. Spears sometimes were used, but they apparently were not very important (see Figure 7-5). For close combat it was customary to use a war club with a stone head bound at one end of a wooden shaft. The shields men carried had a purpose more supernatural than practical, except in defensive circumstances. These circular pieces of bison hide might have bird skins, feathers, or animal tails hanging from them. Either a shield or its leather case was painted with symbols or scenes revealed to its owner in a vision (see Figure 7-6). Men also went into battle with ornamental sticks used to count coup. These were tied together at intervals with skin strings ornamented with quills.

Ideally, each youthful male longed to achieve personal honor in battle and believed that the greatest glory was achieved by dying young in warfare. Yet every effort was made to prevent the death of a Crow in combat, and a war party was never considered successful if it lost a single member. Those who were fearless in battle were persons convinced of their invincibility on supernatural grounds or who were reckless by nature. Still, the positive value placed

Figure 7-5 | George Catlin (1926, vol. 1, 216) wrote of this painting of a Crow warrior, "I have painted him as he sat for me, balanced on his leaping wild horse with his shield and quiver slung on his back, and his long lance decorated with the eagle's quills, trailed in his right hand." (From Ewers 1965.)

on an early death was a recurrent theme in Crow child rearing. Typically, a young man eagerly sought his first opportunity to join a party of raiders. As a novice he performed menial tasks, such as carrying the meat supply and hauling water. He likewise was the butt of jokes as a part of his informal initiation into the life of warriors.

An attack was organized by a raid planner, who usually achieved his position after having a dream or vision that detailed the tribe to be attacked and the booty to be gained. An ambitious warrior not blessed with a personal vision could turn to a shaman and succeed by following the shaman's instructions. Some warriors might doubt an announced leader's abilities and decline to follow him, but recruiting a war party does not appear to have been difficult,

Figure 7-6 | This is one of the finest Crow shields, and it was famous for its power. It belonged to the chief Arapooish and is said to represent the moon. Attached to the left side of the cover are the head and body of a crane. At the right is an eagle feather, and below it is a deer's tail. (Courtesy, National Museum of the American Indian, Smithsonian Institution, N29656.)

especially for previously successful war leaders. Raiders typically set off on foot with a supply of moccasins often carried by dogs. As they approached enemy territory, the scouts were especially watchful. Once an enemy camp was sighted, the war leader performed sacred bundle rituals. For example, the leader of a raiding party might place his sacred bundle on a rock, whistle or sing toward an enemy camp, and then relate how many enemy horses he hoped to obtain. To further ensure success, each participant attached sacred objects to his body and painted himself in an appropriate manner. One or two warriors were chosen to enter the enemy camp, usually late at night, and to drive off as many horses as possible without being discovered. The party made its escape by riding the remainder of the night, all the next day, and the following night before relaxing. As the warriors approached their home camp, they shot guns into the air and paraded the captured horses. The booty belonged to the raid leader, but he freely gave horses to the participants. These raids often were dangerous ventures. If a horse was not captured for each raider, some warriors were forced to return on foot and risked being overtaken by the pursuing enemy. Raiders sometimes went for days without food and rode so long and hard when attempting to escape that their "buttocks were worn out" (Lowie 1935, 222).

As warriors the Crow were daring and merciless enemies. In open battles, especially if a number of Crow were killed, they slaughtered every man and then tortured the wounded to death. Hands and feet were cut off, eyes gouged out, and intestines exposed to be pierced with sharp sticks. The brains and hearts of the dead were hurled in the faces of the living while the victors scorned their victims. It should be added that in defeat Crow warriors suffered a similar fate.

A newly taken scalp was the focus of a three-day celebration. Warriors carrying their weapons and wearing their finest clothing, their faces painted black, danced in a partial circle to the accompaniment of drums and rattles. The scalp was carried on a pole, and the warrior who had made the kill mounted a horse and was led by a chief in the midst of the dancers. That night young men walked around the camp, and at each chief's tepee they sang songs about his particular accomplishments. During the next day the scalp was tied to the bridle of a horse on which a young man rode while beating a drum and singing. When many scalps were taken in a battle, the celebration was far more elaborate and sometimes included a reenactment of the conflict.

Denig (1961) reported that a Gros Ventre girl was captured by the Crow at about the age of ten and became a great chief. As a child she preferred the activities of boys, and her adoptive father encouraged this behavior. She soon was playing with bows and arrows and riding fearlessly. As a youth she was trusted to guard horses. As an adult she always wore women's clothing. When her adoptive father was killed she became the head of his household. Later, in a raid against the Blackfoot, she killed and scalped one enemy and counted coup over another. She came to be known as Woman Chief after she consistently distinguished herself in other raids. Before long she sat as an equal in the council of chiefs. Woman Chief deplored the idea of doing woman's work and obtained first one woman as a "wife" and then three more. Thus she lived as an honored person for twenty years, until she tested a peace with the Gros Ventre and was killed by them after they discovered her origins.

When a man was killed by an enemy, everyone in the camp mourned as the body rested in state outdoors. The face of the corpse was painted; he was clothed in his best garments and was especially honored by members of his military society. They cried and sang over the body to the beating of drums. They pierced their limbs and bodies with arrows or cut themselves with knives. These men also distributed the dead man's property. Relatives took the body to a tree or scaffold for interment and wept. Their period of mourning did not end until a member of the enemy tribe that had killed him was murdered. Thus it was near relatives who most encouraged warriors to avenge deaths.

POLITICAL LIFE Control of the day-to-day Crow social unit or band was in the hands of a man who had performed each of the four honored deeds in war and had demonstrated the qualities of a leader. His authority expanded further if he was generous with booty, a shaman of note, and an able narrator of tales. Thus individual achievement, open to nearly all, was the avenue to honor and prestige in a political context. Tacit agreement determined who was to be band chief, and no formal installation ceremony existed. A band chief decided when a campsite was to be abandoned, where to move, and the placement of tepees. Yet he apparently had little control over people, since he neither judged nor punished in a manner often associated with chiefly powers. It appears that as long as the people who camped together enjoyed good fortune, their chief retained his office. When he failed, he was replaced quietly and informally. One of his most important duties was to appoint the members of a particular military society to take charge of the spring bison hunt. At larger camps the chief appointed an outstanding man as a crier; his duty was to ride among the tepees repeatedly making announcements about matters of public interest and making the chief's opinions known about matters of current concern.

Within a camp or band of the Mountain or River Crow, members of the thirteen clans formed the largest political entities. They dealt with each other as equals, and they recognized no superior authority to which they all were responsible. Feuds between clans were the greatest threat, but intermediaries attempted to settle conflicts as quickly as possible before they became emotionally charged and out of hand. Language, culture, and common social norms unified clans. Crow survival was partially contingent on cooperation among clans for the common good. If a segment of a clan separated from the main body, it could muster comparatively few warriors and would be destroyed by enemies. The tranquillity of camp life in tribal tradition was upset the most when an aggressive person with a small number of related followers became dominant. This was especially true of a person who was regarded as having powerful supernatural guardians. Such individuals might seize the horses or wives of others, but, as Robert H. Lowie (1935) pointed out, such a man was a de facto but never a de jure leader.

The members of the military sodality policing a bison hunt could and did severely punish nonconformity. The worst offense was for men to hunt bison alone or in small groups, because this scattered the herds and made it difficult for others to kill bison on the legitimate communal hunts. Likewise, on a group hunt, if a man broke and charged a herd prematurely, he might scatter the animals and ruin the opportunities of others. These nonconformists might be whipped, their weapons destroyed, and the kill seized. The warrior sodality in charge also had the right to prevent raiding parties from setting forth at inopportune times, and they attempted to settle differences between the people in camp peacefully, especially when a feud threatened to erupt between clans. Disagreements between members of different clans may have been reasonably common, but for one Crow to kill another was almost unknown. Any crime, except murder, could be compensated for with an exchange of property.

When the Crow split into two major bands, the River and the Mountain, it was Arapooish (Arapoosh, Sore-belly, Rotten-belly) who led the River Crow. A brief sketch of his life illustrates the qualities of leadership that he possessed. Arapooish was a retiring and even surly person who said little but spoke in an authoritarian manner. Although he was a relatively retiring shaman, he controlled powerful supernatural forces, and he apparently had many wealthy clansmen. He was fearless in battle. Time and again he successfully raided horses from enemies without any loss of Crow life. He saw to it that the Crow always were on the alert for enemies and that raiders who approached were killed. Arapooish was a confident aggressor and able tactician in the large battles that he planned. In a battle against the Cheyenne, more than 1000 horses were captured, 200 Cheyenne men killed, and 270 women and children captured; the Crow lost 5 men. But Arapooish was a man possessed; when he charged a Blackfoot fortification in 1834 shouting, "One last stroke for the Crow Nation" (Denig 1961, 183), he was killed. Arapooish came to be known as *the* Chief.

RELIGION The basis for Crow supernaturalism centered on personal rapport with a guardian spirit. An unsought spirit aid might reveal itself, but far more often it was gained in a vision quest. All personal glory, power, and wealth ultimately were attributed to valid visions. Thus religion among the Crow was not a tightly integrated system of beliefs with accompanying dogma. In Crow linguistic expression, a vision or a dream of supernatural portent were the same. A youthful male sought a personal spirit aid as he began to emerge into the world of adults. If he was fully successful, he might never seek another vision in his life. Were he to do so, it might be to cure a sick child or in an extraordinary quest for vengeance.

The Vision Quest A vision seeker sometimes, perhaps most often, first purified himself by taking a sweat bath. Ideally he then went to a mountaintop, where he abstained from food and water and wailed. Lightly clad and covered only with a robe at night, he slept until the sun began to rise. The seeker next chopped off the final joint of his left forefinger, placed it on a buffalo chip, and held it up as an offering to the rising sun with an accompanying prayer for glory and success in life. As the blood flowed, he fainted and was unconscious until evening. He could not sleep because of the cold of night. Three nights passed; on the fourth one, with sleep coming late because of the cold, a vision came to him.

Alternative ways of obtaining a vision existed. One man might have another cut slits in his chest or back through which one end of a thong was passed, the opposite end being tied to a pole. The aspirant ran around the pole until he tired; he rested, only to run again and again. He might or might not tear the thong free in his quest. Another means to the same end was to pierce the back with two holes and tie a thong from them to a bison skull that was dragged about in the first stage of the search for power.

A supernatural visitant might assume the form of an animal such as a bear or bison, a bird, an insect, or the earth, moon, or stars. A person could be blessed by association with more than one such power, and literally anything might be revered by an individual. The Sun was the supernatural to whom a direct appeal was made, but it rarely was the source of power received; thus it was not a god worshipped in the usual sense. The supplicant might be taught a sacred song, learn of a symbol that could be represented graphically, or be instructed to follow certain taboos. A feather, a stone with a strange shape, a braided rope, or a weasel skin, among other forms, symbolized the receiver's power and formed the core of a sacred (medicine) bundle. A bundle and its power could be transferred to a near relative after proper instruction or purchased by a nonrelative; thus the control of supernatural forces could pass from one generation to the next. The degree to which any particular bundle was revered depended directly on the fortunes of its possessors.

Tobacco Ceremonialism　The indigenous sacred tobacco known to the Crow as "Short Tobacco" (Lowie 1935, 274) was considered to have inordinate supernatural power. The Tobacco Society included many local chapters, each with distinctive rituals. Crow survival was intimately associated with the sacred seeds and harmony in the natural world. Potential members of a society chapter were instructed in the rituals and formally presented to the group. Typically a married couple was inducted together, and membership normally was for life. The tobacco planter played a key role, and his office was largely hereditary.

The yearly rituals of a chapter began with sowing the seeds in the spring. They built a huge tepee that could accommodate hundreds of people nearby and decorated the interior lavishly. Here the participants ate and danced for three days to music of bells, drums, rattles, and whistles, played in combination. The participants moved off only a short distance each day, indicating their reluctance to leave the sacred plants. To encourage the seeds to germinate, they placed a society member in charge of rainmaking, and he presented valuable property to the rain clouds as a sacrifice. If he was successful, the offerings became his property, and he gained great fame. If he failed, he blamed the other participants for improper behavior during the rituals. In late August members returned to the tobacco plot, harvested the crop, and collected the seeds.

Men alone smoked tobacco (see Figure 7-7). Smoking was most important when making peace with other tribes or during rituals, and shamans smoked when curing severe illness. Even when tobacco was smoked on less ceremonious occasions, the first puffs were dedicated to the earth, heavens, spirits, and the Sun. Each man present took four puffs and then passed the

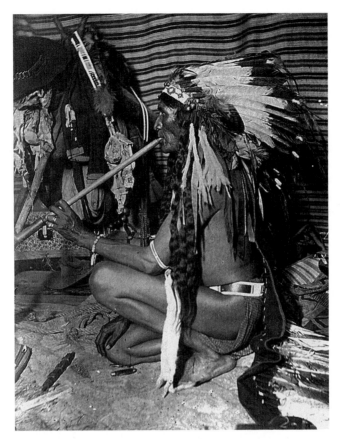

Figure 7-7 | A Crow man in ceremonial costume smoking a pipe. (Courtesy of the Field Museum, Chicago, neg. no. A2790.)

pipe on to the person on his left, because this was the direction in which the Sun moved. Furthermore, each man had personal smoking habits. One man would not smoke if a pipe had touched grass, another would not smoke if women were present, and another would insist on emptying his pipe on bison dung. These details were dictated by individual relationships with guardian spirits.

The Sun Dance The most sacred ceremony focused on the Sun, as a powerful and remote supernatural. A man pledged to perform the rituals following the death of a relative at the hands of an enemy tribe. To host the event involved a private vow to the Maker. The goal was to receive an extraordinary vision that would reveal how the killing was to be avenged. The personal commitment required to hold a Sun Dance was so great and rare that an elderly person may have witnessed only six such dances in a lifetime.

In early historic times the ceremony attracted all tribal members. The vow-maker, called the whistler, and a shaman who owned at least one sacred doll became the principals. A small wooden doll was the vehicle through which the whistler gained his vision. A doll with painted features and painted designs was dressed in skin with attached feathers. This type of doll reportedly led to success for war parties. Prior to the event the whistler fasted and became haggard. Preliminaries included the use of incense, ritual smoking, and the construction of a special lodge a few miles distant. The drama began as the whistler, painted with cross-shaped Morning Star designs and wearing a special kilt, held a wooden hoop with the doll attached at the center. He danced slowly to the lodge while blowing his whistle. Arriving there, he tied the doll at eye level on a lodge pole and neither ate nor drank water until after he received a vision. Other men likewise sought visions. Each such man cut slits in his chest or back and passed a skewer, attached to a line, through the slit and tied it to a lodge pole. Men pulled against the lines until they broke free. The whistler, who was not skewered, gazed intently at the doll and danced as chiefs successively recounted and acted out great deeds of personal valor. The whistler slept in the lodge. The next day he continued to dance before the doll, and he did so day after day until he obtained a vision that he customarily did not reveal. He next ventured forth in quest of the enemy.

Shamans   Physical disabilities and death usually were attributed to supernatural causes such as ghosts or breaking taboos. One category of health care practitioners depended primarily on secular knowledge. They used plant products, lanced a swollen part of the body, or applied a poultice as ordinary treatments. A particular root that was considered a cure-all was rubbed on sores, placed on an aching tooth, or chewed and swallowed to cure a cold. The botanical pharmacopoeia was extensive and appears to have been applied most often in a secular context. Other curers, more properly shamans, had the ability to treat specific traumas because of revelations they received in visions. They might be able to cure snake or spider bites, wounds, or disease caused by a foreign object in a patient's body. Shamans were adept at sleight of hand; they appeared to transform bark into meat or mud balls into beads in either public or private performances. Competitive exhibits of their skills often were dramatic contests. These were men who had the most powerful guardian spirits, and it was primarily in this respect that shamans stood apart from persons who had less potent spirit aids.

Ordinary persons sometimes practiced sorcery to settle grudges against other Crow by supernatural means, but the practice appears to have been relatively uncommon. One technique was to draw the figure of an antagonist along a riverbank near the water's edge, burn incense, and blow smoke toward the figure. As the water washed the drawing away, the victim was expected to die. Other magical practices supposedly could cause lifelong disabilities in the target person. The only sure safeguard against sorcery was considered to be for the victim to have more powerful supernaturals working on her or his behalf.

LIFE CYCLE As the time for a birth approached, the husband, other men, and boys were excluded from a tepee, and the woman was aided by a male or female specialist who was well paid. The woman knelt over padding and grasped two sticks. To hasten delivery she might be given potions or her back might be rubbed with a special preparation. The particular aid used depended on the techniques that the birth specialist had learned in a vision or had obtained by purchase from someone else. A woman present at the delivery cut the umbilical cord, and part of it was encased in a container that hung from the cradleboard of a baby girl and later from the back of her dress. The new mother observed food and behavioral taboos for a brief period, but the father's activities were not restricted. Within a few days and without ceremony, a neonate's ears were pierced with a hot awl; the holes were held open with small greased sticks until earrings could be inserted. Offspring were placed in cradleboards and rocked to sleep with lullabies. Water was poured into the nose of a small child who cried often, and such a child soon learned to stop crying when someone said, "Bring the water!"

A few days after a birth an infant was named, but names were neither sex- nor clan-specific. The father asked a noted warrior to select a name based on one of the warrior's personal achievements and gave the warrior a horse in return. Names often were descriptive phrases; for example, a newborn girl might be named Captures-the-Medicine-Pipe or a boy His-Coups-Are-Dangerous. As a name was given, the infant was tossed into the air four times (four was a sacred number among the Crow), each time higher than the last. Women changed their names when someone with a like name died, and men assumed new names to commemorate brave deeds or to improve their fortunes. Nicknames, often based on unusual behavior, might be more commonly used than formal names. For example, a man who took an old dog with him to carry his moccasins on the warpath came to be called Old Dog as a result.

Adults placed few constraints on the behavior of children. Children might interrupt adult conversations at any time and typically were both forward and self-confident. The freedom of boys was especially boundless. Denig (1961, 154) wrote, "The greatest nuisance in creation is Crow children, boys from the ages of 9 to 14 years. These are left to do just as they please. They torment their parents and everyone else, do all kinds of mischief without either correction or reprimand." Boys swam and played water games, hurled sticks at each other with the ends covered with mud or mud and live coals. Individually or in teams they shot at targets with arrows, and the arrows were stakes for the winner. In the winter boys coasted down hills on toboggans made by covering bison rib frames with rawhide. Every youthful male ate part of a raw grizzly bear heart to bring him strength and a clear head in times of trouble. Thus he could say "I have the heart of a grizzly" in the face of adversity. When meat was plentiful in a camp, boys might cover themselves with mud so that they could not be identified and run into camp where meat was hanging to steal as much as possible before old women chased them away. The thieves cooked the meat away from camp, and the boy who had stolen the best piece ate the choice parts first.

Boys hunted small game, and after a bison hunt they might ride out to kill the calves, bringing home the meat and giving the skins to girls for tepee covers. A pair of boys sometimes became close friends, and the bond could extend into adult life when they fought together and shared the same woman, either as a wife or mistress; these men referred to each other as "Little Father" and were closer than with any other persons.

At about the age of ten, boys and girls began imitating the camp life of adults, an activity called "calfskin tepee." Girls from affluent families had small tepees that they set up at a distance from the camps of their parents. Boys pretended to be their husbands and took food from their families for their "wives." The boys organized themselves in the manner of men, even to the point of kidnapping girls belonging to another group. When the boys killed a coyote or wolf, they returned in triumph with a piece of the pelt as a "scalp," and the girls danced with it in imitation of women dancing with scalps obtained by warriors.

Puberty went unacknowledged for males and females alike, although when a girl or woman menstruated she was prohibited from approaching sacred objects and avoided a wounded man or men preparing for a war party; most persons denied that women were isolated physically during menstruation. Girls appear often to have married before they reached puberty, and while marriage to a person in one's own clan was forbidden (clan exogamy), it also was considered in bad taste, at least in the eyes of some persons, to seek a spouse from the clan of one's father. To marry someone from a father's clan with whom no blood ties could be traced was acceptable although not desirable.

Marital arrangements varied, although the parents of a girl often seem to have had some influence, if only because a daughter was so young when she married. A man might meet a girl while she was alone and propose that they elope, offering her a horse for going off with him. A couple could summarily announce that they were going to live together, or a man might seek the aid of a go-between to make the arrangements. Young men seldom hunted before they married. They slept late and spent most of the day grooming themselves to show off on their horses. They courted girls with flute music and sometimes did not return home until daylight.

The most proper marriage proposal, especially for a woman of virtue, was for a man to offer horses to the girl's brother and meat to her mother; these arrangements produced the most lasting marriages. A man who had offered wealth for his bride had the right to claim her younger sister in marriage (sororal polygyny), and the girls' parents were likely to agree when the first daughter was well cared for. In the early 1800s perhaps half of the men had more than one wife, and apparently a few men had as many as twelve. They did not all live together, and some might simply have been betrothed to him. A woman could marry her deceased husband's brother (levirate), but she would not be forced into the union.

Crow sex life was free and open, especially for men, but women were far from pawns. Men and women alike might have many love affairs and made little or no effort to conceal their feelings and sexual activities; their philandering ways were often noted. When a married woman took offense at the affairs of her husband, she might hold him up to ridicule in songs about his behavior. Men and women alike hurled "a fine variety of beautiful epithets" at each other, according to Denig (1961, 151) and other observers. A woman could leave her husband and take her children, as well as her property, including horses, skins, and the tepee, with her; boys not fully dependent on their mother joined their father. Yet, after a couple had separated, irrespective of the reason, they could not live together again without bringing disgrace on them both. As noted previously, during a particular time each year, a Fox or Lumpwood could abduct and marry another man's wife if she previously had slept with him. If he did seize her, the woman could not return to her husband. Divorce was common, except among virtuous women, and could be initiated by either partner. Just as a marriage was without ceremony, so was a divorce. Men were expected to be unfaithful to their wives; in fact, for a man to keep the same wife for many years was considered unmanly and a source of ridicule. Yet some men were jealous of their wives to the point of always taking a favorite wife along on a hunt and strongly resenting it when she committed adultery.

Male transvestites, or berdaches, were reasonably common among the Crow and were not regarded as abnormal but as a third sex. According to Denig (1961), some boys preferred the company of girls in their preadolescence and eventually were dressed as girls by their parents. They then embarked on a lifetime of female activities and might "marry" a man. It also should be noted that there were sacred aspects of being a berdache. For example, in the Sun Dance certain rituals could be performed only by a berdache.

The hand game was a very popular form of entertainment, with garments and beadwork commonly bet on the outcome. A popular game called shinny (stickball) was played by women in the spring. The object was for the members of two teams to drive a ball to opposite goals by using curve-ended sticks. Another widespread game played by men was hoop-throwing, and they bet on the outcome. The object was to throw a dart through a rolling hoop that might have webbing in the middle. The man whose dart entered the hoop or passed nearest to it won a tally stick.

When someone died, the body was painted, clothed in fine garments, and shrouded in part of a tepee cover. The spirit was told not to turn back, and the body was removed under a side of the tepee to prevent further deaths in the household. Interment was either in the crotch of a tree or on a scaffold above four support poles. After the body had decayed, the bones were sometimes removed and placed in a rock crevice. Mourners from the immediate family pulled out their hair or cut it short, slashed themselves with knives, and often cut off finger joints. The practice of removing a finger was so common that scarcely a person had complete hands. However, men usually did not mutilate their thumbs or the fingers used to draw a bow or shoot a gun. The soul of a person was believed to first linger near the corpse, perhaps giving an owl-like cry, but to later go to the camp of the dead. The Crow had little interest in the fate of souls; although they believed that ghosts might return to harm the living, they also considered ghosts to be a source of helpful visions.

The expectation in this matrilineal society was for material property to be passed down along the female line, going to brothers, sisters, and their heirs rather than to a man's sons. But a dying man's request to pass his property to nonclan members was honored. A man could bequeath horses to his wife or sacred objects to an eldest son. Even when bequests were not made along the maternal line, they usually were made to an immediate family member.

Early History

The Crow soon gained the reputation of being clever, deceptive, and shrewd traders who disdained alcohol, which they called "white man's fool water." The first sustained contacts occurred in the early 1800s with the arrival of adventurous trappers and fur traders (collectively, "mountain men") in search of beaver pelts. Their influence was not great because the area was so inaccessible. A devastating result of visits by whites was the repeated epidemics, especially smallpox, that struck over twenty years beginning in the 1830s. By 1833 their population was about sixty-four hundred.

The rival chiefs, Arapooish and Long Hair, had a disagreement, and the people split into two groups, as previously noted. Just when the Crow were divided internally, the United States began to assert control over the region. A government agent was sent up the Missouri River in 1851 to negotiate the first Treaty of Laramie. Long Hair signed the treaty, but Arapooish refused. Treaty conditions included Crow recognition of the United States and of the federal government's right to regulate trade and intercourse. The Crow further agreed not to harm white Americans. By and large the Crow were faithful subjects, and the eventual protection provided by the U.S. Army probably saved the Crow from extinction at the hands of their Indian enemies.

Father Pierre-Jean DeSmet (1905) was the first Christian missionary to seek out the Crow. He visited them in 1840 and in 1842, being well received on both occasions. They were friendly and admired him, but he had no impact on their lifestyle. After hearing the tenets of Catholicism, one man responded that there were only two Crow men who would not go to hell for killing, stealing, and other non-Christian behavior.

In the first Treaty of Laramie, land was set aside for the Crow in northern Wyoming, southern Montana, and western South Dakota. By agreeing to the conditions of this treaty, the Crow and other tribes involved were granted annuities, and the federal government obtained the right to build forts and roads in the region. The second Treaty of Laramie in 1868 confined the Crow to a reservation south of the Yellowstone River in southern Montana; they have continued to live on a small portion of this area into the present. This treaty established a clearly defined reservation. The town now called Crow Agency became the administrative center of this community in 1884. From the beginning of the reservation period, the federal goal was to destroy the traditional basis for

Crow life. Christian church services were to replace heathen ceremonies, the people were to wear "civilized" clothing and live in log cabins, the men were to become farmers, and the children were forced to attend school (see Figure 7-8). By treaty the Crow obtained highly specific yearly benefits for thirty years. For instance, each male older than fourteen years of age received "substantial woolen clothing, consisting of a coat, hat, pantaloons, flannel shirt, and woolen socks."

Within comparatively few years the Crow were dealt a number of crushing blows. They were forced to abandon the Big Horn Mountains by Indian enemies, and the presence of non-Indians was ever increasing. The most adverse calamity was a precipitous decline in the number of bison as a result of overhunting by whites for pleasure, hides, tongues, and, to a lesser extent, meat. Furthermore, many whites favored the destruction of bison to make way for cattle. By 1883 bison were nearly gone. An immediate result was privation. The people became dependent on Indian agents, who controlled food and goods that were assured by treaty and essential for survival. These agents were powerful and often corrupt, and they withheld aid to those Crow who were uncooperative with federal policies. The presence of whiskey traders nearby also contributed to declining living conditions. Within ten years of passage of the Homestead Act of 1862, whites were surging into Montana Territory seeking land. The new settlers resented the magnitude of Crow holdings. Under pressure from the homesteaders, Congress repeatedly reduced the amount of land

Figure 7-8 | Crow schoolchildren. From left to right: unknown, unknown, Russell White Bear, Henry Shin Bone, Annie Wesley, Addie Bear-in-the-Middle, Fanny Butterfly, Kitty Deer Nose. (Courtesy of the Montana Historical Society.)

set aside for the Crow. Between 1882 and 1904, the size of the reservation was reduced three times. By 1968 only two million acres remained of the eight million acres that the Crow had once occupied. (By the early 2000s over 50 percent of the existing reservation was owned by whites.)

The cultural geographer John W. Stafford (1972, 132) summarized the white attitudes prevailing by the 1900s in terms of "good" and "bad" Indians: "The idea of a good Indian was nurtured. To the 'good' Indian who cooperated by cutting his hair, sent his children to school, and took up farming were given special monetary rewards, wagons, and cattle. Other 'good' Indians were given jobs in the agency. Leaders who cooperated were flattered with trips to Washington. On the other hand 'bad' Indians were threatened with loss of rations."

| Later History

Above all else the attitude of the Crow has become pragmatic. The primary changes appear to date from 1857 when Plenty Coups, then nine years of age, had a vision that anticipated dramatic changes and provided guidance: learn from the mistakes of others and establish peaceful relations with whites. He foretold that the greatest defense of Crow culture would be achieved through education. By adhering to the Crow lifeway as much as possible while adjusting to Euro-American policies and practices, the Crow pursued and realized the vision of Plenty Coups.

FEDERAL CONTROL The most abrupt changes from their historic lifeway date from 1886. By then bison virtually were extinct, and raiding for horses or plunder had ceased as federal control expanded. The Crow Agency was established in 1884 to serve as the single federal administrative center. Before long many Crow families were forced to depend primarily on federal rations for bare survival, leading federal Indian agents to become dictators, pure and simple. The best example was C. H. Asbury. He became the agent in 1919, and with congressional sanction, set about to abolish the core of then existing Crow life by transforming the people into farmers and ranchers. The major vehicle was the 1920 Crow Allotment Act, an outgrowth from the Dawes Act of 1887 (see Chapter 2).

Under its provisions ever-increasing pressure was applied to destroy the essence of Crow life. They were forced to abandon their camp-cluster residence pattern to live on widely scattered family allotments. Asbury also was determined to end the basis for religious life, and to this end he concentrated on Tobacco Society activities. At his instigation the Crow police, who operated under BIA control, broke up Tobacco Society meetings and arrested those men suspected of being religious leaders. They were bound hand and foot and placed on public display at Crow Agency; their punishment included both fines and compulsory labor.

Asbury likewise crusaded against the number of horses on the reservation lest they provide an enduring basis for economic life. In the early 1920s an estimated forty thousand horses roamed the reservation, but Asbury forced the destruction of most of them to make way for cattle and sheep grazing land. The majority of the horses appear to have been shot by cowboys working for white ranchers. The bones of the dead animals were processed for fertilizer and live horses were shipped by rail to canneries. One consequence was that most of the remaining Crow abandoned their roving lives, built log cabins, and settled on allotments. It is difficult for a thoughtful Euro-American to imagine just how devastating this systematic federal control must have been for the freedom-loving Crow. In sum, federal efforts in combination nearly destroyed the core of Crow culture.

Most of the land unalloted to families at this time was declared *surplus* by the government and sold to whites. To compound these travesties, whenever an original owner of an allotment died, the land was divided among the heirs. They received allotments of ever-diminishing size as one generation gave way to the next. By 1967 a large allotment right included only 11 acres, and a small one some 0.014 acre! With such a small landholding, heirs had no option except to lease or sell to whites, who could utilize it by increasing their existing acreage.

The leasing arrangements eventually became an administrative burden for the BIA and an absurdity for the Crow. Federal legislation beginning in 1983 eventually led to the consolidation of fractionated leases. The end result was that, when more than five Crow held a fractionated lease, it was consolidated; if the owners could not agree on the terms, the land reverted to the tribe. The next change occurred when the magnitude of land purchases by whites became alarming. At that point the federal government began to prohibit the sale of land to non-Indians. Between 1961 and 1968 the tribe bought back about fifty-five thousand acres from whites, and that policy has continued. By the late 1990s the outer reservation boundary encompassed about 2.4 million acres. About 0.5 million acres were tribal trust land, and some 1 million acres were allotted to enrollees. Most, but not all, of the remaining land was owned by non-Indians.

CROW FAIR In 1904 an Indian agent launched the Crow Agricultural Fair to encourage farming. Over the years, the Crow Fair, as it is now called, became primarily a showcase for expressing cultural vitality. Eventually "pow-wow culture" was brought into the context of these fairs. Each August a host of Crow families and many Indians from other tribes, plus thousands of Euro-Americans, attend the fair in what is known as the "Tipi Capital of the World." The fair includes indigenous American dances, by Crow and other tribal dancers, an all-Indian rodeo, dance parades, and family reunions. At the parade each morning two Crow veterans of U.S. wars lead the procession as clear recognition that warrior status continues to be respected. Parade participants

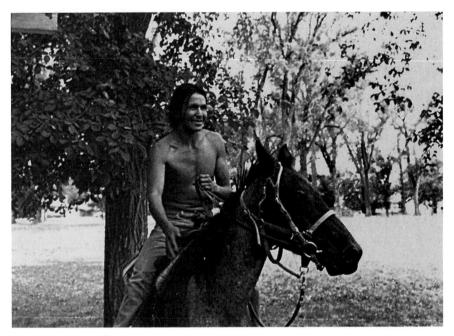

Figure 7-9 | Kevin (Crow Boy) Old Horn in 1985.

wear their finest beaded garments as a symbol of their Indianness. The last day of the fair includes a "giveaway" in which individuals at a public ceremony present gifts to clan aunts and uncles.

The horse remains a focus of cultural identity. Photographs of family members on horseback are often seen on the walls of homes (see Figure 7-9). During the Crow Fair, horses are adorned with the finest beadwork and ridden with pride during the parades. Certainly the horse is no longer economically pivotal, nor is it a clear marker for male prestige. (The last bison hunt was in 1883, and the last coups were counted in 1886 during a Piegan and Dakota raid.)

SUN DANCE A fine example of an old ceremonial complex that disappeared and later was revived is the Sun Dance. The last traditional dance of this nature was held in 1875, but by the 1940s it had been resurrected (see Figure 7-10). Fred Voget (1984) documented the introduction of the Wind River Shoshoni Sun Dance to the Crow. Two individuals were key to the revitalization. William Big Day became disillusioned with the Roman Catholic church. He traveled to Wyoming in 1938 and witnessed the Wind River Shoshoni Sun Dance. Later at one of these dances Big Day reportedly was cured of chest pains by John Trehero, a supernatural specialist of Shoshoni and Mexican ancestry. Big Day pledged to hold a Sun Dance if his adopted son, Heyward, survived a desperate illness. The boy recovered. Trehero helped the Crow reintroduce the dance by giving them his medicine bundles, songs, and the right to hold

Figure 7-10 | A Crow Sun Dance Lodge in the summer of 1994. (Photo by Rodney Frey.)

the dance. As a result, Big Day organized a Sun Dance on the Crow Reservation in 1941. Subsequently over the years the Crow held the dance on numerous occasions. In 1991 Heyward Big Day held a fiftieth-anniversary Sun Dance in honor of his father.

The Shoshoni–Crow Sun Dance became fully integrated into Crow religious life and is now identified as the Crow Sun Dance. It has emerged as a cornerstone for Crow spiritual expression, as from 40 to 120 men and women dancers participate in three or four Sun Dances each summer. Dances typically last three days, and participants offer collective morning prayers for the welfare of all peoples and other prayers especially for family members. In addition, the ill are treated by curers, and individual dancers may receive visions.

PENTECOSTAL CHURCHES The greatest challenge to the Roman Catholic and other churches on the reservation has come recently from evangelical Christians. The following discussion is based on the insightful analysis of Timothy P. McCleary (2000). Although the Pentecostal religion was introduced in the 1920s, its widespread acceptance dates from the 1970s. By 1992 at least one evangelical church existed in every community. Each church is locally controlled, and ministers have been largely local Crow. Differences in creed have produced a variety of sects, with the most extreme ones rejecting traditional Crow culture, as well as its adjustments. By the 1990s Pentecostals had become a dominant force in tribal politics.

The Pentecostal belief system subscribes to a constant struggle between the forces of good (the Trinity, including the Father, Son, and Holy Ghost) and evil (the Devil). This struggle will end with the Second Coming of Christ. The Devil, who is often called "Old Man" in English, cannot be killed. He pursues those persons who have been "saved" and tries to destroy their faith. He is a manifestation of Old Man Coyote, a traditional trickster among the Crow. The ritual of baptism signifies the acceptance of Christ as the only savior, and with it a person becomes "born again" or "saved" and filled with the Holy Spirit. Some Pentecostals believe that a person is not fully saved until he or she is able to speak "in tongues" and interpret the speaking of others as a means of prophecy. Members are warned to be cautious in their beliefs because the Devil constantly attempts to lead them astray. Wisdom is sought through revelations, usually in a vision or dream, and through interpretation of Bible readings. Being saved also involves the gift of faith to resolve problems with confidence, whereas nonbelievers are unable to arrive at a satisfactory solution. Miracles, such as walking away from an accident expected to be fatal, are accepted even though they appear to defy the natural order. The gift of healing is especially prominent. Ministers induce healing by placing olive oil, as Holy Oil, on the forehead of a person who is ill, either as a result of a physical ailment such as diabetes or a psychological maladjustment such as "backsliding."

It would appear that two clusters of negative factors best account for the growth of Crow Pentecostalism. First was the loss of their bison-based economy, which caused profound socioeconomic upheaval. Second was the systematic federal effort to destroy the essence of Crow culture, especially in the religious realm. The nadir of Crow cultural survival had been reached in the 1920s, at about the time a white Pentecostal couple, John and Georgia Forbes, settled in a relatively isolated section of the reservation. They visited Crow at their scattered allotments and generally were well received. Before long some of the Crow scheduled religious meetings in their houses, followed by feasts. These gatherings enabled participants to socialize with their neighbors, which they seldom did now that they lived so far from one another. One Crow woman who attended meetings regularly was Nellie Pretty Eagle Stewart. She was especially distraught over the death of her son and felt greatly comforted by the missionaries. In 1923 Nellie and other Crow attended a revival meeting near Miles City, Montana. It was sponsored by Aimee Semple McPherson, the founder of the Four Square Gospel Church, which was Pentecostal, in Los Angeles. Nellie and other Crow accepted an invitation from McPherson to visit Los Angeles for religious instruction. After brief training, Nellie was ordained by McPherson and told to return to the reservation and establish a Pentecostal church.

One firm basis for the acceptance of Nellie Stewart's leadership was her ordination by McPherson, but there were additional Crow-based reasons for her growing number of followers. Nellie often fasted in the mountains, as Crow visionaries had done in the past. In the process she acquired religious songs of the traditional Crow musical style and integrated them into her services. Some of these songs continue to be sung in the churches today, although following Crow convention, they were her property and could be sung only if given or sold by her to others. Efforts by Nellie Stewart and her followers to establish a church were not realized before she died in 1937, but in 1950 an abandoned cabin at Crow Agency became a Pentecostal church. By then the religion had begun to spread among the Crow, and attendance grew.

At the time of the Crow Fair in 1952 the Pentecostals held a revival meeting. As this practice was repeated, the meeting came to be known as the Jubilee Revival. The original revival leader was a Crow, Harold Carpenter. He appears to have been the originator of pronounced Pentecostal opposition to traditional Crow culture. His impact was considerable, and following his death the leadership role passed to his son, who held the views of his father. The background of Crow ministers varies, but a number of shared influences prevail in their decision to become Pentecostal leaders. They include being instructed at a Pentecostal Bible school, having charismatic and innovative personalities, and most significantly, having had a personal or family illness cured by prayers.

The beliefs of Pentecostals differ in key ways from those of other tribal members. Extremists categorically reject Crow culture in *all* its aspects, including powwows, giveaways, and local craft skills of old. Present-day sweat lodge rituals, medicine bundles, and gambling, especially the stick game, are considered magic (trickery) identified with the Devil (i.e., Old Man Coyote). The concept of Heaven, which had no part in Crow religion of old, is a key belief for Pentecostals, as is faith that the Second Coming of Christ is near at hand. Gradually the Pentecostals have become not only a dominant force in religious life but also a powerful influence on tribal politics.

TRIBAL GOVERNMENT   Historically the earliest form of government was that imposed by federal Indian agents. Although the Crow Agency began operations in 1884, it was not until 1920 that the Crow Allotment Act led to active Crow participation in decision making through a Crow Tribal Business Council. It was partially independent but was indirectly controlled by the BIA.

The next stage was a by-product of the Great Depression (1929–1939) and the failing land allotment programs. Because of these changes, increasing numbers of people moved from their isolated allotments to relatively large and stable community clusters. Most of the people were exceedingly poor; many men entered the wage labor economy by taking jobs or applied for help through the newly established federal relief programs. This pattern continued until World War II. During the war some Crow became members of the armed services, and others worked in defense-related jobs. Their combined experiences led them to create a different form of government in 1948, the Tribal Council. Each enrolled member was granted membership, and quarterly meetings were held for all members to attend and vote on pertinent issues. The council administration included four officers: a chair, a vice-chair, a secretary, and a vice-secretary. They served two-year terms, and between general council sessions tribal business was done by committees. Along with a tribal court, the council governed those internal affairs that were not under the jurisdiction of the BIA. In retrospect, the council government was a cumbersome, ineffective democratic political institution.

The 1950s introduced major unilateral federal changes in Indian policies. The vigorous BIA Relocation Program, which moved many Indians to cities, was intended to reduce reservation poverty levels and the need for federal support. The federal government sought to "get out of the Indian business"; in other words, to withdraw federal support within fifteen years (see Chapters 2 and 15 for details). On the Crow Reservation a separate issue involved the construction of Yellowtail Dam. Opponents and proponents were each adamant. The dam was completed in 1965, but the factional split created over the dam's construction continues into the present. About the time of these tribal disruptions, the Pentecostals became increasingly unified and began to dominate tribal politics. They sought to gain power through a new socioeconomic approach. Edison Real Bird, a candidate for tribal chair, solicited Pentecostal votes from this growing but untapped voting block. With their broad support, he won election in 1968 and 1970. As tribal chair he made virtually all Tribal Council appointments political rewards. This was a critical move, especially because local year-round jobs were few and the unemployment rate was extremely high.

Direct Pentecostal political power was realized with a sequence of Pentecostal chairs, climaxing in the election of Clara Nomee in 1990. She became the first woman elected to the tribal chair. Soon after gaining office she was granted broad and unprecedented authority by the Tribal Council to conduct tribal business between council meetings. She was returned to office for an unheard-of five terms.

In 2000 Nomee ran for another term and lost when her opponents, two male candidates, cited a pending court case against her for the misuse of tribal money. Her ten years as chair, however, had enabled her to control about eight hundred tribal jobs. In this general context, she was correctly accused of making appointments to sustain her power base, which was not unusual in tribal politics. Nomee was decisively defeated by Clifford Birdinground, who was not Pentecostal. During the campaign he said he would not fire the current tribal employees and would stress tribal economic development. He soon fired about 130 employees, however, and before long he was indicted by a federal grand jury for conspiracy, bribery, and theft. He resigned as the chair in 2002.

It became apparent that the Tribal Council government was increasingly ineffective. The unhealed wounds created by construction of the Yellowtail Dam, abundant evidence of corruption under tribal officials, and the failed economic agendas invited radical change. The Tribal Council decided in 2001 that Crow government had spun out of control. Council members proposed a new constitution with executive, legislative, and judicial branches, administrative terms that lasted four years, and a chairmanship limited to two terms. The legislative branch was to consist of three representatives each from six districts.

The new constitution was passed by the council but was challenged by an opposing faction as invalid because the ballot was not secret. The challenge was unsuccessful, and changes were instigated with BIA approval but with bitterness lingering among tribal members.

In 2002 the first tribal chair under the new form of government was Carl Venne, a former law enforcement official and subsequently a counselor at Little Big Horn College. He was not closely identified with any political or religious faction. One of his initial goals was to tighten ambiguities, such as fiscal controls, in the constitution. He strongly advocated greater tribal sovereignty and independence from the BIA. He hoped to create a stable political climate that would encourage investments by businesses and industry on the reservation. He planned to hire employees solely on the basis of their job qualifications and to reduce the number of tribal employees to about four hundred.

LITTLE BIG HORN COLLEGE Schooling of Crow children began as early as 1883, when they were sent to the Carlisle Indian School in Pennsylvania. Somewhat later Crow Agency schools emerged on the reservation, and others, run by Christian missionaries, also were established. The next dramatic change in the local educational system came almost a century later. In 1980 the tribe chartered Little Big Horn College, a community college funded largely by a congressional act to support Indian higher education in isolated areas. The second president was Janine Pease, a Crow who has a PhD degree and who later received a MacArthur Foundation "genius grant." She was primarily responsible for the general success of the college and also managed to obtain funding for a major building program, which was completed in 2003. (Pease apparently was fired in 2000 for political reasons by the Board of Trustees.) Between 1985 and 1997 a large percentage of the local adult population enrolled in courses; the student body was almost exclusively Crow (see Figure 7-11). In 2003 sixteen individuals were awarded Associate of Arts degrees. At that time there were about three hundred enrolled students each semester. Requirements for graduation included Crow language courses and general Crow studies.

| Other Dimensions

By the late 1990s local job opportunities were few, and the unemployment rate on the reservation ranged from about 70 to 80 percent. The major employer was the tribe, with about 600 permanent and temporary employees. The Indian Health Service hospital employed about 250 people, and the BIA had some 120 employees. Furthermore, the Crow casino employed about 65 people, the Little Big Horn College employed 30, and local businesses had hired a comparatively small number of additional persons. In each instance, most of the workers were Crow. It might appear that there were many jobs on the reservation, but such was not the case; nearly half of the Crow had a living standard beneath the national poverty level.

Figure 7-11 | India Hill was a Crow student in general studies at Little Big Horn College in 1996. American Indian history was her major interest.

In recent years, the Crow finally have gained political power in Big Horn County, Montana. This development is partially a result of a county redistricting of voting areas that had favored Euro-American voters. As a result of the change, two of the three county commissioners were Crow by 2000. In many ways the Indian majority is more symbolic than anything else, but it does have practical aspects. For instance, county roads to Indian households are now more likely to be comparable to the roads that lead to the farms and ranches of whites.

The nearby Little Bighorn Battlefield National Monument (the Custer Battlefield until 1991) is a major tourist attraction. It was there in 1876 that soldiers under the 7th U.S. Cavalry and Arikara fought about 2000 Indians, mostly Cheyenne and Sioux. Fewer than 100 Indians were killed in the battle by Custer and his battle group. Custer and 265 of his 450 soldiers died there. In 1881 a monument was erected at the site for Custer and his soldiers. A memorial at the site was dedicated in 2003 to the Indian casualties (Figure 7-12). The battlefield attracts more than 300,000 visitors a year.

As many as 30,000 people visit the Crow Fair held every fall. With so many tourists visiting the area, the Crow decided to launch the Little Big Horn Casino in 1994. Although it has electronic gaming machines, the site is comparatively

Figure 7-12 | Located on the Little Bighorn Battlefield and dedicated in 2003 is the *first* federally funded memorial sculpture honoring Native Americans.

isolated. Furthermore, and with greater impact, legal gambling had been approved in Montana in 1972. Subsequently, "casinos" became common at bars and truck stops in the state. The Crow casino is one of the many nationwide Indian gaming facilities with either no profits or only modest ones.

A major land problem, recognized in recent years, was that the "107 meridian boundary" for the reservation was based on an early and inaccurate survey of the eastern limit. It deprived the Crow of about 46,000 acres and involved the Crow, the state and federal governments, and the Northern Cheyenne. (The western boundary of the Cheyenne reservation abuts the Crow Reservation.) In the final settlement, the Crow received about 40,000 acres and the interest from a $30 million fund earmarked for economic development, education, and programs for Crow youth.

The repeated, abrupt, and far-reaching historical changes in the Crow lifeway have molded contemporary conditions, and they merit review. Initially the Crow were hunters and gatherers who walked from one site to the next to maintain their lifestyle. With the introduction of horses, they rapidly became transformed into highly skilled and mobile bison hunters. This stage ended rapidly with the near extinction of bison. Soon thereafter the federal government confined them to a smaller and smaller reservation so that white settlers could be accommodated. Indian agents decided that the Crow, with a reduced land base of small dispersed land allotments, should become settled farmers and ranchers. This effort largely failed, and most Crow were forced to seek wage labor employment and/or to rely on federal welfare programs for survival. Another unsought change was the arrival of Christian missionaries, who introduced a clear and direct challenge to the traditional belief system. Federal and mission schools emerged to teach children Euro-American ways. Early Crow experiments with self-government had limited success but have slowly matured into the present. All of these things have been major reasons for Crow cultural instability that lasted over a hundred years.

In combination, these cultural changes of direct or indirect Euro-American origin led to major confusion among the people about what it means to be a Crow. One substantial indicator is that by 2003 about 25 percent of the approximately eleven thousand tribal members no longer live on the reservation or even nearby. Suggestively, many of them are integrating into the greater American cultural matrix. Another meaningful change centers on the current usage of their aboriginal language. Language loss is a widely accepted measure of declining cultural vitality for a tribe, and the vast majority of younger people have not learned to speak Crow.

Current religious beliefs illustrate the multiple and sometimes contrasting ways the Crow worship today. By 2003 an estimated 35 percent of the people were identified with the Roman Catholic church and an equal percentage with Pentecostal churches. Twenty percent had become Baptist, and 10 percent were primarily Mormons or Open Bible church members. *At the same time,* however, some 40 percent continued to participate in the Sun Dance, Tobacco Society activities, and sweat lodge rituals. Pentecostals became temporarily successful in the political arena, and some of them continue to reject Crow culture in its entirety. Thus for many Crow, being Christian does *not* conflict with actively participating in traditional and new Crow-related religious life. To a greater or lesser extent, the same applies to many other aspects of their modern reservation life.

| Additional Sources

Plains, volume 13 of the *Handbook of North American Indians,* edited by Raymond J. DeMallie (2001) and published by the Smithsonian Institution, provides the best data base about Indians in this culture area. The Crow discussion by Fred Voget in this volume (695–717) is the best brief presentation about these people. The key ethnographic studies about the early historic Crow are by Robert H. Lowie. Reliable historic accounts by fur traders are by Edwin T. Denig (1961) and Zenas Leonard (1959). Outstanding historical discussions of the Crow include a book by Charles Bradley (1991) and a monograph by C. Adrian Heidenreich (1971). Joseph Medicine Crow was the first Crow to graduate from college, and he is the tribal historian. In a 1992 study, he combines oral traditions and written records to present an insider view of Crow life. The autobiography by Alma H. Snell (2000), who was born in 1923, is an insightful account about Crow life, old and new, plus a love story. Presentation about the new Crow Sun Dance by Fred Voget (1984) includes excellent biographical sketches of the key individuals involved. Thomas Yellowtail (1991) writes about his life, with emphasis on the Sun Dance. The most detailed account about present-day Crow supernaturalism is by John A. Grim (2000). A primary contemporary researcher among the Crow is Rodney Frey (1987); in this important work he emphasizes worldview in modern life. Dale D. Old Horn and Timothy P. McCleary (1995) present a brief and notable account of social life, past and present.

The massacre of Lieutenant-Colonel George Custer and his command at Little Big Horn in 1876 is of some interest in Crow history because Custer's scouts were Crow. A great deal has been written about the Battle of Little Big Horn; the events leading up to the massacre are well described in the journal of Lieutenant James H. Bradley, edited by Edgar I. Stewart as *The March of the Montana Column* (Norman, OK, 1961), and the *Little Bighorn Battlefield* (U.S. National Park Service, 1994) by Robert M. Utley.

| Selected Bibliography

Bonner, Thomas D. 1972. *The life and adventures of James P. Beckwourth*. Lincoln, NE.

Bradley, Charles. 1991. *The handsome people: A history of the Crow Indians and the whites*. Billings, MT.

Catlin, George. 1841. *North American Indians*. 2 vols. London. (Later editions in 1880, 1903, 1913, and 1926.)

Crummett, Michael. 1993. *Sun Dance: The 50th anniversary Crow Indian Sun Dance*. Helena, MT.

Denig, Edwin T. 1961. *Five Indian tribes of the upper Missouri*. John C. Ewers, ed. Norman, OK.

DeSmet, Pierre-Jean. 1905. *Life, letters and travels of Father Pierre-Jean DeSmet, S. J., 1801–1873*. Vol. 1. Hiram M. Chittenden and Alfred T. Richardson, eds. New York.

Donaldson, Thomas. 1886. *The George Catlin Indian Gallery in the U.S. National Museum*. Annual Report of the Board of Regents of the Smithsonian Institution, 1885, pt. 2, appendix.

Ewers, John C. 1965. *The emergence of the Plains Indian as the symbol of the North American Indian*. Smithsonian Report for 1964, 531–44.

Frey, Rodney. 1987. *The world of the Crow Indians: As driftwood lodges*. Norman, OK.

———. 1995. *Stories that make the world: Oral literature of the inland northwest as told by Lawrence Aripa, Tom Yellowtail, and other elders*. Norman, OK.

Grim, John A. 2000. Traditional ways and contemporary vitality: Absaroke/Crow. In *Native religions and cultures of North America,* Lawrence E. Sullivan, ed., 53–84. New York.

Heidenreich, C. Adrian. 1971. *Ethno-documentary of the Crow Indians of Montana, 1824–1862*. PhD dissertation, University of Oregon.

Hoxie, Frederick E. 1989. *The Crow*. New York.

———. 1995 *Parading through history: The making of the Crow nation in America, 1805–1935*. Cambridge, England.

Larocque, François A. 1910. *Journal of Larocque*. Publications of the Canadian Archives, no. 3, L. J. Burpee, ed.

Leonard, Zenas. 1959. *Adventures of Zenas Leonard, fur trader*. John C. Ewers, ed. Norman, OK.

Linderman, Frank B. 1930. *Plenty-Coups*. London.

———. 1932a. *Pretty-Shield: Medicine woman of the Crows*. Lincoln, NE.

———. 1932b. *Red Mother*. New York.

Lowie, Robert H. 1912. *Social life of the Crow Indians*. Anthropological Papers of the American Museum of Natural History (APAMNH), vol. 9, pt. 2.

———. 1917. *Notes on the social organization and customs of the Mandan, Hidatsa, and Crow Indians*. APAMNH, vol. 21, pt. 1.

———. 1918. *Myths and traditions of the Crow Indians*. APAMNH, vol. 25, pt. 1.

———. 1919. *The Tobacco Society of the Crow Indians*. APAMNH, vol. 21, pt. 2.

———. 1922a. *The religion of the Crow Indians*. APAMNH, vol. 25, pt. 2.

———. 1922b. *The material culture of the Crow Indians*. APAMNH, vol. 21, pt. 3.

———. 1922c. *Crow Indian art*. APAMNH, vol. 21, pt. 4.

———. 1924. *Minor ceremonies of the Crow Indians*. APAMNH, vol. 21, pt. 5.

———. 1935. *The Crow Indians*. New York. (Revised, 1956.)

Maximilian, Alexander P. 1906. *Travels in the interior of North America*. In *Early western travels, 1748–1846*, vols. 22–24, Reuben G. Thwaites, ed. Cleveland.

McCleary, Timothy P. 2000. An ethnohistory of Pentecostalism among the Crow Indians of Montana. *Wicazo Sa Review*, Spring, 117–35.

Medicine Crow, Joseph. 1992. *From the heart of the Crow country: The Crow Indians' own stories*. New York.

Nabokov, Peter. 1967. *Two-Leggings: The making of a Crow warrior*. New York.

Old Horn, Dale D., and Timothy P. McCleary. 1995. *Apsaalooke social and family structure*. Crow Agency, MT.

Snell, Alma H. 2000. *Grandmother's grandchild: My Crow Indian Life*. Lincoln, NE.

Stafford, John W. 1972. *Crow culture change*. PhD dissertation, Michigan State University.

Thwaites, Reuben G., ed. 1905. *Original journals of the Lewis and Clark Expedition, 1804–1806*. Vol. 5. New York.

Voget, Fred. 1984. *The Shoshoni–Crow Sun Dance*. Norman, OK.

Wildschut, William. 1960. *Crow Indian medicine bundles*. Contributions from the Museum of the American Indian, Heye Foundation, vol. 17.

Yellowtail, Thomas. 1991. *Yellowtail: Crow medicine man and Sun Dance chief: An autobiography as told to Michael Oren Fitzgerald*. Norman, OK.

8 The Cahuilla: Gatherers in the Desert

His food gave out, his water gave out,
Leave him now, go away from him:
Isilwelnet. [enemy name]
[repeated as many times as desired]

Bury him now, plant him now:
And then they buried him, and then they planted him:
Pehuetematewilwish.

There stands the whirlwind, there stands the whirlwind
Where they burned him, where they burned him:
Puchueulchalmalmia.

Three "enemy songs" among the Desert Cahuilla
collected by Lucile Hooper (1920, 345)

A MAJOR REASON for selecting the Cahuilla to represent the California culture area is the quality of the information available about them. Yet it must be stressed that tremendous variability existed in California Indian lifeways; no individual tribe was "typical." Not only is the ethnographic and historical data about the Cahuilla superior, but over the years they have attracted inordinate Anglo-American attention. In historical context, the Cahuilla gained literary recognition in the novel *Ramona*. Once exceedingly popular, it depicts the life of a Cahuilla woman. Its author, Helen Hunt Jackson (1884), brought southern California Indians to national attention. The Palm Springs group (Agua Caliente Band) have been the focus of attention of bankers, land speculators, lawyers, municipal officials, and judges, especially in the resort city of Palm Springs; this interest has been, above all else, monetary.

Considering the course of Native American history, it might be expected that the Palm Springs Band of Cahuilla are relatively disadvantaged, but nothing could be further from reality. The land allotted to individual band members is valued at *billions of dollars*. In addition, the band owns two casinos, a spa hotel, and other tribal operations. The total assets of the 360 band members are astronomical. "Lo! the poor Indian" clearly is not a phrase that applies to these people.

Three Cahuilla subgroups are recognized: the Desert, Mountain, and Pass populations. In this chapter, the emphasis is on the Desert Cahuilla, who lived in the vicinity of Palm Springs. However, it was not always possible to determine from a source whether a specific trait was expressed in both the general desert area and at Palm Springs. As is true of most ethnographic reconstructions, this chapter does not apply in detail to a single community, but it does represent a composite for the desert dwellers.

Six thousand, or possibly fewer, Cahuilla (kuh-WE-uh) lived in the interior of southern California (see Figure 8-1). They are included in the Uto-Aztecan linguistic family, which is widely represented in the western United States and Mexico. The Cahuilla also are members of the Takic subfamily of languages.

| Aboriginal Life

Cahuilla tradition states that they originally lived in the desert but were forced to flee to adjacent mountains by a great flood, a probable reference to the emergence of the inland sea that once covered much of the present lowland and subsided about five hundred years ago. The San Jacinto and Santa Rosa mountains where they sought refuge consist of steep granite ridges and barren tablelands at medium elevations, but higher up are streams, open meadows, and forests of oak and pine. After the flood subsided, the Desert Cahuilla moved into the Coachella Valley, a desert environment in which cacti, mesquite, and screw beans were economically important plants. The region has very little precipitation, and summer temperatures may reach 120°F. Precipitation, when it does come, is often torrential and causes widespread erosion. Furthermore, severe dust storms may whip across the valley. Some sectors, particularly

Figure 8-1 | The Cahuilla area with major reservations indicated.

in the eastern part of the Desert Cahuilla range, are devoid of vegetation. The Pass Cahuilla occupied the country surrounding San Gorgonio Pass; here were open grassland and some oak groves, as well as desert areas.

ORIGIN MYTH   In the Cahuilla culture, ties with the mythological past were very important. Their well-developed origin myth is as follows. In the beginning, there was no earth or sky or anything or anybody; only a dense darkness in space. This darkness seemed alive. Something like lightning bolts seemed to pass through it and meet each other once in a while. Two substances that looked like the white of an egg came from the lightning bolts. They lay side by side in the stomach of the darkness, which resembled a spider web. These substances disappeared. They were produced again, and again they disappeared. This was called the miscarriage of the darkness. The third time they appeared, they remained, hanging there in this web in the darkness. The substances began to grow and soon were two very large eggs. When they hatched two men emerged, Mukat and Tamaioit. They were grown men from the first and could talk. As they lay there, both at the same time heard a noise like a bee buzzing; this was the song of their mother, Darkness (Hooper 1920, 317).

With this great event the natural world began to emerge as an orderly system; at least this was said to be so by the Iviatim, the descendants of Mukat and Tamaioit, who have come to be known in the ethnographic literature as the Cahuilla (Coahuillas, Kawia), a word that may have meant "masters."

Once the twin creators existed, Mukat reached into his mouth and then into his heart to remove a cricket, another insect, a lizard, and a person. These creatures were charged with driving away the darkness, but they failed. From their hearts the creators removed tobacco, pipes, and a coal to light one pipe. Mukat and Tamaioit argued over which one was born first and which was the more intelligent. Mukat became associated with making things black, and Tamaioit made forms that were white. Together they created the earth, ocean, sun, moon, people, and some plants and animals. Finally Mukat and Tamaioit disagreed so violently that Tamaioit disappeared beneath the ground, taking with him many of his creations. It was then that mountains emerged, the earth quaked, and water from the ocean overflowed, forming streams and rivers. After this Mukat lived in a big house with people and animals who had human qualities. The moon was there as a lovely female who instructed women about marriage, child rearing, and both menstrual and pregnancy taboos. Mukat, who had created her, desired to make the moon his wife. She knew this but said nothing. Since she could not marry him because he was her father, she traveled to her present home in the sky. When she was asked to return, she said nothing; she only smiled. One day, while in a humorous mood, Mukat caused the people to speak different languages. As the sun grew hot, some of these people sought shelter and were transformed into different plants and animals. Those who stayed with Mukat remained human. He told the people how to make bows and arrows and how to shoot at each other, which led to the first deaths. It was about this time, too, that the sun turned people different colors. Those people who were nearest the sun's rays became black people, those who were far away stayed white, and the Indians turned brown because they were in between.

The people became angry with Mukat after he had caused a rattlesnake to bite a friendly little man, the moon woman to leave, and people to kill one another. They decided to kill Mukat but did not know how to do it. Mukat lived in the middle of the big house and only went outside to defecate when everyone was asleep; this a white lizard discovered. One night a frog caught the feces of Mukat in his mouth, and Mukat grew ill. The shamans pretended to try to cure him, but Mukat became sicker. As he was dying, he sang songs and told the people how to conduct a mourning ceremony in memory of the dead each year. After his death, Mukat was cremated, the big house was burned, and the essence of the world was established.

MANUFACTURES AND SETTLEMENTS   In aboriginal times, clothing seems to have been nonexistent, although it is possible that women wore short skirts of plant fiber and men wore breechclouts. A more certain item of apparel was footwear, which consisted of sandals made from mescal fiber pads. Women sometimes wore flat-top basketry hats. They were tattooed on the chin, and certain men, most likely leaders, had their nasal septums pierced and a deer bone inserted in the opening. Males and females wore strings of beads in their pierced earlobes. The beads were thin curved and circular pieces of shell received in trade from the coastal regions of southern California.

Cahuilla villages usually were located near canyon mouths or in a valley where flooding was unlikely. Where water was scarce, settlements clustered near water holes or hand-dug wells. Their dwellings were substantial rectangular structures with fork-top corner posts to receive roof beams. Along the sides and on the beam tops were arranged lengths of brush held in place with horizontal poles (see Figure 8-2). On some houses the brush was smeared with mud, and a layer of dirt was added to the roof. At the front of a house was a ramada or porch constructed like a house but walled only on the windward side. A settlement included a post-and-pole bathhouse built in a shallow pit and probably covered with brush and a layer of earth. A fire was built in the fireplace, and smoke drifted from the doorway until the people were ready to bathe. Cahuilla caches were distinct. They usually were raised above the ground on a pole platform and were made by intertwining small branches; they looked very much like birds' nests some two to four feet high and were used to store plant products (see Figure 8-3). The only other structures were a brush enclosure used for ceremonies and a large enclosure walled on three sides and attached to the house of a male leader. Among the Palm Springs Cahuilla in 1925, the social and ceremonial leader occupied the dance house, which was about forty feet in diameter with walls of fitted boards and a palm-thatched roof. At the back was a room where the sacred (medicine) bundle was kept; in front of the structure was a fenced enclosure.

Figure 8-2 | Palm Springs Cahuilla homestead, ca. 1900. (Courtesy of the Southwest Museum, Los Angeles. Photo #33934.)

Figure 8-3 | A 1907 Desert Cahuilla granary. (Courtesy of the Phoebe A. Hearst Museum of Anthropology, University of California at Berkeley.)

An aboriginal house remained relatively cool even in the hottest weather. The inside was dark from soot on the walls, and natural light filtered in only through the doorway. On one side of the entrance were a woman's food-grinding stones. People the world over who collect seeds as food often used a set of stones to crush the shells. The Cahuilla spread seeds on a flat or slightly concave stone called a milling stone (metate, quern) and pulverized them using a smaller stone called a hand stone (mano, rubbing stone). On the other side of the doorway was a pottery water vessel. Toward the center of the room, fire-blackened cooking pots encircled the fireplace; at the back of the house, blankets and animal skins served as mattresses. Attached to the roof beams or in the thatch were bundles of plants or dried meat for future use. Near every house a section of log set vertically into the ground served as a mortar: the top was flat except that the center was hollowed out a foot or more in depth. A smooth pole some two feet long served as the pestle. The combination was designed to pulverize mesquite beans, an important item in the diet.

Most artifacts around a settlement were made from plant fibers. Baskets, usually fashioned by coiling, often had black geometric designs woven on the sides, the most varied cluster of forms. Among the more common styles were globular baskets used as utensils or containers for small objects and round forms for food or seed storage (see Figure 8-4). Mescal fiber nets used as carrying baskets looked like small hammocks and had loops at each end for cinching cords. A woman carrying a basket passed the cord over her forehead and rested it against the front of her basketry hat.

The only domestic animal, the dog, served as a pet and watchdog rather than an aid in hunting. The dog was not an ordinary pet because it was believed to possess certain supernatural powers. According to Cahuilla belief, dogs could

Figure 8-4 | A Cahuilla woman, Louisa Costa Rice, making baskets for the tourist trade in 1938 at the Soboba Reservation. (Photograph by Maxine and Gerald A. Smith, courtesy of the San Bernardino County Museum and A. K. Smiley Public Library, Redlands, CA.)

understand human conversation but could not speak, and like people, they had souls. In the origin myth, at the time of Mukat's death, the people had only one dog, and among the modern Desert Cahuilla, some dogs still were named after the first dog. Other dog names referred to their appearance or to some behavioral characteristic.

SUBSISTENCE ACTIVITIES   The Cahuilla identified three primary seasons: the budding of trees, hot days, and cold days. Some persons divided the year into eight more specific seasons, each associated with the development of mesquite beans. The beginning of a season arrived when a particular star appeared; this was a moment for rejoicing and a time to make preparations for an appropriate collecting activity. Star watching was especially important in the spring when food supplies might be low and edible plants were ripening. It is estimated that 80 percent of all edibles were harvested within five miles of a village.

The Desert people relied on mesquite beans as their primary staple. The most productive stands flourished near streams and along washes, but the productivity of trees varied by year, and the beans of some trees were favored over others because of their taste. Entire families participated in a harvest, with children climbing trees to dislodge bean pods from high branches. People gathered ripe pods from the ground and artificially ripened immature pods in the sun. They used upright wooden mortars with wooden pestles to grind fresh pods and produce juice for a beverage. The bulk of a harvest was cached and processed later in the year with mortars and pestles or on milling stones. Dried meal, moistened and pressed into cakes, became snacks or food for travelers. Pottery and basketry containers held loose meal that could be processed as a beverage or, more often, be prepared as a mealtime gruel. Screw beans, as an important but secondary staple, grew under the same general conditions as mesquite beans and were processed in the same manner.

Accounts about aboriginal California tribes justly identify acorns as a key staple, but they were comparatively unimportant among the Desert Cahuilla. Patriclans (families related along the male descent line) controlled acorn harvests, and specific families owned particular trees. In the fall, men climbed the trees to dislodge the acorns. Women cracked the acorns between two stones, spread the kernels out to dry for several weeks, and then pulverized them with pestles in stone mortars. To remove the bitter tannic acid, they spread the meal on a loosely woven basket or in a depression made in sand. In either case, grass or leaves were placed in the leaching basin to prevent the meal from washing away. Then they poured water repeatedly over the meal and stirred the mixture. The domestic capabilities of a woman were gauged by her skill in leaching and grinding acorn meal. Finely ground meal was made into cakes and baked in hot coals, while coarse meal was made into a gruel. Acorns that were not ground at gathering time were stored in platform caches.

In addition to the three plants cited, they harvested over one hundred additional plants as edibles. A number of specifics illustrate the diversity. A species of *Chenopodium* grew in well-watered localities. The seeds were collected, ground, and baked in cakes. One of the most important seed-producing grasses was chia, a member of the sage family. They used a seed beater to dislodge the seeds from the whorls onto a flat basket. The seeds were parched and ground to be baked into cakes or mixed with water to make a nourishing drink. When the century plants or agave of the canyons produced stalks, the stalks and "cabbages" were roasted in sand pits heated with stones. To this list of foods could be added many others, but the examples cited suggest the broad range of plants collected and the varied means of food preparation.

Contrary to expectations, the overwhelming emphasis on plant foods did not mean that hunting was neglected nor that the inventory of weapons and traps was impoverished. Adult males trapped animals and also stalked, chased, and intercepted them. The principal weapon was a shaft (self) bow with a plant fiber bowstring. The arrowshafts were vaned with split feathers, and shafts simply sharpened at the point probably were meant for birds and small game. Arrows with cane shafts and wooden arrow points probably were used against large game and enemies; some arrows apparently were tipped with poisons made from rattlesnake venom and other toxic substances. Another weapon was the nonreturning boomerang, commonly called a throwing stick when reported in western North America. It was a flat, curved piece of wood thrown at birds and small game. Hunters also used calls and decoys to lure game near enough to kill with arrows. Additional facilities for taking game included nets set along trails, deadfalls, and snares. Hunting was surrounded by numerous restrictions. For example, the Desert Cahuilla regarded mountain lions and grizzly bears as having powerful spirits and avoided killing them. When a mule deer was killed, people gathered to sing all night and eat the deer the following morning. In general, a man or boy did not consume any of the animals that he killed. Rabbits, squirrels, and wood rats taken by a young boy in a communal hunt usually were given to his mother's family. The kills of an adult male were given alternately to his own family and to his wife's family.

DESCENT, KINSHIP, AND MARRIAGE Many people around the world placed particular stress on either the male *or* female lines to identify their nearest relatives (unilineal descent). As noted in the previous chapter, the Crow emphasized descent traced through females (matrilineal descent). The Cahuilla, however, stressed the male line (a patrilineal descent system). A married couple resided with or near the husband's family (patrilocal marriage residence). A typical Cahuilla settlement centered around a group of males who traced their descent to a *known* common ancestor (patrilineage). Closely related patrilineages with a *presumed* common ancestor composed a larger unit (patriclan), which was the landowning political unit.

In the kinship terminology, a male distinguished among his older and younger male and female siblings and made similar distinctions between his father's brothers and mother's sisters. He employed still other terms for his father's sisters and mother's brothers; these did not take relative age into consideration. A male referred to his father's older brother's and his mother's older sister's son and daughter by the same term as for his older brothers and sisters. Similarly, he referred to the son and daughter of his father's younger brother and mother's younger sister by the same terms as for his younger brothers and sisters. In essence, parallel cousins (children of father's brother and mother's sister) were termed the same as siblings, with the same age distinction as for siblings. For cross-cousins (father's sister's and mother's brother's children), the male–female kin terms were the same but different from those for siblings or parallel cousins. This cousin terminology is of the Iroquois type, while the terms on the first ascending generation are bifurcate collateral. The Iroquois cousin terms make particular sense since moiety exogamy (marriage outside each of the two basic tribal subdivisions) existed. Thus certain near relatives, such as father's brother's children and mother's sister's children, were of one's own moiety and reasonably called brother and sister. Cross-cousins, on the other hand, were of a different moiety and termed differently, but in spite of the terminological difference one could not marry a cross-cousin (see Figure 8-5).

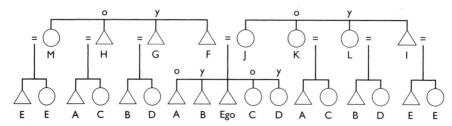

Figure 8-5 | The early historic Cahuilla system of kinship terminology.

SOCIAL DIMENSIONS In the Cahuilla origin myth, Mukat and Tamaioit were associated with the wildcat and coyote, respectively, and all Cahuilla identified with one or the other of these groups (moieties). Among the Desert Cahuilla, the Wildcat moiety included eight clans, and the Coyote moiety consisted of ten clans. In aboriginal times the members of each clan theoretically occupied a single settlement, but in actual fact, persons from a number of clans might live in one settlement. We may presume that at one time all the members of a patriclan lived in a single village. As their number increased and they could not support themselves at the village site, the surplus, most likely members of a junior patrilineage, formed a new village or joined another clan at its settlement. A clan section or patrilineage founding a new village might eventually become so populous that it qualified as a clan, with its own name and leader, or clan "chief," called a *net*. The office of net usually passed from father to eldest son (primogeniture), and it included extremely important obligations. Nets lived in dwellings with dance houses attached and were the trustees of sacred clan bundles. A net directed subsistence activities, settled conflicts between members, represented the clan before other clans, and was responsible for the correct performance of ceremonies.

In sum, the core population of a village consisted of small family groups related through male lines descending from a known common ancestor (patrilineage). In the same settlement might be the members of other patrilineages assumed to have had a common male ancestor (patriclan). Moiety exogamy prevailed, which meant that a Wildcat was obligated to marry a Coyote and vice versa. Persons in opposite moieties maintained a joking relationship and friendly rivalry, along with economic and ritual obligations.

POLITICAL LIFE Hereditary leaders did not exist above the clan level, and in instances in which the activities of one clan impinged on those of another, the differences were resolved by the nets in council. Decisions of a clan as a collectivity were made by the net, who ideally was a man of exceptional abilities. A net was required to know the boundaries of all clan lands, all clan traditions, and a broad range of esoteric facts important to the clan's viability; he also was expected to be a good orator and fair-minded. He did not possess more material property than anyone else, but families presented him with the initial harvest (first fruit) of any plant, which was partial compensation for the time he devoted to clan activities. At the rear of the net's house was a small room in which sacred objects, termed the "heart" of the clan, were kept. Eagle, hawk, and owl feathers were a vital part of each sacred bundle. Clearly, the net, as conveyer of clan knowledge and guardian of the most sacred clan objects, was the paramount leader.

A second important political and religious functionary was the *paha*. His role existed only in certain localities, and his exact duties have not been reported in detail. Apparently, where the office existed, the paha was primarily responsible for ceremonial preparations and the maintenance of order on such occasions. In addition, he was a leader of hunting parties and a spokesman and messenger for a net. Upon his death he was replaced by a son or another close male relative.

Formalized warfare or even feuds with neighboring ethnic groups were rare. To the east the desert area had no permanent occupants as far as the Colorado River; here the aggressive Mohave and Yuma lived. The Cahuilla feared these tribes, although trade with them was limited. The intervening desert was an effective barrier to intensive contacts. The Chemehuevi, who lived to the east along the Colorado River and into the deserts of California, were friendly with the Desert Cahuilla. The southern neighbors of the Desert Cahuilla were the Kumeyaay, but contacts with these people have not been described in any detail and are assumed to have been infrequent.

RELIGION Shamans were responsible for dealing with intermittent disaster and personal trauma, while the net and paha guided ceremonies focusing on the life cycle and belief system. The Eagle-Killing Ceremony belongs to the latter category and was a highlight in religious life.

The Eagle-Killing Ceremony symbolized the continuity of a lineage. According to Cahuilla belief, the eagle was one of the species originally created by Mukat. It was said that the eagle lived forever, and by permitting itself to be "killed" by people it assured them of life after death. Thus, although lineage members died, the lineage would continue as had the eagle as a species. Furthermore, the flight of the eagle symbolized the magical course of shamans when they led human souls to the land of the dead. The ceremony also provided a means of obtaining eagle feathers, essential for replacing ceremonial artifacts that had worn out, been destroyed, or exchanged in previous rituals.

In the higher country controlled by some clans, eagles' nests were closely watched by a clan member. This person notified the others of the clan when the eggs had been laid. A feast was then held, and after the nestlings were well feathered, one was removed and raised in a cage by the net's family. After the bird had grown, festivities were held with the members of a neighboring clan or clans as guests. At the appointed time, special songs were sung about the death of eagles, and dances were performed. The climax came after the eagle was rolled into a ceremonial mat held by the close family members of the net. They danced with the encased eagle and at dawn the bird screeched and died; it probably was gradually squeezed. The bird was skinned, and the net kept the feathered skin in the sacred clan bundle. Some feathers might be made into a ceremonial skirt, and others were kept to adorn images during the Mourning Ceremony.

Among the Desert group the status of a shaman was not hereditary, and a number of practitioners might belong to a single clan. A shaman often was a man who had been ill frequently as a child, and the healer who treated him had become aware of the child's potential as a curer, magician, and seer. As a young man the novice dreamed of a song that became a tangible manifestation of his inordinate powers. Mukat was responsible, in Cahuilla belief, for implanting the dreams and guardian spirits identified with shamans. A novice danced before the people of his clan for three nights and afterward was qualified to pursue his calling. In his dreams, and from other shamans, he eventually learned additional songs, dances, feats of magic, and bewitching methods. In his dreams, too, a shaman learned of herbal cures for particular ailments or, at other times, of harmful or curative spells. Certain creatures, such as the coyote, fox, humming-bird, and owl, were considered to be messengers who brought shamans warnings of impending illness. When not drawing on his pharmacopoeia, the shaman attempted to cure by sucking on the afflicted part of a patient's body. Reputedly, he removed the disease object without breaking the skin. Only a few plants were used in curing, despite the Cahuilla's extensive botanical knowledge and their many uses of plants as food. As a youth a shaman did not receive compensation for his services; but as he grew older and became established, he would charge a fee.

If a shaman became malevolent, he posed a threat to the community. In the latter part of the nineteenth century, one old man was considered the world's most powerful shaman. When shamans exhibited their skills, he always performed last and challenged the others to kill him. None was able to do so because he was protected by spirits on all sides. Finally, the old shaman was told by a man of a different clan to stop killing people. The man who gave the warning was soon struck by a "pain" that no shaman could remove, and he died. Everyone knew that the old shaman was responsible. A man from the shaman's clan and men from other clans met and decided that he must be killed. The executioner was to be the net of another clan because he was strong and brave. This man and another visited the sorcerer and were invited to spend the night. After everyone else was asleep, the net crushed the old man's skull with a stone pestle. At the head of the victim's bed were found a variety of small feathers and the skin of a gopher snake, objects used by the old man to make pains. As they were trampled into the ground, a thunderlike sound was heard. In the morning people came to view the body, and later the same morning the body and the house were burned. This is one of the rare recorded instances in which collective action was taken for the good of all the people.

LIFE CYCLE   At critical times during an individual's life, he or she followed numerous rules, and one of these periods was pregnancy. A future mother refrained from eating any more than necessary; she drank only warm water, ate very little meat, and consumed no salt. In Cahuilla belief, if a pregnant woman ate fruit pecked by a bird, her infant would have sores; if she ate meat from the legs of game, a breech presentation would result; but if she was industrious when pregnant, her offspring would be energetic. These were but three of the rules to insure a safe delivery and a normal offspring. As soon as a woman gave birth and expelled the placenta, she lay in a specially prepared trough dug in the floor of a house. The depression was lined with hot sand, and after the woman stretched out, more hot sand was piled over her body. Here she remained for about ten days, leaving the trough only to urinate and defecate, to have the sand reheated, and to be bathed with hot water each morning. During the month following parturition, the mother remained subject to food taboos, and the father could eat no foods containing salt. A nursing mother did not have sexual intercourse with her husband, for to do so was thought to spoil her milk. She was the object of teasing if she weaned her infant early.

The naming of a child was enmeshed in ritual. After a number of children had been born into a clan, the parents began accumulating food and wealth for a formal naming ceremony. This meant that a child was between four and twelve years of age before he or she was named. A child who had not been named by the age of thirteen would always be known by a nickname. The ceremony was in the father's clan dance house with the couple's clans represented. Female names most often referred to plants or artifacts, whereas males tended to be named after animals, birds, or insects. Amidst singing and dancing, the net held up a child and shouted his or her name three times; the name was repeated by the audience. To prevent an "enemy" clan from learning a child's true name, a disgraceful revelation, and incorporating it in their songs, a net might not say the child's real name. In these instances, a false name would be shouted and the true name revealed in secret. After the namings, food and gifts were distributed to the guests to conclude the ceremony.

When a Desert girl approached adolescence, she was tattooed by her mother's sister as guests from the operator's clan watched. The tattoos were made with cactus thorns pricked in straight or angled lines from the lower lip to the chin, and black paint was rubbed into the wounds. At this time the earlobes of a girl were pierced. When a girl menstruated for the first time, the net summoned the clan of the girl's mother to a ceremony that began in the evening. A fire was built before the net's house to heat the ground, and afterward a trough was dug. The girl was placed in the depression, and her body was covered with hot sand. Throughout the night the members of the girl's clan danced and sang around the pit. In the morning the girl was removed, bathed in warm water, and her head covered with a white paint. For the next three weeks she was subject to food taboos very much like those surrounding pregnancy. The girl stayed in or near the house, and she scratched her head with a special implement rather than her fingernails to prevent her hair from dropping out.

Subsequent menstrual periods were surrounded by the same taboos, and in addition, a married woman was forbidden to touch her husband when she was menstruating. The good health of a couple supposedly depended on how well the woman obeyed these rules.

Some Desert Cahuilla do not appear to have initiated adolescent males, but an appropriate ceremony occurred at Palm Springs. Boys between the ages of ten and eighteen were selected by elders for initiation and taken to a brush enclosure outside the dance house. The boys were secluded there for five days and saw only those persons who brought them special foods. Throughout three nights the old people danced until morning. The climax came on the fourth night when the initiates were brought out and given a drink of cooked jimsonweed, or *toloache* as it is known in Spanish. After taking it, the boys danced briefly, but they became dizzy and were placed in a corner while the older people continued to dance. The following evening the effects of the jimsonweed had worn off, and for the next five nights the boys were taught how to dance, sing particular songs, and behave correctly as adults. This ceremony seems to have symbolized the initiates' death as children and their rebirth as knowledgeable adults. The only forms of body mutilation among males were piercing the ears and the nasal septum. The latter operation was not common and was performed only on young boys with promise as leaders. In the opening at the base of the nose pieces of deer bone were inserted.

When members of different clans assembled, especially for the tattooing of a girl or the piercing of a boy's nasal septum, songs known as enemy songs might be sung. Between clans, especially those geographically removed from one another, a rivalry of unknown origins existed. Members of competing clans composed derisive songs in which they incorporated the personal names of individuals in rival clans. These names had been bestowed by a net in secret, and the fact that they were known to the members of other clans was shameful. First one clan performed and then the other, with victory going to the side mentioning the most names of rivals and heaping the greatest abuse or to the clan whose members were physically able to sing longer. Enemy songs were an obvious means for giving vent to aggressive behavior in a socially approved manner. (These were not comparable to the dueling songs sung by two hostile Eskimos in some sectors of the Arctic.) The joking relationship between moiety members served the same purpose in a friendlier atmosphere.

The Desert Cahuilla marriage pattern included not only moiety exogamy but a prohibition against seeking a spouse from known relatives on either side of the family. Since genealogies were remembered for about five generations, one could marry a distant cousin in the opposite moiety. A thirteen-year-old girl was most likely to wed a man of eighteen from a nearby community. The match was arranged by parents, and after the formalities had been settled, the bride was led into the groom's house (patrilocal residence). She sat facing a corner with her back to the assembled relatives of the groom. The groom then sat next to the girl, and the couple was given food as the boy's relatives ate. When the feasting was over, the couple was considered married, and that night the newlyweds were given a single blanket with the theory that if affection did not bring them together the cold desert night would. A girl who was unhappy in the home of her in-laws might return to her mother's home, but if she did this repeatedly, the presents that had been given were returned and the marriage considered dissolved. The groom and his parents had the right to expect the bride to bear an offspring within two or three years. Failure to do so might annul the marriage and again mean a return of the wedding presents. A man could, if the woman's parents agreed, receive a younger sister of his wife if the latter died (sororate). It was less common for a woman to marry her deceased husband's brother (levirate). Among these people monogamy was the prevailing form of marriage, and familial relationships appear to have been quite stable.

Of all the forms of entertainment, the hand game, called *peon,* played at secular gatherings and during ceremonies was most popular. A team from one village competed against one from another settlement. The goal was for a member of the opposite team to guess which clenched fist held a small bone. Bets were made, and shamans aided their respective sides while women sang at certain times during the game. A mediator kept a fire burning by which the game was played, held the stakes, and settled disputes. A particular game ended when one side had lost all the peons of the four players or had won a series of tally sticks. Then a new game was started, and new stakes were put up. Peon was frequently played throughout the night, and as one player tired, he was replaced by another (see also Chapter 2).

Other games included races between two groups of men. Each group kicked a wooden ball for several miles and then back again to the starting point. The men on each team took turns kicking the ball, and the team that finished first was the winner. Another race took place on the night of a new moon. The first boy to see the moon would call the others, and they would race to a spot where they could swim. After swimming they raced home, and by so doing they supposedly brought good luck in the coming month. Cat's cradles were made by persons of both sexes. This skill had supernatural implications, since the people believed that before a person's spirit could pass into the world of other spirits, it was required to make string figures.

In the routine of adult life, a woman was the outsider in the extended family household of her husband. The husband and wife were expected to be reserved in the presence of others, and the wife generally was retiring when with her in-laws or around men. Ideally, younger persons were thoughtful and unselfish in their dealings with older persons; these values were instilled in children when they were small. Young boys who hunted or collected the first plant products of the season were expected to take them to the aged (see Figure 8-6). The most respected men were nets, pahas, shamans, and outstanding hunters. Women gained the greatest recognition by being curers and as efficient workers.

In early times, death brought immediate destruction of a Cahuilla household: on the morning following the death of a person, the body of the deceased and the house in which the death had occurred were burned. In later times,

Figure 8-6 | Pasqual, a Cahuilla man said to be ninety years old, circa 1890. (Courtesy of the San Bernardino County Museum and A. K. Smiley Public Library, Redlands, CA.)

however, this pattern was modified. When an individual died, the members of his or her and other clans assembled, bringing presents. The body was washed, dressed, and taken to the clan dance house of the deceased. Here the assembled mourners sang over the body throughout the night. If a man had died, the creation narrative was sung; for a woman, a song about the moon was sung, since it was the moon who had originally instructed women. The body was burned the morning following death, and within a week the person's house and possessions were burned.

In the Cahuilla life cycle, a ritual focus on death dominated, not for the cremation of a body but in an annual Mourning Ceremony, their most notable religious observance. In the fall or winter each clan held a seven-day ceremony for persons who had died after the ceremony of the previous year. Months of preparations by a clan net, paha, and other members preceded the event, especially to accumulate food and gifts for the guests. Relatives of a specific clan related to the deceased by marriage arrived, bearing gifts, on a particular night to avoid overcrowding. The commemoration included a narration of the origin myth in which Mukat described the creation of the world and the proper death rituals. During the opening three nights, shamans of the host and other clans sought to communicate with the spirits of the honored dead. In this context a performing shaman commonly placed live coals in his mouth and appeared to swallow them (see Figure 8-7). Throughout the next two nights, the singing of clan songs dominated.

The following night, singers, aided by relatives of the deceased, prepared images of the dead. Nearly life-size figures of reed mat construction were

Figure 8-7 | A Cahuilla shaman, Salvador Lopez, with a live coal from a wood fire in his mouth, photographed in 1963. (Courtesy of the Phoebe A. Hearst Museum of Anthropology, University of California at Berkeley.)

adorned with deerskins. A female figure included baskets decorated with eagle feathers. A male image required an eagle-feather headdress and a bow and arrows. At sunrise on the final day, guests ate and received presents from their hosts. The rituals climaxed in a procession by surviving relatives, who carried the images to a spot near the clan dance house. Somewhat later the images were burned, releasing the souls of the deceased and ending the period of mourning; the names of the honored dead ceased to be used. The rituals concluded as each guest received a string of shell beads from the hosts.

The evidence for the presence of human souls took varied forms. They believed that souls found expression in dreams, and when someone fainted, they inferred that that person's soul was wandering. Similarly, a person might become ill if his or her soul became wayward, and the intervention of a shaman became necessary to return the person's soul to the body. They also believed that the soul left the body months before death. After death a spirit or soul sought passage between the clapping mountains created by Mukat and was questioned by a deathless guardian. The spirits of those who had lived by Mukat's rules passed unharmed beyond the clapping mountains. Those who failed became bats, butterflies, trees, or rocks.

| Historic Changes

The Cahuilla are often classified as Mission Indians, which is not an entirely accurate label. They were not subject to the mission environment in the manner of coastal Indians in southern California, and most Cahuilla had only indirect contact with Roman Catholic missionaries. Neither Pedro Fages in 1772 nor Juan Bautista de Anza in 1774, the first Europeans in the region, made any known impact on these Indians. In 1819 a mission outpost (*rancho*) was founded in the San Bernardino area, but it was not until Mexico secured independence from Spain in 1821 that the interior of southern California began to attract attention. After the San Bernardino rancho was secularized in 1834, it passed into the private ownership of ranchers. The rancho was sacked and burned by marauding Mohave, Paiute, and Yuma in raids on the cattle and horses of the ranchers. Cahuilla participation appears to have been minor. Then in 1847 the United States acquired California. Mormon settlers and Anglo ranchers soon became the dominant outsiders. The Cahuilla were left largely to themselves. Continuing raids for livestock by other Indians, however, led to general hostility among whites toward all Indians of the region.

In 1850 the U.S. Congress sent a special commission to California to negotiate treaties with Native Americans and assign them lands. A treaty arranged in 1852 set aside an area about forty miles long and thirty miles wide for the Cahuilla. The U.S. Senate, however, refused to ratify any of the eighteen treaties with California Indians. Congressional resistance stemmed from a number of factors: the commissioners had committed the government to spend a great deal of money; white Californians vigorously opposed the treaties; and it was thought that some of these lands might contain gold.

In 1852 Edward F. Beale was appointed superintendent of Indian affairs in California, and a report about Indians in the southern part of the state was prepared, possibly by Benjamin Hays. The report noted that numerous members of other nearby tribes were living among the Desert Cahuilla. The elders and many others spoke Spanish by this time. The Indians worked as underpaid laborers and domestics on the ranchos of whites and were frequently intoxicated. The report pointed out that under Spanish law the Indians had rights to their settlements and pasture lands, and in theory the State of California recognized Indian land rights. The report characterized state laws as "*All* punishment. *No* reform!" With congressional authorization in 1853, Beale established a small, short-lived reservation at Tejon between the San Joaquin Valley and Los Angeles. This appears to have been *the beginning of the modern reservation system.* It was not, however, until 1858 that setting land aside for Native Americans became a general federal policy.

In the mid-1850s, Cahuilla men reportedly numbered about thirty-five hundred, including many non-Cahuilla Indians, but they far outnumbered the local white settlers. At the same time leaders among the Cahuilla strived to protect tribal interests in dealing with whites. Leaders such as Juan Antonio and Cabeson, for example, represented their people in the failed treaty of 1852. These Indians were discontented after the federal government failed to set land aside for their exclusive use; they complained that they had not received farm equipment as promised and that whites were trespassing and squatting on traditional Indian lands, as well as taking water and wood. Then in 1863, and again in 1870, devastating smallpox epidemics struck, killing a large but unknown number of Cahuilla. These epidemics destroyed their previous cultural vitality at a time when whites were becoming far more numerous among them and increasingly dominant. Throughout the latter part of the nineteenth century, some Cahuilla worked on the ranches of whites, the men often as cowboys and the women as domestics. The men also tended orchards and vineyards, cut mesquite wood, and labored at salt works. When the Southern Pacific Railroad was being built through the area in the 1870s, they were employed as laborers. They continued to collect products of the desert and farmed some of the better-watered localities.

By the 1870s the cultural norms of the people were moving in new directions. The rule of moiety exogamy declined, and money was substituted for the gifts formerly presented to a bride's family. A girl's family received thirty dollars around 1900, but a generation later a female infant scornfully was termed "a paper," meaning a marriage license that no longer brought a gift. By 1925 clan ownership of farmland remained the rule, but the amount of arable land was small because water was scarce. Changes in dwelling forms were notable because frame houses had replaced the aboriginal type; a frame house was not burned until three members of a household had died. In the desert, a clan dance house continued to be occupied by a net and his family, but it looked different from the houses of old because the roof now was pitched like that of a shed.

Ceremonial life reflected reintegration during the same period. A major shift occurred as unrelated ceremonies were combined with the Mourning Ceremony into a fiesta week. For example, among the Pass Cahuilla in the late 1880s, the Eagle-Killing Ceremony was joined with the Mourning Ceremony; the eagle feathers were used to decorate the images, which were burned two days later. In aboriginal times the people had cremated their dead; under Spanish, Mexican, and Anglo-American influence, they began to bury the dead. Interment sometimes included placing food, clothing, and bedding with the body in the hope that these things would be useful to the spirit if it did not soon find a permanent resting place. Changes in the Mourning Ceremony included dressing the images in manufactured clothing, such as hats and veils. Indian-owned lunch counters sold food and coffee to participants and observers. By 1931 the Mourning Ceremony at Palm Springs had become biennial and was held by alternating clans for the dead of the two previous years. Among the Desert Cahuilla, one of the last nets died in 1958. He had directed local ceremonial life, but when he died, the ceremonial structure, his house, and all of the ceremonial equipment were burned, an end not only to his life but also to the net ceremonials. Today most Cahuilla are Roman Catholic. Funerals continue to be an important rite of passage, however, and at death some personal possessions of an individual are burned as traditional Cahuilla songs are sung.

In the 1990s reservation lands best symbolized Cahuilla identity and their Indianness. In a broader cultural context, some Cahuilla, possibly most youth, were not taught traditional cultural ways, and many were uninterested in their Native American background. Those elders who have such an interest find it difficult to convey to the younger generations. Most Cahuilla no longer speak their language. Their distinct craft skills have declined, but a revival may be emerging. They have not had a ceremonial house since the early 1960s. The last shaman died in 1984, but one woman had learned the ceremonial songs, and she carries out part of the old religious tradition into the present.

The Agua Caliente Band

In the course of Desert Cahuilla history, especially for the Palm Springs Band, land rights have been a dominant theme since the late 1860s. In 1875 the Agua Caliente (Palm Springs) and Cahuilla reservations were established as slight yet meaningful recognition of the plight of these and other Indians in southern California. In 1881 Helen Hunt Jackson published a book entitled *A Century of Dishonor,* a scathing indictment of the treatment of American Indians. Because of her crusading interest in Indians, she was retained to report to the commissioner of Indian affairs about the Indians of southern California. She conducted her study with Abbott Kinney, and their report, partly a chronicle of wrongs against Indians and partly a series of recommendations, was submitted in 1883. This study did not make the impact on Indian policy that Jackson felt was essential, and so she decided to write a novel about the plight of these people. As a novel, *Ramona* was highly successful. It has appeared in at least three hundred English editions. Yet it failed to bring about the reforms Jackson advocated, although it called attention to much that was wrong and helped stimulate reforms in the 1890s (see Figure 8-8).

EARLY LAND DISPUTES   The problem of Palm Springs Indian land rights is complex, and the most critical legal developments must at least be summarized. The modern reservation, created in 1896 under the Mission Indian Relief Act of 1891, set aside thirty-two thousand acres in essentially a checkerboard pattern in and around the town of Palm Springs. The act was based on the Dawes Act of 1887, and the keystone of this act was the allotment of reservation lands to family heads. After twenty-five years an allottee could in theory receive a fee patent to the land and become the legal owner. Allotments were first issued in 1923, and the land per family was limited to 160 acres. Allotments were made irrespective of whether or not the band members agreed with the idea of dividing land into individual parcels. Furthermore, the allotments were not of comparable value. In 1927 allotments were made only to Indians who requested them; nearly half of the members made requests. These allotments consisted not of 160-acre parcels but of packages of a 5-acre parcel of irrigable land, a 40-acre parcel of dry land, and a 2-acre lot in the town of Palm Springs. The 1927 allotments were not approved by the federal government. Meanwhile, the Indian Reorganization Act of 1934 opposed allotments, and the Indians took legal action in the 1930s to force allotment approval. The Indian legal battle reached the U.S. Supreme Court, and in a subsequent decision in 1946 allotments were declared valid. Some allotments were approved in 1949.

Figure 8-8 | The Cahuilla woman Ramona Lubo at her home, probably photographed around 1900. Her life was fictionalized in the novel *Ramona* by Helen Hunt Jackson. (Courtesy of the Southwest Museum, Los Angeles. Photo #24329.)

The ones that were unapproved involved conflicting claims; finally, however, selections were approved for the entire band.

One of the suits involving allotments resulted in a 1950 court decision that allotted lands should be of *approximately equal value,* since this was the original intent of the law. The allotment values, based on 1949 estimates, ranged from about $17,000 to $165,000, with a total value of lands allotted and pending allotment being about $7.4 million. To equalize the allotments, the BIA proposed that a tribal corporation be created and all tribal assets conveyed to it. A bill in 1957 before Congress in essence established a liquidation corporation that could have ended the tribal identity of the Cahuilla involved. It was rejected by Congress.

In 1959 two new bills were introduced in Congress, and these became law. The major provisions of one of them, the equalization bill, were that (1) allotments would be made to all band members who had not received them, but no future-born members would receive allotments; (2) equalizations would be made on the basis of 1957–58 appraised land values, and the cemeteries, Roman Catholic church, hot springs, and certain canyons were to remain tribal reserves not subject to allotment, but all other lands were to be allotted regardless of prior acreage limitations and in proportion to the highest monetary value of the prior allotments. The second bill provided that reservation lands could be leased for a period not exceeding ninety-nine years except for grazing land, which could be leased for not more than ten years. The 1957–58 allotment appraisals ranged from approximately $75,000 to $630,000, in contrast with the 1949 appraisal range of $17,000 to $165,000. Obviously, the land was rapidly becoming fantastically valuable. Even with the passage of the first bill, it was impossible to equalize the allotments fully. Some 80 percent of the band obtained allotments valued at not less than $335,000; the remaining 20 percent of the allotments had values in excess of $335,000. Most of the land was still in trust status by 1962 and thus was not producing income. However, changes in leasing laws made it likely that over the next ten years individuals would derive considerable profit from it. The first large leasing enterprise was the Palm Springs Spa complex at the hot springs. The spa was completed in 1960 at a cost of $1.8 million, and an adjacent hotel, also on Indian land, was completed in 1963. In 1961 the City of Palm Springs purchased lands allotted to eight Cahuilla adults and twenty-two Cahuilla children for $2,979,000, which was shared by the allottees.

WOMEN'S LEADERSHIP ROLE   A notable aspect of all the Palm Springs land disputes is the leadership role assumed successfully by women. When the issues were coming to a climax in 1957, the band included only thirty-two adults and sixty-four minors. At that time there were ten adult men and twenty-two women; of the men, two were in the U.S. Navy, two were over seventy years of age, and two were incapable of handling their own affairs. At this point only two courses of action were possible: either the band could trust the BIA and its lawyer to handle its business affairs completely or the women could assume the role of leaders. The Cahuilla decided to pursue the latter alternative. Aboriginal sociopolitical life had set no precedent for female leadership, except that a woman did occasionally hold an office in trust for a son and old women sometimes were very active in clan ceremonies. The net was always a man, and in the early historic period whites appointed some Indian men to act as intermediaries and later as reservation leaders. These persons often seem to have been clan leaders. A differential rate of adaptation for women and men appears to have developed. Many of the men continued to follow a "collecting" pattern in their economic activities; they worked only sporadically as grape pickers, cowboys, woodcutters, or railroad laborers. In their jobs they interacted most often with other Indians, not whites. Women, by contrast, often worked as domestics in the homes of whites and therefore became much more familiar with the new ways. This was possibly an important reason why women could become the stable core around which the society was reorganized. In 1935 a woman became secretary to the band business committee, and by 1954 an all-woman tribal council had been elected, with Vyola Olinger as chairperson. Mrs. Olinger, who was an active member of the band, was an apt choice. She was intelligent, articulate, and hardworking. Although distrustful of the bureau agents, she

Figure 8-9 | The all-woman Palm Springs Tribal Council in 1955. From left to right are Eileen Miguel, La Verne Saubel, Gloria Gillette, Elizabeth Monk, and Vyola Olinger. (Courtesy of the Agua Caliente Cultural Museum.)

managed to work successfully with them. This was the first all-woman tribal council in the United States, and they resolved the major land disputes with the City of Palm Springs. In 1961 a young man was elected to the council, and this brought an end to the era of all-female political dominance, but it was the women who had handled the vital issue (see Figure 8-9).

ISSUES IN THE 1960S By the early 1960s a small group of determined Indians had gained a settlement, and seemingly the avarice of whites had become just another episode in our blemished past; justice had prevailed. Alas, it was not to endure. In 1967, George Ringwald, a reporter for the *Daily Enterprise* of Riverside, California, wrote a series of articles about the administration of Palm Springs Cahuilla lands and funds. He demonstrated beyond any doubt that greedy whites still were taking grossly unfair advantage of Indians. Among the individuals involved in the immoral and often illegal handling of Palm Springs Cahuilla affairs were BIA personnel, a Superior Court judge, a municipal judge, a former mayor of Palm Springs, a Palm Springs real estate broker, and a host of attorneys-at-law. As a result of Ringwald's journalism the BIA was forced to conduct an investigation into the system of court-appointed guardians and conservators for Indians. It was demonstrated, for example, that a municipal judge and one attorney had, over a seven-year period, collected $485,000 in fees. From 1956 to 1967, approximately 40 percent of the $10.8 million received by eighty-four estates had gone to conservators, guardians, or their attorneys under the supervision of the Riverside County Superior Court. Congressional action in 1968 put an end to the conservator and guardian management of these valuable lands.

A fair-minded person would hope that Palm Springs Indian problems with the BIA, some local developers, and city officials would have ended by the 1960s, but such was not the case. When Palm Springs incorporated as a city in 1938, its governing body included Indian land as part of the city without consulting the Indian owners. The city passed zoning ordinances and a master plan that included control over Indian land in the city. The Palm Springs Indians in turn formed a zoning commission and prepared their own zoning ordinances that did not agree with those of the city. In 1966 the Indians won a judgment against the city with reference to zoning procedures, but by 1972 the city had not made the required modifications. The Indians initiated further zoning litigation, in which they accused the city of preventing the development of Indian land and thereby decreasing its value. The issue finally was settled in 1977 when the U.S. Supreme Court decided, in another case, that neither the state nor its political subdivisions could regulate Indian trust lands.

THE MODERN SCENE   To enhance the value of the land owned collectively by band members, the Agua Caliente Development Authority was formed in 1989, a major administrative innovation. BIA managers in Palm Springs play a major role in leasing land belonging to the band. Their office, the only one in the country funded entirely by the Indians involved, supervised residential and commercial leases as well as the development of Indian land, which comprises about ten square miles in scattered plots within Palm Springs—more land than is held by any other single landowner in the city, about 6,700 acres. Yet the Indians remain confronted with a major problem: allotments and their equity. After allotments were made to 131 band members, the available land for allotments was exhausted. As a result, those band members born after 1959 have no land allotments except by inheritance. Their greatest hope for financial gain is to share in the profits from the development of land held by the band collectively. By the 1980s most original allotments had been sold or subdivided among heirs, so that individual plots tended to be small and scattered. Since developers prefer large land units, numerous owners of small adjacent allotments must agree to the joint lease or sale of their holdings. In the 1990s major developments included the Marquis Hotel and the Canyon Country Club. Above all else, a casino was opened in downtown Palm Springs in 1995 (see Figure 8-10). They also built a second casino in 1999 at nearby Rancho Mirage, closer to Interstate I-10, at a cost of $80 million.

After the federal Indian Gaming Regulation Act became law in 1988, the State of California made it difficult for federally recognized tribes to build or

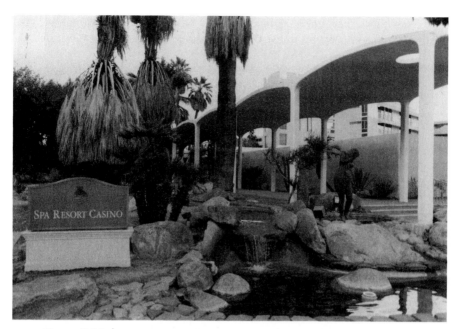

Figure 8-10 | The Spa Resort Casino of the Agua Caliente Band in Palm Springs as it appeared in 2004.

expand casinos. A major reason the state no longer cooperated with tribes was the successful lobbying of Nevada gambling interests. Reportedly, in the mid-1990s about one-third of Nevada casino patrons came from California to spend over $7 billion each year. Despite this opposition, the Palm Springs Cahuilla were able to open their initial casino. In 1998 California Indians sought to change the laws regarding casinos in a statewide ballot measure that passed but was declared unconstitutional by the state courts. A constitutional amendment would be required for Indians to gain greater control of casino activities. Ballot Proposition 1A, the Indian Self-Reliance initiative, was approved by 69 percent of voters in 2000. Highlights of 1A include giving Native Americans the exclusive right to operate gaming in California. A tribe was permitted two thousand slot machines and must share a percentage of the profits with noncasino tribes in the state. Furthermore, casino tribes became obligated to pay "a fair share" to the state, which typically was from 10 to 18 percent of the revenues from slot machines, the most profitable aspect of Indian casino operations.

The emphatic statewide voter support for Indian casinos represented by Proposition 1A abruptly eroded within a few years. When Gray Davis was governor in 2003, he hoped to obtain at least $1.5 billion from casinos to help balance the state budget. In the Davis recall election in 2003, most casino tribes staunchly supported Lieutenant Governor Cruz Bustamante as the new governor, but he was soundly defeated by Arnold Schwarzenegger, who promised to pressure casino tribes to share more of their earnings with the state.

The most prominent Palm Springs Cahuilla band leader, Richard Milanovich, formulated an initiative, Proposition 70, which was supported by most casino tribes for the November 2004 ballot. The goal was to prevent the state government from playing a greater role in new casino compacts, as evident in the paragraph to follow. Proposition 70 sanctioned 99-year compacts, extended the variety of games (e.g., roulette), and eliminated tribal limits on the number of slot machines per casino. A key provision was for casino tribes to pay the same state tax rate as other corporations (8.84 percent). The response of Governor Schwarzenegger was clearly negative. One reason was the casino tribe opposition to his election in the Davis recall ballot. In a public statement about the proposition in San Diego, Schwarzenegger said, "Indians are ripping us off," and he made other negative comments about casino Indians. Casino tribes in turn spent more than $21 million to support the proposition. However, the ballot measure was soundly defeated by about two-thirds of the voters.

In July 2004, the governor, state legislators, and the Department of the Interior approved five revised casino compacts that had been approved by Governor Davis in 1999. These compacts and five others that are pending expire in 2030. They lift the limit of two thousand slot machines for each tribe. The rate of payment to the state from slot machine earnings is on a progressive scale with $25,000 being the maximum for a single machine. Collectively the Indians are to float a $1 billion bond for state transportation projects until 2030. The overall payment total is an estimated $1.5 billion to help resolve state budget problems. Additionally, in the new agreements the state gains authority over casino Indians in tort law (a wrongful act for which a civil action will lie, except one involving breach of contract), environmental regulations, and the right of unions to organize workers, but not the right to strike. Then too, disputes with casino patrons about gaming and with local governments are subject to binding arbitration.

The reaction of Milanovich to the approved and pending Schwarzenegger compacts introduced a new dimension to casino–state relations. Soon after the defeat of Proposition 70, Milanovich said that until the governor apologized for his negative remarks about Indians, the Palm Springs Cahuilla would be unwilling to consider a new compact. Other supporters of the failed proposition emphasized that the existing compacts, with relatively modest payments to the state, are valid for another sixteen years; thus there are no compelling reasons to enter into renegotiated contracts. Another consideration centers on the modest earnings of many, possibly most, casinos that do not have the resources to provide the state with large sums of money on a yearly basis as required in the new Schwarzenegger contracts. By late November 2004 the outcome of state–Indian posturing was unpredictable.

Despite the controversy over casino compacts, a number of interim perceptions merit attention. First, between the years 2000 and 2004, voter support for casino tribes in California eroded rapidly. Inbalance of the state budget was a factor combined with the rapid and vast earnings of highly successful casinos that were widely reported in the media. Second, the essentially anti-Indian position by Governor Schwarzenegger clearly had broad appeal among non-Indians as a durable solution for state budget needs. Third, a defensive casino Indian response to the governor's position, especially the possibility of continuing to operate most casinos under existing compacts, could undermine the new compact total. Fourth, the apparent state success in obtaining more money from ten casinos may encourage other states with casinos to follow suit. Finally, the innovative partial budget solution in California is neither in the spirit nor in the text of the Indian Gaming Regulatory Act of 1988. Minimally one would expect suits in state and federal courts to overturn the existing Schwarzenegger compacts. Considering the purpose of the Indian Gaming Act (tribal economic development and self-determination), it would be best for the federal government to require strict state compliance. Yet this possibility may be impossible if the federal government continues to sacrifice Indian rights to state rights.

The most innovative achievement by these Cahuilla in recent years has been to launch the Santa Rosa and San Jacinto Mountain National Monument. The 272,000-acre site was approved by Congress in 2000. The land is owned or controlled primarily by federal agencies (e.g., Bureau of Land Management and U.S. Forest Service), the state and county governments, and the Indians involved; about 95,000 acres is designated a wilderness area. The monument landscape ranges from valley bottom springs and oases to granite peaks and includes great geological and wildlife diversity. Visitor attractions include scenic canyons and interpretive sites (e.g., Indian culture and natural history), as well as hiking trails and campgrounds. The monument may represent an initial effort to reclaim tribal lands lost to Euro-Americans in the 1870s and later.

Although the Palm Springs Cahuilla are proud of their cultural heritage, it has little impact on their daily lives. No band member speaks fluent Cahuilla, their aboriginal religious ceremonies disappeared years ago, and aboriginal craft skills are no longer retained. The present-day Agua Caliente Cultural Museum Center is a monument to their past. As soon as some $38 million is raised, partially through donations, a fifty-acre museum complex will be established. Despite these and other efforts, traditional cultural losses are pervasive and undeniable. Related cultural activities include an annual Native American film festival and the Agua Caliente Living Traditions, an educational program for the general public that includes crafts. Perhaps efforts such as these will lead to "new cultural traditions."

In 2004 the Agua Caliente Band included nearly four hundred members, most of whom owned allotted lands whose total value was in the billions of dollars. The band understandably is unwilling to release figures about total band assets. At the same time, it must be noted that numerous band members do not have allotments, and therefore the money they receive from the band depends on the collective investments that they share. Thus not all Palm Springs Cahuilla are wealthy. Some rich band members, however, share their riches with those who are less affluent. They may buy them new cars each year, provide them with money for vacations, and pay their medical bills. The Agua Caliente Band reportedly is one of the most wealthy groups of Indians in the United States.

In recent years they have donated millions of dollars to local nonprofit organizations such as police and fire departments, public libraries, and centers for both senior citizens and youth groups. Thus Palm Springs Cahuilla wealth clearly benefits not only their band members but also Euro-Americans in the area.

| Additional Sources

Lowell J. Bean is the most prominent student of Cahuilla life. The best place to begin searching for information about these people is the book by Bean and Lisa J. Bourgeault (1989). *California,* volume 8 of the *Handbook of North American Indians,* edited by Robert F. Heizer (1978) and published by the Smithsonian Institution, includes a Cahuilla summary by Bean, and the volume provides a wealth of information about other California Indians. Bean's 1972 study is an insightful ethnographic reconstruction with considerable emphasis on worldview and values. Bean and William M. Mason (1962) examine Spanish influences in their presentation of the Romero expedition accounts. For traditional Cahuilla material culture, the monographs by Lucile Hooper (1920) and Alfred L. Kroeber (1908) are the best sources. A pioneering ethnobotany study was written by David P. Barrows (1900), and it is supplemented by an article published by Bean and Katherine S. Saubel (1961).

| Selected Bibliography

Barrows, David P. 1900. *The ethno-botany of the Coahuilla Indians of southern California.* Chicago. (Reprinted in Banning, CA, 1967).

Bean, Lowell J. 1963. *Cahuilla ethnobotanical notes.* Archaeological Survey, Annual Report 1962–1963, 55–76. Department of Anthropology and Sociology, University of California, Los Angeles.

———. 1972a. *Temalpakh: Cahuilla Indian knowledge and usage of plants.* Riverside, CA.

———. 1972b. *Mukat's people.* Berkeley.

———. 1991. *Cahuilla landscape.* Menlo Park, CA.

Bean, Lowell J., and Lisa J. Bourgeault. 1989. *The Cahuilla.* New York.

Bean, Lowell J., and William M. Mason. 1962. *Diaries and accounts of the Romero expeditions in Arizona and California.* Los Angeles.

Bean, Lowell J., and Katherine S. Saubel. 1961. *The aboriginal uses of the oak.* Archaeological Survey, Annual Report 1960–1961, 237–49. Department of Anthropology and Sociology, University of California, Los Angeles.

Beattie, George W., and Helen P. Beattie. 1951. *Heritage of the valley.* Oakland, CA.

Ellison, William H. 1922–23. The federal Indian policy in California, 1846–1860. *Mississippi Valley Historical Review* 9:37–67.

Gifford, Edward W. 1922. *California kinship terminologies.* University of California Publications in American Archaeology and Ethnology, vol. 18.

Hooper, Lucile. 1920. *The Cahuilla Indians.* University of California Publications in American Archaeology and Ethnology, vol. 16, no. 6.

Jackson, Helen Hunt. 1881. *A century of dishonor.* New York. (An 1890 edition contains the *Report on the conditions and needs of the Mission Indians of California.*)

———. 1884. *Ramona.* Boston.

James, Harry C. 1960. *The Cahuilla Indians.* Los Angeles.

Kroeber, Alfred L. 1908. *Ethnography of the Cahuilla Indians.* University of California Publications in American Archaeology and Ethnology, vol. 8, no. 2.

Ringwald, George. 1967. *Riverside Press-Enterprise* and *Riverside Daily Press* articles.

Rush, Emmy M. 1932. The Indians of the Coachella Valley celebrate. *El Palacio* 32: 1–19.

Shinn, George H. 1941. *Shoshonean days.* Glendale, CA.

Strong, William D. 1929. *Aboriginal society in southern California.* University of California Publications in American Archaeology and Ethnology, vol. 26.

Transmitting report by Subcommittee on Indian Affairs. State of California, Senate Committee on Rules, Resolution No. 8. Sacramento.

Wilson, Benjamin D. 1952. *The Indians of southern California in 1852.* John W. Caughey, ed. San Marino, CA.

9 The Tlingit: Alaskan Salmon Fishers

Tlingit rattle (from Lisianskii 1814)

The world is rolling around for all the young people; therefore let us not love our life too much, hold ourselves back from dying.

A song about the earth composed by
Dry Bay George (de Laguna 1972, 792)

WE PROBABLY HAVE more information about the Tlingit from early historic to modern times than we have for any other Northwest Coast salmon fishers. The Tlingit are an excellent example of a people in a land of plenty who stressed wealth as well as social achievements within family lines. Yet they were not politically organized at the tribal level; instead, narrowly defined bonds of kinship focused their economic, political, and social lives. Totem poles and potlatches, characteristic of Northwest Coast Indians in general, predominated among the Tlingit. Although Tlingit totem poles usually are assumed to have been an aboriginal characteristic of Northwest Coast Indians, this chapter shows that they were a relatively recent development, quite possibly stimulated by the fur trade.

Tlingit (TLING-kuht) means "the people." Their language belongs to the Nadene family of languages, and they may have numbered about ten thousand early in their history. Tlingit country is a mass of mountains that reach a sea marked by islands, deep bays, and glaciers. This verdant land with its tranquil and turbulent waters had rich exploitative potential. Along the northern third, impressive mountains abruptly meet the sea, and sheltering bays are rare. In the balance of Tlingit country innumerable large and small islands front a fractured coastline. The mild temperatures and heavy precipitation produce a lush and varied vegetation, including stands of red cedar and Sitka spruce. Considering the geographical configuration, it is understandable that travel by boat was far more important than walking, although trails to the interior existed along certain rivers and over low divides and were negotiated for trading or raiding ventures (see Figure 9-1).

| Aboriginal Life

Among all the aboriginal peoples of the world who lived as hunters, fishers, and collectors, those of the Northwest Coast of North America achieved a high level of cultural complexity. Their lifeways were in many respects more complex than those reported among numerous aboriginal farmers. The Tlingit are reasonably typical of these Indians; as was true of other Northwest Coast populations, the richness of their culture was based on the abundance of salmon and the reliability of this major food source.

ORIGIN MYTH According to the Tlingit, the first people simply existed, and no explanation was sought for their origin. Among these people, according to one account, was a woman whose sons were killed by her brother. She decided to commit suicide, but an old man told her to swallow a heated beach pebble. The woman followed his instructions and became pregnant. She bore an offspring, who was Raven in human form. When Raven was older, he visited his uncle despite his mother's warnings that this man had killed his ten older brothers. The uncle attempted to kill Raven, but because of his supernatural powers Raven saved himself. Finally, Raven caused a flood, and all the people perished except for Raven and his mother, who donned bird skins and

Figure 9-1 | Range of the Tlingit Indians.

flew into the air. Raven stuck his beak in the sky and hung there for ten days. After the water subsided, he fell to earth and landed on a heap of seaweed. Raven went to the house of Petrel, a man who had always existed. In a small locked box on which he sat, Petrel kept water, and when Raven was thirsty, Petrel gave him only a little. Raven tricked Petrel into thinking that he, Petrel, had excreted in his bed. While Petrel was outside cleaning his blanket, Raven drank more than his fill of water and then flew to a tree with pitch in it. Petrel built a fire beneath the tree, and the smoke turned Raven from white to black. Later the trickery of Raven released the stars, the moon, and finally the sun into the sky. Raven was a creator or releaser of forces in the world, a culture hero, and an inordinate trickster.

APPEARANCE AND CLOTHING The Tlingit were lean, medium to tall in stature, and their complexion was no darker than those of many persons in southern Europe. Women wore their hair loose and had striking adornments.

Figure 9-2 | A girl in the Yakutat area with earrings, a nose pin, and labret. Sketched by Don Tomás de Suría in 1791. (Courtesy of the Beinecke Rare Book and Manuscript Library, Collection of Western Americana, Yale University.)

From a woman's pierced earlobes hung ornaments of shell, stone, or teeth, and her nasal septum was pierced to receive a bone pin. Each woman also wore a large medial labret (lip plug) inserted through a hole beneath the lower lip (see Figure 9-2). The initial opening was made about the time of puberty and was fitted with increasingly larger labrets until the hole was as much as four inches across; as one observer noted, these women could not kiss. Men wore their hair loose and rubbed it with grease; although their whiskers were not numerous, they were nonetheless plucked. When a male was young, his nasal septum was pierced, and through the opening a small ring was suspended. Men wore ear ornaments like those of the women, and a man of great achievements might have bits of wool or small feathers stuck in several small holes around the outer edge of each ear. Facial paints were worn by men and women on special occasions and as protection from temperature extremes and insects.

Adults of both sexes dressed in long-sleeved shirts of dehaired skin, over which they wore sea otter skin capes with the fur facing outward. The processed skin undergarments of women reached from the neck to the ankles. During severe weather they wore moccasins made by interior Indians or styled after their footwear. Tlingit hats, worn for hunting and ceremonies, were woven from roots or bark and were shaped like a truncated cone with a flat top. Their clothing hardly seems adequate to an outsider, but these people conditioned themselves to accept temperature extremes. They not only bathed in cold or icy waters but also lived in extremely hot winter houses heated by large fireplaces.

SETTLEMENTS   Winter villages were built along bays, inlets, or the lower courses of rivers, near good fishing grounds and where canoes could be landed safely. The square plank-covered houses had gabled roofs. At small villages, houses were built in a line facing the water, but the houses in larger settlements were arranged in rows. The plank-covered floor of the small dwellings was at ground level, but the central area of the larger houses was dug down about three feet. Along the sides at ground level were board- or mat-enclosed compartments for sleeping, bathing, or storage. Around the fire pit were stones to be heated in the fire and placed in containers for cooking food. Hunting and fishing devices were stored overhead along the beams, and fish might be hung from the roof beams to dry. Among the northern Tlingit, in particular, the house of a leading lineage was likely to have decorated wall partitions or panels called heraldic screens. It appears that behind a screen was the apartment of the house chief. Around the entry to a house, or even around an entire village, were palisades to protect the occupants. A bough-covered structure might be leaned against the outer wall of a house or built nearby for women during menstrual periods or childbirth. Pole racks for drying fish were scattered about a settlement, and a short distance away, either toward the forest or sea, were clusters of graves. At summer camps, where they caught their winter supply of fish, families lived in flimsy plank structures, some of which were walled only on the windward side.

MANUFACTURES AND HOUSEHOLD LIFE   Tlingit artistic skills rank high among tribal peoples anywhere in the world. Their manufactures in bone, stone, and wood are justly famous. A wide variety of wooden containers filled a typical aboriginal household. One style was made from a thin plank of cedar that was steamed and bent into a rectangular form, then overlapped and sewn with root. A wooden bottom was fitted into place and a top sometimes added. Some of these boxes had bulging sides that were painted or carved. The largest and most elaborately decorated boxes were for the storage of valuables, and others were used for cooking or food storage. Another common wooden form was made from a single piece of wood and ranged from round to oval to rectangular in outline. To these basic forms were adapted various animal shapes, such as a beaver lying on its back, with its head at one end, legs on the sides, and tail opposite the head. Other household items included dishes, spoons, and ladles of mountain sheep or goat horn. Oval lamps of pecked and polished stone furnished light, as fish or seal oil burned on a moss wick.

Family members gathered around the fire pit to rest, eat, or work during the day. At the fireplace, they prepared meals at irregular times of the day for as many as thirty house occupants. They boiled foods in wooden or woven containers. They poured water into the containers and dropped hot stones in to simmer the meat or fish before putting on the lid. Fish were boiled, roasted, or dried and served as the principal food, supplemented by flesh from land and sea mammals. They also ate shellfish, vegetable products, and fruit, particularly a wide variety of berries. These foods were relatively unimportant; however, shellfish became important in times of food stress. Boiled foods were dipped from their cooking containers in large spoons, which served as plates, and people consumed large quantities of water at meals.

CONVEYANCES   The most important Tlingit manufacture for subsistence activities was the canoe, normally built in the winter when unhurried production allowed men to make attractive and sound vessels. The best wood came from a straight-grained red cedar blown over by the wind or felled by building a fire at the base. A builder would hew and scrape the log with a stone-bladed adz. To spread the sides of the hollowed log he filled the cavity with water and dropped hot stones into it. As the log expanded, pieces of wood were wedged across the gunwales to give the sides the desired degree of flare. The outer sides might be painted with designs and the bow carved. A small canoe carried two or three persons, whereas larger ones held sixty persons and were forty-five feet long. They propelled canoes with paddles and used a long paddle for steering. When not in use, a canoe was covered with mats or blankets to protect it from the sun, and water was sprinkled over the sides. A small canoe made from a cottonwood log was used for fishing and river travel.

Snowshoes were essential for overland mobility during the winter, especially among the Chilkat, who went inland to trade at this time of year. The maple or birch snowshoe frames were heated over a fire and shaped; the netting was made from rawhide thongs. The shoes were about four feet long and ten inches wide at their broadest point, with rounded toes that turned up at the front and pointed heels.

SUBSISTENCE ACTIVITIES   Terrestrial fauna included black and grizzly bears, fox, wolves, wolverine, lynx, and deer on some islands. Scattered caribou herds occupied mainland plateaus, and mountain goats, as well as mountain sheep, frequented the coastal ranges. Smaller species included hare, squirrel, ermine, porcupine, muskrat, and a few beaver. Among the marine mammals were whales, hair and fur seals, sea lions, and sea otter. Of all the fish the most important were the salmon and candlefish (eulachon); halibut, haddock, trout, and herring also were caught. Along the edges of the sea were edible algae, crabs, sea urchins, mussels, and cockles. Avifauna included the bald eagle, raven, owl, and migratory waterfowl that summered in the area.

The subsistence cycle ebbed during the winter, and even March did not offer reliable weather for fishing. Nonetheless, it was during March that the subsistence year began anew. Men repaired canoes, readied fishing gear, and waited anxiously. In calm weather they fished for halibut along the coast fronting the Pacific Ocean. Two men fished from a canoe, maintaining about fifteen lines with baited V-shaped hooks and a wooden floater for each. When they hooked a fish, they paddled to the bobbing float, raised the line, and clubbed the fish to death as it was boated. Trout fishing with baited hooks also was important at this time. Following the breakup of river ice in March, women fished for trout with gill nets of rawhide with inflated bladder floats and stone sinkers. One woman usually paddled a canoe as a second handled the drifting net. They collected clams and mussels in large quantities and either dried and smoked them for future use or steamed them in a pit by pouring water over hot stones and applying a leaf covering. The pelts of fur animals were prime in March; fox, mink, wolf, and river (land) and sea otter all were sought. They trapped some of these animals in deadfalls but hunted sea otter with harpoon darts.

Candlefish were a rich source of the oil that was drunk during feasts but was more commonly served as a dip for dried salmon. These small fish were taken in traps or dip nets in the spring as they ascended rivers. The people began processing these fish by placing the fish and water in a canoe half-buried in the sand. They dropped heated stones repeatedly into the mass, and as the oil from the cooked fish surfaced, they ladled it into wooden containers. In mid-April herring spawned in shallow bays and were so numerous that they could be impaled on sharp tines set in the side of a pole. The tine-studded pole was drawn back and forth in the water, and the pierced herring were shaken off into the canoe. They either were eaten soon after being caught or were strung on ropes and dried.

Auke, Chilkat, and Stikine men traveled inland trading fish oil to Athapaskan Indians in exchange for caribou skins, moccasins, sinew, and lichens to be used for a particular form of dye. During the summer they paddled great canoes south to Haida and Tsimshian country, and in early historic times they ventured as far as Puget Sound in trading canoes. They carried copper from the Copper River and other local products to exchange for dentalia, haliotis, shark teeth, and slaves.

They usually hunted sea mammals with harpoon darts that had a line running from the detachable dart head to the shaft. When an animal was struck, the barbed dart head held beneath its skin, and the shaft was dragged through the water as the animal dove into the water. When it surfaced, the captive was harpooned again or killed with a spear or club. The most important species hunted were dolphin, seals, sea lions, and especially sea otter in early historic times. From the ethnographic accounts it seems that sea mammal hunting was not very important or that inland hunting was important at most settlements. If bears or mountain goats were pursued, they were cornered with the aid of dogs and killed with bone-pointed spears.

In the late summer people collected berries and stored them with candlefish oil in airtight boxes. Salmon eggs, oil, and berries were similarly mixed and preserved. If large land mammals were killed, their flesh usually was cut into strips and sun-dried or else boiled and stored in oil. Some foods were stored for winter at this time of the year, but it was not until September that the winter food supply became a major concern. They took diverse species of salmon during the summer but made no great effort to catch and dry quantities of them until September. The species available included dog (chum), hump-back (pink), king (chinook), silver (coho), and sockeye (red), and these were taken from July through December. The principal salmon-fishing device was a funnel-shaped trap set with the mouth opening downstream. The stream was blocked with a weir, which opened only at the trap. Fish caught in September were cleaned and hung on racks to dry or were smoke-cured in the house. After being dried or smoked, they were bundled and stored. As soon as a house group had obtained enough salmon for the winter, the members left their fishing camp and settled down in their village until April. Very little food apart from shellfish was gathered during the winter months, for this was the season for rituals, feasting, storytelling, and recreation.

In subsistence activities men dominated as the procurers of edibles, and women played the key role in households. The principal wife of the Keeper of the House was responsible for allocating domestic female tasks. The capacity of these women to process food, especially salmon, was a critical factor in the prosperity of a household. As Frederica de Laguna (1983, 81) noted, "The whole Tlingit economy of subsistence and luxury wealth rests ultimately on the stores of dried salmon prepared by the women."

DESCENT, KINSHIP, AND MARRIAGE   In social and political life the *kwaan* (kwáan, kon) represented a key geographical unit. It refers to the people who lived in a particular area. In many ways a kwaan is comparable to a tribe, in which case the Tlingit as a whole made up a "nation." Every kwaan included precise boundaries, and the members of each village controlled the portion its residents exploited. From north to south the first kwaan was Yakutat, with its most important settlement along Yakutat Bay. The most powerful kwaan was that of the Chilkat, with four major villages along the shores of the upper Lynn Canal. One of these, Klukwan, had sixty-five houses and about six hundred res-idents. The only interior group, the Inland Tlingit, lived around a series of lakes and occupied the largest area. The other kwaans, each of which had at least one large village, were the Auke, Taku, Huna, Killisnoo, Sitka, Kake, Kuiu, Stikine, Henya, Tongass, and Sanya.

The people of each kwaan were divided into two groups (moieties) that were traced through female lines (matriclans) and that were represented in each of the kwaans. The moieties were named Raven and Wolf, with the Wolf moi-ety called Eagle in the north; these were in turn divided into named matriclans. The Tlingit associated specific personality characteristics with the moieties. Raven people were expected to be wise and cautious, and the Wolves quick-tempered and warlike. According to Aurel Krause (1885), the clans of the Raven moiety included the Frog, Goose, Owl, Raven, Salmon, and Sea Lion. Clans of the Wolf moiety included the Auk, Bear, Eagle, Shark, Whale, and Wolf. These lists, although far from complete, identify the important clans in early historic times. An outsider, who was not a member of any clan, was addressed as uncle or son-in-law, reflecting his in-marrying status. Within each clan the lineage with the greatest wealth was most influential. Ideally, the leadership of a lineage was passed from a man to his sister's son. Each settlement with a number of clans represented had more than one "chief," but one dominated because of his wealth and personality. A person in one moiety was obligated to seek as a mate someone in the opposite moiety (moiety exogamy); further ramifications of marital arrangements are presented in the section about the life cycle.

Within a village the land was owned by groups of persons who traced their descent to a presumed common female ancestor (matriclan), and land was subdivided among house groups. Plots of ground near houses were owned by the adjacent households, but village paths were common property. Community members as a group cleared the trails, and everyone was free to use the beach. Within the domain of a village, each represented clan had particular localities defined as its own. Unclaimed sectors could be exploited by anyone. A clan, or portion thereof, owned fishing streams; land of a stream's drainage used for hunting; sealing islands; mountains inhabited by mountain goats; ocean banks; berry patches; and house sites. They conceived of ownership in terms of specific spots used rather than as geographical areas exploited.

Each clan recognized a particular settlement as the place of its origin. Although a clan was identified initially with a specific site, by the time of historic contact a number of different clans usually were represented in most villages. If a clan was large in a particular settlement, it was divided into lineages represented by house groups. In theory, the clans of each moiety possessed distinctive titles and associated design motifs that only members could use. These might be lent temporarily to or even usurped by a more powerful clan. Again in theory, only members of the Raven moiety had the right to the raven design, and only those of the Wolf moiety, the wolf design. House names usually were derived from a clan myth, from the clan's name, or by assuming the name of another clan's house for legendary or historical reasons. Moieties were each divided into a number of matriclans that in turn were divided into house groups composed of nuclear families, again related through females.

Nuclear family unity did not exist among the Tlingit because the parents were of different clans and moieties. Because various clans were represented in most areas, geographical groupings acted as a unit only in those rare instances when a feud affected all sections of the clan. A clan had no common leader or unified territory, and even crests were often identified with localized lineages rather than with the clan as a whole. Finally, each clan included persons ranked as nobles, "commoners," and slaves, depending on the social standing of particular lineages.

In the kinship system we find that a single term embraced all the people of the grandparent generation. To these persons the individual was attentive and respectful. The ties between a mother and her son were close even though the son might leave home to live with his mother's elder brother, who was for him the most powerful individual in Tlingit society and his authority figure.

Fathers were considered too lenient to discipline their sons effectively, and of course a father did not belong to his son's clan or moiety. Parents were especially concerned about the welfare of a daughter, who would command a large bride price only if she were well mannered and a maiden; thus she always was watched by someone. A mother's sister was called by a term for diminutive mother and was treated as one's mother. The "little mother" term was extended to all the other women of her moiety in her generation. A mother was aided and advised in raising children by her sister. A father's sister was termed differently from mother and mother's sister, with the father's sister word extended to all women of her moiety in both her generation and descending generations. The father term was unique, whereas the term for father's brother was extended to the other men of his moiety of his generation, as well as the next lower one. A man treated his father's brother with respect, and on rare occasions a girl might marry her father's brother.

A man ideally married his father's sister, and because she was a potential mate, their relationship was always warm. At one's generational level a man distinguished between older and younger brothers, and these terms were extended to the other men of one's generation and moiety. Older and younger male sibling distinctions were highly important because an older brother had the first rights of inheritance, greater authority, and more ceremonial responsibilities. A woman made the same distinction among sisters. There also was a particular term for a man's sister and one for a woman's brother; these were extended to all the members of that sex of the individual's generation and moiety. Brothers were socially and physically close because they were of the same clan and lived in the same house; with a sister a man was supposed to be distant and withdrawn, although he was concerned for her welfare. A mother's sister's children were termed brother and sister, and the boys were raised in the same household as the mother's children. The terminology for the first ascending generation was essentially bifurcate merging, and the cousin terminology was of the Crow type (see Figure 9-3). One overriding principle governed the kinship terminology of the Tlingit: to separate blood relatives in one's own moiety from those in the opposite moiety. The average adult avoided using relationship

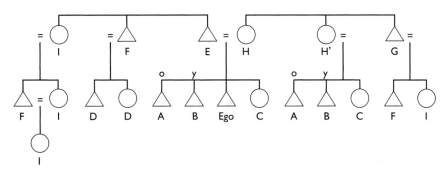

Figure 9-3 | The early historic Tlingit system of kinship terminology.

terms in direct address in everyday conversation for fear of offending someone, as a great deal of emphasis was placed on an exact ranking of individuals. Thus nicknames and given names were in common use. Relationship terms were employed primarily on ceremonial occasions.

SOCIAL DIMENSIONS   The most important social and economic unit was the household, and it had a significant place in the ceremonial life of the clan and moiety. A house group ideally was composed of a male and his brothers, as well as his mother's sister's sons who were classificatory brothers, and the sons of the sisters of these individuals, plus the sons of the daughters of these sisters. All were members of one matrilineage, and there were additionally the in-marrying spouses. A household of this nature functioned as an economic unit, with members working for their common welfare. In particular it was brothers, led by the eldest, the Keeper of the House, who aided one another in feuds, potlatches, and other matters of house group concern. The importance of the Keeper of the House in directing house group life cannot be overestimated. He guided the economic activities of household members and was deferred to by the other men in his residence unit. The house group leader allotted items obtained in trade, was given choice foods, and was freed from any humble form of household labor. It was this man, the eldest brother, who represented the household in ceremonial activities, as well as in clan councils. Furthermore, when he died the rights to his position fell to the next oldest person called brother. In addition to the position of Keeper of the House, the wealthiest of the local household heads in any clan, and thus the ranking Keeper of the House, was designated Rich Man. These men more than any others were responsible for the fortunes of their clan units.

Within a household the Keeper of the House and his principal wife outranked all other members. Older brothers and sisters outranked younger ones, and bastards and slaves ranked lowest. The same system prevailed between the members of a leading lineage and of the secondary ones within a clan. The highest-ranking persons were aristocrats, chiefs, and the wealthy. Their status was based on birth, personal character, accomplishments, age, and either inherited or acquired wealth. "Commoners" as such did not exist; instead, most persons within lineages were junior members who could be ranked against other persons in broadly similar positions. Furthermore, just as households and lineages were ranked against one another within a clan, so it was among the clans of a moiety. The members of lowly clans were poor, whereas those of lofty clans were rich, hosted elaborate potlatches, and had splendid artifacts as clan heirlooms. The leading members of some aristocratic clans reportedly could not sleep at night because they thought so intently about their greatness.

Men clearly were the overt Tlingit leaders, but the importance of women behind the scenes was exceedingly strong, so much so that they may be considered the dominant gender. Judgments by women were critical in trading relations; they were the keepers of household wealth, and they made critical decisions in social life. The prominence of women was in keeping with Tlingit matrilineality. Thus, moiety, clan, and lineage matters were in their firm grasp. Unfortunately, however, their position is not well reported in the early ethnographic record.

In this social setting, based as it was on rank, classes did not exist. Instead, wealthy and prestigious households competed with one another within a clan and beyond it for high status that changed with the fortunes of these units. In the absence of social classes, the rank of a household, a clan segment, or a whole clan relative to another such unit constantly was being reassessed. The comparative wealth and prestige of these units was tested in numerous ways, such as in potlatches and, to a lesser extent, in the erection of totem poles.

CRESTS AND TOTEM POLES Among these people their most valued possessions were clan and lineage crests. Crests were represented on canoes, dishes, ceremonial garments, totem poles, and other artifacts. A crest ideally was carved by a member of the opposite moiety who held a rank equal to that of the individual requesting the item. By preference this would be a wife's brother; if such an individual was not a capable carver, he could hire someone else of either moiety to make the object. The man who was first asked to do the work paid the craftsman and in turn was paid by his brother-in-law. Carvings produced in this manner fulfilled ritual obligations, and the labor was ceremonial. The most important crests for Raven moiety were the raven, owl, and whale. Wolf moiety crests included the eagle, wolf, and bear. Crests represented Tlingit totems that were honored in ritual contexts, but totems were not worshiped.

No aspect of Northwest Coast Indian life has fascinated Westerners more than totem poles. Their size, boldly sculptured figures, and design motifs have made them memorable cultural monuments. Edward L. Keithan (1963), in a comprehensive account of Tlingit poles, identified six primary types.

1. The four main vertical support posts for a house usually were plain, but they might be faced with carved pillars (or panels) bearing clan crests that could include abalone shell inlays. *Carved house pillars* were one of the two prehistoric types.
2. The second prehistoric type was the *mortuary pole*. The pole body was plain. A box was set at the top of the pole in which were placed the cremated remains of the person honored. A crest figure might be carved on the upper portion of the pole. The earliest example was reported in 1791 (see Figure 9-4).
3. A *memorial pole* honored a deceased house group leader and was raised under the sponsorship of a younger brother or maternal nephew of the dead person. Such a pole usually was not erected at the interment site. Its purpose was to honor the deceased and, equally important, to validate the succession of the house group leader.

Figure 9-4 | The earliest illustration of a Tlingit mortuary pole and graves, 1791, for the Yakutat area. (From Malaspina and de Bustamante y Guerra 1885.)

4. A *heraldic pole* was raised at the front and center of a house. A myth or tale associated with the house group was represented by the carved and painted pole.
5. The *ridicule pole* usually was raised to force another house group to settle a debt. One particular example was said to have been erected to shame a white trader for not repaying a potlatch held in his honor.
6. The *potlatch pole* was the most recent type to appear. They were raised to enhance the prestige of a family group that had accumulated and distributed wealth from the fur trade or by working directly for whites (see Figure 9-5).

Totem poles in general did not become commonplace among the Tlingit until the late 1800s. In 1881–1882 one pole was reported among the Chilkat, none among the Sitka or Killisnoo groups; however, they were numerous at one Stikine village. Some observers have suggested that great totem poles may not have been carved until iron-bladed tools became widely available as a result of the fur trade. Yet a well-developed woodworking technology predates the Northwest Coast Indian fur trade.

For the Tlingit, erecting a totem pole was an end in itself. A pole that was carved and raised for a particular purpose was thereafter unimportant as a physical object. As a pole tilted with age or threatened to fall, it was not supported in any manner. Restoration necessitated ceremonial involvements and an outlay of wealth equal to that expended when the original pole was raised, and therefore it was more sensible to erect another pole and bring even greater honor to the house group. Because poles deteriorated rapidly in this damp area and comparatively few new poles were raised after 1900, most have rotted away.

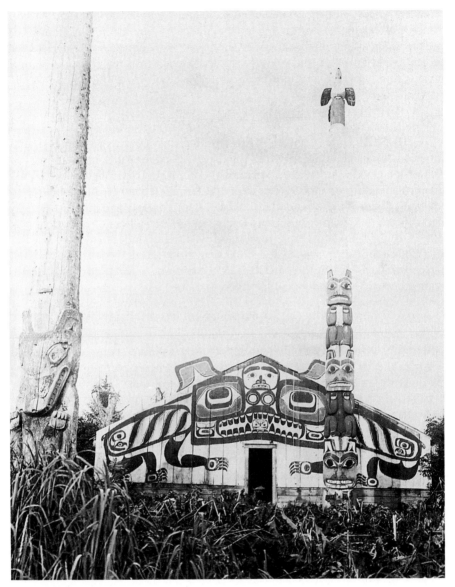

Figure 9-5 | Chief's house with painted front and totem poles in 1899. (Courtesy of the Smithsonian Institution, National Anthropological Archives, neg. no. 43,548-H.)

The totemic symbols exhibited on poles were associated with one or the other of the moieties, with clans, or with house groups. All of the Raven moiety members employed the Raven design as their primary symbol. The Wolf moiety had the Wolf as its chief totem in the south and the Eagle in the north. Not only the actual crests but also the names of animals associated with a clan were important, and their uses were validated through the potlatch system. These honorific names, often drawn from the clan or moiety totems, tended to pass from great-grandfather to great-grandson. The animals associated with a moiety could be killed and eaten by moiety members, however, and the uniform eating habits of all the tribe indicate no taboo on eating one's totemic species.

POLITICAL LIFE Conflicts between Tlingit moieties were common, and modern Tlingit liken these disputes to relations between European nations. For real or imagined injuries, either material goods were exchanged or a life was taken. The nature of a settlement depended on the ability of the guilty to pay and the power of the offended to collect. Minor conflicts eventually were settled at feasts that included property settlements. When a person was grievously offended, the only acceptable retribution was the offender's murder, but this was bound to lead to a retaliatory killing. If those murdered were of unequal rank, there was the further problem of establishing a value for each death. Sometimes when an individual felt badly wronged and had no means to retaliate, he committed suicide, and his relatives then pressed for compensation. On occasion, clan disputes were settled by a duel between warriors who represented each group. Murders were committed by ambush, as were raids against other clans or tribes. The only crimes occurring within a clan were incest and witchcraft, each punishable by death. It should be stressed that overall political unity did not exist within a moiety, and some of the bloodiest feuds were between clans of the same moiety.

Clans conducted raids to avenge deaths and to obtain slaves. Preparations for impending conflict involved fasting and abstaining from all contact with women. In addition, a warrior conditioned himself for combat by bathing in the sea, even at the coldest time of the year, and by being whipped by an older man. As a raiding party traveled, it seized property from camps along the way irrespective of whether the residents were friendly or not. A shaman always accompanied the party and predicted events of the near future. Plans for an attack on an enemy community were kept secret, and the foray was launched at dawn. Rod or skin armor protected a man's body; his face was covered with a mask, and his head with a wooden helmet. All the enemy men who did not escape were killed with daggers; women and children were taken as prisoners. A reprisal attack would be expected to avenge the murders.

Copper-bladed daggers, spears, and war clubs appear to have been the most important weapons. Scalps were taken at times, and the scalped person's head sometimes was impaled on a stick and exhibited. The men in a war party sang of victory as they returned to their village, and the paddle of each warrior killed was propped up at the spot he had occupied in the boat. To bind peace, hostages might be exchanged and kept for a year or longer. Peacemaking followed a pattern of ceremonialism, which climaxed with the exchange of hostages, termed "deer" since they were to behave as timidly as these animals.

In the Northwest Coast cultures, slavery was well established by A.D. 500 and was more complex than elsewhere north of Mexico. Most Tlingit slaves, male and female, were captives in raids or were purchased from peoples to the north and south. Slaves performed the most menial tasks, such as collecting firewood, hauling water, and preparing fish and game for consumption. They represented a major economic asset for their owners, who also gained social prestige by ownership. Also, such slaves might be ceremonially strangled at the discretion of their owners. This usually occurred in connection with a major event, such as the completion of a new house for a high-ranking individual or perhaps at his funeral. Slaves may have represented about 10 percent of the population in early historic times. In addition to slavery by capture, purchase, or birth to a female slave, a local person might become a debt slave, which was of a different order. A poor indebted man who could find no other way out of his situation could offer himself, and as many of his children as necessary, to cancel the debt. Such an individual did not perform menial labor as other slaves, could not be sold, and could be redeemed by clan relatives. At death the body of a slave typically was thrown into the sea.

RELIGION AND SUPERNATURALISM The Tlingit crystallized their knowledge about the natural world and integrated it into a loosely ordered system. They thought of the world as a flat expanse with the sky as a dome above the earth. They believed that everything that existed in all this space was alive: spirits lived on the sun and moon; stars were the lights of distant towns or houses. They identified Venus and sometimes named clusters of stars. A rainbow was thought to be the path of dead souls to the upper world, and the northern lights, human spirits playing. For the Tlingit, everything on earth was possessed by a spirit quality, which had subordinates or helpers; each trait, every fire, and everything that one did had its main spirit and helpers.

Tlingit shamans reputedly were the most powerful on the north Pacific coast, and their effectiveness came from the spirits they controlled. The usual manner in which a clan acquired a new shaman was for the spirit of the clan's shaman to leave his body at death and enter the body of an upstanding clan youth. Nephews who aspired to the position went into trances around the dead man's body, and the one who remained in a trance the longest was most likely to be named the successor. After this supernatural visitation the novice and certain near relatives went into the forest, ate little, and searched for a sign. The most propitious was to see a bird or an animal drop dead; the spirit of this creature henceforth aided the novice. After the young man demonstrated that he had his uncle's power, he inherited the ceremonial equipment.

Shamans controlled the spirits represented on their masks (see Figure 9-6), and although most spirits served specific clans, some could be controlled by any shaman. The latter category included a spirit associated with the souls of persons who were lost at sea or died alone in the forest. The primary protecting spirit was represented as the main figure on a mask, and helping

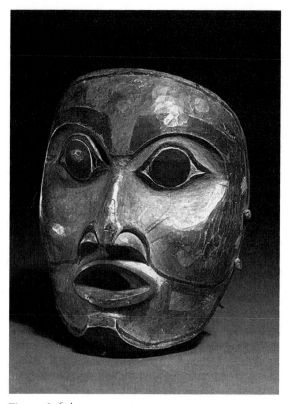

Figure 9-6 | Shaman's mask of painted wood. (Courtesy of the Field Museum, Chicago, neg. no. A98082.)

spirits also might appear. A secondary spirit might be posed around the eyes of a mask, thereby increasing the vision of the primary spirit.

A shaman neither cut nor combed his hair, and about his neck he wore a bone necklace and a small whetstone, the latter used for scratching his head. A shaman owned rattles that had spirit associations and were used in his performances. The split tongues of animals, especially the river otter, and the claws of eagles were sources of power; both appear to have been placed in sacred bundles of cedar bark, grass, and devil's club. After a shaman bathed, he rubbed himself with the bundle, and he used it in all his rituals. Among the spirit helpers were those of the sun, the sea, and the crest animals of the shaman's clan. After summoning his spirit helpers, a shaman cured an afflicted individual by blowing, sucking, or passing an object over the locus of the disease, which drew out the cause. Other services of a shaman included locating food sources and predicting the future. A shaman and his family usually lived in a separate residence, and in the forest near the house was his shrine. From time to time shamans retreated for extended periods to intensify their spirit relationships.

A number of charms appear to have been employed by ordinary persons. Made from parts of plants, they were used in such diverse activities as foreseeing the future, attracting a woman, making one wealthy, or improving hunting abilities. A few additional items seem to have served as secular cures, but these were rare and apparently unimportant. In general, it would appear that curing and supernaturalism were shamanistic matters. It is interesting that salmon, which were the all-important subsistence item, were not dealt with in a sacred manner. They simply were accepted as present and were caught and eaten. Even in Tlingit mythology, salmon play a relatively unimportant role; they seem to have been regarded as a constant part of the environment.

Witchcraft was most often performed by obtaining an item intimately associated with the victim and using it in a representation of the victim in the form desired. If a person became ill, the cause was attributed to sorcery, and the offender was named by the curing shaman. Persons accused of being witches usually were women, children, or slaves. They were tortured to extract a confession or killed if a confession was not forthcoming. An accused witch was bound by clan members and given no food or water for eight days or longer. If the person was a witch and did not confess, death was expected at this point; if the accused confessed, the object or objects used to bewitch a victim were scattered in the sea, and the individual presumably resumed an ordinary status.

LIFE CYCLE Childbearing was prohibited within the mother's home because it supposedly would bring ill fortune to the men of the house. Thus, a birth took place in a shelter never visited by men. During the birth, slaves and a midwife, always a member of the opposite moiety and preferably the woman's husband's sister, aided the woman. Inside the structure a pit was dug and lined with moss, and a stake was driven into the center of the hole. While giving birth, the woman squatted in the pit, holding the stake. After the birth the umbilical cord was cut and placed in a bag hung around the neonate's neck for eight days; the umbilical cord of a boy later was placed under a tree where an eagle had nested to make the boy a brave adult. To prevent a baby from crying repeatedly, the first cry was caught in a container and buried where many people walked so that it would be smothered as the baby grew. The baby was wrapped in skins, with moss for a diaper, and was tied to a board. The mother carried the cradleboard with her or hung it from a roof beam when she was in the house. She placed woodworm burrowings on her nipples so that as the baby nursed she or he would swallow the burrowings and would be neat in later life. A child was nursed for three or four years and was given its first solids after about a year. An infant born to a woman without a husband normally was suffocated. A baby was named after a maternal ancestor; the name itself was taken from an animal associated with the clan. With the birth of a son the parents referred to themselves by the son's name, as the father or the mother of the son (teknonymy).

Children were encouraged to behave in a manner appropriate to adults of the same sex. They were taught to restrain signs of emotion, to be dignified and aloof. They were expected to take cold baths daily from the time they learned to walk and were physically punished if they refused to bathe in the winter. When boys moved to the household of their mother's brother, they were whipped with a switch by this man after bathing and were forced to run up and down the beach. After this exercise, they were instructed by older men in the customs and history of the clan, and they learned certain skills by watching men perform routine tasks. As a boy grew, he came increasingly under the influence of his maternal uncle and performed tasks for this older man rather than for his father. A boy tended to gravitate toward a particular uncle whom he wished to emulate in his exceptional skills relating to carving, hunting, or the supernatural. The uncle gave honorific names to his young charges and taught them clan lore, but no secret initiations took place. The most important nephew was the oldest, for he would inherit from his maternal uncle not only material property and wives but titles as well. Even while young, boys were free to use a maternal uncle's tools with permission. If a mother died, the father was obliged to place the offspring in the custody of the mother's siblings.

When a girl first menstruated, she was confined to a brush-covered shelter or to a compartment in the house behind the heraldic screen. Her face was covered with charcoal, and she was attended by female relatives and a slave if her parents were wealthy. A high-born girl was isolated for a year, and one of lower birth was confined for at least three months. She drank water through a bird-bone tube and went outside only at night, even then wearing a broad-brimmed hat so that she would not taint the stars with her gaze. During isolation her mother instructed her about proper female behavior and taught her clan myths and songs. At the beginning of her confinement, her lip, nasal septum, and possibly her earlobes were pierced by a woman of the opposite moiety. When she came out of seclusion, she wore new clothing, and her slave attendant, if she had one, was freed. The girl would marry soon, and to ensure that she remained chaste she slept on a shelf above her parents' bed. The rank of a person was reckoned through both sides of the family and depended largely on the amount of bride price paid by one's father for one's mother; thus parents attempted to provide a daughter with all the advantages of careful rearing and wealth.

Moiety exogamy was strictly observed, and a match was initiated by the suitor, who used a go-between to approach the girl and her family. If favorably received, he sent presents to his future father-in-law. The most desirable marriage partners, in decreasing order, were a father's sister, brother's daughter, father's sister's daughter, and finally, mother's brother's daughter. In the ideal form of marriage with father's sister, the groom assumed the role of his mother's brother. However, the most common marriage was with a father's sister's daughter, and this was preferred by a young man. Marriage to near relatives served two important functions: to keep wealth concentrated and to provide spouses of nearly equal rank.

A wedding ceremony was held in the bride's house. Here relatives of the groom assembled as he sat in the middle of the floor wearing his most elaborate ceremonial garb. The bride was concealed in a corner of the house and was lured to sit beside the groom by the singing and dancing of the assembled group. The guests were feasted, but this was not a formal potlatch event. A month after the ceremony the couple was considered married. Marriage residence was with the family of either spouse (bilocal), depending on the wealth and standing of the principals. If the couple moved into the man's household, the bride's relatives presented him with property equal to or exceeding the value of that presented by his relatives. A man of wealth might have multiple wives (polygyny), with the first wife holding a rank superior to that of any subsequent spouses; five wives appear to have been the maximum. A woman sometimes had more than one husband (polyandry) but only if the second husband was a brother (fraternal polyandry) or near relative of the first. A widow customarily married her late husband's brother (levirate), and if the deceased husband did not have a brother, his sister's son married the widow. If neither category of individual was available, a widow could marry any man of her former husband's clan. If his mother's brother died, a man was obligated to marry the widow even though he might already have a wife, and he inherited his uncle's wealth. In spite of the ideal that a man should live in the house of his mother's brother, inherit his wealth, and marry his daughter or another person in this line, his father's clan attempted to lure him into its domain. This especially seems to have been true for a boy who had married into the community. When a married woman was seduced, blood revenge might be exacted by her husband, or the seducer might make a property settlement. If the seduction was by a near relative of the husband, the offender was expected to become the woman's second husband.

Gambling was an important pastime among adult Tlingit males, and some men were so addicted that they sometimes lost prized possessions, including wives. The most important form of gambling was a hand game in which one man guessed which hand of an opponent held a uniquely marked stick. The game was played by teams, but only one man of each team handled the sticks at any one time. Other adult diversions included dice games and a ball game in which the purpose was to drive a ball along the tidal flats to the opponent's goal. Boys played a game that involved throwing a stick at a rolling wad of grass. They also wrestled, hunted, and swam for entertainment. A favorite diversion among little girls was to arrange beach pebbles in the form of figures.

In the production of artifacts, the dominant materials worked by women were flexibles such as wool and cedar bark or the root fibers of spruce. Their most famous woven products were Chilkat robes, which were made from mountain goat wool with symbolic patterns produced by using wool dyed black and yellow. A single robe required six months or longer to make (see Figure 9-7). Women also wove baskets, making named patterns of geometric design. Men usually worked hard materials such as red cedar, copper that was pounced and incised, horn, and ivory. They often included symbolic patterns, especially clan crests, as decorative elements on their totem and house poles, canoe parts, and ladles.

Figure 9-7 | Chilkat woman weaving a dance robe. (From Krause 1885, vol. 1.)

Outsiders described the Tlingit (Koloshes) as unlikable. Physicians for the Russian-American Company at Sitka in 1843–44 described the people as follows (Romanowsky and Frankenhauser 1849, 35): "The Koloshes are proud, egoistic, revengeful, spiteful, false, intriguing, avaricious, love above all independence and do not submit to force, except the ruling of their elders." Still, adults were patient and persistent; they never seem to have hurried; and they became angry only with provocation. During the fishing season they worked long hours, but winter was a time for leisure. During the winter women made their famous robes and baskets; in general, women appear to have had less free time than men. The social position and respect that a woman commanded depended on her personality and standing within her clan; a woman with abilities was listened to by men. Women had well-defined rights, and relatives were willing to come to their defense in case of any injustice from the husband's side of the family. An individual, whether male or female, was expected to behave in accord with his or her rank. Persons were of higher rank if their clan was large, wealthy, and powerful. Still, not all such persons were noble in their behavior, in which case they were treated as though they belonged to a lesser clan. Were a person from a high-ranking clan to behave coarsely as judged by fellow clan members, he or she might be killed by them.

Death, as a major aspect of the life cycle, was given elaborate focus in funeral ceremonies, memorial feasts, and especially memorial potlatches. Collectively, these involvements provide insight into the substance and symbolism of Tlingit culture. The conventions surrounding Tlingit dead in the nineteenth century have been reconstructed by Sergei Kan (1983; 1986), who emphasizes the meaning behind the rituals and ceremonies.

A corpse embodied specific qualities and was considered dangerous to lineage members. The flesh was regarded as soft and wet compared with the bones, which were solid and dry. Bones were intermediate between the flesh and spirit; with cremation, bones, which were pure, found release from the polluted flesh. A ghost dwelled with the bones and, by cremation, became warm in the afterlife. The fireplace in a house served as the medium through which to communicate with the deceased of a lineage; burning food and gifts became a means for the living to provide for the dead.

Shortly after a death a body was prepared by members of the immediate lineage. The ghost of the deceased was thought to remain in the dwelling for four to eight days, while the body rested in state at the back of the house surrounded by personal wealth and by lineage and clan possessions. The principal mourners were closely related lineage members who painted their faces black, fasted, and observed other customs as they wailed and sang "crying songs." One important ritual was to burn food and tobacco in the fireplace as offerings to matrilineal ancestors. At this critical time, parental and affinal relatives (members of the opposite moiety) performed routine household activities to free mourners from ordinary and thus polluting concerns. Members of the opposite moiety also visited the mourners each evening to comfort them and received token gifts for their efforts.

Following a wake, the body was removed through a temporary opening made in the back of the house or through the smokehole above the fireplace. Males of the opposite moiety cremated the corpse, and some of the person's possessions were burned. Females of the opposite moiety collected the ashes and bones, which were put in a box and temporarily placed in a grave house. Afterward, the primary mourners bathed, dressed normally, and hosted the first of a series of small feasts for those who had helped them. At these events, food and tobacco again were offered to the matrilineal ancestors of the deceased. This series of small celebrations ended when the spirit of the deceased was believed to have entered the "village of the bones' people," the Tlingit term for a cemetery. The dead usually were buried behind the house of their clan, although the ashes and bones of aristocrats might be placed in mortuary poles. In their afterlife, the dead were believed to follow the lifestyle of their immediate descendants. Obligations to the recently deceased did not end until a new box, a repaired grave house, or a mortuary pole was provided for the remains. This was taken care of by the same group from the opposite moiety that had aided the bereaved relatives throughout the wake.

The memorial potlatch, for which extended preparations were made, was given to compensate moiety opposites for their help at the time of a death. A second purpose was to end the period of mourning, and a third one was to transfer the names and certain items of property of the deceased to a successor.

The word "potlatch" is of European and anthropological origins. The Tlingit word is *kueex,* meaning to call or invite to a ceremony that focused on marriage, death, or the investiture of an heir. The hosts sent delegates near and far to extend formal invitations to named guests. When guests arrived, songs and dances of greeting were exchanged and a mock battle enacted. Although a potlatch spanned only four days, the hosts entertained and fed their guests for about a month. The formalities began as the hosts cried and sang sad or "heavy" songs to indicate that their period of mourning was nearly over. Guests offered condolence speeches, followed by speeches of gratitude from the hosts. The hosts also placed food in the fire for the deceased, who were considered to be present. The tenor of the rituals then shifted, as the guests coaxed the mourners back to a normal state with jokes and "lighter" songs. The climax of the potlatch came when hosts transferred the titles and ceremonial objects of the deceased to his or her successor and to others in the maternal group. The hosts also ceremonially presented gifts to specific guests according to their rank; the number and quality of gifts a person received became a marker of his or her status. Some gifts were burned in honor of lineage ancestors, who were believed to receive the essence of the goods. When the potlatch ended, guests received any excess food and expressed thanks to their hosts (see Figure 9-8).

By the end of a potlatch, the bones and ghost of the honored dead were thought to be at home in the village cemetery, and the person's spirit had reached the "village of the dead." Another noncorporeal entity was believed to return to the living to be reincarnated in matrilineal descendants of the deceased, while names, ceremonial titles, and lineage or clan artifacts went to his or her immediate successor. Sergei Kan (1986, 198) writes, "The rebirth of the deceased and the death's failure to interrupt the continuity of the matrilineal group were dramatically expressed by addressing the new owner of the title or the regalia as if he were the deceased himself."

In analyzing Northwest Coast Indian potlatches, ethnographers often have placed the greatest emphasis on competitive aspects, both within the host group and between the hosts and their guests, as individuals or groups vied for rank, status, and prestige. Competition seems to have been most keen among host lineages of nearly equal rank in their efforts to "grab" a high-ranking name, rather than between hosts and guests. Although this element clearly was

Figure 9-8 | Two Tlingit men in ceremonial garments before 1895. The man on the left wears a painted hide tunic and wooden hat. The one on the right with a nose ring and facial paintings wears a woven dance shirt and holds a rattle. Both men are wearing leggings decorated with porcupine quills. Photograph by Lloyd V. Winter and Edwin P. Pond. (Courtesy of the Alaska State Library; PCA 87-296.)

important, Kan emphasizes that among hosts and guests there also was a major stress on group or individual "love and respect" for ancestors. Finally, reciprocity in different forms was a pervasive aspect of potlatch traditions. Reciprocity between the living and the dead of a lineage or clan and reciprocity between hosts and guests were especially prominent. In sum, a potlatch fostered both competition, to separate, and cooperation, to unite, the participants.

Early History

As early as 1582 a Spanish explorer sailed along the Tlingit coast, but he apparently made no contact with the people. An expedition led by Vitus Bering sailed from Kamchatka in 1741 to determine whether the Asian and North American landmasses were continuous. The ship that Bering commanded anchored off Kayak Island, at the northern fringe of Tlingit country; and although the sailors saw no people, they found a camp with a burning fire. The commander of the other vessel, Alexei Chirikov, anchored off the southern shores of Tlingit country. He sent two boats to investigate the coast, but neither boat returned. Indians later paddled two canoes toward Chirikov's ship but withdrew before making contact. On the return voyage Bering and his crew were forced to winter on what came to be known as Bering Island off the coast of Kamchatka. Here Bering died, but his men returned to Kamchatka the next year with valuable sea mammal pelts. Russian adventurers hastily formed trading and hunting expeditions and sailed to the Aleutian Islands in a quest for furs, especially for sea otter pelts, which were extremely valuable in China. Before many years passed, Russian fur hunters and traders had reached the Alaskan mainland. In the late 1700s competition between European and American trading vessels seeking sea otters expanded.

With increased competition, Russian merchants moved to gain firm control over the north Pacific trade. In 1799 the Russian-American Company was granted a monopoly by Czar Paul I. The company was dominated by one man above all others, Alexander Baranov, who had established the first permanent base on Kodiak Island in 1791. The major fort and trading post were built at Sitka in 1799. As long as Baranov was there, the Indians, who respected his bravery, were afraid to attack. When he left temporarily in 1801, the Indians destroyed the fort and killed the members of the small garrison. Baranov returned in 1804, and founded a hilltop settlement, New Archangel (Sitka). Following Baranov's retirement in 1818 relations with the Tlingit fluctuated with the abilities of the chief administrator. Sitka remained the primary trading center.

Russians and shipborne European or Euro-American traders were most eager to obtain sea otter pelts from the Indians, and they found the Tlingit to be cunning and dangerous hagglers. Furthermore, women were usually at the forefront of commercial transactions. As trade contacts intensified, the people were increasingly selective. They wanted woolen blankets because they were trading away their animal pelt clothing; they also desired firearms and were able to obtain them from non-Russian sources. Standard early trade items included axes, metal containers, tobacco, glassware, and clothing. The Russians never gained political control over the Tlingit. The Russians could only try to minimize the violence around the Sitka area.

Russian-era efforts to Christianize the Tlingit were not very successful because of the strong aboriginal religious system, the limited scope of Russian influence, and the scarcity of clergy. A Russian Orthodox priest made an unsuccessful attempt to vaccinate the people of Sitka against smallpox in 1834.

In 1835 a smallpox epidemic struck. No Russians died, but nearly half of the Tlingit may have perished. When the Indians realized their shamans could not cure the disease, they turned to the Russians for vaccinations.

| Later History

In 1867 ownership of Alaska was formally transferred from Russia to the United States. The ceremony took place at Sitka. The Tlingit were not permitted in Sitka for the ceremonies, but they watched from canoes in the harbor. Russians in Alaska had the option of either returning to Russia within three years or becoming U.S. citizens; nearly all of them left soon after the transfer. For ten years civil government did not exist, and the U.S. military garrisons at Sitka, Tongass, and Wrangell were more often a source of trouble than a means to establish order. The Tlingit clashed repeatedly with the military over Indian deaths that went uncompensated, which led to murders and the destruction or threatened destruction of Tlingit settlements. After the troops departed, the U.S. Revenue-Cutter Service vessels and the collector of customs usually represented legal authority. In 1880 gold was discovered near the present city of Juneau, which brought miners and confusion; still, it was not until 1884 that a civil government began to function in the more populous areas of Alaska.

By the early 1880s, the most obvious changes in Tlingit life were the changes in material culture. Women had stopped wearing the labrets that had begun to go out of fashion fifty years earlier. Bracelets and finger rings made from silver coins became popular. Skin garments rapidly were replaced by cloth clothing, and imported woolen blankets served as capes. Women raised vegetables, especially potatoes, which had been introduced by the Russians. Intoxicants, unknown in aboriginal times, had become an important item of trade. A discharged American soldier taught the people to distill alcohol, and this drink, called *hooch* in English, became extremely popular.

Tlingit settlements became consolidated in the early twentieth century as a result of population decline, pressure by the federal government, and the availability of better boats and engines for greater mobility. Men increasingly built single-family dwellings of finished lumber, resulting in a shift away from house group and lineage solidarity. Women worked as domestics for whites and in salmon canneries. Some men became trappers, commercial fishermen, or laborers in local gold mines. As employees of whites, the Tlingit often found the working conditions intolerable. To be ordered around and required to work scheduled hours was insulting, and yet there was little alternative. Craft skills of old survived largely because of the tourist market.

Slavery remained a highly visible and troublesome issue during the Russian era. By the 1850s Russian influences led to manumissions, but the scope of Russian influence was confined largely to the vicinity of Sitka. Fur traders on American ships sometimes bought and sold slaves. Russian Orthodox missionaries opposed slavery, as did the early American Presbyterian missionaries, but just as in the Russian period, the U.S. government agents were so few for many years they could not achieve general emancipation. The conditions faced by slaves appear to have improved somewhat, and at the funeral feasts of high-ranking Tlingits, slaves now appear to have been more often freed than killed. Freed slaves might be absorbed into the households of their previous owners, but their stigma as slaves remained. The last examples of Tlingit slavery were in the 1890s.

Protestant missionaries largely displaced Russian Orthodox workers to become a powerful influence on Tlingit life. Presbyterians established a mission at Sitka in 1878 and a school in 1880. They found that Tlingit women were more receptive to Christianity than were men. Because women were influential in this matrilineal society, working through them became an important avenue of culture change. Girls attended school more often than boys, and women became interpreters more often than men, which gave them increased standing and influence. Certain biblical messages were readily understood by the Tlingit because of their own beliefs. For example, the sacrifice of Jesus Christ for the sins of humankind was fully comprehensible in terms of compensation. A Tlingit also considered it much better to give than to receive, which was again a Christian ideal, although in a different context. They began, however, to expect rewards for becoming Christian. When asked to attend church, an old Tlingit was likely to respond, "How much you pay me?" Parents also expected compensation for permitting their children to attend school.

Presbyterian mission schools became widespread and a key institution for the introduction of systematic changes. Instruction was in English, and students were punished for speaking Tlingit. It was through these schools that missionaries were most successful in winning converts.

Despite missionary pressures, the potlatch system continued with much of the pageantry and drama of aboriginal times. The predilection for borrowing and imitating the songs, dances, and costumes of foreigners continued. For example, some shipwrecked Japanese arrived at Dry Bay in 1908. The next year Tlingit women displayed a memorable imitation of Japanese clothing and hairstyles. Changes were also evident in the form that potlatch gifts took. Blankets from traders came to be more important than Chilkat robes; silver dollars were a favorite gift item, followed closely by store-bought food. Over the years, the tradition of erecting totem poles continued on occasion (see Figure 9-9).

Expanding Tlingit acceptance of Euro-American technology led to pervasive material culture changes, just as Christian missionaries altered the nonmaterial aspects of life. Russian Orthodox and Presbyterian missionaries alike sought to assimilate the people into mainstream Western culture. After converting people to Christianity, church-centered brotherhoods, as voluntary associations, became a major means to foster culture change. The strength of Tlingit traditions and the small number of Orthodox priests made their mission less than successful. Then too Orthodox influence declined after the sale of Alaska in 1867. The first Orthodox brotherhood was established in 1896, but again, with few church workers, they were unable to make significant progress.

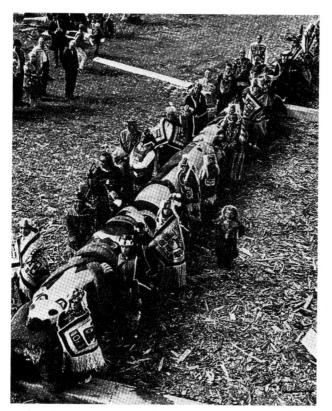

Figure 9-9 | The totem pole erected at the town of Kake in 1971 is 136 feet high and is the tallest pole ever raised. (Courtesy of the Alaska Division of Tourism.)

Following the Russian Revolution in 1917 most priests left Alaska. Orthodox failure paved the way for temporary Presbyterian achievements.

BROTHERHOODS Presbyterian Indian leaders strongly committed to integration into the greater society founded the Alaska Native Brotherhood (ANB) in 1912. By the 1920s chapters (camps) existed in most southeastern Alaskan Indian villages. The Alaska Native Sisterhood, created in 1923, became a parallel organization for women. Their official song was "Onward Christian Soldiers." Eligibility for membership was restricted to English speakers, and the constitutions were printed in English.

The ANB concentrated on gaining rights for Indians equal to those of whites. The Russo–American treaty for the sale of Alaska stated that uncivilized tribes, including most Tlingit and other aboriginal Alaskans, were to be subject to such laws as the United States might pass. With the purchase, no attempt was made to negotiate treaties or to establish Indian reservations, and therefore the citizenship status of aboriginal Alaskans remained unclear. They were not "wards of the government" in the sense of reservation or treaty Indians. They came to consider themselves as citizens, but the whites in Alaska usually regarded them in the same light as Indians in the United States. Until they were declared citizens, the Tlingit could not file on mining claims, a major cause of resentment. The citizenship issue was forced in 1922 by a Tlingit lawyer, William L. Paul, who was extremely active in brotherhood affairs. As a result of Paul's efforts, Alaskan Indians, in theory, had full voting rights before the federal government passed the Indian Citizenship Act of 1924 granting full citizenship to all Indians who were not previously citizens: In the late 1930s he became involved in labor politics and was successful in obtaining collective bargaining for many cannery workers and fishermen in southeastern Alaska. (In 1924 William L. Paul was the first Indian elected to the territorial legislature.) In 1945 the territorial legislature passed an antidiscrimination law.

The original brotherhood goal of doing away with aboriginal customs had been partially realized in the 1950s. The principal target, the potlatch, was regarded as heathen and was deplored; however, as Philip Drucker (1958) pointed out, it was primarily a social, not a religious, ceremony. In reality some potlatch customs emerged within the structure of the ANB. These included addressing persons of the opposite moiety in a ceremonial fashion; fining individuals for infractions; and gift giving by the family of a deceased person for burial services provided by the opposite moiety through the brotherhood. In one sense the ANB served as a new institution through which moieties reciprocated. Furthermore, although the ideal of speaking English continued, the meetings of local chapters sometimes were conducted in Tlingit, especially because the most active members normally were older and less likely to speak English with ease.

Despite Presbyterian missionary success and the neglect of the Tlingit by the Russian Orthodox church, Orthodoxy endured. Two reasons may best account for this. First, although Presbyterians were winning and keeping converts, they were closely identified with the civil government of Alaska that the Tlingit justly regarded as unfair to them. Second, and in response to these circumstances, many Tlingit felt that if they were to become Christians, it was better to be Orthodox, because this church was more tolerant and traditional in its orientation.

LAND CLAIMS SETTLEMENTS   Land and property rights were paramount concerns of the aboriginal Tlingit. Because of this focus, seizure of their land without compensation by outsiders over the years became a growing issue. Russian and early Euro-American settlement was thin, but it was far more widespread in southeastern Alaska than elsewhere in the territory and seldom had a clear legal basis. In 1935 the Tlingit and Haida Indians in Alaska sued the federal government for land losses and sought a settlement of $80 million.

(The Haida live largely on the Queen Charlotte Islands of British Columbia, but some of them had moved to Prince of Wales Island in southeastern Alaska in prehistoric times.) In 1968 the U.S. Court of Claims "settled" their claim by granting them $7.5 million as compensation for the *sixteen million acres* of land involved.

Despite the Alaskan natives' profound distrust of the federal government, the Indian Reorganization Act (IRA) was extended to their homeland in 1936 to establish village councils (see also Chapter 2) that would have limited political power but that could administer meaningful loan programs for fostering community welfare. Few villages in southeastern Alaska voted to come under the terms of the act. Those that did so invested largely in commercial salmon-fishing equipment (e.g., boats) and canneries to provide greater economic vitality. When the canned salmon market declined in the 1970s, however, many villagers defaulted on their loans and moved away to find more promising economic opportunities. Over the years the Alaska Native Brotherhood lost its vitality and began to be replaced in the 1940s by the Tlingit and Haida Central Council, established as the broad-based political organization for the Indians of the region.

When Alaska became a state in 1959, Native Alaskan landrights were acknowledged but not seriously considered. The state obtained title to some 103 million acres from the public domain, with *no* allowance for Native Alaskan claims. Alarm over this situation led to the formation of the Alaska Federation of Natives in 1966 to press for statewide land rights. Years of acrimonious debate finally resulted in the Alaska Native Claims Settlement Act (ANCSA) in 1971. At that time the federal Indian policy nationally was shifting from termination—"getting out of the Indian business"—to tribal "self-determination." Both were meant to result in the eventual assimilation of Indians into the greater society. In Alaska corporate efforts to tap the considerable oil deposits on the North Slope of Alaska could not be accomplished until the Native Alaskan claims were resolved. The basic conflict pitted Alaskan and national political interests against those of Native Alaskan land claimants and their supporters. The resultant ANCSA took the form of a law, *not* a treaty. It did not establish reservation lands to be held in trust by the federal government, nor did it classify Alaska as Indian Country or recognize claims of tribal sovereignty. Instead, it legalized for-profit native public corporations established on a land base to be owned and managed in the future by the people involved. This was meant to resolve a long-standing political issue and hopefully end a pattern of welfare dependency that had become widespread among the Native Alaskans.

One major provision of the ANCSA was that Native Alaskans were to receive fee simple title to 40 million acres of public land, as well as $962.5 million paid to the Alaska Native Fund (ANF) over a period of years, as compensation for extinguished claims. Typically, U.S. citizens in or from Alaska with one-fourth or more Aleut, Eskimo, or Indian genetic heritage were enrolled as stockholders in both village and regional corporations. Those born later received only shares as gifts or by inheritance. In general the regional corporations held mineral rights to village lands. Payments from the ANF to regional corporations were made on a per capita basis; the corporations retained part of the money and turned the balance over to the village corporations. The village corporations were distinct from the IRA village organizations, which retained their legal standing. Furthermore, because each of the regional corporations had a different resource base, such as from oil in the north and timber in the south, potential profits were to be distributed among the corporations.

Tlingit and Haida claims not resolved by earlier court decisions were absorbed into the ANCSA structure. Under the act's terms, the Tlingit and Haida together formed one of the twelve original corporations, which was named the Sealaska Corporation. It received 540,000 acres of land; of this amount the village corporations each received about 23,000 acres, usually near the village and selected to contain old-growth timber. The original act became increasingly involved as its application went forward. In 1976–1977 alone twenty-eight amendments were added by Congress. The tortuous details of the act with reference to southeastern Alaska and its implications by the late 1990s are set forth with interpretive elegance in a book by Kirk Dombrowski (2001).

In 1971 some people had opposed the act, arguing that it was designed to fail and that the land of most Native Alaskans eventually would become directly owned or controlled by the political allies of powerful non-native business enterprises. This negative conclusion has gained in credibility following a complex series of anticipated and unanticipated problems. In 2003 a Nadene Indian leader in Alaska, Gary Harrison, offered the following evaluation of the functioning of the ANCSA. "There are a whole lot of attorneys, accountants, administrators and consulting carpetbaggers who have retired as multimillionaires, and the people still have not received what they were promised." He went on to observe, "The corporations were designed to strip the rights and resources from the people and the land" (Stephenson 2003, A3). Examples from southeastern Alaska reveal the background for Harrison's judgment.

As mentioned earlier, eligible Native Alaskans born after passage of the ANCSA receive no personal shares except as gifts or by inheritance. These "new natives," or "afterborns," are left landless, for whatever the reasons, and they deeply resent their disadvantaged status. Sealaska and the region's village corporations have only one current economic asset, stands of old-growth timber, which for years were harvested under the act without environmental restraints. The timber industry and its allies, including state officials, have used recent settlement act revisions based on changes in the federal tax code to gain handsome profits through tax loopholes for corporations in general. Some of these profits reached shareholders, but many of them are now nonresidents, having left their villages following economic hardships, such as a decline in commercial salmon fishing. They are intent on receiving timber harvest money rather than reinvesting for the sake of continuing village economic vitality.

In starkly general terms, three clusters of contemporary Tlingit are prominently involved in current corporation management. Older persons in particular support and foster those aspects grounded in their traditional culture, although they also are willing to embrace historical changes; thus among them there is a syncretism that combines the old and new. Its elements include speaking Tlingit, continuing clan traditions, and retaining select craft skills. The moderate group tends to be young to middle-aged English speakers who identify with and may actively participate in select and highly visible aspects of their traditional cultural heritage. They also tend to identify with the biannual Sealaska Corporation "Celebration," a four-day event centering on performances of traditional dances by groups from most of the villages. Finally there are those who reject the traditional culture. These are usually younger tribal members who require particular attention at this point because their responses are radically innovative and, to a great extent, appear to result from flaws in the ANCSA.

"You won't find any Chilkat dancers in Heaven." This sentence, or a variation of it, has come to symbolize those Tlingit who reject their cultural background on religious grounds. The rejectors are largely have-nots. Many of them face pressing hardships due to unemployment, low-paying jobs, substandard housing, political impotency, and the abuse of alcohol. Before the mid-1970s most of these Tlingit appear to have been members of Christian churches controlled by missions from afar. Those who reject their Indianness find positive identity in the "new churches." The Assembly of God came first, with the United Pentecostal and Four Square churches following. All became established in Tlingit communities. They either have loose ties with their national organizations or are unaffiliated and self-supporting. The Tlingit who serve as preachers are chosen by the local membership. Congregations tend to be small, and most members habitually interact with one another. There is considerable flexibility in attending services in other new churches, however. Members accept a literal interpretation of the Protestant Bible. They stress the words of Christ, embrace Jesus as their personal savior, and feel guided by the Holy Spirit. They battle against sin, with the consumption of alcohol as a prime example. Services include prayers from the congregation for guidance, testimonies about being saved, and sermons focused on sin and salvation. Prayer meetings and revivals are held, and speaking in tongues occurs at these meetings as well as at Sunday services.

The "Flo Ellers incident" in 1992 was a catalytic episode in younger Tlingits' movement for change. It occurred at an independent Pentecostal church revival where the preacher was a local person and the participants were from other communities. In her quest for salvation, Ellers had become an itinerant preacher who spoke against native beliefs and artifacts as barriers to achieving eternal salvation. (Shortly before this revival, a major ANCSA cash payment to villagers in the area had resulted in local suicides, as well as other deaths associated directly with alcohol.) Immediately following the revival service, participants from other villages apparently reported that years earlier they had burned their cultural artifacts to gain salvation and that a serpent's image arose from the flames. They received permission from Ellers, who was present, and the preacher to burn objects associated with their past. The participants built a fire in an oil drum in the church parking lot. Items thrown into the flames included liquor bottles, unacceptable books and magazines, and jackets bearing a traditionally derived logo associated with the settlement act. They also burned one or more button blanket dance costumes belonging to a local dance group, even though these blankets are not traditional heirlooms. Soon similar fires in other "new church" communities destroyed items considered harmful, including evidence of Tlingit culture. These fires expressed a long-festering dislike of outsiders' culture, as well as disapproval of traditional tribal government. (Precedent had been set in the early American era by Christian missionaries who approved the burning of Tlingit totem poles.) It is conceivable that new church congregations may become a political force among Native Alaskans.

A VILLAGE CORPORATION   No Tlingit village corporation is typical, but Goldbelt Incorporated is less so than most others. It was created for the Auke kwaan ("tribe" in some contexts) in and around Juneau, the capital of Alaska and a major tourist stop. Goldbelt enterprises are increasingly tourist-oriented, but they do provide a good example of Tlingit adaptability to present-day realities.

Auke kwaan had little contact with colonial Russians or with agents of the United States until 1880, when gold was discovered in the Juneau area. The sudden influx of miners, prospectors, and others led the U.S. Navy to establish a local presence to contain white lawlessness. The federal government previously had identified the area as "Indian Country," meaning that trade and intercourse laws, including a prohibition on intoxicants, were in effect. Naval officers in charge recognized some aspects of Tlingit customary law and were impressed by its sophistication. However, before long the Tlingit were restricted in where they could live and were forced to settle at the margins of white-dominated Juneau.

With ever-expanding white control in southeastern Alaska during the early decades of the twentieth century, Tlingit rights became a pressing issue. The Auke were a principal participant in the lawsuit that eventually forced the federal government into a partial settlement of Tlingit land claims in 1959. With the ANCSA of 1971, as revised, a village corporation was permitted to claim 23,040 acres, but there was no block of land in the Juneau area for the Auke to claim. They had to select acreage nearby. Initially they logged a great deal of timber from the area to pay stockholder dividends.

In 1998 their Goldbelt corporation assets amounted to approximately $77 million, excluding the value of their landholdings. The board of directors included five men and three women. The corporation and its subsidiaries employed nearly five hundred shareholders from a total population of nearly three thousand. Alaska had become an increasingly favored destination for cruise ships in the summer months, with Juneau a major stop; in 2000 about 632,000 people visited there. Understandably, Goldbelt management invested heavily in downtown Juneau. By 2003 these included a hotel in Juneau and part ownership in the Mount Roberts Tramway at one end of town. They owned sightseeing vessels for one-day to week-long cruises in the region. Sea kayaking opportunities and whale watching excursions were added to attract greater numbers of tourists. However, the weakening of the national economy began in the early 2000s, and visitor travel to Alaska was curtailed.

FURTHER ISSUES AND DEVELOPMENTS   Thomas F. Thornton (1998) justly wrote that subsistence has been the most contentious issue in Alaskan politics for over twenty years, and this is particularly applicable to Native Alaskans. The problem covers not only the local harvest of wild food resources but the right of local peoples to help determine harvest levels and to exercise general control over their landholdings. Thus subsistence and "sovereignty" are intimately associated. Subsistence issues basically pit people in rural areas against those who live in urban settings. Twenty percent of Alaskans live in rural areas, and about half of them are Natives. The 80 percent who are urban and primarily Euro-American obviously have the greater political power. Two additional sets of statistics further suggest the scope of the conflict. In rural areas during 1994, the average harvest of local edibles was about 375 pounds per person per year, whereas in urban areas it was 22 pounds. Equally significant, 4 percent of the fish and wildlife harvest throughout Alaska in 1990 was for subsistence use; 1 percent was taken by sportspersons and 95 percent went to commercial interests, meaning primarily the fishing industry. Clearly, subsistence has represented only a small fraction of the total harvest.

The legal and political battles over subsistence usage among all interested parties are convoluted, but a brief summary can point up the critical issues. The ANCSA and the Alaska National Interest Lands Conservation Act of 1980 indirectly and directly support Native preference in subsistence matters; about *60 percent* of Alaskan land is under federal control, a crucial statistic. The State of Alaska has argued, however, that it has the right to manage all of its fish and wildlife resources. The federal government agreed to state management of subsistence on federal and state lands *if* it complied with federal laws. The state has not complied, and in 1999 the federal government assumed the responsibility for subsistence management on federal lands. The following year the federal government restricted commercial salmon fishing to ensure a more reasonable catch for rural residents. Although state officials remain distressed over this development, the federal government remains in control.

Native Alaskans have become alarmed by a proposal from Senator Ted Stevens (R-Alaska), an extremely powerful individual in Congress, that recommended the administrative consolidation of the 229 "tribes," mostly villages, who receive federal funds. Given the uncertain economic climate and the federal deficit in 2002, Stevens found the yearly cost of about $500 million for social, housing, health, and other programs for Native Alaskans to be unacceptable. He proposed the formation of statewide regional groups (i.e., a major change in political status) to channel funds more economically. He reasoned that because numerous tribes are very small, most of the federal money was being spent for administration, which was not aiding the people who needed help (i.e., duplicative waste). The Alaska Federation of Natives and the Alaska Inter-Tribal Council considered the proposal as a direct attack by the federal and *state* governments on Native Alaskan self-determination and fear the loss of existing tribal rights and recognition. They suspect that the federal government is prepared to make an essentially unilateral decision that will eventually result in termination of federal responsibilities. Stevens's proposal failed, but many Native Alaskans fear that he may seek alternative means to achieve his goals.

The Westernization of the Tlingit has been somewhat eased by what might be called the "Tlingit factor." This factor comprises three sets of unique circumstances. First is the sophistication of aboriginal Tlingit culture. The second is the fact that they remained essentially free of effective Euro-American political control until the early 1900s. The third is the traditional Tlingit emphasis placed on trade for economic gain; this key value fit comfortably into the Euro-American concept of capitalism. As a result of these factors, the Tlingit could be reasonably discriminating in their acceptance of Western innovations, and they were adept at fitting new ideas into traditional patterns. As a result, selective sociocultural continuity becomes evident (see Figure 9-10).

As previously discussed, the Tlingit people made numerous early adjustments, such as replacing Chilkat robes with imported blankets and using silver dollars in potlatch exchanges to partially replace craft items. The Orthodox and Protestant brotherhoods provide examples of compromises that furthered Tlingit values. For many Tlingit, clan affiliations have lost their meaning, but identity with a moiety remains strong. Kan (1989b, 406) noted that modern potlatches retain many essential elements of the traditional versions. Old age and ritual expertise are now more important to hosting a potlatch than rank status, as in the past. Participation in potlatches, however, has declined. Memorial potlatches to release the spirits of the dead persist and often are ecumenical. Traditional Tlingit, Orthodox, Presbyterian, and Salvation Army participation may all occur in one ceremony, with little or no conflict.

The regional geographical clusters, or kwaans, have retained selective vitality, due in part to their incorporation into the structure of the ANCSA. Thus village corporations such as Goldbelt remain a central factor in assuring Tlingit identity. Similarly, we find that traditional Tlingit artifacts are important identifiers for some clans and house groups. For example, the Eagle Nest House at Sitka has a comprehensive inventory of traditional ceremonial artifacts, and six other clans or house groups have similar holdings. In addition, many craftspersons make Tlingit artifacts for sale to tourists. Some twenty-five highly skilled craftspeople contract with individual buyers to produce artifacts, such as masks, helmets, and house post facings. The best artists may charge as much as $15,000 for a mask. In this general context, some Tlingit singers and dance groups, especially the Naa Ka Hidi Theater, are widely honored for their performance skills, and recognition of these groups continues to expand. Thus Tlingit culture is far from moribund despite its losses.

Figure 9-10 | Tlingit art is especially apparent in Juneau, Alaska. The State Office Building includes the "Old Witch" totem pole made in the 1880s on Prince of Wales Island.

| Additional Sources

The best relatively brief overview about the Tlingit, past and present, is by Wallace M. Olson (1995). The best synopsis is by Frederica de Laguna (1990). The key general source about Northwest Coast Indians is edited by Wayne Suttles (1990) and published by the Smithsonian Institution. An excellent Tlingit ethnography for the late 1880s is by Aurel Krause (1885). The only comprehensive ethnographic reconstruction concerning a kwaan is for Yakutat by de Laguna (1972). Traditional social life at Klukwan is brilliantly described in a monograph by Kalervo Oberg (1973). The best discussion of Tlingit totem poles is by Edward L. Keithan (1963), and the best general work about totem poles is by Marius Barbeau (1950). Bill Holm (1965) provides the most insightful book-length discussion of Northwest Coast Indian art. The ethnohistorical studies by Sergei Kan are valuable, especially *Memory Eternal: Tlingit Culture and Russian Orthodox Christianity through Two Centuries* (Seattle, 1999). A notable but more broad-based study is *The Canoe Rocks: Alaska's Tlingit and the Euroamerican Frontier, 1800–1912* by Ted C. Hinckley (Lanham, MD, 1996).

| Selected Bibliography

Bancroft, Hubert H. 1886. *History of Alaska, 1730–1885. The works of Hubert Howe Bancroft.* Vol. 33. San Francisco.

Barbeau, Marius. 1950. *Totem poles.* Ottawa.

Dauenhauer, Nora Marks, and Richard Dauenhauer. 1994. *Haa Kusteeyí, our culture: Tlingit life stories.* Seattle.

de Laguna, Frederica. 1960. *The story of a Tlingit community.* Bureau of American Ethnology Bulletin 172.

———. 1972. *Under Mount Saint Elias.* Smithsonian Contributions to Anthropology, vol. 7.

———. 1983. Aboriginal Tlingit sociopolitical organization. In *The development of political organization in native North America,* 1979 Proceedings of the American Ethnological Society, Elisabeth Tooker, ed., 71–85.

———. 1990. Tlingit. In *Northwest Coast,* Wayne Suttles, ed., vol. 7, 203–28. *Handbook of North American Indians.* Washington, DC.

Dombrowski, Kirk. 2001. *Against culture: Development, politics, and religion in Indian Alaska.* Lincoln, NE.

Drucker, Philip. 1958. *The native brotherhoods.* Bureau of American Ethnology Bulletin 168.

———. 1965. *Cultures of the North Pacific coast.* San Francisco.

Emmons, George Thornton, with Frederica de Laguna and Jean Low. 1992. *The Tlingit Indians.* Seattle.

Holm, Bill. 1965. *Northwest Coast Indian art.* Seattle.

Hope, Andrew, III, and Thomas F. Thornton. 2000. *Will the time ever come? A Tlingit source book.* Fairbanks.

Jonaitis, Aldona. 1986. *Art of the Northern Tlingit.* Seattle.

Jones, Livingston F. 1914. *A study of the Thlingets of Alaska.* New York.

Kamenskii, Anatolii. 1985. *Tlingit Indians of Alaska.* Sergei Kan, trans. Fairbanks.

Kan, Sergei. 1983. Words that heal the soul. *Arctic Anthropology* 20(2):47–59.

———. 1985. Russian Orthodox brotherhoods among the Tlingit. *Ethnohistory* 32: 196–222.

———. 1986. The 19th-century Tlingit potlatch. *American Ethnologist* 13:191–212.

———. 1989a. *Symbolic immortality: The Tlingit Potlatch of the nineteenth century.* Washington, DC.

———. 1989b. Cohorts, generations, and their culture: The Tlingit potlatch in the 1980s. *Anthropos* 84:405–22.

———. 1991. Shamanism and Christianity: Modern-day Tlingit elders look at the past. *Ethnohistory* 38(4):363–87.

———. 1996. Clan mothers and godmothers: Tlingit women and Russian Orthodox Christianity, 1840–1940. *Ethnohistory* 43(4):613–41.

Keithan, Edward L. 1963. *Monuments in cedar* (rev. ed.). Seattle.

Krause, Aurel. 1885. *The Tlingit Indians*. 2 vols. Jena. Translated edition, Erna Gunther, trans., American Ethnological Society, 1956.

Lisianskii, Urey F. 1814. *A voyage round the world*. London.

Malaspina, D. Alejandro, and Don Jose de Bustamante y Guerra. 1885. *Political-scientific trip around the world* (translated title). Madrid.

McClellan, Catharine. 1954. The interrelations of social structure with northern Tlingit ceremonialism. *Southwestern Journal of Anthropology* 10:75–96.

Niblack, Albert P. 1890. *The coast Indians of southern Alaska and northern British Columbia*. Annual Report of the Smithsonian Institution, 1887–88, 225–386.

Oberg, Kalervo. 1973. *The social economy of the Tlingit Indians*. Seattle.

Olson, Wallace M. 1995. *The Tlingit: An introduction to their culture and history*. Juneau.

Porter, Robert P. 1893. *Report on population and resources of Alaska at the Eleventh Census: 1890*. Washington, DC.

Romanowsky, S., and E. Frankenhauser. 1849. Five years of medical observations in the colonies of the Russian-American Company. *Medical Newspaper of Russia* 6:153–61. St. Petersburg. (Translated from German and reprinted in *Alaska Medicine* 4:33–37, 62–64, 1962.)

Stephenson, Dave. 2003. "Tribalizing" Alaska's Native corporations. *Indian Country Today* (newspaper), June 4, 2003.

Suttles, Wayne, ed. 1990. *Northwest Coast*. Vol. 7, *Handbook of North American Indians*. Washington, DC.

Swanton, John R. 1908. *Social conditions, beliefs, and linguistic relationship of the Tlingit Indians*. Bureau of American Ethnology, 26th Annual Report, 391–512.

Thornton, Thomas F. 1998. Alaska Native subsistence. *Cultural Survival Quarterly* 22(3):29–34.

Veniaminov, Ivan. 1984. *Notes on the islands of the Unalaska district*. Lydia T. Black and R. H. Geoghegan, trans.; Richard A. Price, ed. Kingston, Ontario.

10 The Hopi: Farmers of the Desert

Your beautiful rays,
may they color our faces;
being dyed in them,
somewhere at an old age
we shall fall asleep old women.

Woman's prayer to the sun
for a newborn girl
(H. R. Voth 1905, 53)

THE PUEBLO PEOPLES of the Southwest may best typify Native American lifeways. Massive pueblos, painted pottery, colorful rituals, and kachina dolls characterize these people to most outsiders. Pueblo Indians, such as the Hopi of northeastern Arizona, continue to live in their desert setting, and most of them have clung tenaciously to their Indian identity. The survival of the Hopi as a people is remarkable in light of the forces that have been bent on their destruction over the centuries. As an example of the persistence of their culture, Christian missionaries began working among the Hopi in 1629, but by the 1950s fewer than 2 percent of the Hopi were practicing Christians.

There are additional reasons for devoting a chapter to the Hopi. Nowhere else are Indians so intimately associated with one locality. Nowhere else among Indians do the past and present blend into such a consistent whole. Furthermore, a wealth of information exists about the Hopi. They have long attracted the attention of ethnographers, resulting in excellent studies about their lifeways. The monograph titled *Old Oraibi* by Mischa Titiev (1944) is one of the best ethnographic studies of American Indians.

Pueblo peoples were distinguished from other Native Americans in the Southwest by their emphasis on maize cultivation, social and political complexity, and rich ceremonial life. Yet significant differences existed between the Eastern Pueblos, such as Isleta, Taos, and Zia, and the Western Pueblos that included Acoma, Hopi, and Zuni. Pueblo Indian linguistic diversity suggests that they had varied prehistoric backgrounds, and they differed by region in other ways. The Western Pueblo matrilineal stress contrasted with the patrilineal emphasis in some pueblos to the east. Western Pueblos were theocratic and less centralized than those to the east. Furthermore, kachinas (supernatural beings) were prominent in the west, whereas medicine societies tended to dominate in the east. Clearly it is incorrect to view Pueblo Indian cultures as uniform.*

Hopi (HO-pee), the word that these people apply to themselves, is often translated as "good" or "peaceful." The Hopi language is in the Uto–Aztecan family, and the aboriginal population numbered about twenty-eight hundred. Their Arizona homeland is one of deserts and plateaus with sporadic and unpredictable rainfall (see Figure 10-1). Rainwater from the upland sandstone region seeps into a layer of shale and emerges at the ends of mesas as springs and moist areas. At higher elevations on the mesas, juniper and scattered pinyon grow. This flora is replaced by grassland nearer the valley floors, and in the lower areas desert vegetation, including saltbrush, greasewood, and sagebrush, dominates. In damp localities or along irregularly flowing streams, cottonwoods and willows grow.

| Aboriginal Life

Unlike the peoples discussed in earlier chapters, the Hopi were sedentary farmers whose lives centered in small, stable villages. They, possibly more

---

*See Chapter 1 for evidence about prehistoric Pueblo Indian cannibalism.

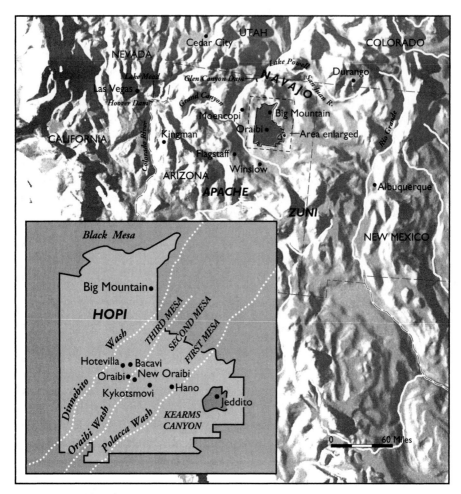

Figure 10-1 | The Hopi Reservation.

than any other Pueblo people, display an appealing continuity with the past. Their ancestors settled in northern Arizona at least a thousand years ago, and the Hopi village of Oraibi (Old Oraibi) is one of the oldest continuously occupied settlements north of Mexico.

ORIGIN MYTH   Each Hopi clan had its own version of a creation story. In primeval times, according to a myth recorded at Oraibi, there was no light or living thing on earth, only a being called Maasaw (Death). Three caves beneath the earth's surface likewise were engulfed in darkness. In the lowest cave people existed in crowded and filthy conditions. Two brothers, The Two, lamented the plight of the people and pierced the cave roof; they grew one plant after another, trying to reach the second world. After a particular type of cane grew tall enough, the people and animals climbed it to the second cave world. This level finally was filled with people, and they ascended to the third cave. Here the brothers found fire, and the darkness was dispelled. Here the people built houses and ceremonial structures called *kivas;* but great turmoil developed when women began to neglect their duties as wives and mothers, preferring instead to dance in the kivas. Finally, the people, along with Coyote, Locust, Spider, Swallow, and Vulture, emerged at the fourth level, which was the earth. They wandered about with only torches to light their way. Together the people and the creatures with them attempted to create light. Spider spun a white cotton blanket that gave off some light. The people then processed a white deerskin and painted it turquoise. This skin was so bright that it lighted the entire world. The painted deerskin became the sun, and the blanket was the moon. Stars were released from a jar by Coyote.

Once the earth was lighted, the creatures realized that the land area was limited by surrounding water. The Vulture fanned the water with its wings, and as the waters flowed away, mountains appeared. The Two made channels for the waters through the mountains, and canyons and valleys were formed. The people saw the tracks of Maasaw and followed them to the east. They caught up with Maasaw, and a girl conspired with him to cause the death of a girl she envied. This was the first death among people, the conspirator was the first witch, and her descendants became the witches of the world. The dead girl was seen living in the cave world below the earth, which had become an idyllic place. The witch caused conflicts with people who had emerged on earth before the Hopi, particularly the Navajo and Mexicans. Another deity helped people by making their maize and other seeds ripen in a single day. Of the two brothers who led the people from the underworld, the younger brother was the ancestor of the Oraibi people. The older brother went east but promised to return when the Hopi needed him. After many generations and in accord with this promise the older brother's descendants, the Bahanas, were to return when the Hopi were poor and in need. The Bahanas would be rich and would bring food and clothing for the Hopi. The Hopi would reject them, but the Bahanas would treat them kindly.

APPEARANCE AND CLOTHING A Hopi girl wore her hair long until she passed through a puberty ceremony; it then was put up in two disk-shaped bundles ("squash-blossom hairdo"), one over each ear. After she married, her hair was parted in the middle and worn long again. A woman's clothing consisted of a wraparound cotton blanket that passed under her left arm and was fastened together over the right shoulder. This garment extended a short distance below her knees, and she wore leggings as well as moccasins. Men wore headbands to control their hair, which might be relatively short or long and knotted behind the neck. Everyday male clothing included a breechclout of deerskin or cotton cloth and a cotton cloth kilt, belted at the waist. A man also might wear deerskin leggings and moccasins or sandals.

Figure 10-2 | The village of Oraibi, with melons and peaches drying on the roof in the foreground. (Courtesy of the Southwest Museum, Los Angeles. Photo # neg. no. 24007.)

SETTLEMENTS AND MANUFACTURES   At the south end of Black Mesa are three tongues of land, and on the westernmost, called Third Mesa, the village of Oraibi is located (see Figure 10-2). This is the community where Mischa Titiev worked, and whenever possible the descriptions will focus there. The pueblo was laid out in a series of eight nearly parallel streets with scattered kivas and a plaza between two streets. In aboriginal times men made the square houses from stones dressed and set in place for the floor and walls. The roof beams were placed on the uppermost course of stones, and the women for whom a house was being built prepared and applied a mud plaster to the inner walls. A woman and her friends completed the roof by adding brushwood, grass, and finally mud. Women owned the dwellings, and new ones were usually built next to the residence of a woman's mother or another close female relative. Houses were often windowless, and no doors opened on the street. They were often multistory, with access through an opening in the ceiling beneath which was placed a notched log ladder. Bin metates (milling stones) of different degrees of coarseness for grinding maize lined one side of a room (see Figure 10-3), and fireplaces completed the furnishings. Rooms without any outside opening were often used for storing food and material goods. A kiva (ceremonial structure) was a rectangular subterranean room entered by descending

Figure 10-3 | A Hopi woman grinding grain in a bin metate. (Courtesy of the Southwest Museum, Los Angeles. Photo # LS. 6035-N42082.)

a ladder from an opening in the roof. The section of the floor where observers sat was slightly raised, and the remaining portion included a fire pit and sipapu, a hole in the floor through which spirits were thought to enter. Along most walls were stone compartments that held sacred objects. At Oraibi there were about fifteen kivas, each owned by a matriclan.

The most elaborate manufactures were textiles, usually woven by men. They carded and spun cotton into thread and wove textiles on looms in their homes or in kivas. The fiber often was dyed black, green, orange, red, or yellow. On a vertical loom suspended between the ceiling and the floor they made square and rectangular cloth for blankets. Belts were made on a waist loom attached to a beam at one end and to the weaver's waist at the other, being held taut with his body. Women wove rabbitskin blankets on vertical looms. The most important textiles woven by men for women were for wedding robes, belts, dresses, and shawls. For themselves, men wove kilts and sashes for ceremonies, and blankets, kilts, and shirts for daily use.

Women made pottery, both undecorated ware for cooking and storage and polished and decorated forms for other uses. They collected clay from nearby deposits, soaked it, and kneaded it into a paste, adding ground sandstone to the paste of utility wares. Long coils were added to a flat clay bottom, and each seam was pinched to join the preceding piece and then obliterated by hand-smoothing. The completed containers were dried, and undecorated utility ware was fired without further processing. If a pot was to be decorated, the woman smoothed and thinned it after drying with a piece of sandstone. Then she moistened and polished it with a stone in preparation for painting. Pottery was painted black, orange, red, white, and yellow, and the prevalent designs were quite similar to those used in early historic times, when old designs were revived after falling out of use. In 1895 an archaeologist excavated an abandoned Hopi pueblo. One of his Indian workmen was the husband of a woman who was widely recognized as one of the best Pueblo potters, Nampeyo. She found the beautifully executed, painted pottery unearthed at the site fascinating and studied the sherds to become familiar with the patterns. She developed a style based on these originals, and it became very popular.

SUBSISTENCE ACTIVITIES   The Hopi farming year began near the end of February, when plots were cleared for planting. The time to sow was established by a Sun Watcher, who based his determination on the occurrence of the sunrise at a particular spot on the horizon. At the stipulated time, the men of a matriclan worked as a unit from planting through the harvest. A married man planted the clan land allotted to his wife and her immediate family. Men owned the crops until the harvest was taken to a wife's house, upon which the harvested food became her property. Farmland at the foot of Black Mesa was watered by ground seepage or from stream overflow (floodwater farming). A farmer prepared a plot by trampling the weeds or cutting them with a broad-bladed implement and breaking up the soil with a pointed stick. Maize, the most important crop by far, was planted in holes made with a digging stick. He dropped ten to twenty seeds into a single foot-deep hole; if a planting did not sprout in about ten days, he might reseed the plot. As plants grew, farmers weeded the plots and loosened the soil about the roots. Fields, about one acre in extent, were not rotated, nor was the maize hilled. They sometimes planted beans among the maize stalks but more often raised them in separate plots. Squash and cotton also appear to have been raised in separate acreage. During planting and harvesting, someone impersonating Maasaw, the God of Death, was usually present. Most other Hopi subsistence activities also were group endeavors, organized by individuals or societies to embrace some or all community members. One cooperative, communal task was to clear sand and debris from village springs that were owned by the Village Chief but used by everyone.

About forty plant species were cultivated in the 1930s. Of this number, five species were aboriginal (kidney and tepary beans, maize, cotton, and squash); four others may have existed prior to Spanish times but more likely were postcontact domestics (Aztec and lima beans, gourds, and sunflowers). Five species were introduced during the Spanish period (chili peppers, onions, peaches, watermelons, and wheat); all others were introduced by Mormon farmers or other Anglo-Americans. The Hopi cared for ten species of wild plants, but they apparently did not sow the seeds regularly. Seeds from two species of wild tobacco were sown when necessary to provide sufficient leaves for ceremonial uses. They used wild dock root for dye and sometimes planted the seeds. Fifty-four different wild plants were eaten, fifty were used to make or decorate artifacts, sixty-five were used medicinally, and forty had ceremonial or magical purposes. Although there is some overlap in these listings, the Hopi obviously used a wide variety of plant species. About two hundred wild flowering plants grew locally, of which half commonly were used.

The primary staple, maize, was the symbol of life to the Hopi, and they grew three varieties. In early historic times the flint variety was important because the hull of each grain was hard and not easily destroyed by weevils in storage. The flint variety was so difficult to grind, however, that it declined in importance. The most popular variety of maize in more recent times had been the flour type, which every farmer grew. They raised sweet corn of two named strains in small quantities.

They prepared maize for consumption in numerous ways. The harvested product was usually stored on the cob and shelled as needed. They made ground maize into gruel, dumplings, soups, and a breadlike product. Hominy was prepared by soaking shelled maize in a mixture of juniper wood ash and water, then boiling the grains and washing them to remove the hulls. Maize also was roasted on the ear, parched, or baked in pits. One important food made of maize, piki, was used as bread. They made it from a finely ground cornmeal mixed with water, using ashes as leavening, and cooked it on a special stone slab over a fire. The stone was heated and greased, and the bluishgray liquid was poured onto it. After cooking, the piki was folded or rolled into "loaves" for later consumption. They often ate it by dipping one end into liquid food and biting off the moistened portion.

Compared with farming rituals, the ceremonial preparations for a hunt were elaborate. The most important species hunted were antelope, cottontails, and jackrabbits. They often hunted rabbits in the late summer, when crops did not require attention. A man organizing a hunt could be from any clan so long as he made prayer offerings to the God of the Hunt. A crier announced the details of the time for the hunt, and the next day the organizer performed further rituals. In the hunt, men formed a surround and moved in until they could kill the encircled animals with throwing sticks (boomerangs, rabbit-killing sticks) or with hurled clubs. The surround was formed repeatedly, and the game continued to be taken until the leader called an end to the hunt. When they returned to the village, each man gave his kill to his mother, sister, wife, or father's sister. The recipient made a ritual offering to the dead animal to restore the game to the God of the Hunt.

Before hunting antelope, deer, and mountain sheep, the organizer, as well as all the others in the party, made prayer offerings, and they practiced ritual smoking. The surround method was used to capture these animals in aboriginal times. The pattern seems to have been to run down and suffocate an antelope. A deer apparently was shot with arrows or clubbed to death but not stabbed. Once again, they made a ritual propitiation of the deceased animal.

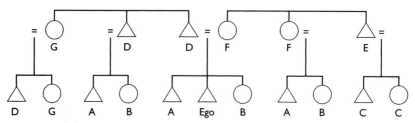

Figure 10-4 | The historic Hopi system of kinship terminology.

Coyote hunts were conducted by kiva members collectively, and as usual they employed the surround technique to catch and kill the animals. After a hunt they took each coyote to a kiva, gave it a lighted corn husk cigarette to placate the animal's spirit, and spoke to it as a child before the owner took the animal home.

DESCENT, KINSHIP, AND MARRIAGE As already indicated, the Hopi traced descent through females (matrilineal), and grooms always joined the households of their brides (matrilocal). Matrilineages were very important in social terms, and matriclans were overwhelmingly important ceremonial units.

A male individual termed his mother the same as his mother's sister and did not distinguish between them in normal conversation. Father and father's brother were termed alike, but mother's brother was termed differently. The designations for females in the first ascending generation paralleled those for males, because father's sister was distinguished from mother and mother's sister (bifurcate merging terminology). This usage is reasonable as mother and mother's sister were of the same clan, and father was in the same clan as father's brother. In the cousin terminology, parallel cousins were termed as siblings, whereas mother's brother's children were termed as one's own children, and a father's sister's daughter was called the same as father's sister. Finally, a father's sister's son was termed father (Crow type cousins) (see Figure 10-4). The most distinguishing characteristic of the cousin term is the ignoring of certain generational distinctions. The kinship terminology provided the framework for lifelong responsibilities, with particular forms of behavior expected in each set of relationships. One of the most bitter overt displays of anger against a relative was to renounce kinship ties.

SOCIAL DIMENSIONS The Hopi knew of no term for household, yet this social unit dominated and guided the life of each individual. A child was born into this unit and retained a strong emotional identity with it throughout life. The household consisted of a core of women—grandmother, daughters, and daughters' daughters—plus unmarried sons and in-marrying husbands. All except the husbands belonged to the same matriclan; also members of the lineage were those males born into the unit but now married and living in the houses of their wives. When a household outgrew its space, a room was added on to accommodate the newer members. This adjacent household retained its ties with the parent matrilineage, held farmland in common, and worshiped a common fetish (sacred bundle). The lineage fetish was in the custody of the oldest female lineage head, and the associated ceremonies were conducted largely by the old woman's brother or son. These ritual obligations were passed down the most direct maternal line. Common lineage problems were discussed at the original lineage residence, and it remained the heart of the matrilineage, sometimes after it was abandoned as a residence. From a leading matrilineage, with the greatest rights and duties, subordinate (daughter) lineages developed. As a daughter lineage grew, it might become socially removed from the original group and lose the underlying ties. The distant lineages would become separate clans if they created new bundles and acquired distinct names. Members of a named group who traced their ties through the same bundle formed a matriclan even though they could not trace connecting genealogical ties.

By 1906, about thirty named matriclans existed at Oraibi, a number that represented splits as well as the possible settlement there of new clans. The names, including Bear, Bow, Butterfly, and Lizard, were linked with happenings in mythological times or referred to clan ancestors. These ancestors were termed *wuya* and might or might not be tangibly represented by a sacred clan bundle. A bundle sometimes included more than one wuya; this led to alternative names for the clan and probably represented the consolidation of two clans. Clans formed nine larger groups (phratries) that were associated with the mythological past but not named; clans of the same phratry possibly stemmed ultimately from the same lineage base. Members of the same phratry shared common ceremonial and landholding interests, and they could not marry within the group (phratry exogamy).

POLITICAL LIFE Overall village control was in the hands of the Village Chief and the War Chief. The Village Chief was from the Bear clan, and a sacred stone in his possession verified his authority. The stone reportedly was brought from the underworld by the legendary village founder. The stone was engraved with motifs, including human figures, and their interpretation was the basis for a division of lands among the clans. The stone was inspected as a part of each Soyal Ceremony that the Village Chief headed (see next section). The Village Chief had not only the greatest sacred responsibilities at Oraibi but important secular duties as well. He settled land disputes, the most important differences between villagers. His sacred duties, in addition to those dealing with the Soyal Ceremony, included offering prayers for village welfare. It was the Village Chief who remained up late each night smoking and musing about pueblo conditions after most people slept. For any critical community matter, his advice was sought, although he could not compel the actions of others. The office of the Village Chief was passed to a brother or to a sister's son after a long period of training. The Village Chief wore no badge of office, but he had a distinctive style of body painting for certain ceremonies and a sacred stick or cane of authority.

The only person at Oraibi with permanent power was the War Chief, who attained his position by being the most outstanding warrior. He had the right to inflict verbal or physical punishment for nonconformity. On occasion, when parties of men were organized for a community project, men as *kachinas* (gods) assembled the workmen and directed their activities. (See the section "The Kachina Cult" later in this chapter.) A lazy man might be reprimanded or in extreme instances beaten by a kachina. The authority and power of the overt leaders *never* extended beyond the village. No means existed for uniting the Hopi as a tribe; in fact, the only time they clearly joined in a common cause was during the Pueblo Revolt of 1680.

The Hopi prided themselves on being a peaceful people who disliked shedding blood, and yet they organized for armed conflict. They fought to defend their pueblo, and the role of a warrior was recognized as dangerous, important, and necessary. In primeval times, when the Hopi reportedly emerged from the underworld, the Kokop and Spider clans introduced a Warrior Society. Every man was a member, but not all were of the same rank. Members were divided into ordinary warriors and stick-swallowers. Boys were trained for warfare with a rigorous program of cold baths, races, archery practice, and early rising. The Warrior Society held a ceremony each fall, using the sacred equipment held by the Spider and Kokop clans. The two days of rituals involved making prayer objects, ritual smoking, offering prayers, and building altars. A war medicine was prepared and drunk, after which one branch of the membership gave exhibitions of stick-swallowing. For the real warriors, those who acknowledged killing and scalping an enemy, a special initiation that involved fasting and secret rituals took place.

Warfare was said always to have been defensive. Men went into battle clad in ordinary clothing but with the addition of caps made from mountain lion skin to which eagle feathers were attached. A warrior fought with a bow and arrows, stone club, spear, and throwing stick. Before a battle the men prayed to Maasaw and to long-dead warriors, and they sang songs to make themselves brave. Armed only with a stone club, the War Chief led them into conflict. A slain enemy was scalped to the accompaniment of a scalping song, and scalps were carried into the pueblo on poles. A Navajo scalp was considered worthless, but one from an Apache or Ute was valued. The permanent resting place for a scalp was in the home of its taker. A scalp was washed with yucca suds and intermittently "fed" by its owner.

RELIGIOUS SYSTEM The Hopi religious system was precise, the ceremonial round was exacting, and the kachinas played a vital ceremonial role. To maintain the balance in nature and to sustain human relationship with the gods, each individual was obligated to contribute to the best of her or his ability. Through this effort an individual expressed a desire to be *hopi,* or good, but being hopi involved more than goodness alone. A Hopi ideally was cooperative, self-effacing, and nonaggressive, and the particulars of such behavior were spelled out in detail. A Hopi had moral and physical strength and good health and accepted collective responsibilities while concentrating on good thoughts; this was the Hopi Way. Conversely, an evil or bad person was *kahopi,* with personality traits opposite those of the ideals.

Central Concepts The basic tenet of the Hopi religion was the continuing relationship between the living and the dead, a duality expressed in many ways. A person not only had a physical body but also a "breath-body," spirit or soul. At death a soul journeyed to the underworld and continued to exist as it had on earth, with the exception that souls consumed only the essence of food. Preparations for the burial of the dead were similar to those for a newborn Hopi: a corpse was sprinkled with cornmeal, bathed, and received a new name. Because of their weightlessness, a soul could rise into the sky, where it would become a cloud to bring rain to the living. Thus, the God of Death, Maasaw, was in essence a god of fertility. The Sun too was a god of fertility in intimate association with the dead: it spent half of its time in the underworld with the dead and half of its time over the earth. Prayers and offerings to the Sun and to the dead were thought to bring earthly blessings. Birth and death formed an endless cycle; in theory, death held no fears because it represented rebirth.

The Sun's daily and yearly cycle in some ways mimicked the human life cycle. Each day on earth began as the Sun left its eastern home in the morning and ended when it set in its western home; thus the Sun gave light to both the earth and the underworld. A yearly cycle began with the summer solstice around mid-June. The summer solstice began the winter season because it was then that the days began to shorten. Summer, quite logically, began about mid-December, as the days grew longer. Earth and the underworld were thought to mirror each other: a summer solstice in one realm was a winter solstice in the other. Furthermore, when a major ceremony was held on earth, a minor one was being performed in the underworld, and vice versa.

Ceremonies The Hopi religious system required a series of annual and biannual ceremonies hosted by particular religious associations. Each important ceremony was controlled by a specific organization that was linked to a different matriclan. Each association was headed by a male elder of the leading lineage in the clan; this lineage also owned a sacred bundle called the "mother" or "heart" of the clan, which consisted of an ear of maize, feathers, and coverings, as well as other sacred objects. Ceremonies were held in a kiva associated with the clan and at times established by phases of the Moon, the location of the Sun when it rose, or the number of days since a previous ritual had ended. The pattern for major ceremonies was similar. The rituals spanned nine days, during which kiva members were not permitted to eat fatty foods, meat, and salt. Sexual activities were restricted before, as well as during, these celebrations. The specifics of the ceremonies included the use of altars and associated wooden, stone, or clay tablets painted with motifs symbolic of animals, clouds, maize, and rain. Sand paintings and certain fluids with a water base likewise were important, and prayer offerings were left at the proper shrines.

The performance of each major ceremony was the responsibility of a secret society, and it was essential for each Hopi to participate actively in the affairs of one or more of these societies. At about nine years of age, boys and girls were initiated into either the Kachina Society or the Powamu Society, the latter being more restricted in membership. Within the next few years, girls also joined one of several women's societies, and boys joined those for men. Occasionally, a woman joined a man's society and vice versa to fulfill a particular role, but by and large the ceremonial societies were divided by gender. The organization of women's societies was similar to that of men's: they were controlled by a lineage in a particular clan, possessed sacred bundles, carried out secret rituals in a kiva, and performed certain ceremonies in public.

The ritual calendar may arbitrarily be considered to begin with the winter solstice or Soyal Ceremony. The Soyal was conceived around that mysterious moment each year when, in Hopi thinking, the sun rises at the same place for four days and the days are shortest. The principal purpose of the Soyal Ceremony, which was conducted by those males who had completed the Tribal Initiation, was to induce the Sun to begin the trip back to its summer home so that it would bring warmth enough for the crops to be planted. The ceremony had the complementary purposes of inducing fertility in women and plants, and participation was villagewide. The typical smoking and prayers were accompanied by the manufacture of a large number of prayer offerings of corn husks, feathers, and prayer sticks. The kachinas performed, and select men and women danced.

The Powamu Ceremony began with the new moon of February and centered on the forced growth of beans in the kiva of the Powamu Society. After the beans sprouted, they were presented by kachinas to the grower's uninitiated offspring, his ceremonial children, and favored relatives. A child to be initiated into the Powamu Society saw some of the sacred rituals for the first time. This new knowledge was not to be revealed, under threat of punishment by men representing kachinas. Initiated children were permitted to impersonate kachinas, to participate in kachina rituals, and to become kachina fathers (ceremonial sponsors). Children who were not inducted into the Powamu Society became members of the Kachina Society.

Another high point in the ceremonial round came in August of every other year when the Antelope and Snake societies joined for a major ceremony. Together they manufactured prayer offerings, then went to their respective kivas to perform secret rituals. Snake Society members collected snakes to become a focal point of a dance. A Snake man held a snake's head with his lips or teeth as he danced around the plaza several times. During the dance another man brushed the shoulders of the snake holder with a "snake whip," a short stick with eagle feathers attached. The man danced with each snake and then released it on the ground at the plaza. Afterward the snakes were gathered in a circle and sprinkled with cornmeal by women and girls of the Snake clan.

Finally, younger men of the Snake Society picked up as many snakes as they could handle and took them to shrines in each of the four cardinal directions. The major goal of the ceremony was for the snakes to carry the message of the Hopi desire for rain to the underworld.

The public performances of Snake Society members have attracted more popular interest among Euro-Americans than any other American Indian ceremony. The reason is that the snake dancers carried prairie rattlers in their mouths as often as they did harmless species and did so with equal ease. Although prairie rattler bites could be fatal, illness or death from snakebite among the dancers was not reported. No evidence suggests that the handlers were immune to snake venom or that the snakes were charmed or drugged. Furthermore, laboratory tests showed that the Hopi did not have an effective antidote for venom. There appear to have been two reasons for Hopi success in handling rattlesnakes. In 1883 a herpetologist visited a kiva in which rattlesnakes were being kept for a dance; he inspected the fangs of one rattler and found them intact. After the dance he sent two of the rattlesnakes that had been used to the U.S. National Museum, and the venom glands were found to contain poison. Thus it would seem almost certain that the fangs were milked before the public ceremony. In 1932 and again in 1951, after a snake ceremony, herpetologists recovered rattlesnakes that had had their fangs removed. These studies suggest that traditionally the Hopi had milked the poison from rattlesnake fangs but that between 1883 and 1932, they began to cut away the fangs. Presumably, as Anglo-American (English-speaking whites) knowledge about rattlesnakes became known to the Hopi, they cut out the fangs to eliminate the risk of poisoning from bites.

The final ceremony of major importance was the Tribal Initiation. Controlled by the Agaves Society, it was held only when this society had at least one candidate for initiation. During this ceremony, adolescent males were initiated into one of four secret societies: the Agaves, Horns, Singers, or Wuwuchim. A male could not be a fully participating adult in Hopi society until he had passed through this initiation. The Tribal Initiation was the most complex of the ceremonies and a cornerstone of Hopi religion. It took place in November at a time established by the Sun Watcher. A new fire was made in the Agaves kiva by the kiva chief, and some embers were carried to the other participating kivas. A figure of Dawn Woman was brought from her shrine and exhibited on top of the kivas until the fifth day of the ceremony, when she was returned to her shrine after "delivering" her offspring. All candidates slept in their kivas. The dances performed on the third and fifth days were clearly associated with fertility; phallic symbols and simulated pregnancies were presented. These events, and many others, symbolized the ritual rebirth of male children into manhood and reaffirmed the integration between the living and the dead.

The Kachina Cult   Once long ago, according to a Village Chief of Oraibi, after the Hopi had departed from the uppermost level of the underworld, they wandered on earth with their gods, the kachinas. They were attacked by

Figure 10-5 | Model of the Prickly Pear Cactus Kachina. (© The Field Museum, Chicago, Neg. A 95940.)

Mexicans, and all the gods were killed. The dead returned to the underworld, and the Hopi divided their ceremonial paraphernalia to impersonate them. From then on, impersonations of kachinas formed the core of Hopi rituals.

When a man wore the sacred apparel of a kachina, he became what he impersonated, and his basketry or leather mask was the most sacred item of his dress. As masks wore out, became soiled, or broke, they were replaced or repaired; however, this did not detract from their sacredness. The chief kachina masks were the only ones reportedly not replaced or duplicated. It was possible also to vary a new kachina mask from the original without impairing its supernatural associations.

Participation as a kachina was open to all village men under the general sanction of the Village Chief, and the activities of the kachinas were under the control of the Badger and Kachina clans. Kachinas were present at Oraibi from the winter solstice until the summer solstice, after which they were supposedly in the underworld except for Maasaw Kachina, representing the God of Death, who was about the earth all year long. Whereas a Hopi adult did not believe that an impersonator was a god but rather a friend of the gods, small children were told that these were actual gods.

Kachina "dolls" have attracted widespread attention from whites, who have collected them avidly for many years (see Figure 10-5). These carvings are stylized renditions of the disguises worn by the men who portrayed kachinas.

They are small painted and adorned wooden images usually made by men prior to kachina performances. The figures were presented to children by kachinas and were considered by them as gifts from the gods. These kachina images were hung from the rafters of the homes to familiarize the children with the many different forms. Although kachina figures frequently are called dolls, this is a misnomer. They were not toys but served mainly to instruct uninitiated children about one aspect of the religious system. The Hopi made more than 240 different forms of kachina figures; they fit into six groups, including chief kachinas, clowns, and runners. A figure was carved from cottonwood tree roots, shaped, and then smoothed before appendages such as ears or horns were pegged in place. A thin layer of white clay was applied, and the clay was painted in vivid colors, the same ones used for the body paintings of real kachinas. Finally, feather adornments often were added to complete the figure.

Sorcery   To the Hopi, community-wide prosperity indicated that each individual had contributed his or her utmost, and the ideals of the Hopi Way thus were achieved. But what about failures? Why was it that during some years rain did not fall, winds dried the soil and blew seeds away, and the streams did not flow with water? Obviously, it was essential to be able to explain why nature sometimes did not respond to the complex ceremonies. The burden of failure was said to rest largely with individuals, persons who were kahopi, thinking evil and doing evil; these persons were sorcerers (witches).

The origin of sorcery was traced to Spider Woman, who caused the first human death. Hopi have reported that they believed a typical village included more witches than ordinary people. Witches might be male or female and from any clan; no one was considered to be incapable of witchcraft. A Village Chief or ceremonial leader might be suspect simply because he held an important office. Any self-assertive person was open to the accusation of being a witch because such behavior was not hopi. One could become a witch either by voluntarily practicing sorcery or by having been unknowingly inducted into a society of witches as a child. In the latter instance, existing witches reportedly carried off a related child while it slept and inducted it into a secret society that followed the pattern of other Hopi secret societies. The initiate was taught the witches' art of assuming the shape of an animal to pursue their nefarious craft by night. The power of a witch was derived from association with an animal familiar, such as a coyote, owl, wolf, or small black ant, from whom the greatest forces of evil emanated; quite logically, sorcerers supposedly possessed "two hearts," their own and that of their animal familiar. Sorcerers reportedly worked evil by sending pestilence to the fields, by causing land erosion, or by driving off rain clouds and replacing them with a conjured windstorm. A witch was not content with destroying crops but killed people as well. Murder probably was the most important activity of a sorcerer because it was believed that he or she extended his or her own life by killing one relative each year. In Hopi belief, a relative was killed or caused to be ill when a sorcerer shot stiff deer hairs, ants, a bit of bone, or some other object into his or her body without breaking the skin.

Ordinary people believed they could best protect themselves against a witch, who was most likely a near relative, by wearing stone arrow points regarded as the ends of lightning flashes associated with the clouds. The Hopi did not attempt to interfere with the activities of witches because they believed that they would die prematurely or encounter misfortune. A witch's spirit supposedly thirsted and hungered for the underworld and approached it by one step a year. The sanctions against a witch were not in this world but in the underworld; when his or her spirit arrived there, it was supposedly burned in an oven and became a beetle.

Shamans Some persons harmed and killed people by supernatural means, but others, shamans, cured people through their special abilities. A society of Hopi curers existed in early historic times, but it became extinct before being reported adequately. In any event, curing specialists relied on pharmacopoeia and massaging techniques. Some shamans were secular healers; they set broken bones and prepared herbs for patients. Their rather complex body of knowledge required specialized training, and a secular shaman was likely to pass his information on to a sister's son. In another category were the shamans who performed supernatural cures. These "two-hearted" individuals were supposed to employ their powers only for curing illness caused by witches. Obviously, such a person would be suspect in a sorcery case and considered a dangerous individual in any event. He would chew jimsonweed root or some other plant to induce a vision that aided in diagnosing the source of a malady.

LIFE CYCLE As might be anticipated, the Hopi stress on fertility led to behavior considered conducive to pregnancy. A woman was supposed to pray to the Sun at each dawn and was thought to be most likely to conceive if she had sexual intercourse while menstruating. Pregnancy was recognized by failure to menstruate, and if a woman suspected that she was carrying twins, she sought a shaman's aid to make the twins one. To bear twins was considered difficult, and it was thought that if both lived one parent would die. A pregnant woman prayed to the Sun and sprinkled cornmeal while she prayed to ease the labor of childbirth. She was active during her pregnancy, and she, as well as her husband, observed diverse taboos.

A woman often gave birth in the same dwelling where she was born. She delivered in a squatting position over a layer of sand; the sand and afterbirth were covered with cornmeal and deposited in a special rock crevice. Following a birth the mother's mother cut the umbilical cord, and before long the father's closest female relative arrived to wash the head of the neonate. This woman was in charge until the naming ceremony twenty days later. Note that the relatives of both parents were involved with a newborn. The father was not present during the birth, and he usually lived in the kiva with which he was identified for forty days after an offspring was born.

An infant was nursed on demand and weaned after two to four years, sometimes longer. After a small child was able to walk, he or she was encouraged to urinate and defecate outside the home; if a child repeatedly defecated in a house, she or he might be scolded or slapped on the head. Because everyone slept in one small room, children soon learned about sex. Sexual activities, including masturbation by children, were accepted with casual regard. Small boys were taught jokes that we would consider obscene, and they told the jokes when performing as ceremonial clowns. Despite this casual attitude, young girls usually were shy, and a licentious person might be called "crazy."

Young children were taught that kachinas were gods, and in this role kachinas encouraged childhood conformity. Children were told that giants were coming to visit, and, if they had misbehaved, they were warned to prepare themselves. Girls were instructed to grind cornmeal and boys to trap small animals. A few days later, giant kachinas arrived at households wearing frightening masks and carrying weapons and baskets with which to carry off wayward children. The kachinas cited a child's specific transgressions—having been previously informed of them by parents—and threatened to seize particular children. Erring little girls offered the kachinas baked cornmeal; it was accepted, but the animals trapped by boys were rejected. Parents defended their children, and finally the kachinas left after receiving a gift of meat from the parents. Obviously the entire community was involved in childhood socialization. Children also had further contact with kachinas during formal ceremonies (see Figure 10-6).

There were no formal puberty ceremonies, but it was customary for boys in their early teens to begin sleeping in a kiva rather than at home. A girl was, however, expected to pass through a ceremony before she married. Each year girls between the ages of sixteen and twenty assembled at the house of a paternal aunt of one girl. The event usually was directed by a female who recently had passed through the rituals, and she was aided by two boys. For most of four days the girls ground maize in a darkened room; they observed food taboos and drank liquids only at midday. The boys organized a rabbit hunt on the third day, and the girls spent most of their time baking piki. Afterward, the girls appeared for the first time with new coiffures termed "butterfly wings" or "squash blossoms." A girl continued to wear her hair in this manner until she married. She was most likely to marry someone from within the community (village endogamy) soon after passing through this ceremony.

Premarital sexual relations between teenagers were expected and were formalized in the *dumaiya*. As a boy began sleeping in a kiva, he was free to roam the pueblo at night and did so wrapped in a blanket so that he could not be easily identified. As the members of his amourette's household slept, he crept in carefully to the side of the girl, who in a whisper asked who it was. The boy answered, "It is I," and from the sound of his voice, the girl identified her caller. If she were willing, which usually was the case since the boy went only where he thought he would be received, he passed the night with the girl, leaving just before daylight. A dumaiya supposedly was secret, but it could not

Figure 10-6 | Young children being introduced into the ceremonial round in a Flute Dance. (Courtesy of the Field Museum, Chicago, neg. no. 7020.)

remain so in a small community like Oraibi. The girl's parents did not interfere if they regarded the boy as an acceptable husband for their daughter. A girl was not likely to have only a single lover, and before long she might become pregnant. If this happened, the girl named the boy she liked best as the father, and the formalities of arranging a marriage were begun. It also was possible for a girl to propose directly to a boy during certain festive or ceremonial occasions. A couple did not court unless they stood in a proper social relationship with one another. A person could not marry another in the same clan or phratry and was not supposed to marry someone from his or her father's clan or phratry, but the latter rule was not observed with care.

After the relatives of a couple approved a match, the girl ground maize for three days at the groom's house to demonstrate her abilities as a homemaker. There was no comparable trial for the groom. While the girl was in the boy's home, his paternal aunts attacked the boy's mother and her sisters with mud and water for permitting the girl to "steal" their "sweetheart." An atmosphere of jovial hostility surrounded the fight. On the fourth morning the couples' hair was washed in one container by their respective mothers and female relatives.

A mingling of their hair symbolized the marital union. Once again the paternal aunts of the boy attempted halfheartedly to disrupt the ritual. After their hair had dried, the couple stood at the mesa edge to pray to the Sun and later returned to the groom's home for a wedding breakfast. They were now man and wife, but they continued to live in the groom's house until the bride's wedding costume was completed by his male relatives and other men who offered to help. The men prepared the cotton and wove two sets of wedding garments, a small robe, and a white-fringed belt; in addition they prepared skins and sewed white moccasins and leggings. During the manufacture of these items the groom's family feasted the workers. After a month or more, the garments were completed; wearing one set and carrying the second in a reed container, the bride returned home. Her husband informally and unobtrusively took up residence in her household. The wedding garments were very important because they reportedly were required for entering the underworld after death.

All Hopi women appear to have married, but such was not the case for men. Indirect pressure was put on a girl by her brothers and her mother's brothers to bring another male into their economic unit. A boy's parents did not encourage him to marry because they then lost him as a productive family member. Any form of plural marriage was prohibited, but many unions were transient. It appears that over 35 percent of the people had from one to eight divorces. The most common grounds for divorce was adultery, followed by what we probably would call incompatibility. Divorce was a simple matter since it was only necessary for a man to rejoin his natal household or for a woman to order her husband from her household. The primary pressures against a divorce came from a girl's family, because they did not relish losing an economically productive male. The mother and her small children continued to reside in their old abode; an older offspring might join either parent.

The social core of a household consisted of a line of females. Within this setting the closest bonds were between a mother and her daughters. Daughters were destined to spend their lives in their mother's home or in an adjacent residence, and eventually they assumed their mother's role. From her mother a girl learned domestic skills and the norms of proper behavior. A mother guided the most important decisions in the ceremonial life of a girl and was likely to have a voice in the selection of her mate. As a girl's menarche arrived, she was instructed by her mother about caring for herself. The girl was not isolated at this time, nor at any other menstrual period; neither was she restricted from participating in ceremonies while menstruating. Were a mother to die, the mother's sister, who was called mother, replaced the biological mother in the girl's affection. Between a mother and her son the social bonds were not as close. A mother indulged an offspring of either sex, but a son in his early teens soon found his identity with a kiva group. A man's natal home remained the residence with which he felt most identified, however. He returned there if divorced and was a frequent caller in his mother's house. Like a girl, a man identified closely with his mother's sister, especially if the mother had died. A father was not overtly important in the upbringing of his children. A father took

Figure 10-7 | An old man and a child. (Courtesy of the Southwest Museum, Los Angeles.)

comparatively little active interest in a son until the latter's tribal initiation. Then the father selected the boy's ceremonial sponsor, which was an important decision. As a boy grew older, his father assumed a major role as his teacher. He imparted farming and ceremonial skills, as well as advice about being hopi (see Figure 10-7).

The maternal uncle of a young boy was the only male of his parents' generation who was of the same lineage and clan as himself. If such an uncle were a ceremonial leader, a boy might follow him in office, which called for systematic training of the youth. A mother's brother was likely to be the most important figure of authority associated with the boy's home, and he did not hesitate to apply discipline. A mother's brother was not all sternness toward his sister's children, however. He often told them myths or tales about their clan and occasionally presented them with gifts. One very warm relationship was between a man's sister and his son. As a small child, a boy soon learned that he was always a welcome guest in this woman's home. Here he received favored foods and frequent demonstrations of love and affection. As he grew older, he took game to his paternal aunt and exhibited his warm feeling toward her. Sexual relations with this aunt and her daughters were possible, and Titiev suspects that in the recent past a youth may have been expected to marry a father's sister's daughter.

As death approached it was said that a person's body became swollen. Youths as well as most adults left the house because they feared being present at the time of a death. The body and hair of a deceased person were washed, and then he or she was reclothed. After a man was wrapped in a deerskin or a woman in her wedding blankets, the corpse was flexed into a sitting position. Prayer offerings were fashioned by the father of the deceased or another male in his clan. A prayer feather was placed beneath each foot and in each hand, as well as over the navel, the supposed location of a person's spirit. The face was covered with cotton, symbolic of the time the dead become clouds, and food and water were placed with the body as sustenance on the journey to the underworld. The body was carried to the cemetery by men from the house of the deceased; here a hole had been dug just large enough to receive the bundled corpse, and soil was spread hastily on top. Men who attended the dead purified themselves afterward by washing in a boiled juniper preparation, and there was a ritual in the household of the deceased to protect members against spirits. The next day the man who had manufactured the prayer offerings took cornmeal and five prayer sticks to the grave. The prayer sticks were supposed to help the person on his or her travels to the land of the dead, and the food was to feed the spirit. A prayer was offered, and the spirit was told not to return for anyone else in the community. Later, household residents washed their hair and smoked themselves over hot coals on which pinyon gum had been placed. All possessions of the deceased were thrown away. A separate cemetery was provided for the stillborn, infants, and children. It was believed that the spirit of an infant did not travel to the underworld but lingered above the house, to be reborn again as a person of the opposite sex. The death of an adult was surrounded with misgivings and fear despite the fact that in Hopi belief most dead were to be reborn into a peaceful world that was an intimate part of the Hopi Way.

| Early History

In July of 1540 the Hopi saw the first Spanish. A small group under Pedro de Tovar arrived from the pueblo of Zuni, where Francisco Coronado, the expedition leader, rested. When de Tovar arrived at an eastern Hopi settlement, he encountered hostility and attacked the village, defeating the Indians. De Tovar then peacefully visited the six other Hopi communities. More lasting contact was made by Juan de Onate in 1598 when the Hopi grudgingly submitted to the authority of the Spanish king. The Spanish hoped to make these people Christians, but Franciscan missionaries did not settle among them until 1629. Churches were built at three settlements, and two more missionaries joined the first three. The Franciscans reported great progress, but the poisoning of one of the priests in 1633 suggests that not all Hopi were contented charges. Vigorous Franciscan efforts to destroy the old Hopi religion led to cruel punishments for backsliding Indians. In 1655 a missionary caught a Hopi performing an "act of idolatry." The man was beaten severely in public and again beaten inside the church; turpentine was applied to his body and ignited, and he died. The missionary was relieved of his post, but no punitive action was taken against him.

In 1650 the Hopi refused to join the other Pueblo peoples in a revolt against the Spanish, but they fully supported the Pueblo Revolt in 1680. Their major contribution was to kill the four missionaries stationed among them. The Hopi indirectly aided the insurrection by accepting refugees from the Rio Grande pueblos when the Spanish struck back. The Hopi feared Spanish reprisals, and three villages were relocated on mesa tops that could be better defended than could their valley bottom settings. The Spanish returned in 1692, and when the Indians willingly swore to support the Spanish king, peace was established. By 1699 the Spanish were in firm control of the Rio Grande pueblos, and this led to a Hopi faction that favored Catholicism to request missionaries from the authorities at Santa Fe. A missionary visited, but after he left, the community was summarily destroyed by the anti-Catholic Hopi faction. The men who resisted were killed; their wives and children were scattered among the remaining settlements. Throughout the 1740s and early 1750s the Hopi thwarted Spanish efforts to bring them under effective control.

Beginning in 1755 the course of Hopi history gravitated increasingly toward accepting the Spanish. When a sequence of dry years exhausted their reserve of food, they were faced with hunger. By 1779 many of them had abandoned their homeland and moved among the Zuni to survive. The next year most Hopi were so scattered that the local population was reduced to about eight hundred persons. In the midst of this struggle came the smallpox epidemic in 1781. In this same year, however, rain was plentiful, and the bountiful crops made it possible for the population to reconsolidate. Pressures by marauding Navajos forced the Hopi to request aid from the Spanish in 1818, but the Spanish, who were faced with their own survival problems, were unable to help. The most striking characteristic of Hopi historical contact with the Spanish was the ability of these Indians to withstand Spanish sociocultural changes, especially in the religious sphere. Hopi resistance against the Spanish evidently was not unanimous, but the pro-Spanish faction seems to have been of minor importance.

Later History

The next serious problem was how to deal with another group of non-Indians who began to enter their country. Among the earliest Hopi and Anglo-American contacts was a conflict in 1834; white trappers raided Hopi gardens and killed about fifteen people. In 1850 the Hopi asked Anglo officials in Santa Fe for help in controlling Navajo intrusions on their grazing lands, but the authorities took no immediate action. Most Hopi took a cautious approach to Anglos. Everyone knew the origin myth in which an elder brother of the Hopi, a Bahana, departed and promised to return when the Hopi were in need. They reasoned that perhaps Anglos were the Bahanas, the prophesied whites; but no one knew for certain how to identify them.

THE RESERVATION   The Hopi were recognized by the federal government in 1870 when the Moqui Pueblo Agency was established, and a mission school was founded in 1874. The Moqui Pueblo Reservation (later changed to Hopi Indian Reservation) was created by an executive order in 1882, but the land set aside was for Indian, not exclusively Hopi, use. The Dawes Act of 1887 resulted in federal pressures on the Hopi to shift from family and community landholdings to individual allotments. Conflicts with the Navajo over grazing lands intensified, as there had been no boundary survey when the Hopi Reservation was established, and Navajo encroachment on Hopi lands continued. Through a series of executive orders the Navajo Reservation came to surround the Hopi, and about 1937 the BIA reduced the area officially designated as Hopi land to about one-fourth its original size, or one thousand square miles.

CHANGES IN THE SUBSISTENCE CYCLE   By the early 1900s, the Hopi economy had undergone major changes. Their primary reliance on maize, beans, and squash continued, but new crops and animals became increasingly significant. The most important new animal was the sheep, and virtually every man had at least a small flock by 1900. Each animal was individually owned, but men herded cooperatively. Sheep were held as wealth and were butchered only for ceremonial occasions. Surplus meat was dried as jerky or dried, pounded, and mixed with fat as pemmican. Cattle were less popular because of their initial cost and because the pattern of allowing them to graze freely led to the destruction of crops. Although people owned horses, they were difficult to maintain. They had to be rounded up each day for pasturing, usually at considerable distance from the village. Like sheep and cattle, horses were individually owned, but men often tended them jointly.

THE RUPTURE AT ORAIBI   The Hopi population in 1890 was about twenty-two hundred, of whom some twelve hundred lived at Oraibi. Oraibi residents were divided into two major factions vis-à-vis Anglos in general and federal agents in particular. The antiwhite faction (conservatives or hostiles) categorically rejected Anglo ways. Their counterpart, the progressive (friendly) faction, made concessions to whites. One critical issue was whether or not the Anglos were the Bahanas, who were to aid the Hopi. The hostile faction claimed that the real Bahanas would speak Hopi and could produce a stone matching the one held by the Village Chief at Oraibi. Obviously the Anglos were not Bahanas, and if the progressives accepted them, the anger of a supernatural would lead to a flood that would end the world. The progressives, on the other hand, traced Hopi difficulties to the underworld and witchcraft rather than to Anglo-Americans. An individual's choice of sides in this conflict

Figure 10-8 | The original caption on this picture reads: "Mosqui Indians Chief Lo-Ma-Hung-Yo-Ma, arrested at Oraibi, November 25th and 26th 1894, for seditious conduct and confined to Alcatraz Island, California, since January 3rd 1895." (Courtesy of the Southwest Museum, Los Angeles. Photo # 20086.)

was influenced by such factors as clan and phratry ties and kinship links to the leaders of the factions.

In 1894 U.S. soldiers attempted to survey Oraibi land and were opposed by the hostiles, which resulted in the imprisonment of the leaders at Alcatraz from January to August of 1895 (see Figure 10-8). Additional factors contributing to the turmoil at Oraibi included disputes about clan farmlands that were being reduced by erosion, the continuing problem of Navajo encroachments on Hopi land, and a smallpox epidemic in 1897–1898 in which many people died. Open factional conflict occurred in September 1906. The conservative leader drew a line in the ground and became the object of a push-of-war. Before the shoving began it was decided that the losers would leave the village. People pushed the man from behind and in front. The conservatives lost, and the same evening about three hundred of them abandoned the settlement with their belongings. They founded a new village, Hotevilla, about seven miles north of Oraibi.

Over the years Oraibi was virtually abandoned, in part because the Village Chief was an extremely quarrelsome and vindictive person. By 1933 only about 109 people remained there. Others founded New Oraibi on the nearby valley floor, or they settled at Moencopi. At Oraibi a complete ceremonial round could no longer be held, but the old Village Chief faced the situation calmly as he aged. He maintained that the time would soon come when everyone would abandon him, and he alone would carry on the Soyal. Then there would be a great famine, and following it, all of the old ceremonies would be reinstituted at Oraibi. Again the village would thrive in all of its colorful glory. The Village Chief waited and waited, and died still waiting.

| Emergence of the Modern Hopi

By the 1940s about four thousand Hopi lived in fourteen settlements. Critical problems included greater soil erosion and a population increase on a land base made smaller by expanding Navajo encroachments. For years the federal government had encouraged herding, and sheep became an essential element in the economy. To remedy the erosion problem federal efforts centered on a dramatic livestock reduction program, which the people resisted, to no avail; and their diet became essentially meatless. Meals typically consisted of maize, beans, potatoes, sugar, and coffee. At Oraibi the kiva-centered life of males declined, and the significance of the nuclear family increased proportionally. This lessened the position of men and strengthened that of women. The net result was the fostering of a previously unheard-of male individualism. Because the Oraibi land base was not adaptable to the accumulation of farmlands or to male control of such lands, ambitious men moved toward wage labor. Another avenue open to individual men was political leadership; however, personal achievement remained disapproved.

One compelling reason why profound changes did not occur earlier and more rapidly among the Hopi was their remoteness from major Euro-American power centers. In sum, Hopi country was not readily accessible to outsiders for many years. Titiev (1972) proposed that abandonment of traditional Hopi life grew in intensity following the construction of paved highways linking Black Mesa with cities and towns in northern Arizona and New Mexico. No longer isolated physically, the Hopi turned outward to the white world. Many people bought automobiles or trucks, ending travel by wagon or on the backs of burros and horses. Men began commuting daily to jobs in nearby towns or weekly to more distant cities, returning to the village on weekends. Some of these men continued to farm clan lands but only on the weekends. Surplus crops now could be transported over highways to be sold at distant markets, and in times of local food scarcity, a staple such as maize could be imported. Good roads also brought increasing numbers of tourists, especially during ceremonies such as the Snake-Antelope Dance.

In its physical aspects, Oraibi underwent less profound but equally far-reaching changes. The number of occupied houses was about the same as in the early 1930s, but larger houses were being built. Cinder block and cement were replacing local stone and adobe as building materials (see Figure 10-9). Outhouses became common, and most people owned store-bought furniture and

Figure 10-9 | Hopi women cleaning corn. (Courtesy of the Field Museum, Chicago, neg. no. 368.)

appliances. The matrilocal marriage residence pattern and clan ownership of houses continued, but a woman no longer shared a household with her mother. When a woman married, she wanted an official American civil or religious ceremony to document the event, because experience had taught that documents were required in any legal dealings with whites. Each bride, even if she married elsewhere, still received traditional wedding garments from relatives.

As is evident from the account of aboriginal Hopi political life, each village was autonomous; there was no tribal-wide political unit. The federal government strongly encouraged them to organize as a tribe under the terms of the Indian Reorganization Act of 1934 (see Chapter 2). Christian Hopi and those employed by the BIA voted to form a tribal governing body, whereas those opposed did not vote. As a result a Tribal Council was created in 1937, but for many years it barely functioned, if at all. By the 1970s, however, it had become increasingly accepted by many villagers.

The consumption of alcohol traditionally was shunned by the Hopi. But some veterans returning from World War II were heavy drinkers, and intoxicants became increasingly popular, with accompanying drunkenness. Social life changed in yet another respect because numerous clans died out and some others were represented only by males. They, too, will become extinct unless outsiders who are members marry into Oraibi. Political life assumed an unprecedented turn when a woman became the Village Chief because the people could not agree on a male successor. Hopi religion has disintegrated, and the Soyal Ceremony is no longer performed. In 1955 at Oraibi the only remnant of this ceremonial event was that two men stayed up all night making prayer sticks for the Sun.

LAND DISPUTE For many years a major land dispute with the Navajo remained unresolved, and bitterness lingers into the present, especially among the Navajo. When the Hopi Reservation was created by executive order in 1882, the order did not specify that the land was for exclusive Hopi use. The Navajo who lived nearby grew rapidly in number and gradually came to occupy much of the land on the reservation that traditionally had belonged to the Hopi. In the 1930s about 1.8 million acres of Hopi land, from a total of 2.4 million acres, were made part of the Navajo Reservation. In 1962 the U.S. Supreme Court ruled that the land detached from the Hopi had in fact been set aside for both tribes; however, the Navajo continued their effective control. In 1974 the Navajo–Hopi Land Settlement Act was passed by Congress to separate the disputed lands, allotting one section for the exclusive use of each tribe. The act also created the Hopi Partitioned Lands, which led to the removal of some ten thousand Navajo from Hopi land and the relocation of about one hundred Hopi from Navajo land. The Hopi also launched a lawsuit for damage to their partitioned land, largely as a result of overgrazing by Navajo livestock. The suit was finally settled out of court in 2000 when the Navajo agreed to a $29 million damage settlement with the Hopi.

MINING: COAL AND WATER In this context the Hopi and Navajo became close allies. The unity originated in 1964 as they negotiated leases with the Peabody Coal Company (PCC), the world's largest coal-mining enterprise (now the Peabody Energy Company). The tribes agreed to strip mining of coal on Black Mesa land owned separately by the tribes and to the tapping of ground water for mining operations. In the lease negotiations the federal government, through the BIA, forced the Hopi and Navajo to accept water and coal contracts well below their prevalent market value. This became a bitter issue for both tribes in subsequent negotations with the federal government.

Traditional Hopi opposed the lease because they feared the mine would poison the earth. Other Hopi noted that their ancestors had mined local coal as domestic fuel. Evidence suggests the mining took place from the 1200s to the 1600s of the Christian era. (This was among the earliest coal mines in the world; why the Hopi ceased operations is unknown.) The Hopi and Navajo accepted the Peabody lease because of all the money involved. The value of the mining operations combined was about $85 million in 2002 from coal sales, taxes, and wages for workers. This money had become an essential source of payment for government services and soon became the backbone of the tribes' economies.

As the mining progressed, the tribes became increasingly alarmed over the amount of water drawn from the Navajo aquifer. It was their only source of safe drinking water, and a lowering of the water table dried up some springs and streams essential for gardens and farms. The Navajo aquifer was receding at an alarming rate, especially since the continuing dry period that began in this sector of Arizona in 1996. Peabody pumped a vast amount of water, about 4000 acre feet a year. (One acre foot is about 325,000 gallons of water, enough to cover a football field a foot in depth.) The water was used primarily as slurry, which is half water and half crushed coal piped some 270 miles to the Mohave Power Station (MPS) at Laughlin, Nevada. Here it is converted into electricity to meet the needs of about 1.5 million homes and businesses primarily in Arizona and California. The major decisions by the Hopi, Navajo, and Peabody about the mine's future must soon be resolved because the coal-water leases expire on January 1, 2006. A complicating aspect is that the pipeline to Laughlin leaks badly and requires upsizing for any future operations. In addition, a court order requires the installation of pollution control equipment at the MPS that would cost over $1 billion.

The pivotal power company involved is Southern California Edison (SCE), the major owner of the MPS, and the California Public Utilities Commission (CPUC) is a primary regulatory body. The Hopi and Navajo nations and Peabody strongly favor the negotiation of a new contract.

By early 2004 the future of coal mining on Black Mesa was unresolved because the Hopi and Navajo have thus far refused to have slurry water drawn from the Navajo aquifer after 2005. A possible alternative source is undrinkable water from the widespread Coconino aquifer on Hopi and Navajo lands in northeastern Arizona, which would require a new pipeline to the mining operations. Another possibility is for the SCE to depend on a new natural-gas-powered plant in California. This alternative is unattractive because it appears that the wholesale price for gas-produced power would be about twice as much as from the MPS, despite the cost of extensive changes required for its continued operation. Furthermore, the pollution control devices at the MPS apparently cannot be completed before the December 31, 2005, deadline, and SCE refuses to address the problem until the water question is resolved. If the MPS is to continue, approval must be obtained from the CPUC, the Department of the Interior, and numerous other parties involved, as well as from the Indians. Unresolved differences are many.

In August 2004, negotiations were reasonably positive. Peabody had applied to federal authorities for one twenty-year permit to mine 670 million tons of coal on Hopi and Navajo lands combined and to draw water from the Navajo aquifer for at least a few more years. (In the present operations, about 300 million tons of coal have been mined and more than 3 billion gallons of water consumed.) New agreements with the tribes would have no time limits, and there would not be a shutdown at the MPS by 2006. Peabody also could process more coal after pollution control and pipeline problems are corrected, by 2007. Federal approval of the basic proposal appears likely.

Nevertheless, unresolved issues remain. One is the adamant protest by some Hopi and Navajo religious leaders and their supporters against Peabody using any Navajo aquifer water. This objection is shared by the grassroots Black Mesa Trust and more broadly based groups, such as the Sierra Club. Yet viable alternatives for the mining of coal do not appear to exist.

By the fall of 2004, other issues loomed, and given all the variables involved, the final results are unpredictable. Will the Hopi and Navajo grant the use of Navajo acquifer water on a temporary basis? If Coconino acquifer water is used, will the Hopi and Navajo receive some of this water for municipal and domestic purposes, as they hope? If Coconino water is used, will the tribes accept Navajo acquifer water, as would be required intermittently as a backup source? What is to be the compensation rate for the Indians for coal, water, and right-of-way fees? Will reclamation procedures for mined areas be acceptable? These are not simple issues.

Coal and water revenues contributed $7.7 million, about 30 percent of the Hopi operating budget in 2004. The anticipated funding problems with the closing of their Black Mesa mine led them to reconsider opening a casino. In a 1995 referendum, the majority of the voters rejected the possibility. Another gaming referendum in 2004 was rejected by about 58 percent of the voters, much the same percentage as in 1995. (The day before the most recent ballot, I talked with Hopi employees when I was at their administrative center. I raised questions about tribal finances if gaming was rejected and the mine closed. Their response consistently was that the Hopi had survived "bad times" in the past.)

| Additional Considerations

By 2002 the number of enrolled Hopi was about twelve thousand. Older Hopi in particular lament the creeping abandonment of their aboriginal language and speak of their current "language crisis." In Hopi homes by 1998 about 80 percent of children spoke English as their preferred language. In the same year about half of the adults between twenty and thirty-nine years of age were unable to speak conversational Hopi, whereas the people older than sixty were still fluent Hopi speakers. Tribal officials concerned about language losses applied for and received a large grant in 2000 for the purpose of saving their language. Their goal was to begin teaching Hopi preschool and kindergarten children in an immersion program at reservation schools. Less intense instruction would continue through the grades, and speaking Hopi would become a requirement for high school graduation. Within a few years they hoped to have a standard language curriculum in all their schools. Initial hurdles include setting teaching standards, allowing for instruction in the different village dialects, and establishing language tests to certify instructors. Some Hope adults agree that this program is worthwhile, but they contend that if a child is not encouraged to speak Hopi as a first language at home, the program may fail.

Accounts by Richard O. Clemmer (1995) and John D. Loftin (1991) examine modern Hopi developments in detail and with sympathetic insight. They each emphasize the conflict between the attraction of traditional Hopi life and the realities of dealing with the federal government in particular and Euro-Americans in general. Loftin (1991, 84–86) views the Hopi situation as "compartmentalization," a temporary suspension of old values while partaking of Anglo culture and adherence to traditional Hopi values in nontraditional ways. Clemmer (1995, 273) suggests that "segregative goals" characterize the Hopi as they try to maintain their unique identity while concurrently adapting Western institutions to their particular needs and desires. The approaches are complementary.

As the subsequent examples indicate, Hopi ambivalence toward Anglos is manifested in many ways. Fundamentally, the Hopi are opposed to tourists visiting their villages, especially during religious ceremonies, and they are distressed when tourists attempt to take photographs. But the Hopi know that tourist dollars improve reservation economic conditions. Therefore, in 1971, they opened the Hopi Cultural Center, which has produced substantial profits for the tribe by selling craft items to tourists. Furthermore, arts and crafts businesses owned by individual Hopi have flourished from the tourist trade (see Figure 10-10). At the same time, because of pressure exerted by staunch

Figure 10-10 | A Hopi from Second Mesa, Alphonso Numkena, makes and sells traditional-style gourd rattles. This 1998 photograph was taken at the Hopi Cultural Center.

traditionalists, villages and ceremonies periodically are closed to outsiders, only to be opened again by Hopi who seek compromise.

By 1986 about 80 percent of the Hopi lived on reservation land, and soon thereafter most homes had electricity from power lines. At Old Oraibi and Hotevilla, however, traditionalists resisted having power lines in their communities. One result was the installation of solar-powered electrical systems for some households. Whereas traditional houses were made from native sandstone and mortar, nontraditional building materials, especially cinder block, now predominate. Newer homes may look like the old type, but they are cheaper to build.

Religious ceremonies are now held largely on weekends because so many people hold wage-earning jobs during the week. In a religious context, the money earned from jobs has been important because food sharing and gift giving are an integral part of ceremonial life. The greater amount of available cash seems to be responsible for an increase in the number of kachina dances performed. Thus adjustments and readjustments continue.

The reservation unemployment rate in 2001 was about 60 percent, and some 27 percent of the inhabitants lived below the national poverty level guidelines. These statistics suggest that life in a typical reservation family was economically stressful. By 2004 about half of the enrolled members, some six thousands had left the reservation to find work either nearby or at distant places. For families who remained on the reservation, their ability to make a living was not as dire as the 60 percent unemployment rate suggests. Many of these families depend heavily on the "informal economy." They raise cattle, sheep, and garden and field crops to meet subsistence needs that could be supplemented by gifts from relatives or friends. At the same time, families had a limited capacity to make cash purchases.

One present-day facet of reservation life, tribal political power, seems to have crystalized into a government largely controlled by a small number of Hopi-speaking families and their allies. As the primary employer, with about four hundred workers, reservation government is a major source of steady income. By dominating the administration, the current leadership cliques are well entrenched. Not so long ago, however, an apolitical middle-age Hopi on the reservation told me that tribal leaders currently speak with "forked tongues." Potentially capable employees, especially those educated younger persons who may not speak Hopi well, often cannot obtain tribal jobs because they do not belong to the "right families" or have the "right connections." To obtain steady and rewarding employment they must relocate. Moving away makes them feel "less Hopi." As a Hopi woman working in Phoenix said, "I want to go back; there is nothing out here for me," yet her prospects for employment if she returns to the reservation are not bright.

Are Anglos the Bahanas? The issue remains unresolved. Yet it is not clear whether prophecies, which are now prominent among the Hopi, were an integral part of their traditional culture or represent a comparatively recent development. Regardless, some Hopi, especially those on Third Mesa, contend that their actual white brother has not returned; they say Anglos are not Bahanas because they have not produced a stone to match the one at Old Oraibi. Hopi who subscribe to this position contend that the descendants of their *real* white brother have yet to appear.

Who is a real Hopi? Contemporary Hopi identity takes many forms, and individuals cannot be separated into the friendly and hostile factions of old. One good reason is that no modern Hopi follows the traditional Hopi Way in all its aspects, if only because a complete round of ceremonial and clan activities no longer prevails. Thus being Hopi is a matter of degree and has countless variations. Can a Hopi also be a member of a Christian church? Are children, many of whom do not speak Hopi, destined as adults not to be "real" Hopi? Is an alcoholic fundamentally kahopi? In an official panel discussion, one man took a broad view of tribal identity: "First a Hopi is honorable, a virtuous person, has humility, possesses humbleness and values. Self respect, discipline and respectfulness to others by treating women and children with special compassion—these are all traits that embody a Hopi" (Martin 1998). It would appear that a compromise of this order will prevail.

In 2003 a Hopi woman briefly became prominent in newspaper articles about the war in Iraq. Army private Lori Piestewa (1980–2003) became the first Native American woman in the armed services to die in combat during a foreign war. Following her death, and in keeping with Hopi tradition, she received a new name when she entered another realm. The Hopi now refer to Lori Piestewa as "Lady Warrior."

| Additional Sources

Two publications in particular provide a good introduction to the Hopi. They are by Ernest and Pearl Beaglehole (1935) and Nancy Bonvillain (1994). The best works about a particular village are Mischa Titiev's studies made at Old Oraibi. Alexander M. Stephen's diary (1936) offers a wealth of information about most aspects of Hopi life, but it is difficult to use. The best biography of a Hopi man was edited by Leo W. Simmons (1942). The best ethnohistory is included in a book by Edward H. Spicer (1962), and Laura Thompson's work (1950) is a superior source of information about the emergence of the Hopi into modern times. One (vol. 9) of the two *Southwest* volumes edited by Alfonso Ortiz (1979), of the *Handbook of North American Indians,* includes a wealth of information about the Hopi and other Pueblo Indians in prehistoric, ethnographic, and historical contexts. The book by John D. Loftin (1991) is an exceptional account of contemporary Hopi religion. Richard O. Clemmer's book (1995) also is an excellent source about the recent past.

| Selected Bibliography

Beaglehole, Ernest, and Pearl Beaglehole. 1935. *Hopi of the Second Mesa.* American Anthropological Association Memoir 44.

Bonvillain, Nancy. 1994. *The Hopi.* New York.

Clemmer, Richard O. 1995. *Roads in the sky: Hopi culture and history in a century of change.* Boulder.

Colton, Harold S. 1949. *Hopi kachina dolls.* Albuquerque.

Cushing, Frank H. 1923. Origin myth from Oraibi. *Journal of American Folklore* 36:163–70.

Dozier, Edward P. 1970. *The Pueblo Indians of North America.* New York.

Eggan, Fred. 1950. *Social organization of the western Pueblos.* Chicago.

Forrest, Earle R. 1961. *The Snake Dance of the Hopi Indians.* Los Angeles.

Geertz, Armin W. 1993. *The invention of prophecy: Continuity and meaning in Hopi Indian religion.* Berkeley.

Hopi Tutuveni. 2001–2004. (Hopi newspaper).

Jones, Volney H. 1950. The establishment of the Hopi Reservation, and some later developments concerning Hopi lands. *Plateau* 23:17–25.

Loftin, John D. 1991. *Religion and Hopi life in the twentieth century.* Bloomington, IN.

Lomatuway'ma, Michael, Lorena Lomatuway'ma, and Sidney Namingha, Jr., with Ekkehart Malotki. 1993. *Kiqotutuwutsi: Hopi ruin legends.* Lincoln, NE.

Martin, E. Bradley. 1998. Cultural awareness activities. *Tutuveni* (Hopi newspaper), September 25, 1998.

Oliver, James A. 1958. *Snakes in fact and fiction.* New York.

Ortiz, Alfonso, ed. 1979. *Southwest.* Vol. 9, *Handbook of North American Indians.* Washington, DC.

Sekaquaptewa, Helen. 1969. *Me and mine: The life story of Helen Sekaquaptewa.* Tucson.

Simmons, Leo W., ed. 1942. *Sun Chief.* New Haven.

Spicer, Edward H. 1962. *Cycles of conquest.* Tucson.

Stephen, Alexander M. 1936. *Hopi journal.* Columbia University Contributions to Anthropology, vol. 23, 2 pts.

Thompson, Laura. 1950. *Culture in crisis.* New York.

Thompson, Laura, and Alice Joseph. 1944. *The Hopi way.* Chicago.

Titiev, Mischa. 1943. *Notes on Hopi witchcraft.* Papers of the Michigan Academy of Science, Arts, and Letters, vol. 28, 549–57.

———. 1944. *Old Oraibi.* Papers of the Peabody Museum of American Archaeology and Ethnology, vol. 22, no. 1.

———. 1972. *The Hopi Indians of Old Oraibi.* Ann Arbor.

Voth, H. R. 1905. *Oraibi natal customs and ceremonies.* Field Columbian Museum, Anthropological Series, vol. 6, no. 2.

Waters, Frank. 1963. *Book of the Hopi.* New York.

Whiting, Alfred F. 1950. *Ethnobotany of the Hopi.* Museum of Northern Arizona Bulletin no. 15.

Yava, Albert. 1992. *Big Falling Snow.* Albuquerque.

11 The Navajo: Transformations among a Desert People

Earth's feet become my feet, thereby I go through life.
Its legs become my legs, thereby I go through life. . . .
Long life-happiness I am wherever I will go.
Before me it is blessed wherever I will go,
Behind me it is blessed wherever I will go,
It has become blessed again, it has become blessed again!

A part of the Blessingway chant, the purpose of which
is to restore harmony and heal (Wyman 1970, 224–25)

THE NAVAJO ARE by far the most populous tribe north of Mexico, and most of them have retained the essence of their traditional lifeway. They numbered nearly 300,000 in 2000, and most of them lived on reservation lands. Equally significant, despite centuries of efforts by Christian missionaries, most Navajo still adhere to their own belief system.

The Navajo are possibly the tribe best known to non-Indians. Their blankets and silver jewelry have been appreciated and bought by generations of Anglo-Americans ("Anglo" refers to English-speaking whites). In recent years about one hundred films and videos have been released about the Navajo, far more than for any other tribe. They also have been studied by anthropologists more often than have any other Indians. Approximately 2600 authoritative articles, books, and monographs (book-length technical reports) had been published about them by 1987. A Navajo family has sometimes been defined as "a man, his wife, their children, and their anthropologist"!

An additional compelling reason to include a chapter about the Navajo (NAV-uh-ho) is their remarkable cultural adaptability. For example, in the early 1860s the U.S. Army sought to subjugate and apparently to destroy them as a people. Soldiers herded most Navajo from their homeland to a distant fort, an infamous episode that the survivors termed the "Long Walk." During the course of their removal many people were purposely killed—including women in childbirth. When the surviving captives were released after five years, they had little more than hope and tenacity. Amazingly, despite continuing trauma, they not only persevered but began to thrive. One key aspect of Navajo history was their relative freedom from political control by Euro-Americans until the early 1900s. Another has been their capacity to adopt the ideas of other peoples and integrate them into their culture. In sum, the modern Navajo possibly are the most remarkable example of cultural adaptation and readaptation among Indians north of Mexico.

Navajo country has both inviting physical beauty and stark cultural reality. Year-round splendor is visible in the colorful canyons and mesas, rock spires, broad valleys, and mountains. Nonetheless, living there requires constantly shifting adjustments. The low and erratic rainfall, sudden torrents from occasional storms, windstorms, the possibility of heavy snowfall, the high salt content of most soils, and expanses with little vegetation posed cultural challenges. In the Navajo portion of the Colorado Plateau, the landscape is high, ranging from about 3000 to 10,000 feet above sea level. At lesser elevations grama grass, a coarse western grass, prevails, but where there is water cottonwood and willows thrive. At higher elevations pine or pine and juniper dominate the mountainsides. A salient climatic feature is the low precipitation, sometimes as much as ten inches a year but more often considerably less. In the many small valleys, groundwater encourages the growth of tumbleweeds, which soon turn brown and blow away. This weed, a thistle, was accidentally introduced to the United States from Europe in 1873.

Fauna played an early and critical role in Navajo economic life. In addition to small game, such as cottontails and jackrabbits (actually hares), antelope and deer were important for food and hides. Bobcats, coyotes, black bears, and wolves were numbered among the predators. One touchstone of Navajo survival has been their capacity to exploit the resources in varied ecological zones.

This chapter is presented in a different format than are those about the other tribes for a number of reasons. First, and most important, the Navajo did not appear as a clearly distinct tribe until around A.D. 1725, some 185 years after the Spanish first arrived in the Southwest. Hence, we cannot examine aboriginal Navajo life in depth. Second, in their historical emergence the Navajo absorbed so many Indians from other tribes that they justly have been identified as "biological and cultural hybrids" by Garrick Alan Bailey and Roberta Glenn Bailey (1986, 15). Third, in the process of assimilating foreign elements, both Indian and European, the Navajo reworked them into a distinct configuration. Their culture cannot be understood without an appreciation of these factors. Therefore, the Navajo are introduced in an ethnohistorical account to emphasize their cultural "layering."

| The Background

The Navajo (Navaho) call themselves Diné, meaning "the people." They identify northwestern New Mexico, their original home in the Southwest, as Dinetah, or "land of the people." The word *Navaho* entered English from Spanish and is possibly derived from a Tewa Indian word that refers indirectly to cultivated fields. Despite a wealth of information about the Navajo, we know surprisingly little about their ancestors before they arrived in the Southwest. In linguistic terms, they belong to the Nadene language family and the Athapaskan subfamily. Most Athapaskans live and continue to live in a vast inland region of northwestern Canada (see Chapter 4) and interior Alaska. The close early historic association between the Navajo and the Apache as distinct populations creates confusion, yet they both entered the Southwest from the north and emerged as a distinct language subgroup, Apachean.

FILTERING SOUTH We justifiably think of human "migrations" as significant movements from one place to another. The migrants usually are numerous and their destination is known. In these terms, the Navajo and many other people did not migrate. Instead, small family groups or bands typically moved from one watershed to the next. They had no distant target destination in mind because they had no knowledge about far-off places. Why did they move? The reasons usually cited are food stress, overpopulation, disease, and internal or external conflicts. The northern ancestors of the Navajo may have responded to each of these conditions on their journey southward. They did *not* move south in search of a warmer land. They were as yet unaware that warmer land existed.

Neither the ancestral Navajo route to the Southwest nor the time of their arrival has been established with precision. When the precursors of the Navajo

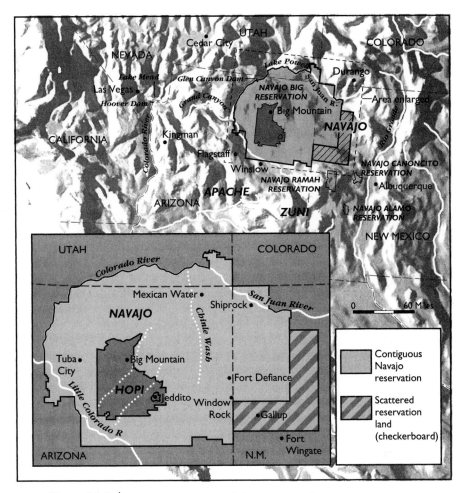

Figure 11-1 | Historic homeland of the Navajo Indians.

lived in the subarctic, they obviously adjusted to local conditions. Probable adaptations included a social life based on small family groups closely related by blood and marriage. Hunting dominated their economy, and their material culture included tailor-made garments and cone-shaped dwellings. They may have begun to leave the far north around A.D. 1000 and may have descended along the eastern flank of the Rocky Mountains. Along the way, perhaps in the Plains, they learned about farming. Shortly before A.D. 1600 they appear to have arrived in Dinetah as a populous Athapaskan group but not as a distinct Navajo tribe (see Figure 11-1). A competing theory suggests that the Navajo presence in the Southwest goes back further. They may have entered the area and intermarried with the Anasazi (prehistoric Pueblo Indians) before A.D. 1100. If so, the blending of Athapaskan and Pueblo cultures into the historic Navajo may have taken place earlier than is generally believed.

THE SPANISH AND PUEBLO IMPACT   The Spanish era in the Southwest began with the Coronado Expedition of 1540 and ended in 1846 with the inception of the Anglo-American era. Reasonably clear evidence of direct Athapaskan–Spanish contact dates from 1582. Initially, relations were friendly, but soon conflict arose over the fate of captives held by the Indians. One of the markers of emerging Navajo culture became evident: they were aggressive and successful raiders for captives, edibles, and loot. Other early markers included trade with varied tribes and the cultivation of maize (corn) as an important food.

Spanish colonialism in New Mexico began in 1598, and Roman Catholic missions soon were established at pueblos; but missions to the Athapaskans failed. Athapaskans were soon raiding both Spanish and Pueblo communities for livestock, which they usually killed for food. In the Pueblo Revolt of 1680, the Spanish settlements were destroyed, some four hundred colonists were killed, and the survivors fled south. In 1692 the Spanish returned in force to reestablish themselves and seek revenge. The Spanish killed many Pueblo Indians and sold captives into slavery. At this juncture, thousands of Pueblo dwellers in New Mexico fled their homes, and most of them sought refuge in Dinetah. Athapaskan contact with these refugees was critical in the emergence of the Navajo. Pueblo refugees introduced weaving, possibly pottery, and a host of religious concepts, including ceremonial masks and sand paintings. Some modern Navajo clans originated at this time by assimilating particular Pueblo populations. From the Spanish they began to learn the complexities of herding goats, sheep, horses, and cattle. It also was from the Spanish that the proto-Navajo began to learn to process metal.

By 1696 the Spanish once again were entrenched in New Mexico, but Indians continued to raid their settlements. The Athapaskans in turn were raided by the Ute Indians, who drove them south and west from Dinetah. During these years, around 1725, Navajo tribal identity was emerging. By the late 1700s they had increasingly turned from hunting and raising maize at homesteads to a more mobile lifestyle, with herding as a major economic focus. The mobility inherent in a herding economy, especially after horses were captured and raised in quantity for riding, enabled the Navajo to become even more formidable raiders. Peaceful negotiations with the Spanish seldom lasted for long, and the same was true after Mexico won independence in 1821. Because the Navajo had no overall political unity, some bands would make peace with the Spanish and Mexicans, whereas other bands continued to raid. The Navajo had become an independent people.

ANGLO-AMERICAN CONTROL   In 1846 the United States seized New Mexico and inherited confrontations with Navajo raiders. In the early history of Navajo relations with Anglos, no date compares with August 31, 1849. An Indian

Figure 11-2 | A watercolor portrait of Narbona made from a sketch on the day he was killed. (Courtesy of the Ewell Sale Stewart Library, the Academy of Natural Sciences of Philadelphia, Ms. Coll. 146, no. 44 Kern.)

agent, along with Colonel John Washington of the U.S. Army and his troops, met with a group of Navajo, including Narbona, a leader who sought peace with the Anglos. A disagreement arose when a Mexican man who was with the troops said he saw a horse that had been stolen from him. Washington demanded that the horse be returned to the Mexican. The Navajo refused and had begun to leave when the soldiers were ordered to fire on them. Seven Navajo were killed, including Narbona, who was shot in the back and scalped. No official action was taken against Washington, and Navajo mistrust of Anglos appears to have intensified (see Figure 11-2).

In the first four years of Anglo-American control of New Mexico, an estimated 450,000 sheep were seized by the Navajo and Apache from Hispanic and Anglo settlements. Neither peace conferences nor military expeditions could stem the raids. The U.S. Army response was to build Fort Defiance deep within Navajo country in 1851. It was attacked unsuccessfully by the Navajo in 1860 and temporarily abandoned in 1861 at the beginning of the Civil War. Until the army returned there in 1863, the Navajo and other Indians, Anglos, and Hispanics fought for revenge, animals, slaves, and booty. By then the Navajo may have had 300,000 herd animals.

THE LONG WALK By the early 1860s the Navajo transformation from hunters and relatively sedentary farmers to mobile herders, raiders, and farmers was well developed. Most Navajo appear to have favored peace with the United States, but they were hostile to many other Indians in the region and to the Hispanics. Unfortunately, federal Indian policy was inconsistent and dominated locally by anti-Navajo military officers. One reason behind the periodic belligerence of the Navajo was that slave traders, including Hispanics, were seizing so many children. Brigadier General James H. Carleton, the commander of the U.S. Army troops, was determined to remove the Navajo from the 30,000 square miles they occupied and relocate them to Fort Sumner (Bosque Redondo) in New Mexico. The Long Walk of some 300 miles, beginning in 1863, was one of the most disreputable actions by the U.S. military against Indians. The army pursued a scorched-earth policy so that the Navajo had little food and few places where they could escape. They were herded to Fort Sumner. Those who could not keep up with the others were shot and killed, whether they were women giving birth, the ill, or individuals who paused to help another captive. About nine thousand Navajo were driven to Bosque Redondo. As many as two thousand Navajo may have avoided capture by the military, but some of them were found by slave traders and sold. At least another two thousand died during the Long Walk or at Bosque Redondo (see Figure 11-3).

Fort Sumner was located in an area without adequate food or water and ill adapted to farming, which was intended to help provision the prisoners. The army was poorly prepared to house and feed so many people in such a bleak setting. The prisoners were homesick; some became desperately ill, and some

Figure 11-3 | Navajo are guarded by a soldier at Fort Sumner following the Long Walk. (Courtesy of the National Archives: U.S. Signal Corps Coll.: 111-SC 87964.)

starved to death. They were raided by their enemies. Navajo boys reportedly went to where horses and mules were corralled, rooted around for undigested corn, and roasted it as food.

The army effort to transform captives into subsistence farmers failed. When they did plant crops, insects, disease, and drought led to repeated crop failures. As a result, the federal government spent more than $1 million a year to provision the captives, but the rations provided made many of them ill. Finally, the government decided to return the Navajo to their homeland because keeping them captive was a financial burden. A treaty was arranged with the cooperation of a prominent leader, Barboncito; it was ratified by the U.S. Congress in 1868. The return trip of the Navajo was not without hardships. Children rode in wagons, some adults rode horses, and others walked.

This is an appropriate context in which to consider Navajo "warfare" in brief. What has been called warfare among them should more properly be termed *raiding;* conflicts typically involved a small number of warriors who approached an enemy covertly to seize livestock. True battles were rare. Men developed many skills to become successful raiders. They became adept at handling bows, riding horses, tracking, controlling livestock, and performing the religious rituals associated with warfare. Men who aspired to be raid leaders underwent a prolonged apprenticeship under an older man who knew one or more highly complex war rituals. A leader organized a small group of family and friends to form a raiding party. As preparation, warriors often had a medicine man (a singer) perform an elaborate ceremony (a sing, or chant way) called the Enemyway. More often, an Enemyway was performed to purify returning warriors and to protect them from ghost sickness as a result of contact with the spirits of slain enemies. A large number of people from a warrior's clan would attend, requiring the warrior's family to slaughter many sheep as food. Outsiders referred to the Enemyway as the "Squaw Dance" because in the social dancing that accompanied the ceremony, women chose dancing partners from among the men.

A small party of raiders set out on foot, hoping to return in a few days with at least as many horses as raiders and driving home a herd of sheep. They never wiped out an enemy's herd, however, so that it would eventually be replenished for future raids.

RESERVATION HISTORY TO WORLD WAR I In their excellent study of the Navajo reservations up to 1975, Garrick Alan Bailey and Roberta Glenn Bailey (1986) described the changes in insightful detail. The original reservation in northwestern New Mexico and northeastern Arizona, created by the treaty in 1868, included about 10 percent of what had been Navajo country before their confinement at Fort Sumner. Because their land base was so much reduced, federal administrators permitted Navajo to live in adjacent areas. The resettlement program encouraged Navajo self-sufficiency because the government feared that they would revert to raiding.

This is not to say that few problems existed along the way. Scattered over about 25,000 square miles, the federal government had little control over the people. The inadequate staff at the administrative centers of Fort Defiance and Fort Wingate led federal agents to appoint "chiefs" to act on their behalf. These charismatic leaders, known to the Navajo as "big men," became powerful because they distributed goods guaranteed by treaty. This arrangement, however, ended in 1879. When some Navajo resumed raiding, the government turned to the big men and hired tribal police to curb the raiders, a combination that was reasonably successful.

After resettlement the people survived by hunting and collecting plant products. Initially, they seldom killed domestic animals for meat. Before long, hunting and gathering depleted local food sources, and goats became an important edible. Goats, who often bore two offspring at a time, were a good source of milk, cheese, and meat. Sheep began to multiply and eventually became the key herd animal, providing meat and wool that was woven into blankets and garments to wear or to trade. Horses, mules, and burros were ridden and provided a source of meat, but cattle were unimportant.

Trade with other Indians and Hispanics flourished and expanded as Navajo blankets became a major item for barter. Trading changed in character once Anglo traders on the reservation were licensed by the federal government in 1868. Initially, the people were poor; annuity payments did not begin to meet their needs. At the same time, local resources were overexploited. A case in point is the supply of skins used for moccasins. The people traditionally killed deer and used these skins to make moccasins, but hunting pressure soon depleted the deer population. Neither goat nor sheep skins were acceptable substitutes. At this time, however, Navajo sheep herds were increasing rather rapidly, and as a result they were able to exchange sheep wool, both with other Indians and at trading posts, for buckskins. Around this time, too, the Anglo-American demand for wool was increasing, and the railroad, which reached western New Mexico in 1881, provided an economical means to ship raw wool east to be processed. Before long the wool trade expanded dramatically, and trading posts both on and near the reservation became numerous and relatively stable enterprises.

By the early 1890s the Navajo owned an estimated 1,700,000 sheep and goats; they were also considered the best weavers in the region. Their blankets had long been a premium craft item, but they also produced a variety of other woven products, such as ponchos, saddle blankets, sash belts, and women's dresses, both for their own use and for trading. They made use of changes in weaving materials and techniques introduced by Anglos, including commercial yarns and dyes and manufactured wool cards (to straighten tangled fibers and thus prepare the wool for spinning). These developments increased and modified the productivity of women, who were the weavers. A new market arose after a railroad was built through the southern sector of their country, thereby introducing tourists as customers for blankets and silverwork.

The Navajo learned the rudiments of silverwork from the Spanish, and the quality of Navajo jewelry grew in the 1870s as the inventory of production tools improved. In addition to and equally important as its appeal to the tourist trade, silver jewelry became a significant way for the Navajo to concentrate their wealth. In the 1880s they developed a pawn system with traders. Silverwork was pawned for goods in times of economic stress and was redeemed as individuals became more affluent.

Navajo assimilation into the greater Anglo-American society became a long-range federal policy. Under the terms of the 1868 treaty, schools were to be provided for children, but the dispersed nature of the Navajo population and the limited federal resources allotted made this goal unrealistic. The Presbyterians founded a day school at Fort Defiance in 1869, but it was a failure, as was a local boarding school. Only a small number of children attended the Carlisle Indian School in Pennsylvania during the 1880s, in part because the people objected to sending their children so far away. By 1892 there were about 18,000 Navajo, but less than one hundred children attended school. Around this time only about fifty Navajo spoke English, and fewer still could read and write. Formal education obviously had failed to this point.

In the late nineteenth century a multitude of events over which the Navajo had no control impinged on their lives. The federal government granted land to railroads in a checkerboard pattern, along a right-of-way in the vicinity of Navajo lands. The eventual illegal exclusion of Navajo from public lands, the arrival of Anglo and Hispanic farmers and herders in their midst, and an expansion of the cattle industry by whites each had negative consequences. Furthermore, an increase in the Navajo population, expansion of their herds, and overgrazing by Navajo and non-Navajo stock created environmental problems.

The last decades of the nineteenth century proved a disaster. With the national economic Panic of 1893, livestock and wool prices fell precipitously. Repeated dry years and heavy snowfalls in Navajo country led to an alarming decline in goat and sheep herds; droughts resulted in crop failures. Many Navajo went hungry or starved despite considerable government aid. These hard times continued into the early 1900s. Overgrazing and competition with outsiders for land meant that most Navajo could no longer depend primarily on herds as their subsistence base. They developed alternative economic strategies. Gradually they improved the breeding stock of sheep, intensified farming activities, and turned increasingly to wage labor as an income supplement.

Federal control over reservation life became far more intense in the late 1800s. The General Allotment Act (Dawes Act) of 1887, as discussed in Chapter 2 and elsewhere, was a concerted federal effort to destroy the reservation land base and assimilate Indians into the general population. The act had relatively little immediate impact on the Navajo, but federal domination increased as six regional administrative centers were created by 1909. Additionally, in the early 1900s the political appointees in charge of Indian reservations began to be replaced by career civil servants, who usually were more rigid in furthering federal policies. Federal agents sought to eliminate childhood marriages, plural marriages, and other "vices," but with poor results.

Navajo–Anglo conflicts varied from one sector of the reservation to another because of localized conditions. Throughout much of the reservation, Indians complained about their inability to graze stock on public lands and their restricted access to water. They were also concerned that the size of the reservation was inadequate for their needs, especially compared with the areas traditionally exploited. Reservation crowding became more acute as the population increased; by 1900 there were about 21,000 Navajo. The land problem was partially and temporarily alleviated by repeated expansion of the reservation. By the 1910s some Navajo claimed land allotments under the Dawes Act despite strong opposition from local whites, who anticipated that one day the reservation would be abandoned by the federal government and they would be able to homestead most of the land. When Arizona and New Mexico became states in 1912, Anglo political power vastly increased at the expense of Indians.

As mentioned previously, Navajo blankets had long been a major craft item both for personal use and to trade with other Indians. Blanket designs include patterns based on Pueblo Indian, Spanish, and Navajo designs (see Figure 11-4). By the 1890s, with the encouragement of trading post owners, weavers began to produce textiles for the Anglo market. Rug weaving soon had a major impact on reservation economic life following changes in weaving styles. An early "rug" measured about four by six feet, and many actually were blankets or ponchos sold as rugs by traders. The Santa Fe Railroad and the Fred Harvey Company were instrumental in fostering the Anglo passion for Navajo crafts. Navajo rugs and, to a lesser extent, silverwork designed for the Anglo market began to be sold in stores that featured Indian crafts. In 1903 the Navajo may have sold as many as 50,000 blankets and may have earned as much as $350,000 from their sale. The market continued to expand until around 1920, then declined during the Great Depression.

Traditional Life

The preceding summary of Navajo ethnohistory before World War I points up a major problem when attempting to describe their "traditional life." Over more than two hundred years of Navajo tribal identity, the people changed repeatedly and dramatically. First they were hunters, farmers, and raiders who shifted to herding and then to herding supplemented by wage labor, which becomes increasingly prominent. In becoming "Navajo" they were profoundly influenced by the Spanish, Pueblo Indians, and Anglo-Americans, as previously emphasized. No comprehensive Navajo ethnography appeared until after they began to be dominated by the federal government. Hence, a "typical and traditional year" cannot be presented. Instead, the account in this chapter represents a mixture of customs both old and relatively new. The

Figure 11-4 | This Early Classic–style poncho was made before 1860. A Navajo woman probably spent more than a year in its manufacture. (Courtesy of the Southwest Museum, Los Angeles, Photo #42671.)

emphasis in this ethnographic reconstruction is on the decades surrounding the year 1900.

ORIGIN MYTH Numerous varying Navajo accounts record their creation and emergence as a people. Narrators of and listeners to these tales accept the legends as legitimate, despite the textual differences. The myth recounted here represents a composite and differs significantly from some versions. Initially, we should note that the word used by the Navajo for themselves, Diné, literally means "Earth Surface People." They contrasted with the Holy People, who once lived beneath the present earth surface. Holy People are termed Yei; they exist at the zenith and nadir of the celestial sphere and at points of the compass. The Yei are associated with many things: features on the landscape, the weather, plant life, and some animals. The Yei are not gods in our sense because they may either help or hinder the people; to control them in rituals is a cornerstone of Navajo religion, crystallized in the Blessingway.

In a series of twelve stratified worlds beneath the earth lived the Holy People, but discord, usually resulting form witchcraft, forced them into one higher world after another. At one point men and women could not reconcile their differences and lived separately, but finally they learned to live together. In the last of the underworlds, a flood forced the Holy People to escape to the earth's surface. It was here that death originated.

The Yei created natural objects. They also originated the Earth Surface People, commonly referred to as "the ones with five fingers." The Earth Surface People were the ancestors of the Navajo and other peoples. The Holy People taught the Navajo how to live. The Holy People also were the parents of Changing Woman, the most prominent individual in Navajo mythology, who is identified with the earth itself. Changing Woman later conceived miraculously by the Sun and gave birth to two sons, the Twin Monster Slayers, who killed earthly monsters. The sites of these slayings are prominent features on the landscape. In this way the natural world was created.

APPEARANCE AND CLOTHING   Traditionally the hair of adults and children was brushed back, folded, and tied in place. Men followed a newer custom of keeping their hair in place with a rolled handkerchief in which they carried small items, such as tobacco and coins. Adults wore large silver earrings and locally made necklaces of silver or turquoise beads; alternatively, they might obtain coral or shell beads from traders. Silver bracelets likewise were popular, as were belts made from heavy silver disks strung on leather straps.

Around 1900, new apparel styles were displacing older ones. However, low-cut moccasins with rawhide soles remained the universal footwear. White man's shoes were taboo; they could not even be touched. Similarly, some older people thought that garments manufactured by whites would produce illness if worn. This restriction began to disappear as factory-made yard goods, Pendleton blankets, and shawls became more readily available. Both sexes wore knit stockings. Navajo blankets were worn and used as bedding, but their use declined as blankets became a popular tourist item.

Traditional woolen dresses were being displaced by homemade calico dresses or hand-sewn blouses and skirts. On special occasions a woman wore a heavy knee-length woolen tunic with border designs and knee-length leg wrappings of goat or buckskin. The tunic was held in place with a woven girdle. Apparently, velveteen blouses and satin skirts did not become popular until the 1920s. Men wore pants of wool or calico, calico shirts, and leggings of dyed deerskin held in place with garters of woven thread. On special occasions their leggings or pants were trimmed with buckskin fringes and silver buttons.

SETTLEMENTS AND MANUFACTURES   As the people became less mobile in the early 1900s, they created new dwelling types and modified old ones. The standard traditional winter house, or hogan, continued to dominate. It was cone-shaped and about fifteen feet in diameter. The frame consisted of three interlocking forked posts at the center that extended to the outer walls; a pair of additional posts and poles formed an entrance that always faced east. Pieces of wood and poles were placed against the frame, and the structure was covered with mud or earth. A shallow interior excavation became the floor, and a storage shelf extended around the inner walls. Smoke from a central fireplace escaped from a hole near the dwelling peak. Aboriginal American Indians did not make chimneys over fireplaces. Early in the 1900s an improvised metal flue began to be fashioned above a fireplace to draw smoke from the room. They also bought metal stoves from traders or fashioned homemade stoves from oil drums. A small number of houses included Anglo-style tables and chairs, but otherwise there were no furnishings. People worked and slept on sheepskins.

Another traditional hogan type had four interior posts to support crossbeams and a post and pole entryway. The frame was covered with small poles, bark, and, finally, packed earth. This flat-topped dwelling type was intimately associated with ceremonies. Hogans competed with new forms of housing that included log cabins, inspired by Anglos, and jacal dwellings of Hispanic origin; a small number of families occupied frame houses with either flat or gabled roofs.

Summer and temporary campsites consisted of improvised shelters. They included lean-tos, ramadas (open porchlike structures), and windbreaks, or tepee-style structures covered with canvas. Another prominent structure at a camp or winter settlement was a sweat house. This was a tepee-shaped structure with a pole frame covered with cedar bark and then with dirt. Rocks were heated in a nearby fire and transferred inside the structure for the bathers. A settlement also included wooden enclosures for securing livestock (see Figure 11-5). They also employed various items for the animals, such as saddles, quirts, lassos, and hobbles for horses and imported baby bottles of glass for feeding newborn lambs.

Imported artifacts were becoming increasingly popular. Iron axes had replaced those made from ground stone, and knife blades flaked from chert or chalcedony long ago had given way to imported metal knives. Near a homestead were looms on which women produced woven goods. Some people made and used clay cooking pots, but most containers were of metal and bought at trading posts. Locally made baskets and pottery were primarily produced for religious ceremonies, although some families continued to use relatively flat coiled baskets as food dishes.

Farming equipment of old, such as wooden digging sticks and wooden weed cutters, were being displaced by imported shovels and hoes. To harvest wild seeds a person might use a clublike wooden flail, and he or she could remove kernels of corn from a cob by striking one ear against another. For grinding corn and other grains, they used a lava slab metate and round stone mano. These, however, were giving way to the hand gristmills that traders stocked.

Figure 11-5 | A Navajo camp as it appeared in 1944. (Photo by C. E. Purviance. Courtesy of the Museum of Northern Arizona.)

Roasting pits provided a traditional means for cooking meat, ears of corn, and ground cornmeal products.

Horses and burros had become beasts of burden, but some people continued to use tumplines as an aid for carrying firewood, water containers, and other heavy loads. A tumpline was a strap made from buckskin or wool that could be slung over the forehead or across the chest of a male or female bearer to help support a burden. This form, however, appears to have been a relatively recent introduction. To carry water, they coiled sumac twig splints to form a somewhat globular basket that had loop handles near the top and that was covered with pitch. Goatskin water bags were a recent addition to their material inventory.

THE SUBSISTENCE ROUND   By the 1910s the economic round continued to depend most heavily on herd animals. Wealth, prestige, and security were linked primarily to the ability to meet the needs of livestock. The insightful discussion of Navajo stock by James F. Downs (1972) based on his fieldwork in the early 1960s is the primary source of information about herding in earlier decades.

One characteristic of Navajo pastoralism was their dispersion into small family groups at homesites. But as the population expanded, pressure on grazing land intensified. A key to their success was an ability to meet the particular needs of cattle, goats, horses, and sheep in thoughtful combination. Efficient herding depended in part on having at least a few horses, and owning them increased one's social status. In practical terms, to keep at least one horse at a living site was highly desirable. A hobbled or tethered horse nearby provided immediate mobility for meeting various needs, especially for locating animals that had strayed. Yet keeping horses at hand meant that they must be fed and watered on a daily basis.

Sheep were most important as a food source, but they could also be converted into money, and they provided a major source of personal satisfaction. The care of sheep dictated the texture of Navajo life. Sheep required daily attention, but they also were the most domesticated and the least intelligent of the livestock raised. A herding instinct leads sheep to follow one another; a stray sheep is defenseless and will die of hunger, thirst, or predation, especially by coyotes. Sheep are nervous and react to the behavior of one another. To counteract this characteristic, a few goats usually were added to a herd because goats are more curious and self-reliant; they calmed and led the sheep. A small number, even hundreds, of sheep and goats could be managed by one person, adult or child, because after they were driven to grass the animals could be ignored. In sum, sheep required a great deal of care but were readily controlled.

Yet sheep herding itself was demanding. Herders typically moved their flocks to high country in the summer and to lower land in the winter, a pattern termed transhumance. A heavy snowfall forced a family to dislodge the snow so that animals could graze, and cold winds made it difficult to find grass. Spring lambing required careful attention. Lambs were separated from a herd and tended at a homesite to increase the survival rate. Sheep were grazed on open range, penned each night, and taken out to feed shortly before dawn. This pattern may have originated in years past when other Indians raided Navajo herds. In addition, most Navajo feared the dark because of religious beliefs. Sheep were also penned during the heat of the day because in hot weather they would stop and refuse to eat or move despite vigorous efforts by a herder. The proximity to water was another crucial factor in the tending of sheep. Finally, if nearby land became overgrazed, a family was forced to move at least temporarily to more distant pasturage.

During World War I, the sizes of sheep and cattle herds increasingly responded to the market demands for lamb and beef. Cattle were raised to sell. Most families owned a few animals, but they were rarely slaughtered as food. Those families that placed at least some emphasis on cattle were constrained by a number of factors. Most important, a single cow required about four times as much rangeland as a sheep or goat. A few cows could be grazed together with sheep, but herds of cattle tended to stray widely. Considerable effort might be required to locate such animals and to drive them back again, especially if a man did not have a horse. Considering the importance of sheep as food, the fluctuations in cattle prices, and the far greater emotional identification with sheep, it becomes clear why cattle assumed secondary importance.

The only other important domestic animal was the dog. Often, each family member owned a dog and viewed it with considerable affection. One practical reason for owning a dog was to help herd sheep. Dogs usually aided a herder moving sheep in a particular direction, but they were not trained in the manner of Anglo sheep dogs. Perhaps the most important role of dogs was to keep coyotes away from sheep. They also served as scavengers around a homestead. Dogs were hungry most of the time and contributed to sanitation around a home by eating cow, horse, and human feces.

The arid nature of Navajo country meant that it was ill suited for intensive farming. At reasonably well-watered sites, family members, especially women, were largely responsible for raising maize and squash as dietary supplements. Alternatively, a family might exchange sheep or sheep wool at a trading post or with the Hopi for maize, flour, and fruit. Planted fields were preferably near a homesite, but might be several miles away when the distant land was better suited. Despite the labor expended on clearing land, planting seeds, and controlling weeds, crops often failed for lack of moisture; or the seeds might wash away with heavy rains. After a few years the yield of a plot declined abruptly, and the process was repeated.

In another context, maize cultivation served a critical need unrelated to food. Corn pollen was considered an exceedingly sacred plant product, an idea borrowed from Pueblo Indians. Pollen was placed in small bags and used to bless individuals, animals, and hogans; it played a crucial role in all religious rituals.

DESCENT, KINSHIP, AND MARRIAGE   Descent was traced through females and included about sixty named matrilineal descent groups (matriclans). These clans in turn were grouped into about fifteen unnamed phratries. A primary purpose of the clan and phratry was to regulate marriage. No one could marry into one's own clan, the clan of one's father, or a clan in the same phratry. Members of the same clan tended to be widely dispersed, and, possibly as one result, neither clan chiefs nor clan councils existed. A prominent man in a clan might influence the lives of nearby clan members and persons representing other clans in the vicinity; thus his authority was territorial and not based on clan affiliations per se. Furthermore, when a person traveled to another part of Navajo country, he or she could expect food, shelter, and other forms of aid from members of the same clan, irrespective of whether or not the persons had ever met previously.

Navajo kinship terminology not only is changing but also varies from one segment of the population to another. The version discussed is possibly the most widely prevailing system. A child was "born in" the mother's clan and regarded all the females of the mother's clan as "mothers." Whenever necessary for clarity of meaning, a person would identify a biological mother as his or her "real mother." A child likewise was "born for" the father's clan, and the males of this clan were "fathers." In addition, those *born for* a father's clan were siblings, whereas those *born in* a mother's clan were children. Mother and mother's sister were termed alike because they were women of the same clan. Similarly, father and father's brother were termed alike. Different terms existed for father's sister and mother's brother. The terms for the first ascending generation are bifurcate merging.

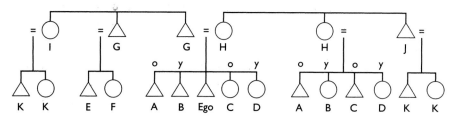

Figure 11-6 | The early historic Navajo system of kinship terminology.

For siblings and mother's sister's children, distinctions were made by age and gender, and all were termed alike (e.g., an older sister and mother's sister's older daughter were both in a sense "older sisters"). Cross-cousins were termed alike with no gender distinction, and parallel patrilateral cousins were distinguished by gender. The terminology for cousins is basically Iroquois (see Figure 11-6).

The kinship terminology provided the framework for lifelong responsibilities, with particular forms of behavior expected in each set of relationships. Mother's brothers had important responsibilities toward their sisters' children, especially their sisters' sons, since many of the duties of raising children fell to the mother's brother. Adults who acted irresponsibly were said to bring shame on their families and, in fact, to act as if they had no families. Brother–sister relationships often overrode those of wife–husband in long-term importance.

Some relationships required polite, almost bashful, behavior, as was required of younger kin in dealings with older relatives. Women had high status and could address any man as "my son," whereas a man might address any woman by the more respectful term, "my mother." Daughters acted politely toward fathers. Intermediaries were often called upon to communicate with relatives who deserved extreme respect. When a brother married, his sisters might interact with him through their children or his wife. The social distance between a man and his mother-in-law was so great that a son-in-law was obliged to avoid her—he never spoke to her or remained in the same building or even in her vicinity. By contrast, relationships between a mother and her children were said to be "easy," warm, and affectionate. Sons enjoyed similar relations with their fathers. Some family ties were so familiar that joking was allowed, as between sisters and their unmarried brothers. In some relationships the joking could be of sexual content, as between cross-cousins or between a mother's brother and his sisters' sons.

A young couple was expected to live with the family of the wife's mother (ideally matrilocal residence). Despite this expectation, a newly married couple might live for a time with the husband's family unit (actually bilocal residence). Any number of factors determined the residence of a couple, such as whether a family could accommodate the newcomers or whether a family required the help of another male. For a couple to move back and forth before they settled down was not uncommon. As the population continued to grow, however, and the land base remained relatively stable, increasing numbers of couples lived apart from their parental families, especially when the husband had a wagelabor job.

POLITICAL LIFE   The Navajo did not emerge as a distinct tribal entity until about A.D. 1725. Furthermore, incipient political integration was initially thrust upon them following the treaty of 1868. It was then that the federal government appointed charismatic leaders, Navajo "big men," whom the administrators called "chiefs." This effort was largely unsuccessful. These points were made earlier, but they bear repeating to introduce more recent political developments.

In 1899 the federal government began to create regional administrative centers on the reservation, and soon thereafter career civil servants began to replace political appointees in Indian administration. These changes, as mentioned previously, meant that the United States was in a better position to assert greater political control over the people. As in the past, men who were appointed as "leaders" were those who did not actively oppose federal policies. There were thirty such appointees in 1900. In some sectors of the reservation, councils were organized that functioned on an intermittent or regular basis, but they were above all else the tools of Indian agents. Yet some agents opposed Navajo councils and sought instead to deal directly with individual Indians. These devices prevented the people from developing a unified political base. Even when an elected Navajo Tribal Council was launched in 1923, the purpose was to serve the interests of oil companies in lease negotiations. Broader Navajo interests were not considered.

RELIGION   The Holy People ("gods"), as Navajo precursors, have a dominant role in the mythology and belief system, as evidenced in their origin myths. As supernatural beings the Holy People are dangerous and powerful. Equally important, they are not especially sympathetic to people. Yet they may be induced to restore harmony in human life that results largely from inappropriate behavior. A major goal literally is to compel the Holy People to restore balance in the universe. The Holy People are not worshiped as gods in a Christian sense; instead harmony is regained after people meet their proper ritual obligations. This presentation of Navajo religion is in the present tense because most of the people continue to accept their traditional belief system.

As noted by Leland C. Wyman (1983) in a masterful synthesis of the Navajo ceremonial system, these people have neither a word nor phrase comparable to the English word "religion." And yet religion is the best English word for their configuration of beliefs and practices, which expands far beyond the usual definition. As Wyman (1983, 536) wrote, "[t]hey regard the universe as an orderly all-inclusive, unitary system of interrelated elements. The tiniest object, being, or power, even minute insects; the most stupendous, the great mountains that bound the Navajo country and the thunder and lightning that crash above them; and man himself—all have their place and significant function in the universal continuum."

In Navajo thinking, the natural and supernatural blend into one another. A key to understanding and dealing with the Holy People is embodied in an inherent conflict between evil and good. To achieve a balance in life by dealing with these forces simultaneously is a persistent goal. Many potential sources of evil prevail, such as whirlwinds, lightning, human ghosts, and particular animals, especially bears, coyotes, and snakes. Likewise, breaking taboos, excessive gambling or sexual activity, and out-of-the-ordinary behavior in general can disrupt balance and harmony. Therefore, the world is a dangerous place and every reasonable effort is made to avert contamination. Disharmony results in the anticipation of illnesses, or illness itself, and is to be avoided for the well-being of herd animals, farmlands, and other aspects of living.

One word, *hozho,* expresses the most fundamental Navajo value. Collectively hozho includes concepts of beauty, harmony, goodness, normality, and success. When disharmony or imbalance prevail, hozho is restored in varied ways, ranging from prayers to immensely complex ceremonial configurations. If hozho is not restored, it is a result of human failings. In broader context, and unlike the Pueblo Indians, the Navajo have neither religious societies nor a rigid ceremonial calendar to achieve and sustain general well-being. Instead the focus is on individual specialists with specific capabilities. They usually are men called *singers,* an indication of the emphasis on singing, a key activity in meeting ritual obligations. A singer's attention usually centers on a specific patient in a particular context. Any beneficial results aid not only the patient but also his or her family, a local group, or sometimes the Navajo in general.

A tyro (novice) singer typically serves an extended apprenticeship under the guidance of an older established practitioner. For a major "chant" a tyro must learn hundreds of songs precisely, long and involved prayers, the use of plant medicines, the preparation of drypaintings (sand paintings), and involved ritual procedures. A singer specializes in one or more chants because of the breadth and depth of knowledge required for a major chant; specific chants are identified as "chantways."

Major chantways are numerous, varied, and distinct in purpose and procedure. So much variability is involved that Karl W. Luckert (1979, 7) suggests that each chantway might be regarded as a "minireligion." At the same time, chantways share many common elements. Ideally they are held in a circular hogan with an entrance to the east—the direction from which good arrives. A smokehole at the center of the roof is for the exit of evil. A chantway is held for two, four, five, or nine nights. The sacred bundle of a singer may include rattles, whistles, fossils, animal claws, and many other forms, each with its particular significance. Maize pollen is an especially holy substance employed in many contexts. It is tossed in the air during prayers and applied to consecrate or sanctify people, artifacts, and animals. In a chantway drypaintings are likely to be included, and over five hundred highly symbolic designs have been reported. Most of them illustrate two or more Holy People on rainbow-bars to represent their means of movement or on black bars representing the earth. A chantway ends with a prayer and song to negate the ill consequences of any errors in the rituals.

The Blessingway is one of the two cornerstones in the ceremonial system. Its goal usually is to promote harmony (hozho), achieve well-being, and result in a fruitful life. Blessingway rites include dedicating a new hogan, validating a marriage, aiding a woman in childbirth, and protecting livestock. This chantway usually begins at sundown and lasts two nights and one day. (Time is determined by nights, from sundown to sundown, not by days.) The opening night is devoted to songs and prayers by the participants while the person who is the focus of the rituals holds a medicine (sacred) bundle at his or her chest. The buckskin bundle includes small containers of earth from four sacred mountains, prayer sticks, and small packets of pollen. Additional songs and prayers are performed during the day, and the rituals end with songs during the final night.

The second cornerstone, originally designated the Enemyway, was designed to protect warriors from the ghosts of slain enemies. It evolved into a cure for illness thought to be caused by the ghosts of non-Navajo; it is grouped with Evilway (Ghostway) ceremonies. The Evilway is unusual because it spans from three to five nights, because it has more than one singer in charge, and because rituals are held in different localities.

As a cultural institution, traditional religion clearly was, and remains for many Navajo, a prominent aspect of life. Yet some people, possibly not very many, appear to achieve personal goals by witchcraft and sorcery. Inordinate envy of others may be the most prominent characteristic attributed to witches. Likewise, a witch might seek vengeance for real or imagined wrongs, strive to obtain wealth beyond normal means, or seek to harm someone based on pure malice. Witches are feared and despised because they are presumed to cause illness, death, and disharmony. To combat their evil requires constant vigilance. Protection is gained in songs and prayers, in plant and animal substances, and especially in the ownership of ceremonial artifacts. Extreme care is required in disposing of any body substance (e.g., feces, urine, menstrual blood) or body materials (e.g., hair, nail clippings) that could be used in sorcery by a witch. Partial security is achieved by being among trustworthy relatives and friends. Caution is required in large crowds that include strangers. People also prefer to be in the company of others at night.

Witches are usually considered to be male, or sometimes a childless woman; they are intimately associated with death and the dead. Witchcraft is reportedly learned from a parent, grandparent, or less often from a spouse. A powderlike poison made from the flesh of corpses, which has the appearance of pollen, is said to be their primary weapon. Witches usually are thought to go forth at night in animal skins, especially those of wolves. A witch might drop poison through the smokehole of a hogan to infect a victim. Another possibility is to blow poison in the face of a person in a large crowd. Strange noises at night suggest the presence of a witch, and their tracks are said to be like those of animals, only larger; they might be traced a long way to a hogan.

Someone suspected of witchcraft could be called to a meeting by his accusers and led there, tied by a rope, for questioning. When confession was not soon forthcoming, he was tied down, deprived of food and drink, and not allowed to relieve himself. Confession meant recovery for the victim unless the person was near death. Within a year a witch was expected to die with the same symptoms as his victim. A witch who did not confess was killed as an approved form of capital punishment. When a witch went undetected, he eventually was expected to be killed by lightning.

Are Navajo witches real? The comprehensive study of their witchcraft by Clyde Kluckhohn (1944) addressed the question. In one sector of Navajo country nearly every family possessed medicine against witchery in the form of a specific antidote, animal gall. Individuals have been accused of witchcraft in private and in public; some people think they have been bewitched. If, in Navajo thinking, an illness is inexplicable, witchcraft is suspected by at least some persons. Witch fear is real, and accused witches have often been murdered. Kluckhohn concludes that witchcraft is practiced, but there is no certainty that all of the traits associated with witches exist.

When men take sweat baths, usually about once a week, two purposes are served: to cleanse one's body and to worship. The relatively small semisubterranean bathhouse at a homestead has a low entrance. Rocks are heated in a nearby fire and transferred on a shovel to a corner of the sweat house. Before entering a bath, naked adult males tie a string about their prepuce (foreskin); it is considered dangerous not to do so. It is an indication that a boy has gained adult status when his father or an uncle shows him how to apply the prepuce string. After bathers crowd into the room, the entrance is covered. The men begin by singing songs to bring good fortune in cycles of four, eight, or more depending on the bathers and their tolerance of the extreme heat. Women formally bathed after men, but this practice appears to have declined.

The formalities of chantways and their crucial role in dealing with the natural and supernatural realms represent one aspect of religious behavior. A second dimension pervades ordinary daily life. Each day the oldest male in a household group greets the rising sun with a sacred song and by dropping maize pollen in the four cardinal directions. As James F. Downs (1972, 98) noted, "[t]hroughout the day that follows, the routine is accompanied by endless and almost unconscious acts of ritual." The lives of these people are enveloped in songs with varying degrees of sacredness. The words might be barely audible or sung in a loud voice. Singing is common during such activities as driving sheep, doing farm work, collecting wood, and spinning, weaving, or cooking. In each instance the goals are to aid and to protect the singer, household members, and their possessions.

LIFE CYCLE Ethnographic gems are unusual, and a flawless one is exceedingly rare. The autobiography of Left Handed, a Navajo male born in 1868, is a stellar example. Compiled by Walter Dyk (1938) and published as *Son of Old Man Hat,* the book recounts the life of Left Handed from his childhood until after he married, at about the age of twenty. The narrative style is compelling, as are the particulars. Although it is rash to depend on one man's view of growing up, a number of examples from his account ring true and provide details usually unrecorded or muted in a standard ethnography. In addition, at least some Navajo had the capacity to remember the precise wording of conversations for many years and thus provide another dimension of reality. Some events from Left Handed's childhood are described later in this section.

Children were valued by the Navajo, but no elaborate ceremonies accompanied birth. Corn pollen was sprinkled over a baby's head immediately after delivery. The baby then was bathed, wrapped in a blanket, and "shaped" by a midwife's kneading and molding. Within the first day of life, his or her ears were pierced. The afterbirth and everything stained with blood was buried, burned, or wrapped in a bundle and hidden in a tree to prevent a witch from using these items to harm the offspring. The umbilical cord was buried in the sheep corral or somewhere else near a family home so that the person's mind would be rooted to the family land. Although children were named, they were typically addressed by kin terms. Babies could be several months old before a name was chosen. They were indulged and kept in close physical contact with their mothers to nurse on demand. A baby's mother, as well as the other members of a household, were responsive to his or her needs and cries, and the baby was often held and cuddled.

A neonate spent most waking hours strapped with cotton cloths to a cradleboard, which could be carried easily. After a few months, he or she spent less and less time in the cradleboard and gradually learned to walk. A baby's first laugh led to gift giving and was a sign that his or her time in the cradleboard had ended. The person who first made a baby laugh was responsible for organizing a celebration.

Children could breast-feed until they were three or four years old or a sibling was born. Toilet training was not begun until a child could talk and typically was a slow and gentle process. Children decided what and how often to eat and when or where they would sleep. It was not unusual for a family to rearrange its plans to accommodate a child's wishes. Children seldom, if ever, were spanked or reprimanded; instead they were encouraged and taught with stories. They grew up feeling confident, loved, and valued and soon learned to respect those who were older. Small boys and girls helped with camp responsibilities by hauling water or firewood. Lambs were often given to children to raise. It was while herding that a child learned to value some measure of silence and solitude.

Left Handed was raised by his mother's sister and her husband, Old Man Hat. The family initially had few sheep and moved often from one semi-isolated hogan to another in search of pasture for the animals. Thus in his formative years Left Handed was primarily under the direct influence of his sociological parents above all others. They often provided formal guidance about growing up. Left Handed was told repeatedly to run each morning for good health and a long life. Old Man Hat said time and again that Left Handed should go to bed late at night and rise before the sun. By the time he was twelve he ran early in the morning, at midday, and in the evening. He put sand in his moccasins so his feet would toughen and he would be able to run in sand or snow.

Left Handed's life centered on herding sheep, and he was introduced to the task while quite young. He herded in the morning and evening near the family hogan. Because he was afraid, he stayed in the middle of the herd where he felt safe. Before long he learned to avoid soft ground in which the sheep might sink and not to allow the sheep to stray. By the time he was about eleven years old, he had a large sheep herd and many horses under his care.

As a child the daily cycle of the sun puzzled Left Handed. He did not ask about it but reasoned that the sun came up and went down in the same pattern each day. He thought that where the sun set, there must be many suns, or else they melted and disappeared. As he thought about the seasons, he wished for summer when it was cold and for cold when it was hot. He reasoned that when it was cold where they were living, they should return to the place they had been when it was warm. Similarly, when he was young he heard about the concept of a year, and it troubled him (e.g., one year as opposed to many years). He came to think that a year must have a body like an animal and he wanted to see it, but he never was able to see a year.

Sex puzzled Left Handed as a young child. He wondered, for example, why a girl had no penis. Did their parents cut them off? He asked his mother, who said that girls and boys were born as they are. When out herding, he met girls who also were tending sheep, but his mother told him to stay away from them. She said that girls and women had teeth in their sexual organs and could bite off his penis. He knew this was not so for sheep and reasoned that it possibly was true only for human females. It might be noted that the idea of a toothed vagina occurs in the mythology of many different people around the world.

The *Kinaalda,* a Blessingway rite, honored a girl's transition into adulthood. During her initial menstruation she was especially vulnerable to adverse influences. For four days she was the center of ritual attention as relatives, friends, and guests gathered to sing and help ensure her success as an adult. Subdued and somewhat withdrawn, the girl remained in the family hogan, but left there to gather wood at dawn, run, and demonstrate the adult ethic of hard work. Her mother and maternal relatives prepared food, and on the fourth day the initiate distributed it to everyone and was congratulated.

A formal institutional means prevailed for a young woman to seek a husband following her Kinaalda. Loosely termed a "Squaw Dance," it originally was a part of the Enemyway chant. Usually held in the summer in comparatively recent times, the overt purpose was for a medicine man to treat an ill person. The patient's immediate relatives enlisted the aid of distant relatives to host the four-day event. Curing was thought to be most successful when many guests attended, and they sometimes numbered in the hundreds. An unmarried woman dressed in her finest garments and, wearing her best jewelry, selected a dance partner who could not easily refuse her and was obligated to dance with her on subsequent nights. This courtship pattern was accompanied by a great deal of joking, and a girl might elect to dance with a married man.

A woman clearly had considerable influence in the selection of a spouse but hesitated to ignore the feelings of her mother and other maternal relatives. When an agreement had been reached, livestock was presented to the family of the bride (bride price) by the groom's family. The wedding ceremony at the bride's hogan was simple and concluded with a feast for the guests. Plural marriages were also common. If a man had multiple wives, they most likely were sisters (sororal polygyny), and each wife had a separate hogan. The levirate and sororate also were customary.

Ideally, social and economic life centered around a "head mother," her stock, farmland, hogan, and the adjacent land that the family used. With her or close by lived her unmarried children, daughters and their husbands, and the children of these couples. Thus an ideal homestead consisted of matricentered hogans. The core residents were persons born into the matrilineage of the head mother. The stability of a homestead might be disrupted when the head mother died. In that case, her daughters might move away to found their own homesteads and in turn become head mothers. A less serious disruption occurred when an in-marrying husband was divorced by his wife or vice versa. In either case, the former husband left, usually to rejoin his mother's family at least temporarily; his children remained with their mother.

The nuclear family was the basic socioeconomic unit, and it was deeply enmeshed in kinship or marriage ties with other local families. A neighborhood ideally was dominated by extended family members of the core matrilineage. Additional matrilineage relatives probably lived at more distant localities. In combination, these matrigroups might form an "outfit." The term also has been applied to a more extensive territorial unit that did not have a strict basis in kinship; in this sense an outfit may be a comparatively recent development. In sum, social life focused on matricentered lineages.

Domestic tasks such as child care, cooking, and sewing occupied the time of women, who also were responsible for weaving blankets and rugs for household use, trade, or sale. Women, men, or children might herd sheep, but men focused on herding. Men not only had responsibilities to their children, wife, and wife's family but also to their mother's and sisters' families in which the men had grown up. As members of their own clans, sisters' children received special attention from the men. Men helped arrange the marriages of their nieces and nephews and instructed them in clan responsibilities and religion. Men usually were the ones who dealt with outsiders for the family. Few responsibilities fell to the nuclear family alone; parents were responsible for clothing their children, and fathers worked to build up herds of livestock for their sons.

Divorce was easy and could be initiated by either gender. Putting a husband's saddle outside the hogan indicated that a wife had terminated a marriage, and the man returned to his mother's home. A woman retained all property and custody of the children, since they were members of her clan. A decision to divorce was not difficult for Navajo women, who depended on their extended families, rather than their husbands. A woman could also rely on her brothers and other relatives to help raise her children.

The Euro-American stereotype of American Indians is that they are stoic and devoid of humor, but nothing could be further from reality, at least for the Navajo. In his study of Navajo humor, W. W. Hill (1943) found that it was rich and varied. A popular category of humor was based on accidental or ridiculous episodes. For example, a man might lie about his relationship with a woman, and she might accuse him of the lie in public. In another instance, a person caught stealing would have the stolen property in hand. Thus the offender appears ridiculous, and the episode might be told and retold to the enjoyment of the listeners. Practical jokes also were popular. For instance, when a horse race was scheduled for the following day, the horse that was a sure winner might be stolen the night before, ridden until it could hardly walk, and then returned to the corral of the owner. There also were what we might call "numbskull jokes." When a sheep was slaughtered, for instance, a man was told to obtain salt to process the meat; he might spend four days obtaining the salt.

Foreigners, especially Anglos, provided a basis for humor. When numerous Anglo tourists were watching a ceremony, a Navajo said he thought there must be many transvestites among whites since so many women wore trousers. Although the Navajo did not ideally approve of sadistic humor, it nonetheless existed, especially with reference to individual physical or behavioral characteristics. Nicknames such as Ugly Woman, Scum of Coyote Ear, and Hunchback are examples. Vulgar humor was also common, such as asking a man with a big belly how long it had been since he had seen his penis. Institutionalized humor, including "joking relationships," a form usually noted by ethnographers, was well developed among the Navajo.

Humor provides a fitting context in which to consider personality differences. The Navajo are well known for their individualism and flexibility; ideally, each person spoke for herself or himself. This behavioral variation extended to all aspects of their culture. One woman, for example, might consider a joke laughable, while another could regard the same joke as vulgar if not obscene. Or one man might take offense and become violently angry if a practical joke was played on him, whereas another would regard the joke as very funny. Admittedly, within any particular culture individual personality differences would be expected; the Navajo represent an extreme in their individual behavioral differences.

Within a homestead and beyond it, respect for and deference to the aged, rich or poor, prevailed. Old persons with the greatest number of children and grandchildren were held in highest regard. As conveyers of complex socioreligious traditions across the generations, the aged fulfilled a critical role. The Navajo probably feared death no more or less than most peoples around the world. Although death was not a focal point of life, the dead were dreaded and feared. The ghost of a person embodied the evil aspects of his or her life, including ghosts of individuals regarded as good in life. Failure of the living to behave properly in any context invited a human ghost to enter the body of a living person to bring illness or other trials that upset the balance in life. Thus it was wise to have as little to do with the dying and dead as possible, be they relatives, friends, or enemies. To prevent contamination of a hogan a special structure might be built for a dying person; otherwise a hogan was abandoned. Quickly and without ceremony a dead person was buried with the artifacts that she or he valued in life. Ghosts were associated with darkness, and as a result the Navajo had a deep-seated fear of venturing forth at night.

| The Comparatively Recent Past

As historical changes are considered further, one variable in particular merits attention: the proximity of Navajo and Westerners to each other. Navajo autonomy prevailed during the Spanish and Mexican eras because the people were so scattered and far from the administrative centers. And so it was during the early Anglo era. Anglo expansion became more persistent as wagon trails were developed and as railroads penetrated the region. Nonetheless, most of the reservation remained isolated. Much of the country was so rugged that most travel was on horseback. Remote sectors did not become accessible until adequate roads were built. In realistic terms, road construction began on a modest scale in the 1910s. As the network expanded, not only were Anglos able to reach distant places, but also local Navajo could travel afar with much greater ease. The popularity of wagons was followed by Navajo ownership of automobiles and trucks. Yet by the early 1930s many Navajo continued to depend on travel by horseback or horse and wagon.

Road access contributed to the construction of day schools in more isolated localities, and as the people came to realize that formal education for their children was desirable, school attendance was more regular. Proselytizing by Christian missionaries became more widespread, though ineffective. With increasingly dependable roads, greater numbers of men either sought year-round jobs at distant towns or expanded their pattern of seasonal work on distant farms and ranches owned by whites. Roads and highways thus became enablers and facilitators. Yet it was not until after 1950 that more remote sectors became accessible by paved roads or highways.

NEW TRAUMA: LIVESTOCK REDUCTION   A number of environmental concerns began to arise in the early 1900s. Both the Navajo population and their herds were perceived as increasing at a dramatic rate, even though herd numbers probably were relatively stable. But because the Navajo eventually were forced from nonreservation public lands that they traditionally had exploited, the impression was created that the number of livestock was increasing. From 1900 to 1934 the reservation land base was expanded several times in an attempt to keep pace with this presumed growth. In terms of actual use, however, the land base had declined. Nonetheless, livestock reduction became a major federal goal.

Flocks, especially of sheep, were growing rapidly, and land erosion in the semidesert became alarming. The federal government began to encourage stock reduction in the mid-1930s and became coercive by 1937. By then most livestock was owned by comparatively few individuals, and they were the target of the most drastic reductions. One result was that livestock ownership by wealthy and poor persons alike suffered, and so it was into the 1940s. Thus wealthy individuals were unable to host ceremonies, and, equally as important, most people could not make a living from their livestock holdings. The herding economy was essentially destroyed, and people were forced to turn to wage labor jobs, which were few, and to depend heavily on government welfare programs. Most people were poor and felt helpless, and hozho clearly was out of balance, which was psychologically devastating.

WORLD WAR II   The Navajo considered World War I to be a white man's conflict and assumed a passive attitude; no more than perhaps a dozen individuals served in the military during the war. They could not be drafted because they did not become U.S. citizens until a congressional act was passed in 1924. Early in World War II, many Navajo did not register for the draft because they distrusted the federal government; some people thought that registration had a connection to stock reduction. After the Japanese attack on Pearl Harbor, however, their attitude changed, and most of them supported the war effort. By the end of the war about 3600 Navajo had served in the armed forces. About 15,000 others held war-related jobs locally and elsewhere. In 1945 the total Navajo population was about 59,000.

The most famous Navajo during World War II were the approximately four hundred "Code Talkers" in the U.S. Marine Corps. A film about their achievements, *Windtalkers,* appeared in 2002. Searching for a code that the Japanese could not easily decipher, the military turned to Navajo servicemen. The code was used in Pacific-area campaigns largely to report the location of enemy artillery and to direct fire at it from marine positions. The code itself consisted of isolated Navajo words; the first letter of each word was translated into English to spell out the message in English. In the assault on Iwo Jima, over eight hundred transmissions were made without error. The Japanese were never able to break the code, and the success of the Iwo Jima campaign was attributed in large part to the Code Talkers. (During World War II, the U.S. Army had Choctaw, Comanche, Hopi, and Lakota [Sioux] Code Talkers, and during World War I Choctaw speakers served the same purpose.)

World War II impinged on Navajo life in other ways as well. The federal government reduced its presence and influence on the reservation, and stock reduction programs were not enforced. More important, after the war, returning veterans and civilian war workers who held jobs off the reservation were far better able to cope with the white man on Navajo terms.

THE NATIVE AMERICAN CHURCH   The Navajo began to participate in the "peyote cult" in the mid-1930s (see also Chapter 2). Its successful introduction was in part a reaction to the BIA livestock reduction program and a result of the growing hostility toward whites in general. Despite vigorous opposition from some Navajo, state and federal officials, and Christian missionaries, the church has thrived. Membership statistics are unreliable, but it appears that by 1951 about 13 percent of the people were church members. In 1972 from 40 to 60 percent of adults and children out of a population of about 130,000 were members.

A church leader is termed a Roadman (Road Chief, Peyote Chief). An aspiring Roadman is trained by an established one and begins to hold services when he considers himself capable. No formal creed exists, and there is variability in details of beliefs and rituals. An important prohibition, however, is the consumption of alcoholic beverages. Church members share a belief in the same supreme being and employ peyote for its psychotropic impact as a medicine and as a source of spiritual enlightenment achieved through prayer. (Peyote is not addictive, nor do users crave it.) The goals of a particular church service vary widely. Frequently a meeting is held to cure physical or psychological illness. Less often the purpose is to achieve economic success, counteract witchcraft, sanctify marriage, honor the dead, or celebrate holidays such as Christmas or the Fourth of July. A specific service is sponsored by someone out of harmony with the universe and with his or her spouse.

Services begin in the early evening and end the following morning. They are held in either a hogan or a Plains-type tepee. Prayers, smoking cigarettes, singing, and eating peyote are dominant, and in essence each represents prayer. Ritual equipment provided by a Roadman include an ornamental cane, eagle feather fans, a bunch of sage, whistle, and drum. An altar of sand is made with a crescent moon symbol of the Peyote Road of Life, and a four-stick fire is built at the center of the structure.

As David F. Aberle (1966), the foremost authority about the Native American church, repeatedly has noted, the church gained prominence as a reaction to long-term oppressive conditions of reservation life. Surprisingly, perhaps, the peyote church supplements the traditional religious system; the church represents a comparatively new means to cope with adversity. In many contexts, the Native American church supplements the goals of traditional Navajo religion.

THE NAVAJO NATION EMERGES   Stock reduction and World War II provided a partial background for a virtual cultural revolution beginning in the 1950s. It was then that reservation mineral resources—coal, gas, and oil—began to be exploited intensively to supply power to the rapidly growing population centers in the west. By the 1960s the tribe was receiving an average of $14 million a year in bonuses, leases, and royalties from mineral resources, including uranium and vanadium (a mineral used in vanadium steel). The interest from tribal monies was more than $4 million in 1975.

The Navajo Tribal Council began to be controlled by the tribe rather than by the BIA in the 1950s, when it gained the right to allocate money earned from mineral resource development. The tribe likewise gained control over their police and the management of grazing land. Navajo court judges were elected rather than appointed by the BIA. Before long the council created its own infrastructure as a way to gain far greater authority over education, housing, and health services.

Following World War II people became increasingly mobile as better roads were built and motor vehicle ownership expanded. Wage labor, year-round and seasonal, off and on the reservations came to dominate the economy, together with a significant welfare supplement. Livestock ownership was becoming concentrated in the hands of fewer stockmen with larger herds, but there was no decline in the total number of animals. Rug production declined, while silverwork for sale to tourists remained modestly profitable. Before long the trading posts of old disappeared or became convenience stores.

Formal education developed so slowly that by 1945 the median attendance figure for adult schooling was about one year; understandably, most of these people did not have basic English skills. In the late 1940s a serious federal effort was launched to make schooling for children far more widely available. By the late 1970s reservation day schools, boarding schools, and public schools provided nearly all children with at least some formal education. Before 1950 few students had completed high school, but by the end of the 1960s the rate had improved, and higher education began to become available. The first Indian tribal college was launched by the Navajo themselves in 1968—the Navajo Community College (now the Diné College). Soon thereafter, universities in the region began offering programs to further Navajo higher education. By 2000 they had eight college campuses and tribal centers for higher education.

As is evident in this synopsis, Navajo culture became transformed in an erratic pattern. In the early 1900s direct control of the people and their lifeway diminished in fits and starts, depending on the degree of federal intrusion, national and regional economic conditions, and the accompanying Navajo responses. The extraction of reservation mineral resources beginning in the 1920s and the eventual control gained over much of Navajo life by the Navajo Nation president and the Navajo Nation Council heralded a new era that continues into the present.

| Modern Developments

The capital of the Navajo Nation is Window Rock, Arizona. Reservation land includes over 27,000 square miles. It is dominated by the "Big Rez" in Arizona, New Mexico, and Utah. Additional holdings include the Alamo, Canoncito, and Ramah reservations in New Mexico. Despite the size of the land base, there are so many residents that the herding and farming economy of old supports relatively few families. Concurrently, the exploitation of mineral resources has become a major source of tribal income, but coal and uranium mining have also been disadvantageous. The lease and royalty arrangements were unfavorable, whereas open-pit mines and polluting power plants have been environmentally destructive. Another major problem has been a lowering of the water table to produce slurry to transport crushed coal to power plants. Uranium mining led to illnesses and deaths from radiation as a result of unsafe conditions. It was not until 1995 that the tribe gained greater control over mining operations, royalties, and related matters (see also Chapter 10).

In 1990 the tribal government was reorganized to include executive, legislative, and judicial branches; the office of tribal chief was replaced by a president. The smallest administrative units are the 110 Chapters. The Navajo National Council consists of eighty-eight members (Council delegates) based on Chapter population size, and they are elected to four-year terms. An enrolled tribal member was required to have at least one-quarter Navajo genetic heritage and at least two generations of direct ancestors who were enrolled Navajo. Allowance was also made for adoption or persons raised off reservation lands to become members of the Navajo Nation.

The land dispute with the Hopi, outlined in the previous chapter, continues as a source of conflict. As a result of a 1977 agreement, some two thousand Navajo families on the Hopi side of the dividing line were to leave their homes and be relocated (see Figure 11-7). By 1997 most families had signed

Figure 11-7 | Jenny Manybeads was among the many Navajo to be relocated as a result of the Navajo–Hopi land dispute. (Photo by Paul Natonobah, 1993. Courtesy of the Gallup *Independent* newspaper.)

accommodation agreements with the Hopi. The families who signed have the right to live on Hopi Partitioned Lands under Hopi and BIA administration for seventy-five years. About a dozen families refused to sign an agreement, and they were, in theory, to be evicted in the year 2000. Historically, the Navajo have been on friendly terms, both socially and economically, with the Hopi. One unfortunate result of the land dispute is that now there is a great deal of bitterness on both sides. The Navajo, however, do permit the Hopi to take eagles for ceremonial purposes from Navajo lands.

An educational policy statement by the Navajo Nation in 1984 emphasized the critical importance for all schools to teach Navajo to ensure lasting cultural vitality. There is tribal concern that this goal has not been achieved, even though Navajo is spoken more than any other indigenous language north of Mexico. In 2003 most Navajo speakers were older than thirty-five; fewer than half of the children entering kindergarten could speak Navajo. It appears that they will lose their language unless the support from parents and tribal leaders becomes far more effective in the near future. Language immersion programs exist in some of the schools, but comparatively few children are involved.

ALCOHOL All interested parties currently agree that alcohol abuse is *the* major Navajo problem. In the early 1800s Mexican traders began selling alcohol to the Navajo on a limited localized basis. Following the Long Walk and Navajo confinement at Fort Sumner, the federal government established a small and clearly inadequate reservation in 1868, and men who lived there soon began working at railroad construction sites in the region. At the associated saloons, these Navajo workers drank with the others, even though this was contrary to federal laws. During this association with Anglos, the Navajo seem to have developed the pattern of binge drinking that the Anglos followed. They also adopted the Anglo belief that a drunken person was not responsible for his or her behavior. In somewhat isolated areas, bootleggers began operating freely, and trading posts stocked intoxicants for sale to Indians. Widespread heavy drinking did not become a pattern until the late 1930s, when it was at least in part attributable to stresses brought about by the federal stock reduction programs. Another reason for an increase in heavy drinking was the newly accepted view that heavy drinking, which was costly, was a sign of wealth. At large social gatherings it was the well-to-do persons who drank an abundance of alcohol. Other people drank to excess as a way to lose their shyness. Since the 1920s problem drinking appears to have been one response to a land base that is inadequate for making a living despite the repeated major expansions of the reservations by the federal government as the population grew.

An additional reason that some present-day adults have become alcoholics appears to stem from the federal education system. In the 1920s young girls and boys in expanding numbers were sent to off-reservation boarding schools. This continued into the 1970s. Children were not only torn from their families but also became obligated to follow a rigid Euro-American routine. Infractions of rules could be, and frequently were, punished by whippings and other forms of physical and sexual abuse. One study suggests that in later life these children were far more likely to have drinking problems, more severe for women than men, than non-boarding-school students. Present-day boarding schools provide a far better environment. They are close to the students' homes, and home visits by students and school visits by families are relatively frequent. This lessens the stress of the school years, as does the prohibition of any abuse of children at schools.

The Navajo Nation prohibits intoxicants on reservation lands, yet according to law enforcement agents, virtually all arrests are directly attributable to alcohol. Murders, suicides, spouse and child abuse, and highway accidents are depressing examples. Bootleggers range widely to sell intoxicants from their pickup trucks. Since 2002 federal, Arizona, and tribal officials have coordinated intense operations against bootleggers with considerable success. Another approach being tested is to demonstrate in the courts that liquor wholesalers and retailers adjacent to the big reservation have deliberately violated tribal prohibition by selling to known bootleggers. Despite the vastness of the reservations, the Navajo have only 250 Indian police officers. This will change as the U.S. Department of Justice's $5 million grant to the Navajo in 2002 results in training and hiring more police and obtaining new equipment to provide greater effectiveness. Although this depiction of alcohol problems among the Navajo is bleak, one must note that the percentage of Navajo who are problem drinkers is no greater than the current national average.

In recent years the Navajo have debated legalizing intoxicant sales at tribal stores on the reservations. One goal was to put bootleggers out of business and develop a new source of revenue. A committee of the Navajo National Council consulted the White Mountain Apache Tribe in 2004 because that tribe had legalized the sale of intoxicants on their reservation in 1954. The Apache purpose was to undercut bootleggers and avoid fatal accidents among people buying intoxicants at off-reservation stores. Over the years they have earned a great deal of money from liquor sales, but bootleggers persist. Furthermore, the suicide rate is extremely high, and about 60 percent of juvenile court cases are alcohol related. The White Mountain Apache experience does not provide an encouraging model for the Navajo.

REPATRIATIONS In 1990 the U.S. Congress enacted the Native American Graves Protection and Repatriation Act. It established a process for public and private museums, colleges, and universities that receive federal funds to repatriate Native American skeletal remains and artifacts. The return of human remains for appropriate reburial has become an issue to be decided by individual tribes, and the Navajo response is revealing. The tribe was contacted by about 350 institutions concerning pertinent human remains and artifacts in their collections. The enduring ambivalence of many Navajo about the dead posed a problem for the tribal leadership, especially because the collections included thousands of skeletal remains. Tribal leaders concluded that any re-burial, to be meaningful, should be where the body originally was interred, but this would be impossible or difficult in many instances. Therefore they decided not to seek the return of skeletal remains nor any accompanying grave goods. Regarding most other artifacts, such as rugs and jewelry, they felt that these items were purchased legally and need not be returned. Medicine bundles, however, represented a major concern. It was considered desirable to return them if similar items continue to be used by medicine men; they would be rein-tegrated into appropriate ceremonies. The return of religious objects associated with abandoned ceremonies was not thought desirable, nor did they feel it was fitting for the tribe to curate them.

There are exceptions concerning the return of artifacts with special reli-gious and historical significance. As previously discussed, the Navajo were forced from their homeland in the early 1860s by the U.S. Army. Some people managed to escape and settled in a rugged sector of southern Utah. Among them were two medicine men responsible for three bison-hide shields of reli-gious importance. In 1926 an amateur archaeologist found three carefully wrapped shields buried on federal land in a Utah rock shelter. He turned the shields over to the National Park Service, and they were exhibited at a national monument. In 2001 a Navajo medicine man claimed that they were the long-lost shields. Park Service investigators found his evidence compelling, and in 2003 the shields were returned to the Navajo Nation, which accepted them gratefully.

GAMING The national recession beginning in the early 2000s has been especially stressful for minorities, including the Navajo. Many families began depending heavily on food stamps and other direct federal aid programs. Some Navajo felt that a new enterprise would be desirable, and they seriously considered opening a limited number of casinos. Chapters (local government districts) with favorable casino sites supported gaming. In 1994 and 1997 refer-enda, the people voted against casinos. Irrespective, the council voted in 2000 to make six chapters exempt from the existing gaming prohibition and the fol-lowing year created the Navajo Nation Gaming Ordinance as required by the federal government for casino tribes. The council also approved gaming com-pacts with Arizona (2002) and New Mexico (2003). However, two ambiguous gaming measures were placed on the ballot in 2004; one was approved and the other was disapproved. Thus the future of Navajo casinos remained uncertain.

COAL & WATER The strip mining of coal from Indian lands on Black Mesa involves contracts between the Peabody Energy Company and both the Hopi and Navajo, who owned the land involved. The background, general is-sues, and recent developments are addressed in Chapter 10, about the Hopi. However, by 2003 the Navajo were taking a somewhat different stand from that of the Hopi. In that year the Navajo National Council voted overwhelmingly for a resolution to end pumping water from the Navajo aquifer to provide slurry for coal mining operations when the present contract expires in 2005. The council contended that the needs of thirty thousand Navajo and Hopi for this water far outweighed the financial benefits derived from the Peabody contract. This was a major decision by the Navajo National Council because the Navajo government depended heavily on royalties from water and coal and on Peabody's employment of tribal members. As noted in the Hopi chapter, it appears that coal mining on Black Mesa will cease by 2006 if Navajo aquifer water is to be used on a permanent basis. However, if hydrological and environmental studies prove positive regarding the use of Coconino aquifer water, the mining may continue, assuming that the many other problems cited in the previous chapter also are resolved.

TOURISM   The Southwest has long been a major tourist attraction because of its majestic scenery and the fascination many outsiders feel for the Indian peoples and their lifeways. In 2002 some 2.5 million persons visited the Navajo reservations. A study of tourism at the "Big Reservation," as reported in the *Navajo Times* (August 21, 2003), made the Navajo more fully aware of the existing impact of tourists. They have been contributing more than $100 million a year to the economy, and some thirty-five hundred Navajo have benefited economically from these outsiders. Most of these visitors were traveling elsewhere but stopped at the big reservation because they had never been on a reservation. The greatest number of visitors from the United States lived in California; one in five came from foreign countries, especially England and Germany. Based on their experience, tourists commonly said they would recommend a visit to friends and relatives because the Navajo were so friendly. Navajo officials have long realized that tourists represented an "untapped gold mine," which this study demonstrated.

A particular attraction for tourists has been the opportunity to buy attractive locally made products such as baskets, blankets, and especially jewelry. The Spanish metalworking tradition introduced around 1850 by Mexican metalworkers provided the Navajo with the technical background for skillfully crafting silver jewelry. When confined at Fort Summer later, some of them learned to work metal at the blacksmith shop and started crafting jewelry from brass and copper. After settling on their initial reservation in 1868, they found silver coins useful as a major source of metal, and by 1890 they were incorporating turquoise settings in their products. Heavy silver personal jewelry soon became visual evidence of a person's wealth. Also, a number of local trading posts had opened by 1889, and in times of economic stress, the Navajo could pawn their jewelry. Soon after 1900 rugs were the items most often purchased by tourists. It was not until the Navajo made more lightweight and less expensive silver jewelry (e.g., rings, bracelets, and belt buckles) that this market grew among Anglos. When trading posts declined in number during the 1970s, specialty stores in urban centers and elsewhere became major sales outlets for local Indian crafts. Navajo roadside stands for sales to tourists also have become popular (see Figure 11-8).

In recent years reportedly Indian arts and crafts have in fact been made by non-Indians and sold as genuine, especially in the Southwest. The problem

Figure 11-8 | David Tsinnie, in this 1998 photograph, is a Navajo artist living in the Coconino District of Arizona.

expanded as false Native American arts and crafts were produced commercially in foreign countries, imported to the United States, and sold by unscrupulous dealers as being authentic Indian. The foreign-made items cost comparatively little to produce and are sold for much more than their actual value. Some imported items are so well made that only experts are capable of identifying them as forgeries. The sale of reproductions is costing indigenous American craftspersons millions of dollars in income each year, and buyers are deceived. The Indian Arts and Craft Act passed by Congress in 1990 was designed to resolve the basic problem. Major provisions are that legitimate Indian arts and crafts can legally be made and sold by members of tribes recognized by the federal government or other formally recognized groups (e.g., states). Tribes are encouraged to register their trademarks with the U.S. Patent and Trademark Office. The act has proved difficult to enforce because Indian arts and crafts are sold in so many different places and under widely variable circumstances. The federal Indian Arts and Crafts Board oversees the act's general enforcement. A private watchdog organization, the Indian Arts and Crafts Association, is especially concerned with making certain that proported indigenous American products are genuine.

| Additional Issues and Concerns

One economic possibility is to replace the Peabody coal mining operation and resume mining uranium on reservation land. The Nuclear Regulatory Commission has issued a license but apparently did so based on faulty evidence. The Navajo have strongly opposed the proposal. One compelling reason is that uranium previously was mined on the reservation. As a result, a tailing dam failed in 1979 and released some 94 million gallons of acid waste-water and 1100 tons of radioactive tailings into a local river system. The premature deaths of miners and others in the area have been attributed to cancer cases resulting from the earlier mines. Alternative options are to negotiate short-term leases with gas and oil companies for greater exploitation of these reservation resources.

Most land on the Navajo reservations is held in trust by the federal government, although exceptions exist (e.g., individual Indian allotments and state leases). In many ways the dominance of trust lands is a blessing; it means that land is not owned by outsiders. At the same time, this creates disadvantages for economic development, because private businesses, whether owned by Navajo or Anglos, must lease land from the Navajo government. The leasing process, however, is a difficult and time-consuming process because there are so many regulations and approval is required by numerous Navajo Nation agencies, divisions, and offices. As a result a relatively small number of businesses exist (e.g., shopping centers, motels, fast-food restaurants, and a professional building complex). Thus businesses near the reservations dominate the economy. As Trib Choudhary (n.d., [2], p. 13) has noted, the "leakage of

Figure 11-9 | In the Navajo Nation the Mexican Water administrative unit (chapter) is among the poorest and most isolated chapters. They numbered 7,235 in the 2000 census. The median family income was $12,667.00 in 1999, when some 60 percent of the people lived beneath the poverty level. Their subsistence economy was based on farming plus herding cattle and sheep. Most youthful residents had left because there were so few jobs in the locality. The previous Navajo national president never visited this chapter, and the same was true for the current president by 2004. The people have no public electrical power system, the homes typically are of inferior quality, and the unpaved roads are poorly maintained. Attendance at chapter meetings is poor, and voter turnout is low. Few enrolled members run for offices because they virtually have abandoned hope for positive changes. The Mexican Water employees in 2004 (left to right) included Renae Keith, Jerry Tsosie, and Tina L. Begay.

Navajo dollars to border towns" is vast. About 70 percent of reservation Navajo money is spent in off-reservation communities. The personal income total in 2001 was some $1.3 billion a year. For years the Navajo Nation has sought to create a more business-friendly environment, and it recently took a major step forward by approving the Local Governance Act. This act enables chapters (regional political jurisdictions) to gain partial control over business lease rates.

As noted initially in this chapter, the Navajo are the most populous tribe in the United States whose members live primarily on reservations. In bringing this chapter to a close, it is fitting to include a statistical survey pertaining to their lives in the recent past (see Table 11-1).

TABLE 11-1. Navajo Nation demographic statistics from 2000 to 2001 and select comparisons with the general U.S. population

---

Enrolled member total in 2001
    250,010
Navajo total in all states, including persons with other ethnic identity
    298,215
Major metropolitan areas with greatest Navajo populations
    Phoenix, AZ, 9034
    Albuquerque, NM, 6958
    Gallup, NM, 5730
    Farmington, NM, 5399
    Flagstaff, AZ, 3703
Dominant Languages
    5–17 years old
      Navajo only, 31,967
      English only, 24,524
    18 and older
      Navajo only, 88,520
      English only, 17,027

Families
    38,162 (average household size, 3.77)
Income aggregate sample in 1999
    Self-employed, $23,454,300
    Public assistance, $24,982,200
    Grand total, including other sources (e.g., Social Security, retirement income),
      $1,304,041,800
Per capita income
    $7269 (U.S., $21,587)
Families living below the poverty level
    42.90% (U.S., 12.38%)
Education (25 years old or older)
    No schooling completed, 12.16% (U.S., 1.44%)
    High school graduate (including equivalency), 26.32% (U.S., 28.63%)
    Bachelor's degree, 4.66% (U.S., 15.54%)
    Doctoral degree, 0.23% (U.S., 0.96%)
Veteran status
    7689

Note: Unless otherwise noted, the information is for the year 2000 (Choudhary n.d. [1], n.d. [2]; U.S. Department of the Interior 2001).

Over the years Native American newspapers have been founded to better inform their membership. These publications commonly print articles critical of the tribal government for illegal decisions, cronyism, nepotism, and general political corruption. In response, accused leaders may fire the editor, dismiss reporters, and in extreme cases have the police shut down the operation. The editors of the *Navajo Times* were fired six times since 1961. In 2003 the Navajo National Council created Navajo Times Publishing, Inc. and the *Navajo Times* became the *first* independent tribally controlled Indian newspaper.

Additional Sources

Peter Iverson (1990) provides a brief book-length historical and ethnographic overview, whereas James F. Downs (1972) describes life in one community. Longer standard works are by Clyde Kluckhohn and Dorothea Leighton (1946) and Ruth M. Underhill (1956). The best ethnohistory is by Garrick Alan Bailey and Roberta Glenn Bailey (1986), and Gladys A. Reichard (1950) is the standard source about religion. The second *Southwest* volume (vol. 10) of the *Handbook of North American Indians,* edited by Alfonso Ortiz (1983) and published by the Smithsonian Institution, includes excellent chapters about most historical and ethnographic aspects of Navajo life. The book about the Navajo and alcohol by Stephen J. Kunitz and Jerrold E. Levy (1994) is excellent, as is the volume by Willow R. Powers (2001) about trading posts. Recent systematic, detailed, and highly reliable statistical information about Native American tribes in the United States is rare. The Navajo are an exception thanks to Trib Choudhary (n.d. [1]; n.d. [2]).

Selected Bibliography

Aberle, David F. 1966. *The peyote religion among the Navaho.* Chicago.

———. 1981a. Navajo coresidential kin groups and lineages. *Journal of Anthropological Research* 37:1–7.

———. 1981b. A century of Navajo kinship change. *Canadian Journal of Anthropology* 2:21–36.

———. 1993. The Navajo–Hopi land dispute and Navajo relocation. In *Anthropological approaches to resettlement: Policy, practice, and theory,* 153–200. Boulder.

Adair, John. 1944. *The Navajo and Pueblo silversmiths.* Norman, OK.

Bailey, Garrick Alan, and Roberta Glenn Bailey. 1986. *A history of the Navajos: The reservation years.* Santa Fe.

Benedek, Emily. 1992. *The wind won't know me: A history of the Navajo–Hopi land dispute.* New York.

Bingham, Sam, and Janet Bingham. 1984. *Between sacred mountains: Navajo stories and lessons from the land.* Tucson.

Brugge, David M. 1994. *The Navajo–Hopi land dispute.* Albuquerque.

Choudhary, Trib. n.d. [1]. *Navajo Nation data from US Census 2000.* Support Services Department, Division of Economic Development, the Navajo Nation. Window Rock, AZ.

———. n.d. [2]. *2002–2003 Comprehensive economic development strategy of the Navajo Nation.* Support Services Department, Division of Economic Development, the Navajo Nation. Window Rock, AZ.

Downs, James F. 1972. *The Navajo.* New York.

Dyk, Walter. 1938. *Son of Old Man Hat.* New York.

Dyk, Walter, and Ruth Dyk. 1980. *Left Handed: A Navajo autobiography.* New York.

Frisbie, Charlotte J., and David P. McAllester. 1978. *Navajo Blessingway singer: The autobiography of Frank Mitchell.* Tucson.

Henderson, Eric. 1989. Navajo livestock wealth and the effects of the stock reduction program of the 1930s. *Journal of Anthropological Research* 45:379–403.

Hill, W. W. 1943. *Navaho humor.* General Series in Anthropology no. 9.

Iverson, Peter. 1990. *The Navajos.* New York.

Jett, Stephen C., and Virginia E. Spencer. 1981. *Navajo architecture: Forms, history, distributions.* Tucson.

Kelley, Klara B. 1993. A rebuttal to some negative stereotypes of Navajos and misconceptions about Navajo history and Navajo–Hopi relations. Typescript. Window Rock, AZ.

Kelly, Lawrence C. 1968. *The Navajo Indians and federal Indian policy: 1900–1935.* Tucson.

Kluckhohn, Clyde. 1944. *Navaho witchcraft.* Papers of the Peabody Museum of Archaeology and Ethnology. vol. 22. (Reprint in Boston, 1967).

Kluckhohn, Clyde, and Dorothea Leighton. 1946. *The Navaho.* Garden City, NY. (Other edition: 1974).

Kluckhohn, Clyde, W. W. Hill, and Lucy Wales Kluckhohn. 1971. *Navaho material culture.* Cambridge, MA.

Kunitz, Stephen J., and Jerrold E. Levy. 1994. *Drinking careers: A twenty-five year study of three Navajo populations.* New Haven.

Lamphere, Louise. 1977. *To run after them: Cultural and social bases of cooperation in a Navajo community.* Tucson.

Luckert, Karl W. 1979. *Coyoteway.* Tucson.

Lynch, Regina H., and the Rough Rock Demonstration School Navajo Curriculum Staff. 1993. *A history of Navajo clans.* Chinle, AZ.

McNitt, Frank. 1970. *Navajo wars.* Albuquerque.

Navajo Times. 2001–2004. (Navajo newspaper).

Ortiz, Alfonso, ed. 1983. *Southwest.* Vol. 10, *Handbook of North American Indians.* Washington, DC.

Parmon, Donald. 1976. *The Navajos and the New Deal.* New Haven.

Powers, Willow R. 2001. *Navajo trading: The end of an era.* Albuquerque.

Reichard, Gladys A. 1928. *Social life of the Navajo Indians.* New York.

———. 1950. *Navaho religion: A study of symbolism.* New York.

Spicer, Edward H. 1962. *Cycles of conquest.* Tucson.

Tamir, Orit. 1991. Relocation of Navajo from Hopi partitioned land in Pinon. *Human Organization* 50:173–78.

Underhill, Ruth M. 1956. *The Navajos.* Norman, OK.

U.S. Department of the Interior, Bureau of Indian Affairs, Office of Tribal Services. 2001. *American Indian population and labor force report.* Washington, DC.

Walters, Frank. 1950. *Masked gods: Navaho and Pueblo ceremonialism.* Chicago.

Witherspoon, Gary. 1975. *Navajo kinship and marriage.* Chicago.

Wyman, Leland C. 1970. *Blessingway.* Tucson.

———. 1983. Navajo ceremonial system. In *Southwest,* Alfonso Ortiz, ed., vol. 10, 536–57, *Handbook of North American Indians.* Washington, DC.

12 The Iroquois: Warriors and Farmers of the Eastern Woodlands

Great Spirit, who dwellest alone, listen now to the words of thy people here assembled. The smoke of our offering arises. Give kind attention to our words, as they arise to thee in the smoke. We think of thee for this return of the planting season. Give to us a good season, that our crops may be plentiful.

A portion of the Planting Ceremony speech of the Seneca that is typical of ceremonial prayers (Morgan 1954, vol. 1, 188)

ANTHROPOLOGISTS HAVE LONG had a special fondness for the Iroquois, and not without good reason. They were the subject of the first essentially modern account of an aboriginal people, written by the Jesuit missionary Father Joseph F. Lafitau and published in 1724. However, because this work first appeared in French, it did not make an immediate impact on Americans. Then in 1851 Lewis Henry Morgan published a book about the Iroquois that became a model for ethnographic reports.

The Iroquois have also been of special interest because they played a prominent role in shaping the North American colonial empires of the British and French. From colonial times to the present, distinguished members of Iroquois tribes have been known to the people of Canada and the United States. During the colonial period, Hendrick was an outstanding Mohawk military leader and warrior, Joseph Brant was a Mohawk warrior and politician, and Red Jacket, a Seneca, was a great orator. Kateri Tekakwitha, a Mohawk born about 1656, was beatified by the Roman Catholic church in 1980. General Ely S. Parker, a Seneca, served as secretary to General Ulysses S. Grant and drafted the terms of peace at Appomattox, Virginia, that ended the American Civil War. Jay Silverheels (Harold I. Smith), a Mohawk, was better known as Tonto of "Lone Ranger" fame, and the famous runner Tom Longboat was an Onondaga. The Iroquois, famous in war and politics and representative of the Northeast culture area, have retained their identity with a rare resilience, but now their battles are most often fought in courtrooms.

The Iroquois (pronounced IR-uh-kwoi in the United States and IR-uh-kwa in Canada) are considered a tribe or as nations. The original "Five Nations" were the Cayuga, Mohawk, Oneida, Onondaga, and Seneca. The Tuscarora in North Carolina spoke a closely related language. Following wars with white settlers, they moved north to join the other Iroquois in 1722 or 1723 to form the "Six Nations."

The origin and meaning of the word *Iroquois* is unknown. The aboriginal core population lived largely in northern and western New York State, where each tribe occupied an oblong strip of country (see Figure 12-1). Collectively at the time of early historic contact, they may have had a minimum population of ten thousand. The Iroquois belong to a distinct language family, Iroquoian, and each of the Six Nations has its own language. The Cherokee language belongs to the same family.

| Early Historic Life

One major difficulty in assembling Iroquois sources is to separate ethnographic information about the Iroquois in general from that about a single tribe. The problem cannot be successfully resolved because we do not have parallel information about all of the tribes. The descriptions to follow represent a composite view stressing the Mohawk and Seneca. A second major problem is that systematic ethnohistorical accounts date largely from the nineteenth century into the present. Therefore, it is difficult to place early Iroquois history in an acceptable perspective.

Figure 12-1 | Area of early historic Iroquois occupation.

ORIGIN MYTH Iroquois origins are reported in at least forty accounts, most of which were recorded in the comparatively recent past. The content exhibits considerable variability, although the overall plots are reasonably consistent. The account to follow is a composite synopsis.

The primeval world was a sea of water, enveloped in darkness. Aquatic animals represented the only form of life. The earliest humans lived in a sky dome among the clouds, where a great tree grew that always bloomed. Their lives mimicked later life on earth. The pregnant daughter of the Great Chief, Sky Woman, was told by her father to follow the tree roots to the world below and establish the earth. Fire Dragon in the sky hole gave her maize, a mortar, a pot, and a firebrand so that she could cook food. Sky Woman dropped through the hole. Various aquatic species dove in the sea to find land, and each of them failed until Muskrat was successful. He brought soil to the surface that expanded to become the earth that was supported on the back of Turtle. Waterfowl flew up from the water to cushion the fall of Sky Woman. The earth was small, but by walking about, she caused it to grow beyond her sight. In time she bore a daughter who soon matured. Sky Woman's daughter was visited by a man, and she subsequently gave birth in a normal manner to a male, Sapling (Older Brother, Good Twin). His twin, Flint (Younger Brother, Evil Twin), emerged from his mother's armpit, and she died as a result. In his grief, Sapling created the sun from his mother's face and obtained the moon and stars from her breasts. Sapling created mountains and rivers in an orderly pattern, he created earth people and forests, planted crops, and became the source of well-being. Flint created darkness to drive the sun westward, jumbled the mountains, and made the rivers crooked; monsters, weeds, and species to attack plants were included among his creations. Eventually, Sapling defeated Flint, who lives in a vast cavern from which he persists in sending forth evil.

SETTLEMENTS AND MANUFACTURES   In the early 1600s the Iroquois occupied ten major towns. These settlements, joined by major and minor trails, clustered along an east–west line. After about ten years, communities were relocated as the productivity of nearby farmland declined, firewood became scarce, and the dwellings began to decay. Palisades enclosed a settlement (see Figure 12-2). The well-known longhouse, up to 130 feet in length and 16 feet wide, had a framework of poles and a dome-shaped roof, and overlapping sections of bark covered the basic structure. At each end of a longhouse a bark door hinged at the top provided access. A partitioned section adjacent to each entry contained maize and other provisions. Small matrilineal families occupied as many as twenty apartments in a large longhouse, and each family had a fireplace. An apartment included high and low platforms covered with bark, reed mats, and skins on which people worked, lounged, and slept (see Figures 12-3 and 12-4). Oblong openings at intervals in the roof admitted light and allowed smoke to escape from the fires; bark slabs covered these spaces during storms. Additional village structures included underground caches for maize or dry meat, and temporary tepeelike dwellings had bark covers.

These people wore deerskin garments sewn with bone awls (not needles) and sinew thread. A woman wore a waist-to-ankle underskirt highlighted along the lower border with porcupine quill designs. Over the skirt was a long dress fringed along the sleeves and at the bottom. Short leggings and moccasins completed her typical attire. A man wore a shirt with fringed sleeves and a knee-length kilt belted at the waist, fringed at the bottom, and decorated with

Figure 12-2 | This engraving of the principal Onondaga community in 1615 withstood attack by Samuel de Champlain and his Indian allies. Located between a pond outlet and streams for defense, a series of palisades, some as high as thirty feet, provided further protection. The settlement covered some six acres, with the longhouses arranged in blocks. (From Morgan 1881.)

quill designs. They also wore long fringed leggings and quill-decorated moccasins.

The relative stability of community life facilitated the accumulation of varied artifact types, and flexible materials dominated in their manufactures. They favored bark for storage and maple sap containers, as trays for mixing meal, and as ladles. Woven baskets were made but had limited use. Animal skins commonly accommodated household items, and a skin bag that hung from a man's belt contained most of the artifacts required when traveling. They ate soup and hominy from wooden ladles with deep bowls. Food commonly was cooked or stored in grit-tempered and fired pottery. Surprisingly, perhaps as a technological bias, they produced relatively few artifacts from stone, despite its abundance. Chipped (flaked) arrow points and ax blades represented important examples of those they did make. Stone processed by grinding and then polishing produced mortars and adz blades.

Figure 12-3 | Model of an Iroquois settlement with a longhouse under construction. (Courtesy of the Rochester Museum and Science Center, Rochester, NY.)

Figure 12-4 | Model of one portion of a Seneca longhouse. (Courtesy of the Rochester Museum and Science Center, Rochester, NY.)

Items for transport represent a final major cluster of artifacts. Winter travel over deep snow involved the use of short, yet broad, snowshoes with hickory frames laced with babiche. Traveling along a trail with a burden led to the development of pack frames made from hickory that fitted the bearer's back; support for a load was provided by a chest strap, tumpline, or the combination. Canoes were the dominant means of water transport. A vessel could be from twenty to forty feet long with a slight upturn at the bow and stern. The rounded ribs of ash were covered with red elm or hickory bark attached to ash gunwales. They used a single-bladed paddle.

SUBSISTENCE ACTIVITIES   The Iroquois diet consisted primarily of three sacred domestic plants, maize, beans, and squash, collectively termed the Three Sisters. Women, as the primary cultivators, cleared the land and thereby became the owners of specific plots. They planted, controlled the weeds, and harvested crops. A digging stick and a hoe with a scapula blade served as their primary tools. The singular importance of maize is indicated by the identification of at least fifteen varieties. Women likewise collected wild plant foods, including over thirty fruits and about fifty additional plant products ranging from roots to leaves. Dependence on wild plants for food became critical when the corn and bean crops failed. They also planted tobacco, which seeded itself. Following the first frost the leaves were picked and dried for use. Tobacco use was confined to the elbow pipe made from fired clay; a man often kept his tobacco supply in a weasel-skin pouch attached to his belt.

Between fall harvests and midwinter, some families dispersed over settlement lands, especially to capture deer. The most productive means to take an individual animal was with a spring-pole snare that lifted a deer into the air by its hind legs. Communal deer hunts likewise prevailed as men drove deer between converging lines of brush, at the base of which bowmen were concealed. A snare set along a bear trail included a heavy pole to pin down an animal and prevent escape. Alternatively, a bear might be tracked a long distance and killed with arrows. A big game animal killed near a residence was hauled there on an improvised bark toboggan. Otherwise, it was butchered at the kill site, the bones removed, and the meat fire-dried for transport in bark containers.

In the spring some families scattered, occupying temporary camps to collect maple sap and hunt and fish. They set nets made from shredded bark for quail and pigeons. Alternatively, as women planted crops, husbands and sons harvested birds and fish near the village. Men guided fish with sticks into cone-shaped traps set in rapids or ripples. After the spring subsistence activities, men devoted most of their time to ceremonies, council meetings, and warfare.

For a morning meal, the only one scheduled during a day, men ate before women and children. Otherwise people ate when hungry, but a woman offered food to any visitors and to her husband when he returned from a day's activities. For meals, maize was the chief food, and hominy gruel, called *sagamite,* an Algonquian word, was the basic staple. To prepare it a woman first boiled maize kernels in water with wood ash to remove the hulls. She then ground the kernels with a pestle and mortar, sieved the meal, and formed it into loaves to be boiled in water. Additional maize dishes included succotash, roasted corn, and boiled corn. Meat, soup, and wild plant products rounded out the standard diet.

DESCENT, KINSHIP, AND MARRIAGE A longhouse was occupied by women of a matrilineage, their in-marrying husbands, and their children (matrilineal and matrilocal). The matrilineages were joined into fifteen named matriclans; among these were the Bear, Beaver, Deer, Hawk, Turtle, and Wolf clans. The clans of the Cayuga, Onondaga, Seneca, and Tuscarora were divided into moieties. The Mohawk and Oneida had only three matriclans. The Turtle and Wolf clans formed one moiety, and the Bear the other. The matriclans cut across national lines so that members of the Wolf clan, for example, were found in each tribe, in different villages within a tribe, and in one or more households within a settlement. The moiety division once was said to have formed the exogamous unit; any combination of marriages between persons of opposite moieties was permitted. By Morgan's time only clan exogamy and matrilineal descent prevailed. Inheritances were bequeathed by a man to his brothers, his sister's children, or some other person in his matriclan. The importance of the clan cannot be overestimated in Iroquois society; not only was it the property-holding unit, but it was empowered to invest, and renew if necessary, political leaders. Members cooperated in economic and political life and judged disputes with other clans. Furthermore, each clan had a common burial ground, held religious ceremonies, and could adopt outsiders.

In the kinship terminology, a person referred to her or his father and father's brother by the same word, and called the mother the same as mother's sister. There were separate and different words for father's sister and mother's brother (bifurcate merging terms). The words for parallel cousins (father's brother's or mother's sister's children) were the same as for biological brothers and sisters, but cross-cousins (father's sister's or mother's brother's children) were called "cousins." This is a cousin terminology that has come to be known as the Iroquois type (see Figure 12-5). By extension, all individuals of one's matriclan, irrespective of their tribal affiliations, were drawn into the system as blood relatives. The basis of Iroquois political life was an extension of household and community kinship ties at the tribal and national levels.

SOCIAL DIMENSIONS The Iroquois have often been characterized, especially in older writings, as one of the best examples of a matriarchy, but this is an unfortunate label. It does not appear that they were overtly controlled by women. Because the Iroquois were matrilineal and matrilocal and because women were a very powerful political force, it certainly is appropriate to label the Iroquois as a matricentered or matrifocal society. The position of Iroquois women in the early seventeenth century, and probably for many earlier years,

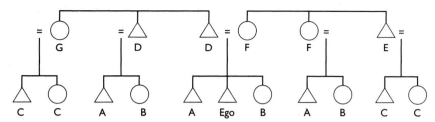

Figure 12-5 | The early historic Iroquois system of kinship terminology.

was well summarized by Lafitau (1974, 69): "In them [women] resides all the real authority: the lands, fields and all their harvest belong to them; they are the soul of the councils, the arbiters of peace and war; they hold the taxes and the public treasure; it is to them that the slaves [captives] are entrusted; they arrange the marriages; the children are under their authority; and the order of succession is founded on their blood."

The Iroquois clearly distinguished between the activities of men and women, and no close bonds other than family ties joined members of the opposite sex. Men sought the company of men, and women preferred to associate with other women. The primary duties of women were to care for children; to plant, cultivate, and harvest crops; to collect wild food products; and to prepare meals. Men concentrated their energies on hunting, politics, and warfare. The behavioral ideals for each sex were set forth in their oral traditions, and children were taught these values by their parents.

When a woman died, her farmland, along with her domestic property, usually was inherited by her children, although she might will them to other persons. A man's property normally was passed to his matrilineage, whose members disposed of his separate dwelling or apartment in a longhouse as well as his other material goods. The members might keep some items by which to remember the deceased. A man too could will his property to his wife or children if he made his desires known before a witness (see Figure 12-6).

An analysis of historical references to Tuscarora personality characteristics by Anthony F. C. Wallace (1958) provides what possibly are general traits of aboriginal Iroquois. Their "demandingness," which Wallace thought masked their extreme dependency, was best exhibited in their expectations of others; they never ceased, it seems, to expect goods and services. The same attitude was reflected in their use of intoxicants introduced by Europeans; their desire apparently knew no limits in early historic times. They blamed the difficulties resulting from intoxication on the white traders or on the rum itself but not on the person drinking it. Another striking characteristic of the Tuscarora and other Iroquois was the absence of fear of heights.

DREAMS Wallace (1958) studied early historic records about Iroquois dreams and found that the meanings they attached to dreams were in some respects similar to ideas developed by Sigmund Freud. The Iroquois in general

Figure 12-6 | A 1724 illustration of an Iroquois burial. (From Lafitau 1974.)

believed that dreams expressed inner and symbolic unconscious desires, which if frustrated could cause psychosomatic illness. An individual could not always interpret his dreams properly, in which case he consulted a shaman versed in such matters. The dreamers most often mentioned in the literature were adolescent boys who embarked on vision quests, warriors who feared torture, and the ill who feared death. The young boys had dreams of the visitation form, according to the twofold Iroquois dream classification of Wallace. In these, the supernatural communicated with the dreamer, bestowing power such as good fortune in hunting or war or some other inordinate ability. One of the most important powers given was a capacity to predict the future. Symptomatic dreams told one of the desires of his soul. Wallace (1958, 244) wrote that "the only way of forestalling realization of an evil-fated wish was to fulfill it symbolically. Others were curative of existing disorders, and prophylactic only in the sense of preventing ultimate death if the wish were too long frustrated. The acting out patterns can also be classified according to whether the action required is mundane or sacred and ceremonial." It was under the compulsion of fulfilling a symptomatic dream that men were tortured by their friends, sought some material object even if it meant great hardships, held traditional but special ceremonies, or introduced a new ritual.

In summary, Wallace's (1958, 247) concluding paragraph is best quoted.

> The culture of dreams may be regarded as a useful escape-valve in Iroquois life. In their daily affairs, Iroquois men were brave, active, self-reliant, and autonomous; they cringed to no one and begged for nothing. But no man can balance forever on such a pinnacle of masculinity, where asking and being given are unknown. Iroquois men dreamt; and, without shame, they received the fruits of their dreams and their souls were satisfied.

ENTERTAINMENT   Diversion in the form of games of chance and skill played an important part in Iroquois religious and social life. The contests were between individuals or teams organized within a community or beyond it, including different tribes. The teams generally seem to have been divided along clan lines. These people were avid gamblers, and betting on the outcome of a game was intense: a man might gamble all of his property on the outcome of a game. The favorite game was lacrosse, played on a field about 450 yards long. Each of the six to eight players on a team carried a crook that had netting strung from the curved end to about halfway up the stick; the ball could be moved only with this racket. The object was to drive a deerskin ball from midfield through the opposing team's goal, which consisted of two poles near each other at one end of the field. The rules allowed a variation from five to seven in the number of goals necessary to win a game. Another game was to throw a javelin through a rolling hoop or to throw it farther than an opponent.

The snow snake game was played mainly by men. The snow snake was a thin, smoothed hickory shaft some six feet in length, with the forward end increased in diameter and slightly upturned. There were up to six players, with three to a side, and each hurled his snow snake across a snow surface. The game was scored according to the distance achieved until the specified number of points had been reached by one side. The snow boat game was based on the snow snake principle. A snow boat, constructed from a solid piece of beech wood, looked like a round-bottomed vessel with an upturned bow. The boat had small feathers at the top of the stern and an oblong central opening in which was placed an arched piece of wood hung with rattles. On a hillside each player trampled a runway in the snow, iced the depression, and propelled two or three boats down the chute and as far as possible across the snow below.

POLITICAL LIFE   In standard accounts about the Iroquois, they are noted for their political acumen, best reflected in the Iroquois League (League of the Longhouse). Traditionally, the League is presented as a powerful, essentially unified force in colonial and later times, but this image is a distortion. Despite the towering contributions of Lewis Henry Morgan (1851) to Iroquois studies, he did not fully understand some key developments. One reason is the nature of the evidence available. European and Euro-American accounts are uneven, and, although rich at times, they may also be poor or nonexistent at other times. Iroquois oral traditions committed to paper are relatively recent and can be contradictory. A recent study by the historian Daniel K. Richter (1992) provides a new, tightly reasoned interpretation of Iroquois political evolution. His findings dominate the following presentation.

According to Iroquois legends, the intensity of warfare within the Five Nations, and with other tribes, produced "mourning wars," a widespread Native American response to the killing of relatives. Warriors among the Iroquois, at the instigation of female relatives, raided enemies for captives who were either ritually executed, as a part of the mourning process, or adopted by a family in mourning to replace the deceased. All too often mourning wars led to ongoing feuds. After the closely spaced deaths of his daughters, an Onondaga, Hiawatha, became distraught and wandered about in a forest. Here he met Deganawida, a person of supernatural origins. Deganawida taught Hiawatha how to remove his grief, and thus eliminate mourning wars; his teaching came to be identified as the Good News of Peace and Power. Together Hiawatha and Deganawida successfully introduced the new doctrine among the Five Nations. This led to the formation of a Grand Council of some fifty leaders, sachems selected by females representing leading matrilineages within the matriclans of the Five Nations. These men were chosen based on specific qualities; each sought goodwill, peace, and harmony. The Great League of Peace and the Grand Council gave rise to the Iroquois League, which was, and remains, largely a ritual institution in which comparatively few organizational changes have occurred.

When the League originated is unclear. Dates between A.D. 1400 and 1600 have been favored by historians; it clearly existed by the 1660s. According to Seneca oral tradition, the League was founded soon after a total eclipse of the sun. Barbara A. Mann and Jerry L. Fields (1997) propose that this eclipse occurred on August 31, 1142. It well may be, however, that the League formation was not a single event but a gradual process, irrespective of any proposed date for its creation.

At the annual Grand Council meetings, a central ceremonial involvement of the sachems, Words of Condolence, was held to honor those of their number who had died. Older women in leading matrilineages of the matriclans of deceased sachems selected the successors. The pertinent ceremonies sought to replace a mourning war with "mourning peace." In the seventeenth and eighteenth centuries, the Iroquois League did *not* represent a central government with unified policies or goals and the means to achieve them. Peace itself was a primary purpose, and they lacked institutional means to prevent raids and warfare. Sachems could only seek to dissuade potential war parties from being launched. Thus League sachems were incapable of dealing with Europeans in diplomatic or political contexts.

To obtain European trade goods on a reliable basis became an early historic Iroquois challenge, accompanied by the power struggle among European colonizers. The Mohawk began trading with the Dutch at Fort Orange (Albany) in the 1610s, and eventually all Five Nations traded there with relative security. Algonquians to the north and east obtained European goods from the French based in Quebec before the Iroquois did, which prevented full Iroquois participation in the fur trade. Nor did they have a locally abundant supply of beaver, a key item in the trade; but beaver were plentiful in Algonquian country. The Iroquois plight compounded as diseases of European origins spread among them; by the 1640s contagions had killed about half of the Five Nations people. Women who had lost family members to enemies inspired a response to these hardships. Women encouraged war chiefs and warriors to seek revenge for relatives killed. As a result the Iroquois preyed on Algonquian traders among the French along the St. Lawrence River. The Iroquois sought guns and ammunition, beaver pelts, as well as captives to satisfy mourning women. The adoption of captives, replacing dead Iroquois, became a major factor contributing to Iroquois survival. Their success by the 1650s led to attacks on neighboring tribes. The French response was to launch concerted military attacks against the Iroquois, which forced them to make peace with the French in the 1660s. All of this produced a revival of mourning wars and destruction of the Great League of Peace. The Iroquois League and its Grand Council could not cope with these developments.

The Iroquois Confederacy evolved as a political and diplomatic solution. By the mid-1600s, French and Iroquois tension began to be dealt with by councils at the village level. The grassroots male leaders included varying numbers of war chiefs, knowledgeable old men, and, secondarily, sachems. In deliberations, Great Peace rituals with an emphasis on peace, condolence, oratory, and gift exchanges became incorporated into Confederacy organization. By the 1660s village leaders met among the Onondaga to address common concerns in war councils that were not as yet distinct from the League. Unified positions among the Five Nations could not be achieved; quite to the contrary, community representatives sought to further their own particular political goals.

Following treaties with the French in 1665–1667, Jesuit priests worked among the Five Nations in a concerted effort to convert them to Catholicism. One result was the emergence of a faction favoring the French, and some of them moved to Canada. Their opposition was driven toward the English sphere in New York and to the Anglican church. By the late 1600s the Iroquois were deeply divided. The French–English factionalism produced increasing unity within the English faction, and the Confederacy formally emerged as distinct from the League, although key League rituals remained. By the 1690s the Confederacy councils met frequently. The leaders were not League sachems but Five Nation community leaders who often sought neutrality. The end result was a series of treaties with the French and their Indian allies in 1701. In the early eighteenth century the Iroquois raided widely, especially to the south, and adopted the remnants of numerous tribes to increase their core population. Confederation cohesion was destroyed by the American Revolution, in part because the Six Nations (by then the Tuscarora were included) could not achieve a unified position toward the colonists and the British. In New York State by 1797 the modern Iroquois reservations were established by treaty, although they are much smaller than originally. Illegal seizures of Iroquois land by white settlers in the nineteenth century produced the small present-day reservations and a decline of the Confederacy.

In sum, the Iroquois Confederacy emerged from the Iroquois League, in part because the latter could not meet political needs in dealing with Europeans in the seventeenth century. The League was not a political monolith. To draw attention to the League–Confederacy distinction is more than an academic exercise in understanding early Iroquois and colonial history.

Wampum played a significant role in Iroquois history. The word *wampum* is an Algonquian term for a string of white beads. Among the Iroquois wampum served as a currency and was made into belts. A convention required that one or more gifts must accompany important decisions, and wampum emerged as the most appropriate gift to bind a treaty or other agreement with foreign Indians or Europeans. An Onondaga chief was the Keeper of the Wampum. A topic of importance was "talked into" the bead pattern memorized by the keeper and learned by his successors. Iroquois wampum is known only from historic sites, usually those dating after the sixteenth century. Their wampum appears to be primarily or exclusively a historical development.

Intermittently the question is raised about the possible impact of Iroquois political organization on the origins of the U.S. Constitution. Some scholars contend there was none, because the American colonists did not really understand Iroquois political life. It also has been noted that the Iroquois system of government did not appear in written form until the 1800s, in which case they could have borrowed concepts from the U.S. Constitution. Yet Iroquois sachems were present at meetings as the Declaration of Independence was being formulated. This leads other historians to contend that the Iroquois contribution was substantial. Evidence for a causal link is inviting but not nearly as conclusive as the proponents imply. The debate is reviewed in a volume edited by José Barreiro (1992).

WARFARE It is fitting initially to examine some of the Iroquois conventions in warfare and place them in perspective. Methods of war among Europeans and Indians in eastern North America during the seventeenth and eighteenth centuries are briefly compared. The best study is by Thomas S. Abler (1992).

Scalping the dead, or sometimes the living, was a custom of the pre-Columbian Native Americans. Whites quickly learned to scalp enemies. Scalping was unknown in Europe, although decapitating enemies and exhibiting their heads was reasonably common. For Indians, scalps usually had sacred associations, but this was not true of heads taken by Europeans. Cannibalism among eastern Indians was practiced, and it usually had sacred associations (e.g., to gain the supernatural power of a slain enemy). It was not practiced in Europe, nor did Europeans adopt this Indian custom.

Torture in Europe was well known, not only to obtain confessions but also as a part of public executions to entertain English or French crowds. For example, in Paris in 1757 some prisoners to be hanged might first have their hands cut off or their tongues cut out. In this context, Iroquois torture techniques, soon to be described, may seem a little less barbaric.

Although not politically sanctioned in Europe, the rape of women was and remains a part of the European warfare complex. Indian warriors in eastern North America do *not* appear to have raped captive women. The evidence, slim as it may be, certainly suggests that the practice was unknown. One possible reason was that sex and warfare were incompatible ideas to warriors; they were considered to be separate domains. However, the rape of Indian women by whites occurred not infrequently.

It must finally be noted that on occasion the French in Canada during the latter seventeenth century tortured Iroquois prisoners as public spectacles.

Warfare was *the* paramount Iroquois interest, irrespective of the goals of the League. Accounts about their war complex postdate the introduction of European firearms, and therefore the aboriginal patterning is reconstructed. Apparently early historic war parties were large, organized by chiefs in council and led by war chiefs and shamans; these were "public wars." After about 1640 guns began to replace the bow and arrow and war clubs as weapons. The famous tomahawk apparently was not an aboriginal Iroquois weapon but was known among the eastern Algonquian, from whom it was derived. The blade was hafted in the manner of a modern hatchet. Metal tomahawks soon were manufactured in Europe for the Indian trade, and they often had a pipe integrated in their design (see Figure 12-7). Early historic war parties most often were composed of young, ambitious men who sought glory in "private wars," irrespective of the wishes of chiefs in council.

Near the center of each settlement was a war post, and a chief who sought to organize a fighting party whooped about the village, stuck a red tomahawk adorned with red feathers into the war post, and danced around it. Any man willing to join the party participated in the dance. After a band of warriors had been organized, women began preparing food for the venture. The standard fare was very dry, pulverized maize mixed with maple sugar and placed in a bearskin bag. A war chief customarily led a raiding party, and each was organized as a small contingent that might join one or more similar units. The units had no overall commander; each party leader was responsible for his group. Participants were free to act according to their personal feelings, and proper behavior could not be dictated. Before the warriors departed, at their camps, and on their return trip, they painted symbols on trees representing the number of raiders, the destination of the war party, and the outcome of the raid. When the combatants returned, the authority of the temporary leader ended. Because warfare focused the lives of men and brought them glory and prestige, the organizer of a war party could recruit a following easily. The Iroquois considered themselves at war with all Indians with whom they had no alliance; thus, there always were potential victims.

Figure 12-7 | An aquatint of an Iroquois warrior in 1787; note the war club, ax, and tomahawk. (Courtesy of the Library of Congress.)

When a returning war party passed through a League village, its captives were forced to run the gauntlet naked, and according to Cadwallader Colden (1755, vol. 1, 9), "the Women are much more cruel than the Men." As the warriors approached their home village, they sounded a war whoop and danced as they led their captives. At the war post they were welcomed and praised by an elder. In reply, warriors narrated their exploits and performed the War Dance. Captives were repatriated only under extenuating circumstances. A man either was adopted into the tribe or was tortured to death. The one exception was to free an extremely brave enemy warrior. If the warriors had lost one of their number to an enemy, the Iroquois widow could adopt any male prisoner to take the place of her husband. First, however, he was obliged to run a gauntlet to his new home. The women and children lined up with whips, and the potential adoptee ran between the lines. If he stumbled and fell, he was considered an unworthy person and was killed; if he ran the lines successfully, he became a member of the tribe.

The fact that widows had first choice concerning the fate of captives has been cited as evidence that women were important in decision making. In addition, there are records of women inducing men to go on war parties or restraining them under certain circumstances. Evidence such as this has led to the generalization that Iroquois society was dominated by women. In a review of ethnohistorical writings about the status of Iroquois women, Cara B. Richards (1957) concluded that they gained dominance in relatively recent times. She notes that early reports state that the fate of captives was determined by the captor and the council. If a woman disagreed with their decision, she could not take effective counteraction until after the captor and council released the prisoner. Later in time the release of a prisoner by the council became an unimportant formality, indicating increased female authority. One factor leading to the expanding importance of women in decision making may have been the instability in village life after the introduction of firearms and the subsequent increase in mortality among warriors.

Nathaniel Knowles (1940, 188) reviewed the treatment of prisoners by the Iroquois. Among the techniques were: "applying brands, embers, and hot metal to various parts of the body; putting hot sand and embers on scalped head; hanging hot hatchets about neck; tearing out hair and beard; firing cords bound around body; mutilating ears, nose, lips, eyes, tongue, and various parts of the body; searing mutilated parts of the body, biting or tearing out nails; twisting fingers off; driving skewers in finger stumps; pulling sinews out of arms; etc." Only the Onondaga tortured young and old, male and female; the other tribes reserved their tortures for men. The usual practice, except for a person slated for possible adoption, was to begin abusing a captive soon after he was taken and to begin his systematic torture when he arrived in the settlement of the captor. The prisoner was forced to run around inside a longhouse as young men burned him, primarily on the legs, until he fainted. As he was slowly being tortured, he was expected to sing about his lack of fear. After a captive fainted, he was revived and the tortures repeated. Care was taken to see that he did not die from the tortures because he was to mount a platform at dawn. Here he was bound so that he could move about and was tortured more before the entire community. When the captive was very near the point of dying, he was stabbed to death or his head was smashed. Normally the body of a tortured person was cooked and eaten.

RELIGION For the Iroquois, the world was occupied by a host of invisible spirits. The most powerful deity was the Great Chief, who created people, other animals, plants, and forces for good in nature. The Great Chief indirectly guided human affairs but could not be appealed to directly. He was capable of countering the Evil Twin by applying his energies, and people passed through life between these competing fraternal deities. Among the lesser supernatural controlling forces for good was the Thunderer, who was capable of bringing rain or exacting vengeance, especially against witches. Associations of the Thunderer with productivity are reflected in prayers offered to him when crops were planted and thanks expressed after a harvest. The Spirit of the Winds commanded the winds and therefore could either help or harm people. The Three Sisters, the spirits of maize, beans, and squash, were conceived as lovely women and collectively called Our Life. Everything that aided people, including particular plants, fire, and water, had its spiritual associations. Some spirits assumed human form and were assigned specific obligations, and all bore the general name the Invisible Aids. It was possible to communicate with the lesser spirits for good by burning tobacco, as it was thought that through this medium prayers and special needs could be made known to the gods. Gratitude was expressed in thanksgiving statements.

The Evil Twin controlled a host of lesser spirit beings who brought pestilence to people and to crops, but few of these forces were systematized in the thinking of the Iroquois. One organized group of evil supernaturals was the False Faces, who were able to send death and destruction. They existed as contorted and evil-appearing faces and lived in out-of-the-way places; it was thought that anyone who chanced to see them would become paralyzed.

The most dreaded antisocial actions were believed to be performed by witches in league with the Evil Twin. Anyone could conceivably assume the form of an animal, bird, or reptile in his or her desire to do evil. Witches were supposedly difficult to detect because they transformed themselves into inanimate objects at will. Witches were thought to have a society with regular initiations; to become a member an initiate supposedly had to kill his or her closest friend by supernatural means. Anyone who saw a witch practicing was free to kill him or her, and the normal punishment for unconfessed witches was death. It was possible to establish at a council meeting whether someone was a witch; if the accused confessed and promised to reform, he or she was freed.

Religious specialists, or Keepers of the Faith, were chosen by female and male elders of the matriclans and were expected to serve when requested. Both sexes were represented in nearly equal numbers, and all members held equal rank. Each was invested by being given a new name announced at the next general meeting of the nation. Their primary duty was to arrange and conduct the main religious ceremonies; sachems and chiefs were ex officio Keepers of the Faith. Among their other duties was the censuring of antisocial behavior; the strongest form of censure was to report serious transgressions to the tribal council. A person could choose to relinquish the obligations of Keeper of the Faith by assuming his or her old name.

In addition to the belief system just described, another critical aspect of religious life was intimately associated with a highly personal guardian spirit that appeared in a vision to an awake person rather than in a dream. Such a spirit appeared to be comparable to the Algonquian concept of *manitou*, a supernatural force. An Iroquois sought this spirit by going into seclusion after fasting and meditating. It could have a specific capacity, such as to bring success in hunting or in raids against enemies. Tangible evidence of acquiring a spirit aid in a vision included recognizing an object or objects required in a personal medicine bundle.

Major Ceremonies   The Iroquois held six major religious ceremonies; in sequence of occurrence they were the Maple, Planting, Strawberry, Green Maize, Harvest, and New Year's (Midwinter) ceremonies. The first five were similar in many respects, as in sharing the common feature of public confessions prior to group observances. During these confessions, confessors held a string of white wampum as a symbol of sincerity. The audience did not pass judgment on transgressions, but it was expected that future behavior would reflect renewed purpose and intent. On the day of any ceremony, sacred rituals were held in the morning. The religious aspects included speeches by the Keepers of the Faith about the precedent and purpose of the ceremony, offerings of burnt tobacco, prayers, and thanksgiving speeches. In the afternoon and evening, social festivities included dances and feasting. One of the most popular dances was the Feather Dance, which included not only a dance but accompanying songs of thanksgiving.

The seven-day New Year's Ceremony usually was held in early February. Before the rituals began, people who had dreamed went from house to house asking the residents to guess the nature of their dreams. When someone suggested a reasonable text and meaning for a dream, the dreamer ceased his or her quest for an interpretation. If the accepted text and its meaning included statements about the future behavior of the dreamer, she or he was obligated to behave as directed. Jesuit missionaries who witnessed the dream procedure in 1656 recorded it as a violent affair, with the dreamer threatening and actually destroying a great deal of household property until he or she was satisfied with an interpretation.

The formal New Year festivities, designed to drive away evil, were launched by two Keepers of the Faith disguised in skin robes and adorned with corn husks. On the first day, they visited each household on two separate occasions to announce the purpose of the ceremony and to sing a song of thanksgiving. The same day one or two white dogs, symbolizing purity, were sacrificed and hung from a pole. On the second day the Keepers of the Faith dressed as warriors and visited each household three different times to perform rituals that included prayer and song. The third and fourth days were devoted to dancing and visiting among the people. At this time, groups of boys, accompanied by an old woman carrying a basket, visited each house. The boys danced, and, if given presents, they all moved on. If no gifts were forthcoming, they stole whatever they could. If they were caught, they returned what they had taken. On the fifth day the sacrificed dog or dogs were placed in the council house and a speech was made about their dedication to the Great Spirit; later the dog or dogs were burned in a fire to carry a message of contrition to the Great Spirit. The Thanksgiving Dance was held on the sixth day, and gambling dominated the final day. Note that midway through and at the end of the ceremonies, time was set aside for entertainment, possibly as a relief from the intensity of the religious obligations.

FALSE FACE SOCIETY Their masks were inspired by mythological beings and creatures seen during dreams. A mask was carved from a living basswood tree and portrayed one of about a dozen facial types. As the most distinguishing feature, some had crooked mouths, others a smile, some a protruding tongue, and so on (see Figure 12-8). They might be painted black, brown, red, or white. Another type of mask was made from braided and sewn corn husks. These represented important farming and hunting deities. Corn-husk masks also could be differentiated according to facial features. The society probably existed in each village to prevent and cure illness. People became members either by being cured of illness by the false faces or by dreaming about false faces. The rituals involved abnormal and often violent behavior. They might

Figure 12-8 | Two ceremonial items: a False Face mask and a cow horn rattle, shown by a dancer on his traveling rounds to private homes before a ceremony in the longhouse. (Photo by Annemarie A. Shimony, circa 1970.)

act like babies, dance and cry out wildly, destroy property, smear people with feces, or act in other unconventional ways.

Early in the history of Indian–missionary contacts, meaning the 1660s, Roman Catholic missionaries described the Iroquois response to the increasing availability of rum and brandy. Whenever possible, these Indians drank to become intoxicated, especially when in the company of other tribal members, and they acted as though they were possessed. In extreme instances they murdered friends, relatives, and strangers. Typically there were no reprisals because alcohol, not the individuals involved, was blamed. Maia Conrad (1999) examined the context of their drinking during the late 1600s. This was before the beaver trade collapsed, which meant the Iroquois could readily obtain intoxicants in trade. At this same time, epidemics of exotic diseases led to famines and contributed to an abrupt population decline. Furthermore, the Iroquois sustained heavy casualties in conflicts with the French and other Indians, which contributed to their loss of political power in the northeast.

Standard anthropological and historical accounts about Iroquois drunkenness associate it at least indirectly with the individual vision quest described previously. Conrad, however, found that drunken behavior represented a direct development from the traditional False Face Society activities connected with dreams, not with the visions of individuals. As the reader, you may judge Conrad's interpretations as relatively insignificant, yet in ethnohistorical context the study is an innovative approach to a contentious aspect of Iroquois culture.

Most preceding chapters about specific peoples include sections about the life cycle, but early systematic ethnographic information of comparable scope about an Iroquois tribe does not appear to exist.

| Later History

The final political drama in which the Iroquois participated was the American Revolution. Most Iroquois appear to have been loyal to the British, who sought their active support following the Declaration of Independence in 1776. The rebels hoped for Iroquois neutrality, but the Confederacy could not achieve a unified position. Among the Mohawk and Onondaga there were both loyalist and rebel factions, whereas the Cayuga and Seneca supported the loyalists; the Oneida and Tuscarora in theory were neutral but aided the rebels. Following early Iroquois and loyalist victories, in 1779 rebel troops destroyed Iroquois communities, crops, and grain caches to end their effectiveness. Many Iroquois fled to Canada, abandoning their traditional lands forever.

In Canada some Mohawk settled near Montreal, where they were given land. When peace was achieved, no mention was made of the Indian participants and their future. In recognition of Mohawk aid, the British granted a prominent leader, Joseph Brant, land along the Grand River that flows into Lake Erie. A portion of this area is the modern Six Nations Reserve. Separate treaties were made between the Six Nations and the United States, in which the

Oneida and Tuscarora, who had remained relatively neutral in the conflict, were permitted to retain much of their land, but the other nations, who had aided the British, were forced to relinquish claim to most of their land.

THE NEW RELIGION In addition to the political influence of Iroquois tribes, a second major influence was the emergence of the "New Religion." It originated with a Seneca prophet. His revelations occurred at Burnt House in northwestern Pennsylvania, a small land grant from the Quakers where one of their missionaries recorded what happened. In 1799 Handsome Lake appeared to be near death when he had a vision. By then generations of Iroquois had become addicted to the excessive consumption of intoxicants. In an initial vision three men told Handsome Lake that the Great Chief was displeased by the drunkenness and that if he recovered he was not to consume intoxicants. In a second vision the Great Chief apparently talked with Handsome Lake, who went into a trance and was thought to have died. Yet he recovered some seven hours later to reveal what he had learned. Among the revelations was that Handsome Lake was not to consume alcoholic beverages and was to abandon all dances except the Green Corn Ceremony. Children were to respect their parents, and, if people agreed, it was proper to accept whites as teachers. Finally, Handsome Lake was told that he was to return among the living and that he would see no more of these things until he died; in death he would return to this setting if he behaved properly.

When Handsome Lake recovered, he began preaching his doctrine, which came to include the rejection of schools and a return to a subsistence-based economy. In 1802 his cause received American support when Handsome Lake went to Washington, D.C., with other Iroquois and President Thomas Jefferson condoned his teachings. Partly because of this official sanction, Handsome Lake became an acknowledged prophet. From the time of his recovery until his death, Handsome Lake visited Seneca communities to influence the behavior of others. By 1807 his fame as a prophet had spread widely among the Iroquois and to other eastern tribes. When the War of 1812 began, the Iroquois had learned their lesson, and most of them did not participate. Handsome Lake in particular preached neutrality because of his continuing close ties with the Quakers. In 1815 the prophet moved to Onondaga, and it was here that he died the same year.

As Merle H. Deardorff (1951) noted, the Handsome Lake revelations, the Good Message, came to be joined by a body of teachings that included biographical material, prophecy, law, parable, and anecdote. Believers called the entire system the New Religion. The Good Message was not the only basis for the New Religion; some of the more important changes proposed in the revelation had been initiated before Handsome Lake's trances. If the text of the revelations had been the only document to survive, Handsome Lake might have been assumed to be a great innovator; but from the diaries of the Quaker missionaries it is obvious that the revelations were in step with what were recognized and pressing problems at Burnt House. Although much of the Handsome Lake doctrine was influenced by Quaker and earlier Jesuit missionaries and although some aspects were novel, these teachings also had deep roots in Iroquois religious life of old. The emphasis on confession, the continuity in honoring traditional gods, and the prominence of the annual ceremonial round are examples. Furthermore, the Iroquois had long placed considerable emphasis on prophetic dreams, and this too was a critical element in the Handsome Lake revelations. Unlike many other Indian prophets, Handsome Lake was willing to adapt his basic ideas to accommodate Quaker beliefs and to accept certain material aspects of white culture, such as farming methods. This flexibility contributed to the stability of Iroquois life in his time and unquestionably aided the long-term survival of the Good Message. Soon after Handsome Lake's death, other Christian missionaries proselytized among the Seneca, and the Indians labored in council to establish a uniform approach to religion. The time-honored pattern of unanimity, however, could not be achieved, and by 1820 the New Religion had separated from other Iroquois religious systems.

The Good Message was not recorded systematically until 1845, and no single text became standard. By 1949 the New Religion was being taught in ten ceremonial structures, each termed a longhouse, on the meeting circuit of the Six Nations. Most of the preachers required four days to relate the Good Message. The Tonawanda Longhouse was called symbolically the Central Fire, and here were kept the most sacred strings of wampum that had belonged to Handsome Lake.

The New Religion includes the following tenets: the prohibition of intoxicants; obedience of children toward their parents and care of aged parents; faithfulness of married couples; reproval of gossiping or boasting; killing of witches; awareness of a hell for sinners and heaven for persons who have lived good lives or repented of having lived evil lives; and the acceptance of the ways of whites save for schools. As has been noted by Edmund Wilson (1960, 87), the New Religion "has a scope and a coherence which have made it endure as has the teaching of no other Indian prophet, and it is accepted at the present time by at least half the Iroquois world as a source of moral guidance and religious inspiration."

OTHER CHANGES   The course toward modern Iroquois life was set in the early nineteenth century. Many of those Iroquois who sympathized with the British had moved to Canada, and the ones in the United States had settled on small reservations. Each of these two major groups had its own chiefs, councils, and wampum, and each became increasingly involved in reservation or reserve politics and relationships with the respective governments. In the early 1800s the Iroquois in both countries continued to hunt over broad areas that reached beyond their boundaries and to plant traditional crops in old ways. However, as increasing numbers of white settlers occupied nearby land, Iroquois life began to change in basic ways.

The ability of the Indians to hunt profitably declined as the supply of game diminished; furthermore, they no longer could move from one area to another as the productivity of their farmland declined. Consequently, they turned increasingly to plow agriculture, farming in the manner of whites. In New York State, the Iroquois depended heavily on annuities derived from the sale of land to obtain items of material culture such as blankets, guns, and farming equipment. Annuity payments unquestionably eased their transition to a more sedentary lifestyle. The greatest threat to their security was continued encroachment of whites on their lands; another concern was the conflict arising from the pull of traditional Iroquois culture and the attractions of white culture. This inevitably caused factions to develop on reservations and reserves that have continued into the present.

| The Six Nations Reserve

By the end of the American Revolution, Iroquois men were scattered widely in the western provinces of Canada and the western United States. Most of them worked for the North West and Hudson's Bay companies, especially as canoemen in the fur trade. Some of these Iroquois, however, were freemen as trappers and traders, and small groups have maintained their separate identity in western Canadian provinces. Other Iroquois, especially Cayuga and Seneca, who had settled in Ohio, were forced to move to Indian Territory under the Indian Removal Act of 1830 and to live on a reservation in northeastern Oklahoma. There likewise is an Oneida reservation in Wisconsin. From about 1870 to 1881 Iroquois from the Six Nations Reserve in Ontario, especially Cayuga, moved to the Oklahoma reservation and remained there. The emphasis now shifts to the Six Nations Reserve in Canada for three good reasons. The reserve is the most populous Iroquois stronghold up to the present, each tribe is represented, and an account about the reserve by Annemarie A. Shimony beginning in the 1950s is superior.

As compensation for land lost in New York State following the American Revolution, the Mohawk war chief, Joseph Brant, received an original tract of about 675,000 acres along Grand River from the British. In 1784–1785, about 1,450 Iroquois began to settle there and were accompanied by nearly 400 persons from other tribes who lived among the Iroquois.

Brant justifiably claimed that the land grant reflected British recognition of Iroquois national sovereignty, and he felt free to do as he wished with the land. Soon he had sold about half of the acreage to whites. He felt that white farmers in their midst would encourage Indian men to farm. The Mohawk, Oneida, and Tuscarora lived largely along upper Grand River and became known as the Upper Tribes. Many had been Christianized before migrating to the reserve, and they were as a group reasonably responsive to becoming more like white Canadians. Down the river were the Lower Tribes, the Cayuga, Onondaga, and Seneca, who retained a far more traditional way of life and the Good Message of Handsome Lake.

By 1956 the reserve population, most of whom were Mohawk and Cayuga, numbered about sixty-five hundred. They lived on scattered homesteads, and individual holdings were inherited by members. The stress placed by Euro-Canadians on inheritance through males confused the traditional Iroquois matrilineal descent system. Inheritance rights, like individual rights to band membership, were calculated patrilineally according to the Canadian authorities but matrilineally by the Iroquois. Another difference was that Canadians considered the nuclear family an important social unit, and their emphasis on it robbed the clans of important functions. A newly married couple on reserve land now lived either with the husband's or wife's relatives only until they could establish an independent household (neolocal residence). The exogamous nature of the matriclans continued to be observed by some people, but others felt it was acceptable to marry anyone to whom close genealogical ties could not be established. The matrilineages remained important in selecting leaders, but disputes arose over which were the leading lineages with the vested rights. Members of the leading lineages of a clan most often made an effort to retain their clan ties so that they would not lose their political and religious authority. A real difficulty, however, stemmed from the fact that even some conservative families could no longer trace their clan affiliations.

THE NEW RELIGION   Four local congregations formed the organizational base for the New Religion, each centered at a different longhouse. The Central Fire was the Tonawanda Longhouse in New York State. Here preachers on the longhouse circuit were invested, but the Central Fire had no jurisdiction over the Home Fires. The rituals of the four longhouses were essentially the same. Each longhouse had wampum to validate its legitimacy, and the particular one to which a person belonged was determined by matrilineage ties and by its proximity. Longhouses were the traditional rectangular wooden buildings, usually with doors and wood-burning stoves at each end and with benches along the walls.

Longhouse leaders were Keepers of the Faith or deacons, as they more commonly were called. Each longhouse had a leading male and female Keeper of the Faith, chosen on the basis of merit. They guided all longhouse functions. With a breakdown of the clan structure, Keepers of the Faith as a group had an increased voice in community affairs. A second longhouse functionary, the Keeper of the Fire, was the guardian of the longhouse wampum. His moiety and clan affinities were unimportant, but he had to be a staunch believer in the New Religion. The wampum was symbolic of the longhouse traditions, and the people believed that Canadian officials sought to destroy the wampum and thereby eliminate the longhouses. The final longhouse leader was the Speaker, who presented traditional and extemporaneous speeches to the congregation. Such persons did not hold a formal office, nor were they usually preachers on the longhouse circuit. A Speaker was required to have a talent for public speaking and knowledge of traditional speeches.

A longhouse served many functions in the members' efforts to resist becoming like other Canadians. The organization fulfilled social, medical, economic, and political needs. Social gatherings included softball or lacrosse games, raffles, and dances. Organized social activities sponsored outside the longhouse usually were closed to longhouse members by their own dogma. The longhouse ceremonial round was rich in detail; it was based on the Handsome Lake revelations, as well as the aboriginal planting and harvest ceremonies and the old and new means for curing. An important aspect of almost any longhouse function was the recitation of a formal address of thanks to the Great Chief for the continued life of the persons attending and thanks to the participants for attending. In all longhouse activities the ritual and social language was Iroquois; speaking English was disapproved in any context. To the members, participation in longhouse events gave real purpose to life and at the same time offered a systematic philosophy for living. People were encouraged to remember the teachings of Handsome Lake and to live good lives. At times the younger members were told not to imitate such fashion extremes of whites as high-heeled shoes and low-cut dresses for girls. Neither should one listen to the radio, watch television, or drink intoxicants, for such behavior was not in keeping with the New Religion. Behind it all was the real fear that the longhouse members would become carbon copies of their white Canadian neighbors. The conflict of values seems often to have led to trauma at the time of death for those individuals who had at some time followed forbidden white ways.

For members of the New Religion and other Iroquois as well, there was a deeply rooted focus on death. Death supposedly could be caused by failure to accept a time-honored view about the spirit world, by showing a lack of respect for plants or animals, or by failing to hold rituals as directed. Furthermore, the dead had great power over the living, and to neglect them was an invitation to disease and death. In general, it was thought that souls resided in a pleasant upperworld or else suffered punishment. Souls bent on evil could assume animal forms, but ordinarily they were nonmaterial or a light vapor. All of this concern with death and the dead necessitated the proper performance of obligations to the dead.

The sachems, who were either Christians or members of the New Religion, represented traditional authority and formed the official political body of the Six Nations Reserve until 1924. The longhouse sachems considered that their Christian counterparts were not legitimate officeholders unless they had been invested at a longhouse ceremony, which was comparable to raising up a sachem in the old League. With respect to Canadian officials, the sachems were divided over whether or not they favored closer rapport. In 1924 some World War I veterans, especially those from the Upper Tribes, formed a group known as the Progressive Warriors and sought Canadian recognition of an elected council. During an ensuing investigation of Six Nations Reserve affairs, the sachems would not present their case to Canadian representatives; thus, the government heard from only the "progressive" faction, which supported elected chiefs. The Canadians decided in favor of elected leaders, since they received little cooperation from the sachems, who represented the traditional confederacy council. An elected council was installed in 1924; the New Religion sachems were locked out of the council house, and Royal Canadian Mounted Police officers enforced the government's decision. The supporters of the Six Nations Confederacy were bitter against the Canadians, as well as against their factional opposites, and the bitterness continues to the present. In an ethnohistorical account about the relatively recent past on the reserve, Sally M. Weaver (1972) has noted that the confederacy council refused to disband after the elected council was instituted and continued to hold regular meetings in the hope of being reinstated as the only legitimate authority.

RECENT DEVELOPMENTS ON THE RESERVE   A major issue is the identity of a status Indian (a registered member of the reserve). In 1998 there were about 20,000 status Indians enrolled on the reserve, and about 50 percent of them lived there. Of this total, 24 percent became members as a result of the 1985 Canadian government Bill C-31; it reinstated band membership to women who had married non-native men. However, under current Canadian government policy a child with one C-31-status parent *cannot* pass membership on to his or her children, and about one-half of the children have only one status parent. If this trend continues, there soon will be *no status Indians*. Understandably, the Six Nations government is very concerned about this possibility, and it plans to change the current status determination with Canadian government approval.

Furthermore, the elected government passed a by-law in 1986 stating that only registered band members could live on the reserve. If a band member files a formal complaint that a non-band member lives there and the complaint proves to be valid, the person must leave the reserve within forty-eight hours. The Ontario courts have accepted the Six Nations residency law. It must be emphasized that these Native Americans are legally defined as *allies* of the Crown, not *subjects* of the Crown, irrespective of Canadian law. The Six Nations own their land; it is not Crown land. To have their own residency laws on the reserve represents one effort to be more fully self-governing. The long-festering reserve residency requirement continues. In 2003 a survey was made of band opinion, but it was not helpful because so few people responded. Another effort was made in a survey by an outside consultant; however, the results were not released by the band council. By 2004 the old by-law still prevailed; it is considered later in the chapter.

In another context, the Canadian government has transferred the funding and partial control of some programs to the Six Nations band council. By 1994 the band had received nearly C$21 million from the federal government and nearly C$8 million from the provincial government. Most of this money supported the band council government, infrastructure, and social services. Thus they gained greater local administrative power.

By the late 1990s, elected band council members were far less sympathetic to Canadian government policies than they had been in 1924. The traditional leaders as hereditary chiefs have maintained a "shadow government" on the reserve. In some contexts, the traditional council leaders—with considerable authority but no formal power—support the positions of the elected leaders in a more united effort to gain autonomy. One ongoing problem is that the federal, provincial, and local Canadian governments have refused to recognize the hereditary council. One instance in which the two councils are united is an effort to establish a traditional Iroquois justice system on the reserve despite Euro-Canadian opposition.

For most band members, a disturbing development emerged in 1988 when a militant group, the Warrior Society, began patrolling the reserve as non-legal police. The hereditary and elected chiefs alike denounced the Warriors, and the patrols soon ceased. By 1994 they had few members and sympathizers, perhaps a total of forty individuals. One major problem, however, is that the Warriors, like the hereditary chiefs, seek far greater independence from Canadian government control. Both groups seek an Iroquois government. The Warriors, however, have been involved in smuggling alcohol, guns, tobacco, and drugs from Iroquois reservations in the United States. Some smugglers on the reserve are multimillionaires. Legitimate leaders fear that Warrior activities will undermine the basis for band control and will provide the Canadian government with reasons for abrogating the rights of Six National Reserve members. In a real sense Warrior activities are compatible with the traditional Iroquois emphasis on warfare; what they do is dangerous and akin to the early historic "private wars." The massive Warrior smuggling activities from the United States involved U.S. Mohawk at the St. Regis Reservation and at least $687 million U.S. dollars. In 1999 some twenty-seven participants, Indian and non-Indian, pleaded guilty to or had been convicted of felonies from investigations in the United States.

In 1997 an estimated 9,500 Iroquois lived on the reserve, and they have been increasingly concerned about the perpetuation of Iroquois culture. The Woodland Cultural Centre at Brantford includes a museum, archives, and numerous programs that stress traditional Indian life (see Figure 12-9). One major fear is that their aboriginal languages will become extinct. In 1998 at the Six Nations Reserve no one spoke Seneca or Tuscarora, and the other Iroquoian languages combined were probably spoken by fewer than 350 persons. Most important, longhouse ceremonial texts are traditionally delivered in an Iroquoian language, and about 50 percent of the reserve residents are members of a longhouse. Although a local radio station, CKRZ, includes Iroquoian-language texts and programs, these efforts do not appear to be very effective in language instruction. In 1986 concerned parents launched a program to teach Mohawk and Cayuga at a small number of reserve schools, and by 2004 twelve reserve residents spoke fluent Mohawk.

The Six Nations Reserve is among the strongest centers for the perpetuation of traditional Iroquois culture in Canada and the United States. Their sense of Indian identity is much greater than it was twenty years ago, and it

Figure 12-9 | Erik Bruce Isaacs, a Cayuga, won the "Typical Indian Baby" award at the Six Nations Fall Fair in 1983. (Courtesy of the *Brantford Expositor.*)

continues to grow after each confrontation with Canadian authorities. The Six Nations willingly concede little to Euro-Canadians, not only because the reserve residents own the land they occupy but also because they continue to consider themselves "allies of the Crown," not its subjects.

A far-reaching positive change for the Grand River band's cultural development has resulted from money received by the largest Indian-managed casino in Canada. It is Casino Rama, opened in 1996 on Chippewa land at Orillia, Ontario, reasonably near Toronto. By 2004 it had an annual payroll of nearly C$96 million. The profits are shared among Ontario Indians. The Grand River reserve profits have run into the millions. The band's Rama Trust has made grants to fund health service training, training for employment, and technological training.

A widespread and powerful weapon at some Canadian reserves (and U.S. reservations) is the authority given to an elected band or tribal leader to fire employees who appear to pose an administrative threat, who dissolve committees or boards, who appoint political allies, and who commit other abuses of power. The present-day Grand River reserve administration provides a relatively modest example.

In 2001 the first woman elected to head the Six Nations Band Council for the Grand River reserve was Roberta Jamieson, a lawyer. She fired the land research employees who were involved in a major case and also reconstituted the band gaming commission to gain greater control over its activities. While serving as the elected head, Jamieson ran for leadership of the National Assembly of First Nations, the advocacy organization for indigenous Canadians. She refused, however, to take a leave of absence as chief to campaign and managed to ensure that she was paid her salary as band leader at the same time. She failed in her bid for this elected post but set a record for a leader's travel expenses in one year. The same year, 2003, Jamieson was removed from a House of Commons committee meeting by security personnel for creating a disturbance. These and numerous other of Jamieson's political activities appalled many, possibly most, reserve residents, but she managed to retain her position.

In 2004 Jamieson and the elected Six Nations council proposed a ballot measure about the long-festering residency issue. The ballot supported residence "permits" for nonband members to live on the reserve. The Six Nations Confederacy Council (representing the traditional historic Iroquois government) encouraged people not to vote because the band council had no legitimate authority over membership requirements, the land, treaty obligations, and related issues. About 6 percent of the voters cast ballots in support of residence permits; 123 voted for them, and the opposition vote was 590. Thus, as in the recent past, only band members can legally live at the Six Nations Reserve. This was a clear victory for Confederacy members and their sympathizers. Confederacy advocates contended that Jamieson sought to undermine the pre-1924 authority of the Confederacy council. The residency ballot represented a no-confidence vote on Jamieson and her administration and calls for their resignation (see articles in *Tekawennake* and *Turtle Island News,* 2002–2004; these are Canadian Iroquois newspapers).

A major widespread moral scandal in Canada centers on the treatment of First Nation students in residential schools. Beginning in 1863 strenuous efforts were made to suppress aboriginal cultures by forcing indigenous Canadian children between the ages of four and eighteen to attend a residential school. Nearly one hundred of these schools were operated by churches under contract with the federal government until the 1960s. Children routinely had their heads shaved on admission, were issued uniforms, and were closely regimented and forbidden to speak their native languages. In essence residential schools were meant to reduce children's participation in their traditional culture.

In the early 1990s the uncovering of widespread physical, psychological, and sexual abuse of children over the years became widely reported. Ottawa apologized for the abuses and established a C$350 million Residential Schools

Healing Fund. Nationwide, by 2003 some twelve thousand former students had filed lawsuits against the federal government and those churches that had managed the schools. The federal government is to set aside C$1.7 billion to help settle the claims, with Ottawa paying 70 percent of a claim. The balance is to be paid by the churches that managed the cited schools. The Anglicans and Presbyterians agreed to pay their 30 percent of any proven claim, but negotiations remained pending with the Roman Catholics and other denominations. To avoid lengthy court battles Ottawa has proposed "fast-track" settlements. Upon application a plaintiff could have her or his case reviewed by a panel of former judges and lawyers for an individual settlement ranging up to C$195,000 for severe cases on the "meat chart." At the current rate of settlements, an estimated fifty years will be required to settle all the claims, with a cost of at least C$1 billion for legal bills apart from the actual settlements. Thus far one thousand fast-track settlements have been made, and twelve have been resolved through court procedures.

Six Nations children, along with those from other tribes, attended the Mohawk Institute Residential School operated by the Anglican Church of Canada near Brantford from 1834 to 1969. A woman who was a student there in 1968 reported that she used one word of greeting in an Iroquoian language, and her punishment was to be beaten with a tack-studded belt on her neck, back, and legs. By 1998 more than eight hundred former students at the school had launched a class-action suit against the church involved and the federal government.

A key objection by First Nation peoples is that there is no current means to resolve claims based on language and cultural losses at residential schools. They are accepted by Ottawa as separate and legitimate, but a settlement process has not been established.

A long-term negative result of the treatment that Indian children received at residential schools over the generations is that, as adults, many raised their children in the pattern they learned from residential schoolteachers and supervisors. Residential school graduates often purposefully did not teach their children an Indian language or Indian ways so that they would not suffer similar trauma in school. It also has been established that adults who attended residential schools as children have a high rate of substance abuse, suicide, and emotional problems compared with other Canadians.

SKYWALKERS The word "skywalkers" refers to Indian ironworkers, especially Mohawk, who construct skyscrapers, bridges, and other high steel structures. Since the late 1940s ethnographic and popular accounts have praised their inordinate success in this dangerous occupation. The best overview of the skywalkers is by Richard Hill (1987), an ironworker.

Traditionally, as discussed earlier in this chapter, warfare was a primary focus among Iroquois men, but warfare diminished rapidly following the War of 1812. Some of the men became canoemen in the fur trade—a dangerous occupation, especially when in enemy country. This trade, however, began to decline about 1900. Adventurous men were next drawn to the timber industry; rafting logs through fast water and rapids was hazardous work. At about the same time, other men became farmers, and still others began to travel about New England selling Indian medicines.

Reports about the Mohawk dating from colonial times suggest that at least some men did not fear heights. They were observed crossing deep creeks by walking fearlessly on small poles and had been seen casually striding along the ridges of gabled houses. Some outsiders have suggested that an absence of a fear of heights was inborn, but it seems more likely that the ability was learned. The Mohawk began to work iron systematically in 1886, when a cantilever bridge, known to them as the "black bridge," was built across the St. Lawrence River and buttressed on the Caughnawaga Reserve. In exchange for building rights, the contractor agreed to hire Mohawk for unskilled jobs. The Indians were unhappy with this arrangement and could not be kept off of the bridge as it was being built. It soon appeared that they were unafraid of heights and were pleased with the new experience. Finally a few men were hired, and they proved to be excellent workers. Three crews reportedly were trained on the black bridge. In the construction of a bridge of this nature, precut and drilled beams and girders were hoisted in place with a crane or derrick, temporarily bolted and plumbed, and then riveted. The Mohawk became members of riveting crews, both the most dangerous and the most lucrative work.

By 1907 there were more than seventy skilled Mohawk ironworkers. Thirty-eight were working on the Quebec Bridge across the St. Lawrence River near Quebec City. On August 19, 1907, while still under construction, the bridge collapsed, killing ninety-six workers, thirty-three of whom were Mohawk. Bridge work then took on a new meaning; because it obviously was dangerous, it became an attractive type of employment to Mohawk men. Mohawk women, however, insisted that the gangs of ironworkers hire out on many different projects so that another disaster could not devastate so many families at the same time (see Figure 12-10).

Over the years, some Mohawk who attempted to become ironworkers failed because they feared heights or found the work unappealing. To others, however, it was exciting work, and the comparatively high wages were especially attractive. In the early 1900s Mohawk and other Iroquois men began working on jobs in the United States and established skywalker colonies in such cities as Buffalo and Brooklyn in New York State. They were among the modern urban Indian populations. Following World War II, Iroquois from each of the U.S. reservations and Canadian reserves had become skywalkers. By the late 1980s there were about 130,000 ironworkers in the United States and Canada, of whom about 7000 were Indians. Although Indians, especially Mohawk, are the best known skywalkers, they obviously represent a minority of the persons, including some women, who work in high steel. (The first steel-framed skyscraper dates from 1886.) Despite their smaller numbers, it appears that

Figure 12-10 | Stan Hill, a Mohawk ironworker in 1973. (Courtesy of Richard W. Hill, Sr.)

Indian skywalkers are maimed or killed in accidents at about the same rate as non-Indians.

In a search for the reasons behind Mohawk success as ironworkers, Morris Freilich (1958) learned that Mohawk men were not free from fear of heights but that they concealed their fear in order to behave as warriors and prove their courage. Also, work in high steel was highly compatible with many essential features of the old Mohawk way of life. The men left home to work for extended periods as they had left to hunt and fight in aboriginal times. There was danger and possible death in what they did, just as there had been of old. When a man returned, he could boast of the tall buildings on which he had worked, just as he once had boasted of his skills in combat. The modern steelworker was subject to little authority, and if he was displeased he could quit his job, just as he formerly had been able to drop out of a war party. These and other parallels lent support to the traditional status of the male in a nontraditional setting. Yet when an ironworker retired, he was likely to return to a reservation or reserve. His adjustment to an uneventful and sedentary life was difficult. One response was to readopt Indian ways, to the point of refusing to speak English, and to become deeply involved in local social life and politics.

| Nationalism and Sovereignty

As the twentieth century progressed, the Iroquois increasingly asserted their nationalism. In World War I, the Iroquois in the United States, as a separate entity, declared war on Germany. In Canada, the people of the Six Nations Reserve had a forceful confrontation with the Royal Canadian Mounted Police in 1924 to assert their national sovereignty. In both countries, the Iroquois tend not to vote in non-Indian elections as a means of emphasizing their separate identity. In New York State, the Iroquois have forcefully resisted efforts by state officials to intervene in their affairs. Predictably, in the United States the Iroquois have avoided paying state and federal income taxes and fought varied efforts to use reservation lands for the St. Lawrence Seaway, the Power Authority of New York State, and the relocation of highways or the building of dams. These disputes have often been complicated by the fact that elected leaders cooperate with the whites, whereas hereditary leaders continue to support the Iroquois Confederacy (see Figure 12-11).

In Canada the Liberal government of Prime Minister Jean Chrétien introduced the First Nations Governance Act in 2003 to replace the Indian Act of 1971. Typically, opposition from First Nation bands and tribes has ranged from strong to vehement. One good reason is that there has been no meaningful input from aboriginal Canadians. Equally important, the proposed act was regarded by the First Nations as regressive because it violated treaties and legislation and would result in erosion of the structure of their tribal and band governments. Only one bill associated with the new act had passed Parliament by the time Paul Martin became the Liberal party prime minister in 2003. At the onset of his administration Martin stated that the federal–native relationship had been "severely poisoned" by the previous government. Martin said aboriginal issues would be a major focus of his administration, with an emphasis on improving their economic conditions.

The new Liberal administration was considered untrustworthy among First Nations tribes by mid-2004. Martin reintroduced a bill in Parliament from the previous administration, an optional property tax on reserve lands. First Nations have good reason to believe passage of the bill (C-23) would become mandatory because of the elaborate administrative network proposed. In essence, the property tax would be comparable to municipal and provincial taxes and thereby reduce federal government responsibility and liability. Whether C-23 will pass or not is unclear, but it is a foreboding omen. On the positive side of Martin's agenda is a plan to better fund the Urban Aboriginal Strategy to aid status Indians who live off their reserves.

In the United States greater fairness toward Indians emerged in the 1970s. In 1976 the Seneca of the Allegheny Reservation signed an agreement with New York State *as equals*. This was the first time since the early 1800s that the state had recognized the sovereign or national status of the Seneca. To build

Figure 12-11 | This statue of Joseph Brant was unveiled at Brantford, Ontario, in 1886. In a 1990 protest, the blindfold over Brant's eyes and the sign symbolized a major confrontation with the Canadian government. At the Oka Reserve, Quebec, the Mohawk contested the proposed construction of a golf course on an Iroquois burial ground. The conflict peaked in a standoff between the Iroquois and Canadian military forces. The golf course was not built. (Courtesy of the *Brantford Expositor.*)

a highway through the reservation, the state attempted to exercise its power of eminent domain, but the courts, including the U.S. Supreme Court, held that the state had no right to condemn reservation lands for the highway. As a result, the state negotiated with the Seneca and received an easement of, but not title to, 795 acres of land. In return the state agreed to pay $2 million, give the Indians *title* to 795 acres of land from the adjoining Allegheny State Park, and provide other benefits.

The Iroquois have long been adamant in asserting that the governments of Canada and the United States must acknowledge their distinct national identity and deal with them as a sovereign nation on the basis of negotiated treaties. In the recent past, the federal government of the United States had refused to entertain the concept of "nations within a nation," but as indicated in the previous paragraph, the federal courts began to be far more sympathetic to sovereignty cases in the mid-1970s (see also Chapter 2).

Among the Iroquois, other Indians, and Euro-Americans alike, Indian gaming has been and remains a divisive issue. Some Iroquois favor it, whereas others are clearly opposed. One of the early establishments for Indian gaming was built on the Oneida Reservation in New York State, and the circumstances merit review. Public bingo was launched in 1975, but the prize money awarded was in greater amounts than the state permitted. The operation was soon closed by county authorities. However, this effort helped launch gaming on reservations and led to many court cases before gaming finally was sanctioned by the federal government (see also Chapter 2). In 1993 the eleven hundred Oneida opened another gaming facility, the Turning Stone Casino. Soon after opening, the casino was employing about fifteen hundred people and beginning to attract some seven thousand visitors each day. Within a few years, gaming profits revolutionized the quality of reservation life. By 1996 some elderly people who had never dreamed of having adequate housing began to occupy up-to-date dwellings funded by gambling profits, as well as by Department of Housing and Urban Development funds. They built a new health care clinic, day care center, and recreational center for young people. Before the casino operation, only two Oneida had attended college; soon after, thirty-eight received scholarships. Furthermore, the Oneida have been buying available local farmland; as a result, the original 32-acre reservation includes nearly four thousand acres (see also Chapter 15). As the Oneida leader Ray Halbritter said (McAuliffe 1996, 8), "Our future depends on our ability to take care of ourselves, not on our ability to get anybody else to look out for us by either giving us money or having a law that protects you. We've really got to, number one, develop our own empowerment. Gaming gives us one step in that direction."

| Additional Sources

The book by Lewis Henry Morgan (1851) remains a standard Iroquois source. The first systematic study is by Joseph François Lafitau; it was translated and edited by William N. Fenton and Elizabeth L. Moore (1974; 1977) and remains an ethnographic classic. Daniel K. Richter (1992) examined the League and Confederacy in colonial times. The most comprehensive relatively recent ethnographic study about the Six Nations Reserve is by Annemarie A. Shimony (1994). Nancy Bonvillain (1992) provides a relatively brief book-length overview of the Mohawk; Barbara Graymont (1988) does the same for the Iroquois in general. The Seneca ethnohistory by Anthony F. C. Wallace (1970) is superior. Lawrence M. Hauptman (1981; 1986) examines the relatively recent past in perceptive detail. Uneven presentations about the Iroquois are included in *Northeast,* volume 15 of the *Handbook of North American Indians,* edited by Bruce G. Trigger (1978) and published by the Smithsonian Institution. The writings by Fenton about various aspects of Iroquois life are superior.

| Selected Bibliography

Abler, Thomas S. 1992. Scalping, torture, cannibalism and rape. *Anthropologica* 34:3–20.

Barreiro, José. 1992. *Indian roots*. Ithaca, New York.

Biggar, H. P., ed. 1925. *The works of Samuel de Champlain*. Vol. 2. Toronto.

Bonvillain, Nancy. 1992. *The Mohawk*. New York.

Colden, Cadwallader. 1755. *The history of the Five Indian Nations of Canada*. 2 vols. London.

Conrad, Maia. 1999. Disorderly drinking: Reconsidering seventeenth-century Iroquois alcohol use. *American Indian Quarterly* 23(3–4):1–11.

Deardorff, Merle H. 1951. *The religion of Handsome Lake: Its origin and development*. Bureau of American Ethnology Bulletin 149, 79–107.

Fenton, William N. 1940. Problems arising from the historic northeastern position of the Iroquois. *Essays in Historical Anthropology of North America*. Smithsonian Miscellaneous Collections, vol. 100, 159–251.

———. 1941. *Tonawanda longhouse ceremonies: Ninety years after Lewis Henry Morgan*. Bureau of American Ethnology Bulletin 128, 140–66.

———. 1951a. *Locality as a basic factor in the development of Iroquois social structure*. Bureau of American Ethnology Bulletin 149, 35–54.

———. 1951b. *The concept of locality and the program of Iroquois research*. Bureau of American Ethnology Bulletin 149, 1–12.

———. 1951c. *Iroquois studies at the mid-century*. Proceedings of the American Philosophical Society, vol. 95, 296–310.

———. 1957. Long-term trends of change among the Iroquois. In *Cultural stability and cultural change*, 30–35. American Ethnological Society.

———. 1998. *The Great Law and the Longhouse*. Norman, OK.

Freilich, Morris. 1958. Cultural persistence among the modern Iroquois. *Anthropos* 53:473–83.

Graymont, Barbara. 1988. *The Iroquois*. New York.

Hauptman, Lawrence M. 1981. *The Iroquois and the New Deal*. Syracuse, NY.

———. 1986. *The Iroquois struggle for survival*. Syracuse, NY.

Hill, Richard. 1987. *Skywalkers*. Brantford, Ontario.

Knowles, Nathaniel. 1940. *The torture of captives by the Indians of eastern North America*. Proceedings of the American Philosophical Society, vol. 82, 151–225.

Lafitau, Joseph François. 1974. *Customs of the American Indians compared with the customs of primitive times,* William N. Fenton and Elizabeth L. Moore, eds. and trans. Vol. 1, Toronto, 1974. Vol. 2, Toronto, 1977.

Lydekker, John W. 1938. *The faithful Mohawks*. Cambridge, England.

Mann, Barbara A., and Jerry L. Fields. 1997. A sign in the sky. *American Indian Culture and Research Journal* 21(2):105–163.

McAuliffe, Dennis, Jr. 1996. For many Indian tribes, the buffalo are back. *Washington Post National Weekly Edition*. March 18–24, 8–9.

McKenney, Thomas L., and James Hall. 1933. *The Indian tribes of North America.* Vol. 1. Edinburgh.

Mitchell, Joseph. (*See* Wilson, Edmund.)

Morgan, Lewis Henry. 1851. *League of the Ho-De-No-Sau-Nee or Iroquois.* 2 vols. New York. (Editions published in 1901 and 1904 were edited and footnoted by Herbert M. Lloyd and were reproduced in 1954 by the Human Relations Area Files.)

———. 1881. *Houses and house-life of the American aborigines.* Contributions to North American Ethnology no. 4.

Parkman, Francis. 1892. *A half-century of conflict.* 2 vols. Boston.

———. 1901, 1902. *The conspiracy of Pontiac and the Indian war after the conquest of Canada.* 2 vols. Boston.

Richards, Cara B. 1957. Matriarchy or mistake: The role of Iroquois women through time. In *Cultural stability and cultural change,* 36–45. American Ethnological Society.

Richter, Daniel K. 1992. *The ordeal of the longhouse: The peoples of the Iroquois League in the era of European colonization.* Chapel Hill, NC.

Shimony, Annemarie A. 1994. *Conservatism among the Iroquois at the Six Nations Reserve.* Syracuse, NY. (First published in 1961.)

Snow, Dean R. 1996. *The Iroquois.* Cambridge, MA.

Tekawennake. 2002–2004. (Canadian Iroquois newspaper).

Thwaites, Reuben G. 1898. *Travels and explorations of the Jesuit missionaries in New France.* Vol. 13. Cleveland, OH.

Trigger, Bruce G., ed. 1978. *Northeast.* Vol. 15, *Handbook of North American Indians.* Washington, DC.

Turtle Island News. 2002–2004. (Canadian Iroquois newspaper).

Wallace, Anthony F. C. 1951. *Some psychological determinants of culture change in an Iroquoian community.* Bureau of American Ethnology Bulletin no. 149, 55–76.

———. 1958. Dreams and the wishes of the soul: A type of psychoanalytic theory among the seventeenth century Iroquois. *American Anthropologist* n.s. 60:234–48.

———. 1970. *Death and rebirth of the Seneca.* New York.

Weaver, Sally M. 1972. *Medicine and politics among the Grand River Iroquois.* National Museum of Man Publications in Ethnology, no. 4.

Wilson, Edmund. 1960. *Apologies to the Iroquois.* (Includes a reprinting of "The Mohawks in High Steel," by Joseph Mitchell.) New York.

13 The Eastern Cherokee: Farmers of the Southeast

*My companions, men of renown, in council, who now sleep
in the dust, spoke the same language [antiremoval] and I
now stand on the verge of the grave to bear witness to their
love of country. My sun of existence is fast approaching to
its setting and my aged bones will soon be laid in the bosom
of this earth we have received from our fathers who had it
from the Great Being above. When I sleep in forgetfulness,
I hope my bones will not be deserted by you.*

Woman Killer, a man reportedly over eighty years of age in
1830, arguing against selling Cherokee land at the time of their
pending removal from North Carolina (Strickland 1977, 379)

HISTORICALLY IN THE Southeast culture area, the dominant tribes were the Cherokee, Chickasaw, Choctaw, and Creek. Along with the Seminole, who emerged in historic times, these people collectively are identified as the Five Civilized Tribes. The Cherokee occupied the largest area, whereas the Creek initially dominated in the political sphere. Choctaw and Chickasaw influence declined rather rapidly as Euro-Americans became established in the region. Each tribe held land coveted by white settlers. The Indian Removal Act of 1830 led to most of these Indians being resettled in Indian Territory (Oklahoma). The illegal seizure of their homelands and private property, accompanied by calculated cruelties, characterized the years of their displacement. Some Cherokee, however, hid in the Great Smokey Mountains and avoided removal. This chapter first concerns Cherokee life before removal and then concentrates on those who remained in North Carolina. They represent the largest aboriginal tribe that continues to live in their southeast homeland. Interestingly, the present-day Eastern Cherokee domain is *not* a reservation in the usual sense because the land was purchased for them after the removal act. The position of women in Cherokee life is emphasized. Their dominance as artifact makers and as the providers of most food is notable in combination. Women likewise play a dominant role in religious life and an influential one in political life. These aspects of Cherokee culture early in their history are vividly presented by Theda Perdue (1998).

People, Population, and Language

The archaeological record suggests that the ancestors of the Cherokee (CHER-uh-kee) occupied the Southeast culture area for thousands of years. At the time of historic contact, they may have numbered 22,000. Cherokee is a corruption of Tsalagi, the Choctaw–French term for the Cherokee, which they adopted for themselves. Originally they called themselves "the principal people," and they clustered largely in western North Carolina (see Figure 13-1). Their language belongs to the Iroquoian family, and their nearest linguistic relatives are the Iroquois. They occupied four regional groups separated by rugged terrain, which led to a certain degree of isolation that is reflected in dialectic differences. The Eastern Band of Cherokee Indians numbered about 13,300 in 2003, and they owned about 57,000 acres in North Carolina. (The Cherokee population primarily in Oklahoma was almost 282,000.)

Early Historic Life

The Cherokee were not described in reasonable detail until the mid-1700s, and since their ties with traders and other whites were well established by then, an aboriginal baseline ethnography was never assembled. The description that follows therefore focuses on their early historic life.

ORIGIN MYTH The earth once was a great island of water floating on a sea of water. In primeval times animals existed above the sky vault, which

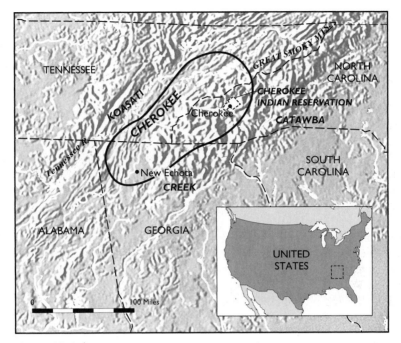

Figure 13-1 | Aboriginal range of the Eastern Cherokee Indians.

became crowded, and they wondered what was beneath the water. Water Beetle volunteered to explore the water, and after diving to the bottom it surfaced with soft mud. As the mud expanded it became the earth and was suspended to the sky and above it with four cords, one in each cardinal direction. Because the earth was soft, various birds were sent to find somewhere to land. Each failed until Great Buzzard flew low over the earth. As he tired his wings struck the earth over what would become Cherokee country, and many valleys and mountains were created. After the earth dried, animals came down from above into darkness, which led to the sun's creation.

The arrival of animals and plants on earth was followed by a human brother and sister. The brother struck his sister with a fish and told her to reproduce, and an offspring was born in seven days. She reproduced in this manner time and again until the number of people grew alarming. Then it was deemed that a fertile woman should bear one offspring a year, and this pattern continues. When the earth ages and wears out, the suspension cords holding it up will break and the earth will sink into the sea.

CLOTHING AND APPEARANCE   As was true for other Indians in the Southeast, the Cherokee made most clothing of deerskins sewn with sinew thread. A man's basic garment was a breechclout, and women wore knee-length skirts. Their moccasins were of deerskin, and they wore bison-skin robes during cold

Figure 13-2 | Three Cherokee men during a visit to England in 1762. (By permission of the British Library.)

weather. (In early historic times bison were scattered throughout most of the United States and from Mexico into Canada.) Capes for summer wear had feathers attached to a fiber base. Buckskin shirts and cloth boots were added in early historic times. The most distinctive personal adornment was the ear decoration of males. A section of the outer border of each ear was cut free, stretched, and wound with wire to hold it in an expanded arc (see Figure 13-2). This aboriginal practice declined in popularity when silver jewelry became popular in the late 1700s. Wealthy persons wore collarlike bands of clamshell beads around their necks. Youthful warriors were tattooed by pricking the skin with a needle and rubbing bluish coloring in the openings. Designs of animals, flowers, and geometric forms were tattooed on the chest or muscular parts of the body. All the hair was plucked from a man's head except for a scalp lock at the back; it was decorated with beads or feathers. Women apparently drew their hair back into a very long bundle held with ribbons.

SETTLEMENTS AND MANUFACTURES In reasonably early historic times, the Cherokee lived in scattered settlements because relatively level plots of ground suitable for cultivation were scarce. They built communities near streams and rivers to have access to fish and to game that was attracted to water and also for religious reasons. A large settlement might encompass 450 acres, but a typical community covered a much smaller area. Matrilineal families owned dwellings, storage facilities, and a nearby menstrual hut. The rectangular summer house had pole framing, a gabled bark-covered roof, and walls of poles interwoven with branches and covered with mud. A large winter house was constructed much the same way. Within both types were platforms along the walls, and heat and light were provided by firewood in fireplaces; neither type had windows or a chimney. The most imposing structure was the council house used for religious, social, and political purposes; some of these buildings accommodated five hundred people. A council house was seven-sided, framed with logs, and had a roof supported by concentric circles of interior posts. The entire structure was covered with earth except for a narrow doorway and a smokehole at the center of the roof. Inside were benches and a central fireplace.

Women were the primary artifact makers. They possessed diverse craft skills combined with patience and hard work. Their superior glazed pottery included cooking pots, bowls, dishes, and food-storage vessels. It required highly technical skills and hours on end to produce baskets woven from swamp cane, food and garment containers, sieves, household mats, and additional items. Deerskins and gourds fashioned into receptacles held water, honey, or bear oil. The women appear to have made pipes from soapstone, and they were avid smokers. Women supplied their households with water and firewood. These obligations, combined with food preparation and caring for children, meant that they typically worked hard most of the year.

The physical labor of women in artifact production had no realistic counterpart among men. Men made large dugout boats, the major conveyance, from logs as long as forty feet. To hollow a log, they burned one side and chipped away the charred wood. These boats were some two feet wide, straight-sided, and flat-bottomed, and they could carry as many as twenty people. Wood-framed canoes covered with bark had far less importance. Men likewise fashioned their weapons for the hunt and warfare—bows and arrows, spears, and clubs.

SUBSISTENCE ACTIVITIES Women planted, tended, and harvested crops, the primary staples. Each matrilineal household had a field at the edge of a settlement. Men cleared and burned small trees and brush; they girdled large trees to kill them as a later source of firewood. Women planted three varieties of maize in small hills, and among the hills sowed bean, gourd, and squash seeds. The bean vines grew up the maize stalks, and the leaves of the gourds and squash helped retain moisture in the soil. Women hoed the most troublesome weeds, and throughout the growing season elderly women sat atop platforms in the fields to scare off predators, such as crows and raccoons. In addition, women gathered a wide variety of wild edibles, including berries, leaves, and seeds. Honey locust tree and sugar maple sap were processed as sweeteners.

While women farmed in the summer, men at a settlement gambled and lounged before traveling widely as warriors to confront enemies. Men hunted with self bows and reed arrows tipped with bone or fish-scale points. The most important big game included white-tailed deer and black bear, and bison and elk were available in some sectors. The most important game bird was wild turkey, hunted for its meat and, equally important, its feathers. They harvested small game and small birds with darts shot from blowguns, a widely prevailing weapon in the Southeast that probably was introduced from Mexico or the Antilles. Men fished with hooks, leisters, and traps, and they set traps for game and birds. The only aboriginal domestic animal was the dog, but Europeans introduced chickens, hogs, horses, and new crops such as potatoes and watermelons.

GENDER IDENTITY   Early Western observers, meaning European men, customarily wrote that Cherokee men were lazy and that servile women slaved for them. The two previous sections of this chapter may suggest that women were subservient, but clearly this was not the case. Largely unbiased observers noted that women were willing and cheerful workers who had an advantageous position because they controlled the fruits of their labor, especially crops, for general welfare. In mythology and in fact, women played a critical role that balanced that of men. The word "balance" was, and in part remains, central to gender relations. The division of labor was theoretically rigid, but in actuality men and women consistently aided one another. Men, irrespective of their social standing, helped clear the fields that women planted. Women turned to medicine men to produce rain for crops in time of droughts. Men depended on the women who accompanied them on extended hunting trips and raids to fulfill their gender roles. Religion and social relations focused in large degree on the harvest of maize, especially the Green Corn Ceremony, in which women as the providers played a central role, as is discussed later. No remotely comparable ceremonial recognition was accorded the contributions of men for their skills as hunters and fishermen.

DESCENT, KINSHIP, AND MARRIAGE   Descent was traced through females (matrilineal), and a person was prohibited from marrying a member of his or her own matriclan (clan exogamy) or father's clan. A man's preferred mate was from his father's father's or mother's father's clan. After a man married and moved to another settlement (matrilocal residence), he still was regarded as a member of the clan of his birth. The members of a localized clan segment made certain that a spouse was mourned properly and that men fulfilled familial obligations. Violations led to public whippings by the women of the clan involved. A widow was expected to marry her deceased husband's brother (levirate), and a widower was supposed to take his deceased wife's sister as a spouse (sororate).

The aboriginal Cherokee kinship terminology reportedly was of the Crow system, meaning that the cousin terms were of the Crow type and descent was matrilineal. In this cousin terminology, a father's sister's daughter and mother's

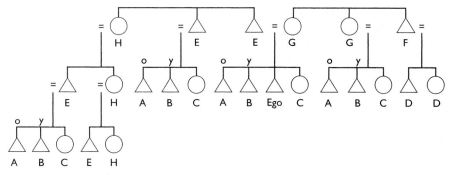

Figure 13-3 | The early historic Cherokee system of kinship terminology.

brother's daughter were termed differently from each other and from sisters or parallel cousins (mother's sister's and father's brother's daughters). However, a father's sister's daughter was classed with father's sister. With respect to the words for aunts, the term for mother and mother's sister were the same, but a separate term existed for father's sister (bifurcate merging parental generation terminology). The kinship terms made it possible to distinguish precisely the four matrilineages that were most important to an individual: those of mother, father, mother's father, and father's father (see Figure 13-3).

SOCIAL DIMENSIONS Eighteenth-century Cherokee households usually consisted of a number of nuclear families related through females (matrilineal extended family). Ideally, the household included an elderly couple, their daughters, the daughters' husbands, unmarried males born into the household, and the daughters' daughters. The mutual obligations of household members and their relationship with the members of other such units were defined with precision. A father taught his son to hunt, but a mother's brother, who lived in another household, was a child's disciplinarian. An in-marrying male was respectful toward his in-laws but was expected to joke with his wife's brothers and brothers-in-law; through the jokes of others, one became aware of erring ways. In-marrying males retained close ties with their natal households and the clans of their birth, yet a household's members formed the most closely cooperating economic unit in the society.

In social and political terms, matrilineages were less important than matriclans. Members of the same clan in a band acted collectively. Apparently seven named clans (Bird, Blue Paint, Deer, Red Paint, Twister-Long Hair, Wild Potato, and Wolf) were represented in each village, and members of a clan cooperated closely at the village level. The seven clans in a settlement allotted farmlands to member households and regulated marriage. Another important obligation of a clan was to settle disputes with the members of another clan. The most serious crime was murder. If someone killed a person in another clan, all local members of the murderer's clan were held responsible, and all males of the dead person's clan were obligated to seek revenge. Preferably the offender himself was killed in revenge, although one of his clan mates might be substituted.

In the drift of history, early and contemporary sources suggest basic continuity in the ways that individuals deal with one another. Thus the information in this paragraph is in the present tense. I begin with inappropriate behavior. Included is any form of overt and direct aggression or hostility in face-to-face contacts. Parsimony with one's property, time, and especially food are singularly undesirable. Particularly anathema are assertive and boastful persons. The reactions to undesirable behavior are powerful weapons—gossip, withdrawal, and turning to witchcraft are prime examples. In general, misfortune, such as bad luck, is anticipated for aggressive persons. The opposites of all these traits are encapsulated in the anthropological label for Cherokee behavior, the Harmony Ethic. In essence, when dealing with others a good person is friendly but not innocent in being generous, helpful, and understanding. Quite obviously, to coerce others has no place in the Harmony Ethic.

Among the Cherokee and other Indians in the Southeast, stickball, the generic game from which lacrosse is derived, was a popular sport (see also Chapter 12). Every player carried a stick that had a small loop and a pocket attached at the end. The object of the game was to carry a small ball across the goal of the opposite team. The ball could be carried in one hand, in the mouth, or in the mesh pocket of the stick. Any means, including the use of the stick, could be employed to obtain the ball; injuries, both purposeful and unintended, were difficult to prevent. They quite reasonably called the game "the little brother of war." Stickball games were social events but included many ceremonial aspects. For example, a man was not to have sexual intercourse with his wife for at least seven days before participating in a game, and if she was pregnant, he could not play. Several shamans were active for each side, and a rite was performed at running water. On the night before the game a dance was held, magic was invoked against opponents, and other rituals took place. During a game itself, each side tried to disable the best players on the other team.

POLITICAL LIFE Early in their history, Cherokee political life was well organized, although it was localized and did not unite the tribe as a whole. This political organization changed as it was affected by both British influences and inclusion of warriors.

Early Organization A large village or a number of small ones formed a political aggregate, or band, of from 350 to 600 persons. As a group approached the larger number, the tendency was for a portion to separate and organize as a new unit. In the early 1700s some sixty settlements were represented by about thirty-five bands. Each band was politically autonomous. Control was in the hands of a council of elders, both female and male, the heads of clans, and representatives of two organizations, called the Whites and Reds, that stood in opposition to one another. The Whites symbolized peace, and members were traditionally old, passive, and mild-mannered. White chiefs achieved their goals through diplomacy and reached decisions by consensus. The Reds, by contrast, symbolized war; members were expected to be young, active, and impetuous. Reds generally were young males who had married into a village and thus occupied a marginal position within the social system. As Reds aged, they became associated with the Whites and gradually found themselves integrated into community life.

Each fall, after the Harvest Ceremony and before rekindling a sacred fire, a white flag flew over the council house to indicate that the community was in control of the Whites. At an assembly, seating arrangements were by age, gender, and clan. Deliberations were guided by a general council composed of elderly men, called Beloved Men, and by priests. There was also an inner council of seven Beloved Men, one from each clan. Topics for discussion typically included relations with other Indians and non-Indians, matters of war and peace, and trade. With the priests as arbitrators, any question put before a council was stated and restated until a consensus was achieved. Apparently the members of each clan attempted to reach a unified position, but if it became clear that a clan could not support an emerging consensus, they withdrew to avoid open conflict.

A council served one large settlement or a cluster of smaller communities, but no larger political structure united the bands or the tribe. Each village was an independent political entity that sought to live in harmonious relations with other such units. Fred Gearing (1962, 83) has reasoned that prior to 1730 the Cherokee comprised a "jural community," meaning that they were united by cultural and social ties. The members of one village might cooperate with those in another, and they appear never to have fought each other, although they were often at war with adjacent tribes. Some villages were more important than others because of their strategic location, the learning of their priests, or the importance of a secular leader, but no village appears to have been dominant for very long. Conflict between Cherokee villages most likely developed if a man killed someone from another village. This was a matter to be resolved by the members of the clans involved, and because each clan was represented by fictive brothers in every other village, these ties, and the ideals of proper behavior in times of disputes, were enough to avert open conflict.

British Influences   In 1730 the village council functioned as it had in the past, but British colonial administrators, because the Cherokee spoke a common language, began to view them as a single political unit rather than an aggregate of independent villages. Thus, when a raiding party attacked a white frontier settlement, all of the Cherokee were held responsible. To avoid reprisals, a tribal government began to form. The first person with political authority beyond the village level was Moytoy, an Overhill Cherokee, who presumably was a war chief. He was crowned "Emperor" of the Cherokee in 1730 by the British. The Overhill settlements had long been influential, and they became more important as the military effectiveness of the Chickasaw declined.

This placed the Overhill communities on the French frontier and led to their strategic importance to the British and Cherokee alike. The influence of Moytoy was not acknowledged among all Cherokee, but his political office was widely recognized as legitimate. A smallpox epidemic in 1738–1739 seems to have killed about half of the people, which led to greater power shifting to political leaders. With the death of Moytoy in 1741, his son Amouskositte became the leader. Presumably, it was he who threatened to destroy a Cherokee village and kill all the inhabitants if they did not kill a man who had murdered a trader. The pressure to take action against the murderer had come originally from the governor of South Carolina, who threatened to cut off trade to the Cherokee. Without arms and ammunition they would have been unable to defend themselves against the French and their Indian allies. Thus the actions of any one village began to be subordinated to broader interests.

In this and other episodes, particular individuals emerged as spokesmen for the Cherokee, but only in dealing with alien powers. By 1753 a priest state was beginning to emerge, roughly paralleling the village-level organization. The capital settlement was the residence of the most notable leader and the chief priest. Other leaders from representative villages met there to deliberate. The major problem was how to prevent warriors from launching raids. The tribal council could punish raiders after the fact but had no institutionalized network to prevent raids. The inability of Amouskositte's successor to curb raids against frontier settlements led to a war with the English from 1759 to 1761. The destruction of numerous villages forced the Cherokee to sue for peace. Raids continued to be a problem, however, and as white settlers boldly began farming Cherokee land, retaliatory raids increased.

Influence of Warriors   By 1768 the Cherokee had decided to include outstanding warriors among the decision makers at the tribal council meetings. Heretofore warriors had played an integral part in council decisions only during preparations for conflict and when actually at war. Although the tribal council in theory remained opposed to reprisal raids, integrating the warriors into the tribal political organization meant that any activities they undertook would be legitimate. The American Revolution and the opening of Kentucky to white settlers split the Cherokee into two factions. Most young warriors sided with the British and were armed by them; the old men only sought peace. Decades of raids by warriors such as Dragging Canoe led American military forces to destroy nearly all Cherokee settlements, but the people were not destroyed. When their villages were burned, they fled to the mountains, and after the conflict they returned to reestablish farming communities. Although they repeatedly were forced to give up land, in 1800 they still held title to about forty-three thousand square miles, about half of it in Tennessee and the remainder in adjacent sectors of Alabama, Georgia, and North Carolina.

WARFARE   Among the aboriginal population, armed conflict meant primarily raids against enemies who had killed a Cherokee. The purpose was to

Figure 13-4 | Pencil drawings of Cherokee men by George Catlin. (Collection of The New-York Historical Society, neg. no. 33072.)

avenge a death so that the person's soul could finally be at ease. A raiding party typically included a few warriors related to the deceased who set out to kill or capture one or more persons of the tribe responsible for the death. By the early 1700s much of Cherokee energy focused on raids and war as a direct and indirect result of white contact. When a council decided to make war, a red flag was raised over the council house, and the Reds began their preparations. Rituals by priests, fasting and dances by warriors, narrations of heroic deeds, and ritual bathing were all involved. An oration by the war speaker preceded the formal departure of a war party. When venturing forth, the warriors were elaborately painted red and black. The war club, with a projection at one end, was either hand-held or thrown. Warriors also used bows and arrows and spears when fighting. In early historic times, the metal tomahawk of European manufacture was popular, but these and earlier weapons were replaced by imported firearms and knives as they became available (see Figure 13-4).

Native American women typically did not fight tribal enemies, although exceptions are reported, especially in the Southeast culture area. Among the Cherokee, women and warfare had a well-established institutional basis. As noted earlier, obligations based on gender had become comparatively rigid;

a clear exception was women and warfare. War parties could include women to perform camp chores, such as hauling water and preparing food. Yet a relatively small but distinct number fought in the manner of men and became War Women. Some ethnographic sources use this term as an alternative to Beloved Women, a good indicator that among females a War Woman occupied a unique position. If one were captured by an enemy and survived to return home, she underwent the same purification rituals as a man under like circumstances.

Relatively little is known about War Women, with the partial exception of Nan-ye-hi (Nancy Ward, d. 1822). In 1750, during a Cherokee–Creek conflict, she had accompanied her husband, and when he was killed, she fought with his gun. Her subsequent achievements as a warrior are poorly known. It is clear, however, that she achieved prominence as a diplomat, evidenced by an oration she gave during negotiations with a U.S. treaty commission in 1785.

This is a fitting context in which to report why the status of War Women declined rapidly in the early 1700s. As the Cherokee became increasingly dependent on the British for trade goods, especially guns and ammunition, they became British allies against the French and enemy Indians. One result was an expanding importance of European methods of warfare. The old pattern, for a few Cherokee warriors to seek revenge for the death of one of their number, declined. European warfare did not include females as fighters, and, whenever possible, battles dominated over raids, with obvious implications for War Women. Equally important, in European warfare men were killed, and women and children became captives.

RELIGION The power of blood, deeply ingrained in their belief system, found a major focus in female physiology: menstruation, childbirth, and menopause. Women were isolated during their periods, and restrictions and taboos accompanied pregnancy and childbirth. Unlike the widely held belief in Western societies, women were not considered unclean during menstruation; quite to the contrary, they possessed extraordinary qualities. In one myth, a stone-skinned cannibal approached a settlement. As he came nearer, a medicine man had menstruating women stand at intervals along the path. The cannibal became weaker and weaker. As he passed the last woman he collapsed and was killed. In this general context, menstrual blood was regarded as an unborn offspring, and with childbirth a new generation arose. In sum, the fertility of women was pivotal in life itself, embodying a combination of danger and power.

By the 1700s, as religious life began to be recorded in reasonable detail, the Green Corn Ceremony dominated. It was intimately associated with women, the maize harvest, and rebirth of the Cherokee as a people for the coming year. Preparations began in late September with feasting, extinguishing household fires, cleaning homes, and preparing the square ground (plaza) where nonconforming men could not enter. Warriors and Beloved Women fasted for a short period, and then these women prepared a sacred emetic for warriors to consume and thereby purge themselves of physical and spiritual pollution. Presentation of the new maize crop by Beloved Women was the unifying ritual. A priest received the crop, kindled a new fire symbolic of renewal, and placed maize in the flames for a feast. People confessed their transgressions since the last Green Corn Ceremony, such as unpaid debts, grudges, and adultery, which were forgiven by the onlookers. The square ground then became the center for feasting and dancing. Lastly, people painted their bodies with white clay, a symbol of peace and well-being, and ritually bathed in a river. An explicit goal was to begin life anew and thereby sustain the Harmony Ethic.

As European contacts intensified in the 1750s, traditional ceremonies were consolidated or abandoned. Following the American Revolution, families tended to occupy scattered homesteads, as towns no longer provided adequate defense. As a result of this and other conditions, clan unity diminished, along with a cohesive identity as Cherokee that previously was reinforced in collective rituals and ceremonies. The Green Corn Ceremony survived for a time, but without the unifying qualities of old.

Early History

The expedition led by Hernando de Soto may have passed through a Cherokee community in 1540, but not until the late 1600s were white intrusions relatively common. Firearms and other trade goods became available about 1700, and shortly thereafter traders settled among them. It was not long before the Cherokee were embroiled in hostilities with white colonists from the eastern seaboard, and old rivalries with other Indians intensified. In a series of conflicts with English colonists in 1759–1761, many settlements were destroyed, and the Cherokee were defeated. Soon thereafter intrusions by white settlers became increasingly common, and the Cherokee were forced to give up large sectors of land. In the American Revolution, they understandably fought on the side of the British because white settlers posed the greater threat. An alliance with the British, however, led to the repeated destruction of their settlements. When peace was made, some Cherokee decided to settle west of the Mississippi River because they felt that whites would never be satisfied in their desire for more land. Most Cherokee remained, however, and became prosperous farmers, even organizing a government modeled after that of the United States. Yet pressures by whites for land never ceased.

When George Washington initiated a policy of Indian assimilation in 1789, he expected the process to be completed within fifty years for all Indians east of the Mississippi River. Assimilation was to be achieved by teaching English to Indians, introducing the farming methods of whites, and imposing the concept of private land ownership. In 1794 the Cherokee signed a treaty of peace with white Americans. This was meant to end the bitter conflict that for twenty years had destroyed the aboriginal basis of Cherokee culture and had sapped the energies of the surviving Indians. Many of them concluded that the selective adoption of white ways was not only desirable but also essential for survival. However, the process of Indian assimilation was hampered by the anti-Indian attitude of many whites along the frontier.

Missionaries were to play a key role in Christianizing and "civilizing" the Cherokee. The first series of Protestant missionaries arrived among them in 1799. As the historian William G. McLoughlin (1984) noted in his seminal study of early missionary activities among the Cherokee, their resistance to becoming Christian was far greater than the missionaries had anticipated. Before long these Indians tried to revive their religion of old, but with little success. In the early 1800s the Cherokee were still adopting white ways on a selective basis and at their own pace, but the Jacksonian era that began in 1828 brought changes in federal policies toward Indians, and it became increasingly difficult to sustain traditional cultural ways.

SLAVERY   Before sustained contacts with Europeans, the hereditary type of slavery was unknown among these people, but the institution shared significant parallels with the treatment of prisoners from raids and warfare. Captive men most often were tortured to death by Cherokee women, whereas captive women and children faced different fates. They could either become members of a family by forced adoption and later be accepted into the tribe by a governing council, or they became quasi-slaves. Expanding contacts with the customs of British traders, settlers, and colonial administrators led to Indian adoptions of both whites and blacks captured in raids. In sociopolitical context these individuals became slaves, meaning that they had hereditary subordinate status in Cherokee society. Thus the aboriginal treatment of prisoners led to the subsequent adaptation of slavery, especially of blacks. The Cherokee used their black captives also to purchase firearms and ammunition, especially from the British. Some Cherokee, in turn, became enslaved by whites and learned European farming methods during their captivity. Following their escape or repatriation by treaty, they were able to introduce new agricultural practices and use their own slaves more effectively. Soon the Cherokee were called "Slave Catchers" as a result of their success in capturing slaves for sale or to work on their farms. Because Cherokee women were the primary cultivators of crops, they fully supported black slavery to lighten their labors. Men, now freed from agricultural involvements, also valued slaves, as they were now able to devote more time to hunting, warfare, trapping furbearers for trade, and to a new economic venture, capturing more blacks, who had expanding economic value.

When the American Revolution began in 1775, many supporters of the British colonial government (Tories) settled, with their slaves, among sympathetic Cherokee. They allied with the Indians in raiding rebel farms, killing and scalping men, women, and children, and seizing black slaves. The American rebels in turn sent an army into Cherokee country to destroy their towns and either kill the slaves or capture them for sale. The traditional Cherokee farms were on lands held in common by matrilineal family groups. As their slave population grew, the land was divided into individual farms that depended heavily on black slaves for success. By the early 1800s there was no Indian op-position to the enslavement of blacks or persons of mixed genetic heritage. When formal hostilities between the Cherokee and the U.S. ended by treaty, slaves and other properties seized by these Indians were to be restored to the federal government, but this provision was not broadly honored. By this time Cherokee farms had become widely scattered, and whenever feasible they had adopted the plantation economy of southern whites. Slaves in particular be-came symbols of wealth. Blacks might be freed by their Indian owners under special conditions, or they might be adopted into the tribe as "black Indians." By the late 1820s the Cherokee owned about thirteen hundred black slaves. When the Civil War erupted, most Cherokee supported the Confederacy, be-cause of both their location and their similar economic life.

NEW GOVERNMENT The Cherokee Nation founded in 1827 was modeled after the government of the United States, with executive, judicial, and legisla-tive branches. A capital with buildings in the Euro-American architectural style was constructed at New Echota, Georgia, in 1825. Shortly before the nation was founded, Sequoya (George Gist), who was of Cherokee and white ancestry, presented to the leaders a proposal for writing their language. In 1809 Sequoya had become impressed with the importance of writing, and he had originated a system whereby symbols represented syllables in the Cherokee language (see Figure 13-5). After the syllabary was adopted in 1821, the vast majority of the

Figure 13-5 | Sequoya (circa 1760–1843) originated the Cherokee syllabary adopted by the Cherokee Nation in 1821. (Corbis.)

Cherokee soon became literate. The syllabary served to preserve traditions by allowing the Cherokee to transcribe their sacred formulas and to record their own history. A print shop was established at New Echota, and a bilingual newspaper appeared in 1828. By then they were numbered among the Civilized Tribes. Their population was about 13,500, in addition to nearly 150 white men who had married Cherokee women and about 75 white women who had Cherokee husbands.

THE TRAIL OF TEARS Of all the Indian policies enacted by the United States, none was more heartless than "removal." In 1830 the U.S. Congress passed the Indian Removal Act, which provided for the relocation of all Indians in the southeastern states and the Ohio River drainage to Indian Territory (Oklahoma). The act was strongly supported by President Andrew Jackson, whose goal, at least in part, was to prevent the inevitable destruction of these Indians at the hands of whites. Cherokee resistance was strong but largely unsuccessful. They had adopted "civilized" ways, which was disconcerting to politicians in Georgia who yearned to bring their productive lands under state control. In 1829 the Georgia legislature passed a law making much of the Cherokee Nation land into state holdings. Under terms of the law, all previous federal legislation and regulations were to be null and void. In addition, Indians were prohibited from testifying in court cases involving whites, and prohibitions were established against interference with removal plans. About this time, gold was discovered on Cherokee holdings, and the governor declared that all gold-bearing lands belonged to the state. The actions of the Georgia legislature led to the famous *Worcester v. Georgia* case, which reached the Supreme Court in 1831. The court judgment, under Chief Justice John Marshall, was that the federal government, not the state of Georgia, was responsible for the Cherokee. Illegal seizures of land and other property by whites, conflicting policies of the Indian leaders, intrigue by unscrupulous whites and Indians, and harassment by state representatives finally led to the 1835 Treaty of New Echota and Cherokee removal.

Before the Cherokee treaty leading to their "legal" removal, gross injustices were perpetrated by citizens and representatives of the state of Georgia. Indians were forced from their lands at bayonet point, they were removed in chains without due legal process, they were sold intoxicants in violation of federal regulations, and their movable property was often stolen with impunity. A state law prohibiting a Cherokee from employing a white was used as a pretext for seizing plantations; these then were distributed to whites by lottery. The Cherokee were allowed by law to transfer land only to the state. When some families finally were forced to leave Georgia, much of the property they carried with them was seized and their money extorted. Food and shelter during the forced migration often were inadequate or nonexistent, and the weakened emigrants were struck by cholera, along with other diseases. Yet, by 1838 when all of these people were supposed to be gone, only two thousand had been deported; the other fifteen thousand still believed that somehow they would not be driven from their homeland. Such was not the case. About seven thousand soldiers under General Winfield Scott moved against the Cherokee, who had previously been disarmed. Scott ordered that within a month's time every Cherokee must be moving westward. Soldiers went from house to house, forcing people to leave at once. Often the Indians were not allowed to take anything with them, and they were impounded in stockades until they could be shipped west. Their journey to Oklahoma is known to the Cherokee as the Trail of Tears; about four thousand people died as a direct result of their forced removal. This episode in American Indian history is the saddest of the sad.

Later History: The Eastern Band of Cherokee

During the forced removal by the federal government, at least one thousand conservative Cherokee successfully hid in the mountains. Nonetheless, well into the 1840s federal and state officials encouraged them to move west to Indian Territory; small numbers relocated there at that time and later. The most important white advocate for the Eastern Cherokee was William H. Thomas, a businessman, attorney, and the adopted son of a chief. He became a state legislator and helped persuade government officials to permit the remnant population to remain in the region. Yet his financial reverses and mental instability produced greater periodic turmoil. The local Cherokee could not legally own land, which was bought for them by Thomas and others. This land came to be known as the Qualla Indian Boundary. The State of North Carolina recognized the Cherokee as legal residents in 1866, and soon thereafter federal recognition was achieved. Following lengthy and complex legal battles, the title to Qualla Boundary land, some seventy-three thousand acres, was granted to the Eastern Cherokee collectively in 1874. They incorporated as the Eastern Band of Cherokee in 1889 and were acknowledged by the state. With revisions, this incorporation document remains a primary basis for their government. As their legal status evolved, it became a curious and confusing combination of state and federal jurisdictions. Band members voted and paid taxes to the state and were likewise considered wards of the federal government. A major problem was state land taxes; their inability to pay these led to the sale of some holdings. The only major band resource, timber, was harvested to pay some tax debts.

The 1887 passage of the Dawes Act and separate efforts to allot Oklahoma Indian lands led to rumors that Eastern Cherokee land was to be allotted. A long-standing complaint, and one that would recur, was that some whites used devious means to become tribal members in the hope of obtaining land. Some whites reportedly became "five-dollar Indians" by paying this amount as a bribe to be entered on the roll. The enrollment of these whites, in addition to the children of white–Indian marriages, has, over the years, meant that there are a significant number of "white Indians."

Figure 13-6 | A North Carolina Cherokee home in 1888. (Courtesy of the Smithsonian Institution, National Anthropological Archives, neg. no. 1000-B.)

A concerted effort by the federal government to further "civilize" these people introduced schools that were managed by Quaker missionaries until 1893. The Quakers succeeded in upsetting the pattern of Indian life, but not nearly as much as did their educational successors in the BIA. The pattern of formal education under the BIA was for a child to attend a day school through the fourth grade and then attend a local boarding school through the ninth grade; his or her education was completed at a distant boarding school such as the one for Indians in Carlisle, Pennsylvania. The goal of compulsory education helped destroy traditional Indian life; children were punished for speaking Cherokee, chained to their beds if they repeatedly ran away, and forced to learn white ways.

In the late 1800s a new source of income emerged as timber companies bought large tracts of land to harvest hardwoods. Mill towns and railroads penetrated sectors to transport and process logs. Cherokee men found seasonal employment in logging and with railroad companies for relatively short-term economic gain. The old forests were cleared of timber by the 1930s, and the related jobs disappeared.

By the early 1900s, following years of trauma and uncertainty, the lives of Qualla Boundary residents became more stable (see Figure 13-6). The *gadugi,* a free labor company, became a prominent cooperative enterprise and a source of pride. It was represented in most communities as a dozen or so men who formed a company to help one another with farming and other activities; they could likewise borrow money from the treasury. As they began hiring themselves out to whites around 1910, however, these companies became taxable

Figure 13-7 | Booger Dance mask. (Courtesy of Museum of the Cherokee Indian.)

by the state, and they began to disappear. Subsistence farming remained the basis of the economy, but by the late 1920s stock-fencing laws and a chestnut blight led to a decline in hog production, a significant source of meat. The standard of living decreased at a time when the population was growing. An eventual positive economic factor was an expansion of the local road network to provide access to wage labor jobs, although jobs were few, and the living standard declined.

Continuity with the past was provided by a wide variety of dances associated with ceremonies. Prominent among these was the Booger Dance. The word *booger* has the same root in English as the word *bogy,* meaning goblin. In its Cherokee meaning it approximated the concept of ghost and was represented on dance masks as caricatures of foreigners (see Figure 13-7). It appears as though the dance was originally performed to induce men to join war parties and to dilute the harmful spirits of foreigners. By the 1930s, the dance had lost its religious associations and portrayed whites and blacks. Performers, usually men, danced in a circle, frightened children, and joked with adults in the audience who stood in a proper joking relationship.

In retrospect, *the* most dramatic change in Eastern Cherokee life since the Trail of Tears began in the 1920s and continues relentlessly into the present. It is tourism. It began in 1914 with the annual Cherokee Indian Fair (now the

Cherokee Fall Festival) attended by the local population. Then as the system of regional roads improved in the late 1920s, the fair attracted expanding numbers of tourists. Of paramount importance, in 1926 the federal government established the nearby Great Smoky Mountains National Park. Land for the park was transferred to the federal government from the states of Tennessee and North Carolina in 1934, and the park was dedicated in 1940. Before the formal dedication, tourists visited the park, and their number increased dramatically as a system of paved roads was developed following World War II.

The most important Cherokee-crafted items for sale were baskets produced by women, and this remains true into the present. It cannot be overemphasized that by the late 1800s, baskets provided the most reliable income source for innumerable families, especially during economically stressful times, such as when the timber industry declined. The basketry tradition slowly changed in response to the market, including widely available nontraditional materials. Most every home included basketmakers who worked throughout the year to feed and clothe family members. Eventually the Qualla Arts and Crafts Cooperative set high standards for the baskets they marketed. In response to tourist desires, baskets are usually now richly ornamented, and the small ones sell best.

The contrast between those Cherokee who followed the essence of their traditional way of life and those who were becoming more involved with Euro-American ways became especially evident in the 1950s. The differences are highlighted in the following summary, which owes a great deal to the notable presentation by John R. Finger (1991).

Indianness had become best associated with being a full-blooded Cherokee accompanied by a configuration of cultural characteristics. The dichotomy between "full-bloods" and "white Indians" was expanding. Full-bloods "looked like Indians," and they subscribed to the Harmony Ethic. Being generous and kind to others, withdrawing from potential conflict, and minding one's own business fostered harmony. For example, the officers in a surviving gadugi worked in an egalitarian manner. Decisions reflected common consent. Because overt disagreements ran counter to their values, in a voting situation individuals ideally either cast an affirmative vote or did not vote.

People of full Cherokee heritage customarily lived in relatively remote communities. They spoke Cherokee at home but could converse in English; many children learned Cherokee as their first language. These "true Indians" represented possibly one-fourth of the population. Family heads farmed less often than they had previously and sought wage labor jobs instead. Young men sporadically worked at unskilled jobs in cities, and military service was common. Householders often lived in log cabins and had wood-burning stoves and privies; many did not have electricity; telephones were rare and automobiles few. Christian church membership represented a major involvement with the supernatural, yet shamanism continued.

The "new" Cherokee may or may not have a significant genetic heritage quantum, but among them the use of their aboriginal language was in rapid decline. Their homes usually were of frame or cinder block construction, and numerous households had electricity, television sets, telephones, and indoor plumbing. They typically lived in increasingly accessible communities in which the roads were paved and the ownership of automobiles was common.

Among both population segments, the old system of kinship terms had changed. Cherokee terms were employed in a manner compatible with English usage. In other words, the terminology that had made it possible to identify relatives based on their matrilineage and clan had been modified for bilateral application. The regulation of marriages by clans waned. Common-law marriages became a standard practice, and illegitimate offspring were not stigmatized. Notably, young adults with a minimum of Indian heritage tended to marry persons with a greater quantum to ensure the Eastern Cherokee rights for their children. Nuclear family households became more common, but a significant number of households consisted of small extended families, especially among conservative families. It may be that the larger households represented continuity with the old matrilocal residence pattern.

In the 1950s, to improve economic conditions, a concerted effort was made by the BIA and the band to attract small manufacturing plants on unused band lands. The inducements for companies included long-term leases, tax and other incentives, and the availability of an underemployed labor force. The goal was to achieve year-round employment, but many potential workers did not place an emphasis on material wealth and objected to the on-the-job discipline. The program was moderately and temporarily successful. One later major manufacturing venture by the band was the 1986 purchase of a mirror-producing company. It was not as successful as they had hoped, and in 1999 its sale was being negotiated.

Another change that had a reservation-wide impact was the program of formal education. By 1954 road access to remote communities was improving rapidly, and boarding schools were abandoned. In the 1970s the Cherokee High School opened and began to offer a comprehensive Cherokee language program. The Eastern Cherokee assumed direct control of the school system from the BIA on the Qualla Boundary, and in 1998 a language immersion program was launched for kindergarten through sixth grade.

Federal efforts, especially the "Great Society" programs of President Lyndon B. Johnson and the "War on Poverty" in the 1960s, created greater Cherokee dependency, as well as many benefits. House construction and renovation increased, day-care centers were built, and social programs expanded. The federal emphasis on tribal self-determination beginning in 1975 represented a major change in the band administration as members obtained increasing control from the BIA.

In 1972 the Eastern Cherokee met in general council for the first time since 1838. They gathered to decide whether they should accept nearly

$2 million from the federal government for *25 million acres* of land lost to whites and other injustices. They agreed to receive the settlement and divided the money among the band members. Each person, some 7200, received about $250 each. This settlement finally resolved an old grievance, and other factors were beginning to favor them as well.

| The Contemporary Scene

As previously noted, tourists are a dominant factor in Cherokee life. In 1999 the Great Smoky Mountains National Park attracted more than 10 million visitors, and the town of Cherokee in the Qualla Boundary was host to many of them. Nearly sixty motels operate there, in addition to innumerable restaurants and craft shops. Initially, the white-owned Cherokee Historical Association was largely responsible for major tourist promotions in the town, including the presentation of the outdoor drama *Unto These Hills,* which began in 1950. Some Cherokee have been distressed by the manner in which their history is presented in this play. They are depicted as having been simple savages until their Great White Father, William H. Thomas, and white missionaries saved them and their land. Other major attractions are the white-owned Museum of the Cherokee Indian and Oconaluftee Indian Village, managed by the Cherokee Historical Association. Many tourist-oriented shops have an official greeter dressed in Plains Indian attire, who for a fee can be photographed next to a totem pole, a tepee, or a tourist (see Figure 13-8).

A long-standing Cherokee objection to the tourist-oriented enterprises has been to the long-term leases given to non-Cherokee business owners. Although small numbers owned businesses, Indians usually held low-paying service jobs. A major band response was to launch Cherokee Bingo in 1982, which later became Tribal Bingo. Initially, Indian and non-Indian management of questionable integrity produced modest profits. By 1987 the band more fully controlled bingo, earned nearly $1 million that year, and paid for nearly one-third of band government expenses. The bingo operation, with the highest jackpots anywhere in the country, attracted busloads of players from cities throughout the eastern United States and eastern Canada. After expansion, the bingo hall held over one thousand players and employed about two hundred workers.

The success of bingo led to a far greater gaming operation. Harrah's Cherokee Smoky Mountains Casino opened in 1997, with an initial fifty thousand square feet of gaming space, soon expanded by ten thousand square feet. The contract gave Harrah's a management fee of *27 percent* of net revenues. The fee subsequently was reduced to 15 percent and is scheduled to be 7.5 percent in 2005, which would be one of the lowest percentages for any Indian casino. A band ordinance established that 50 percent of the net profits from gaming were to be distributed to enrolled members on a per capita basis. The remaining 50 percent supported band government and diverse social and health programs.

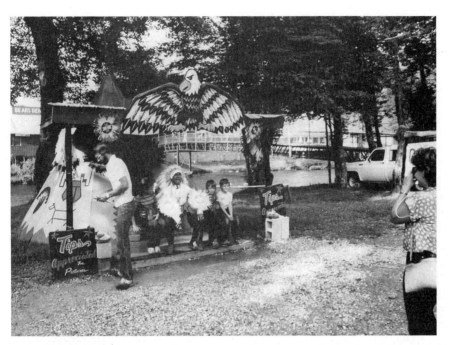

Figure 13-8 | Millions of families visit Cherokee, North Carolina, each year, and many enjoy taking a picture of their children with an Indian. This photograph was taken in 1984.

In 2003 each of the approximate 13,300 enrolled band members received $6000 from casino profits (see Figure 13-9). In 2002 the council approved a casino expansion that would include a second hotel tower. The cost was to be $115 million, and it was completed in 2004. Casino profits have been a major catalyst for positive changes in the recent past, according to the Principal Chief, Leon D. Jones, in a 2002 interview (see Figure 13-10). The tribal government has been able to greatly expand its services to the people and is now a major employer, with some 800 workers, of whom about 100 are not band members. Individual payments from casino profits have made a significant impact on families by enabling them to buy new homes and improve older ones. The band also has been able to acquire nearby land to meet expanding housing needs. Jones also stressed that for many years band members were forced to leave the Qualla Boundary to further their education and could not return to work because employment opportunities were so few. The casino operation has changed that unsatisfactory condition, enabling many educated band members to return. This has contributed to a greater workforce stability, as well as a new opportunity for personal lifestyle satisfaction.

In a different context, the band signed a compact in 2003 with the Indian Health Service for local control over the Cherokee Indian Hospital and also

Figure 13-9 | The entrance to Harrah's Cherokee Casino, Cherokee, North Carolina, in 2002.

Figure 13-10 | Leon D. Jones was elected Principal Chief of the Eastern Band of Cherokee Indians in 1999. He previously had served on band committees and was the Tribal Court Magistrate for twelve years. This is a 2002 photograph.

made a land exchange with the Great Smoky Mountain National Park, enabling the Cherokee to build a school in a locality where it was badly needed. For a federal agency to approve such an exchange is unusual, and it is an example of Eastern Cherokee sovereignty being formally acknowledged.

Eastern Cherokee band lands now include about fifty-seven thousand acres. They own the land, and it is held in trust by the federal government; court decisions have established that their acreage is not subject to state taxes. A major issue for about one hundred years has been, "Who is a 'real' Cherokee?" Social and political factionalism continues. Behind the factionalism is the matter of Cherokee genetic heritage; persons of full heritage are likely to be more traditionally oriented than any of the others. Enrollment has been confined to the descendants of persons who had one-sixteenth or more Cherokee heritage in a 1924 roll, some of whom now have one-thirty-second Cherokee heritage, or none at all in the case of white Indians on the 1924 roll. Membership currently is closed except to the newborn of members.

An outline of recent developments in band government helps illuminate the problem. The key governing document for the Eastern Band is the 1889 State of North Carolina charter and its amendments. As noted earlier, these Indians became responsible to both the state and federal governments, leading to jurisdictional and other disputes. For instance, in the early 1980s a band constitution was proposed that would restrict the roll and be far more progressive than the original charter. Voters defeated the proposal. At about the same time, some 60 percent of the band members had less than one-half Cherokee genetic heritage, suggesting that the proposed constitution was not acceptable to most persons of mixed heritage and white Indians. Two years later the band council proposed that the chief and vice-chief could be elected from the band membership and not be required to have at least one-half Cherokee heritage as had been provided in the original charter. In addition, a band member with insufficient Cherokee heritage for enrollment would have the same benefits as his or her enrolled parents or from the estate of parents. These proposals were accepted by voters, representing a victory for people of mixed-heritage and white Indians. The Harmony Ethic apparently led numerous traditionally oriented members not to cast ballots. Another constitution was proposed and voted on in 1999. It would negate the state jurisdiction and resolve the many administrative ambiguities, such as their court system having no jurisdiction over non-Indians. It was overwhelmingly rejected. A reasonable conclusion is that the confusion in the original charter served the best interests of mixed-heritage Cherokees, white Indians, and at least some traditionalists.

For many years, political issues had focused to a great extent on local problems confronting small communities as voting units. The Harmony Ethic of old is increasingly under pressure from new realities in tribal politics. Cooperation, consensus seeking, persuasion and compromise, fair treatment, and working together are words and phrases still used by tribal politicians. At the same time, these politicians openly, and sometimes forcibly, accuse one another of fraud, of using political office for personal gain, of political favoritism, and of similar infractions. For example, in 1997 the board appointed by the principal chief to exercise control over gaming resigned en masse to protest a tribal council decision. The council chose to reinstate the daughter of a council member who had been fired from her job at Tribal Bingo. The board members acted in terms of the Harmony Ethic—they withdrew when they could not support the council decision. The principal chief refused their resignations while at the same time unsuccessfully seeking replacements for them. Thus the give and take, compromise and openness, of this and many other decisions in the Cherokee political process reflects a vigorous vitality.

| Additional Sources

The best starting place probably is the short book by Theda Perdue (1989). The best comparative study about the Cherokee and other Indians in the Southeast is by John R. Swanton (1946). The relatively early historical study by James Mooney (1900) is a standard source. The book about Cherokee women from 1700 to 1835 by Perdue (1998) is superior. The recent historical accounts by John R. Finger (1984; 1991) are excellent. William O. Steele (1977) examined early English and Cherokee relations. Fred Gearing's (1962) analysis of Cherokee political developments merits careful study.

Enslavement of blacks among the Cherokee is detailed in a book by R. Halliburton, Jr. (1977), and among Native Americans in a book edited by James F. Brooks (2002). The Sequoya syllabary is detailed in a book by Margaret Bender (2002). The works by Harriet J. Kupferer (1966), John Gulick (1960), and Sharlotte Neely (1991) examine continuities with the past and relatively recent culture change.

| Selected Bibliography

Adair, James. *See* Williams, Samuel Cole.

Anderson, William L., ed. 1991. *Cherokee removal: Before and after.* Athens, GA.

Bender, Margaret. 2002. *Signs of Cherokee culture: Sequoyah's syllabary in Eastern Cherokee life.* Chapel Hill, NC.

Brooks, James F., ed. 2002. *Confounding the color line: The Indian-Black experience in North America.* Lincoln, NE.

Cherokee One Feather. 2001–2004. (Eastern Cherokee newspaper).

Coe, Joffre L. 1961. *Cherokee archaeology.* Bureau of American Ethnology Bulletin 180, no. 7.

DePratter, Chester B. 1991. *Late prehistoric and early historic chiefdoms in the southeastern United States.* New York.

Ehle, John. 1988. *Trail of Tears: The rise and fall of the Cherokee Nation.* New York.

Finger, John R. 1984. *The Eastern Band of Cherokees: 1819–1900.* Knoxville.

———. 1991. *Cherokee Americans: The Eastern Band of Cherokees in the twentieth century.* Lincoln, NE.

Fogelson, Raymond D., and Paul Kutsche. 1961. *Cherokee economic cooperatives: The gadugi.* Bureau of American Ethnology Bulletin 180, no. 11.

Gearing, Fred. 1962. *Priests and warriors.* American Anthropological Association Memoir 93.

Gilbert, William H. 1943. *The Eastern Cherokee.* Bureau of American Ethnology Bulletin 133, 169–413.

———. 1965. Eastern Cherokee social organization. In *Social anthropology of North American tribes,* Fred Eggan, ed., 283–338. Chicago.

Goodwin, Gary C. 1977. *Cherokee in transition: A study of changing culture and environment prior to 1775.* Chicago.

Gulick, John. 1960. *Cherokees at the crossroads.* Chapel Hill, NC.

Halliburton, R., Jr. 1977. *Red over Black: Black slavery among the Cherokee Indians.* Westport, CT.

Hill, Sarah H. 1997. *Weaving new worlds: Southeastern Cherokee women and their baskets.* Chapel Hill, NC.

Kilpatrick, Anna Gritts, and Jack F. Kilpatrick, eds. 1966. *Chronicles of Wolfetown: Social documents of the North Carolina Cherokees, 1850–1862.* Bureau of American Ethnology Bulletin 196, no. 80.

King, Duane H., ed. 1979. *The Cherokee Indian nation: A troubled history.* Knoxville.

Kupferer, Harriet J. 1966. *The "Principal People," 1960.* Bureau of American Ethnology Bulletin 196, no. 78.

Leftwich, Rodney L. 1970. *Arts and crafts of the Cherokee.* Cullowhee, NC.

Malone, Henry Thompson. 1956. *Cherokees of the old south: A people in transition.* Athens, GA.

McKenney, Thomas L., and James Hall. 1933. *The Indian tribes of North America.* Vol. 1. Edinburgh.

McLoughlin, William G. 1984. *Cherokees and missionaries, 1789–1839.* New Haven.

Mooney, James. 1900. *Myths of the Cherokee.* Bureau of American Ethnology, 19th Annual Report, pt. 1, 3–548.

Neely, Sharlotte. 1971. *The role of formal education among the Eastern Cherokee Indians, 1880–1971.* M.A. thesis, University of North Carolina at Chapel Hill.

———. 1978. Acculturation and persistence among North Carolina's Eastern Band of Cherokee Indians. In *Southeastern Indians since the removal era,* Walter L. Williams, ed., 154–73. Athens, GA.

———. 1991. *Snowbird Cherokees: People of persistence.* Athens, GA.

———. 1992. Adaptation and the contemporary North Carolina Cherokee Indians. In *Indians of the Southeastern United States in the late twentieth century,* J. Anthony Paredes, ed., 29–43. Tuscaloosa.

Perdue, Theda. 1989. *The Cherokees.* New York.

———. 1998. *Cherokee women: Gender and culture change, 1700–1835.* Lincoln, NE.

Reid, John Phillip. 1970. *A law of blood: The primitive law of the Cherokee nation.* New York.

Speck, Frank G., and Leonard Broom. 1951. *Cherokee dance and drama*. Berkeley and Los Angeles.

Steele, William O. 1977. *The Cherokee crown of Tanaassy*. Winston-Salem, NC.

Strickland, Rennard. 1982. *Fire and the spirits: Cherokee law from clan to court*. Norman, OK.

Strickland, William. 1977. Cherokee rhetoric. *Journal of Cherokee Studies* 2:375–83.

Swanton, John R. 1946. *The Indians of the southeastern United States*. Bureau of American Ethnology Bulletin 137.

Williams, Samuel Cole, ed. 1930. *Adair's history of the American Indians*. Johnson City, TN.

14 The Natchez: Sophisticated Farmers of the Deep South

Dance générale.

A great number of years ago there appeared among us a man and his wife, who came down from the sun. Not that we believe that the sun had a wife who bore him children, or that these were the descendants of the sun; but when they first appeared among us they were so bright and luminous that we had no difficulty to believe that they came down from the sun.

A priest described the origin of the Great Sun and his lineage (Le Page du Pratz 1947, 312)

ALONG THE EASTERN bank of the lower Mississippi River developed the most elaborate Indian cultures reported to the north of Mexico. Nowhere else were similar heights of cultural complexity reported. In essence, the Natchez had achieved a chiefdom level of sociopolitical development. Fortunately, their aboriginal culture was recorded in considerable detail, unlike those of other Indians in the area who probably exhibited comparable complexity. Natchez political life was dominated by a royal family, and the people had inordinately complex religious and social conventions. In addition, their relations with the French passed through well-defined stages that were often similar to European–Indian historical contacts elsewhere.

The word *Natchez* is apparently derived from a French interpretation of the name of their settlement, called Naches, but these people called themselves the *Thécoel*. The language of the Natchez (NACH-uhz) is an isolate, meaning that it had no widely accepted ties with any other language. It is interesting to note that although the women spoke the same language as the men, women were said to "soften and smooth their words, whereas the speech of the men is more grave and serious" (Le Page du Pratz 1758, 312). Because the French learned the language from women, their pronunciation was feminine and ridiculed by both Natchez men and women. At the end of the seventeenth century, the Natchez numbered about thirty-five hundred, and in 1720 they could assemble twelve hundred warriors, including refugees they had absorbed and the Tiou (Tioux), who were a dependent people (see Figure 14-1).

| Aboriginal Life

The Natchez clearly stand apart from all the Indians reported on in earlier chapters. Natchez social conventions, political organization, and religious institutions survived into historic times, whereas other mound-building Indians in the Southeast with similar cultures soon disappeared. It is assumed, and with good reason, that the Natchez had deep prehistoric roots in the Southeast. Fortunately, one careful observer, Antoine S. Le Page du Pratz, Dutch by birth, lived among the Natchez from 1720 to 1728 and learned to speak their language. His observations are superior and form the primary basis for the following account.

ORIGIN MYTH   The mythological beginnings of the Natchez offer special insight into the form of sociopolitical structure that they developed. According to tradition, a man and his wife entered an already established community to the southwest of historic Natchez country. The newcomers were so bright in appearance that they seemed to have come from the sun. The man said he had noted that the people did not have effective means for governing themselves and that he had come from the sky to instruct them. He told the people about the Great Spirit and what they must do to please him. Among the rules of behavior were a series of prohibitions: do not kill except in self-defense; do not have sexual intercourse with a woman not one's wife; do not steal, or lie, or

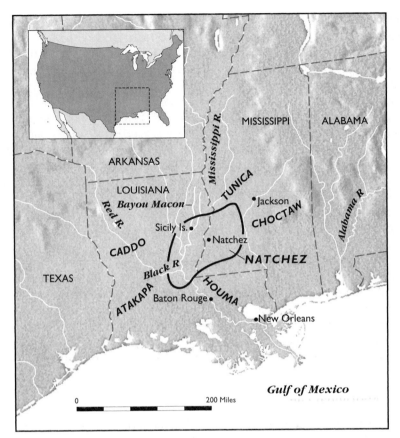

Figure 14-1 | Aboriginal range of the Natchez Indians.

become intoxicated. (Alcoholic beverages do not appear to have existed in this area until early historical times.) Finally, he said that the people should give freely of what they had to those in need. After hearing these rules of conduct, the people agreed to their wisdom and asked the man to be their leader. He said he would do so only under certain conditions. Among these were that the people must obey him but no other and that they must move to another country, to which he would lead them; finally, he set forth the rules for selecting his successor. He said too that they should build a temple in which the leaders could communicate with the Great Spirit. In the temple would be an eternal fire that he would bring from the sun. The people agreed to these and other conditions, and the sacred fire was brought from the sun. This man then became the first Great Sun.

APPEARANCE AND CLOTHING The Natchez were striking in appearance, according to the French. Their proud air and noble bearing became the

American Indian stereotype among Europeans. Le Page du Pratz (1947) described them as 5½ feet or more in height, lean, sinewy, with rectangular features, coarse black hair, and black eyes. To him they were "naturals," but to other French observers they were "savages." As infants their foreheads were flattened by the straps that held them in cradleboards. A woman wore short bangs in front and bound her long hair in a mulberry thread net with tassels at the ends. Her ears were pierced, and from each large hole hung an elongated shell ornament. Around her neck she might wear strings of small stones or perforated shell disks. Around a man's head was a band of short hair. A few hairs were allowed to grow long at the crown, and white feathers were worn in these scalp locks. Often the young Natchez dandies painted themselves red and wore bracelets made of steamed deer ribs bent in circles and then polished to a high luster. They might carry fans of turkey tail feathers, and they wore necklaces of stone beads like those of the women. The people plucked their axillary hair, and the men plucked their whiskers.

The tattoos of these people were impressive in their diversity and complexity. Youthful males and females were tattooed with lines on the face. Persons of the nobility and warriors were elaborately tattooed on the body, head, and limbs. The patterns were of serpents, suns, and other undescribed forms. Warriors who had slain an enemy were permitted to tattoo themselves as evidence of their kills, and for a brave deed a man had the right to tattoo a war club on his shoulder with a sign beneath symbolizing the people involved in his conquest. The tattooing method was to prick the skin until blood flowed freely and then rub charcoal, red pigment, or blue pigment into the openings. Warriors pierced their earlobes and expanded the holes until they would hold decorative plugs about an inch in diameter.

Males younger than twelve years and girls younger than nine went without clothing. An older girl's primary garment consisted of a short fringed skirt made from the threads of mulberry inner bark. An adult woman wore a deerskin that was fitted about the waist and reached the knees. Some high-status women wore cloaks of netting made on a loom from mulberry inner bark. The netting was covered with overlapping rows of bird feathers. In cold weather a woman wore a cape, probably of skins, that passed under her right armpit and fastened over the left shoulder. Ordinary men wore skin breechclouts that were belted and colored white; breechclouts of nobles were black. The leggings of men reached from their thighs to their ankles, but they wore skin moccasins only when traveling. In cold weather a man wore a poncholike shirt of deerskin that was sleeved and reached below the knees. In severe weather a bisonskin robe with the hair intact and facing inward was worn. Deerskin garments were sewn with sinew after an awl was used to pierce the skins. Class distinctions in dress and adornment included elaborate tattoos for the nobility, feather-covered mantles for noblewomen, and black breechclouts for the chiefs or nobles. Infants of the nobility wore two or three pearls about their necks. These ornaments were taken from the temple and were returned when a child was about ten years old.

SETTLEMENTS AND MANUFACTURES   The main area of Natchez settlement was along the eastern bank of the Mississippi River near the present city of Natchez, but the Natchez also seem to have controlled adjacent land on the western bank of the river. During the French period, the main settlement area was a rolling plain of black soil covered with grasses, hickory forests, cane thickets in the low-lying areas, and adjacent pine or hardwood forests. There were reportedly five communities. Grand Village, the principal settlement and the one that may have been termed Naches, was the residence of the Great Sun and other officials. Nearby settlements included Grigras, a community of refugees among the Natchez, Hickory, Flour, and White Apple. These designations possibly were neighborhoods around Grand Village, the only site identified with certainty; it has been partially excavated.

In the center of Grand Village was an open plaza measuring 250 by 300 paces with a flat-topped mound at each end. On top of one mound was a temple, and on the other was the home of the Great Sun. The temple mound was about eight feet high, relatively steep on three sides, and sloped gently to form a ramp on the side toward the open plaza. The temple on top probably was about thirty feet long and somewhat narrower. This structure was built of thick logs ten feet in height and plastered on the outside with mud. The roof was ridged, and three large wooden figures of birds adorned the peak. Entered through a rectangular doorway, the temple was divided into two rooms. A perpetual fire burned in the larger outer room, and on a nearby platform was a cane coffin containing the bones of the most recently deceased Great Sun. In the inner room were two special boards with unidentified items attached. The wooden box that contained the stone statue of the first Great Sun probably was kept here. Reportedly, he turned himself into stone because he feared that his remains would be tainted if placed in the ground. The bones of other persons probably were stored in this room.

The home of the Great Sun was on an earthen mound some eight feet high, and the house itself was twenty-five feet wide and forty-five feet long. All other houses were at ground level, but the eight homes nearby were larger than the other houses. At the death of a Great Sun his house was burned, and the same mound probably was increased in size and used as a foundation for the home of his successor. The houses in general appear to have been square, rectangular, or, less often, round. Their straight walls were not less than fifteen feet high, and they had rectangular doorways but no windows. Hickory timbers were embedded in the ground at the four corners; they were bent over at the tops and tied to form a dome. Along the sidewalls similar poles were embedded in the earth, bent, and tied to the primary dome branches. Poles forming the inner walls were tied in place, and the inner as well as outer walls were spread with a clay and moss plaster and covered with split cane mats. The roof was covered with a mixture of sod and grass and topped with cane mats. In the winter the inhabitants built a fire for warmth. Recent experiments in a reconstructed Natchez dwelling suggest that the fire drew air *into* the building, and the smoke filtered out through the roof. It appears that the houses may have been scattered widely. Somewhere near a village were raised platforms on which the bodies of deceased persons were placed. A woven mat smeared with mud covered the body; the head of the individual was left uncovered so that food offerings might be placed beside it. After the flesh had decayed, the bones were moved to the temple.

A number of household artifacts were reported among the Natchez, and others were excavated from a historic site. Within the cane-walled dwellings were household goods not usually reported north of Mexico. The most prominent furnishings were beds made from poles and cane with bearskins over the frame, a bison skin cover, and log pillow. When relaxing during the day, the people sat either on the beds or on short-legged wooden stools. Pottery vessels were commonly used, including some with shallow bowls decorated with incised scrolls or meanders. Some large pots held up to forty pints of bear oil. A wide variety of cane basketry included sieves of various grades for sifting maize, containers for small items of adornment, and hampers for maize. Knives were made from split sections of hard cane, and stone-bladed axes served for heavy woodworking.

For water transportation, they used both rafts and canoes. Rafts were used to carry relatively light loads and were made from bundles of cane lashed together. For transporting heavy loads, large canoes were made from hollowed-out cypress or poplar logs. The interior of the log was removed by controlled burning, after which the charred wood was chipped away. These dugout canoes were some forty feet long, had three-foot beams, and could carry up to twelve tons.

SUBSISTENCE ACTIVITIES   Cultivated crops were the most important source of food; hunting and fishing clearly were secondary. A farm plot was cleared of cane, which was dried and burned, and the ground was broken up with an L-shaped mattock of hickory. Maize was planted by making holes in the ground with a digging stick and dropping a few grains of corn into each hole. The Natchez probably cultivated their crops with a hoe made by hafting a bison scapula blade at right angles to a wooden handle. The principal cultigen was maize, and from two varieties some forty named dishes were prepared in the Natchez area. Maize was mixed with beans, smoke-dried, ground into meal, prepared as hominy, or parched. Ground meal was made into cakes that were roasted in ashes, baked, or boiled in water. Additional crops included squash and beans, while two species of wild grass were cultivated along riverbanks. The Natchez consumed walnuts, chestnuts, and acorns, but these were not important dietary items. There were no set mealtimes except for feasts. When an ordinary meal was served, the males, including those who were very young, ate before the females.

A primary reason the French established plantations in the Natchez region was for the cultivation of tobacco. The Indians had raised tobacco in aboriginal times, and the people were described as avid smokers. They smoked pipes of unknown form and inhaled the smoke. Smoking was not merely a pleasant activity; pipes and smoking played an important part in events surrounding war and peace.

Hunting was most important in the fall, and deer sometimes were pursued by about a hundred men at a time as a sport. Once they had located and surrounded a deer, men forced the animal to run back and forth until it was exhausted. It was taken alive to the Great Sun or his representative, who killed it and divided the meat among the leaders of the hunt. In ordinary hunting a man wore a deer disguise when animals were cautious and imitated the deer's call to attract an animal. Hunters used self bows of locust wood strung with plant fiber or twisted sinew. Arrows of cane or wood had feather vanes and heads made from splinters of bone, garfish scales, stone, or a fire-hardened shaft tip. Cane-shafted spears were tipped with flint points and used when hunting large game such as bear, bison, and deer. When a kill was made near a settlement, the hunter returned with the choice parts and sent his wife to retrieve the remainder of the animal. Meat was either cooked or smoke-dried for future use. They ate bear meat only if it was lean, but bears were killed when they were fat to obtain the oil. These animals were smoked out of their holes in trees, and if a cub was found, it was sometimes taken alive to the village and tamed. The only domestic animal of the Natchez was the dog. It was used to tree turkeys so that they could be killed with arrows. Fishing was a less important means of obtaining food than either farming or hunting. Among the fishing devices were gill nets made from organic fibers and fish arrows that had pointed bone tips and wooden floats attached by a cord to the shaft. They also used hooks, and the species they took most often were suckers and catfish.

SOCIOPOLITICAL DIMENSIONS   For years the accounts of Natchez sociopolitical life had been confused and contradictory. Thanks to Douglas R. White, George P. Murdock, and Richard Scaglion (1971), particulars about their descent and ranking system have been clarified. The Great Sun ruled as a divine king and administered Grand Village. He appointed administrative officers, including the Great War Chief, a supervisor of public works, the leader of temple ceremonies, and others. The Great Sun also appointed the War Chief in each of the other major villages.

The Suns constituted a royal family, and in 1700 they numbered seventeen individuals. Members of the royal family were obligated to seek a commoner as a spouse. Inheritance was through the matrilineal line for the royal family; it was extended to only three collateral generations. The fourth generation of collaterals became Nobles, and three generations after that they became Stinkards (commoners). Furthermore, the male children of Noble men became Honored men; women could only achieve Honored status as the wives of Honored men. The Honored title could not be passed on to either male or female children; thus there were no Honored women by birth. The summary of descent and rank provided by White, Murdock, and Scaglion (1971, 373) follows:

Parent(s)	Offspring
Sun mother	Sun rank, Noble class
Sun father	Noble class
Noble mother	Noble class
Noble father	sons: Honored rank, commoner class
	daughters: Stinkard (commoner) class
Honored father	Stinkard (commoner) class
Stinkard parents	Stinkard (commoner) class

The sons of highest rank, from oldest to youngest, held the key political offices. Noble men in turn filled subordinate offices, and Honored men also appear to have served in lesser offices. As will later become apparent, under special conditions, a male commoner could be elevated to the rank of an Honored person.

WARFARE Judging by the respect the French gave the Natchez, it is apparent that their military power was considerable. A Great War Chief was in charge of warfare. Ideally, it appears, warfare was controlled at the tribal level. The rationale for aggression might be real—for instance, another tribe may have been hunting on Natchez land—or an offense might be fabricated. Subordinate to the Great War Chief were three grades of combatants: apprentices, warriors, and old warriors. Old warriors played a critical role in military matters, and one of these men led a delegation to confront a potential enemy. They carried a peace calumet but offered no gifts so that they would not be thought of as appeasers. A delegation of this nature was usually well received, gifts were presented to them, and the matter was closed. If this effort failed, the Natchez prepared for war.

To prepare for combat, the military hierarchy performed numerous formal rites and ceremonies that lasted for three days. A pole with a war calumet attached, representing the enemy, was raised near the house where the plans were being formulated. The Great Sun, lesser war chiefs, warriors, and old warriors met, and the Great War Chief described the grounds for launching an attack. The opinions of the old warriors were decisive. If the presentation was accepted as valid, they proceeded with preparations for combat. Each warrior painted his body in different colors and carried a bisonskin shield and war club into combat. A meal was prepared of coarse food to remind warriors that they did not require dainty edibles, and later a dog was roasted for ceremonial consumption. Subsequently, as an act of purification, a war drink that was a powerful emetic was drunk by each man, who then vomited violently. The three-day ceremony also included dances, recitations of personal achievements in warfare, and the singing of death songs.

A war party could include as many as three hundred warriors, who traveled only by night. If they interpreted any sign as an ill omen for an attack, the men returned to their villages, despite all of the preparations. Similarly, if they met an unanticipated enemy party, they withdrew. Attacks were launched at daybreak. The intent was to kill and scalp as many men as possible and to take one male captive, along with all of the women and children. If an enemy had been forewarned and had prepared a defensive position, the Natchez searched for hunting parties to attack. Whenever possible, a Natchez killed in combat was scalped by his comrades to prevent an enemy from obtaining a Natchez scalp. The raiders returned home in honor if they had taken a living enemy man as a captive. On their return, the Great War Chief would compensate the families of any warriors lost in battle.

Back in their own village, the warriors planted two poles in the ground if a male captive had been taken; on them a crosspiece was lashed near the ground and another somewhat higher than a man's head. The captive was stunned with a blow at the base of the skull and was scalped by his captor. The victim's naked body was tied in spread-eagle fashion on the pole frame (see Figure 14-2). The young persons in the assembled throng gathered canes and lighted them; the first flaming cane was applied to the captive by his captor. The torturer was free to apply the cane anywhere he chose, and it was most likely to be on the arm with which the victim had best defended himself. The victim was then burned by the others as he sang his song of death. Some sacrificial victims were reported to have sung for seventy-two hours without pause before dying. However, not all captive males were dealt with in this manner; if a young woman whose husband had been killed claimed the captive, he was given

Figure 14-2 | The plan of a fort and illustration of methods of torture. (From Le Page du Pratz 1947, vol. 2.)

to her as a husband. Captive women and children had their hair cut short and became the servants of their captors.

When an attack was anticipated, the Natchez usually decided in council to defend themselves rather than appease the aggressors. They warned outlying families to join the main group and posted guards at the approaches to their settlements. Another defensive move was to build palisaded fortifications. Forts were rather complex structures built around a tall tree that served as a watchtower. The trunks of trees were stripped of branches and were set in the ground to reach a height of about ten feet. The palisades were arranged in a roughly circular form with an overlap at the ends. Inside were structures to protect the women and children from arrows. The entrance was protected by towers, and in the passage to the outside were placed brambles and thorns. When an attack was imminent, emissaries carrying a peace calumet were sent to enlist the aid of friendly peoples. In the meantime the Great War Chief cited in council the reasons for defending themselves. He sought the support of warriors by reminding the older ones of their honor and pointing out the vengeance they could obtain and by holding out for youths the hope of glory.

Warriors who had distinguished themselves were given new names by the Great War Chief. These denoted particular levels of achievement in warfare. For example, the name Great Man Slayer could be claimed by a warrior after he had taken twenty scalps or ten prisoners. A warrior also might tattoo his body to commemorate an achievement and might be elevated to Honored status.

RELIGIOUS SYSTEM   The Natchez religious system was a formalized network of beliefs, ceremonies, and dogma maintained by specialists who devoted all their time to supernatural matters. They were priests in a generic sense and served as guardians of the major temple. One of these men explained Natchez religion to Le Page du Pratz. The latter recorded that they believed in an all-powerful Great Spirit who created all things good and was surrounded by lesser spirits that did his bidding. A particularly malignant spirit led the spirits of evil, but because it was tied up forever by the Great Spirit, it could do no great harm. The Great Spirit reportedly molded the first man from clay, and the figure grew to the proportions of a normal man. It was believed that woman probably was created in the same manner, but because man was created first, he was stronger and more courageous.

The reigning Great Sun, the highest authority on earth, combined the qualities of a god and a king. His power and authority over things religious were paramount, and his decisions were very important in secular matters. In this theocratic state, all religious, social, and political control was, in theory, in the hands of this individual. The Great Sun was surrounded by warriors and retainers wherever he went. When he traveled about, he was carried on a litter by eight warriors (see Figure 14-3); in his dwelling he sat on a small wooden throne. The Great Sun was distinguished in his dress from others; for example, his normal headdress was a net covered with black feathers and bordered in

le transport du Grand Soleil

Figure 14-3 | The Great Sun being carried on a litter. (From Le Page du Pratz 1947, vol. 2.)

red decorated with white seeds; hanging from the top of the headdress were long white feathers in front and shorter ones behind. Lesser Suns appear to have worn similar headpieces.

The core of religious life was a sacred temple fire tended by eight elders; two of them cared for the fire continually, and they were killed if they permitted the fire to go out. When ordinary persons walked in front of a temple, they put down any load that they might be carrying and extended their arms toward the temple as they wailed loudly. The same type of behavior was displayed when they passed before the Great Sun. The Great Sun visited the temple daily to make certain that the fire still burned, and each morning at sunrise he faced the east, bowed to the ground, and wailed three times. With a special calumet he blew smoke first toward the rising sun and then in each of the other cardinal directions. Thus the Great Sun venerated the sun and was in turn venerated by all other persons in the tribe. What we see is a direct line of continuity from the past functionally linked to the Great Spirit, the Great Suns, and an eternal fire.

| Ceremonies

The annual ritual calendar focused on edibles, the temple, and the Suns. A new year began in March, and each of the thirteen months was named for the most important food identified with the previous month. Seeds were blessed at the temple before they were sown, and family heads presented the first harvest of edibles (first fruit ceremony) to temple guardians for the Great Sun to distribute at his discretion. A feast was celebrated at the beginning of each month by a person of Sun rank, and following ceremonies and ritual acts, the Great Sun received gifts while on his throne.

The seventh month, Great Corn, celebrated the first harvest of maize and climaxed their annual celebrations. Warriors had planted ceremonial corn in virgin soil, tended the crop, and stored it in a granary some distance from the settlement. Villagers assembled at the cache for the arrival of the Great Sun on his litter adorned with flowers. For the prolonged ceremonies, a special dwelling on a raised platform was built for the Great Sun, and other temporary housing accommodated the other assembled families. A new fire was kindled by rubbing sticks together, and corn was presented first to a Sun woman and then to the others. After cooking the sacred crop people feasted, heard orations, and danced to torch light throughout the night to the accompaniment of music played on a drum and gourd rattles. Women danced in the opposite direction to men (see Figure 14-4), and individuals from the audience replaced tired dancers. A violent and highly competitive ball game highlighted the next day's activities; the purpose was to drive a ball to an opposite goal. One team of warriors, led

Figure 14-4 | A dance scene. (From Le Page du Pratz 1947.)

by the Great Sun, wore headdresses of white feathers, and their opposites, led by the Great War Chief, wore red feathers. The winning team received gifts from the captain of the losing team and could wear their headdresses until the game was played again. Following the contest warriors performed a war dance, and the festivities concluded after all of the maize had been consumed.

Apart from the temple cult, a host of spirits prevailed, possibly as lesser agents of the Great Spirit. The honey locust tree, for example, represented supernatural power, and beneath one such tree near the Grand Village temple sacred firewood was cached. Lightning appears to have had religious associations, and a deep-seated fear of snakes was common. Because moisture was all important for crops, the Suns and all others fasted for rainfall.

SHAMANS These specialists appear to have functioned independently of the Sun-centered theocracy. A man or woman who aspired to become a shaman went into isolation for nine days and consumed only water until a spirit aid appeared. During the power quest, the seeker reportedly acquired particular skills. Subsequently, the practitioner filled a small basket with objects such as owl heads, animal teeth, small stones, and spirit aids. A shaman who did not cure a patient might be killed, but successful treatment brought material gain. One cure included making an incision at the locus of an illness and sucking blood from the wound. When the shaman spit blood into a container, he or she spit not only blood but also a foreign object such as a piece of wood, straw, or leather; the illness was attributed to this item.

The more mundane treatment of illness, possibly by other practitioners, likewise prevailed, with plant products making up at least some medicines. In this context Le Page du Pratz cited repeated examples in which French physicians were unsuccessful, whereas their Natchez counterparts cured either the same or other patients.

LIFE CYCLE Soon after babies were born, they were tied to a cradleboard, and strips of deerskin were bound over their foreheads to flatten them. The cradleboard was placed in a bed beside the baby's mother. Infants were smeared with bear oil to keep flies off and to make them supple. When nearly a year old, infants were encouraged to walk; they were nursed until they weaned themselves or until the mother again became pregnant. As children grew they came under the influence of an elder male in their extended family; this man counseled all the nuclear families within his group. A child termed this man father, but he might be a great-grandfather or even a great-great-grandfather. Children were discouraged from fighting with the threat that they would be sent away from the Natchez. Boys were encouraged to exercise and gradually acquire adult skills from about the age of twelve, and the gender division of labor was instilled at this time. Hunting, fishing, fighting, some farming, and the manufacturing of most artifacts were male activities. Carrying home game or fish, most of the farming, preparing food, and manufacturing clothing, baskets, or pottery were female responsibilities, along with raising children.

Following puberty, youths were free to have sexual intercourse, and girls apparently did not bestow sexual favors without material gain. A potential husband was proud of the amount of property his bride-to-be might accumulate in this manner. Males did not marry until they were about twenty-five, but females appear to have been somewhat younger. Once the couple decided to marry, the man went before the heads of their respective families to be questioned. If no close blood ties existed and if the pair loved each other, the elders sanctioned the marriage. On the wedding day the woman was led by the elder of her family, and followed by the remainder of her family, to the home of the man. Here they were greeted and invited into the house, where, after a pause, the elders of both families asked the couple whether they loved each other and were willing to be husband and wife. The ideals of domestic harmony were set forth, the couple exchanged vows, and a gift was made to the bride's father. The bride's mother handed her a laurel branch to hold in one hand and an ear of corn to hold in the other hand. She gave the corn to her husband, and he said, "I am your husband," to which she answered, "I am your wife." Finally the husband told his wife, "There is our bed, keep it tight," which was an injunction against committing adultery. After a special meal the couple and their guests danced from early evening through the night. This description of a marriage by Le Page du Pratz does not specify whether or not these customs were observed by everyone. The need for such clarification is evident, because other descriptions of Natchez marriages differ from this form.

Most marriages were monogamous, and a couple established an independent household (neolocal residence). Yet plural marriages prevailed among the nobility, and sororal polygyny was the most common form. A man with many wives lived with one or two of them and visited the others at their natal homes. In polygynous households, the wife who bore the first offspring supervised the other wives. Divorce was extremely rare for most persons, but an upper-class woman married to a common man was free to take other husbands (polyandry). Furthermore, such a woman could have her husband put to death if he committed adultery. This is an unusual form of the double standard of morality. Berdaches (transvestites) were reported, but their position in the society is not clear.

The writings of Le Page du Pratz and a few others convey the essence of the ideals that guided adult life. Tribal unity did not prevail during the brief historical era, and there is good evidence of a power struggle among leading upper-class persons that influenced intervillage affairs. Some communities were friendly to the French, whereas others were hostile, suggesting that the Great Sun could not, or did not, effectively control all the members of his lineage. Yet it appears that villagewide harmony existed and that the upper class did not abuse its power. The people in general were honorable in their dealings with each other and with the French. Recall that in the myth about the acceptance of the first Great Sun, certain specific rules of behavior were stated; they were maintained insofar as possible by the priests and the upper class in general.

One of the most vivid descriptions by Le Page du Pratz was of the funeral for the Great War Chief, Tattooed Serpent, who was the brother of the Great Sun and nearly as powerful. When he died everyone was greatly distressed because each brother had vowed to kill himself at the death of the other. The temple guardians urged Le Page du Pratz, who was influential among the Natchez and a friend of the Great Sun, to avert the leader's potential suicide. Le Page du Pratz and other whites went to the home of the Great Sun and talked with him. The Great Sun was deeply grieved over the death of his brother but was successfully restrained from committing suicide.

At the house of Tattooed Serpent, his corpse lay on the bed he had occupied while alive. His face was painted red, and he was clothed in his finest garments, including a feather headdress. Beside the bed were his weapons and the peace calumets he had received during his life. From a pole stuck into the ground hung forty-six linked sections of red-painted cane representing the number of enemies he had killed. Gathered around the body were his "chancellor," physician, chief domestic, pipe bearer, two of his wives, some old women, and a volunteer from among the noblewomen, all of whom were to be killed as a part of the funeral ceremony. The next day included a Dance of Death and two rehearsals for the deaths of persons to be killed. At about this time, two commoner parents each strangled one of their offspring out of respect for Tattooed Serpent; by doing so they were raised to noble standing and would not be killed when the Great Sun died. Some warriors also had apprehended a common man who had been married to a Sun woman but had fled at her death to avoid being killed. His capture once again slated him for death, but three old women related to him offered themselves to be killed in his place. The man in turn was elevated to the upper class by the women's sacrifice.

On the day of the funeral, the "master of ceremonies" was painted red above the waist and wore a garment about his waist with a red and white feather fringe. On his head was a crown of red feathers, and he carried a red staff with black feathers hanging from the upper part and a crosspiece near the top. When this impressively arrayed individual approached the house of the deceased, he was greeted with "hoo" and by wailing indicating death. A procession formed behind the master of ceremonies; he was followed by the oldest warrior carrying the staff from which hung the red cane rings and a war pipe that reflected the honor of the dead man. These men were in turn followed by six temple guardians who carried the body on a litter (see Figure 14-5); then came those who were to be killed, each accompanied by eight relatives who served as executioners. Each of these relatives was subsequently freed from the probability of being killed at the death of the Great Sun and seemingly was raised to Honored status. The procession circled the house of the deceased three times, and then the litter bearers walked in intersecting circles to the temple. The dead child was thrown repeatedly in the path of the bearers and retrieved by its parents. After the body of Tattooed Serpent was placed in the temple, the sacrificial victims, their hair covered with red paint, were drugged with tobacco and strangled. Within the temple the two wives of Tattooed Serpent and two men were buried in the grave with him. The other victims

Mort et Convoi du Serpent pique

Temple.

Figure 14-5 | The burial of Tattooed Serpent, brother of the Great Sun. (From Le Page du Pratz 1947.)

were buried elsewhere, and the funeral ended by burning the home of Tattooed Serpent.

With a great man's death, pomp, pageantry, and human sacrifice unrolled; the death of a Sun was a tragic highlight to life. The number of persons killed at the funeral of Tattooed Serpent unquestionably was fewer than would have been considered fitting before the French arrived. For other people to die was of lesser moment, and yet any death was surrounded with further deaths. When an outstanding female Sun died, her husband, a commoner, was strangled by their eldest son. Then the eldest surviving daughter ordered twelve small children killed and placed around the bodies of the deceased couple. In the plaza fourteen platforms were erected, and on each was a man who was to die during the funeral. These men danced before the house of the deceased every fifteen minutes and then returned to their platforms. It was said that after four days the March of the Bodies ritual took place. The dead children previously had been placed outside the dead woman's home, and with them were the live victims. The woman was carried out on a litter, and the small bodies were dropped repeatedly before the procession so that by the time the litter reached the temple the corpses of the children were in pieces. After the woman's body was inside the temple, the fourteen victims were strangled, but not before they had received water and wads of tobacco that drugged them into unconsciousness. The living mourned for an important deceased person by weeping for four days. In general, mourners cut their hair but did not paint their faces, and they avoided public gatherings. The temporary grave was on a raised platform. A shelter of branches formed a vault over the body, and there was an opening at the end near the head where food was placed. The mourners grieved at the grave each day at dawn and at sunset for a month. After the flesh had decayed, the bones were placed in a basket in a temple.

The custom of executing persons at the death of the Suns and other upper-class individuals may seem barbaric and senseless, but they believed that it had very real advantages to the individuals involved. In their belief system, one's spirit under such circumstances would accompany the deceased upper-class person to the world of the dead and serve him or her there in perennial happiness. The same future awaited all others who observed the rules of the society during their lifetimes. It was thought that a person who had broken the rules of the people would go to a place covered with water; naked, she or he would be bitten by mosquitoes and have only undesirable foods to eat.

Tattooed Serpent's Oration

Only a few short years following the dramatic burial ceremonies for Tattooed Serpent, the Natchez were nearly extinct. It seems fitting to record a speech that Tattooed Serpent made to Le Page du Pratz (1947, 40–41) after a war with the French and shortly before the Natchez were destroyed.

> I did not approve, as you know, the war our people made upon the French to avenge the death of their relation, seeing I made them carry the *pipe of peace* to the French. This you well know, as you first smoked in the pipe yourself. Have the French two hearts, a good one to-day, and to-morrow a bad one? As for my brother and me, we have but one heart and one word. Tell me then, if thou art, as thou sayest, my true friend, what thou thinkest of all this, and shut thy mouth to everything else. We know not what to think of the French, who, after having begun the war, granted a peace, and offered it of themselves; and then at the time we were quiet, believing ourselves to be at peace, people come to kill us, without saying a word.
>
> Why . . . did the French come into our country? We did not go to seek them: they asked for land of us, because their country was too little for all the men that were in it. We told them they might take land where they pleased, there was enough for them and for us; that it was good the same sun should enlighten us both, and that we would walk as friends in the same path; and that we would give

them of our provisions, assist them to build, and to labour in their fields. We have done so; is not this true? What occasion then had we for Frenchmen? Before they came, did we not live better than we do, seeing we deprive ourselves of a part of our corn, our game, and fish, to give a part to them? In what respect, then, had we occasion for them? Was it for their guns? The bows and arrows which we used, were sufficient to make us live well. Was it for their white, blue, and red blankets? We can do well enough with buffalo skins which are warmer; our women wrought feather-blankets for the winter, and mulberry-mantles for the summer; which indeed were not so beautiful; but our women were more laborious and less vain than they are now. In fine, before the arrival of the French, we lived like men who can be satisfied with what they have; whereas at this day we are like slaves, who are not suffered to do as they please.

| Recorded Natchez History

Andrew C. Albrecht (1946) identified six phases of Natchez history, a framework that I have followed. The *first phase* is represented by contacts with European explorers. Initial exploration of the region in 1542 was by the Spanish under the command of Hernando de Soto, who died that year. The next year the expedition survivors rafted down the Mississippi River and were attacked by Native Americans, quite possibly by the Natchez. Far more important was a French expedition in 1682 led by Sieur de La Salle. The Natchez graciously hosted these explorers but were not overawed by them. La Salle smoked a peace calumet with the Natchez and was cautious in dealing with them.

A *second phase* began as missionaries and fur traders from Canada in 1698 launched the era of European exploitation. French colonials arrived from the south in 1700 under the leadership of Pierre de Iberville. He established friendly relations with the Natchez at Grand Village and wrested political control of the region from the French Canadians to establish a separate French colony. English traders from the Carolinas, however, soon began to influence the Natchez at some of their settlements. Competition between European nations produced discord among the Natchez.

The *third phase* began in 1713 with the establishment of a French trading post in Natchez country. A wealthy speculator, Antoine Crozat, was granted a monopoly of all the trade in Louisiana, with the stipulation that he bring slaves from Africa and settlers from France. A trading post was built, but intrigue by English traders led Natchez sympathizers to attack the fort, plunder, and destroy it. As a result the French found themselves in a tenuous position. Their solution was to subjugate the Natchez.

The *fourth phase,* military control, began in 1716 when Jean de Bienville, with a small force, tricked the Natchez and was able to seize and kill those who had murdered Frenchmen and plundered the trading post. The Natchez agreed to peace with the French and aided in the construction of the stockaded Fort Rosalie, built to the west of their villages and overlooking the Mississippi River.

Relations temporarily stabilized, with the Natchez controlling their settlements and a small French garrison representing the outpost of an empire.

The *fifth phase* began with the arrival of French colonists in 1720 under the sponsorship of John Law, a Scottish businessman. He obtained the right from the French government to colonize and trade in the region. The colonists established small, scattered plantations, a good indication that Natchez relations were congenial. The colonist to whom we are most indebted for our knowledge about the Natchez was, as mentioned earlier, Antoine S. Le Page du Pratz. From him we learn that the French were provided land and food by these Indians. In turn they received guns, powder, lead, intoxicants, and cloth, a satisfactory arrangement for both parties. Then in 1723 at Fort Rosalie an old Natchez warrior was killed needlessly by a soldier, and his murderer went unpunished by the fort commander. In retaliation the Natchez killed some French settlers. Peace was reestablished within a few days, but a course toward further hostilities had been set. After the peace the French attacked White Apple, demanding and receiving the head of a leader who had been hostile to them. The Natchez could not understand this deception by the French and subsequently avoided contact with them.

At this crucial point in Natchez–French relations two Natchez deaths occurred that quite possibly led to temporary Indian disorganization. In 1725 the younger brother of the Great Sun, Tattooed Serpent, died, and three years later the Great Sun died. Thus, in 1728 a young and inexperienced Great Sun was in power. In the next year, 1729, a new commander of the Fort Rosalie garrison decided quite arbitrarily that he required the land of White Apple for settlement. When he told the Natchez leader of the community to forfeit the village, the Noble refused, and the commander became furious. The Natchez parleyed to decide a course of action. They concluded that because the French were becoming more numerous, were corrupting the Natchez youth, and were breaking their promises, the French should be destroyed.

The *sixth phase,* the final one, was the Natchez revolt and their destruction as a tribe. In 1729 the pro-English Natchez faction attacked Fort Rosalie and the French plantations. They may have killed two hundred colonials and took women, children, and black slaves hostage. The next year the French attacked two Natchez forts in which hostages were held. In the conflict neither side prevailed, and a truce was arranged. The Natchez released their captives, and the French moved back to the Mississippi River from Grand Village. Then the Natchez slipped across the Mississippi River, ascended the Red River to the Black River, and built a fort at Sicily Island. In 1731 a French and Indian force was sent against them, and about two hundred, including the Great Sun, were forced to surrender. These Natchez were sold into slavery in the West Indies.

The Indians captured by the French at Sicily Island were primarily women and children. The main body of warriors escaped and intermittently raided French settlements for the next five years. Eventually they became refugees among the Chickasaw, Cherokee, and Creek. With the Indian Removal Act of 1830 the majority of Native Americans in the Southeast were forced to relocate

Figure 14-6 | Nancy Taylor, one of the last Natchez speakers, in 1908. (Courtesy of Smithsonian Institution, National Anthropological Archives, Swanton Book IV 180-A.)

in Indian Territory, including most Natchez survivors. In 1907 Swanton located some Natchez near Braggs, Oklahoma, in the southwestern part of the Chero-kee nation; five of the individuals he found still knew some of the language (see Figure 14-6). In 1934, when Mary R. Haas worked among the Natchez living near Braggs, she found that only two Natchez speakers had survived among the postremoval Oklahoma Cherokee. Today a few rituals are pre-served in Cherokee and Creek communities into which Natchez survivors in-termarried. The descendants of these Natchez identify themselves as Cherokee or Creek and no longer perform these rituals in the Natchez language (Moore 1994, 371). Today in Natchez, Mississippi, the Grand Village of the Natchez has been reconstructed as a state park.

In 1747 Natchez survivors living among the preremoval Cherokee peti-tioned the colonial government in Charleston, South Carolina, to become "set-tlement Indians." They were given land near Charleston along the Edisto River.

Figure 14-7 | Matthew Creel and Andy Spell, Edisto-Natchez-Kusso Indians, at their festival in 1992. (Photo by Gene Joseph Crediford, © 1999.)

Today in South Carolina the 450 people in the communities of Four Holes and Creeltown are petitioning for federal acknowledgment as the Edisto-Natchez-Kusso Indians (see Figure 14-7). As an independent tribe, however, the Natchez are extinct, like so many Native American tribes.

| Additional Sources

The best comparatively brief and insightful account of Natchez ethnography and ethnohistory is by Jim Barnett (1998). The most worthwhile firsthand account is by Antoine S. Le Page du Pratz (1947), the primary source for this chapter. For additional details and a comparative view of the Natchez and other Indians in the Southeast, the best source is the 1946 publication by John R. Swanton.

| Selected Bibliography

Albrecht, Andrew C. 1946. Indian–French relations at Natchez. *American Anthropologist* n.s. 48:321–54.

Barnett, Jim. 1998. *The Natchez Indians.* Mississippi Department of Archives and History. Natchez.

Blumer, Thomas J. 1994. Edisto. In *Native America in the twentieth century: An encyclopedia,* Mary B. Davis, ed., 181–82. New York.

Crediford, Gene Joseph. 1993. *Those who remain: Native Americans in South Carolina 500 years after Columbus.* Columbia, SC.

Fogelson, Raymond D., ed. (2004). *Southeast.* Vol. 14, *Handbook of North American Indians.* Washington, DC.

Ford, James A., and Clarence H. Webb. 1956. *Poverty Point, a Late Archaic site in Louisiana.* Anthropological Papers of the American Museum of Natural History, vol. 46, pt. 1.

Haas, Mary R. 1939. Natchez and Chitimacha clans and kinship terminology. *American Anthropologist* n.s. 41:597–610.

Le Page du Pratz, Antoine S. 1947. *The history of Louisiana.* Paris. (Published in London, 1758; reprinted in New Orleans, 1947.)

Moore, John H. 1994. Natchez. In *Native America in the twentieth century: An encyclopedia,* Mary B. Davis, ed., 370–71. New York.

Neitzel, Robert S. 1965. *Archaeology of the Fatherland site.* Anthropological Papers of the American Museum of Natural History, vol. 51, pt. 2.

Swanton, John R. 1946. *The Indians of the southeastern United States.* Bureau of American Ethnology Bulletin 137.

Taukchiray, Wesley DuRant, and Alice Bee Kasakoff. 1992. Contemporary Indians of South Carolina. In *Indians of the Southeastern United States in the late twentieth century,* J. Anthony Paredes, ed., 72–101. Tuscaloosa.

White, Douglas R., George P. Murdock, and Richard Scaglion. 1971. Natchez class and rank reconsidered. *Ethnology* 10:369–88.

15 Overviews

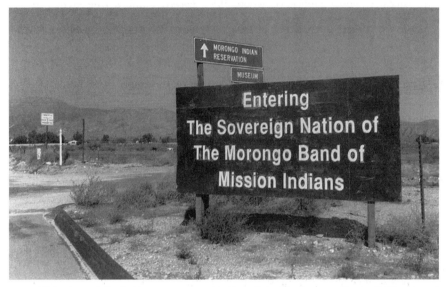

This sign marked the entrance to the Pass Cahuilla Reservation in California during 1997.

Survival = Anger × Imagination. Imagination is the only weapon on the reservation.

The Lone Ranger and Tonto Fist Fight in
Heaven (Sherman Alexie 1993, 150.
Courtesy of The Atlantic Monthly Press.)

THE TWO OPENING chapters of this text survey the background of modern Native American life north of Mexico. The twelve tribal chapters describe particular Indian lifeways for each of the culture areas. This final chapter provides overviews of those recent developments that may lead to profound changes in the future of Native American cultures and concerns current issues.

It may seem strange to begin by considering Indian gaming operations, yet no other Indian-related topic is as timely among Indians and non-Indians alike. Equally pertinent, the existence of Indian casinos expands in importance beyond the gambling at its base. It affects the realities of tribal sovereignty, states' rights, state finances, the wealth of highly successful Indian casinos versus the continuing poverty on many reservations, and related concerns.

| Indian Casino Highlights

By 2004 an end to the constantly expanding number of Indian casinos was beyond the horizon. Their success has numerous labels: "the new buffalo," "Indian revenge," "Indian catch-up," and "a rags to riches story." Yet the wisest Indians and non-Indians alike, including anthropologists, had no inkling of what would happen.

Here is brief summary. During 2002 legal gambling (gaming) in the United States amounted to about $70 billion. This total was dominated by commercial gambling (e.g., casinos and racetracks), $24.2 billion; state lotteries, $19.5 billion; and Indian gaming, $14.5 billion. Gross revenues for all Indian gaming approached $17 billion in 2003. Indian casinos represent about 35 percent of the national casino industry market share, compared with 28 percent for state lotteries and 21 percent for commercial gambling.

A good indication of nationwide interest in this widespread development is seen in two lengthy articles in *Time Magazine:* "Special Report: Indian Casinos," coauthored by Donald L. Barlett and James B. Steele (December 16 and 23, 2002). The reactions of Native American tribal newspapers to these reports were highly critical. They considered them unfair because the authors emphasized the questionable financial backing of some casinos and failed to fully credit the positive aspects of casino operations. Just as the Barlett and Steele articles had a negative bias, however, the Indian newspaper responses focused primarily on the positive results. The U.S. population in general views Indian gambling establishments from a similar combination of positive and negative viewpoints.

The Indian Gaming Regulatory Act (IGRA) was passed by Congress in 1988 to foster tribal economic development and self-determination; these primary goals must be kept firmly in mind. Shortly before the gaming act passed, the average per capita income on reservations was $4478, less than a third of the U.S. national average; the Indian unemployment rate could exceed 50 percent.

The IGRA concerns gaming on "Indian lands" held in trust by the federal government, meaning primarily on reservations in states in which gambling is legal. Indian gaming is the most regulated in the United States, which indicates how restrictive Congress was in formulating the act, at least partially as a result of pressures from gambling interests in Nevada and New Jersey.

The federal classification of Indian gaming under the act merits review to help clarify the key issues. Class I gaming involved traditional social games often associated with ceremonies; it is regulated by a tribe. Class II includes games permitted and regulated by a state and in conformity with federal laws. These include bingo, card games, lotto, and pull-tabs approved by tribal ordinance and regulated by a tribe, as well as by the National Indian Gaming Commission (NIGC). Class III gaming is permitted in a state that allows legal gaming and includes games of chance other than bingo. It requires an enabling tribal ordinance, as well as a formal tribe–state compact (agreement). This is casino gambling. Class II and III gaming facilities combined numbered 377 in 2002, operated by 220 tribes in 28 states. As the gaming act has been implemented, the distinction between these classes of gaming has become somewhat blurred.

It is essential to elaborate on the foregoing outline of the act. The IGRA applies only in states with legal gambling and does *not* include a provision permitting states to control Indian casino operations. States may, however, assess casino tribes for directly related infrastructure and administrative costs. In these qualifying states a gaming compact must be negotiated by Indians with the state's governor and approved by its legislators. Existing legal gambling interests, such as state lotteries and racetracks, are of a different nature from casinos but nonetheless represent entrenched opposition to Indian enterprises. States often have failed to negotiate with Indians who desire casinos in the "good faith" required by the IGRA, which has resulted in court cases against state governments. These typically are settled by signing compacts. They usually include provisions for "revenue sharing" with states as the price for launching and maintaining casinos. Many Indians consider this to be *extortion*, but they find it in their best interest to acquiesce because the act requires mutual agreement. This is a profound intrusion on tribal sovereignty, which becomes confrontational with state governments.

The gaming regulatory act *requires* that a portion of casino profits be devoted to tribal well-being. In 2003 most of the net revenue was for police and fire protection, economic development, housing, education, and the care of children and elderly persons. In California a portion of the profits must be set aside for sharing with tribes without casinos.

Some indigenous populations would like to open casinos in states in which gambling is illegal (e.g., Arkansas, Indiana, and Utah). These Indians contend that their sovereignty makes them independent of state laws and that the IGRA is obstructionist by restricting gaming to states where it is legal.

The NIGC is the federal agency regulating Indian casinos. By statute the commission checks on casino financing to make certain that criminal organizations are not involved, and it conducts background checks on key employees. The commission is also charged with reviewing management contracts, setting limits on investor profits, and overseeing other aspects of the operations. The NIGC has not uncovered any major examples of corruption, and the same applies to tribal and state audits. Tribal governments spent in excess of

$230 million in recent years to regulate their gaming establishments. However, in the legal non-Indian gambling industry, an estimated 6 percent of revenues is lost to criminals. The loss percentage is unavailable for Indian casinos. In 2004 the Federal Bureau of Investigation and numerous other federal agencies launched studies centered on Indian casino theft, embezzlement, fraud, and possible influences by criminal organizations.

Indian casino growth has been so rapid and successful that gambling revenues at Atlantic City and Las Vegas have begun to level off. Slot machines provide an estimated 80 percent of Indian casino revenues, which means their number is a critical factor with respect to potential profits, and may be controlled through tribal–state negotiations. The expansion of casinos had created nearly 500,000 jobs by 2004, with an estimated 75 percent of the workers being non-Indian.

Major predictors of Indian casino success tend to be relatively few and quite specific with respect to the location. An ideal site is on reservation land connected to a major metropolitan area by one or more interstate highways. Having no other reservations close enough to become competitors will ensure greater profits. Alternatively, a rural area near a busy freeway or major highway is an attractive location. Far less desirable are sites with interstate access to a nearby major city but with other casinos close by. The Albuquerque region is an example. Numerous Pueblo Indian reservations, such as Acoma and Sandia, have casinos in relatively close proximity. Along with the resultant profit sharing, this has led to highly competitive local billboard advertising, as well as a growing impact on the area's infrastructure.

One of the world's most profitable casinos, Foxwoods, is owned by the Mashantucket Pequot in Connecticut. Its gross revenues exceeded $1 billion in 2002. The state receives 25 percent of the slot machine take. Between 1993 and 2003 the Pequot paid $1.6 billion to the state as their contract required. They also donated $10 million to the National Museum of the American Indian in Washington, D.C., and they regularly make significant monetary contributions to the welfare of disadvantaged Indian tribes, especially those in the northern Plains.

California is the major center for Indian casinos, in part because the state is large, populous, and has the greatest number of federally recognized tribes. Of the 109 California tribes, 61 have casinos. These operations, with their related enterprises such as lodging and dining facilities, earned a total of some $3.6 billion in 2002. In the San Diego region, five of the nine casinos were established by 2001, making this the fastest growing legal gaming area in the country. Additional casinos were in the planning stages by 2004. The irony of ironies is that prior to the Indian casino boom, San Diego area "Mission Indians" had small and inadequate reservations, the people were dismally poor, and they attracted no meaningful positive interest by either the state or the local non-Indian population. Now they have substantial incomes, and they have built enough political power to affect local elections, thereby expanding their power even more.

The manner in which a state spends the money earned in a compact with a casino tribe varies widely. Arizona, for example, received about $85 million in 2003, none of which went into the state's general fund, as is common elsewhere. Twelve percent went directly from casino tribes to nearby towns and cities. Other amounts were primarily used for statewide education, gaming regulation, and problem-gambling programs. The percentages going to a state government vary because they are negotiated independently by each state and the tribes involved there.

In recent years Native American business enterprises have increased dramatically. According to recent census data, Native American businesses grew by 84 percent compared with 7 percent for other U.S. firms. Inherent Indian advantages include their land ownership, the ability to regulate taxes, and a typically underemployed workforce. Other contributing factors that have been growing include sufficient capital for investments, expanding technological abilities, and capable leadership. One major cornerstone now is the association with casinos. On or near casino sites are opportunities for profitable restaurants and hotels, shopping malls, golf courses, and powwow settings. Casino tribes also are increasingly invested in other businesses, such as real estate developments, racetracks, and banks.

In addition to diverse and clearly constructive projects to further tribal well-being, nearly fifty gaming tribes make yearly payments to each enrolled member. Because these are based on casino earnings, they vary from year to year. The gaming act does not require public disclosure of casino finances, but some figures are available. The huge stipends paid by a *small number* of casinos are most often cited in the media as examples of casino profits and their distribution. Two unverified examples during the early 2000s are Mystic Lake Casino and Hotel in Minnesota, with an enrollment of 326 and yearly stipends of as much as $1 million per individual; and Table Mountain Casino in California, enrollment about 115 with stipends of about $180,000. The small enrollments naturally lead to larger personal payments. Far more often stipends are modest, such as those of the Spirit Mountain Casino in Oregon, with an enrollment of about 4700 and payments of up to $5000 a year.

The wording of a tribal constitution recognized by the federal government is critical in defining membership (enrollment). In the American West, tribal enrollment usually has been based on blood quantum, which typically varies from one-half to one-sixteenth. It appears to have become the prominent criterion after the Dawes Act of 1887 established a minimum of one-quarter Indian blood as a general federal standard. In the East and Midwest, however, tribal identity is more likely to be based primarily on descent enrollment (lineal ancestry) recorded in census reports accepted by the BIA; to these tribes the percentage of Indian blood is not pertinent. These different means for Indian identification have major effects on the lives of individuals and their families. Why? Because in many tribes about half of all marriages are currently with non-Indians, and the rights of descendants are diluted in one case but not the other. An example of the problem follows.

A constitutional amendment proposed recently by the enrolled members of the Flathead Indian Reservation in Montana, a casino tribe, deals with the issue. They voted in 2003 on whether to continue to identify new tribal members based on Indian blood quantum or to abandon this criterion and open the enrollment to all the descendants of tribal members. The blood quantum law had produced growing numbers of "split families." For instance, assume first that two brothers each have one-quarter Indian blood (the minimum acceptable amount for tribal membership). The offspring of a brother who married a woman with a quarter or more Indian blood would become eligible as tribal members, but if the other brother married a non-Indian, his children could not become tribal members because their blood quantum would be too low. The people overwhelmingly voted to retain the existing blood law after a demographic study found that ignoring blood quantum and basing membership on historical tribal membership would allow the present population of about 7000 to double rapidly. Projections suggested that by 2025 there would be more than 24,000 members. With the existing blood quantum law retained, however, the current population number, which has already peaked, will decline rather rapidly. A proposed solution was to discourage marriages with nontribal members, in which case the population could remain relatively constant. The procedure employed by the Flathead reservation members illustrates the capacity of present-day reservation Indians to determine their own standards of enrollment.

Before the tribes had casinos, they could not imagine ever having substantial independent political clout at the local, state, and national levels. That has changed and probably will grow in impact. Wealthy tribes now contribute millions of dollars to influence causes important to them. An example is the $11 million they contributed in 2003 to recall Governor Gray Davis in California. Another example is working with state and local governments to finance infrastructure improvements beneficial to the establishment of new casinos. Casino tribes also may make major contributions to tribes seeking to launch casinos in other states. Furthermore, they have developed the lobbying skills necessary to influence national legislation and for the election of candidates they support in state and national elections.

A backlash against Indian casinos has expanded as they have proliferated and become increasingly successful. One national issue centers on the millions of dollars wealthy casino tribes continue to receive from the federal government. Some tribes voluntarily return this money to the government for distribution to poor tribes, but this does not satisfy objectors. Regardless, $15 billion was generated by gaming and directly related wages by casino tribes; $2.2 billion was paid in federal income taxes and $2.5 billion paid into Social Security in 2003. The same year the federal government saved $1.2 billion from reduced Indian welfare programs and unemployment benefits. Finally, Indian gaming tribe income per capita increased more than 50 percent from 1990 to 2000.

One localized problem for a casino tribe is actual or potential highway congestion. A tribe often absorbs the cost of changes to provide better access.

Some non-Indians also feel that a casino in their midst will create a "Nevada-like atmosphere," and conversely local political jurisdictions fear that wealthy casinos, such as Foxwoods, may buy up all the land in the region, an unexpected twist of fate that would be legal but disturbing to the local non-Indians.

Another reason local governments object to Indian casinos is that they simply do not understand the nature of tribal sovereignty and its far-reaching implications. Tribes are not required to comply with state and local laws, such as those about smoking, union representation of employees, building standards, and environmental policies because of their sovereign status. These issues were not apparent until "casino culture" emerged. States may and do seek to include restrictive provisions in gaming contracts with tribes, or tribes may work out cooperative approaches to differences as an aspect of public relations.

Objections to casinos are sometimes based on fear that local problems will be created by addicted gamblers. This concern has restricted any form of legal gambling in many states for years, especially if a religious group backs the complaints. Yet a 2003 study of legal gambling suggests that fewer than 2 percent of the general population become addicted gamblers. However, 2 to 3 percent may become problem gamblers within a few years following the introduction of legal gambling.

A 2003 Roper survey brings out some specific differences in gambling versus nongambling lifestyles that are of tangential interest in this respect. In their home lives, people who make bets are more likely to pay their credit card bills each month (61%) compared with most others (52%) and are more likely to save for retirement (50% vs. 40%). Their household income is greater than the general population ($50,716 vs. $42,228). They favor slot machines (74%), and women are somewhat more likely to gamble than men are.

In general, casino tribes find their new positive status rewarding in a number of different ways. They have achieved a far greater degree of self-determination, self-sufficiency, and economic security than ever before in their history—precisely the goals of the original IGRA. Their success gives them a new pride in being Indian, and this appears to be accepted by non-Indians. Casinos likewise provide the opportunity for more tribal members to find work on their reservations, which fulfills their desire to support themselves within an Indian setting. They also like being able to enlarge or fund new Indian museums or reconstruct village sites as a tribute to their traditional culture.

But what about noncasino tribes? Has their economic status changed? They constitute about 40 percent of the tribes in the lower forty-eight states. A specific example is California, which anticipates a $9 billion general fund debt by the end of 2004. To help resolve this financial pitfall, the state plans to make a dramatic reduction in Indian welfare programs, basing the decision, at least in part, on the wealth of highly successful casino tribes. Yet most casinos in the state do not yield vast returns, and they are largely ignored in most media reports. Furthermore, most Native Americans who live in California are not enrolled members of a tribe within the state; in fact, many of them are members of tribes that are unrecognized at present by the federal government. The point is that states, especially California, are attempting to ease their budget woes by "taxing" casino tribes as they would business corporations.

| Federal Administration

In the United States, federally recognized tribes, bands, and other Native American groups have been under the direct control of the Department of the Interior (DI), especially the Bureau of Indian Affairs (BIA), since 1824. The BIA has had primary but not exclusive responsibility, either directly or indirectly, for ongoing Indian well-being, especially for those tribes living on reservations. The basis for this bureau responsibility rests largely on treaties, congressional legislation, executive orders, administrative decisions, and federal court judgments. If the bureau fails in fulfilling its responsibilities, Congress ultimately is held accountable for correcting inadequacies. It is essential to keep in mind that decisions bearing directly on Native American life often emerge because of differing political agendas (e.g., Democrats or Republicans, as well as East and West). A brief review of select issues follows.

First, some reservations have evolved into "welfare states" because their economic potential was poor from the time they were first established. Present-day Indian dependency has many aspects that the federal government has had to address; examples include health benefits, relief programs, housing and education in general, job training, law enforcement, and environmental decisions. In dealing with these issues, the BIA shares responsibility with other government agencies, a situation that has led to an inefficient bureaucratic jungle. Second, as a firmly entrenched bureaucracy, the bureau's primary focus has been to expand its own self-interests as opposed to its obligations to further programs to better the quality of Indian life. Third, the bureau has assumed management of reservation resources (e.g., coal, oil, timber) based on federal legislation and administrative decisions. Fourth, administrative continuity within the bureau is inhibited by basic changes in federal policies, including termination of federal responsibilities by stealth. It is fostered by the states' rights agenda of the George W. Bush administration. Each of these configurations may seem desirable or undesirable to Indians or non-Indians alike, depending on their general political philosophies or perceived personal benefits.

To receive funds and benefits from federal programs, the Indians involved must accept any accompanying management procedures. By 1975 the federal government made it possible for tribes to assume far greater management control at a local level (i.e., self-determination). The Hopi exemplify the results. By 2003 their enrollment was about twelve thousand, about half of whom lived on or near the reservation. The number of administrative units requiring local management was extensive. Yet because many residents were either quite young or old or could not participate for other reasons, the population pool for positions was relatively small. Grounded in the Hopi Tribal Constitution, tribal government included an election board, enrollment department, judicial branch, budget committee, tribal management department, and housing authority. Teams became responsible for water rights, energy, law enforcement, and land. This list, although far-reaching, does not include all of the administrative network. Irrespective of how capable and devoted administrators might be, each aspect of government required complex decision making and careful follow-through. Many Hopi have made careers of working for the tribal government, the primary employer on the reservation. In sum, the Hopi increasingly have learned to deal with Euro-American bureaucrats, but there may be considerable variability in their success from one Hopi administration to the next.

The Hopi example illustrates how, under this self-determination policy, some tribal governments have become radically transformed. By the early 2000s numerous tribes had an increasingly firm grip on administrative procedures and had developed valuable expertise. This in turn has facilitated more equitable federal–tribal relationships. Nonetheless, the federal government may still legislate Indian issues without seeking or allowing critical tribal input. Recent examples of decisions providing mutual benefits can be found in government-to-government dealings, although they are not numerous. This encouraging change includes some land exchanges advantageous to both tribes and the federal government. A small number of tribal and federal comanagement agreements involving tribal and federal lands have been implemented. Furthermore, improved understanding by local tribal leaders about the practicality of new and existing programs may aid agencies to be more successful in setting up new agreements. In some cases cooperative Indian involvements may result in more de facto tribal control.

Additional positive developments merit note. Management of the Indian Health Service hospitals has been assumed by tribal governments on most reservations with hospitals. In similar fashion federal grants support tribally administered programs that previously were under total BIA control. The responsibility to manage money from the bureau, the Department of Housing and Urban Development, the Department of Justice, and other federal agencies has been turned over to tribes.

Self-determination management successes are muted by disruptive tribal politics on some reservations. Problems often arise when newly elected leaders replace successful program administrators with far less qualified, or unqualified, persons for political reasons. The traditional historical struggle on a reservation between "conservative" and "progressive" factions has fractured and deepened into numerous other segments that conflict and disrupt tribal unity. These include long-standing family rivalries, deep-seated religious differences, and opposing views on the exploitation of reservation resources. Indigenous language speakers may be separated from those who speak English only, or from others who speak both languages. Another separation between younger and older voters may occur, and there can be serious differences between enrolled members who live on or near a reservation and those living afar. Then, too, political corruption ranging from the abuse of power, cronyism, and nepotism to graft and theft can disrupt reservation harmony. A "typical" reservation family may inherently distrust its local government, a condition not unknown among "standard American" families.

Intermittently, since the BIA was originated in 1824, it has faced charges of corruption, graft, and incompetence that have been proven. No previous scandal compares in scope, however, with current accusations that the bureau has been failing to properly administer Indian trust accounts over the course of many years. The Dawes Act of 1887 made the bureau responsible for transfers of trust land (e.g., through inheritance), but the system was not designated to handle lease income payments until later, when Congress declared the bureau to be responsible for handling these payments as well as Individual Indian Monies (IIM) from land sales and leases, grazing rights, logging operations, gas and oil production royalties, water rights, and other contracts. Not only was the BIA not prepared to do so, but these issues also became increasingly complicated over the years. Finally, in the 1990s, it became apparent that the bureau had failed to distribute the income from trust land payments to the Indians involved for an *unknown* number of years. The BIA now has been confronted and acknowledges that its record-keeping has been so inadequate that, besides not making payments, a part of its IIM funds probably have been lost, stolen, or not collected. It also appears that IIM funds have even been used to reduce the national debt! Furthermore, it may be impossible to obtain a full accounting at this point because some files and e-mail messages have been illegally destroyed, and others cannot be located. In sum, the bureau lacked the ability from the late 1800s to record trust transactions efficiently and to make the legitimate payments.

No one knows the total amount unpaid over the years to the approximately 387,000 beneficiaries. Since 1887 legal Indian recipients may have been deprived of about $13 billion. An estimated $2.4 billion is unaccounted for between 1973 and 1992 alone. A trust fund reform act was passed by Congress in 1994 to resolve these problems, which have continued into the early 2000s. A major court challenge to the DI for lack of progress in a class-action suit centering on IIM was made by Elouise Cobell of the Blackfeet Nation and others. The federal judge in charge of the case, Royce C. Lamberth, harshly criticized the DI for resisting IIM reform by its evasive action intended to protect its own interests. In 2003 Lamberth issued a "structural injunction" ruling that a historical accounting by the DI was required. This accounting is to go back to 1887 and is to specify the funds and interest due to the Indians. The DI also must demonstrate that it is complying with court-appointed supervision. The DI is forbidden to make any stay of the injunction pending appeals. Lamberth will remain in charge of the case through 2009, when his authority will end.

A possible way to resolve the Cobell suit has been proposed recently in Congress. The Senate Committee on Indian Affairs, under the chairmanship of Ben Nighthorse Campbell (R-Col.), began to explore a partial solution of the mishandling of IIM accounts by congressional action. In general terms, settlement mediators would attempt to resolve trust account settlements without full documentation, but any Indian could contest his or her settlement through an appeal. Another alternative would be for an Indian to pursue his or her settlement as a part of the Cobell case.

The plot thickened after Lamberth's injunction. A "midnight rider" (last-minute attachment) was added to the DI appropriation bill to prohibit for one year a full historical accounting of IIM; the cost of this delay would be in the billions of dollars. Despite strong opposition to this attachment, the bill passed and was signed by the president. Senator Campbell probably could have fought against the midnight rider successfully, but he did not. He apparently felt that the rider was not all that bad if it forced the Cobell litigants to resolve their differences within a year. This proved to be the consequence. In April 2004 the federal government appointed two widely respected lawyers as mediators, and the lead plaintiff, Elouise Cobell, accepted them. Thus it appears that the case may be resolved without being tried in court.

Because most reservation Indians have badly needed these funds to which they were entitled, the BIA's handling of the IIM accounts obviously has been tragic. Innumerable Native Americans have died in poverty when they could have lived far more comfortably if they had received the money due to them on a regular basis over the years. In terms of personal finances, many reservation Indians live today in debt as a direct result of nonpayments. Individuals have lost ownership of their ranches, have been denied loans, and have not obtained clear titles for some land sales, all because of bureau failings.

Not surprisingly, the BIA has promised to reorganize as a result of the scandal. It has decentralized its operations by establishing regional offices to address local issues more promptly and effectively. One Native American reaction has been to wonder whether the changes will simply add yet another complicating bureaucratic administrative level that may make the BIA more inefficient than in the past.

| Urban Indians

The Indian population has undergone numerous changes since its first contact with Euro-Americans. For example, during and shortly after colonial times, some became "invisible Indians," as they abandoned their aboriginal ways and blended into the Euro-American matrix surrounding them.

The recognized Indian population reached its all-time low between 1890 and 1900, when the population total in the United States was about 250,000. This small number of survivors compares with an estimated 7 million some five hundred years earlier. In 1900 urban Indians in the United States represented about 0.4 percent of the total Native American population. At that time years of exploitation by Westerners and intermarriages with non-Indians had reoriented the lifestyles of most tribes as they sought accommodations with whites for survival. Working for whites indirectly (e.g., the fur trade) and directly (e.g., wage labor) had become common. Second, intense daily contacts with non-Indians became far more common during World War II, when indigenous Americans served in the armed forces and earned civilian job experience during the shortage of factory workers. By the end of the war, these individuals were far more capable of dealing effectively with Euro-Americans than they had been in the past. Third, soon after World War II, the federal government decided to "get out of the Indian business" by terminating the status of some reservations and establishing a timetable to abolish all reservations.

Beginning in the 1950s, the BIA Relocation Program (RP) was designed to assimilate Native Americans rapidly into the American mainstream by moving them to urban settings. The program was launched in 1952 and had involved over 100,000 Indian participants when it ended in 1973. The RP was justified by federal officials because the resource base on most reservations could not support the growing numbers of impoverished families without relying on ever-increasing federal aid. Difficult living conditions had become endemic; local jobs generally were few, low paying, and often temporary, which resulted in extremely high unemployment rates and low annual incomes. The RP was designed to provide an opportunity for these people to live more satisfying and productive lives by becoming part of more economically stable urban populations. Change in that direction had begun when some twenty-five thousand Native Americans left their reservations to become members of the armed services during World War II and about twice that number went to work in war-related industries away from their reservations. The BIA anticipated that formal relocation efforts would expand on this pattern and would be successful.

When the program was launched, participating Indians received direct aid under the supervision of relocation officers as they resettled in major urban areas such as Chicago, Denver, and Los Angeles. By the time the program was expanded to other cities, however, its inadequacies were becoming apparent. There was a high return rate to reservations because Indians did not have the essential skills to obtain any but the lowest-paying jobs in the postwar civilian world. Consequently, on-the-job training, vocational training, employment assistance, and other programs were added to help ensure greater economic success. The majority of those willing to relocate were young, single males hopeful of earning adequate income in a city.

Despite the added federal assistance, the overall relocation success rate appears to have been more modest than the glowing reports by the BIA indicated. "Culture shock" struck many relocatees as insurmountable. On an individual basis, most of them kept to themselves or were surrounded by other Indians, could not overcome their poor educational background, and retained cultural values that set them apart as a distinct urban minority. This was true especially of those who "looked like Indians." Furthermore, they most often lived in inadequate housing scattered through poor areas. Their urban poverty turned out to be no better than their reservation poverty. (In the early 1960s I planned to study relocated Indians in Los Angeles. However, I soon realized that I could not cope emotionally with their living conditions. One family with numerous children remains fixed in my memory. They lived in a garage under conditions that were unbelievable; the only positive factor, in my mind, was that they had each other.)

The RP did not succeed to the extent anticipated by its innovators. Most of the participants had lived segregated lives on reservations; they did not adapt readily to their new environment. Any contacts they had with whites typically were highly structured, sporadic, and generally confusing or upsetting to them. The BIA sometimes had relocation quotas, and because of that, clearly maladjusted individuals might be encouraged to relocate by tribal officials. Other young males looked at government sponsorship to live in a city as a new adventure that could be ended at any time. Young Indians in particular were unaccustomed to rigid, time-focused work routines, and job absenteeism was commonplace among them. Racial prejudice by whites clearly made them uncomfortable, and among Indians themselves those with mixed racial heritage commonly looked down on full-bloods and vice versa. An inability to speak standard American English was another handicap that led to diminished feelings of self-worth. They missed the buffering ties of family life, as well as the comfort that came from social and religious activities on their reservations. They might make visits home frequently, in part because they were homesick. Their deep attachment to a reservation landscape had no replacement in an urban setting. Many of these people, possibly most, felt alienated in an essentially hostile foreign setting. Many who remained in this environment became alcoholics, and the suicide rate was astronomical.

Nevertheless, thousands of Native Americans found the RP to be an inviting and successful escape from poverty. They sought to become upwardly mobile and were open to change. To ease the transition, Indian centers were set up in many cities so that relocatees could socialize and receive help with adjustment problems. Powwows and craft fairs became popular and were the most visible socializing aspect of urban Indian life.

A study of the Relocation Program by Donald L. Fixico (2000) provides vital source material. His summary statement in the book (p. 25) is particularly valuable:

> Ironically . . . the majority of Indians who moved to urban areas suffered socially, economically, and psychologically. In many cases, urban Indians have traded rural poverty on reservations for urban slums. Their survival in urban areas, however, yielded hope and a brighter future for their offspring. Indian youths growing up in an urban environment often become teachers, lawyers, doctors, and other professionals. It is an unfortunate fact, however, that success in the white world is costing them their native culture. Today Indians continue to experience difficulties in substituting traditional values for white American materialism and competition in the modern world.

By the early 2000s about two-thirds of the Native American population in the United States, somewhat more than 2 million people, lived in urban areas. At that time they had become the most widely distributed ethnic minority in the country. These facts in themselves should help to negate the Indian stereotype of the past. Those who have moved to urban settings, as well as those whose casinos enable them to, have a far different lifestyle than they did in the past. Their living conditions in cities have gradually improved, and their job skills have now become more socioeconomically rewarding. Considerable numbers of them are being successfully absorbed into the greater American cultural matrix. Some continue to retain their tribal identity, although tribal bonds have tended to diminish as they establish a new identity with other urban Indians in general. Others continue to hope or dream of permanently returning to their reservations. This has become an economically viable possibility for some members of casino tribes and for others whose reservation economies had improved because of other assets.

The impact of the Relocation Program lingers on, as in Portland, Oregon, and vicinity where Lakota (Teton) and Ojibwa Indians in particular were resettled. By 2004 more than thirty-one thousand Indians lived there, both relocatees and Indians who arrived on their own. Their homes were widely scattered, which tended to inhibit a strong sense of mutual identity as Native Americans. In general, the problems of urban populations still existed. In the Portland example, about 8 percent of the people were homeless, and about half of the families reportedly lived 200 percent below the poverty level. Domestic violence was prevalent, and foster care for many children was given in non-Indian households.

To help resolve these and other difficulties, a grassroots organization began to emerge in 1975—the Native American Youth Association—which was funded largely by federal, state, and county money. By 2004 the staff of thirty was aided by many volunteers, most of whom were Native Americans. Two primary goals appear to have dominated: the formal education of youth and the instilling of a positive identity as Indians. Programs included tutoring children during the school year, as well as a recently established six-week summer school session centering on math, science, and writing. Indian-oriented field trips, such as contributing to the restoration of salmon spawning grounds and a clamming trip sponsored by the Coos Indians, have been held. Youth programs in the recent past have involved more than five hundred young people. The concern of the leaders is to enhance the lives of the next generation of urban Indians.

| Unrecognized Tribes

Some 130 tribes with a total population of about 130,000 remain unrecognized by the federal government in the United States. They are concentrated largely in the eastern states and California. Federal recognition is *not* essential to be considered a tribe or band, but obtaining formal federal status is necessary to obtain most federal benefits. Unrecognized tribes usually have few members who live in or near their historic territory and typically have been ignored by the federal government because of their small size, location, or historical background. Most tribes gained formal recognition by treaty, statute, or executive order to create a land base and benefits. Since 1978 the DI's Branch of Acknowledgment and Research has been the primary means of obtaining recognition. The tribes were obligated to document their historical continuity as an indigenous population. This usually is a long, involved process that is difficult for a small group to complete. An act of Congress is an alternative means of formal recognition, but this requires powerful political supporters.

A recent example is the struggle of the Timbisha, a Western Shoshone population living in the Death Valley region of California. They received federal recognition with its benefits in 1983 but had no land commitment. Congress approved the Timbisha Shoshone Homeland Act in 2000 and granted them 314 acres of land in the Death Valley National Park, plus partial management responsibilities for additional land and limited water rights. In another, somewhat different instance 4500 acres of federal land were transferred to the San Ildefonso and Santa Clara pueblos in New Mexico in 2003. The land had been formally declared "disposal property" by the Bureau of Land Management, which facilitated the title transfer.

The longest quest for full federal recognition that remains unresolved is still being pursued by the Croatan Indians, now known as the Lumbee, who are concentrated in the Robeson County region of North Carolina. Their cultural and historical background includes a mix of fiction and reality, fancy and tradition, and speculation of unprecedented complexity.

Scottish settlers first moved into the region in the early 1730s to establish farms and plantations, but an early and seemingly reliable report about the presence of the Lumbee dates from 1790. It mentions a small number of ancestral members of the Lumbee as "free white" residents and others as "free persons of color," the latter being a description often referring to Indians and blacks who were not slaves. Following the pattern of Scottish settlers, the Lumbee established legal claims to scattered plots of farmland. Before long they began to be described by outsiders as a unique population, and eventually the state recognized them as distinct from whites, free blacks, and other Indians. They reportedly had a genetic background that included white, Cherokee, Tuscarora, and other Indian tribes. The Lumbee spoke Old English rather than an indigenous language. Their garments, houses, crops, some domestic animals (e.g., chickens), and farming methods clearly had emerged from a European background. Furthermore, numerous English surnames prevailed among them. The most logical explanation for Lumbee origins, which may be wrong, is that they were descended from the "Lost Colony," which consisted of 117 colonists whom Sir Walter Raleigh settled on Roanoke Island in 1587 and who abandoned the area before 1590. According to some historians, the people moved and became the core Lumbee population.

As antebellum white supremacy crystallized, the Lumbee launched guerrilla raids against their southern white neighbors. In the Reconstruction Era following the Civil War they became politically active as a separate population. In 1885 a sympathetic state legislator presented evidence to support the claim that the original Lumbee were descended from the Lost Colony population that had mixed with local Indians. As a result of this legislator's efforts, the state formally recognized the Lumbee as Indians. The people realized that the best means to improve their lives was through high-quality education, and they refused to attend schools for blacks. After becoming well established at the town of Pembroke in the 1880s, they were instrumental in founding and improving schools funded by the state. Ultimately their interest in education led to the present-day Pembroke State University. The state changed their name to the Lumbee Indians of North Carolina in 1951. Congress recognized their Indian status in 1956 but nonetheless refused to grant federal wardship. Subsequently they attempted unsuccessfully to gain full federal recognition with the customary benefits. A renewed effort for full recognition was launched by Senator Elizabeth Dole (R-NC), and congressional hearings were held in 2004 about the issue. Some Indians and non-Indians still contend that the Lumbee are not "real Indians." The Eastern Band of Cherokee Indians oppose Lumbee recognition. They propose, as do others, that the more than fifty thousand Lumbee seek their status change through the BIA recognition process. By November 2004, federal recognition had neither been approved nor denied.

Unsettled issues surround the status of aboriginal Hawaiians. Historically the territory, and then the state, assumed a primary responsibility of programs for the Native Hawaiian administration. They do not have agreements comparable to those basic to federal–tribal relations in other states, nor have they established a clear legal status with respect to their land and its resources. In fact, some of these people contend that the U.S. Government has *no* legal basis (e.g., treaty) for controlling them. In 2001 the U.S. Supreme Court ruled against the state policy that gave aboriginal Hawaiians preferential voting rights on racial grounds with respect to elected positions for the state Office of Hawaiian Affairs. This court decision plays a part in continuing negotiations. A proposed settlement bill had not been approved by Congress by October 2004. One major provision would grant federal recognition of Native Hawaiians as a governing entity. Congressional resolution appears to center on racial issues, a land settlement, and monetary compensation for lost lands.

| Diabetes and Native Americans

In 1999 some ten million cases of diabetes were diagnosed in the United States, and an estimated six million more cases were undiagnosed. Two primary forms of diabetes are generally identified. Type 1 usually, but not always, develops in young people whose bodies have stopped producing insulin, which is required to metabolize food into energy. (Two Canadians, Frederick G. Banting and Charles Best, first produced injectable insulin from beef pancreases in 1922.) Type 1 is rare, possibly about 8 percent of all cases. People with Type 2 diabetes are not insulin dependent, but most require pills or insulin to remain healthy. Type 2 typically appears among adults, although it is increasingly common among young people. Individual lifestyle affects the development of Type 2, although a genetic factor is also involved in any diabetes. Failure to self-manage this chronic disease may result in serious consequences (e.g., amputations, blindness, kidney failure, and heart attacks).

Type 1 diabetes does not seem to occur in Native Americans, but their risk for Type 2 is high. They had a moderate diabetes rate before the 1950s, but since then it has risen to epidemic levels. In the late 1980s the age-adjusted Indian death rate from diabetes was 2.7 times the rate for the general U.S. population. Among the Pima Indians in Arizona in the 30–64 age bracket, the death rate in the 1980s was about 500 per 1000, one of the highest rates recorded. A longitudinal study suggests that the Pima incidence may be attributed to their high-carbohydrate diet and lack of exercise, both conditions that began to prevail as they became affected increasingly by Euro-American culture.

In 1996 an estimated 9.0 percent of Native Americans in the United States who were age twenty or older were found to have diabetes, compared with 4.2 percent for non-Hispanic whites. By 2003 the Indian Health Service, as well as state health agencies, had launched widespread and intensive prevention and treatment programs that have lessened diabetic problems among reservation Indians. Tribal newspapers and newsletters now frequently include general articles about diabetes, and many public notices are posted about local prevention classes and clinics. Particular attention is paid to high-risk individuals, such as pregnant women, who have not received adequate medical attention in the past. The scope of the diabetes control campaign appears to be growing as funding increases, leading to more positive results.

Indians as Environmentalists

The "Noble Savage" characterization of Native Americans living north of Mexico gained prominence in the late 1700s, especially in its artistic and literary expressions. In recent years, this "good Indian" image has grown, and Indians are widely thought of as "the first American environmentalists."

Examples of conservation practices among aboriginal Indians are widely reported in ethnographic accounts. Fishermen leaving openings in weirs for some fish to escape is one example. Some beaver trappers also left a few animals in a lodge to reproduce. Concurrently, and in varied contexts, aboriginal Americans might not have had the technological capacity to seriously disrupt the natural balance. For instance, their relatively short gill nets, made from rawhide or plant fibers, produced comparatively modest harvests, especially when compared with the long modern nets made from cotton or synthetic fibers.

Environmentalists today forcefully and avidly condemn the burning of tropical rain forests throughout the world to produce farmlands. In eastern North America, however, indigenous Americans typically and systematically burned vast areas to produce arable land. The same was true for Euro-American pioneers, whether they were settling in Ohio or Oregon. Furthermore, it was commonplace for Indians to burn grasslands to drive out animals that could be killed for food. Native Americans were thorough vegetation burners, just as are many other peoples throughout the world.

Most Euro-Americans today probably think that Indians harvested only enough fish, game, and birds to provide necessary food and raw materials. This was both true and untrue. Did some Indians also kill animals needlessly? The answer is a clear and resounding "yes." However, we must step back and place such killings in their context.

Although not everyone would agree, a good argument can be made that killing per se is learned behavior. Assuming this is so, the sooner a child in a society of hunters learned to kill nonhuman species, the greater the person's survival potential. Thus, when a small child found a nest of ducklings and systematically pulled live birds apart, the process became a learning experience. The child could be praised, not reproved, by adults. In sum, among hunters killing became a way *to* life and a way *of* life.

It is not difficult to document the destruction of game by Native Americans in early historic times. Chipewyan examples dating from the 1770s will suffice. Samuel Hearne (1958), on his travels from Churchill along western Hudson Bay to the Coppermine River and the Arctic Ocean, reported Chipewyan wastefulness soon after their first contact with the British. He reported that caribou were so abundant that Indians "frequently [killed] great numbers merely for the fat, marrow, and tongues" (p. 75); "[i]ndeed, they were so accustomed to kill every thing that came within their reach, that few of them could pass a small bird's nest, without slaying the young ones, or destroying the eggs" (p. 76); and caribou "were very plentiful on the whole way [south]; the Indians killed great numbers of them daily, merely for the sake of their skins" (p. 127). Despite these quotes, it must be added that the Chipewyan believed, based on their creation myth, that game would always be abundant (see also Chapter 4).

Not only was the reckless destruction of animals reasonably widespread in aboriginal times among some Indians, but the practice expanded exponentially as they received firearms in the emergence of the European fur trade. Indians contributed to the near extinction of sea otter and greatly reduced the beaver and musk ox populations. Furthermore, destructive harvests have continued into the present. Why is this practice, as selective as it might be, not generally known? One answer is that modern ethnographers do not publish information about overkills, of which they are fully aware. Their rationale is to protect Native Americans from law enforcement agents and others. As Shepard Krech III (1999) suggests in his study of Indians as environmentalists, it may be that the prevailing contemporary view of Indians as ecologically caring was *borrowed from* Euro-Americans in the recent past.

| Tribalism

Tribalism refers to a unique sense of ingroup identity, which distinguishes the lifeway of one tribe from another. In early historic times, the Indian sense of tribal identity ranged from strong to weak and essentially nonexistent, depending on economic, political, and other factors. Tribal identity sometimes gave way to tribal alliances in unsuccessful attempts to avoid Euro-American domination. Following the establishment of reserved lands for Native Americans, tribalism often grew stronger as relations with whites stabilized. Indian identification with a particular tribe, whether weak or strong, represents the modern face of tribalism, irrespective of how similar or different their culture may be from its early historic configuration.

By the early 1900s ethnographers and many older Indians alike lamented the decline in traditional tribalism. This remains true at present, with a far greater sense of cultural losses. Modern expressions of tribalism are highly varied. At one extreme are tribal members who have abandoned their tribal identity by "going white." In the 1980 federal census, about one-fourth of Native American respondents did not list any tribal affiliation. An opposite extreme is represented by traditionalists, the "real" Indians, who usually live on or near their reserved lands and seek to retain or to revitalize their distinct identity. Between these extremes are innumerable alternatives suggested by the following examples. An Indian family might move to an urban area but retain close ties with their reservation, returning often to participate in social and religious activities. Alternatively, a young adult raised on a reservation might abandon tribal conventions. Later in life, he or she might begin to identify primarily with his or her tribe, especially in religious aspects. Another common pattern is for an individual or family to leave a reservation or region repeatedly to obtain work and periodically return home.

An additional gauge of a decline in tribalism is the number of aboriginal languages that continue to be spoken north of Mexico. By 1995 about half of the four hundred aboriginal languages were extinct, as previously noted (see Chapter 1). The same year forty-six tribal languages continued to be spoken by many adults and substantial numbers of children. They include Cherokee, Cree, Hopi, Inuit (Eskimo), Navajo, and Yuit (Eskimo). Traditional cultural ways are likely to persist among tribes with the greatest language vitality.

Tribal cultures possibly have their greatest strength among relatively isolated populations that have retained their indigenous languages and that depend heavily on local food resources and in tribes for which Euro-American control is a comparatively recent development. Some modern Eskimos meet these criteria. For instance, in the early 1990s at Holman, an Inuit community in the Northwest Territories of Canada, the aboriginal language continued to be spoken, but with declining proficiency by younger residents, especially those raised in nontraditional households. In general, most children were more fluent in English than in Inuit. Some twenty years previously, little English was spoken there. The material culture at Holman was dominated by imported manufactures, including television sets, washing machines, dryers, and freezers. Likewise, decreasing numbers of settlement youth were interested in traditional subsistence pursuits. Why? Some of them lacked the essential hunting skills or the economic ability to purchase the required equipment. Wage labor jobs had greater appeal, and store-bought foods were preferred by some youth over traditional edibles. Then, too, introduced sports, such as basketball and hockey, represented compelling interests. Somewhat similar studies exist about Eskimo high school students in northwestern Alaska and in the Bristol Bay sector. In the early 1990s most of these students living in towns, and nearly half of the villagers sampled, expected to leave their communities *permanently*. Students typically characterized life in their home settlements as "boring." Anticipated out-migration by students who expected to attend college was higher than for other students. I suspect that these responses of modern youthful Eskimos in Canada and Alaska are similar to those of most other relatively isolated Native Americans.

Although physical isolation unquestionably is a significant factor contributing to the relative vitality of Native American cultures, other variables demand recognition. Especially prominent is the impact of the electronic age and its potential in fostering tribal *and* intertribal identity. This influence is in part reflected in the television programs received by isolated households. Some videos, especially those made by Indians or reproduced from public television, encourage Native Americans in the United States to learn more about what is happening among the First Nations in Canada and vice versa. It appears, too, that the Internet is becoming a prominent means for Indians to communicate with members of their own and other tribes for a personal exchange of information. Additionally, and possibly just as important, individuals may access information on the Internet that is far more difficult to obtain by other means. As younger Native Americans in particular acquire the required skills, the Internet may have a lasting impact on their lives.*

| National Museum of the American Indian

On September 21, 2004, grand opening ceremonies were held to launch the National Museum of the American Indian, a Smithsonian Institution museum located along the National Mall in Washington, D.C. Unlike any other major museum in the United States, Native American consultants played an important role in the building design, landscape, and exhibit content. The displays are drawn from the 800,000 objects pertaining to indigenous Americans in the vast Smithsonian collection. The exhibits represent peoples in the Western Hemisphere with an emphasis on the United States.

The design of the museum building has been widely praised as being boldly innovative, while the landscaping represents varied ecological settings and symbolic associations with indigenous Americans (see Figure 15-1). The galleries feature exhibits about diverse ethnic groups, their histories, and present-day developments. Additional interior features include a conference center, theaters, educational workshop areas, a place where craftpersons can build boats, stores selling Indian-made artifacts, and a cafe.

| Tribal Sovereignty

Before the arrival of European settlers in what was to become the United States, it was all Indian domain. Today Native Americans control less than 3 percent of their original holdings. Land losses resulted from international

---

*Pan-Indianism (pantribalism) is presented in Chapter 2.

Figure 15-1 | The National Museum of the American Indian.

European laws as they were applied to the New World. Initially the tribe–federal relationship was reasonably equitable. Yet treaties were based on Euro-American political conventions; tribal concepts were not seriously considered. On a regional basis the first major heartless displacement occurred in the southeastern states with the Indian Removal Act of 1830. Indigenous American lands were illegally seized or bought for a pittance (see Chapter 13). As white settlers ventured westward treaty after treaty consistently diminished what had been exclusively Indian Country.

Following the Removal Act, tribes came to be identified as "domestic dependent nations," a far cry from their original status as free peoples. They were forced to cede land, along with much of their political autonomy, to federal authorities in exchange for treaty benefits and other arrangements that they usually did not seek but could not prevent. This pattern dominated for nearly a hundred years. Tribes were made subject to laws at the discretion of Congress, and most often without serious Native American consultations or approval.

Congress maintained its power but shifted its basic policy in 1953. Public Law 280 enacted in that year enabled Congress to unilaterally terminate major federal obligations to some reservations, including those with valuable natural resources desired by private corporations (e.g., timber for lumber). The states involved gained unprecedented control over the lives of the Indians involved. (See also the relocation program presented earlier in this chapter.) Also in the 1950s, Congress established a timetable to terminate *all* reservations. As Native

Americans became more politically sophisticated following World War II, they eventually challenged federal termination efforts, as has been noted. During that time period, the national political climate was becoming more sympathetic to Indians, and by the 1970s a new "self-determination" policy came to the fore. The congressional goal was to enable tribal governments to strengthen their ability to achieve far greater political and economic security on the reservations with federal help. This effort climaxed (unintentionally) with the flood of Indian casinos from the 1990s into the present. Greater financial resources at the reservation level led to relative autonomy among some of the tribes involved.

Reservation tribes are now reasserting limited tribal sovereignty based on the text of treaties, treaty-related developments, and evolving congressional legislation. Reservation tribes now regulate the use of some of their lands, benefit from restricted powers of taxation, and have limited judicial authority. They may *not* go so far as to make treaties with foreign powers or alienate land without federal approval, nor do they have jurisdiction over major crimes committed on Indian lands. Furthermore, Congress and the federal courts have crafted limits to economic changes that develop on reservations, and they restrict the authorization of tribes to deal with non-Indians who live, work, or visit on reservations. The federal government also treats land owned by enrolled members differently from lands it holds in trust for tribes.

Historically states have had clearly defined jurisdiction in Indian Country; their authority has been strictly limited by federal laws and tribal sovereignty. Currently, however, the federal government is relaxing its control in several areas. Non-Indian organizations in some states are attempting to develop their own political agendas with respect to reservation Indians. A recent example is One Nation, a private organization that began gaining momentum in Oklahoma during 2003. It opposes Indian economic rights based on their sovereignty and has been supported largely by the extractors and marketers of petroleum products, by water companies, and the Oklahoma Farm Bureau. One Nation leadership contends that because Indians pay no state taxes and receive federal support, they have economic advantages over other Oklahoma residents. If One Nation or similar organizations gain political power, the status of reservation Indians may move in new directions.

Another attack on tribal sovereignty was seen recently in an effort by Senator Ted Stevens (R-Alaska) to directly challenge the existing federal–tribal interface by turning control of law enforcement, judicial obligations, and housing responsibilities over to the State of Alaska. His effort apparently has failed, but it is in keeping with the George W. Bush administration's efforts to indirectly turn select administrative matters over to states.

As indicated earlier, states are now becoming the most persistent and avid opponents of Indian rights because they cannot tax federal trust lands, nor can they impinge forcefully on reservation life. State control over tribes is included neither in the U.S. Constitution nor in treaties. Over the years a plethora of state disputes have been argued in state and federal courts. Relatively recent cases illustrate the growing diversity of state challenges.

In 2003 the city of Sherrill, New York, began eviction proceedings against Oneida Nation members for unpaid property taxes. A federal court ruled that the property involved was on traditional Oneida land recognized in a treaty. It was within their historic reservation illegally seized by the state and thus not subject to city (or state) taxes in part because the tribe has continued to maintain a trust relationship with the federal government.

In California the state Board of Equalization ruled in 2002 that tribal governments were not required to pay state or local taxes on sales in restaurants on their reservation land. Opponents argue that this ruling was an open invitation for Indians to establish malls and shopping centers on their lands, which would give them obvious economic advantages over other California competitors.

Casinos have created a special problem because the tribes must, by federal law (IGRA), deal with state governments to obtain gaming compacts. This produces a new sovereignty issue. State governments and their citizens often are unaware that tribes have greater governmental rights on their reservation lands than do states. States and tribes are not equal. Nevertheless, debt-ridden states seek more money from tribal casinos to balance their budgets. They contend that the Indians involved are obligated to pay their "fair share" of state expenses.

At present, some state–tribal relationships are unquestionably positive. In Maine, for example, state and tribal governments have consulted about common concerns as far back as the 1820s. Following lengthy disruptions, the process was revitalized and expanded in 1975. In 2002 the Penobscot and Passamaquoddy nations each had a nonvoting member in the state house. These Indian representatives could sponsor pertinent bills and speak to pending legislation of concern to their people. The arrangement has worked out well. In another context these tribes sought to open a $650 million casino in southern Maine in 2003, but the ballot proposal was overwhelmingly rejected by voters.

A long-term problem between states and tribes with reservations has been the mutually exclusive law enforcement jurisdictions. For instance, BIA officers have no legal power over non-Indians who commit major crimes on reservations. One solution is to cross-deputize BIA, country, and state officers to more effectively handle criminal cases. For reservation Indians, this is a sovereignty issue, because a state would thereby gain power over an aspect of reservation life. Non-Indian cases go to state courts, and Indian cases are decided at a tribal court for relatively minor crimes.

Issues involving law enforcement and court jurisdictions on or off the reservation, that is, tribal, state, or federal officers' authority over Indians and non-Indians committing crimes on the reservation and tribal, state, or federal court jurisdictions, have long plagued authorities. Overlapping powers have led to inevitable disputes between the Indians and the agencies involved, as well as among the agencies themselves.

A case of importance in this regard recently reached the U.S. Supreme Court as *United States v. Lara* in 2004. The case had gone to tribal court first. At that level it was the trial of Billy Jo Lara, an Indian enrolled in a Chippewa reservation but married to an enrolled Siouan and living with her on her reservation. Based on his misconduct, Lara was expelled from this reservation but did not leave. He assaulted tribal and BIA police when they arrested him for not leaving. Lara pleaded guilty to assault and served ninety days in a tribal jail. The federal government in turn moved to prosecute him because a BIA officer was involved. Lara's defense was the double-jeopardy clause in the U.S. Constitution (the government cannot try a person twice for the same crime).

Over the years Congress and the courts came to accept the "inherent sovereignty" of tribes based on their political conventions shortly before the arrival of Europeans among them. Nevertheless, the United States eventually assumed "plenary and exclusive power" over Indian nations. Thus federally recognized tribes are regarded as subordinate to the United States as a nation. In 1990 the U.S. Supreme Court ruled in the *Duro* decision that nonmembers of a reservation could not be prosecuted for minor crimes on another reservation. Subsequently Congress passed the *"Duro*-fix" by restoring authority over minor crimes by nonmembers from another reservation. The court thus affirmed the inherent power of tribes in a limited context, with major crimes remaining under federal jurisdiction. The Supreme Court rejected Lara's double-jeopardy argument, ruling the tribal decision as separate from the federal issue in this case.

The seven-to-two ruling by the justices represents a significant victory for tribal sovereignty. As such, it is important because it is a narrow stopgap remedy as far as addressing the more sweeping issues of Indian sovereignty. In a forward-looking summary statement about *Lara* by Rebecca Adamson (2004), president of the First Nation Development Institute, suggests, "We might find that the federal government cannot regulate the tribes through ordinary domestic legislation and simultaneously maintain that tribes are sovereign in any meaningful sense."

What the future holds regarding Indian sovereignty is unsettled. *When and how* did the federal government gain political control over issues involving its agents' actions on reservations? This question has not been addressed. Do tribal courts have jurisdiction over minor crimes committed on reservations by non-Indians? This is a fervent hope of reservation tribes in general. Will Congress and the federal courts now seek to redefine Indian sovereignty? If so, new restrictions could be placed on the earlier definition of "inherent sovereignty" with respect to Indian casinos and other contexts. This is a distinct possibility. Furthermore, most present-day justices of the court are conservative in political outlook, and two of them are close to retirement. Justice John P. Stevens was 84 in 2004, and Chief Justice William H. Rehnquist was 80. The timing of retirements and the choice of their replacements are both political issues of major concern among Indians. With the political status of Indians in a greater state of uncertainty as a result of *Lara,* the issue of sovereignty remains decidedly unsettled.

| Summarizing Thoughts

Indigenous Americans are not cultural imperialists; they do not seek to make outsiders into Indians. Yet many non-Indians in the United States seek, for self-satisfying reasons, to re-form Indians into their own images. Some Indians, past and present, have worked to record and preserve their old lifeways, as have historians and anthropologists. To more fully understand, appreciate, and help perpetuate Native American cultures are surely noble goals for both groups of modern Americans. Lest we forget, most non-Native Americans remain uninvited, albeit powerful, intruders into this country. Minimally, we should strive to do Native Americans no greater harm.

| Additional Sources

As noted for Chapter 2, the best widely available and authoritative source about Native American relations with Euro-Americans is volume 4 of the *Handbook of North American Indians,* edited by Wilcomb E. Washburn (1988) and published by the Smithsonian Institution. Washburn (1996) also published a thoughtful analysis about Native American life in the recent past.

The most comprehensive reports about current issues confronting indigenous Americans appear in tribal newspapers. Prominent examples include the *Navajo Times* (Window Rock, AZ), *Tutuveni* (Hopi, Kykotsmovi, AZ), and *Tekanwennake* (Six Nations, Ohswekan, Ontario, Canada). A national weekly newspaper about present-day developments is *Indian Country Today* (Canastota, NY).

Major studies about youthful Eskimos are by Richard G. Condon, Peter Collings, and George Wenzel (1995) and by Lawrence C. Hamilton and Carole L. Seyfrit (1993; 1994). Pioneering studies about urban Indians are by John A. Price (1968; 1978), and especially Donald L. Fixico (2000). The volume about urban Indians edited by Susan Lobo and Kurt Peters (2001) is especially valuable for the highly varied case studies. Robert Jarvenpa (1985) provides an historical overview of Native American adaptations in Canada and the United States. Sharon O'Brien (1989) examines the development of tribal governments in the United States, as does Frank Pommersheim (1995). Dean H. Smith (2000) is the author of a thoughtful analysis of approaches to Native American socioeconomic developments in the recent past. Carole Goldberg (1997) presents the background to tribes unrecognized by the federal government, with emphasis on California Indian groups. Karen I. Blu (1980) details Lumbee history.

| Selected Bibliography

Adamson, Rebecca. 2004. *Lara* case is a call to the ramparts. *Indian Country Today,* May 12.

Baca, Lawrence R. 1988. The legal status of American Indians. In *History of White–Indian relations,* Wilcomb E. Washburn, ed., vol. 4, 230–37. *Handbook of North American Indians.* Washington, DC.

Blu, Karen I. 1980. *The Lumbee problem: The making of an American Indian people.* New York. (Reprint in Lincoln, NE, 2001).

Condon, Richard G. 1981. *Inuit behavior and seasonal change in the Canadian Arctic.* Ann Arbor.

Condon Richard G., Peter Collins, and George Wenzel. 1995. The best part of life. *Arctic* 48(1):31–46.

Fixico, Donald L. 2000. *The urban Indian experience.* Albuquerque.

Goldberg, Carole. 1997. Acknowledging the repatriation claims of unacknowledged California tribes. *American Indian Culture and Research Journal* 21(3):183–190.

Hamilton, Lawrence C., and Carole L. Seyfrit. 1993. Town-village contrasts in Alaskan youth aspirations. *Arctic* 46(3):255–63.

———. 1994. Coming out of the country. *Arctic Anthropology* 31(1):255–63.

Hearne, Samuel. 1795. *A journey from Prince of Wales's Fort in Hudson's Bay to the Northern Ocean.* London. (Other editions: Dublin, 1796; Toronto, 1911; Toronto, 1958).

Indian Country Today. 2000–2004. (National newspaper about indigenous peoples).

Jarvenpa, Robert. 1985. The political economy and political ethnicity of American Indian adaptations and identities. In *Ethnicity and race in the U.S.A.,* Richard D. Alba, ed., 29–47. Boston.

Krech, Shepard, III. 1999. *The ecological Indian: Myth and history.* New York.

Lobo, Susan, and Kurt Peters, eds. 2001. *American Indians and the urban experience.* Walnut Creek, CA.

O'Brien, Sharon. 1989. *American Indian tribal government.* Norman, OK.

Pommersheim, Frank. 1995. *Braid of feathers: American Indian law and contemporary tribal life.* Berkeley.

Price, John A. 1968. The migration and adaptation of American Indians to Los Angeles. *Human Organization* 27:168–75.

———. 1978. *Native studies, American and Canadian Indians.* Toronto.

Smith, Dean H. 2000. *Modern tribal development: Paths to self-sufficency and cultural integrity in Indian country.* Walnut Creek, CA.

Stevenson, Marc G. 1997. *Inuit, whalers, and cultural persistence.* Toronto.

Washburn, Wilcomb E., ed. 1988. *History of White-Indian relations.* Vol. 4, *Handbook of North American Indians.* Washington, DC.

———. 1996. The Native American renaissance, 1960–1995. In *The Cambridge history of native peoples of the Americas,* Bruce G. Trigger and Wilcomb E. Washburn, eds., vol. 1, *North America,* pt. 2, 401–473. New York.

Wunder, John R., ed. 1996. *Native American sovereignty.* New York.

Appendix A
A Sample of Widespread
Artifact Types

BASKETRY Native American women utilized three primary basketry weaves—coiling, twining, and plaiting—at the time of early historic contacts.

The coiling method was most prominent among tribes in western North America. Coiled baskets have two basic components: the horizontal coil (warp), or foundation, and a more flexible vertical coil binding strip (weft). Coils commonly were fashioned from small bundles of grass fibers sewn together with a binding strip (see Figure A-1). The sewing process was repeated until the desired shape and size were realized. The finished artifacts included bowls for food, containers for small objects, dippers, burden baskets, and hats.

Twining, which dominated among Northwest Coast peoples, also occurred widely in the western United States. Making a twined basket involved using vertical warp elements, often rods, as a foundation and joining adjacent rods by means of horizontal flexible weft strips (see Figure A-2). Both twined and coiled baskets, if they were tightly woven, could be used to process edibles for consumption. After food and water had been placed in a basket, hot stones were added to cook the food. The stones were stirred to prevent the bottom of the basket from burning. Twined water bottles were tightly woven and could be covered with pitch. Fish traps and baskets designed to collect edibles also were made with the twining method, but these were woven more loosely.

Plaited basketry commonly resulted in a checkerboard pattern; no distinction prevailed between the warp and weft elements (see Figure A-3). Plaiting dominated in the eastern United States in the production of baskets, bags, and mats. In sectors of the Northwest Coast and Southwest culture areas, plaited mats dominated. For bags or mats, plant stems or rushes often were

Figure A-1

Figure A-2

Figure A-3

split or flattened. They might be made into a checkerboard pattern, although numerous other patterns were used to provide variety.

TOOLS Some tools used by Native Americans include the rodent tooth knife, the semilunar knife, the crooked knife, and the adz.

The rodent tooth knife was widely used. It was commonly made from a beaver incisor because of the durable, chisel-like cutting surface of the tooth. The tooth typically was inserted into a wooden handle and lashed into place (see Figure A-4). This knife type served primarily to hollow out wooden artifacts or to cut grooves in their surfaces. The back of the tooth could be used to make the final polish on a wooden artifact, and the tooth sides could be used to sharpen the blades of other knives. Like the adz and the crooked knife, the rodent tooth knife was drawn toward the user when cutting.

A semilunar knife blade usually was made from flaked or ground stone and wedged into an antler or wooden handle (see Figure A-5). An Eskimo form, called an *ulu* by some Eskimos, is becoming a generic term for the type. The Eskimo ulu was a woman's knife and varied widely in size according to its purpose (e.g., sewing, butchering big game). The type occurred commonly in the Arctic and Subarctic and sporadically elsewhere. For example, in the Lake Superior region, the blade was fashioned from cold-hammered copper. In historic times metal saw blades were remade into ulu blades.

The crooked knife apparently originated after heat-treated metal was obtained from exotic sources, especially from European traders. The narrow bent iron or steel blade, from which the knife receives its name, might be made from a barrel hoop, imported trap, or scrap metal. The blade was riveted, lashed, or wedged into a handle of wood, antler, or other material (see Figure A-6). The type became a widespread woodworking tool for finishing wooden artifacts after they were blocked out with an adz. This knife type continues to be used by Native American craftspersons.

The adz dominated as a woodworking tool. Contrasting with an ax, whose blade is set parallel to the handle, an adz blade is set at right angles to the handle. In a typical wooden or antler adz handle, the blade was either lashed directly on top of the handle or, as in Figure A-7, held in a separate socket. Depending on the shape, which varied widely, adzes produced coarse to relatively fine woodwork and could also be used to fell trees. The latter purpose usually was avoided, although standing dead trees might be burned at the

Figure A-4

Figure A-5

Figure A-6   Figure A-7

base and the charred sections chipped away with a heavy adz. Logs were preferably obtained as fallen trees or as driftwood. In colonial America the adz once was a primary woodworking tool. One advantage of an adz for careful woodwork is that it is drawn toward the user, and the blows can be more precise than those of an ax. Contemporary Native American craftspersons typically continue to use adzes with metal blades for woodwork.

WEAPONS   Some weapons used by Native Americans include the bow and arrow, the fish spear, the toggle harpoon, and the double-headed toggle harpoon.

Surprisingly perhaps, the bow and arrow appear to have been invented only once in prehistory. The earliest secure evidence is from Europe, some 10,500 years ago. The combination was introduced to the Arctic culture area about 4000 years ago and to the contiguous states during the Christian era. At the time of historic contact, the bow and arrow were nearly universal north of Mexico. The earliest bows had wooden shafts (self bow) with attached bowstrings. The earliest composite bow, such as the one in Figure A-8, arrived in the Arctic from Asia around A.D. 800. This type usually was fashioned from sections of antler or wood that were tied or glued together; lengths of sinew

Figure A-8

A   B

Figure A-9

were sometimes tied on the back of the bow (composite, sinew-backed bow) or added to the back of a self bow (sinew-backed self bow).

Arrowheads typically were made from antler, stone, or bone and attached to either a foreshaft or directly to the shaft. The base (nock) of an arrow usually included feathers (fletching).

In general, ethnographic accounts report that an archer's target usually was quite close; thus great skill was required when approaching prey on foot or waiting at a concealed location. The advantage of the composite or sinew-backed bow was that it typically had greater thrust than a self bow.

The fish spear (leister) was widely used except in desert and semidesert areas. Two basic types were common, each with a long handle, and are shown in Figure A-9. One form had two or more similar barbed points (A). After a fish was struck, the barbs held it fast for retrieval. Multiple points increased the likelihood of striking the prey. Another form had a central point and two flexible prongs, each with a separate point (B). After a fish was impaled on the central point, the lateral points held it in place for retrieval. In the far north fish spears often were used at holes in ice where the water was clear and still. In the eastern and western sectors of North America, but not in the far north, leisters were used from boats at night, and fish were speared by torchlight.

The toggle harpoon, used primarily by Eskimos, held but did not kill aquatic species (e.g., seals, walrus, whales). It was the most technologically complex weapon in aboriginal North America; a Greenland type included more than thirty parts. The illustrated example on the left in Figure A-10 was for taking seals on sea ice. The stone-pointed ivory harpoon head (a) was joined to the foreshaft (b) and tied to the shaft (c); an icepick (d) was bound at the shaft base. The line (e) attached to the harpoon head was handheld or, for other harpoon styles, attached to flotation devices. As a seal entered a breathing hole (shown on the right in Figure A-10), the harpoon was thrust (B),

Figure A-10

0   .5   1 ft.

Figure A-11

and the head cut into the animal's flesh and toggled (A) as the seal attempted to escape (C). The hunter played the seal with the line until it was exhausted and then pulled it to the ice hole to kill with a knife. For narwhal hunting from a kayak (D), the harpoon head was attached to a sealskin float and drag anchor (E) to tire the whale, which was eventually killed with a lance. (Original drawings by Patrick Finnerty.)

The double-headed toggle harpoon was widespread along the Northwest Coast and western California and was used primarily to take salmon. At the top of a long wooden shaft were diverging foreshafts of different lengths with a toggle head at the end of each one (see Figure A-11). Each toggle of bone or horn was bound as a unit and tied to the shaft with a short line. This harpoon often was used at river eddies in which fish congregated to rest or feed. A harpooned fish was landed by raising the shaft. The use of diverging heads increased the probability of striking a fish. A barbed spear was not as effective against large fish because the barbs often tore free from the flesh; this occurrence was less likely with a toggling harpoon.

NETS To harvest fish, Native Americans used two types of nets—dip nets and gill nets.

A dip net for fish was widely used by aboriginal North Americans. The cone-shaped net was usually attached to a wooden hoop that kept the netting open at the mouth. Made from thong or fiber lines, the mesh size depended on the species sought (see Figure A-12). These nets were typically employed directly in streams or rivers, at weirs, or from platforms built at an eddy or other

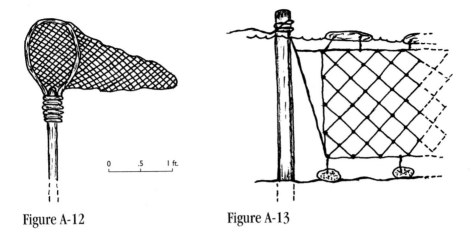

Figure A-12   Figure A-13

spots where fish congregated. With a migrating species such as salmon, hundreds of fish could be harvested in a single day.

The gill net had a relatively limited distribution and was probably most popular in the Northwest Coast culture area. The netting, of thongs or fiber, looked like a modern tennis net and had wooden floats and stone sinkers (see Figure A-13). Small fish swam through the netting, and large fish would bump against the netting and back off. A fish of the proper size, however, could not swim through the netting and was held fast by its gills. These nets typically were short and fragile, and they required careful maintenance. Gill nets also might be set from boats and drifted down a river; they are termed drift nets. Somewhat similar to a gill net were the nets used on land in British Columbia for deer or elk. Seines are similar to gill nets but have very small mesh. They were usually manipulated by two or more persons along a shoreline or riverbar and drawn to the shore or bank where the catch was collected.

TRAPS Native Americans used the fish weir and trap and numerous types of snares to obtain their quarry.

The fish weir and trap dominated along the Northwest Coast and was most effective for taking migratory species, especially salmon. A trap was fashioned from wooden splints bound in place with fiber lines. This trap for salmon faced downstream in a waterway; at right angles to it was constructed a weir (fence-like arrangement) of poles and brush (see Figure A-14). Fish ascending the waterway swam into the trap, and a funnel-shaped opening to the trap prevented most fish from escaping. This type of trap could be set beneath ice. They were sometimes made in sections and reached an overall length of about fifteen feet. The obvious advantage of a trap of this nature was that it harvested most fish ascending a stream or river.

Numerous varieties of snares were widely used, depending on environmental conditions and the potential quarry. It was desirable to set snares across

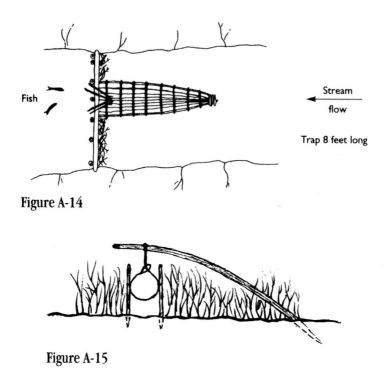

Fish

Stream

flow

Trap 8 feet long

Figure A-14

Figure A-15

a game trail, as in Figure A-15. This type was made from thong or fiber, with a noose at one end and an attachment at the other end. The noose opening size and height depended on the species sought, for example, rabbit or ground squirrel. As the prey stuck its head into the opening, the noose tightened and choked the animal to death. In still water another variety might be used for waterfowl. Multiple snares floated in a wooden, hooplike frame and held the feet of prey, such as ducks. Alternatively, stout and more elaborate snares trapped big game, such as bears. Snares usually were not tended by a person and thus operated all of the time, an advantage for capturing nocturnal species or potentially dangerous animals.

Appendix B
Resources about Native Americans

At the close of each chapter, an "Additional Sources" section provides an initial guide to further information about the topics and tribes presented. However, the range of subjects pertaining to Indians is so vast that your particular interests may not be accommodated. This guide to sources is more expansive but overlaps with the chapter listings.

ENCYCLOPEDIAS If you know comparatively little about the scope of cultural anthropology, one source in particular will be helpful. It is the four-volume *Encyclopedia of Cultural Anthropology,* David Levinson and Melvin Ember, eds., 1996, New York.

For an introduction to most topics, encyclopedias concentrating on Native Americans may be the best place to begin, although the quality of particular entries varies widely. Some of them are *Native America in the Twentieth Century: An Encyclopedia,* Mary B. Davis, ed., 1994, New York; *Encyclopedia of North American Indians,* Frederick E. Hoxie, ed., 1996, New York; *Native American Tribes,* Sharon Malinowski and Anna Sheets, eds., 1998, New York; *American Indians,* Harvey Markowitz, ed., 1995, Pasadena, CA.

SOURCE BOOKS The following works concentrate largely on present-day organizations, such as museums, tribal governments, libraries, and federal agencies: *Native Americans Information Directory,* Julia C. Furtaw, ed., 1993, Detroit, MI. *The Native American Almanac,* Arlene Hirschfelder and Martha Kreipe de Montaño, eds., 1993, New York. To learn about individuals involved before 1900, a source is *Who Was Who in Native American History: Indians and Non-Indians from Early Contacts through 1900,* Carl Waldman, 1990, New York. The topical diversity of the following book by Jack Utter is conveyed in the subtitle: *American Indians: Answers to Today's Questions,* 2001, Norman, OK.

ARCHAEOLOGY The best overview about the prehistory north of Mexico is the college textbook *Ancient North America,* Brian M. Fagan, 1995, New York. For details the following sources are especially recommended: *Archaeology of Prehistoric Native America: An Encyclopedia,* Guy Gibbon, ed.,

1998, New York; *Historical Dictionary of North American Archaeology,* Edward B. Jelks, ed., 1988, Westport, CT.

TRIBAL ETHNOGRAPHIES The best published bibliographic source by far about specific tribes is *Ethnographic Bibliography of North America,* George Peter Murdock and Timothy J. O'Leary, 4th ed., 1975, New Haven, and the supplement, 1973–1987, by M. Marlene Martin and Timothy J. O'Leary, 1990, New Haven.

ETHNOLOGICAL COMPARISONS If you are interested in the regional cultural variability among aboriginal North Americans, including those in Middle America, a key source is *Indians of North America,* Harold E. Driver, 1961, Chicago. Among the subjects examined are house types, garments, crafts, music, art, warfare, social life, and religion.

IN-DEPTH REGIONAL AND TOPICAL STUDIES The multivolume *Handbook of North American Indians,* William C. Sturtevant, gen. ed., Smithsonian Institution, Washington, DC, is an excellent source. Not all twenty volumes of this monumental work have yet appeared. The published volumes are as follows: v. 4, *History of Indian–White Relations,* 1998; v. 5, *Arctic,* 1984; v. 6, *Subarctic,* 1981; v. 7, *Northwest Coast,* 1990; v. 8, *California,* 1978; vols. 9, 10, *Southwest,* 1979, 1983; v. 11, *Great Basin,* 1986; v. 12, *Plateau,* 1998; v. 13, *Plains,* 2001; v. 14, *Southeast,* 2004; v. 15, *Northeast,* 1978; and v. 17, *Languages,* 1996.

NATIVE AMERICAN ACCOUNTS *Native American Testimony: A Chronicle of Indian–White Relations from Prophecy to the Present, 1492–1992,* Peter Nabokov, ed., 1991, New York. *Growing Up Native American,* Patricia Riley, 1993, New York. The lengthy Nabokov book (474 pages) provides an ethnohistorical survey of indigenous American writings about their lives in specific and general terms. The Riley volume focuses on accounts by twenty-two Indians about their lives in the 1800s and 1900s. Together these books provide a timely and excellent review.

LAW *American Indian Law Deskbook,* Conference of Western Attorneys General, 2004, Boulder. This is the third edition of a standard work. An historical approach to the legal status of Indians, including the recent past, is presented in *Braid of Feathers: American Indian Law and Contemporary Tribal Life,* Frank Pommersheim, 1995, Berkeley. The same general topic is examined with particular insight in *Uneven Ground: American Indian Sovereignty and Federal Law,* David E. Wilkins and K. T. Lomawaima, 2001, Norman, OK.

STEREOTYPES Euro-American cultural imperialism and its impact on Native American images encapsulates the theme of *Selling the Indian: Commercializing and Appropriating American Indian Cultures,* Carter J. Meyer and Diana Royer, eds., 2001, Tucson. Indians in popular culture also are examined in *Playing Indian,* Philip J. Deloria, 1998, New Haven. Although focusing on adornments, *North American Indian Jewelry and Adornment: From Prehistory to the Present,* by Lois S. Dubin, 1999, New York, includes a discussion of broader material culture changes, which makes it especially helpful.

RACE   *One Drop of Blood: The American Misadventure of Race,* Scott L. Malcomson, 2000, New York. The book examines Indian, African American and Euro-American relations in historical context with engaging insight. *African Americans on the Western Frontier,* Monroe L. Billington and Roger D. Hardaway, eds., 1998, Niwot, CO. Concentrating on historical developments from 1865 to around 1910, chapter topics include blacks as soldiers, cowboys, and slaves and all-black towns.

LANGUAGES   *The Languages of Native North America,* Marianne Mithun, 1999, Cambridge, UK, is the most notable one-volume study of languages to the north of Mexico. This lengthy book is the most comprehensive comparative survey, and it probably will become the standard study for many years.

CASINOS   *Indian Gaming: Tribal Sovereignty and American Politics,* W. Dale Mason, 2000, Norman, OK, includes historical survey about Indian gaming followed by a discussion of casinos in New Mexico and Oklahoma. It quite possibly is the best survey of the subject. The most controversial casino is Foxwoods in Connecticut. The machinations of the Indians involved, the financial backers, and the politicians are little short of astounding. Two books about these developments are biased but revealing: *Revenge of the Pequots: How a Small Native American Tribe Created the World's Most Profitable Casino,* Kim I. Eisler, 2002, New York, and *Without Reservation: The Making of America's Most Powerful Indian Tribe and Foxwoods, the World's Largest Casino,* Jeff Benedict, 2000, New York.
    Tourism and Gaming on American Indian Lands, Alan A. Lew and George A. Van Otten, eds., 1998, New York. The authors, in broad and narrow outlooks, emphasize the impact of tourists and casinos on reservation life, past and present.

RODEOS   *Riding Buffaloes and Broncos: Rodeo and Native Traditions in the Northern Great Plains,* Allison F. Mellis, 2003, Norman, OK. Despite the regional emphasis, this book is among the best studies of rodeo history.

TIMELY TOPICS   *Contemporary Native American Cultural Issues,* Duane Champagne, ed., 1999, Walnut Creek, CA. This work deserves particular attention if you seek information about current developments ranging from gender issues to visual media and health.

LITERATURE *Native American Literature: Boundaries and Sovereignties,* Kathryn W. Shanley, ed., 2002, Vashon Island, WA. For novels a key source is *The Native American in Long Fiction: An Annotated Bibliography,* Joan Beam and Barbara Brandstad, 1993, Walnut Creek, CA.

THE INTERNET For U.S. Federal Government sources, consult the *Internet Blue Pages,* Laurie Androit, 1998, Medford, NJ. A more general source is *The Internet Directory,* version 2.0, Eric Braun, ed., 1996, New York.

Key U.S. Government websites are as follows:

Department of Commerce—Census Bureau—American Indian Data
  http://www.census.gov/population/www/socdemo/race/indian.html

Department of Interior—Bureau of Indian Affairs
  http://www.doi.gov/bureau-indian-affairs.html

Department of Interior—Bureau of Land Management—Guidance for Native American Consultation
  http://www.blm.gov/nhp/efoia/wo/handbook/h8160-1.html

Department of Interior—Office of American Indian Trust
  http://www.doi.gov/oait

Department of Interior—Office of the Special Trustee for American Indians
  http://www.ost.doi.gov

Department of Justice—Office of Tribal Justice
  http://www.usdoj.gov/otj/otj.html

Department of Labor—Indian & Native American Programs
  http://www.wdsc.org/dinap

Environmental Protection Agency—American Indian Environmental Office
  http://www.epa.gov/owindian

Federal Emergency Management Agency—Draft American Indian and Native Alaska Policy
  http://www.fema.gov/library/frgn019.htm

U.S. Representatives Internet Law Library—Indian Nations and Tribes
  http://law.house.gov/31.htm

U.S. Senate—Committee on Indian Affairs
  http://www.senate.gov/~scia

One informed nongovernment website is the National Congress on American Indians at *www.ncai.org.* Another is the Native American Rights Fund at *http://www.narf.org.*

Native American Resources, found at *http://www.nativeamericans.com/resources.htm,* provides an extensive list of resources with wide-ranging topical coverage.

ETHNOGRAPHIC FILMS AND VIDEOS   The account about "the last wild Indian in North America," discovered in California in 1911, is widely acclaimed and titled *Ishi, the Last Yahi*. A classic documentary, released first in 1922 and filmed by Robert Flaherty, is about Eskimos (Inuit) along the eastern shore of Hudson Bay and titled *Nanook of the North*.

The best source is the Audio-Visual Services, Pennsylvania State University, *www.medianet.libraries.psu.edu*.

FEATURE FILMS   Two comparatively recent films are especially notable and widely available in video stores. Each is a poignant, sad, and humorous account of modern Indian life. *Pow Wow Highway* is regarded by many Indians as the best film about the contemporary scene. Sherman Alexie, of Spokane and Coeur d'Alene ancestry, wrote and coproduced *Smoke Signals,* released in 1998, which has received numerous awards.

Glossary

acculturation (culture contact, transculturation) represents the changes in the culture of a people resulting from contacts with other peoples; the Native American response to Euro-Americans is an example

agriculture the cultivation of field crops with the aid of plows and draft animals

Anglo (Anglo-American) English-speaking whites; the term is used most commonly in the Southwest

artifact (artefact) any object of human workmanship

babiche thin, dehaired strips of animal skins; used primarily as binders

Bahana the Hopi word for the mythological older brother of the Hopi, whose descendants would someday return when the Hopi were in desperate need

band a small, family-oriented group of aboriginal foragers; the word is now used in Canada and the United States to identify some federally recognized groups of Native Americans, for example, the Six Nations Band

bannock (fry bread, Indian bread) in Native American context, refers to white flour and baking powder mixed with water and fried in grease

baseline ethnography the description of a tribe before the members had significant contact with representatives of a literate society; thus the time frame varies widely by geographical area

berdache traditionally identified as a physiological male who assumes the behavior, dress, and status of a woman; more recently defined as a physiological male *or* female who assumes the behavior, dress, and status of the opposite sex; the terms "man-woman," and "woman-man" appear to be gaining favor

biculturation combining the traits of one culture with those of the members of another culture; for example, a modern Crow Indian shares in both Crow and Euro-American culture at the same time

bifurcate collateral kinship terms (for parents and their siblings) an uncle, aunt, mother, and father are each given separate terms

bifurcate merging kinship terms (for parents and their siblings) father and father's brother are called by one term, mother and mother's sister by another term, but mother's brother and father's sister terms are distinct

bilateral descent relatives are traced through both the male and female lines; the descent system used in the United States today

bilocal residence   the establishment of residence by a married couple with or near either the husband's or the wife's parents

booger mask   a Cherokee term, with the same root as the English word "bogey"; refers to enemies depicted on dance masks

bow, composite   *See* composite bow

bow, self   *See* self bow

bow, sinew-backed   *See* sinew-backed bow

bride price   an alternative term for bridewealth

bride service   a groom must work on behalf of a bride's family for an indefinite or established length of time

bridewealth   material property presented by a man, or a man and his kin group, to reward a woman's family for the loss to her natal group and to legitimize a marriage

bull-roarer   usually a piece of wood tied to the end of a cord that is twirled to make a roaring sound; the sound produced may have supernatural implications

calumet   a Native American ceremonial pipe smoked in religious contexts or on state occasions, such as to validate a treaty

cariole   a French word to refer to a toboggan with side panels and stanchions at the back; the cariole is a French innovation. *See also* toboggan

cat's cradle   a string tied at the ends and looped around the fingers of both hands to form a cradlelike pattern; as the string is manipulated different patterns emerge; may involve two persons

charismatic person   an individual with an inordinate personal capacity for leadership

Chilcat robe   a woven woolen dance robe made by Chilkat (Tlingit) women

clan   a unilineal descent group in which relatives are traced primarily along the male or female line to a presumed common ancestor; thus matriclans and patriclans

Code Talkers   Navajo in the U.S. Marine Corps during World War II who used Navajo words as a code in frontline radio transmissions in the Pacific campaign

composite bow   sections of antler or horn glued together to form a bow; it may be backed with strands of sinew as one type; *see* Appendix A for an example

composite family   represented by a woman and multiple husbands or a man with multiple wives

count coup   a means of exhibiting bravery in warfare by striking or touching a live enemy; associated primarily with Plains Indians

cousin terms

Crow type: father's sister's daughter and mother's brother's daughter are termed differently from sisters and parallel cousins, but father's sister's daughter is termed the same as father's sister and/or mother's brother's daughter is termed the same as brother's daughter

> *Eskimo type:* parallel and cross-cousins are termed the same but with a separate term from those used for siblings; this is the cousin terminology used in the United States
>
> *Hawaiian type:* parallel and cross-cousins are termed the same as siblings; thus "uncles" and "aunts" are termed the same as "mother" and "father"
>
> *Iroquois type:* father's sister's daughter and mother's brother's daughter are called by the same terms, but different terms are used for parallel cousins and for sisters
>
> *Omaha type:* father's sister's daughter and mother's brother's daughter are called by terms different from each other and different from those used for parallel cousins and sisters; however, father's sister's daughter is termed the same as sister's daughter and/or mother's brother's daughter the same as mother's sister

cross-cousins   the children of siblings of the opposite sex; father's sister's children and mother's brother's children

Crow-type cousin terms   *See* cousin terms, Crow type

cultural blindness   a trait that appears to be illogical in its cultural context; for example, the long, slim olive jars in the United States today that make it difficult to remove the olives

cultural relativism   the view that any human behavior occurs in the context of a particular culture and should be considered within that framework; for example, societies have different cleanliness standards

culture area   a geographical sector of the world whose occupants exhibit more cultural similarities with each other than with the peoples in other culture areas

deadfall   a trap with a baited and triggered entry and a weight above that falls on an animal when it attempts to take the bait; especially useful against bears

descent, bilateral   *See* bilateral descent

descent, unilineal   *See* unilineal descent

Dinetah   the Navajo word for their traditional homeland in the Southwest

dip net   a bag-shaped net with rigid support around the mouth and a long handle used to scoop fish or other aquatic species from the water; broadly similar to a butterfly net used in the United States; *see* Appendix A for an example

dumaiya   the Hopi word applied to a young man who secretly visits a young woman in her home at night to have sexual intercourse

encomienda   a land grant in the Southwest given to Spanish colonists as a reward for services rendered; included control over resident Indians

endogamy   marriage to someone within a defined group, for example, band or village

Eskimo-type cousin terms   *See* cousin terms, Eskimo type

ethnocentrism   the attitude that one's own culture is superior compared with all others; an example is to regard your own religion as superior to all others

ethnographic present the use of the present tense when describing past forms of behavior; a literary device to convey the vitality of an ethnographic account

ethnography a descriptive framework for behavioral information about a population at a particular point in time, usually a year

ethnography, baseline *See* baseline ethnography

ethnohistory the presentation and interpretation of ethnographic information in historical context

ethnology the systematic comparison of cultures to establish how and why they are similar or dissimilar

ethos the guiding beliefs, standards, or ideals that characterize a people; the Harmony Ethic of the Cherokee is an example

extended family the families of two or more siblings that are joined over two or more generations

False Face Society an Iroquois sodality whose members were primarily curers

fandango a lively Spanish dance accompanied by fast music popular in Spanish America and integrated into traditional Native American social or ceremonial events, especially in the southwestern United States

first fruit (first harvest) the ceremonial distribution of an initial harvest for a plant product or an animal species

First Nations a designation in Canada for their Eskimo (Inuit), Indian, and Métis populations

fish trap an arrangement of stones or wooden splints, often funnel-shaped, set in conjunction with a weir to capture and hold, but not kill, fish; *see* Appendix A for an example

Five Civilized Tribes the Cherokee, Chickasaw, Choctaw, Creek, and Seminole

foragers people who depend on wild species for food; they hunt, fish, and collect plant products for a living

gadugi the Cherokee term for a free labor company, a sodality

generational kinship terms (for parents and their siblings) the father term is extended to uncles and the mother term is extended to aunts

gill net a fishing device that looks somewhat like a tennis net with floats attached at the top and weights at the bottom; as a fish of appropriate size attempts to swim through the mesh, it is caught by its gills; may be used to entangle other species, such as beaver; *see* Appendix A for an example

hand game *See* stick game

Harmony Ethic the Cherokee ideal for people to be nonaggressive and generous with one another

harpoon, toggle-headed *See* toggle-headed harpoon

Hawaiian-type cousin terms *See* cousin terms, Hawaiian type

hogan the Navajo word for their pole-framed and earth-covered types of dwellings

hominy   from an Algonquian word that now refers to a food prepared from kernels of corn whose shells have been removed

hooch   a distilled alcoholic beverage originally made by Indians

hopi   a Hopi term for a person who is good, honorable, and nonaggressive

horticulture   the small-scale cultivation of domestic plants with a hoe and digging stick

hozho   the Navajo word that means balance, beauty, goodness, happiness, harmony, and health

Indian   an aboriginal or indigenous (as opposed to an immigrant) inhabitant of the Americas; an American Indian or Native American

infanticide   the killing of a newborn offspring, or sometimes a young child

Iroquois-type cousin terms   *See* cousin terms, Iroquois type

kachina doll   the small-scale representation of mythological, ancestral, or historical figures; the figures are not "dolls" as toys but are designed to teach children the differences among the many types of kachinas

kahopi   a Hopi word for a person who is dishonorable and aggressive

kayak   a skin-covered Eskimo vessel with an enclosed deck designed to accommodate one person; the boat is framed with wood and/or antler

kinaalda   the Navajo word for the ceremony that a girl underwent at her menarche

kindred   close bilateral relatives along the male and female lines; a kindred is ego-centered, meaning that a particular kindred is shared only by biological siblings; the kindred is an important kin group in the United States today

kiva   a Pueblo Indian ceremonial structure that is often beneath the ground

kueex   the Tlingit term for a potlatch

kwaan   a major geographical area identified by the Tlingit; comparable in many ways to a "tribe"

labret (lip plug)   an artifact, often made from wood, worn in a perforation above, below, or at the sides of the lips; multiple labrets may be worn

leister (fish spear)   often with multiple barbed heads; *see* Appendix A

levirate   the marriage of a woman to her deceased husband's brother

lineage   a consanguineal kin group with descent traced along either the female or male line from a known common ancestor

lineal kinship terms (for parents and their siblings)   father's brother and mother's brother are given one term, father's sister and mother's sister are given a different term; both terms are different from those for parents; this is the "uncle" and "aunt" classification used in the United States today

lip plug   *See* labret

Long Walk   the forced removal beginning in 1863 of Navajo to Fort Sumner (Bosque Redondo) by the U.S. military; the captives remained there under military control until 1868

manitou   an Algonquian word for a supernatural force

mano   *See* milling stones

material culture the physical objects made and used by a people; the products of technology; examples include tools, weapons, garments, dwellings, and art objects

matriclan relatives traced through the female line to a presumed common ancestor

matrilineal descent relatives traced through the female line

matrilocal residence the establishment of residence by a married couple within or near the wife's mother's household

medicine bundle (sacred or spirit bundle) a packet of sacred objects for an individual or for a group such as a clan

menarche the initial menstruation of a female

metate *See* milling stones

Métis the term widely used in Canada to refer to a person of mixed Indian and non-Indian ancestry

milling stones used to pulverize seeds or animal materials in the preparation of edibles; the base stone may be termed a milling stone, metate, or quern; the hand-held stone may be termed a hand stone, mano, or rubbing stone

mnemonic to aid memory; for example, tying a string around a finger

moiety when a society at the highest level is divided into two and only two social groups, each of these is termed a moiety; for example, if a tribe had six clans, one moiety might consist of the members of clans A, B, and C while the opposite moiety would consist of the members of clans D, E, and F.

moiety exogamy the convention that an individual must marry someone from the opposite moiety

money a medium of exchange with a standardized value

neolocal residence the establishment of a separate residence by a married couple apart from the husband's or wife's parents

neonate a newborn human offspring less than twenty-eight days of age

net the male leader of a Cahuilla clan

nuclear core family a nuclear family plus one or more outsiders (e.g., wife's mother, husband's cousin)

nuclear family same as the basic or elementary family; a person, the person's spouse, and their dependent offspring

oki an Iroquois term for a personal guardian spirit

Omaha-type cousin terms *See* cousin terms, Omaha type

paha a male ceremonial leader among some groups of Cahuilla

Pan-Indianism or pantribalism; a sharing of traits among the members of different tribes, for example, apparel, dances, foods, and ceremonies

parallel cousins the children of siblings of the same sex; father's brothers' children and mother's sisters' children

patriclan a group of families related primarily through males to a presumed common ancestor

patrilineage a family line that is traced primarily through males to a known common ancestor

patrilineal descent   relatives traced through the male line

patrilocal residence   the establishment of residence by a married couple within or near the husband's family's household

pemmican   a Cree word that refers to dried pulverized meat and fat used mainly as food for travelers

peon   a guessing game played by the Cahuilla

personal kindred   blood relatives of a person of his or her generation, as well as junior and senior generations; the convention that prevails in the United States at present

phratry   two or more associated clans that recognize common unilineal ties

piki   a Hopi word for finely ground cornmeal mixed with water and ashes and cooked on a heated stone slab

polyandry   a form of marriage in which a woman has two or more spouses at the same time

polygamy   a form of marriage in which the participants have two or more spouses at the same time

polygyny   a form of marriage in which a man has two or more wives at the same time

potlatch   from the Nootka word "gift"; a ceremonial occasion in which wealth is displayed and gifts presented to honor a person and validate the claim to a title

powwow   a Narraganset word originally referring to the activities of shamans; presently used to refer to a public Indian gathering that focuses on feasting, dancing, other performances, and the sale of Indian craft items

primogeniture   preferential inheritance by the firstborn male or, less often, by the firstborn female

religion   a minimal definition proposed by Edward B. Tylor in 1871 is "the belief in Spiritual Beings"; a more detailed definition by Melford E. Spiro in 1966 is "an institution consisting of cultural patterned interaction with culturally postulated superhuman beings"

rites of passage   rituals performed in response to status changes affecting the life of an individual (e.g., birth, marriage, death)

sachem   based on an Algonquian word and used widely to refer to a hereditary male leader; the head of a matriclan among the Iroquois is called a sachem

sacred bundle (medicine or spirit bundle)   a packet of sacred objects of an individual or a group, such as a clan

sagamite   an Algonquian word applied to corn porridge; a hominy gruel

seine   a small-meshed net the ends of which are drawn together to enclose fish

self bow   a bow made from a wooden shaft

shaman   a word from the Tungus in Russia; a part-time specialist in the supernatural; "shaman" does not mean sha*man,* a shaman may be male or female; the plural is shamans

sinew-backed bow   a wooden bow shaft or composite bow strengthened with strips of sinew along the back; *see* Appendix A for an example

skywalker   a term used to refer to Indians, especially Mohawk, who work in high steel

slave   the subordinate status of a person that is passed on to his or her descendants; a captive in warfare, an individual purchased, or the child of an indebted person often were slaves

sliding historical baseline   the beginning of history on a regional basis; for example, in area A historic contact with Euro-Americans may have taken place in A.D. 1600, whereas in area B it came in A.D. 1800; the time difference is ignored when establishing the beginnings of written history in the respective areas

snare   a running noose of babiche or other strong material, firmly anchored (e.g., to a bush or tree) to hold a bird or other creature that is caught in the noose; *see* Appendix A for an example

sodality   a secondary, special-purpose association with either voluntary or involuntary membership

sorcery   the use of power gained with the assistance or the control of evil spirits; witchcraft is the use of sorcery

sororal polygyny   a form of marriage in which a man marries two or more women who are sisters

sororate   the marriage of a man to the sister of his wife, either while he is married to or after the death of his first wife

stick game (hand game)   involves skill and chance by two teams accompanied by drums and songs; it is widely popular in the western states and western provinces; the game is based on score counters resulting from the manipulation of "bones"

surround   a structure often made from stone or poles and brush into which big game was driven to become impounded and killed by other means

sweat bath   bathing in the heat produced by coals from a fire or fire-heated stones for pleasure and/or for a supernatural purpose; often a small structure; water may be placed on stones to produce a steam bath

taboo (tabu)   a Polynesian word meaning "sacred"; it commonly refers to something that is both sacred and forbidden

taiga   a moist subarctic forest dominated by conifers

teknonymy   naming a parent after a child, often the firstborn; for instance, if the child's name is Alfred, his mother is called "Alfred's mother"

throwing stick (boomerang, missile stick, rabbit-killing stick)   used to hurl at birds or small game to stun or kill; the self-returning boomerang did not exist in North America

toboggan   an Algonquian word; a flat-bottomed conveyance usually made from thin strips of wood bound together and bent upward at the front; *see also* cariole

toggle-headed harpoon   a weapon, typically associated with Eskimos, designed to pierce the skin of an aquatic species and then to toggle (somewhat in the manner of a button passing through a buttonhole); a harpoon usually holds but does not kill prey; *see* Appendix A for an example

toloache   from a Nahuatl word adopted by the Spanish; among the Cahuilla it refers to a narcotic, jimsonweed, used by some Cahuilla in a male initiation ceremony

tomahawk   an Algonquian word for a light stone ax used as a weapon; following European contact a tomahawk head was manufactured from metal as a trade item and could include a pipe bowl at the head

totem pole   a pillar facing or pole with carved and painted symbols representing a clan and based on mythological or historical events

Trail of Tears   the Cherokee term for the removal of most Indians from the Southeast to Indian Territory in the 1830s

trait   an act, object, or thought identified with a specific culture; examples include shaking hands (an act), a pencil (an object), and doomsday (a thought)

transhumance   the seasonal movement of livestock by herders from one altitude to another

transvestite   a person who adopts the clothes of the opposite sex and often behaves in the manner of the opposite sex; *see also* berdache

travois   a French Canadian word for a conveyance consisting of two trailing poles with a platform for a load; a travois was initially pulled by a dog and later by a horse

tribe   in general, a small-scale society with a name, dialect, and a territory, but without central political authority

tunraq   protective spirits that Eskimo (Inuit) shamans attempt to control

tupiliq   dangerous Eskimo (Inuit) spirits that were especially hostile toward people and capable of causing illness or death

umiak   a large open wood-framed and skin-covered Eskimo boat

unilineal descent   relatives are traced through the female line (matrilineal) or the male line (patrilineal)

universalism   the approach to human behavior based on the acceptance of value categories applicable to all cultures

value   a shared concept of what is desirable or undesirable

vanes   feathers attached near the base of an arrow shaft to help guide an arrow in flight

village endogamy   marriage to someone within one's own community

wampum   based on an Algonquian word for a string of white beads; the bead patterns of a wampum belt were "talked into" as a means of keeping records; for example, a particular bead pattern might refer to a tribe, whereas a second bead pattern might refer to the place of a treaty arrangement

weir   an obstruction of stone, brush, or other material across a stream or river to block the progress of fish; it may form a dam and be used with fish spears or have openings for fish traps; *see* Appendix A for an example

witchcraft   employing sorcery; sorcery is the use of power gained with the assistance or control of evil spirits

Yei   the Navajo word for their mythological Holy People

Pronunciation Guide*

Aleut   AL-ee-oot
Algonquian   al-GON-kin
Amouskositte   ah-mos-ko-SIT-tee   (early Cherokee leader)
Anasazi   Ah-nuh-SAH-zee   (archaeological tradition in the Southwest)
Apache   uh-PATCH-ee
Apsáalooke   ap-SOO-laa-ka   (Crow name for themselves)
Arapooish   AARLA-push   (Crow leader)
Auke   AA-kay   (Tlingit geographical unit)
babiche   bah-BEESH   (strip of skin used as a binder)
Bannock   BAN-uck   ("Indian bread")
berdache   BEHR-dash   (transvestite, "man-woman" or "woman-man")
Blackfoot   BLAK-fut
Cahuilla   kuh-WEE-uh
calumet   KAL-u-meht   (ceremonial pipe)
cariole   KAHR-ee-ool   (type of toboggan)
Caughnawaga   gon-na-WAH-ga   (Iroquois reserve)
Cayuga   ki-YOO-guh
Cherokee   CHER-uh-kee
Chickasaw   CHICK-uh-saw
Chinook   shi-NOOK
Chipewyan   chip-uh-WI-uhn
Chippewa   CHIP-uh-wah
Coeur d'Alene   kur-duh-LANE
coup   koo   (touching an enemy in warfare)
Crow   KRO
Deganawida   da-gon-na-WEE-dah   (cofounder of the League of the
   Iroquois)
Diné   di-NAY   (the Navajo's name for themselves)
Dinetah   di-NAY-tah   (Navajo homeland)
dumaiya   doo-MIY-yuh   (Hopi courting practice)
gadugi   gah-DOO-gee   (Cherokee free-labor company)
Gros Ventre   grow-VAHN-truh
Haida   HI-duh

*AUTHOR'S NOTE: Some aboriginal languages have sounds that are quite different from those
of American English.

Hiawatha   hi-uh-WAW-ta   (cofounder of the League of the Iroquois)

Hidatsa   he-DOT-suh

hogan   HO-hwahn in Navajo; HO-gon in English   (Navajo dwelling)

hooch   hootch   (distilled alcoholic beverage)

Hopi   ho-PEE in their language; HO-pee in English

Hupa   HOOP-uh

Huron   HYUR-on

Inuit   IN-yoo-it

Inuktitut   in-Nook-t-toot   (Inuit name for their language)

Iroquois   IR-uh-kwoi in the United States; IR-uh-kwa in Canada

kachina   kaht-SEE-nuh in Hopi; ka-CHE-na in English   (Hopi mythical, ancestral, or historical supernatural)

kahopi   kah-HOH-pee   (Hopi word for a dishonorable person)

Karok   KAH-ruke

kinaalda   ki-nahl-DAH   (Navajo term for a girl's puberty ceremony)

Klukwan   KLUCK-ahn   (Tlingit village)

Kootenai   KOOT-nee

kueex   qu-EEX   (Tlingit word for potlatch)

kwaan   QU-aan   (major Tlingit geographical unit)

Kwakiutl   KWAH-kee-oo-tel

Lumbee   LUM-bee

Maasaw   maah-SAHW   (Hopi god of death)

Manitou   MAN-i-too   (a supernatural force)

Mohawk   MO-hawk

Moytoy   MOY-TOY   (early Cherokee leader)

Mukat   MU-kat   (one of the twin Cahuilla creators)

Naa Ka Hidi Theater   naa-kah-HIDI   (Tlingit performance group)

Nampeyo   naum-PEH-yoh   (Hopi woman)

Nan-ye-hi   nan-YEE-hee   (Cherokee name for Nancy Ward)

Natchez   NATCH-is

Navajo   NAV-uh-ho

net   net   (a Cahuilla clan leader)

Netsilik   NET-silik

Oconaluftee   oh-KOE-nah-LUF-tee   (reconstructed Cherokee settlement)

Ojibwa   o-jib-WAY

Oraibi   oh-zhiy-VHEE in Hopi; oh-rye-be in English   (Hopi village)

pah   PA-ha   (a Cahuilla leader)

parfleche   PAHR-flehsh   (container made of folded skin)

Passamaquoddy   pah-suh-muh-KWOD-ee

pemmican   PEHM-i-kehn   (dried meat as food for travelers)

Penobscot   puh-NOB-scot

peon   pe-ON in Cahuilla   (Cahuilla guessing game)

piki   PEE-kee   (a Hopi ground cornmeal "bread")

poncho   PAHN-choh   (garment)

potlatch   POT-lach   (ceremonial wealth display and gift giving)

Powamu poh-WAH-moo (Hopi ceremony)
Powhatan pow-HAT-un
Seneca SEN-uh-kuh
Sioux SUE
Soyal soh-YAHL (Hopi ceremony)
Tamaiot tim-a-YO-hwit (one of the twin Cahuilla creators)
Tekakwitha, Kateri de-ga-GWEE-ta, ga-de-LEE (Mohawk, beatified by
    the Roman Catholic church)
Tlingit THLING-kuht
Tododaho ta-do-DAH-hoe (Onondaga sachem)
Tohono O'Odham to-HO-no o-O-tahm (Papago)
Tuscarora tusk-uh-ROAR-uh
Wuwuchim woo-WOO-thim (Hopi secret society)
Wuya WOO-yuh (Hopi clan ancestors)
Yei yay (Navajo mythological Holy People)
Yupik YOO-pik (Eskimo linguistic group)
Zuni ZOO-nee

Name Index

Abel, Louison (Chipewyan), 123
Aberle, David F., 368
Abler, Thomas S., 394
Abraham, Eneas (chief; Lower Kootenai), 160
Abraham, Paul (Lower Kootenai), 159
Adamson, Rebecca, 492
Albrecht, Andrew C., 464
Alexie, Sherman (Spokane and Cour d'Alene), 60, 507
Amouskositte (Cherokee), 428
Amundsen, Roald, 95
Androit, Laurie, 506
Antonio, Juan (Cahuilla), 256
Arapooish (chief; Crow), 214, 217, 224
Asbury, C. H., 226–227
Axtell, James, 66

Babbitt, Bruce, 198
Bailey, Garrick Alan, 342, 347, 378
Bailey, Roberta Glenn, 342, 347, 378
Balikci, Asen, 88, 94, 102
Banks, Dennis (Chippewa), 56
Banting, Frederick G., 484
Baranov, Alexander, 292
Barbeau, Marius, 303
Barboncito (Navajo), 347
Barlett, Donald L., 470
Barman, Jean, 67
Barnett, Jim, 467
Barreiro, José, 394
Barrows, David P., 266
Battiste, Marie, 67
Beaglehole, Ernest, 338
Beaglehole, Pearl, 338
Beale, Edward F., 256
Beam, Joan, 506
Bean, Lowell J., 266
Bear-in-the-Middle, Addie (Crow), 225
Beebe, Wilber (Blackfoot), 53
Begay, Tina L. (Navajo), 376
Bell-rock (chief; Crow), 212
Bender, Margaret, 444
Benedict, Jeff, 505
Bennett, Robert L. (Oneida), 60
Bennion, Lynn J., 59
Bering, Vitus, 292
Best, Charles, 484
Bielawski, Ellen, 135

Bienville, Jean de, 464
Big Day, Heyward (Crow), 228, 229
Big Day, William (Crow), 228, 229
Billington, Monroe L., 505
Birdinground, Clifford (Crow), 232
Birket-Smith, Kaj, 102
Blu, Karen I., 493
Bodmer, Karl, 49, 50
Bonvillain, Nancy, 338, 416
Boucher, Alfred (Chipewyan), 131
Boucher, Joe (Chipewyan), 131
Bourgeault, Lisa J., 266
Bowler, Alida, 192
Bradley, Charles, 236
Bradley, James H., 237
Brando, Marlon, 54
Brandstad, Barbara, 506
Brant, Joseph (Mohawk), 382, 401, 404, 415
Braun, Eric, 506
Briggs, Jean L., 84, 92, 93–94, 102
Brodeur, Paul, 67
Brooks, James F., 444
Brunton, Bill B., 168
"Buffalo Bill" (William F. Cody), 50
Bush, George W., 32, 476, 490
Bustamante, Cruz, 263
Butterfly, Fanny (Crow), 225

Cabeson (Cahuilla), 256
Cadman, Charles, 5
Campbell, Benjamin Nighthorse (Northern Cheyenne), 60, 478–479
Carleton, James H., 346
Carpenter, Harold (Crow), 231
Castillo, Edward D. (Cahuilla and Luiseño), 64
Catlin, George, 49–50, 206, 213, 429
Champagne, Duane, 505
Chattaway, Thurland, 5
Chatters, James C., 29
Chirikov, Alexei, 292
Choudhary, Trib, 376–377, 378
Chrétien, Jean, 414
Clemmer, Richard O., 335–336, 338
Cobell, Elouise (Blackfeet), 478–479
Cody, William F. ("Buffalo Bill"), 50
Cohen, Felix S., 67
Cohen, Lucy K., 67

Colden, Cadwallader, 396
Collings, Peter, 493
Columbus, Christopher, 2, 34
Condon, Richard G., 493
Conrad, Maia, 401
Cooper, James Fenimore, 5
Coronado, Francisco, 327, 344
Creel, Matthew (Edisto-Natchez-Kusso), 467
Crosby, Alfred W., Jr. (Northern Cheyenne), 29
"Crow Boy" (Kevin Old Horn; Crow), 228
Crozat, Antoine, 464
Crum, Steven J. (Western Shoshone), 171, 174, 200
Curtis, Charles (Euro-American and Kaw), 60
Custer, George, 234, 237
Cutler, Charles L., 29

Damas, David, 102
Dann, Carrie (Western Shoshone), 198
Dann, Dewey (Western Shoshone), 198
Dann, Mary (Western Shoshone), 198
Dauenhauer, Nora (Tlingit), 64
Davis, Gray, 263, 264, 474
Davis, Mary B., 503
d'Azevedo, Warren L., 199–200
De Acosta, Joseph, 11
De Anza, Juan Bautista, 256
Deardorff, Merle H., 402
De Champlain, Samuel, 382
Deer, Ada (Menominee), 60
Deer Nose, Kitty (Crow), 225
Deganawida (Onondaga), 392
de Laguna, Frederica, 275, 303
Delgamuukw (Earl Muldoe), 42
Deloria, Philip J., 505
Deloria, Vine, Jr. (Standing Rock Sioux), 60–61, 67
De Mallie, Raymond J., 236
De Montaño, Martha Kreipe, 503
Denig, Edwin T., 208, 215, 221, 223, 236
De Onate, Juan, 327
DeSmet, Pierre-Jean, 157, 224
De Soto, Hernando, 431, 464
De Suría, Don Tomás, 271
De Tovar, Pedro, 327
Dickanson, Olive Patricia, 67
Dole, Elizabeth, 484
Dombrowski, Kirk, 298
Downs, James F., 354, 361, 378
Dozier, Edward P. (Santa Clara Pueblo), 64
Dragging Canoe (Cherokee), 428
Driver, Harold E., 504
Drucker, Philip, 296
Dry Bay George (Tlingit), 268
Dubin, Lois S., 505
Du Ponceau, Peter S., 21
Dyk, Walter, 361–362

Echo-Hawk, Walter (Pawnee), 61
Eggan, Fred, 114

Eisler, Kim I., 505
Eliot, John, 21, 35, 36
Ellers, Flo (Tlingit), 299–300
Ember, Melvin, 503
Eric the Red, 12
Erikson, Leif, 12
Ewers, John C., 49

Fagan, Brian M., 29, 503
Fages, Pedro, 255–256
Fenton, William N., 416
Fields, Jerry L., 392
Figgins, J. D., 13–14
Finger, James R., 438, 444
Finnerty, Patrick, 500
Fixico, Donald L., 67, 481, 493
Flaherty, Robert, 507
Fletcher, Alice, 64
Forbes, Gloria, 230
Forbes, Jack D. (Lenape and Powhatan), 29, 64
Forbes, John, 230
Franklin, Benjamin, 40
Frantz, Klaus, 67
Freilich, Morris, 413
Freud, Sigmund, 389
Frey, Rodney, 210, 236
Fumoleau, René, 135, 136
Furtaw, Julia C., 503

Gallatin, Albert, 21
Gearing, Fred, 427, 444
Gibbon, Guy, 503–504
Gibbons, Jim, 199
Gillespie, Beryl C., 118, 136
Gillette, Gloria (Cahuilla), 261
Gist, George (Sequoya; Cherokee and Euro-American), 433–434, 444
Goddard, Ives, 21, 29
Goldberg, Carole, 493
Gone-to-the-Spirits (One-Standing-Lodge-Pole-Woman, Qanqon; Lower Kootenai), 153–155
Grant, Ulysses S., 382
Graymont, Barbara, 416
Great Sun (Natchez), 447, 449, 451, 453, 454, 456–459, 460, 461, 465
Great War Chief (Natchez), 453, 454–455, 456, 459, 461–464
Grim, John A., 236
Gulick, John, 444

Haas, Mary R., 466
Hagan, William T., 19, 66
Halbritter, Ray (Oneida), 416
Hall, Mary (Western Shoshone), 193
Halliburton, R., Jr., 444
Hallowell, A. Irving, 6
Hamilton, Lawrence C., 493
Handsome Lake (Seneca), 402–403, 404, 406
Hardaway, Roger D., 505

Harjo, Joy (Creek), 61
Harney, Corbin (Western Shoshone), 197
Harrison, Gary, 298
Harvey, Fred, 350
Hauptman, Lawrence M., 416
Hayes, Ira Hamilton (Pima), 61
Hays, Benjamin, 256
Hearne, Samuel, 106, 112, 113, 118, 120, 124, 486
Heidenreich, C. Adrian, 236
Heizer, Robert F., 266
Helm, June, 20, 135
Hendrick (Mohawk), 382
Henry, Patrick, 40
Hensley, William L. (Eskimo), 61
Herrington, John B. (Chickasaw), 61
Hertzberg, Hazel W., 48, 49, 66
Hewitt, John N. B. (Euro-American and Tuscarora), 64
Hiawatha (Onondaga), 392
Hill, India (Crow), 234
Hill, Richard, 411
Hill, Stan (Mohawk), 413
Hill, W. W., 365
Hinckley, Ted C., 303
Hirschfelder, Arlene, 503
Hodge, Frederick W., 62
Holm, Bill, 303
Hooper, Lucile, 239, 266
Hoover, Herbert Clark, 60
Houston, James, 97
Howard, James H., 49
Hoxie, Frederick E., 503

Iberville, Pierre de, 464
Ike, Felix (Western Shoshone), 199
Ingstad, Helge, 12
Isaacs, Erik Bruce (Cayuga), 409
Iverson, Peter, 378

Jackson, Andrew, 434
Jackson, Helen Hunt, 240, 258, 259
Jamieson, Roberta, 410
Jarvenpa, Robert, 136, 493
Jefferson, Thomas, 21, 402
Jelks, Edward B., 504
Johnson, Lyndon B., 57, 439
Jones, Leon D. (Cherokee), 441, 442
Jones, William (Euro-American and Mesquakie), 64
Jorgensen, Joseph G., 45–46
Joseph (chief; Nez Perce), 1

Kan, Sergei, 289–291, 302, 303
Keesing, Felix M., 19
Kehoe, Alice Beck, 66
Keith, Renae (Navajo), 376
Keithan, Edward L., 279–280, 303
Kinney, Abbott, 258
Kiuki (Lower Kootenay), 138
Kluckhohn, Clyde, 361, 378

Knight, Stan (Western Shoshone), 195
Knowles, Nathaniel, 397
Kral, Michael J., 101
Krause, Aurel, 275, 303
Krech, Shepard, III, 486
Kroeber, Alfred L., 19, 20, 266
Kunitz, Stephen J., 378
Kupferer, Harriet J., 444

"Lady Warrior" (Lori Piestewa; Hopi), 338
Lafitau, Joseph F., 382, 389, 416
La Flesche, Francis (Omaha), 64
Lamberth, Royce C., 478–479
Lara, Billy Joe (Chippewa), 492
La Salle, Sieur de, 464
La Violette, Forest E., 168
Law, John, 465
Left Handed (Navajo), 361–363
Leighton, Dorothea, 378
Leonard, Zenas, 236
Le Page du Pratz, Antoine S., 448, 450, 456, 459, 460, 461, 463, 465, 467
Levinson, David, 503
Levy, Jerrold E., 378
Lew, Alan A., 505
Lewis, Oscar, 19
Li, Ting-Kai, 59
Lobo, Susan, 493
Loftin, John D., 335–336, 338
Lo-Ma-Hung-Yo-Ma (chief; Hopi), 330
Lomawaima, K. T., 504
Lone Ranger (Clayton Moore), 5, 382
Long, David Alan, 67
Longboat, Tom (Onondaga), 382
Longfellow, Henry Wadsworth, 5
Long Hair (chief; Crow), 205, 224
Lopez, Salvador (Cahuilla), 255
Lowie, Robert H., 216, 236
Lubo, Ramona (Cahuilla), 259
Luckert, Karl W., 359
Luke, Christopher (Lower Kootenay), 165–166
Lytle, Clifford M., 67

Malcomson, Scott L., 505
Malinowski, Sharon, 503
Mann, Barbara A., 392
Manybeads, Jenny (Navajo), 370
Markowitz, Harvey, 503
Marlar, Richard A., 29
Marlowe, Evelyn (Chipewyan), 133, 135
Marshall, John, 434
Martin, M. Marlene, 29, 504
Martin, Paul, 414
Martinez, Julian (San Ildefonso Pueblo), 61
Martinez, Maria Montoya (San Ildefonso Pueblo), 61
Mason, Otis T., 25
Mason, W. Dale, 67, 505
Mason, William M., 266
Mather, Cotton, 10

Matonabbee (Chipewyan), 112, 113–114, 118
May, Philip A., 59
McCleary, Timothy P., 229, 236
McDonald, Jerry N., 29
McGuire, Randall H., 46
McJunkin, George, 13–14
McKee, Christopher, 168
McLoughlin, William G., 432
McNickle, D'Arcy (Flathead), 63
McPherson, Aimee Semple, 230
Mead, Margaret, 18
Means, Russell (Sioux), 56, 61
Medicine Crow, Joseph (Crow), 236
Mellis, Allison F., 505
Meyer, Carter J., 504–505
Miguel, Eileen (Cahuilla), 261
Milanovich, Richard (Cahuilla), 264
Mills, Kerry, 5
Mithun, Marianne, 505
Momaday, N. Scott (Kiowa), 61
Monk, Elizabeth (Cahuilla), 261
Mooney, James, 444
Moore, Clayton (Lone Ranger), 5, 382
Moore, Elizabeth L., 416
Morgan, Lewis Henry, 18, 382, 388, 391–392, 416
Moses (Lower Kootenai), 157
Moytoy (Cherokee), 427–428
Muckle, Robert J., 168
Muldoe, Earl (Delgamuukw), 42
Murdock, George P., 29, 453–454, 504

Nabokov, Peter, 504
Nampeyo (Hopi), 312
Nan-ye-hi (Nancy Ward; Cherokee), 430
Narbona (Navajo), 345
Neely, Sharlotte, 444
Nijhuis, Michelle, 200
Nomee, Clara (Crow), 232
Numkena, Alphonso (Hopi), 336

Oberg, Kalvero, 303
O'Brien, Sharon, 67, 493
Ogden, Peter S., 184
Okalik, Paul (Inuit), 99, 100
Old Horn, Dale D. (Crow), 236
Old Horn, Kevin ("Crow Boy"; Crow), 228
Old Man Hat (Navajo), 362–363
O'Leary, Timothy J., 29, 504
Olinger (Ortner), Vyola (Cahuilla), 260–261
Olson, Wallace M., 303
One-Standing-Lodge-Pole-Woman (Gone-to-the-Spirits, Qanqon; Lower Kootenai), 153–155
Ortiz, Alfonso (San Juan Pueblo), 64, 338, 378
Oswalt, Wendell H., 102

Parker, Ely S. (Seneca), 382
Pasqual (Cahuilla), 254
Paul, William L., Sr. (Tlingit), 61, 296

Paul I (czar), 292
Paul III (pope), 33
Pearce, Roy H., 19
Peary, Robert E., 70
Pease, Janine (Crow), 233
Pembroke, Timothy R., 168
Perdue, Theda, 420, 444
Petalesharo (Pawnee), 49, 50
Peters, Kurt, 493
Piestewa, Lori ("Lady Warrior"; Hopi), 338
Plenty Coups (chief; Crow), 226
Pommersheim, Frank, 493, 504
Pond, Edwin P., 291
Pond, Peter, 118
Powell, John W., 21
Powers, William K., 49, 66–67
Powers, Willow R., 378
Powhatan (Powhatan Indian), 33–34
Pratt, Richard H., 47
Pretty-shield (Crow), 202
Price, John A., 493
Prucha, Francis Paul, 67

Qaggutaq, Patrick (Inuit), 98
Qanqon (One-Standing-Lodge-Pole-Woman, Gone-to-the-Spirits; Lower Kootenai), 153–155

Rabesca, Mary Louise (Chipewyan), 124
Raleigh, Sir Walter, 483
Rasmussen, Knud, 93, 102
Reagan, Ronald, 39, 57
Real Bird, Edison (Crow), 232
Red Jacket (Seneca), 382
Rehnquist, William H., 492
Reichard, Gladys A., 378
Reid, Harry, 199
Rice, Louisa Costa (Cahuilla), 245
Richards, Cara B., 397
Richter, Daniel K., 392, 416
Riley, Carroll L., 13
Riley, Patricia, 504
Ringwald, George, 261
Rogers, William Penn Adair (Will Rogers; Cherokee), 61
Roosevelt, Franklin D., 191
Ross, John, 94–95
Royer, Diana, 505
Russell, Charles M., 49

Saint-Marie, Buffy (Cree), 54, 61
Sampson, Will (Creek), 61
Saubel, Katherine S. (Cahuilla), 266
Saubel, La Verne (Cahuilla), 261
Saum, Lewis O., 19
Scaglion, Richard, 453–454
Schaeffer, Claude E., 155, 168
Schwarzenegger, Arnold, 263, 264–265
Scott, Winfield, 435
Sequoya (George Gist; Cherokee and Euro-American), 433–434, 444

Seyfrit, Carole L., 493
Shanley, Kathryn W., 506
Sharp, Henry S., 136
Sheets, Anna, 503
Shimony, Annemarie A., 404, 416
Shin Bone, Henry (Crow), 225
Silverheels, Jay (Harold I. Smith, Tonto;
    Mohawk), 5, 382
Simmons, Leo W., 338
Smith, David M., 136
Smith, Dean H., 493
Smith, Harold I. (Jay Silverheels, Tonto;
    Mohawk), 5, 382
Smith, James G. E., 113, 136
Smithson, James, 62
Snell, Alma H. (Crow), 236
Spell, Andy (Edisto-Natchez-Kusso), 467
Sperlin, O. B., 168
Spicer, Edward H., 338
Spiro, Melford E., 87, 515
Squirrel, Pierre (chief; Chipewyan), 119
Stafford, John W., 226
Steele, James B., 470
Steele, William O., 444
Stephen, Alexander M., 338
Stevens, John P., 492
Stevens, Ted, 301–302, 490
Stevenson, Marc G., 102
Steward, Julian H., 173–174, 200
Stewart, Edgar I., 237
Stewart, Nellie Pretty Eagle (Crow), 230–231
Stone, John Augustus, 5
Sturtevant, William C., 29, 62, 504
Suttles, Wayne, 303
Swanton, John R., 19, 20–21, 444, 466, 467

Tattooed Serpent (Natchez), 461–464, 465
Taylor, Nancy (Natchez), 466
Tekakwitha, Kateri (Catherine; Mohawk),
    382
Temoka (chief, Te-Moak; Western
    Shoshone), 186, 187, 192
Temoke, Frank (chief; Western Shoshone),
    170
Thomas (Lower Kootenai), 157
Thomas, David H., 200
Thomas, William H., 435, 440
Thompson, Laura, 338
Thornton, Russell, 29
Thornton, Thomas F., 301
Thorpe, James Francis (Mesquakie and
    Sauk), 61–62
Three Moons (Lower Kootenai), 156, 157
Titiev, Mischa, 307, 310, 326–327, 331, 338
Tonto (Harold I. Smith, Jay Silverheels;
    Mohawk), 5, 382

Trehero, John (Mexican and Shoshone),
    228–229
Trigger, Bruce G., 416
Tsinnie, David (Navajo), 375
Tsokkope (chief; Western Shoshone), 186
Tsosie, Jerry (Navajo), 376
Turner, Paul R., 66
Turney-High, Harry Holbert, 168
Tybo, Jim (Western Shoshone), 174
Tylor, Edward B., 87, 515

Underhill, Ruth M., 378
Utley, Robert M., 237
Utter, Jack, 503

van den Steenhoven, Geert, 86, 102
Van Otten, George A., 505
VanStone, James W., 120–121, 124, 135
Venne, Carl (Crow), 233
Vitoria, Francisco, 33
Voegelin, C. F., 21
Voegelin, F. M., 21
Voget, Fred, 228, 236

Waldman, Carl, 503
Walker, Delward E., Jr., 168
Walker, Joseph R., 184–185
Walking Coyote, Samuel (Kalispel), 4
Wallace, Anthony F. C., 389–391, 416
Ward, Nancy (Nan-ye-hi; Cherokee), 430
Washburn, Wilcomb E., 19, 44, 66, 493
Washington, George, 431
Washington, John, 345
Weatherford, Jack, 29
Weaver, Sally M., 407
Wenzel, George, 493
Wesley, Annie (Crow), 225
Weyer, Edward M., 102
White, Douglas R., 453–454
White Bear, Russell (Crow), 225
Wilkins, David E., 504
Wilkinson, Charles, 67
Williams, Robert A., 66
Wilson, Edmund, 403
Wilson, Jack (Wovoka; Paiute), 47, 189
Winter, Lloyd V., 291
Wissler, Clark, 25
Witt, Shirley Hill (Mohawk), 64
Woman Chief (Crow and Gros Ventre), 215
Woman Killer (Cherokee), 419
Wovoka (Jack Wilson; Paiute), 47, 189
Wyman, Leland C., 358

Yellow Bird, Michael (Arikara), 29
Yellowtail, Thomas (Crow), 236
Yowell, George (Western Shoshone), 189
Yowell, Raymond (Western Shoshone), 198

Subject Index

Note: Numbers followed by "g" refer to glossary entries. Numbers followed by "fn" refer to footnotes.

Aboriginals (Canadian indigenous peoples), 41
Absaroka (Apsáalooke; Crow), 203
Acculturation, 18, 63, 509g
Acorns, 246
Adena culture, 16
Adoption, 85, 91, 228, 362, 393, 396, 455–456
Advocates for Indigenous California Language Survival, 24
Agaves Society (Hopi), 319
Agriculture, 509g
Agua Caliente Cultural Museum Center (Cahuilla), 265
Agua Caliente Development Authority (Cahuilla), 262
Alaska Federation of Natives, 297, 302
Alaska Inter-Tribal Council, 302
Alaska National Interest Lands Conservation Act, 301
Alaska Native Brotherhood, 295–296, 297
Alaska Native Claims Settlement Act, 297–299, 300, 302
Alaska Native Fund, 297–298
Alaska Native Sisterhood, 295
Alcoholic beverages
    Cahuilla, 256
    Chipewyan, 125–126, 127, 130
    Crow, 224, 225
    general, 9, 58–59
    Hopi, 332
    Iroquois, 389, 401, 402, 403, 406
    Lower Kootenai (Kootenay), 157, 162, 165
    Natchez, 449
    Navajo, 368, 371
    Tlingit, 293, 299–300
    Western Shoshone, 196
Alcoholics Anonymous, 59
Aleuts, 7, 70fn, 71. See also Eskimos
Algonquian languages, 21
Allegheny Reservation, NY, 414–415
Allegheny State Park, NY, 415
American Indian Movement, 56, 61
American Indian Religious Freedom Act (U.S.), 56
American Revolution, 41, 393–394, 401, 404, 428, 431, 432–433
Amulets, 88, 91, 321

Anasazi culture, 16, 343
Anglican Church of Canada, 411
Anglican missionaries, 393, 411
Anglo (Anglo-American), 509g
Antelope (pronghorn), 178, 181, 191, 208
Antelope Society (Hopi), 318
Appomattox, VA, 382
Apsáalooke (Absaroka; Crow), 203
Archaic cultures, 16
Arikara Indians, 234
Armor (warfare), 149, 282
Artifact, 509g
Assembly of God church, 299
Astoria (trading post), 154
Atlantis (Antillia; presumed lost continent), 10
Audio-Form company (Indian language instructions), 24

Babiche, 75, 109, 111, 387, 509g
Bahanas (Hopi supernaturals), 309, 329, 337–338, 509g
Band (political unit), 509g
    Cahuilla, 258–262
    Cherokee, 427, 435–440
    Chipewyan, 105, 113, 127, 130, 131
    Crow, 206, 216, 217
    Iroquois, 407, 410
    Lower Kootenai (Kootenay), 147, 148, 158, 164, 166–167
    Navajo, 344
    Netsilik, 84, 85–86
    Western Shoshone, 185
Bannock, 122–123, 509g
Bannock War, 188
Barren Grounds, 105–106, 110, 117
Baseline ethnography, 18, 509g
Basketmaker culture, 16
Basketry
    archaeological, 14, 16
    Cahuilla, 242, 244
    Cherokee, 423, 438
    Chipewyan, 108, 109
    general, 495–496
    Hopi, 320, 323
    Iroquois, 385
    Lower Kootenai, 143, 145
    Natchez, 452

Navajo, 353
Tlingit, 272, 288
Western Shoshone, 175, 176, 177
Bath. *See* Sweat bath
Battle Mountain Colony, 191–197
Battle Mountain Colony Smoke Shop, 196
Beans
　Cherokee, 423
　general, 16
　Hopi, 313
　Iroquois, 387
　Natchez, 452
Bears, 80, 208, 221, 247, 274, 387, 424, 453
　as supernaturals, 115, 150–151
Beloved Men (Cherokee), 427
Beloved Women (Cherokee), 430–431
Berdache, 153, 154, 223, 365, 460, 509g
Beringia (land bridge), 13–14
BHP Billiton Diamonds Inc., 132–133, 135
Biculturation, 509g
Bifurcate collateral (kin terms), 509g
Bifurcate merging (kin terms), 509g
Big Horn County, MT, 234
Bilateral descent, 509g
Bill C-23 (Canada, 2004), 414
Bill C-31 (Canada, 1985), 407
Bilocal residence, 510g
Bingo. *See* Gaming
Bison (American buffalo), 2–4, 141, 208,
　216, 225, 228, 421–422, 424, 453
Blackfoot (Blackfeet) Indians, 155, 215
Black Mesa Trust, 335
Blacks (and Indians), 7, 432–433
Blessingway (Navajo), 352, 360, 363
Blowgun (Cherokee), 424
Board of Equalization, CA, 491
Board of Indian Commissioners (U.S.), 41
Bonners Ferry Centennial, 160
Bonneville Power Administration (U.S.), 163
Booger Dance (Cherokee), 437
Booger mask, 437, 510g
Book of Mormon, The, 6
Boomerang. *See* Throwing stick
Bosque Redondo, 346
Bow types
　composite, 208, 510g
　general, 497–498
　self, 111, 145, 246, 424, 453, 515g
　sinew-backed, 178, 515g
Boy Scouts of America, 5
Braggs, OK, 466
Branch of Acknowledgment and Research
　(U.S.), 482–483
Bride price, 286, 364, 510g
Bride service, 510g
Bridewealth, 222, 510g
British Columbia Treaty Commission, 164
British North American Act, 163
Buffalo. *See* Bison
Buffalo Bill's Wild West Show, 50

Bull-roarer, 510g
Bureau of American Ethnology, 62, 64
Bureau of Indian Affairs (U.S.)
　anthropologists' relationship, 64–65
　Cahuilla, 259, 260–262
　Cherokee, 436, 439
　creation, 39, 41
　criticisms, 41, 45–46, 478–479
　Crow, 226–227, 231–232, 233
　Hopi, 329, 332, 333
　Lower Kootenai, 158
　Navajo, 368, 369, 371
　programs (general), 39, 46, 48, 57, 60, 64–
　　65, 473, 476, 477, 478, 480–481, 484,
　　491, 492
　Western Shoshone, 185, 186, 188, 191,
　　192, 193–194
Bureau of Land Management (U.S.), 173,
　191–192, 197, 198, 483
Bush man, 128

California Public Utilities Commission, 334
Calumet, 510g
Camp Fire Girls, 5
Canadian acts regarding Indians, 8–9, 41–
　42, 58, 164
Cannibalism, 16, 82, 112, 179, 394
Canoe. *See also* Kayak
　bark covered, 108, 119, 143–144, 145, 387,
　　423
　canvas covered, 122
　dugout, 273, 452
　skin covered, 108, 112
Caribou
　Chipewyan, 109, 110–112, 120, 122, 131,
　　133, 134
　Lower Kootenai, 146
　Netsilik, 78, 80–81
　Tlingit, 273
Cariole, 122, 510g
Carlisle Indian School, PA, 39, 47, 62, 188,
　233, 349, 436
Carson Indian Agency, 192
Casino Rama (Canada), 409
Casinos. *See* Gaming
Cat's cradle, 253, 510g
Cattle, 157, 188, 225, 227, 256, 329, 337, 349,
　355, 369
Central Pacific Railroad, 191
Century of Dishonor, A (book), 258
Changing Woman (Navajo supernatural), 352
Char (fish), 78, 80
Charismatic person, 85–86, 113, 348, 358,
　510g
Cherokee Bingo (Tribal Bingo), 440
Cherokee Fall Festival, 438
Cherokee High School, 439
Cherokee Historical Association, 440
Cherokee Indian Fair, 437–438
Cherokee Indian Hospital, 441

Cherokee Indians (general), 37
Cherokee Nation (1827), 433–434
Cheyenne Indians, 217, 234
Chiefs. *See also* War Chief
  Cahuilla, 248
  Cherokee, 427–428, 435, 441, 442
  Chipewyan, 120, 131
  Crow, 212, 216
  general, 40
  Hopi, 312
  Iroquois, 395, 408
  Lower Kootenai, 148, 156
  Natchez, 453–456, 459
  Navajo, 348, 358
  Western Shoshone, 181
Child Tax Credit (Canada), 96, 127, 128
Chilkat robe, 287, 288, 294, 299, 302, 510g
Chippewa (Ojibwa) Indians, 39, 482
Cholera, 434
Church of Jesus Christ of Latter-Day Saints.
  See Mormons
Circle (Round) Dance (Western Shoshone),
  181, 190
Civil War (U.S.), 345, 382, 433, 483
CKRZ (Canadian radio station), 408
Clan, 510g
Clovis lithic complex, 14
Coal mining, 333–335, 373–374
Cobell suit (about Individual Indian Monies;
  U.S.), 478–479
Coconino aquifer, 334–335, 374
Code Talkers (Navajo), 367, 510g
Coeur d'Alene Casino, 54
Community-Based Monitoring report, 133–
  135
Composite bow, 208, 510g
Composite family, 510g
Constitutional Act (Canada, 1982), 164
Continental Congress, 40
Corn. *See* Maize
Coss Indians, 482
Count coup, 149, 211, 212, 510g
Court of Indian Offenses (U.S.), 57–58
Cousin terms
  Crow type, 209, 277, 314, 424–425, 510g
  Eskimo type, 125, 180, 511g
  Hawaiian type, 83, 146, 511g
  Iroquois type, 114, 247, 357, 388, 511g
  Omaha type, 511g
Coyote
  Cahuilla (moiety), 248
  Crow, 204–205, 230, 231
  Hopi, 309
  Lower Kootenai, 141
  Western Shoshone, 174, 182
Cree Indians, 105, 109, 117, 120
Croatan Indians. *See* Lumbee Indians
Cross-cousins, 511g
Crow Agency, MT, 224–225, 226–227, 231
Crow Allotment Act, 226, 231
Crow Business Council, 231

Crow Fair, 227–228, 234
Crow-type cousin terms, 209, 277, 314, 424–
  425, 510g
Cultural blindness, 109, 511g
Cultural relativism, 65–66, 511g
Culture area, 25, 70, 511g
Custer Battlefield National Monument (Little
  Bighorn Battlefield National Monu-
  ment), 234, 235
Custer Died for Your Sins (book), 60

Daily Enterprise (newspaper), 261
Dance of Death (Natchez), 461
Dances, 85, 86, 125, 181, 318, 395, 396, 399,
  426, 431, 437, 454, 458, 461, 462
Darkness (Cahuilla supernatural), 241
Dawes Act (U.S. Dawes Severalty Act, Gen-
  eral Allotment Act)
  Cahuilla, 258–260
  Cherokee, 435
  Crow, 226, 227
  general, 8, 39, 43–44, 45, 473, 478
  Hopi, 329
  Navajo, 349–350
  Western Shoshone, 190
Dawn Woman (Hopi supernatural), 319
Deadfall, 111, 146, 179, 247, 274, 511g
Death Valley National Park, 483
Declaration of Independence (U.S.), 394, 401
Deer, 145, 179, 181, 208, 247, 273, 313, 387,
  424, 453
Delaware Indians, 37, 38
Delgamuukw case (Canada), 42
Department of Housing and Urban Develop-
  ment (U.S.), 194–195, 477
Department of Indian Affairs (Canada), 42
Department of Indian Affairs and Northern
  Development (Canada), 42
Department of Justice (U.S.), 372, 477
Department of the Interior (U.S.), 11, 41, 60,
  264, 476, 478–479, 482–483
Descent
  bilateral, 82, 114, 125, 146, 180, 439, 509g
  matrilineal, 209, 224, 275–276, 314, 356,
    388, 424, 514g
  patrilineal, 246, 247, 515g
  unilineal, 517g
Desert culture, 14–15
Diabetes, 484–485
Diamond mines (Canada), 100–101, 132–135
Diné College (Navajo Community College),
  369
Dinetah (Navajo homeland), 342, 343, 344,
  511g
Dip net (for fish), 511g
Disease. *See* specific diseases
Distant Early Warning station (U.S. radar
  unit), 96
Divorce
  Cahuilla, 253
  Chipewyan, 116–117

Crow, 223
Hopi, 325
Lower Kootenai, 153
Natchez, 460
Navajo, 364–365
Netsilik, 93
DNA test, 8, 11
Doe (Lower Kootenai supernatural), 141
Dogrib (Ticho) Indians, 42, 117, 132
Dogs and dog traction
Cahuilla, 244–245
Cherokee, 424
Chipewyan, 107, 109, 110, 120, 122
Crow, 214
Iroquois, 399
Lower Kootenai, 143, 150
Natchez, 453, 454
Navajo, 355–356
Netsilik, 78, 79, 80
Tlingit, 274
Dominion of Canada, 41–42, 163–164
Drypaintings (Sand Paintings), 359
Duck Valley Indian Reservation, 187, 188, 198
Dumaiya (Hopi custom), 323–324, 511g
Duro "fix" (U.S. Supreme Court decision), 492

Eagle-Killing Ceremony (Cahuilla), 249–250, 257
Earth (Lower Kootenai supernatural), 149
Earth Surface People (Navajo), 351–352
Eastern Pueblos, 307
Edisto-Natchez-Kusso Indians, 467
Education (formal)
Cherokee, 436, 439
Chipewyan, 128–130, 131
Crow, 225–226, 233
general, 43, 47–48, 58, 61–62, 480, 482
Hopi, 335
Iroquois, 402, 408, 410–411
Lower Kootenai (Kootenay), 159, 162, 166–167
Lumbee, 484
Navajo, 349, 366, 369, 371, 372
Netsilik, 96, 99–100
Tlingit, 294
Western Shoshone, 188, 194, 196
Ekati Diamond Mine, 132–133
Elko Colony, 192, 194
Emetics, 430–431, 454
Encomienda (Spanish land grant), 35, 511g
Endeavour (U.S. spacecraft), 61
Endogamy, 125, 511g
Enemy songs (Cahuilla), 252
Enemyway ("Squaw Dance"; Navajo), 347, 360, 363
Environmentalists, 485–486
Epidemics. *See* specific diseases
Eskimos, 7fn, 43, 70fn. *See also* Aleuts; Inuit; Yuit
Chipewyan, 113–114

Eskimo-type cousin terms, 125, 180, 511g
Ethnocentrism, 65, 511g
Ethnographic present (literary device), 512g
Ethnography, 17–19, 512g
Ethnohistory, 19, 512g
journal, 19
Ethnology, 18, 512g
Ethos, 512g
Evil Twin (Iroquois supernatural), 397–398
Evilway (Ghostway; Navajo), 360
Exogamy, 222, 252, 257, 286
Extended family, 512g

False Face Society (Iroquois), 398, 400–401, 512g
Family Allowance (Child Tax Credit; Canada), 96, 127, 128
Famine. *See* Starvation
Fandango (Spanish dance), 190, 512g
Farming
Cahuilla, 256, 257
Cherokee, 423, 430–431, 436
Crow, 226–227
general, 44
Hopi, 312–313
Iroquois, 387, 401, 404
Lower Kootenai (Kootenay), 146, 157, 158, 166
Natchez, 452, 457–458
Navajo, 356, 366, 376
Western Shoshone, 175
Feather Dance (Iroquois), 399
Federal Bureau of Investigation (FBI), 56, 472
Feuds. *See* Warfare
Fire Dragon (Iroquois supernatural), 384
First Doer (Crow supernatural), 205
First fruit ceremony, 249, 457, 458, 512g
First Nation Development Institute (U.S.), 492
First Nations (Canadian indigenous peoples), 2, 5, 10, 41–42, 130, 164, 411, 512g
First Nations Governance Act (Indian Act; Canada, 2003), 42, 414
Fishing devices
arrows, 453
general, 498, 500–501
harpoons, 179, 274
hooks, 80, 111, 146, 179, 274, 424, 453
impaler, 274
leister (impalers, pronged), 78, 80, 95, 112, 424, 513g
nets (dip, gill), 95, 111–112, 122, 146, 179, 274, 453, 511g, 512g
traps, 144–145, 179, 274–275, 387, 512g
weirs, 80, 81, 144–145, 179, 274–275, 517g
Five Civilized Tribes, 420, 512g
Five Nations (Iroquois), 38
Flathead Indian Reservation, 474
Flathead Indians, 155
Flathead Post, 155

Flint (Iroquois supernatural), 384
Folsom lithic complex, 14
Foragers, 512g
Fort Defiance, 345, 348, 349
Fort Hall, 187, 188
Fort Orange, 393
Fort Rosalie, 464, 465
Fort Ruby, 186, 187
Fort Sumner (Bosque Redondo), 346, 374
Fort Wingate, 348
Four Square Gospel church, 230, 299
Foxes (Crow sodality), 211
Fox (Mesquakie) Indians, 37–38
Foxwoods Resort Casino, 52, 472
Fred Harvey Company, 350
Free labor companies (gadugi; Cherokee), 436–437
Frobisher Bay (Iqaluit, Nunavut capital), 98, 99
"From the Land of Sky Blue Waters" (song), 5
Fur trade. See Trade and fur trade

Gadugi (Cherokee), 436–437, 512g
Games (noncommercial). See also Hand game
   ball, 253, 458
   card, 125, 126
   guessing, 117, 181
   skill, 148, 181, 223, 253, 287
Gaming (bingo, casino)
   Cahuilla, 262–264
   Cherokee, 440–441
   Crow, 234–235
   general, 45, 59–60, 482, 490, 491
   Hopi, 335
   Iroquois, 409, 416
   Lower Kootenai (Kootenay), 159–163, 167
   Navajo, 373
General Allotment Act. See Dawes Act
Generational kinship terms, 512g
Ghost Dance, 47, 155, 189
Gill net, 512g
Girl Scouts of America, 5
God of the Hunt (Hopi), 313
Goldbelt Incorporated (Tlingit village corporation), 300–301
Good Message (Iroquois), 402–403, 404
Good News of Peace and Power (Iroquois), 392
Grand Council (Iroquois), 392, 393
Grandfather Sweathouse (Lower Kootenai supernatural), 153
Grand Village (Natchez), 451, 453, 464, 465, 466
Great Buzzard (Cherokee supernatural), 421
Great Chief (Great Spirit; Iroquois supernatural), 384, 397, 402, 406
Great Depression (U.S., 1929–1939), 191, 231, 350
Great League of Peace (Iroquois), 393

Great Salt Lake Desert, 177
Great Smoky Mountains National Park, 438, 440, 443
Great Society Program (U.S. federal program), 439
Great Spirit
   Iroquois, 299
   Natchez, 449, 456
Green Corn Ceremony
   Cherokee, 424, 430–431
   Iroquois, 399, 402
   Natchez, 458
Greenland, 12, 43
Grizzly Bear Ceremony (Lower Kootenai supernatural), 146, 150–151
Gross Ventre Indians, 215

Haida Indians, 296–297
Handbook of North American Indians (1978–), 62
Handbook of North American Indians North of Mexico (1907–1910), 62
Hand game. See Stick game
Harmony Ethic (Cherokee), 426, 431, 438, 443–445, 512g
Harpoons, 79–80, 274, 498–500
Harrah's Cherokee Smoky Mountains Casino, 440–441
Harvest Ceremony (Cherokee), 427
Hawaiians (aboriginal), 484
Hawaiian-type cousin terms, 83, 146, 511g
Hell Gate Treaty, 156
Hiawatha (poem), 5
Hidasta Indians, 208
Historia natural y moral de las Indias (book), 11
Hogan (Navajo dwelling), 353, 356, 512g
Hohokam culture, 16
Holman, NWT (Canada), 487
Holy People (Navajo supernaturals), 351–352, 358, 359
Home brew. See Alcoholic beverages
Home Department of the Interior (U.S.). See Department of the Interior
Homestead Act (U.S.), 185–186, 225–226
Hominy, 385, 452, 513g
Hooch, 293, 513g
Hopewell tradition, 16–17
Hopi Cultural Center, 336
Hopi Indians
   hopi (goodness), 316–317, 513g
   and Navajo, 333, 370–371
Hopi Partitioned Lands, 333, 371
Hopi Tribal Constitution, 477
Hopi Way (ethic), 317, 321, 338
Horn Society (Hopi), 319
Horses
   Cherokee, 424
   Crow, 203, 206, 207–208, 212, 215, 227
   Hopi, 329
   Lower Kootenai, 141

Navajo, 344, 348, 354, 366
    Western Shoshone, 185
Horticulture, 513g
House Concurrent Resolution 108 (83rd Congress), 39, 46
House Made of Dawn (book), 61
Hozho (Navajo concept), 359, 360, 513g
Hudson's Bay Company, 95, 100, 118, 121, 128, 130, 156, 184, 404
Humboldt Trail, 185
Humor. *See* Joking

Igloo, 76
Indian (defined), 2, 4–5, 6–9, 167, 513g
Indian acts (Canada), 8–9, 41–42, 414
Indian Affairs (U.S.). *See* Bureau of Indian Affairs
Indian Affairs Branch (Canada), 122, 126–127
Indian and Northern Health Services (Canada), 128
Indian Arts and Crafts Act (U.S.), 375
Indian Arts and Crafts Association (U.S.), 375
Indian Child Welfare Act (U.S.), 48
Indian Citizenship Act (U.S.), 8, 39, 191, 296
Indian Claims Commission Act (U.S.), 39, 46, 193, 198, 199
Indian Country (U.S.), 44–45, 300, 489, 490
Indian Gaming Regulatory Act (U.S.), 39, 60, 262–265, 470–471, 475, 491
Indian Health Services (U.S.), 161, 233, 441, 477, 485
Indian image (stereotype), 49–51
Indian Killer (book), 60
Indian Removal Act (U.S.), 37, 39, 404, 420, 434, 465–466, 489
Indian Reorganization Act (Wheeler–Howard Act; U.S.)
    Cahuilla, 258–259
    general, 39, 44, 58, 64
    Hopi, 332
    Tlingit, 297, 298
    Western Shoshone, 192
Indian Self-Determination and Education Assistance Act (U.S.), 39, 57, 194, 490
Indian Self-Reliance initiative (California), 263
Indian Service (U.S.). *See* Bureau of Indian Affairs
Indian sovereignty. *See* Sovereignty issues
Indian Territory, OK, 404, 420, 434, 466
Individual Indian Monies (U.S.), 478–479
Infanticide, 91, 94, 112, 184, 285, 513g
Influenza, 121, 155
Inter-American Commission on Human Rights (Organization of American States), 198
Internet, 488
Intoxicants. *See* Alcoholic beverages
Inuit (Eskimoan linguistic group), 7fn, 70fn. *See also* Eskimos

Inuktitut (Eskimoan language), 99–100
Invisible Aids (Iroquois deities), 398
Iqaluit (Frobisher Bay, Nunavut capital), 98–99
Iroquoian language family, 382, 420
Iroquois Confederacy, 393, 394, 401, 410
Iroquois League, 391–394
Iroquois-type cousin terms, 114, 247, 357, 388, 511g

Jimsonweed, 252, 322
Joking, 84, 147, 213, 252, 323, 357, 364–365, 425, 437
Jubilee Revival (Crow), 231

Kachina (Hopi), 316–321, 323, 337
Kachina Cult (Hopi), 319
Kachina "dolls," 320–321, 513g
Kachina Society (Hopi), 318
Kahopi (evil, bad; Hopi), 317, 513g
Kalispel Indians, 4
Kaw (Kansa) Indians, 60
Kayak, 75, 77, 81, 513g
Keeper of the Fire (Iroquois), 405
Keeper of the House (Tlingit), 275, 278
Keeper of the Wampum (Iroquois), 394
Keepers of the Faith (Iroquois), 398–399, 405
Kennewick Man, 11
Kinaalda Ceremony (Navajo), 363, 513g
Kindred, 513g
Kinship terms (for parents and their siblings)
    bifurcate collateral, 83, 114, 147, 247, 509g
    bifurcate merging, 114, 180, 210, 314, 356, 388, 425, 509g
    lineal, 513g
Kiva, 309, 310–311, 314, 319, 323, 513g
Kolosches (Tlingit), 288
Koniag (Eskimo tribe), 70fn
Kootanae House (trading post), 154, 156
Kootenai Casino Powwow, 160, 161
Kootenai Reservation, 157, 168
Kootenai River Inn, 159
Kootenai Tribe of Idaho, 158
Kootenai Valley Resource Initiative, 163
Kootenay District Council (Canada), 164
Ktunaxa/Kinbasket Tribal Council (Canada), 164, 167
Kueex (Tlingit potlatch), 289–291, 513g
Kwaan (Tlingit geographical unit), 275, 513g

Labret, 271, 513g
Lacrosse, 223, 391. *See also* Stickball
Lamanites, 6
Languages (Indian), 21–24, 487
L'Anse aux Meadows, Newfoundland (Norse site), 12
Lara (U.S. Supreme Court case), 492
League of the Iroquois (Longhouse), 391–394, 395
Leister, 78, 80, 95, 112, 424, 513g

Levirate, 147, 180, 222, 253, 287, 364, 424, 513g
Lineage, 513g
Lineal kinship terms (for parents and their siblings), 513g
Lip plug, 271, 513g
Little Bighorn Battlefield National Monument, 234, 235
Little Big Horn Casino (Crow), 234–235
Little Big Horn College (Crow), 233
Local Governance Act (Navajo), 377
Locust (Hopi supernatural), 309
Lone Ranger and Tonto (radio and television programs), 5
Lone Ranger and Tonto Fistfight in Heaven, The (book), 60
Long Walk (Navajo), 341, 346–347, 513g
Looms, 288, 311, 353
Lost Colony, 483–484
Lost Tribes of Israel, 10
Lower Kootenay Band (Canada), 165, 166
Lower Kootenay Indian Reserves (Canada), 164–165, 168
Lower Tribes (Iroquois, Canada), 404
Lumbee (Croatan) Indians of North Carolina, 483–484
Lumpwoods (Crow sodality), 211
Lutheran missionaries, 43
Lutselk'e. See Snowdrift
Lynx (Lower Kootenai supernatural), 141

Maasaw (Hopi supernatural), 308–309, 312, 316, 317
Maize (corn)
  Cherokee, 423
  general, 16
  Hopi, 312–313, 331
  Iroquois, 387
  Natchez, 452
  Navajo, 344
Maker (Crow supernatural), 205, 219
Malaria, 36–37
Manitou, 120, 398–399, 513g
Manners, Customs and Conditions of the North American Indians (book), 50
Mano and metate. See Milling stones
March of the Bodies (Natchez), 463
Marine Mammal Protection Act (U.S.), 100
Marriage residence
  bilocal, 125, 180, 287, 357
  matrilocal, 113, 114, 147, 180, 314, 332, 357, 424
  neolocal, 125, 405, 460
  patrilocal, 84, 93, 247
Massachuset Indians, 21, 36
Material culture, 514g
Matriarchy, 388
Matriclan, 514g
Matrilineal descent, 514g
Matrilocal residence, 514g
Measles, 36, 155

Medicine bundle, 514g, 515g. See also Sacred bundle
Medicine man. See Shaman
Menarche, 514g. See also Menstruation
Menstruation
  Cahuilla, 242
  Cherokee, 430
  Chipewyan, 116
  Crow, 222
  Hopi, 325
  Lower Kootenai, 152
  menarche, 92, 325
  Netsilik, 92
  Tlingit, 272, 286
  Western Shoshone, 184
Mesquakie (Fox) Indians, 37–38
Mesquite beans, 245–246
Metamora (play), 5
Metate. See Milling stones
Métis, 10, 42, 514g
Mexican War for Independence, 35, 256, 344
Mexican Water (Navajo political chapter), 376
Milky Way (Lower Kootenai supernatural), 149
Milling stones, 177, 244, 310, 353, 514g
Missile stick. See Throwing stick
Mission Hill (Lower Kootenai reservation), 157
Mission Indian Relief Act, 258
Mission Indians, 472
Mississippian tradition, 17
Mnemonic device, 394, 514g
Mogollon culture, 16
Mohave Power Station, NV, 334
Mohawk Institute Residential School (Canada), 411
Moiety, 514g
  Cahuilla, 247–248, 252
  Iroquois, 388
  Tlingit, 275–276, 279, 289, 296
Moiety exogamy, 514g
Money (indigenous), 514g
Monte Verde (site in Chile), 14
Moon (supernatural)
  Hopi, 317
  Lower Kootenai, 141
  Netsilik, 73, 88
Moose, 120, 131
Moqui Indians. See Hopi Indians
Moqui Pueblo Agency, 329
Moqui Pueblo Reservation, 329
Mormons, 6, 185, 236, 256
Morning Star (Crow), 220
Mourning Ceremony (Cahuilla), 250, 254–255, 257
Mourning peace (Iroquois), 392
Mourning wars (Iroquois), 392
Mukat (Cahuilla creator), 241–242, 245, 249, 250, 254, 255
Museum of the Cherokee Indian, 440

Muskrat (Iroquois supernatural), 384
Mystic Lake Casino and Hotel, 473

Naa Ka Hidi Theater (Tlingit), 302
Nadene Indians, 15, 105, 269, 342
Naming
  Cahuilla, 251
  Chipewyan, 116
  Crow, 221
  Hopi, 322
  Lower Kootenai, 151
  Navajo, 362
  Netsilik, 88, 91
  Tlingit, 285
National Aeronautics and Space Administration (U.S.), 61
National Bison Range, MT, 4
National Indian Gaming Commission (U.S.), 471–472
National Museum of the American Indian (U.S.), 62, 488
National Park Service (U.S.), 373
Native America Calling (U.S. radio program), 24
Native American (defined), 2, 4–5, 6–9
Native American church, 48–49, 56, 65, 368
Native American Graves Protection and Repatriation Act (U.S.), 39, 56, 372–373
Native American Rights Fund (U.S.), 61
Native American Youth Association, 482
Navajo aquifer, 334–335, 373–374
Navajo blankets (ponchos, robes, rugs), 348, 350, 364
Navajo Community College (Diné College), 58, 369
Navajo–Hopi Land Settlement Act, 333
Navajo (Navaho) Indians
  general, 39–40
  and Hopi, 373–374
Navajo Nation, 368–369, 377
Navajo National Council, 369, 370, 373–374, 378
Navajo Nation Gaming Ordinance, 373
Navajo Times (newspaper), 374, 378
Navajo Times Publishing Inc., 378
Navajo Tribal Council, 358, 369
Neolocal marriage residence, 514g
Neonate, 514g
Net (Cahuilla leader), 248–249, 260, 514g
Nets (for land species), 145–146, 179, 247, 387
New Echota, GA (Cherokee), 433–434
New Religion (Iroquois), 402–403, 405–407
New Year's Ceremony (Iroquois), 399–400
Nishga (Nisga'a), 42, 164
Norse, 12, 43
Northern Athapaskan Indians, 105, 118
Northern Cheyenne, 235
Northern Lights (Lower Kootenai supernatural), 149
Northern Paiute, 171, 189, 191

North West Company, 118, 154, 156, 404
Nuclear core family, 125, 514g
Nuclear family, 514g
  Cherokee, 439
  Chipewyan, 116, 125
  Iroquois, 405
  Natchez, 459
  Navajo, 364
  Netsilik, 83, 85
  Tlingit, 276
  Western Shoshone, 179–180
Nuclear Regulatory Commission (U.S.), 375–376
Nunavut (Inuit territory), 42, 98–99
Nunavut Tourism, 100

Oconaluftee Indian Village, 440
Office of Hawaiian Affairs (state office), 484
Office of Indian Affairs. *See* Bureau of Indian Affairs
Ojibwa (Chippewa) Indians, 39, 482
Oki (Iroquois spirit), 514g
Oklahoma Farm Bureau, 490
Old Man Coyote (Crow supernatural), 204–205, 230, 231
Old Oraibi (monograph), 307
Omaha-type cousin terms, 511g
One Flew over the Cuckoo's Nest (book, motion picture), 61
Oneida (Nation) Reservation, 416, 491
One Nation (private organization), 490
One Who Made Everything (Crow supernatural), 205
Open Bible church, 236
Oregon Territory, 156
Organization of American States, 198
Our Life (Iroquois deity), 398
Outfit (Navajo group), 364
Overland Route, 185

Pacific Fur Company, 154
Paha (Cahuilla leader), 249, 514g
Paiute Indians, 47
Palisades, 272, 384, 385, 456
Panic of 1893 (U.S.), 349
Pan-Indianism (pantribalism), 46–49, 56, 514g
Parallel cousins, 514g
Parfleche, 209
Parka, 73–74
Partnerships (Netsilik sharing), 85
Passamaquoddy (Nation) Indians, 55–56, 491
Patriclan, 514g
  Cahuilla, 246, 247, 248
Patrilineage, 247, 514g
Patrilineal descent, 515g
Patrilocal residence, 515g
Peabody Coal Company (Peabody Energy Company), 333–334, 374
Pembroke, NC, 484

Pembroke State University, 484
Pemmican, 109–110, 515g
Pend d'Oreille Indians, 4
Penobscot (Nation) Indians, 55–56, 491
Pentecostal churches, 229–231, 232, 236, 299
Peon (Cahuilla game), 253, 515g
Pequot Indians, 472
Personal kindred, 82, 515g
Petrel (Tlingit supernatural), 270
Peyote, 48–49, 368
Peyote Road of Life (Navajo), 368
Phratry, 209, 315, 324, 515g
Piki (Hopi bread), 313, 323, 515g
Pima Indians, 485
Pine Ridge Reservation, 56
Pipes. See Tobacco
Poisons, 247, 327, 360
Polar Eskimos, 70
Polyandry, 87, 92, 180, 287, 460, 515g
Polygamy, 92, 515g
Polygny, 92, 113, 180, 222, 287, 364, 460, 515g
Populations (general), 9–10, 21
Potlatch, 280, 289–291, 294, 296, 515g
Pottery
    archaeological, 16, 312
    Cahuilla, 244
    Cherokee, 423
    Hopi, 311
    Iroquois, 385
    Natchez, 452
    Navajo, 353
    Western Shoshone, 178, 181
Powamu Society (Hopi), 318
Powhatan confederacy, 33
Powwow, 515g
    Crow, 227–228, 231
    general, 52–54, 481
    Lower Kootenai, 160–161
Presbyterian missionaries, 293–295, 296
Primogeniture, 248, 515g
Private wars (Iroquois), 395
Proclamation of 1763 (British), 41
Progressive Warriors (Iroquois), 406–407
Prophet (Cult) Dance, 155, 156
Public Law 280 (U.S.), 39, 46, 489
Public wars (Iroquois), 395
Pueblo Indians, 16
Pueblo revolts, 35, 316, 344
Puha (spirit power; Western Shoshone), 178, 182, 197
Pumpkins (squash), 16, 387, 423
Puritan missionaries, 35

Quaker missionaries, 34, 402–403, 436
Qualla Arts and Crafts Cooperative, 438
Qualla Indian Boundary (Eastern Cherokee reservation), 435–444
Quebec Bridge, 412

Rabbit-killing stick. See Throwing stick
Radio (Indian-related programs), 24

Rafts (conveyances), 108, 452
Raids. See Warfare
Rama Trust (Iroquois; Canada), 409
Ramona (book), 240, 258
Raven (Tlingit)
    moiety, 275–276
    supernatural, 269–270
Red Power movement, 56
Red River Rebellion (Canada), 42
Reds (Cherokee moiety), 426–427, 429
"Red Wing" (song), 5
Religion (defined), 87–88, 515g
Relocation Program (U.S.), 232, 480–481
Removal policy (U.S.). See Indian Removal Act
Reservation Blues (book), 60
Residential Schools Healing Fund (Canada), 410–411
Revenue-Cutter Service (U.S.), 293
Rites of passage, 90–91, 92, 152, 183–184, 254, 515g
Roadman (Navajo religious leader), 368
Roman Catholic churches and missionaries
    Cahuilla, 255, 257
    Chipewyan, 118, 120, 125, 127, 128
    Crow, 224, 228, 236
    general, 33, 35, 36
    Hopi, 327–328
    Iroquois, 382, 393, 411
    Lower Kootenai, 157, 163
    Navajo, 344
    Netsilik, 95
Royal Canadian Mounted Police, 95, 127, 128, 407, 414
Royal Proclamation of 1763 (British), 163
Ruby Mountains Forest Reserve, 190
Russian-American Company, 288, 292
Russian Orthodox Greek Catholic church, 292, 293, 294–295, 296

Sachem (Iroquois leader), 392, 406–407, 515g
Sacred bundle (medicine bundle, sacred packet), 515g
    Cahuilla, 243, 249
    Crow, 214, 218, 228–229, 231
    Hopi, 315, 317, 318
    Lower Kootenai, 149–150
    Natchez, 459
    Navajo, 359, 360, 373
    Tlingit, 284
Sagamite (hominy gruel), 387–388, 515g
Salmon, 274–275, 285, 293, 297
Sand painting (drypainting), 359
San Idlefonso Pueblo, 483
Santa Clara Pueblo, 483
Santa Fe, NM, 35, 328, 350
Santa Fe Railroad, 350
Santa Rosa and San Jacinto Mountain National Monument, 265
Sapling (Iroquois supernatural), 384

Scalp (or scalping)
   Crow, 212, 215, 222
   Hopi, 316
   Iroquois, 394
   Lower Kootenai, 142, 149
   Natchez, 455, 456
   Navajo, 345
   Tlingit, 282
Schools. *See* Education
Screw beans, 246
Sea Goddess (Netsilik), 73, 88, 89
Sealaska Corporation, 298–299
Seals, 78–80, 85, 89, 95, 100
Seine, 515g
Self bow, 515g
Shaman, 515g
   Cahuilla, 242, 249, 254
   Cherokee, 424, 426
   Chipewyan, 115, 128
   Crow, 213, 217
   Hopi, 322
   Iroquois, 390, 395
   Lower Kootenai, 150–151, 153, 155
   Natchez, 459
   Navajo, 347, 359, 363
   Netsilik, 85, 88, 89–90, 95
   Tlingit, 282, 284–285
   Western Shoshone, 178, 181, 182–183
Sheep
   Crow, 227
   Hopi, 329, 337
   Navajo, 345, 348, 349, 355, 367, 369
Sherrill, NY, 491
Sierra Club, 335
Silverwork, 348–349, 352, 369, 374–375, 422
Sinew-backed bow, 178, 515g
Singer (Navajo shaman), 347, 359, 363
Singer Society (Hopi), 319
Sipapu (Hopi spirit entrance), 311
Six Nations (Iroquois), 41, 382, 393–394
Six Nations Confederacy (Canada), 407
Six Nations Reserve (Canada), 401–402,
   404–410
Sky (Lower Kootenai supernatural), 149
Skywalker, 411–413, 516g
Sky Woman (Iroquois supernatural), 384
Slaves and slavery, 516g
   blacks, 432–433
   Cherokee, 432–433
   Iroquois, 389
   Natchez, 464, 465
   Navajo, 344, 345
   Tlingit, 276, 282, 283, 293–294
   whites, 483
Sled, 77, 78–79
Sliding historical baseline (chronological
   skewing), 20–21, 516g
Smallpox
   Cahuilla, 256
   Cherokee, 428
   Chipewyan, 118–119

   Crow, 205, 224
   general, 34–35, 36
   Hopi, 328
   Lower Kootenai, 155
   Tlingit, 292–293
   Western Shoshone, 187
Smithsonian Institution, 62, 488
Smoke Signals (motion picture), 60
Snake-Antelope Dance (Hopi), 331
Snake Society (Hopi), 318–319
Snares, 110, 111, 179, 247, 387, 501–502, 516g
Snow boat (Iroquois game), 391
Snowdrift (Lutselk'e), NWT (Canada), 120–
   135
Snowhouse, 76
Snowmobile, 96
Snowshoes, 109, 145, 273, 387
Snow snake (Iroquois game), 391
Soapstone (artifacts), 76, 91, 93, 97–98, 423
Society of Friends. *See* Quaker missionaries
Sodality, 211, 216–217, 516g
Songs, 86, 152, 215, 228–229, 257, 289, 359,
   360, 361, 399, 454, 455
Son of Old Man Hat (book), 361–362
Sorcery. *See* Witchcraft and sorcery
Sororal polygyny, 516g
Sororate, 147, 180, 253, 364, 424, 516g
Southern California Edison (power com-
   pany), 334
Southern Pacific Railroad, 257
South Fork Reservation, 192
Sovereignty issues
   Canada, 96, 98–99, 101, 126–127, 130,
      132, 163–164, 167–168
   Cherokee, 435, 443
   Crow, 224–225
   general (U.S.), 38–40, 55–56, 57–58, 475,
      488–491
   Hopi, 327, 329, 333, 335
   Iroquois, 407
   Lower Kootenai, 157–159
   Navajo, 344–347, 349–350, 370–371,
      372–373
   Tlingit, 293, 295–299, 301–302
   Western Shoshone, 185–188, 190–191,
      193, 197–199
Soyal Ceremony (Hopi), 315, 318, 331, 333
Spanish land grants. *See* Encomienda
Speaker (New Religion; Iroquois), 405
Spider Woman (Hopi supernatural), 309, 321
Spirit Mountain Casino, 473
Spirit of the Winds (Iroquois supernatural),
   398
Spokane House (trading post), 154
Squash (pumpkins), 16, 387, 423
Squaw Dance (Enemyway; Navajo), 347, 363
Starvation, 82, 86, 91, 93, 112, 117, 119, 144,
   179, 349, 401
Steam bath. *See* Sweat bath
Stickball (shinny), 223, 231, 426. *See also*
   Lacrosse

Stick game (hand game), 53–54, 55, 148, 180–181, 223, 516g
Suicide, 91, 94, 101–102, 282
Sun (as a supernatural)
  Crow, 218, 219–220
  Hopi, 317, 322, 325, 333
  Lower Kootenai, 141
  Natchez, 448–449
  Navajo, 352
  Netsilik, 73
Sun Dance (Crow), 205, 219–220, 223, 228–229, 236
Suns (Natchez royalty), 453–454
Sun Watcher (Hopi), 319
Surround for game, 110, 208, 313, 387, 516g
Swallow (Hopi supernatural), 309
Sweat bath, 142–143, 153, 175, 183, 231, 236, 243, 353, 361, 516g
Sweathouse Spirit (Lower Kootenai supernatural), 153
Syllabary, 95, 433–434

Table Mountain Casino, 473
Taboo, 516g
  Cahuilla, 242, 247, 251–252
  Cherokee, 424, 425, 426, 438
  Chipewyan, 120
  Crow, 218–219, 220, 221
  Hopi, 317, 325
  Iroquois, 395, 403, 406
  Lower Kootenai, 147, 151, 152
  Natchez, 448–449
  Navajo, 352, 357, 359
  Netsilik, 88–89, 94
  Tlingit, 280, 282, 286
  Western Shoshone, 178, 179, 184
Taiga, 516g
Tamaiot (Cahuilla creator), 241–242
Tammany (opera), 5
Tattoos, 75, 94, 242, 251, 252, 422, 450, 456
Taxation (U.S.), 44–45, 57
Teknonymy, 285, 516g
Te-Moak Bands of Western Shoshone Indians, 173, 192, 194, 198
Te-Moak Tribal Council, 199
Te-Moak Western Shoshone Housing Authority, 195
Tepee
  Chipewyan, 107–108
  Crow, 206, 221
  general, 51
  Lower Kootenai, 142
Termination of federal obligations to Indians (U.S.), 39, 46
Thanksgiving Dance (Iroquois), 399
Thécoel (Natchez) Indians, 448
Three Sisters (Iroquois deities), 387
Throwing stick (boomerang, missile stick, rabbit-killing stick), 247, 313, 516g
Thule culture (Eskimo), 15
Thunderer (Iroquois supernatural), 397–398
Ticho (Dogrib) Indians, 42, 117, 132

Timbisha Indians (Western Shoshone band), 483
Timbisha Shoshone Homeland Act, 483
Time Magazine, 470
Tlingit and Haida Central Council, 297
Tobacco
  Cahuilla, 242
  Cherokee, 423
  Crow, 218–219
  general, 45
  Hopi, 313, 314, 315, 318
  Iroquois, 387, 398, 399
  Lower Kootenai, 146
  Natchez, 452–453, 461, 463
  Navajo, 368
  Netsilik, 95
  Tlingit, 289, 292
  Western Shoshone, 175, 178, 196–197
Tobacco Society (Crow), 218–219, 226, 236
Toboggan, 108–109, 110, 146, 175–176, 221, 387, 516g
Toggle-headed harpoon, 516g
Toiyabe National Forest, 190
Toloache, 252, 517g
Tomahawk, 395, 396, 429, 517g
Torture, 215, 285, 390–391, 395, 397, 455
Totem poles, 279–282, 294, 295, 300, 517g
Tourists, 97–98, 100, 293, 336–337, 348–349, 369, 374–375, 437–438
Trade and fur trade
  Cherokee, 428, 430, 431, 432
  Chipewyan, 118–120, 121, 122, 131
  Crow, 208, 224
  general, 36
  Hopi, 331
  Iroquois, 392–393, 401
  Lower Kootenai, 148, 156
  Natchez, 464
  Navajo, 344, 348
  Netsilik, 95, 96, 97, 100
  Tlingit, 274, 278–279, 280, 292
  Western Shoshone, 184–185
Traditional Cultural Property (Bureau of Land Management; U.S.), 197
Trail of Tears (Cherokee), 434–435, 517g
Trait, 517g
Transhumance, 517g
Transvestites, 153, 154, 223, 365, 460, 517g
Travois, 206, 517g
Treaties (general), 38–40, 55–56, 256
Treaty Number 11 (Canada), 126
Treaty of Guadalupe Hidalgo, 185
Treaty of Laramie, 224–225
Treaty of Ruby Valley, 186–187
Tribal Bingo (Cherokee), 440
Tribal Council
  Crow, 231–232
  Hopi, 332
Tribal Initiation Ceremony (Hopi), 318, 319
Tribalism, 486–488
Triballly Controlled Community College Assistance Act (U.S.), 58

Tribe (defined), 19–20, 517g
Tuberculosis, 36, 187
Tunraq (Netsilik spirit), 89, 517g
Tupiliq (Netsilik spirit), 90, 517g
Turning Stone Casino, 416
Turtle (Iroquois supernatural), 384
Twin Monster Slayers (Navajo supernaturals), 352
Two, The (Hopi supernaturals), 308–309
Two-Year-Old-Goose (Lower Kootenai supernatural), 145

Umiak, 517g
Unilineal descent, 517g
United States v. Lara (2004), 492
Universalism, 66, 517g
Unrecognized tribes (U.S.), 482–484
Unto These Hills (play), 440
Upper Tribes (Iroquois; Canada), 404, 406
Uranium mining, 369–370, 376
Urban Aboriginal Strategy (Canada), 414
Urban Indians (U.S.), 479–482
U.S. Constitution, 394, 490, 492
U.S. Supreme Court, 57, 59–60, 198, 258–259, 415, 434, 484, 492
Utah Territory, 185
Uto-Aztecan language family, 171, 240, 307

Value, 517g
Vanes, 517g
Vikings. *See* Norse
Village Chief (Hopi), 319–320, 321, 329–331, 333
Village endogamy, 517g
Vision quest and visions
    Crow, 205, 213, 220, 221, 229, 230–231
    Iroquois, 390, 401
    Lower Kootenai, 148, 149
    Western Shoshone, 182
    Tlingit, 283
Vulture (Hopi supernatural), 309

Wampum, 394, 399, 403, 405, 517g
War Chief
    Cherokee, 427–428
    Hopi, 312, 315–316
    Iroquois, 395
    Natchez, 453, 454–456
War Dance (Iroquois), 396
War Department (U.S.), 40–41
Warfare (feuds and raids)
    Cahuilla, 249
    Cherokee, 427, 428–430
    Chipewyan, 113–114, 115
    Crow, 208, 212–216, 217
    Hopi, 316
    Iroquois, 394–397
    Lower Kootenai, 148–149
    Natchez, 454–456, 465–466
    Navajo, 347
    Netsilik, 85

Tlingit, 282
    Western Shoshone, 181, 185
War of 1812, 39, 402, 411–412
War on Poverty (U.S. federal program), 439
Warrior Society
    Hopi, 316
    Iroquois (Canada), 408
War Women (Cherokee), 430
Water (Lower Kootenai supernatural), 149
Water Babies (Western Shoshone supernaturals), 182
Water Beetle (Cherokee supernatural), 421
Water Girl (Western Shoshone supernatural), 174
Weather God (Netsilik), 73, 88
Weir, 517g
Wells Colony, 192
Western Pueblos, 307
Western Shoshone Defense Project, 198
Western Shoshone Distribution Act, 199
Western Shoshone National Council, 198
Wheeler–Howard Act (U.S.). *See* Indian Reorganization Act
White Knives (Western Shoshone band), 187
White Mountain Apache Indians, 57, 372
Whites (Cherokee moiety), 426–427
Whooping cough, 36, 155
Wife abduction, 92, 116–117, 180, 182, 211
Wildcat (Cahuilla moiety), 248
Wild West Show, 50
Windtalkers (motion picture), 367
Witchcraft and sorcery, 516g, 517g
    Cahuilla, 250
    Crow, 220
    Hopi, 309, 321–322
    Iroquois, 398
    Lower Kootenai, 151
    Navajo, 360–361, 362, 368
    Netsilik, 87
    Tlingit, 282, 285
    Western Shoshone, 182
Wolf (Tlingit moiety), 275–276, 279
Wood Buffalo National Park (Canada), 4
Woodland Cultural Centre (Canada), 408
Woodland culture, 16
Worcester v. Georgia (U.S. Supreme Court decision), 434
Words of Condolence (Iroquois), 392
World War I, 8, 191, 231, 350, 355, 367, 406, 414
World War II, 332, 367, 368, 412, 480, 490
Wounded Knee, SD, 56, 61
Wuwuchim Society (Hopi), 319
Wuya (Hopi concept), 315

Yakama Nation Legends Casino, 55
Yei (Navajo Holy People), 351–352, 517g
Yellowknife Indians, 105
Yellowstone National Park, MT, 4
Yellowtail Dam and Reservoir, 232
Yuit, 70fn. *See also* Eskimos; Inuit; Yupik
Yupik (Eskimoan language), 71

PACIFIC
OCEAN

1 Clatskaine
2 Molala
3 Coosans
4 Oregon Athapaskans:
   Applegate, Chasta
   Costa, Cheto, Galice,
   Tututni, Upper Coquille,
   Upper Umpqua
5 Takelma
6 Karok
7 Wiyot
8 Chilula, Hupa, Whilkut
9 Chimariko
10 Mattole

11 Cahto
12 Eel River Area: Lassik,
   Nongatl, Sinkyone,
   Wailaki
13 Yana
14 Yuki
15 Nomlaki, Patwin
16 Konkow
17 Lake Miwok
18 Coast Miwok
19 Wappo
20 Kitanemuk
21 Tataviam
22 Mohave
23 Cupeño

CHINOOKANS
TILLAMOOK
ALSEANS
SIUSLAWANS
KALAPUYANS
YUROK
POMO
COSTANOAN
ESSELEN
SALINAN
CHUMASH
GABRIELINO
LUISEÑO
IPAI
KUMEYAAY
QUECHAN
MARICOPA

COLVILLE
LAKES
KOOTENAI
BLACKFOOT
GROS VENTRE
ASSINIBOINE
COLUMBIAN
SPOKANE
KALISPEL
COEUR d'ALENE
FLATHEAD
CROW
HIDATSA
MANDAN
ARIKARA
SAHAPTIN
NEZ PERCE
CAYUSE
NORTHERN SHOSHONE
CHEYENNE
TETON
PONCA
PAWNEE
KLAMATH
NORTHERN PAIUTE
BANNOCK
EASTERN SHOSHONE
BESAWUNENA
MIWOK
WESTERN SHOSHONE
UTE
ARAPAHO
NAWATHINEHENA
YOKUTS
SOUTHERN PAIUTE
WALAPAI
HAVASUPAI
HOPI
NAVAJO
JICARILLA
ZUNI
SHASTA
KLAMATH
YAVAPAI
WESTERN APACHE
PIRO
COMANCHE
WINTU
ACHUMAWI
CHIRICAHUA
MESCALERO
ATSUGEWI
MAIDU
NISENAN
WASHOE
TOHONO O'ODHAM
PIMA
xx
JEMEZ
B
C
A
TANO
LIPAN
SOLANO
OWENS VALLEY PAIUTE
ZUNI
ACOMA
LAGUNA
TOMPIRO
PECOS
D
MIWOK
YOKUTS
TUBATULABL
PIRO
COAHUILTECO
KAWAIISU
CHEMEHUEVI
SERRANO
HAVASUPAI
WALAPAI
YAVAPAI
CAHUILLA

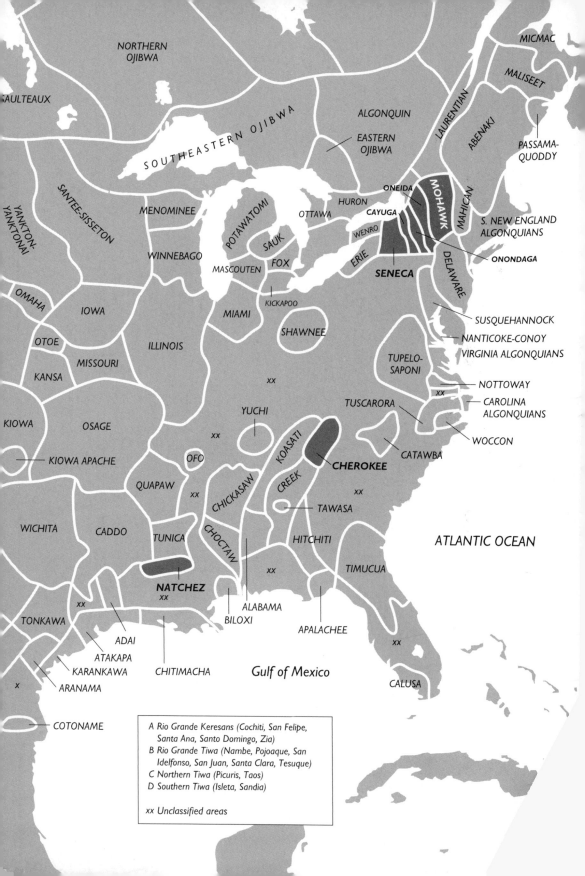

NORTHERN OJIBWA

MICMAC

MALISEET

GAULTEAUX

SOUTHEASTERN OJIBWA

ALGONQUIN

EASTERN OJIBWA

LAURENTIAN

ABENAKI

PASSAMA-QUODDY

SANTEE-SISSETON

MENOMINEE

POTAWATOMI

OTTAWA

HURON

ONEIDA

MOHAWK

MAHICAN

S. NEW ENGLAND ALGONQUIANS

YANKTON-YANKTONAI

CAYUGA

WENRO

DELAWARE

ONONDAGA

WINNEBAGO

SAUK

FOX

ERIE

SENECA

MASCOUTEN

OMAHA

IOWA

MIAMI

KICKAPOO

SHAWNEE

SUSQUEHANNOCK

NANTICOKE-CONOY

VIRGINIA ALGONQUIANS

OTOE

ILLINOIS

TUPELO-SAPONI

KANSA

MISSOURI

xx

NOTTOWAY

xx

KIOWA

OSAGE

YUCHI

TUSCARORA

CAROLINA ALGONQUIANS

KIOWA APACHE

xx

OFO

KOASATI

CHEROKEE

CATAWBA

WOCCON

QUAPAW

xx

CHICKASAW

CREEK

xx

WICHITA

CADDO

TUNICA

CHOCTAW

TAWASA

HITCHITI

ATLANTIC OCEAN

NATCHEZ

xx

ALABAMA

xx

TIMUCUA

TONKAWA

xx

BILOXI

APALACHEE

ADAI

xx

ATAKAPA

KARANKAWA

CHITIMACHA

Gulf of Mexico

CALUSA

ARANAMA

x

COTONAME

A Rio Grande Keresans (Cochiti, San Felipe, Santa Ana, Santo Domingo, Zia)
B Rio Grande Tiwa (Nambe, Pojoaque, San Idelfonso, San Juan, Santa Clara, Tesuque)
C Northern Tiwa (Picuris, Taos)
D Southern Tiwa (Isleta, Sandia)

xx Unclassified areas